EDUCATIONAL PATTERNS AND CULTURAL CONFIGURATIONS

The Anthropology of Education

EDUCATIONAL POLICY, PLANNING AND THEORY
Series Editor: Don Adams, University of Pittsburgh

EDUCATIONAL

PATTERNS

AND

CULTURAL

CONFIGURATIONS

The Anthropology of Education

JOAN I. ROBERTS

SHERRIE K. AKINSANYA

DAVID McKAY COMPANY, INC./NEW YORK

EDUCATIONAL PATTERNS AND CULTURAL CONFIGURATIONS:
THE ANTHROPOLOGY OF EDUCATION

Developmental Editor: Nicole Benevento
Interior Design: Angela Foote
Cover Design: Jane Sterrett
Production and Manufacturing Supervisor: Donald W. Strauss
Composition: Automated Composition Service, Inc.
Printing and Binding: Hamilton Printing Company

Library of Congress Cataloging in Publication Data

Main entry under title:

Educational patterns and cultural configurations.

   (Educational policy, planning, and theory)
   Bibliography: p.
   1. Educational anthropology—Addresses, essays,
lectures. I. Roberts, Joan I. II. Akinsanya,
Sherrie K.
LB45.E25   301.2'1   75-42021
ISBN 0-679-30291-3

For Susan, Darren, Jodi, and Scott

Acknowledgments

"Some Demands of Education upon Anthropology" by Nina C. Vandewalker is reprinted from *American Journal of Sociology*, Vol. 4 (1898), by permission of *American Journal of Sociology*. Copyright © 1898 by The University of Chicago Press.

"Ethnic Factors in Education" by Edgar L. Hewett is reproduced by permission of the American Anthropological Association from the *American Anthropologist*, Vol. 7, No. 1 (1905).

"Education, Conformity, and Cultural Change" by Franz Boas is reprinted from *Anthropology and Modern Life* by Franz Boas. By permission of W. W. Norton & Company, Inc. Copyright 1928 by W. W. Norton & Company, Inc. Copyright renewed 1956 by Norman Boas. Copyright 1932 by W. W. Norton & Company, Inc. Copyright renewed 1960 by Helene Boas Yampolsky. Copyright © 1962 by W. W. Norton & Company, Inc.

"Native Education and Culture Contact" by Bronislaw Malinowski is reprinted with permission from *International Review of Missions*, Vol. 25 (1936).

"Primitive Education" by Margaret Mead. Reprinted with permission of the publisher from the *Encyclopedia of the Social Sciences* edited by Edwin R. A. Seligman, Editor-in-Chief, and Alvin Johnson, Associate Editor. Volume 5, pages 399–403. Copyright 1931, 1959 by Macmillan Publishing Co., Inc.

"An Anthropological Framework for Studying Education" by Thomas J. La Belle is reprinted from *Teachers College Record*, Vol. 472, No. 4 (May 1972), by permission of the *Record* and the author.

"Education in Anthropology: Areas of Common Concern" by Solon T. Kimball is reprinted from *Anthropology and the Behavioral and Health Sciences*, Otto von Mering and Leonard Kasdan, eds. By permission of the University of Pittsburgh Press. © 1970 by the University of Pittsburgh Press.

"An Anthropological View of Urban Education," by G. Alexander Moore, Jr., is reprinted from *Education and Urban Society*, Vol. I, No. 4 (August 1969), pp. 423–439 by permission of the Publisher, Sage Publications, Inc.

"A Cross-Cultural Outline of Education" by Jules Henry is reprinted from *Current Anthropology*, Vol. 1, No. 4 (July 1960), by permission of *Current Anthropology*. Copyright © 1960 by The University of Chicago Press.

"The Socialization of Juveniles in Primate and Foraging Societies: Implications for Contemporary Education" by John D. Herzog is reproduced by permission of the Council on Anthropology and Education from the *Council on Anthropology and Education Quarterly*, Vol. 5, No. 1 (February 1974).

"From Omnibus to Linkages: Cultural Transmission Models" by George D. Spindler is reproduced by permission of the Council on Anthropology and Education from the *Council on Anthropology and Education Quarterly*, Vol. 5, No. 1 (February 1974).

"Where We Are and Where We Might Go: Steps Toward a General Theory of Cultural Transmission" by Frederick O. Gearing is reproduced by permission of the Council on Anthropology and Education from the *Council on Anthropology and Education Quarterly*, Vol. 4, No. 1 (February 1973).

"Structures of Censorship, Usually Inadvertent: Studies in a Cultural Theory of Education" by Frederick O. Gearing, with Allan Tindall, Allen Smith, and Thomas Caroll, is reproduced by permission of the Council on Anthropology and Education from the *Council on Anthropology and Education Quarterly*, Vol. 6, No. 2 (May 1975).

"Another Route to a General Theory of Cultural Transmission: A Systems Model" by Marion L. Dobbert is reproduced by permission of the Council on Anthropology and Education from the *Council on Anthropology and Education Quarterly*, Vol. 6, No. 2 (May 1975).

"Controls, Paradigms, and Designs: Critical Elements in the Understanding of Cultural Dynamics" by Arthur M. Harkins is reproduced by permission of the Council on Anthropology and Education from the *Council on Anthropology and Education Quarterly*, Vol. 6, No. 2 (May 1975).

"On the Analog between Culture Acquisition and Ethnographic Method" by Jacquetta Hill Burnett is reproduced by permission of the Council on Anthropology and Education from the *Council on Anthropology and Education Quarterly*, Vol. 5, No. 1 (February 1974).

"Methods of Study" by William Whyte is reprinted from *Street Corner Society* by William Whyte. By permission of The University of Chicago Press. Copyright © 1955 by The University of Chicago Press.

"The Methodology of Participant Observation" by Severyn T. Bruyn is reproduced by permission of The Society for Applied Anthropology from *Human Organization*, Vol. 22, No. 3 (1963).

"Grounded Theory and Educational Ethnography: A Methodological Analysis and Critique" by Louis M. Smith and Paul A. Pohland is reprinted by permission of the authors. Copyright © 1969 by Louis M. Smith and Paul A. Pohland.

"The Ethnography of a Japanese School: Anthropological Field Technique and Models in the Study of a Complex Organization" by John Singleton is reprinted from a paper presented at the Annual Meeting of the American Anthropological Association, 1968. Reproduced by permission of the author.

"Event Description and Analysis in the Microethnography of Urban Classrooms" by Jacquetta Hill Burnett is reprinted from a paper presented at the Annual Meeting of the American Anthropological Association, 1968. Copyright © 1969 by Jacquetta H. Burnett. Reproduced by permission of the author.

"Interaction and Adaptation in Two Negro Kindergartens" by Carol Talbert is reproduced by permission of the Society for Applied Anthropology from *Human Organization*, Vol. 29, No. 2 (Summer 1970).

"Ceremony, Rites, and Economy in the Student System of an American High School" by Jacquetta Hill Burnett is reproduced by permission of the Society for Applied Anthropology from *Human Organization*, Vol. 28, No. 1 (Spring 1969).

"A Proposal for the Unification of Secondary School Courses through Anthropology" by John H. Chilcott is reprinted from *The Clearing House*, Vol. 36, No. 7 (March 1962), by permission of the publisher. Copyright © 1962 by *The Clearing House*, Fairleigh Dickinson University, Teaneck, New Jersey.

"Anthropology and World History Texts" by Rachel Reese Sady is reprinted from *Phi Delta Kappan*, Vol. 45 (February 1964), by permission of the publisher. Copyright © 1964 by Phi Delta Kappan, Bloomington, Indiana.

"Cross-Cultural Teaching of Science" by Francis E. Dart and Panna Lal Pradhan is reprinted from *Science*, Vol. 155 (10 February 1967), pp. 649-656. Copyright 1967 by the American Association for the Advancement of Science.

"An Experimental Ninth-Grade Anthropology Course" by Paul Bohannan, Merwyn S. Garbarino, and Earle W. Carlson is reproduced by permission of the American Anthropological Association from the *American Anthropologist*, Vol. 71, No. 3 (1969).

"Anthropology and Teacher Education" by Elizabeth M. Eddy is reproduced by permission of the Society for Applied Anthropology from *Human Organization*, Vol. 27, No. 1 (1968).

"Anthropology and an Education for the Future" by Margaret Mead is reprinted from *The Teaching of Anthropology* edited by David G. Mandelbaum, Gabriel Lasker and Ethel M. Albert. Originally published by the University of California Press, 1963; reprinted by permission of The Regents of the University of California.

Contributors

Sherrie K. Akinsanya is a professor of anthropology and education at the University of Maryland, Eastern Shore.

Franz Boas is now deceased; he was a professor of anthropology at Columbia University, New York City.

Paul Bohannan is a professor of anthropology at Northwestern University, Evanston, Illinois.

Severyn T. Bruyn is a professor of sociology at Boston College, Chestnut Hill, Massachusetts.

Jacquetta Hill Burnett is a professor of intercultural education in the Bureau of Education Research at the University of Illinois at Urbana.

Earle W. Carlson is on the faculty at Northwestern University, Evanston, Illinois.

John H. Chilcott is a professor of anthropology at the University of Arizona, Tucson.

Francis E. Dart is a professor of physics at the University of Oregon, Eugene.

Marion L. Dobbert is a professor of anthropology and education at the University of Minnesota, Minneapolis.

Elizabeth M. Eddy is a professor of sociology and anthropology at the University of Florida, Gainesville.

Merwyn S. Garbarino is a professor of anthropology at the University of Illinois at Chicago Circle.

Frederick O. Gearing is a professor of anthropology at the State University of New York at Buffalo.

Arthur M. Harkins is a professor of education at the University of Minnesota, Minneapolis.

Jules Henry is now deceased; he was a professor of anthropology at Washington University, St. Louis, Missouri.

John D. Herzog is a professor in anthropology and education at Northeastern University, Boston, Massachusetts.

Edgar L. Hewett is now deceased; he was in the Bureau of Ethnology, Washington, D.C.

Solon T. Kimball is a graduate resident professor of anthropology at the University of Florida, Gainesville.

Thomas J. La Belle is a professor in the Department of Education at the University of California at Los Angeles.

Bronislaw Malinowski is now deceased; he was a professor of anthropology at the University of London and at Yale University.

Margaret Mead is curator emeritus, American Museum of Natural History and special lecturer in anthropology, Columbia University, New York.

G. Alexander Moore, Jr. is a professor of anthropology at the University of Florida, Gainesville.

Paul A. Pohland is in the Department of Education/Administration at the University of New Mexico, Albuquerque.

Panna Lal Pradhan is a professor of psychology at Tribhuwan University, Kathmandu, Nepal.

Joan I. Roberts, a specialist in anthropology and social psychology of education, was previously a professor at the University of Wisconsin, Madison.

Rachel Reese Sady is an anthropologist who works at Hastings-on-Hudson, New York.

John Singleton is a professor of educational anthropology at the University of Pittsburgh.

Louis M. Smith is a professor of education at Washington University, Saint Louis, Missouri.

George D. Spindler is a professor of anthropology at Stanford University, California.

Carol Talbert is a professor of anthropology at Syracuse University, New York.

Nina C. Vandewalker is now deceased; she was on the faculty of Milwaukee State Normal School.

William Whyte is a professor in the School of Industrial and Labor Relations, Cornell University, Ithaca, New York.

Preface

For many years, anthropologists have studied the kinship systems and patterns of enculturation of the young; but the specialized field of anthropology and education began to flourish only recently. The two books presented here—volume 1 on the anthropology of education and volume 2 on anthropological studies of education—together form an overview of the critical work done in this field.

The two volumes derive from bibliographic research that extended over a five-year period of time. Major bibliographic sources consulted include the *Education Index*, the *International Bibliography of Social and Cultural Anthropology*, the *Psychological Abstracts*, the *Review of Educational Research*, the *Sociological Abstracts and Index*, and the *Social Science and Humanities Review*.

In addition, the *Review of Anthropology* and all pertinent individual bibliographies appended to major works were examined. From these sources thousands of references were located and reviewed. Out of this large collection, only about seven hundred fifty met our criteria for inclusion in the final bibliography. This sharply defined collection is part 6 of the first volume. In it, all references are listed in chronological order, extending from the first statement in 1898 to those in 1975. The references for 1974-75 although incomplete, are included as they became available during the stages of preparation of this book for publication. The first draft of the bibliography, now revised for publication, was informally distributed by the Council on Anthropology and Education.

From the works chosen, we selected an initial set of those considered most important to represent the field as it has emerged over time. More importantly, we wanted the selection and organization of these materials to define the major parameters of the discipline. The first and all subsequent reorganizations of articles proved too long for publication in even two volumes, but the books that have been produced, although considerably shortened, should prove useful in clarifying the field of anthropology and education.

For those familiar with this area of research, some older studies will be quickly recognized. Our decision was to choose the best, not necessarily the most recent work. For those who are accustomed to an organization by cultural world areas, articles may seem unevenly distributed. We can only say that such organization yielded a useless product because the research itself is extensive in some areas and negligible in others. We would have preferred an organization around major cultural processes. This, given the state of the field, proved to be a premature organizational scheme.

The work of several competent scholars could not be included because of space limitations and organizational strictures. Although we cannot name the many authors we considered, we refer the reader to the bibliography for the publications of the following scholars: Wilfred Bailey, Roger Barker, Ruth Benedict, Howard Becker, Lyman Bryson, John Collier, Malcolm Collier, Yehudi Cohen, Lambros Comitas, Loren Eisley, Fred Eggan, Meyer Fortes, Estelle Fuchs, Herbert Gans, Marcus Goldstein, Nancy Gonzalez, Ward Goodenough, Bruce Grindal, Melville Herskovits, Philip Jackson, Landa Jocano, Vera John, Felix Keesing, George Kneller, Bud Kleif, Anthony Leeds, Philip Leis, Thomas Leemon, Oscar Lewis, Rhoda Metraux, Nancy Modiano, Ashley Montagu, Marie Montessori, Grace

Nicholson, Morris Opler, Alan Peshkin, George Pettit, Annette Rosenstiel, Seymour Sarason, Herbert Thelen, Charles Valentine, Anthony Wallace, Thomas Williams. In all cases, the bibliographic references and the articles chosen for inclusion were selected on the basis of the following criteria: first, the extent to which culture was the organizing concept; second, the degree of reliance on fieldwork methodology; third, the use of anthropological concepts in analyses; fourth, the inclusion of formalized education systems in relation to culture; fifth, the involvement of the author in the discipline of anthropology or in the concepts and methods basic to the field.

Neither book incorporates the literature on informal learning, or more broadly, on enculturation. The extensive literature in this area requires a separate volume. Although some of the finest work in the field of anthropology and education has been done on enculturation, we have confined ourselves to the works directly concerned with some aspect of formalized education. For a representative collection of the ethnographic studies of enculturation, we have compiled a Chronological Bibliography in the first volume of the critical studies conducted by anthropologists who have described the actual processes of growing up in different cultures throughout the world.

An examination of these and other anthropological studies will be incorporated in a textbook, *The Ethos of Learning*, to be published by David McKay Company, Inc., in the near future. It is hoped that this text, when combined with *Educational Patterns and Cultural Configurations* and with *Schooling in the Cultural Context*, will offer the overview necessary for an understanding of the fundamentals of the newly emerging field, anthropology of education. A field in which we would not have been involved were it not for the generous support of Solon Kimball, Elizabeth Eddy, Alexander Moore, Beatrice and Robert Miller, and Louise Sweet.

Contents

Part I

An Overview of Anthropology and Education

Introduction

Joan I. Roberts

HUMAN BEINGS ARE DISTINGUISHED from all other species by their capacity to create culture and to transmit it to their young. Cultural transmission depends on that faculty peculiar to the human species, the ability to use symbols. Through the ability to symbolize, we can learn those attributes and products of human societies which then become transmissible by mechanisms other than biological heredity or genetic properties. Both anthropologists and educators are therefore vitally concerned with culture, the ways of living developed by a group of people, and with cultural transmission, the processes of continuing and enlarging the cumulative heritage between generations. Thus learning must stand as a concept basic to enculturation, the process of becoming a functioning member of a particular group of people.

Although the field of anthropology and education has begun to develop only recently as an entity within the area of cultural anthropology, its roots are deep in the Western philosophical tradition, first appearing during the Enlightenment, when religious dogma began to give way to scientific explanations of human origins and existence. John Locke, stressing the relationship between the environment and human thought, said: "Whence has all the materials of reason and knowledge? To this I answer, in one word, *experience*. In that, all knowledge is founded; and from that it ultimately derives itself."[1] Claude Helvetius extended this idea: "The inequality of minds is the effect of a known cause and that cause is the difference in education."[2] Later, Jacques Turgot claimed: "Possessor of a treasure of signs which he has the faculty of multiplying to infinity, he is able to assure the retention of his acquired ideas, to communicate them to other men,* and to transmit them to his successors as a constantly expanding heritage."[3] For these philosophers, enculturation expressed through the rational capacities of the human brain was critical to understanding how a group of people comes to take on distinctive ways of thinking basic to their mode of living.

In the nineteenth century the emphasis on progressive rationality gradually became subject to biological factors in species survival, as articulated by Charles Darwin and expressed in social context by Herbert Spencer. But it was Karl Marx and Friedrich Engels who subordinated the world of ideas into a mutually interactive system composed of three parts: (1) the economic base, (2) the social organization (particularly legal and political structures), and (3) the social consciousness or ideology. To Marx and Engels, the "omnipotence of education," again conceived of in the broader sense of enculturation, was critical to adaptations for reproductive success that depended on the technical and economic processes responsible for biosocial survival.

*The word *man* as a generic term for the human species is an unacceptable usage to the editors. Because the materials presented here are quoted from other sources, however, the term, when used, cannot be modified.

1

Primarily confining themselves to Western cultural history, Marx and Engels looked to nineteenth-century anthropologists for confirmation of the materialist conception of culture in other areas of the world. From Morgan, they derived stages of evolution presumed to characterize different cultural eras; Tylor, whose work could not be as easily restated into a materialistic mode of evolution, was largely ignored.[4] In one of the earliest definitions of culture, Tylor saw it as that complex whole which included knowledge, belief, art, morals, law, custom, and any other capabilities and habits acquired by man as a member of society.[5] This definition held limited interest for the productive bases proposed by Marx and Engels in their explanation of cultural evolution.

Nearly a century later, after hundreds of clarifications of the concept, definitions still contain Tylor's concerns while incorporating the physical basis of human life. Here, for example, is one such definition:

> By culture as such we mean all the ways of life that have been evolved by men in society. By a particular culture we mean the total shared way of life of a given people comprising modes of thinking, acting and feeling which are expressed in religion, law, language, art, and custom as well as material products such as houses, clothes and tools. From another perspective we may regard a culture as the learned and shared behavior, thoughts, acts and feelings of a certain people together with their artifacts—learned in a sense that this behavior is transmitted socially rather than genetically, shared in that it is ascribed to by the whole population or some part of it.[6]

Although this definition still does not detail cause-effect linkages as to how, when, and where cultures came into existence, several assumptions remain consistent with those of anthropologists in the previous century. These assumptions are critical to anthropology and education.

First, it is assumed, on the basis of ethnographic evidence, that culture is a complex whole in which structure and function are interrelated. This holistic unity of society is, unfortunately, often lost in the training of educators as they confront a welter of discrete stimulus-response bonds and behavioral modification programs. The traditional social scientific emphasis in education derives from psychology with its concern for the individual; too often, it ignores the context in which the person exists. Even the individual may lose the holistic quality of a complex organism, becoming instead a fragmented collection of traits presumably created by the search for pleasure and the avoidance of pain. In contrast, the concept of the person in a cultural context forces educators to deal with complex wholes, sharply focusing attention on the unique qualities of human life that make culture possible. Without intentionality emerging out of awareness of being aware and without the complex human brain creating complicated schemata of the world, there could be no human learning, no enculturation, and no culture.

The second component of a definition of culture that has been sustained over time is the fact that culture is acquired. Culture not only possesses order but it is also a process which extends throughout the entire life span of any individual. Anthropologists have seldom been caught in the trap of developmental psychology which, until recently, has formulated the socialization process as a phenomenon of childhood. To study a complex whole requires that cultural acquisition is observed from birth to death. We not only learn how to live, but also how to die. Furthermore, acquisition of culture, at any point in the human cycle, is learning in all activities of life. Thus, schooling is only one portion of the learning process when defined as enculturation.

The acquisition of culture over the life span as a variegated phenomenon details the third component of this definition. The multiple means developed to raise children within a number of very different kinship systems is no longer a matter of conjecture. But in the training of educators, ethnocentrism, or self-centered assumptions regarding the "correctness" of one's own pattern of enculturation, is too often fostered. This makes it difficult to know of other forms of cultural transmission or, if they are known, to see them as other than curious, "deviant," or aberrant behaviors enacted by groups of people who need to adjust to a "normal" nuclear family or to "proper" methods of child rearing.

Although the acquisition of culture is universal, it is highly differentiated according to the conditions that have formed a particular societal pattern. Cultural relativism within universal needs of the human species is thus a fourth characteristic of any anthropological definition of culture. Within the biological and ecological constraints set for the species, an astounding variation in cultural patterns has developed.

The educator untrained in the comparative understanding of these patterns may assume that "primitive" cultures are simply inferior versions of Western civilization. This assumption was rampant in the previous century when certain evolutionary schemes were infused with the concept of "progress" culminating in the "highest" stage of development—i.e., the writer's own Western society. There is no longer any reason to believe that so-called primitive cultures are simplistic. A quick look at their complex kinship patterns, for example, is sufficient to rid an educator of such illusions.

The concept of culture when applied to education insists, then, on perceiving the learner as a complicated person living in a complex human environment who acquires through enculturation over the entire life span the total shared way of life of of a given people. This is accomplished through a variety of socialization techniques that express relative solutions to universal needs of the human species within the constraints of the physical world.

HISTORICAL DEVELOPMENT OF ANTHROPOLOGY AND EDUCATION

To understand the culture of any group of people, one must understand their historical lineage. By analogy, we can say that to know the intellectual culture of a particular field of inquiry, we must understand the origins and development of the ideas proposed within the periods in which they were written.

The field of anthropology and education has a peculiar history, peculiar in the sense that previous thinkers enunciated the primacy of education in the molding of human existence while few anthropologists directly engaged in the study of educational institutions. In part, this can be attributed to the lack of institutionalized "schooling" in the cultures studied. This, however, is a weak argument since socialization can readily be conceived of as patterned educational practices. It is, therefore, quite likely that the absence of such studies may reflect a bias inherent in the Western intellectual tradition, one that assumed educators to be inferior intellects whose practitioner's arts were unworthy of concentrated consideration. Furthermore, the field of education—formal or informal—has, within the last several decades, been predominantly populated although never controlled by women. In Western cultures this may have been sufficient reason to place education beyond the realm of "serious" scholars. Even if this bias were absent, the overwhelmingly large number of males in anthropology practically precludes an investigation of certain women's activities because male and female cultures are not open equally to men and women researchers.

In short, cultural biases inherent in the culture of intellect may account for the peculiar lack of attention to anthropology and education. Indeed, the study of child-rearing patterns as a specialized anthropological subfield did not achieve prominence until Margaret Mead and other female anthropologists questioned the relation of enculturation to adult modal personalities through assessments of child-rearing practices within the context of widely differing sex roles for women and men. As Robin Fox points out in his book *Kinship and Marriage*, most studies of kinship systems focused neither on the internal dynamics of family functions nor on childhood education, but rather on the degree to which kinship interrelated with or even formed the political, legal, or economic power structures of cultures.

On the other hand, given these general trends in the field, it is gratifying to note that a number of statements were published over the last seventy-five years. (Most of these, however, can be traced to the last two decades, the period of time in which the field became a recognized area of knowledge.) Franz Boas, probably the most influential American anthropologist of this century, was probably the first to write on anthropology and education when in 1898 he discussed the teaching of anthropology at the university level. However, Boas, in his essay, was more concerned with legitimizing the field within the institutional structure of academic disciplines than with expressing the relationship between anthropology and education.

It was, in fact, an unknown scholar, Nina Vandewalker, who in the same year was to make the first application of anthropology to education. In her article, the opening chapter in part II, she states that the process of education "must be considered from the anthropological standpoint as well as from the psychological, as has been the case hitherto." She points out that anthropological investigation has been confined almost wholly to the phenomenon of adult life, with the child practically left out of consideration. Working with the evolutionary theory of Morgan, she argues that the recapitulation of ethnic experiences in the individual should parallel the development of major cultural epochs. (Although this is now a discredited assumption, Vandewalker was sophisticated in her adaptation of extant evolutionary conjecture to the education of children.) On safer ground, she insists on the anthropological study of childhood, predating by sixty years Mary Ellen Goodman's *The Culture of Childhood*, a beginning attempt to see the world through the child's eyes. Vandewalker goes on to stress the child's need to have knowledge of other children in different cultures, predating by decades most of the application of anthropology to curriculum. For the practitioner, she claims that a series of type studies of child life among representative peoples in different stages of ethnic development would be "a veritable boon."

Turning again to evolutionary theory, she emphasizes the fact that these studies must, however, be organized so that the "significance of the whole may be realized." Stressing cultural interrelatedness, she insists that the study of single characteristics of children out of cultural context is useless; children in any cultural epoch must be studied in relation to their origins and development over time. For this reason, she charts cultural stages as theorized by Morgan. She is not fooled into believing that cultural development has been uniform and homogeneous, however, noting that all groups need not pass through all phases and concluding that "the urgency of present needs is sufficient to make the attempt at placing available data in better working form of some value, while something more fundamental is being worked out."

It is interesting that in this short article Vandewalker grasped the need for a study of the culture of childhood; the need for an organized set of studies of children, embedded in their own cultures; the need for an overarching organization of culture in historical time; the need to understand the effects of culture contact on children; and the implications in all these for the organization of curriculum. This she did at a small midwestern normal school, removed from the "prestigious" institutions of her time.

Edgar Hewett, almost a decade later, again deals with the need for pedagogy to derive its facts from anthropology: "On the clear apprehension of the relation of contributory sciences of biology, psychology, sociology, and anthropology to pedagogy depends the efficiency of the educational system." This interdisciplinary stress will continue to dominate anthropology through the decades ahead. In his article, the second in part II, Hewett reflects on the disparities between the aims of education and the values of American culture: the individualistic ideal predominates yet the teacher is trained to emphasize the interests of society. (Incongruity between cultural values is a theme later elaborated by Ruth Benedict and Margaret Mead, among others.) Deriving his ideas from Herbert Spencer, Hewett resolves the contradiction: "On the general acceptance of this fact of the identity of individual and social interests depends the happy adjustments of most of our social, economic, political, and educational problems."

Using this assumption, he claims that the aim of education is to make better cultural citizens, presumably because "the mutual interests of individual and state can best be achieved in this manner." He uses "ethnic mind," now a discredited term, to indicate the force of culture on the acts of individuals within societal groups.

Turning to cultural transmission, Hewett predates urban education by sixty years, saying "the teaching of forty children of a single race [used in the broader sense of ethnicity] is a comparatively simple problem. But the teacher in an American City school may have under her instructions representatives of half a score of ethnic divisions with ethnopsychic characteristics that are as distinctive as are their physical differences. The teacher must know that children of different cultures look upon questions of honor, morality and decency out of separate ethnic minds." Stating a fact that was then radical and is now the major thesis of urban educators, he maintains that ideas and ideals that have been rooted for ages in the cultures of individuals cannot and should not be eradicated in a generation.

However, it was not until after the decimation of Native Americans and the conquest of the Phillipines that Americans began to question their role as colonialists and cultural eradicators. This question is central to the rest of Hewett's paper. Emphasizing the cultural integrity of colonized peoples, as have other anthropologists who followed him, he speaks in their behalf: "The reservation Indian school is successful so far as its ideal is to make of the Indians better Indians. Unhappily Americanization is often thought to be education." He quotes the superintendent of Indian schools who states that the Indian looks upon the tribe or family as the primary unit while the American values most the individual; that the Indian is richest who gives most, the American who keeps most. Citing these characteristics, the administrator concludes, "against these odds the Indian schools are pitted." Hewett responds, "Might it not have been better if the Indian schools had never been *pitted against* these conditions at all, but rather, devoted to the cultivation of just what could be found in the Indian that was worthy of stimulation?!"

Turning to the Filipinos, he again takes up the cudgels in their behalf. For example, he predates the continuous controversy over language usage in the schools, questioning the value of replacing Spanish and original tribal languages with English: "Let us not inaugurate another 'century of dishonor' by malpractice on another alien race. There is really no need for haste. It is hardly time to put the Filipinos to school to us. Let us go to school to them for awhile."

Hewett reflects Boas, whose theoretical concern stressed cultural relativity; Vandewalker relies on Morgan's theory of evolution. This shift in theoretical orientation mirrors the new directions in anthropology during this time span. Although Hewett is overly caught up in geographical determinism, he nevertheless precedes by half a century the pleas for cultural integrity and for children's rights to retain and expand their own heritages in schools adapted to their own needs.

In 1928, Boas, in *Anthropology and Modern Life*, devoted a chapter to education in a book marked by historical particularism, a theoretical orientation that deplored biological, geographical, or economic determinism. Placing his emphasis on full descriptions or ethnographies of particular societies, he directed attention away from the evolutionary model so dominant in the previous century. Combining physical and cultural anthropology, Boas detailed the physical characteristics of children as related to social class, race, and ethnicity. He was predated in this effort by Marie Montessori, who in 1913 had published *Pedagogical Anthropology*, a book based on physical anthropology and medicine and applied to an analysis of slum children in Italy.

The more important portion of Boas' work derives from cultural anthropology. Working with the problem of cultural determinism, he draws on his early field work among the Eskimo, showing that a highly individualistic social life does not negate cultural restrictions that determine behavior: ". . . since all alien forms of behavior are unknown to them, it never enters into their minds that any different way of thinking and acting would be possible, and they consider themselves as perfectly free in their actions." Contrasting Eskimo and American cultures, he shows that the cultivation of religious and political values in the training of the young results in similar restrictions in courses of thought or action. He concludes that the individual freedom presumed to be fundamental to democracy is hardly the case in the actual schooling received by children. As Hewett before him, Boas pinpoints the incongruities in values and behaviors within education: "They instill automatic reactions to symbols by means of patriotic ceremonial . . . too often through the automatic reactions to the behavior of the teacher that is imitated. At the same time, they are supposed to develop mind and character of the individual child."

Moving to an analysis of cultural determinism and social class, he points to the lack of freedom in all strata, deriding the sharp distinctions between higher and lower classes and contending that those in the upper classes may, in fact, have less freedom to question cultural values because they have most to lose. To him, "the freedom from thought by convention may be less in what might be called the educated classes than in the mass of people."

Nationalism, to Boas, is the extreme of cultural determinism which he deplores: "The history of humanity points in the direction of a human ideal as opposed to a national ideal." Foreshadowing C. P. Snow's *Two Cultures and the Scientific Revolution*, he also points to the extreme occupational differentiation in industrial society, noticing the difficulty in communication created by education which is presumed to make the educated more rational. For these and a number of other reasons, Boas believes that the masses in modern city populations may be less subject to the influence of traditional teaching and less strongly attached to the past; thus they may respond more quickly to the urgent demands of the future. In this, he antedates the urban educational crises and reforms by decades. His concern for freedom from traditional thought through the demise of restrictive enculturation reaches culmination, years later, in Mead's *Culture and Commitment*. Implicit throughout Boas' thinking is the assumption that knowledge of cultural alternatives makes freedom possible and that education must incorporate such knowledge if cultural determinism is to be avoided.

By 1930, Mead summarizes, in the *Encyclopedia of Social Sciences*, a comparative analysis of primitive education, a task urged by Vandewalker almost forty years before. Mead's short synopsis follows on her ethnographies in the South Pacific, published in *Growing Up in New Guinea* and in other books and articles. Fresh from the investigation of child-rearing patterns, she is eminently qualified to begin her lifelong series of writings on anthropology and education. In the next article in part II, Mead stresses a relativistic point of view, an emphasis that will extend consistently in her works over the next forty years. Both she and other students of Boas continue to focus on the patterned wholeness of culture and on the distinctive processes of child rearing, sex-role definitions, and family functioning that lead to adult personalities associated with particular cultural themes.

In her article, Mead states that a variety of theories and practices characterize enculturation processes. These may center around respect for property, ritualistic patterns of etiquette, or any of the many themes selectively emphasized in different cultures. The social responsibilities demanded of children also vary: at one extreme children are seen as small adults with heavy duties and at the other their infancy is prolonged and their duties are light. The importance of the child's role in the community by levels of maturity is differentially evaluated as well. Sex roles may also be sharply demarcated or softly blurred.

Methods for emphasizing culturally accepted behaviors vary too. Punishment may be corporal, supernatural, or rely on shame or guilt. These methods depend, in turn, on the pace at which acquisition is expected to occur. This relates to the role of kin in socialization, the extension of the biological family, and the rankings within kinship grouping.

Clearly, systems of education in primitive societies display a fascinating set of variations. These become even more complex when societies are in contact with other cultures. Malinowski, in the last article in part II, is primarily concerned with the education of colonized peoples within the context of acculturation or cultural contact. As social changes whirled throughout the world, anthropologists became increasingly involved, not with the pristine culture untouched by external influence (if there ever was such a culture), but by the processes of reciprocal borrowing between or unilateral impositions upon groups. The concept of diffusionism was primarily concerned with the documentation of cultural "traits" and the distribution and spread of these among groups. The concept of culture contact or acculturation, in contrast, often focused on migratory or conquered groups in proximity to each other.

Bronislaw Malinowski, in South Africa in 1936, speaks within this context. In contrast to Hewett, he assumes the colonial policy will continue and that the colonized groups will remain, at least for some time, subservient. Although he can be accused of sustaining a colonial mentality, he nevertheless shows more courage than most as he expresses himself within the context of his time. His remarks are atypical of the attitudes of a number of colonialists who form his audience.

Malinowski, as Hewett before him, argues for the integrity of culture and the relative values of different cultures. But his position is not as radical as Hewett's. Malinowski's primary concern is accommodation between groups. He forces the educator to perceive that through schooling, "we not only give but we also take away. What we take away is their knowledge of their own tribal tradition, of their own moral values and of their own practical skills . . . leading to the disintegration of a primitive society because it estranges a number of individuals from the traditions still controlling the rest of the tribe." He continues with a warning: "To create a supply of coloured people educated and skilled, and at the same time to curtail by legal and social action any demand for them, leads to a very dangerous situation." Believing sheer economic necessity and not racism the cause of this state of affairs, he, nevertheless, states that the anthropologist is obliged to present the native point of view and its relevance to the well-being of both Europeans and Africans.

Malinowski begins his defense of Africans by attacking presumed genetic race differences in intelligence as measured by brain size or by intelligence tests. In this, he joins a long and bitter controversy extending over two hundred years of white academic life. He stands in the environmentalists' camp, believing that the overwhelming evidence is that the better the education, the better the product. Malinowski sees the African standing in no-man's land, between two worlds, to neither of which he fully belongs: "In short, his cultural birthright has been taken from him, and instead of it what have we given him?" Since an African education for Africans can be better obtained from the tribe, he concludes that Western schooling must prepare natives for contact with Europeans and at the same time produce the minimum of disintegration in tribal groups. To do this, Europeans must learn the indigenous systems of education: the rites of passage, the etiquette standards, the obligations and duties of kinship, the sex roles, the age grades, the ordinary lives of families. Nevertheless, he maintains that, although education is larger than schooling, educational institutions can be justified only as preparation for contact with "us"—the white colonizer.

RELATION OF ANTHROPOLOGY TO EDUCATION

There is at this time no explanatory system that approximates a theory which would encompass the logical interconnections between anthropology and education. Although a systematic set of concepts is lacking, there is increasing agreement on key linkages. Over the last forty years, anthropologists have delineated substantive areas, pinpointed concepts, and engaged in cultural analyses of education. As early as 1937, Felix Keesing published *Education in Pacific Countries*, a book arising out of a conference convened to apply anthropological knowledge to educational problems. In 1939 Lyman Bryson detailed the potential linkages between museums and schools, specifying the educational uses of archeological and cultural evidence and artifacts. Within the next two decades, Fred Eggan, Morris Opler, Theodore Brameld, Solon Kimball, and others contributed papers and books which attempted to show the relevance of anthropology to education through the application of significant cultural concepts to the learning process. In 1955 George Spindler published *Education and Culture*, a collection of papers that grew out of a conference of anthropologists and educators. His own introductory articles added to the growing agreement on the concepts basic to cultural analyses of education.

Within the last decade increasing clarity was achieved. As Thomas La Belle notes in the first article in part III, the formation of the Council on Anthropology and Education (CAE) in 1968 served to accelerate the push for more sophisticated relational linkages. However, La Belle remains within a substantive framework focusing on enculturation and schooling, reemphasizing the fact that formal education is only one form of the broader enculturation process. As others before him, he deplores the assumption that schooling is synonymous with enculturation. Noting the widely held belief that schooling provides continuity of cultural tradition, he suggests that out of formal education arise discontinuities that are patently obvious. He considers the school as the locus for cultural learning, stressing that the meaning for participants can be conveyed through an analysis of the explicit, planned objectives and activities compared with the implicit, unplanned, or even unrecognized learning that actually occurs. In this, he again follows a consistent tradition in anthropology in which cultural assumptions are often found to be recognized only partially. They form a matrix for living so pervasive as to be "only natural" to the participants, thus filtering their perceptions of the bases of their own beliefs and actions.

Cultural disparities may become readily apparent in those situations where ethnic groups directly interact. This contact forces a clarity about the meaning of daily rituals expressed in organized schemes for the "correct" use of institutionally defined time and space within schools. La Belle's interest in identifying subcultural referent groups, as they exist in varying stages of assimilation and urbanization, flows logically from his analysis of implicit and explicit learning. The classroom is the scene of much of the interaction of ethnic groups in educational institutions; thus, La Belle calls for microethnographies that detail the traditions of learning groups and trace the cultural meaning for participants. Finally, he sees the anthropologist applying his or her knowledge of cultural conflict to the processes of change. Taking a typical anthropological stance, he views bilingualism as an organizer of experience and conceptualization as a qualitative pattern of culturally expressed thought processes. Thus, individuals in culture conflict will speak and think in distinctive ways.

Solon Kimball, in contrast to La Belle, chooses one key concept, cultural transmission, as the core from which to link cultural concepts to educational processes.

As in his earlier work, he continues to translate educational problems into anthropological concepts, reaching for a new clarity in describing cultural behavior within patterned social systems.

Arguing that anthropology provides a strategic view of learning, school, and community, he points to the accumulating body of knowledge that depicts the incongruous values underpinning the transmission of culture. Educators, he believes, are less likely to perceive these inconsistencies. Structurally, he emphasizes peer groups as the filters through which the young attempt to achieve cultural integrity. And, again, he stresses the strategic anthropological understanding of this process for educators who may simply view such informal groups as intrusions into the adult-planned program.

Redefining educators' concerns in cultural terms, Kimball nevertheless sees that anthropologists themselves must integrate their overview by bringing together theories of learning, culture, organization, and social change to provide the linkages in an explanatory system that would provide logical coherence to analysis.

Alexander Moore, basing his thinking on the works of Kimball, Conrad Arensberg, and James McClelland, proceeds in part III to analyze education in urban communities by applying organization and community theories. Contrasting schools in Main Street small towns of earlier decades with those in urban centers of today, he pictures the unity of public and private worlds expressed in the Main Street schools with the disjunction between private and public worlds drawn by urban schools. The metropolitan school functions to prepare students for a public world of strangers where impersonal knowledge and personal survival skills in corporate structures are paramount objectives. To Moore, it is therefore not surprising that the school is run as an impersonal corporation. Although the explicit educational ideology masks this reality, the logic of hierarchy and the ideal of "efficiency" permeate the learning environment.

Especially for those caught in the throes of social change, these organizational structures create conditions that mitigate against agrarian migrants who are not prepared for impersonal production lines. Victims of cultural disjunctions, they come to be seen as deficient in intellectual, conceptual, verbal, and cognitive capacities. Suffering, presumably, from low self-esteem and exhibiting "limited" role repertories, they and not the system are expected to change. But the system reinforces their status, teaching them to know their place in the assembly line while they struggle against poverty in preparation for a corporate life they do not understand.

From the application of two theories to a particular form of education, we turn to the most fully developed outline of education to be produced by an anthropologist. Jules Henry, in the next article in this section, presents what is essentially the beginnings of a taxonomy. Lacking sets of logically subsumed concepts, he nevertheless characterizes educational personnel, processes, and products in a set of twelve crucial questions derived from field-work observations. Relying primarily on his research in middle-income American schools, he tries, with some success, to compare the categories cross-culturally.

Henry asks, first, on what does the educational process focus? From the large number of foci listed he suggests, as one example, that all education provides learners with a world view of their own culture. He identifies five world views that are implicitly or explicitly taught: isolate-static; communicate changing; hostile or pacific; near-distant geographical positioning of places studied; temporal position in the present, past, or future. Another focus is on the use of the mind. Here, Henry suggests that a culturally standardized perceptual universe is taught, one that requires disjunctions by a selective process acting as a filter.

Henry's second question is: How is information communicated? Sampling only a few of the many processes listed he comments on the extent to which different cultures give children tasks beyond their capacity, noting that American schools with competitive values may cause "jamming of the machine," as evidenced in blackboard paralysis. Still another example of the transmission of information deals with the significance of symbolic learning in which objects, not as single items but as components of object systems, come to take on particular importance. In this he would concur with Boas, who deplored the overemphasis on nationalistic symbols that narrow cultural alternatives for the young. A final example of processes involved in imparting information deserves considerable attention. Henry speculates on the extent to which various cultures emphasize watching, listening, and doing. His comparisons between literate and preliterate societies imply some serious problems for Western cultures in the education of their young.

The next question is straightforward: Who educates? Erroneously assuming sex-neutered education in Western cultures, he nevertheless finds sex differences. These, in turn, may relate to kin and nonkin as teachers. Considering social class and ethnicity, he concludes that, in general, the teaching group struggles to maintain and strengthen its own position. If we add sex castes and age grades to this statement, some startling implications are apparent.

Turning to the next question, Henry considers the attitude of the enculturated: How does the person being educated participate? As one example, he contrasts the boredom and resistance found among children in literate societies with the absence of these reactions in preliterate societies. The corollary question is: How do the educators participate? Although a number of the processes listed seem culturally bound to Western schooling, one, ridicule, is apparently noticeable cross-culturally. Henry then poses the interesting problem that even such consistency must be subjected to a further question: Who has the right to ridicule?

Henry's next query is typically anthropological: Are some things taught to some and not to others? He concludes that sex, age, social class, and religion all determine, in part, what one is allowed to learn. As a lesson in the problem of cultural bias that anthropologists must constantly fight against, it is interesting to note that Henry's sex-caste bias shows when he states that sex unity is sought by dividing what each sex can learn. If this were the case, racial unity would be achieved by continuing to limit blacks to menial tasks while teaching whites technical and professional skills.

These issues relate to still another question pertaining to discontinuities in the educational process. Assumptions regarding the propriety of learning at different ages seem culturally universal, but just what is learned and how soon it is learned remains a variegated phenomenon. Sex-typed learning is also discontinuous; and Henry points out that "forbidden knowledge" will probably be learned anyway, unless fantasies based on adult illusions sustain a distorted perception of cultural imperatives.

Discontinuities are related to the next question: What limits the quantity and quality of the information a learner receives from a teacher? An interesting limitation in literate cultures is the perception of time, which unduly pressures both learner and teacher. That time is money in American society creates a commodity approach to enculturation. As a final irony, Henry points to the fact that knowledge growth is always accompanied by a growth of ignorance. The implications of this statement are of far-reaching consequence for enculturation.

Every society must channel the learning process so that students attend to the acquisition of their culture. What forms of conduct control are used to shape and maintain attention? Order and discipline are differentiated by Henry. The extent to which American educators share his clarity is questionable. Discipline for the morality of decorum rather than the decency of human life may result from confusion between order and discipline.

Finally, in two last questions, Henry considers the products of education: What is the relation between the intent and the results of education? and, What are the self-conceptions that seem to be reinforced? To answer the first question we must return to the century-old anthropological question: What is the relationship between explicit and implicit culture? In his work Henry has, over several years, insightfully revealed unintended learning. For example, American children are often taught the value of competition; but this may cause them to hope for the failure of their peers—hardly a lesson in sportsmanship that teachers would explicitly espouse. In answer to the question on self-conceptions, a cultural emphasis on shame or guilt will, in part, determine the self-conceptions of learners.

From this catalog of questions and lists of empirically observed data, a large number of tentative generalizations are possible. In embryonic stages they are available in the outline presented. They have yet to be formulated in a manner that would provide cohesive linkages and lead to explanatory systems that would order logically the relation between anthropology and education.

Within the last five years, the search for adequate theories has picked up momentum. Two important symposia sponsored by the Council on Anthropology and Education have generated alternative explanatory schemes, some of which are presented in the remaining articles in this section. In the current thinking, Henry's taxonomic approach has been temporarily set aside; instead of working through the logical connections inherent in his outline, there is a move toward the postulation of generic, organizing concepts. These preliminary probes into a complicated territory begin with John D. Herzog's speculative attempt to project a model which incorporates what is known about human beings as primates. Quoting Sherwood L. Washburne, he states: "A view of traditional European education from the vantage point of the primatologist suggests that the school system is based on a series of traditional mistakes . . . . To the student of monkey behavior, schools seem grounded in ignorance of the human beings they are trying to teach . . . . Through a profound misunderstanding of the nature of primate biology, the schools reduce the most intelligent primate to a bored and alienated creature."

What generalizations from primate behavior are possible? Herzog reviews the research and delineates the following principles of primate socialization: (1) the primacy of early learning; (2) the critical function of play as the major channel for acquisition of information; (3) the importance of the social group and its geographical niche as the *actual* learning environment; (4) the central role of peers and slightly older playmates as the most influential socializers; (5) the existence of a period of freedom from adult responsibility; (6) the importance of *all-at-once* learning as a result of fortuitous or arranged intense *emotional experience*; (7) the prevalence of environmentally embedded learning and the relative paucity of direct and deliberate instruction.

Why have humans departed from these socialization processes? Herzog believes the industrialization of society makes it dangerous for children and makes children dangerous to it. Technological shifts require cheap, safe places to store young people who will learn the cognitive skills and behavioral characteristics—docility, punctuality, reliability—needed by industry. Although Herzog's is far from an integrated set of postulates, he is on the track of elements basic to a theory of cultural transmission.

In the next article, George D. Spindler traces his efforts, along with those of Louise Spindler, to discover a viable explanatory system. The omnibus approach, culminating in Jules Henry's *Outline*, is accepted because it calls attention to phenomena but rejected because it does not clarify the relations between them. Turning to socialization models, he finds their breadth too amorphous. Models attempting to incorporate cultural change and stability again orient but do not explain. The Spindlers then postulate a model of cultural compression and discontinuity to detail the points in the life cycle at which a narrowing or widening of cultural alternatives occurs. But the terms of the model are too all encompassing, making distinctions difficult. Moreover, it does not adequately deal with both macro and micro societal levels.

Faced with the thorny problem of creating a theory that applies to both individual and cultural processes, the Spindlers return to earlier work on cultural change in which multiple acculturative adaptation within individuals and communities was postulated. Discarding the earlier use of the Rorschach technique, they develop a new instrument to get at perceptions of social reality which lead to alternative courses of action. The Instrumental Activities Inventory, which combines cultural change and transmission, attempts to get at individual perceptions of societal patterns that pertain to cultural universals.

The Spindlers now propose: (1) that a cultural system operates as long as behaviors produce predictable results; (2) these behaviors are instrumental to goals associated with desired life style; (3) the relationships between activities and goals are instrumental linkages; (4) systematized, interrelated linkages constitute the core of a cultural system; (5) the cultural belief system supports the credibility of linkages; (6) the educational system maintains them by teaching what they are, how they work, why some work better than others, why some do or do not work in certain relations, and why everyone cannot have the same instrumental choices. This results in an individual cognitive structure that is a working model of the cultural system. Identity is a cathexsis with certain instrumental linkages central to presentation of self. During rapid cultural change, linkages weaken; alternatives are recognized and become creditable and eventually operable.

An alternative scheme is presented by Fred O. Gearing whose work in the Project in Ethnography in Education is presented in the next two articles that represent thinking in progress on a general theory of education. Gearing believes that a cultural system consists of an array of diverse but interlocking equivalences of meaning which are variously transacted in the recurrent encounters of group members. Cultural transmission presumably consists of such transactions, particularly those between adult and nonadult. In all encounters, interaction involves persons whose individual cognitive maps fit or do not fit in varying degrees. These mappings change during an encounter. The anthropologist's job is to determine the content of each cognitive map, the kinds of fit between maps, and the changes in them during transaction.

The content of cognitive maps includes the patterning of *setting* or situations, the categorization of perceptions in a *natural science logic*, the mapping of positions or *social identity*, and the organization of expectations, the *agenda* about how the encounter will unfold. Agenda involves the positioning of self in the course of the encounter. *Equivalence* refers to the degree of correspondence between perceptions and between predictions.

Transaction is the process by which maps change in kind and direction through communication which leads to the exchange of one boundary for another, or the creation of boundaries previously nonexistent, or the elaboration of existing boundaries. Cultural transmission primarily involves *elaboration* of the content of cognitive maps. In contrast, changes in the connections among parts, the mapping of logic, involves the *exchange* of one logic for another, i.e., Piaget's analysis of the developmental shift from concrete to abstract thought. Presumably, cultural transmission can be conceived of as predominantly elaboration of content boundaries and exchange of logical boundaries to approximate those of adults.

In his second article, Gearing states that every person moves through two or more worlds of meaning. In all these worlds, the regularly recurring events form an educational system in which the newcomer becomes an old hand. Because every person gets many educations, cultural transmission can be understood only when coexisting educational systems are comprehended. Gearing then presents concepts which presumably apply equally well to all systems, making it possible to bring seemingly different phenomena into a single explanatory system.

Gearing focuses on the information imparted in each system. To him, information is conceived of as property displayed by some and not by others. Education is the elimination of inappropriate displays of information. In dyadic and triadic transactions, each person negotiates through linguistic, paralinguistic, proxemic, and kinesic channels. These negotiations can be studied in the displays, the manifest content, and in dances, a term used to denote the synchronization of positioning which parallels displays. Dyads (pairs) can be analyzed as to identity attributes, such as race or ethnicity, which are shared or not shared. Protocols are formed out of multiple events described as routines enacted by old hands in recurring patterns of display and dance. Routines by old hands constitute a macro *equivalence* structure, a pooling of information selectively distributed. Routines between old hands and newcomers constitute a macro *transactional* structure, an arrangement of rites of passage by which newcomers are initiated.

In his theory Gearing relies on small-group interaction and interpersonal events which evidently add together in combinations to form a *cultural system*. He excludes the viability of the concept of culture and assumes that the ethos of a people can be derived from interpsychic processes. Marion L. Dobbert in the next article argues for culture as more than the sum of the parts, believing that ethos can be analyzed through general systems theory. She sees Gearing's constructs as useful as a sub-component of her own model. But to her, Gearing has created a transaction theory of information-sharing processes, not an explanation of culture transmission. Dobbert presents a complex model which accounts for several complicated sets of subsystems in which information is important only because it serves to maintain the viability of the cultural system. In her complex diagram, the structural components of culture are detailed. What seems needed is a further delineation of interconnecting lines as the *processes* which interconnect complex subsystems.

Arthur M. Harkins radically departs from the previous anthropologists in his concepts. He starts with a well-founded warning to the inexact sciences to stop emulating the physical sciences and suggests that social scientists search for new forms of sociocultural experiments in which prediction is derived from the control of *real* variables, not artificially contrived experimental manipulations. Assuming that the future and past are *now*, he believes that alternative interpretations of the past and alternative projections of the future can lead to cultural pluralization of the present, to alternative cultural presents. To Harkins, cultures are purposive cybernetic systems controlled by and controlling themselves through information flow; similarly, humans are simultaneously the products of culture and cultures are the products of humans. Cultures are, therefore, subject to design and redesign. Harkins asks, How will technology interact with cultural futures that can be conceived of in the present? He then considers three cultural scenarios that may be consciously brought into being: a fixed knowledge system, a limited learning opportunity system, or an open information system.

In contrast to Harkins, Jacquetta Hill Burnett moves away from an abstract to a concrete approach to theory. She points to the analog between ethnographic method and cultural acquisition: Anthropologists in the field must produce a model which distinguishes between acceptable and unacceptable cultural behaviors. The task for the fieldworker is similar to the child's; by inference and instruction, the researcher must acquire a comprehensive knowledge of both implicit and explicit cultural rules which guide behavior and produce appropriate actions. How the ethnographer goes about this task is the critical theoretical question. Burnett puzzles over the manner in which anthropologists code and decode another culture, and she seeks the rules by which they make logical connections in a new environment. Although there are limitations to her analogy, it is an interesting attempt to interweave theory with method.

ANTHROPOLOGICAL METHODS OF STUDYING EDUCATION

Central to anthropological investigations is field work, which involves careful descriptions or ethnographies of the cultures studied and leads eventually to controlled comparisons between and among cultural entities. Perhaps the most important contributions of anthropology to education are: first, the insistence on direct observation of human beings within their own settings; second, the demand for understanding these worlds through the perceptions of those actually living in them; third, the requirement that the researcher adapt to the worlds inhabited by the persons studied. With no imaginative stretch nor logical difficulty, it is rather simple to draw an analogy between the field worker and the educator.

This analogy may surface while reading William Whyte's article, which begins part IV. Here we watch a "hard" data scientist slowly realize the value and need for a "soft" data approach. Whyte originally intended to engage in a survey study, using questionnaires, of an Italian lower-income community in Boston. After his initial efforts, however, he found that he could "examine social structure directly through observing people in action." By analyzing multiple groups, one could reach an understanding of the social organization of a community.

Stumbling out of remote and distant "objectivity" into close but controlled "subjectivity," Whyte talks candidly of learning the meaning of field methodology as he collected his data. For him as for all anthropologists, entry into the society was his first problem. Fitting into the culture while maintaining an investigator's role is difficult at best, and impossible without cultural informants—persons who become, in competent ethnographic research, almost co-researchers on the "inside." Whyte honestly acknowledges his debt to his key informant, and notes that he had lived as a researcher in the neighborhood for eighteen months "before he knew anything." Language, whether professional jargon, ethnic dialect, Italian, or first generation American, is another problem for anthropologists. Whyte directly faced these communication problems. But, he notes, that educators in the neighborhood had not similarly adapted themselves.

Establishing trust by learning the values expressed in etiquette rules, Whyte cast aside formal interviews and listened first, instead of asking questions. Only after achieving an intelligent grasp of the culture did he begin to understand the questions that should be asked and the circumstances under which he should ask them. Dealing with lived experience, he began to realize the problems in the organization of field notes; "soft" data are rich in complexity and voluminous in quantity. Deriving generalizations from these is, of course, the ultimate problem for anyone who wishes to understand the meaning of human behavior. In Whyte's warm account may be found the anthropologist's methodological approach to understanding people.

Severyn Bruyn, in the article that follows, systematizes Whyte's personalized account. Quoting Florence Kluckhohn, the social role of observer in the field requires "conscious and systematic sharing, in so far as circumstances permit, in the life activities and on occasion, in the interests and affects of a group of persons." Enmeshed in the culture, the field worker changes with his or her experiences even while balancing both detachment and involvement. As an outsider, the anthropologist must establish a social role to provide a rationale that gives meaning to his or her presence. Within this role, the field worker is interested in the people as they are, not as the observer thinks they ought to be from a standard of his or her own. Ultimately, the observer becomes a part of the socialization procedure, learning new behaviors and standards of conduct.

Obviously, such a role could also serve as a model for educators, particularly those working with subcultural groups with which they are unfamiliar. What is not so obvious to educators or psychologists or even sociologists is the scientific justification for the field-work approach to the study of human life. Bruyn makes clear the historical bases of "inner and outer perspectives" on the nature of social scientific research. The outer perspective assumes that the study of behavior or conduct is adequate to produce knowledge about social life. The inner perspective insists that understanding can be achieved only by participating actively in the life of the observed and gaining insight through introspection. Although both perspectives are used, relative emphasis on one or the other correlates with different philosophical problems. Determinism, as applied from physical to social sciences, does not account for the fact that all factors are to some extent causes in themselves. What is cause and what is effect depends on the perspective of the viewer. Telic principles are inherent in the inner perspective because it assumes that all peoples have aims and some knowledge about the means to achieve them. Emphasis on the importance of synthesis compared to analysis also varies with perspective. In field work, identification with the people studied coupled with the search for unifying principles causes a constant interplay of logic. Field work is based on the assumption that analysis leading to cause-effect hypotheses must be preceded by synthesis derived from the integration of knowledge involved in identification with those studied.

Bruyn, after discussing problems of validity and reliability, provides minimal guides to observation in the field. These again can be used by teachers, who can readily see the relevance of such principles of participant observation in the classroom. Competent teachers probably already follow such guidelines, even though they may be unable to explicate them in a logical or scientific manner.

One of the more recent attempts to systematize field methodology is expressed by Paul Glaser and Anselm Strauss in their book *The Discovery of Grounded Theory: Strategies for Qualitative Research*. Their ideas are applied to anthropology and education by Louis M. Smith and Paul Pohland in their article in part 4. Studying computer-assisted instruction, Smith and Pohland generate theory through their observation of people in the school setting. They evaluate the usefulness of four postulates: fitness (close correspondence to the realities of the substantive areas studied); understanding (comprehension by the people being observed of the relevance to them of the data abstracted); generality (selection of categories that, while abstract, remain sensitive to the lived reality); and control (the balance achieved to reach predictions in multiconditional and changing situations).

Smith and Pohland also deal with a criticism often leveled at field workers: the presumed incapacity to generalize qualitative data from one group to another. Theoretical sampling and observer teams are urged as checks on the generalizations made. Finally, comparative analysis of groups makes it possible to detect commonalties that appear cross-culturally.

The flexibility required in field research means that constraints imposed by "preplanned, routinized, arbitrary criteria" can largely be avoided. In this connection the authors note: ". . . unless one can communicate the totality of the setting, both the "outsiders" and the "natives" have legitimate cause for questioning one's concepts, hypotheses, and theories."

Essentially, anthropologists work within a different time sequence with cycles of observation, collecting, coding, categorizing data, and theorizing interweaving throughout the entire research period. These processes alternate, feeding back on one another, leading to varied and repeated checks on generalizations *throughout* the research.

Educators and educated should be able to see the relevance to themselves of this form of research since the generalizations emerge *directly* out of their *own* situations. The quantitative research processes and products so frequently imposed on teachers and students often seem (and frequently are) remote from the actual experience in schools. It is not surprising, therefore, that such research is sometimes soundly rejected by those in schools and by parents and kin in the surrounding communities. A considerable portion of the research on black children and their families embodied in studies conducted by Jensen, Moynihan, and others sheds more light on academic ethnocentrism than on those actually involved in the enculturation process.

In contrast to these researchers, John Singleton's article discusses his research in Japanese schools which are, from his perspective, communities interacting with other communities in the city. From participant observation, formal interviews, and institutional documents, he traces the interconnections among school, family, and teacher union within the status system. Through participant observation, Japanese reliance on status differentials to obtain "contributions" from families indicates a distinctive use of social structure to support formal education. Through interviews, he discloses the cultural conflicts between union membership and Buddhist beliefs. From interactional analysis, he observes the heavy emphasis on ceremony and ritual within education. In all, he consistently shows that the flow of instruction is affected by culture contact between schools and other institutions which, as they change, determine, in part, internal operations within education.

In tracing the complex interweaving of institutional life, Singleton refuses to see the school as an isolated entity, choosing instead to research networks of role relationships within educational systems as they adapt to community changes. However, his brief narrative of techniques used to obtain information does not detail specific methodological problems.

In Jacquetta Hill Burnett's work, the next article in this section, we see an anthropologist working with two particular techniques to study the microethnography of classrooms as they exist in urban communities. In the metropolis, neighborhood and community boundaries are often hard to delineate. To surmount this problem, Burnett adapted network and event analysis to education. Researchers followed Puerto Rican and non-Puerto Rican students, both in and out of the school, through their daily routines, mapping linkages with acquaintances, friends, and kin. To obtain meaningful patterns, these egocentric networks were conceptualized as accounts of events: putting network observations into clusters in the stream of behavior provided the general contours of recurrent patterned relations among school, household, and peer groups. Burnett says that as time moves through its cycle, objects, actions, and messages interrelate to produce activities, some of which become salient, forming events. Thus networks come to be ordered by events that can be studied through people's perceptions of the purpose and significance of them. Contrastive purposes and meanings can then be compared between cultural groups to detect points of cultural conflict.

The precision of comparisons is heightened by the typology of events in terms of temporal and spatial scheduling, overlap in purpose, and inclusion or exclusion of particular participants. These characteristics may be conceived of as serial, contingent, or complex arrangements that recur on a regular or irregular basis. Some events are nonrecurrent; these too may be analyzed. Such descriptions of event types presented in terms of the time cycles in which they occur serve to detect and describe patterns in the enculturation process. Moreover, as Burnett suggests, the main advantage to researchers is their consistency of orientation in the categories used to observe educational phenomena. Thus, Burnett's work sustains the ethnographic emphasis on field work while exemplifying the current attempts to systematize observations.

In the next article in this section, Carol Talbert retains the anthropological emphasis on the longitudinal study of people in their own habitat. At the same time, she systematizes her observation of interactions as they are ecologically patterned in space and time. Blending field and experimental techniques, she observes and then methodically records the interaction of teachers and black children in kindergarten classes. Because of her longitudinal approach, she is able to discover the increase of negatively toned responses and a concomitant decrease of positive responses to children as the school year procedes. From her ecological perspective, Talbert identifies three groups of learners which she categorizes according to their peripheral placement in relation to the teacher. Combining ecological and longitudinal methods, Talbert discovers interactional consistency: if a child who enters kindergarten in September engages in minimal interaction and starts school in a peripheral position, one can predict that the same pattern of interaction and status will be found at the end of the year. Although interesting, Talbert's findings are not connected, at this time, to a particular theoretical orientation.

In contrast, Burnett, in the last article, blends careful observation with a theory of ritual behavior which she uses to identify and clarify the meaning of cyclical regularities in high school life in a small community. Although ritual is usually associated with "primitive" cultures, Burnett found that rites of passage and rites of intensification can be found in observed school events. Rituals, or the collective actions required by custom, appear in groups which arise out of age-grade status, subject matter and curriculum, and interschool sports events. Within a four-year cycle, the annual cycle is organized around ceremonial occasions which provide practice in the patterns of associational life expected of adults within American society. Burnett's findings are of practical use to educators who wish to view education from a different perspective.

APPLYING ANTHROPOLOGY TO EDUCATION

Although anthropologists have served as advisers to and staff members in educational systems, their applications in the literature are primarily concerned with curricular innovation. In the first three articles in part V, this orientation is evident. John Chilcott proposes a unification of secondary school courses through anthropology. The breadth of anthropology—cultural, physical, and archeological—is unique among intellectual disciplines today. The cultural focus on the total environment literally forces an integration of significant contributions from many different disciplines. To Chilcott, this atypical organization of anthropology provides a model for the reorganization of badly fragmented curricula.

Looking first at social science studies, Chilcott zeroes in on the most widely taught subject matter, history. To him, history emphasizes people in time; anthropology emphasizes people in time and space. History, when taught from a cultural perspective, can never disintegrate into memorized series of military, political, and religious personages and events. The anthropological emphasis on dominant cultural areas and on the *total* complex arrangements for living simply precludes a nonintegrative approach. Chilcott further argues that only a comparative analysis of *total* ways of life can provide the knowledge needed to understand the current world situation. To know the multiple patterns of human existence is to understand the place of one's own culture within the whole of life's patterns.

In the biological sciences, Chilcott claims that students are taught 10,000 of approximately 500,000 years of human development, excluding some 490,000 years of evidence. Thus the biological unity of humanity is obscured; students do not understand the biological and cultural adaptations that occurred over thousands of years. Human genetics, racial origins and characteristics, human ecology, and the material basis of culture should provide organizational linkages with the social sciences.

Even the humanities are discussed. Literature is described as divorced from oral traditions, from mythology—in short, from its connections with cultural traditions. Just as literary works of Western origin are focal in English courses, so are artistic works of musicians and artists limited to a narrow spectrum. Chilcott would see the humanities integrated with social and biological sciences in an organization that would provide the linkages necessary to perceive the whole of knowledge.

Rachel Sady reinforces Chilcott's conclusions regarding history as it is currently taught. Analyzing the content of widely used "world" history textbooks, she questions *whose* world is taught? She concludes that the texts distort history, that the titles of the book are actually misleading:

> A typical world history starts off with the birth of the earth, skips quickly through the beginnings of life, and then goes on to discuss early man and the

development of early civilizations. Once Greece is reached, the chapters march on with Western civilization, and the rest of the world is held in abeyance until "discovered" by Europeans, of course. In brief, the main content of a typical text follows one life-line of Western civilization.

As previously obscure cultures demand a place in the councils of nations, historians engage in patching operations to include non-Western societies. Lacking anthropological knowledge, these patches are unseamed even in the definition of culture. Culture is the "total way of life of a people" and history is, in anthropological terms, a study of the forms and changes in how people act, value, and judge their existence. But to the historians, culture, even if correctly defined initially, is eventually used to mean the cultivated artistic or intellectual products or lives of people: "We are not asked to admire whole cultures, we are asked to admire the 'culture' as fine arts."

When this basic understanding is absent, it is not surprising that culture is conceived of as precivilization. Nor is it surprising to find that there is no differentiation between ideal culture, life as it is supposed to be lived, and actual culture, life as it is daily lived. As a consequence, minority groups receive stereotypic treatment, with ethnocentric attitudes, even though well-intended, apparent. Similarly, "progress" toward a better life based on technological efficiency is a basic cultural bias. Nowhere is there a reconciliation between destructive wars and peaceful progress in "advanced" civilizations. Instead a part of Western culture is generalized to the whole. Cultural change must inevitably suffer from superficiality, with innovation, diffusion, recasting, and integration of borrowed elements absent. Descriptions of changes, but not the processes of change, abound.

Turning to science curriculum, Francis Dart and Panna Lal Pradhan shift emphasis from materials to the minds of those receiving material. They are particularly concerned with the wholesale imposition of the Western either-or logic of science on students in developing countries: ". . . the teaching of science is singularly insensitive to the intellectual environment of the student." Studying indigenous concepts of cause and effect among ethnic groups in Nepal, they ask: How does the student *experience* natural phenomena? What do they see controlling or manipulating these? What do they believe are the origins of their knowledge?

Although some variation is found, there is considerable overlap among students in tribal groups in their dualistic acceptance of *both* folk-oriented and school-oriented knowledge. The "real world" is thus interpreted with presumably contradictory explanations. Knowledge is seen by many as a closed body of information which the authors try to explain by reference to rote-memorization techniques prevalent in schools. One can argue that cause-effect can, in fact may, move in the opposite direction, with schools reflecting world views of knowledge. Similarly, the authors acknowledge the students' understanding of native technology and the abstractions inherent within usage. But they do not see their own biases when discussing the presumably "nonrational" cognition of students. Nevertheless, they point to a useful conclusion: the degree of stress in the acculturation of the young in non-Western societies will decrease if the science curriculum is organized with respect for the indigenous perceptions of reality with particular reference to dualistic conceptions of cause and effect.

We turn now to efforts of anthropologists to present nonbiased world views to students and teachers. For three years, Paul Bohannon and his associates taught an experimental anthropology course for ninth graders. Surprisingly, they adopted the school rituals with little change in timing or procedures; for example, grades were given on notes taken from lectures. They even trained the students to outline notes. Thus, curricular innovation is reported since it is the central experimental change. As might be expected, the course is interdisciplinary in content. Furthermore, in keeping with the inductive approach, ethnographic studies are introduced first and theories are discussed on demand of students as they express the need for explanation and chronological organization. Moving to human origins, the stress on increasing complexity and specialization in civilized cultures offsets the student tendency to perceive preliterate cultures as earlier, simpler versions of their own culture. The purposeful push away from ethnocentrism continues as they move to a comparative study of non-Western civilizations.

The investigators repeatedly note the student proclivity for adult materials and their rejection of watered-down anthropological sources. Mary Ellen Goodman explicates the American tendency to underrate the intellectual capacities of children. Bohannon seems to support this analysis but explains it by saying that the students were creating techniques for living as adults through their study of multiple cultures. In concluding comments, the researchers turn their attention to training teachers, finding greater resistance among competent teachers who simply want to enrich already successful courses. The obvious impossibility of "patching" is clear. The solution, however, is again a typically American one: extend the length of training.

Elizabeth Eddy is one of the few anthropologists who has written specifically on teacher education and anthropology. Focusing on an issue that is peripheral in Bohannon's report, she asks two questions in her article: What areas of anthropology are most relevant? and, How is anthropology, often derived from preliterate cultures, to be presented as significant to students in modern technological society? To deal with these questions is difficult because of the stumbling blocks inherent in the educational systems: the middle-class focus on the individual out of cultural context, the factory model with stimulus-response learning theory as the process of acquisition, the tendency to select research studies congruent with prevailing practice, and the professional provincialism of educators who follow educational folklore and tradition. Unable to provide complete answers to her questions at this time, she does, however, suggest that the outsider's view of local educational worlds may provide a basis for decisions as to what is to be taught in the most relevant manner.

Margaret Mead broadens Eddy's perspective, considering the role of anthropology in the liberal education of university students in all areas of training. Defining anthropology as a uniquely situated discipline, she sees it as a humanity, a social science, a biological science, a historical discipline—in brief, the essence of liberal education, peculiarly fitted to the task of integrating diverse knowledge. Education for the future must deal with gaps between understanding the past, present, and future; between research and statemanship; between science and art; between knowledge of things in contrast to people; between increasing awareness of the external world and decreasing awareness of the inner world; between ethnocentric, narrow racial and class identities compared with membership in one species. To bridge these gaps, according to Mead, requires the field experience that provides the possibility of integration:

> Along with this integrative, concrete, experimental training, there go certain basic assumptions: the psychic unity of mankind, as one species, with the expectation that because man is one species, all forms of his cultural behavior must have been invented or borrowed; the recognition that all cultures, as systems of learned behavior within which groups have been able to reproduce and protect themselves over several generations must be accorded a basic equal dignity; the insistence that no behavior, no item, no artifact, can be understood except in a complete ecological context; the expectation that in order to behave like an anthropologist one must be prepared to "go into the field."

To Mead, anthropologists are not preoccupied with whether their work looks and sounds like "science." Field work focuses attention on disciplined awareness of all of life as research matter, the complexity of which impels one to search for the meaning of even the smallest, seemingly incidental, moments of life. The educated person must know the shape of knowledge, the imprint of the whole, regardless of the details retained. To her, teachers can learn, at least, to understand the integration of human life on earth, the contours of which give patterned meaning to fragmented facts. Whether applied anthropology can also be grasped by undergraduates remains for Mead an unanswered question. Thus we must return to Eddy's two questions to find an answer. Optimistically, Mead concludes: ". . . the anthropologist does not say: 'We do not know,' but rather we do not know *yet.*'"

In anthropology and education we are beginning the adventure into the application of ideas which may spark a new perception of what enculturation is all about. We are beginning to know some things; others we do not know *yet.*

NOTES

1. John Locke, *An Essay Concerning Human Understanding* (Oxford: Clarendon Press, 1894), p. 122.
2. Claude Helvetius, *On Man* (Paris: Mme Ve lepetit, 1818), p. 71.
3. Jacques Turgot, *Plan for Two Discourses on Universal History* (Paris: Guillaumin, 1844), p. 627.
4. For an analysis of dialectical materialism as it relates to anthropology, see chapter 8 in Marvin Harris, *The Rise of Anthropological Theory* (New York: Thomas Y. Crowell, 1968).
5. Edward B. Tylor, *Primitive Culture* (London: J. Murray, 1871), I: 1.
6. George F. Kneller, *Educational Anthropology* (New York: John Wiley, 1965), p. 4.

Part II

The Historical Development of Anthropology and Education

1 / Some Demands of Education upon Anthropology

Nina C. Vandewalker

The current emphasis upon the genetic method of study has focused attention upon many subjects that would otherwise have but a limited interest. As an end in itself, anthropology is of interest to the few; as a means of interpreting other sciences, an acquaintance with its leading facts and principles is indispensable to the many. But even from the standpoint of means the circle of interest is widening. Heretofore the genesis of industries or institutions has been studied mainly for the purpose of gaining an insight into the product of development; with the progress of analytical thought the emphasis of interest is placed upon the process, as a means of gaining principles of interpretation. As a result, anthropology has come to have a significance for lines of thought upon which it was formerly thought to have but little bearing.

Until recently, education has run in the grooves of tradition, but the past twenty-five years have seen the breaking up of old ideals and methods, and an attempt to reconstruct both anew, not only on the basis of psychology and ethics, but on that of the social sciences as well. The emphasis on the social aspects of education is a marked feature of the present time. But the consideration of education from this broader standpoint demands a broader basis of tributary sciences, both for the building up of scientific pedagogy, and for the practical administration of educational affairs. As a social institution, the school cannot be efficiently directed without a knowledge of social agencies in general, nor can education as a social process be effectively furthered without an insight into the nature of the general processes of development. Hence sociology has become a necessary factor in the teacher's equipment.

But if education thus looks to sociology for insight, it recognizes that sociology itself finds that insight in no small degree in anthropology, and that many questions of both practical and theoretical import can only be solved, if solved at all, by the help of that science. The question of parallelism between the development of the individual and that of the race, with the consequences assumed by the culture epoch theory that such a parallelism must determine the sequence of thought in the school curriculum; the extent and character of the recapitulation of race experiences and interests in the individual; the relation of motor activity to intellectual development in the individual and in the race, with its consequences for education; the function of play in development, and its bearing upon the educational process— all these must be considered from the anthropological standpoint as well as from the psychological, as has been the case hitherto. From the practical side, also, anthropology is coming to have an increasing significance for education, both directly and indirectly.

That the present status of anthropological science is such as to furnish pedagogy the needed assistance will hardly be claimed. Pedagogy needs many anthropological data not yet obtained; it needs also principles of interpretation which must be derived from those facts organized in such a way as to yield their pedagogical significance. It may be claimed that the science itself is not yet sufficiently organized to furnish interpretive principles, but as long as the interest is focused on facts only, this will remain so. It is true that interpretation must be based on a broad foundation of facts, but the mere accumulation of data is insufficient. That observation and interpretation are mutually interpretive is a recognized principle in modern psychology. Its application to anthropological investigation has not been sufficiently recognized. Are the anthropological data insufficient to give an insight into the different phases of human development? The organization of those thus far obtained into a working body of knowledge will hasten their accumulation.

It is evident that the value of anthropological data to any science seeking the aid that anthropology can give will depend on the organization of the data from the standpoint of the science that seeks it. The facts of anthropology have received synthetic treatment from many standpoints, those of social and industrial development in particular. The syntheses made by Morgan, Spencer, Ward, Giddings, and others are of great value to all, but to sociology in particular, because written on the basis of a sociological interest. But while such a synthesis is fundamental, and hence of general value to education, a further synthesis is needed, within the organization already effected, of such data as have a direct bearing upon education. What has been done meets a general need; the specific need remains to be met by a synthesis of anthropological data from the educational standpoint so arranged as to show their educational significance. To indicate what these specific needs are, with some suggestions as to how they may be met, as a result of personal experience in directing elementary school work, is the purpose of this paper.

Thus far, anthropological investigation has been confined almost wholly to the phenomena of adult life, the child in race history being left practically out of consideration. Where child life has received any attention it has been in connection with some phase of adult life, such as the status of woman, or tribal customs, and but seldom from an interest in the facts of child life in themselves. Since the adult in the early stages of race development is in many respects comparable to a child, and the general progress from savagery to civilization has been a progress from mental and moral infancy to maturity, the facts of adult life among the people in the different ethnic stages are of great value to the educator, as a means of giving an insight both into the nature of developmental processes, and into the natural sequence of interests and intellectual and emotional attitudes. A brief but reliable history of race development from the educational standpoint is greatly needed.

But this is not enough for educational purposes. Childhood has usually been considered as something static—the same in savagery and in civilization. But a little reflection will show that the activities and psychical processes of the primitive child must have been as much simpler than those of the child of modern culture as the activities and processes of the adult in savagery were simpler than those of a Gladstone or an Edison, the product of modern civilization. If there is any reason, then, for studying the psychical evolution of man from the standpoint of anthropological data, there is as good a reason for studying the evolution of childhood. This is true on the external as well as on the internal side. A study of the characteristics, the status, and the conditions of child life, in its relations to the sum of the life activities, during the successive stages of race development—an anthropological history of childhood, in short, would be an invaluable contribution to modern educational literature, giving an insight into the principles underlying the educational process, and throwing light on development in general. If the prolongation of the period of infancy has been the means of raising man from the infancy of primitive life to the maturity of civilization, is not such a study of childhood during the steps in the process worthy of the study of mankind? Chamberlin says: "The position of the child in the march of civilization, and the influence of the child idea upon sociology, mythology, language, and religion, would be a valuable contribution to modern thought, for the touch of the child is upon them all, and the debt of humanity to little children has not yet been told."

This need from the side of theoretical pedagogy suggests the practical necessities of the schoolroom along similar lines. Every teacher knows that the interest of children is in no way so effectively aroused as through the consideration of other children. Does it seem difficult to teach the geography of South America, or China, or Africa in a vital way? Approach these countries through the avenue of their child life, and a live interest will not be lacking. This shows why such books as *Seven Little Sisters, Children of the Cold, Ten Boys from Long Ago to Now*, and *Hiawatha's Childhood* are educational classics, and perennially interesting, though the correctness of the data may be questioned in some instances. But what applies to geography applies equally to other lines. Many schools have adopted the culture-epoch theory in a modified form, as a basis of the curriculum, emphasizing the industrial and artistic activities in the race epochs instead of confining the attention to the literary products of the epochs only. The teachers who are working out these new and original methods are greatly handicapped by the lack of available data concerning the periods in question, even from the standpoint of adult activities. To such, an anthropological history of childhood, or a series of type studies of child life among representative peoples in the different stages of race development, would be a veritable boon. At present the teacher who is trying to work on such original lines must either be a specialist in anthropology, which is hardly likely, or she must manufacture facts in the absence of reliable data.

But the organization of anthropological material would have a value more far-reaching still. Sociology and economics, until recently confined to the college or the university, are claiming a place in the curriculum of the secondary schools. But there is no reason whatever why a foundation of the most practical character for both sociology and economics should not be laid in the elementary school, by means of the lines of work suggested. Type studies of race development at its different stages, with emphasis on the social and industrial activities, would furnish the best possible means of interpreting modern conditions, and of appreciating the elements of value in social and industrial relations. With the teacher properly equipped, much could be done in the grammar schools, with but little additional effort, that must at present remain undone. Were the facts so organized as to be accessible to the pupils through reading and reference work, even more could be accomplished. The needs may thus be grouped under three heads—those of the educational specialist who needs a scientific treatment from the standpoint of principles; those of the intelligent teacher who needs reliable and available data; and those of the pupil who needs suggestive and interesting reading matter that will have a permanent value.

Several attempts to collect anthropological material relating to child life have been made within the last few years, those of Ploss and Chamberlin being best known. Many isolated facts could also be collected from the general literature of the subject. The material already collected needs reorganization, however, before it can yield its highest value for educational purposes. The usual method of investigation has been to select some one phase of life process, some one activity or relation, and trace it from its genesis in race history to its maturity at the present time. This method has its value from the standpoint of results and is a necessary stage in the evolution of a completed method. The life process is a unity which, like any other, must be analyzed, the attention being focused successively upon its different elements, in order that the significance of the whole may be realized. But unless the unity as such be kept in mind, with the purpose it is to serve as a means to further insight, there is danger of getting lost in the analysis. Thus far the emphasis in anthropological investigation has been placed on tracing the different elements in the life process one by one, from their genesis to their present state, to the neglect of the return movement, the placing these elements in their true relation to each other and to the ethnic periods. Hence the elements in question have been suspended in a vacuum, and have not been serviceable, since they lacked relations. For educational purposes a cross section of any one ethnic period showing all the life activities in their relations would serve a better purpose than a longitudinal section showing one activity during many. The plan pursued isolates the facts by separating them from their many relations, and thus destroys their value. The method suggested would group the available facts of a given period and, by placing them in their natural setting, would give them a double significance. The work done thus far has been the first stage in a complete method, but the second must follow closely upon the first, both for the sake of the science itself as well as for those to which it is tributary. The same criticism may be made on much of the work in child study. The study of many children with reference to a single characteristic, isolated from its setting in heredity and environment, is the first stage in a complete method. The study of all the characteristics of one period in child life, in their natural relations, is its necessary completion. The child-study movement is doing much to make a future history of childhood from the anthropological standpoint possible, but, like anthropology itself, it needs to work from the synthetic standpoint if its results are to be of the highest value for educational purposes.

As a possible basis for the organization needed, the accompanying chart of anthropological development (see Fig. 1.1) is suggested, as a framework in which to place material already available. To the writer its value is twofold. It gives the general facts of race development in a convenient form, and in so doing it affords a basis for comparing the development of the race with that of the child at the present time, from the standpoint of activities and processes. It thus meets, in a slight degree, one of the needs of the present. The ultimate purpose of its construction, however, was to suggest a principle on the basis of which the facts of child life might be organized, and thus become available for educational purposes. With the general view which the chart affords continually in mind, the facts of child life will be constantly seen in their true relation to the social and industrial conditions of the period in which they occur. Their true setting in the activities and interests of the period being obtained, as well as their sequence in culture history, true interpretation becomes possible.

Since the framework is of some importance if the results are to have validity, it demands further consideration. No credit for originality is claimed either as to form or organization. The general form was suggested by the chart of social organization in Small and Vincent's *Introduction to the Study of Society*. The division into stages is that adopted by Morgan, and that of masculine and feminine activities that suggested by Mason. It is a graphic representation, for convenient reference, of data already collected and in the relations they occupy in the works of the authors mentioned.

Any schematic representation of this character is open to criticism on the basis of inadequacy. The difficulty of representing the facts of geological, paleontological, or anthropological development progressively is that the successive stages are seldom if ever found in nature in their true relations, that many gaps occur for which the missing links cannot be found, and hence the whole is but a skillful piece of patchwork which may mislead instead of instruct. This is particularly true of anthropological data, since customs and institutions may disappear as the result of conquest or imitation of other forms. Visualization has a value, however, in spite of the possibilities of error, and such value is relied upon in the construction here presented.

Objections are usually made to the drawing of distinct dividing lines between the periods of development, but such lines must be understood as indicating general

Activities	PERIOD OF SAVAGERY — LOWEST STATUS	PERIOD OF SAVAGERY — MIDDLE STATUS	PERIOD OF SAVAGERY — UPPER STATUS	PERIOD OF BARBARISM — LOWEST STATUS	PERIOD OF BARBARISM — MIDDLE STATUS	PERIOD OF BARBARISM — UPPER STATUS	CIVILIZATION
Organization of Domestic, Economic, Educational, and Religious Activities.							
4. Shelter.	Trees.	caves, temporary huts.	Huts and wigwams in clusters.	Communal houses and village stockades.	Houses of adobe and stone. Lake dwellings.	Houses of durable material.	Cities, with gates and battlements. Temple architecture.
3. Clothing.	Leaves, bark, grasses, skins	Means—bone needles, knives, scrapers.		fur, hair, wool, tanned deer skin, cotton, linen.		Finger weaving, spinning, etc. Loom with shuttle.	
2. Care of Children.	Education by imitation, cooperation.			Instruction at puberty in traditions of group and environment.	Organization of schools with rites and ceremonies.		
Feminine Activities.							
1. Preparation of Food.		Means—hot stones, shell. Roasting, boiling, drying, smoking of fish and game.	spoons, knives, horn implements,	Making pottery, pottery vessels. Boiling in kettles, baking.	Decoration of articles made. weaving baskets and other necessary articles. Native cereals—gathering and storing, grinding, cooking, etc. Planting, cultivating domesticated plants. Caring for milk, making cheese, etc.		
Social Organization requiring both sexes.							
Form of Family.	Monosyllabic language. Social activity unorganized and undifferentiated.	Fetish worship. Syllabic language. Family and clan not fully differentiated.	Totem worship. Discontinuous monogamy. Gentile organization of society.	Nature and ancestor worship. Patriarchal organization of society.	Organization of priesthood. Monotheism. Inflected language. Patriarchal family.	Monogamic language. Monogamic family.	Property organization of society.
Masculine Activities.							
1. Getting of Food.	Means—clubs, fish, game. Fruit, roots, nuts,		Bow and arrow. spears, hooks, harpoons, nets, traps.	implements—hammers, arrows, saws, drills. cereals, milk, and other animal products.			
2. Defense.		Means—clubs, stones, spears. Defense against animals and human enemies.	Bow and arrow, shield, sling, wooden sword.	Bow and arrow, shield, sling, wooden sword.		Metal plate armor,	Iron implements, sword of iron.
Organization of Military, Judicial, Political, and Commercial Activities.							
3. Trade and Transportation.		Barter of crude materials,	Means of transportation, canoes of	Backs of women and animals, sledges. bark and tree trunks. implements, pemmican, products of fields and herds.	Medium of exchange, wampum, Native copper, bronze, etc.		Ships, wagons, chariots. cattle, etc.
Form of Life and Representative Peoples.	Life arboreal, absorbed in food process. No people found in this state during historic times.	Life wandering, over larger area. Some surplus for advance. Australians and Polynesians, when discovered.	Hunting life, with larger surplus. Athapasean Indians of Hudson Bay, when discovered.	Life becoming organized, and settled. Indian tribes east of the Mississippi, when discovered.	Village Indians of Mexico, New Mexico, Central America, and Peru. Ancient Britons in the Eastern Hemisphere.		Grecian tribes of the Homeric Age; Italian tribes before the founding of Rome; Germanic tribes of the time of Caesar.

Discovery of Fire. · Invention of Bow. · Invention of Pottery. · Domestication of Plants and Animals. Stone and Adobe Houses. · Smelting of Iron. · Invention of Phonetic Alphabet.

FIGURE 1.1 Chart of Anthropological Development.

transitions only. Development has not been uniform, and while certain activities, modes of life, and materials may have predominated in one period, these either persisted with diminished emphasis into the next, or they were gradually transformed into related ones, continuing in connection with the new forms upon which the emphasis is placed.

A similar criticism is likely to be made on the division of labor on the basis of sex. This division holds in general for the prehistoric period, though there were many lines in which both sexes shared, the predominance being, however, on the one side or the other. Thus, while man was the main food producer, woman shared in this to some degree, her activities being especially connected with the vegetable kingdom. Since man's activities along this line were connected mainly with the animal kingdom, the particular habitat, as predominantly animal or vegetable, determined largely the male or female preponderance in procuring the food supply. So, too, man shared in the feminine activities of preparing food and providing shelter, and in the education of the boys when the proper age was reached. It is worthy of note that the feminine activities passed over into the hands of men as they became organized, in the later stages of development. The arts, language, and religion, on the other hand, had a social, not a sex origin.

In addition to the points mentioned it must be kept in mind that race development has not been uniform and homogeneous, and that progress from cultural infancy to the maturity of civilization cannot be traced in any one people. Many peoples are still in their earliest or savage state; others have progressed into some phase of barbarism, while relatively few have attained cultural maturity. Hence, at any historic period peoples could have been found in many or all of these stages, with infinite gradations between. Thus the North American Indians, when discovered, represented in different localities the status of savagery, and two distinct subdivisions of the state of barbarism. It must also be remembered that, while there has been a general similarity in the modes of life and the development of institutions among the peoples that have passed through the stages in question, there has by no means been uniformity. Thus the hunting, the pastoral, and the agricultural stages are generally considered as necessarily successive with all peoples that have passed beyond them. But the North American Indians who reached the borderland of civilization passed immediately from the hunting to the agricultural stage, since the American continent contained no animals suited to domestication. In Europe and Asia, on the contrary, where all the animals that have been domesticated were found, the pastoral period was prolonged and continued in connection with the agricultural until civilization was attained. Hence, if a view of the whole process of development is desired, representative peoples from the different ethnic periods must be selected for purposes of study.

It may be claimed that on this basis no ultimate principles of interpretation can be derived, since it is impossible to determine what is due to the peculiar genuis of a people, and what to universal characteristics. Thus the development of the Hebrews throws but little light on that of the Greeks, and that of the American races has undoubtedly as little in common with that of European stocks as have the first-mentioned races. The force of this argument is not denied, but the value of accurate data concerning the life activities of each is not thereby lessened. It must be remembered that no ultimate value is claimed for the synthesis suggested by the authors who furnish the data. The urgency of present needs is sufficient to make the attempt at placing available data in better working form of some value, while something more fundamental is being worked out.

While the purpose in making the chart was that mentioned above, the mere arrangement of the facts of anthropological development has suggested a new interpretation of the culture-epoch theory, the correspondence between the stages in the development of the individual and the three great stages in the development of the race being too significant to escape attention. The fundamental interests in both the individual and the race grow out of the food process; hence the fundamental activities are determined by these fundamental needs. The intellectual and moral life assumes organized form on the basis of the activities in question, both in the individual and in the race. A comparison between the individual and the race from the intellectual side only, a passing from sense perception to reason, lacks foundation without a consideration of the social and industrial life of which it is the outgrowth. The parallelism frequently traced on the moral side, from blind impulse to moral freedom, is likewise of little value when taken out of its setting in the whole life process. It is because the culture-epoch theory in its current form is confined to the historic peoples only, neglecting the ages of accomplishment that lay back of these, and in whose light the historic peoples must be interpreted, and because the whole industrial and, to a great extent, the social development is ignored, and that the theory is inadequate to the purposes it should serve. By the adoption of the theory from the anthropological standpoint both objections would be met. The working out of the theory on the anthropological basis will be given in a future paper.

The services that anthropology can render the educational cause are thus many and varied. Education can no longer be isolated; it is identifying itself more and more closely with the general movements of the time. In this movement anthropology is destined to play an increasingly important part. If the peculiar character of the present educational need will in any degree stimulate anthropological research; if it can give it a new direction and focus; if it can create a wider interest in it on the part of the general public, it can in part repay the services it hopes to receive at the hands of that science.

2 / Ethnic Factors in Education
Edgar L. Hewett

The eminent place accorded education in our social organization makes imperative the closest investigation of every factor in educational practice. Instruction is a scientific work of the highest order. Pedagogy has no special body of facts or phenomena of its own as material for investigation; it depends for its structure on the conclusions of contributory sciences. Its "sphere of influence" being coextensive with all human welfare, no necessity exists for examining limits, but emphasis must constantly be placed on organization. On the clear apprehension of the relation of the contributory sciences of biology, psychology, sociology, and anthropology to pedagogy depends the efficiency of the educational system.

Before proceeding to the direct investigation of the subject announced in the title, it will be necessary to consider briefly the results of the long discussion of the aims of education. The keen analysis to which this question has been subjected in recent years does not disclose any real antagonism between the individual and the social aims. In practice in American schools the individualistic ideal is unquestionably predominant, notwithstanding the fact that in the great majority of our schools for the training of teachers, emphasis is placed on the interest of society, and the normal school that gives no place to the social sciences in pedagogical training is not in the professional class. A just conception of the relation between the individual and society affords no ground for placing especial emphasis on the interests of either.

In every normal individual of any stage of culture there exists a feeling that the activities which yield him the greatest satisfaction are those which involve the interests of his fellow men. He finds no happiness in habitual isolation. For the pleasure of association with his kind he submits to the social will. In primitive stages of culture he unconsciously accepts the esthetic, the economic, the social, the religious traditions of his tribe. In civilized society he does not surrender his consciousness to the group. He examines and criticizes social conditions; seeks to accelerate or retard social progress; strives to establish, annul, or modify customs and beliefs; pits his individual reasonings against public motives, opinions, and acts; yet withal submits to what society sanctions. But while apparently emphasizing the interests of society, he knows that society is the great efficient agent for benefitting, developing, perfecting himself. Its interests are his interests. In the self-renunciation incident to social service he realizes his highest happiness and highest individual perfection. His individualization and his socialization proceed simultaneously by like processes. Antagonism to the social order carried to the extent of destructiveness is an aberrant condition. On the general acceptance of this fact of the identity of individual and social interests depends the happy adjustments of most of our social, economic, political, and educational problems.

Since an individual aim in education, standing for the highest development of the powers of the one, and a social aim, emphasizing the interests of the many, proceed by simultaneous and similar processes to a common end, it is not necessary to accept any dictum as to the educational aim. It is individual, social, ethnical. A sound, commonplace aim to keep in view in educating Americans is *to make better Americans*; in educating Indians *to make better Indians*; in educating Filipinos *to make better Filipinos*; and it should especially be noted that when the term is applied to the process of improving any race or group or individual that is not formally praying to be absorbed into the citizenship of the United States, it in no sense implies *to Americanize*.

The phenomena of the four sciences previously mentioned as contributing data for the scientific study of education are so interdependent that they cannot be definitely separated. The purpose of this paper is to examine anthropological facts and conditions which are vital in the development of the American system of public education. But I am aware that some of the material chosen for consideration may justly be claimed to be in the domain of psychology, and all of it in sociology. This delightful elasticity and inclusiveness of our several sciences is not altogether regrettable. The crossfire to which a proposition that falls within these overlapping spheres of influence is subjected, compels a certain agility and alertness not incident to the study of closely isolated and definitely limited sciences.

It is possible that the use made in this paper of the term "ethnic mind" may not be acceptable to experimental psychologists. While not in accord with the extreme views of many European scholars on this subject, I accept the opinions of Wundt and Brinton that ethnic psychology is a valid science—a branch of the great unmapped field of anthropology that awaits close investigation. The hypothesis of an ethnic mind is most serviceable in the study of culture history, constructive sociology, and race pedagogy. Any needed justification of its use will, I hope, be accomplished as we examine causes and conditions of ethnic development.

It is a trite saying that "the teacher must understand human nature" but we do not always consider the vast significance of that requirement. It presupposes all the usually expected knowledge of man as an individual, with all his physiologic and psychic characters and the immediate effect thereon of meterologic and dietetic influences. It demands an understanding of the modifications affected by society on individual psychic states. Furthermore, it requires a comprehension of the environmental influences that have worked through the ages to affect man's distribution over the globe, to control his occupations and social organization, and to compel the thoughts which dominated his primitive life and fixed in every group of savage men a unified, collective, psychic state. The individual was a cipher. He lived, worked, thought, prayed as did his tribe. Nature was as regardless of the individual in humanity as in the lower life forms. An ethnic mind, an ethnic character, a race of men was the goal. Fixed environmental conditions compelled men to certain activities, to certain beliefs and customs, equally coercive whether true or false, good or bad. Such was the fatalistic yet effective discipline by which nature shaped men into ethnic groups, by virtue of which we have Hun or Gaul, or Apache or Hopi. Such was the origin of ethnic mind—"a blind, unreasoning, natural force" that rules primitive men absolutely and to a marked degree dominates the acts of civilized nations. The investigation of these phenomena is the province of anthropology; the determination of their use in education is the province of pedagogy.

The teaching of forty children of a single race is a comparatively simple problem. But the teacher in an American city school may have under her instruction representatives of half a score of ethnic divisions with ethno-psychic characteristics that are as distinctive as are their physical differences. The work of the teacher is to Americanize all these elements; to inculcate our best ideals of personal and civic righteousness; to eradicate as far as possible ideals that are foreign or adverse to our own. This is a complex process. The street does its part. The general exercises of school and class advance the unifying process. That day is lost in which the teacher finds no occasion for upholding some ideal of lofty patriotism, of civic virtue, of family life, of personal honor. But daily the necessity arises for dealing directly with individuals who fail to come under the influence of the collective spirit, with whom lawlessness (which may be a misunderstanding of our social order) or incipient crime (which may be but lack of comprehension of our ideals of decency) and the disasters incident to conflict with law or prevailing ethnical sense, seem inevitable. The teacher must know that Italian and Bohemian, and Celt and Hebrew, and Anglo-Saxon and African look upon questions of honor, morality, and decency out of separate ethnic minds under the coercion of centuries of fixed racial customs and ideals. What is to us criminal tendency may be but a survival of a custom which, in the view of a more primitive race, was a strictly moral act. Much that we call evil, malevolent, was in primitive mind altogether beneficent. What is to us an indecent act is often in primitive practice a religious rite. A case of stubborn resistance to a necessary truth may be a matter of racial difference of opinion. So countless perplexing problems of the teacher root in ethnic mind and can be solved only when the ethnic factors in the equation are duly considered and the inheritance from savagery or foreign national life is given its proper value.

Before considering further the educational aspects of the subject, let us inquire into some fundamental causes of static racial conditions. As previously indicated in this paper this must be primarily an inquiry into the influence of physiographic environment on the human mind.

Dr. Edwin G. Dexter has shown, in an eminent contribution to psychological knowledge, the influence of definite meteorological conditions on mental states. These researches pertain to the immediate psychic response to weather influences, and the results are such as to suggest an important application in the study of racial character development under the influence of fixed climatic conditions. I believe that Dexter's method might be extended to the field of racial psychology with excellent results.

Ample facilities exist for the study of this subject by direct observational methods. We may select one element of human nature that is practically universal, namely, the religious element, and see how science accounts for its variations. Race religion is almost as persistent as race physiology. All people have beliefs concerning the supernormal. Speaking in a very general sense, these beliefs constitute their religion. It is a peculiarly fruitful field of study, with abundance of material for investigation. The religious ideas of primitive men are preserved in myths, in symbolic ornament, in pictography in its various forms, in games, the interpretation of which calls for the keenest insight of which the anthropologist is capable. The system of religious thoughts of every primitive tribe is embodied in ritual which can be studied by direct observation.

A remarkable series of field studies on the Hopi Indians of Arizona by Dr. J. Walter Fewkes of the Bureau of American Ethnology, extending over a period of twelve years, the results of which are embraced in numerous contributions, afford such a comprehensive exposition of the evolution of the religion of one primitive tribe in response to climatic influence that, with his kind permission, I quote here at some length his own words on the subject:

> In physical features this province [Tusayan] is a part of the great arid zone of the Rocky mountains. On all sides it is isolated by a dreary extent of mountains, mesas, and arid plains about 6,000 feet above the level of the sea. No permanent streams of water refresh these parched canyons or fields, and the surroundings of this isolated tribe, organic and inorganic, belong to those characteristic of desert environment. The rains are limited in quantity—liable to fail at planting time. Springs of permanent water are small and weak. . . . Uncompromising as was the soil for agriculture, the resources of the hunter were much less, and in this region man was forced to become an agriculturist. . . . He adopted the life which environment dictated, and accepting things as they were, worked out his culture on the only possible lines of development.
>
> Accepting the inevitable, man's ritual became a mirror of that part of his environment which most intimately affected his necessities. The irregularity of the rains, and the possibility that the corn may not grow, developed the ritual in the direction indicated. In a bountiful soil which never fails the farmer, where the seed dropped in the ground is sure to germinate, and the rains are constant, no ritual would originate to bring about what was sure to come. But let natural processes be capricious, awake in a primitive mind the fear that these processes may not recur, let him become conscious that the rains may not come, and he evolves a ritual to prevent its failure. . . . The cults of a primitive people are products of their necessities. . . . The two needs which sorely pressed the Hopi farmer were rain to water his crops and the growth and maturity of his corn. My problem, therefore, is to show by illustrations that the two components, rain making and growth ceremonials, characterize the Tusayan ritual, as aridity is the epitome of the distinctive climatic features of the region in which it has been developed. . . .
>
> In Tusayan the Great Plumed Serpent is a powerful deity to bring the rain, and is associated with lightning, his symbol. By simple observation the untutored mind recognizes that rain follows lightning, and what more natural than that it should be looked upon as the effect. He therefore worships lightning because of this power. The course of the lightning in the sky is zigzag as that of the snake, both kill when they strike. The lightning comes from the sky, the abode of the sun and rain god, and the simple reasoning of the Tusayan Indian supposes some connection between the lightning, snake and rain. The sustenance of the primitive agriculturist comes from the earth, and if the soil is nonproductive the sun and rain are of no avail. The Tusayan Indian thus recognizes the potency of the earth and symbolically deifies it as the mother. Consequently earth goddesses play important roles in his mythology. . . . No better ceremony could be chosen to illustrate the effect of the arid environment than the well-known Snake Dance, the most weird rite in

the Tusayan calendar. This dance occurs every summer on alternate years in five of the Tusayan villages, and although a dramatization of an elaborate sun-serpent myth, is so permeated by rain ceremonials that it has come to be an elaborate prayer for rain. . . .

The reptiles are believed to be elder brothers of the priests, and they are gathered from the fields on four successive days to participate in the ceremonies. It is believed that these reptiles have more power to influence supernatural beings than man, and as the acme of the whole series of nine days' observances they are thrown in a heap on the ground in a circle of sacred meal, and the chief of the Antelopes says a prayer to the struggling mass, after which they are seized by the priests and carried to the fields commissioned to intercede with rain gods to send the desired rains. In fact, the whole series of rites which make up the snake celebration is one long prayer of nine days' duration. . . .

Another component of the Tusayan ritual which occurs each year in the month following that in which the Snake Dance occurs is the ceremony of the women priests for the maturation of the corn. I refer to the September rites called the Lalakonti, celebrated by a priesthood of the same name.

The ceremony for growth of the crops, which is practically for the harvest of maize, is directly the outgrowth of those climatic conditions which have made the Tusayan people agriculturists. A failure of this crop means starvation, and maize is far from a spontaneous growth in those desert sands. Hence the elaborate nature of the appeals to the supernatural beings which control this function. This great ceremony is naturally of special concern to women, the providers. . . .

The influence of arid climatic conditions is shown in the character and intent of symbols. The conventional figure of the rain clouds and falling rain is depicted more than any other on various paraphernalia of worship. It is painted on the altars, drawn in sacred meal on the floor of his sacred rooms, or kivas, embroidered on ceremonial kilts.. . . . By a natural connection it is often replaced by figures of animals or plants associated with water. The frog and tadpole appear when the rain is abundant, and for that reason the priest paints the figures of these animals on his medicine bowl, or places effigies of it on the altar. . . . The dragonfly which hovers over the springs, the cottonwood which grows near the springs, the flag which loves the moist places, becomes a symbol of water. Water itself from the ocean or from some distant spring, in his conception, are all powerful agents to bring moisture. There can be but one reason for this—the aridity of his surroundings. The clouds from which rain falls are symbolized by the smoke from the pipe in his ceremony, and he so regards them. He pours water on the heads of participants in certain ceremonials, hoping that in the same way rain will fall on his parched fields. Even in his games he is influenced by the same thought, and in certain races the young men run along the arroyos, as they wish the water to go filled to their banks. . . .

The necessities of life have driven man into the agricultural condition and the aridity of the climate has forced him to devise all possible means at his control to so influence his gods as to force them to send the rains to aid him. Wherever we turn in an intimate study of the ceremonials of the Tusayan Indians we see the imprint of the arid deserts by which they are surrounded, always the prayer for abundant crops and rains for his parched fields.[1]

In thus attempting to epitomize briefly some results of this investigation, I have done scant justice to the eminent student who conducted it. In this series of researches principles are derived which are capable of wide application. There is no reason to doubt that the same method will show that primitive social organization, economic systems, and aesthetic life are in great measure results of definite physiographic environment.

Everything in human nature must be regarded as a product of growth. Ideas and ideals that have been rooted for ages in the ethnic mind can not and should not be eradicated in a generation. Biology has demonstrated that no appreciable increment of brain power can be effected in the lifetime of an individual. Ethnology has shown how ideals of religion, of welfare, of morals that have become ingrained in racial character, along with color of skin and shape of skull, are likewise persistent under the artificial environment of civilization. With a race a thousand years are as yesterday with an individual. Nature will not be hurried.

There are facts that are particularly applicable to the great task to which we have set ourselves in the education of alien races. The education of the Indian is a work that we have had on hand for many years, and much diversity of opinion exists as to the value of our results. Apparently the idea of educating the Indian away from his native environment is losing ground. The transplanting of isolated specimens of primitive races to a totally new environment has never been productive of happy results. The reservation Indian school is successful so far as its ideal is to make of the Indians better Indians. Unhappily, Americanization is often thought to be education.

Probably no one will be considered better qualified to express the ideals that have dominated our Indian educational policy and to speak of the difficulties which have beset it than Dr. W. H. Hailmann, for some years national superintendent of Indian schools. Dr. Hailmann says:

> There can be no doubt that *an education which inculcates the tastes and establishes the ideals of current civilization constitutes the proper first step in the work of introducing the Indians into American citizenship.* It is equally evident that the cultivation of these tastes and ideals is well nigh impossible under the conditions and influences of tribal life on Indian reservations.
>
> The mere recital of a few of the leading differences between the two civilizations will sufficiently emphasize these difficulties. *The Indian civilization looks upon the tribe or family as a unit; with us it is the individual. With the Indian he is richest who gives most; with us it is he who keeps most.* The Indian claims hospitality as a right until the means of the host are exhausted; and this hospitality is freely granted. To the Indian land is as free as the water he drinks; proprietorship continues only so long as the land is tilled or otherwise in use. The Indian prizes the worthless pony, whilom his companion and friend in the lost occupations of the chase and war. The cow is to him only a poor substitute for the buffalo; he knows nothing of her value as a giver of milk and a breeder of cattle. *Woman in Indian civilization is a producer and possesses in full Indian life an economic value and independence to which in our civilization she is largely a stranger. His religious rights and ceremonies afford the Indian, in addition to a certain degree of spiritual elevation, opportunities for intense social enjoyment for which he looks in vain in the new civilization.* Add to this that *the wants of the Indian are few and easily gratified by simple forms of homely skill in which the industries and other acquirements of the Indian school find little application;* that chiefs and medicine men in the very nature of things look with distrust and disdain upon a civilization which robs them of power and influence; that time-honored tradition imposes upon the young Indian silence and obedience—and you have an array of adverse conditions which is appalling.
>
> Against these odds the Indian schools are pitted.[2]

Might it not have been better if the Indian schools had never been *pitted against* these conditions at all, but rather, devoted to the cultivation of just what could be found in the Indian that was worthy of stimulation? Like ourselves, the Indian possesses many traits that are worthy of the highest nurture and, like ourselves, many for which the world would be better if eradicated. A system of practical education must recognize in the subjects to be educated, potentialities worthy of development. If such potentialities do not exist, then education will be futile. That the Indian is a worthy subject for education, all will agree, but that his potentialities are along the lines of our peculiar culture is not disclosed by history or ethnology. He takes rather kindly to education, but resists the overthrow of his religious and social customs. The need for the overthrow of these (with few exceptions) is not apparent.

I know of no persistent attempt on the part of government or philanthropy to develop the inherent Indian character by stimulating him to the perfection of his own arts, his own social institutions, his own religion, his own literature. When the Indian wants citizenship and prays for absorption into the body politic, then will be time to Americanize. After centuries of contact with us he chooses to remain an Indian. Candid investigation from his point of view as well as ours might lead us to approve his choice. At great cost to childhood we have learned that about all we can do for the young mind is to stimulate, direct, accelerate, or retard its unfoldment. All that we attempt to impose on it that is foreign to its nature can only work to its detriment. It is likewise with a race that is in its childhood. Its development must be from within. An ethno-educational experimental station on the reservation of one of our most isolated tribes, which should have for its task the development of Indian character (which is inherently noble) along strictly Indian lines ought in a few generations to yield us definite knowledge on the subject of educating and governing primitive races.

We are now attacking an ethno-educational problem of enormous proportions, the education of some millions of subjects in the Philippine Islands. In the evolution of our national life, our frontier has moved westward to the other side of the earth. We are in possession of a new domain, peopled mainly by the Malay race, consisting of numerous tribes in every stage of culture from absolute savagery to semicivilization. Of these ethnic groups, none of which approaches the Caucasian race, we know but little. With their customs, morals, ideals, religious beliefs, modes of reasoning, which have arisen and become ingrained through ages of relation to definite conditions, we are just beginning to become acquainted. We are carrying to them an exotic civilization, developed under environment as different from theirs as it is possible for this planet to afford. We propose to prepare them for self-government, and to that end have placed over them, in slightly modified form, our highly specialized American public school system, our only guide to the efficacy of this, when imposed upon other races, being the results of our experience with the American Indians.

The purposes and expectations of the government in this respect are officially set forth in the report of Dr. David P. Barrows, General Superintendent of Education for the Philippine Islands, under date of September 15, 1903.

> The definite purposes in introducing this educational system are unique in the history of colonial administration. Professedly, openly, and with resolute expectation of success, the American Government avowed its intention through public schools to give to every inhabitant of the Philippine Islands a primary, but thoroughly modern education, to thereby fit the race for participation in self-government and for every sphere of activity offered by the life of the Far East, and to supplant the Spanish language by the introduction of English as a basis of education and the means of intercourse and communication.[3]

In justification of this purpose Dr. Barrows says:

> Such an educational plan would never have been practicable had it not been in fact the demand of the Filipino people themselves. Thoroughly American

as our school system is, it represents the ideas which theoretically command the desires of the Filipino. His request was for free, secular schools, open to all inhabitants and teaching the English tongue and the elementary branches of modern knowledge. Again we are told that the Filipino father is desirous that the intellectual advance of his child should be unaffected by ecclesiastical control, and that the instruction of the church shall be separate from that of the school. . . . For common intercourse, as well as for education, the Filipino demands a foreign speech. To confine him to his native dialect would be simply to perpetuate that isolation which he has so long suffered and against which his insurrection was a protest. Opponents of English education find no sympathizer among the Filipino people.

These desires, if accurately portrayed, reveal on the part of the Filipino people a profound insight into the causes and conditions of both individual and national progress—an intelligence already equal to that of the most enlightened nations, and difficult to reconcile with other statements made in the same discussion, of which the following are examples:

The race lends itself naturally and without protest to the blind leadership and cruel oppression of its aristocracy. . . . It is in these rural spots that the great mass of the population finds its home. These are the centers of ignorance, the resorts and recruiting ground for the ladrones, and they perpetuate the ignorance and poverty of the race, which has remained constant for three hundred years.

It is somewhat difficult, too, to share the buoyant enthusiasm of Dr. Barrows for the value of the English language to the Filipino:

It is without rival the most useful language which a man can know. It will be more used within the next ten years, and to the Filipino the possession of English is the gateway into that busy and fervid life of commerce, of modern science, of diplomacy and politics in which he aspires to shine. Knowledge of English is more than this—it is a possession as valuable to the humble peasant for his social protection as it is to the man of wealth for his social distinction. If we can give the Filipino husbandman a knowledge of the English language, and even the most elemental acquaintance with English writings, we will free him from that degraded dependence upon the man of influence of his own race which made possible not only insurrection but that fairly unparalleled epidemic of crime which we have seen in these islands during the past few years.

The above statement of occupations in which the Filipino aspires to shine should be considered in connection with the following statements as pointing to some obvious conclusions concerning him as a subject for education:

American investors and promoters in the Philippines at the present moment are deeply disgusted with the Filipino as a laborer and are clamorous for the introduction of Chinese coolies. They claim that the Filipino hates and despises labor for itself, will not keep a laboring contract, and cannot be procured on any reasonable terms for various enterprises in which Americans desire to invest effort and money. When, however, we looked a little more closely into the demands of these men, it is apparent that what they really want here is a great body of unskilled labor, dependent for living upon its daily wage, willing to work in great gangs, submissive to the rough handling of a boss, and ready to leave home and family and go anywhere in the islands and to labor at day wages under conditions of hours and methods of labor set by their foreign employers. . . . Now, the Filipino detests labor under these conditions. It is probably true that he will not work in a gang under a "boss," subjected to conditions of labor which appear to him unnecessarily harsh and onerous.

These are interesting conditions, pointing to entirely different lines of development from those possible to the Chinese and Japanese and to a commercial civilization, with a leaning to science, diplomacy, and politics, yet unsupported by any sturdy laboring class comparable to our Irish and Italian citizens who have made possible our vast mining, railroad building, and other great constructive enterprises.

It must be admitted that our present knowledge of the Filipino does not warrant very deep convictions with reference to his future possibilities. His habitat is the zone that has not produced sturdy civilized races. Climate and physiography are decidedly against him. He is of a race, the Malay, that has as yet produced no strong ascendant ethnic groups. Ethnology has little to promise in his favor.

There is really much in science and history to guide us in this matter—enough to teach us that it is questionable whether we can prepare any primitive people for self-government by placing them under our institutions. Every nation on the globe that is fit for self-government prepared itself for it by centuries of racial experience.

I do not wish to be understood as being opposed to an educational policy for the Philippine Islands, but I do regard it as premature and wasteful to establish there a public school system in advance of any considerable scientific knowledge of the mind and character of the Malay race. A number of educational experiment stations there, where for some years educational policy, based on the ascertained capability and desires of the people, could be carefully wrought out and the best of their young people stimulated to lead in their intellectual and social life, thus developing such inherent qualities of leadership as may exist, would be economical and sensible, would determine if there are any strong ascendant ethnic groups and develop the methods by which the racial potentialities could be brought out. Such a policy is fraught with no possibility of injustice to our subjects. These people have waited some thousands of years for Americanism. Let us not inaugurate another "century of dishonor" by malpractice on another alien race. There is really no cause for haste. It is hardly time to put the Filipinos to school to us. Let us go to school to them for a while. We can learn much from them that will be for their good and ours. We should study the social order, the religious beliefs, the ethnic mind of these subjects, and accept the fact that we have here a problem in which we must count results by generations and not by years.

These are conditions which suggest a wide extension of the functions of the Bureau of American Ethnology and of the Bureau of Education. Our vast educational interests call for some constructive statesmanship. The present system is wasteful and inefficient. Education in the Philippines was organized by the War Department and is conducted by the Philippine Commission. The Office of Indian Affairs shapes a policy of Indian education. The Bureau of Education takes care of all educational interests not otherwise let out. It is difficult to understand how, under any consideration of efficiency, economy, or businesslike management, such a system should be tolerated. This condition is best known to those who have been intimately connected with it. I quote again from Dr. Hailmann's monograph on Indian Education:

> The direction and supervision of the Indian schools rest with the Indian office which, in its turn, is under the direction and supervision of the Secretary of the Interior. In the Indian office the details of the work are intrusted to the education division, now probably the most important division under its control. The education division consists of a chief clerk, with a corps of subordinate clerks, stenographers and copyists. To this division all reports are made; by it all directions and orders are drafted and issued.

The education division is aided in its work by the superintendent of Indian schools and by five supervisors, assigned in their work to five districts respectively. These officials constitute a branch of the Indian school service which occupies a very uncertain position, which can be designed neither as subordinate nor as coordinate, and which in its effectiveness depends wholly on the force of character of the incumbents and the good will of the commissioner. They have duties, but no rights; and even their efforts to perform these duties may be rendered practically nugatory by the ill-will of the education division or of the commissioner.

This is a statement of the condition in one of our several great uncorrelated departments of education. The American people claim to have supreme confidence in our democratic educational system. They would look with favor upon a more definite recognition of education by the national government, and the organization of the educational system upon an equal footing with commerce, agriculture, and war. No executive department of government has in its care interests more vast and important than our combined educational interests would be. The organization of these interests demands the elevation of the Bureau of Education to the status of an executive department.

The conclusions of this paper may be summarized as follows:

1. Ethnic mind, character, ideals, and motives are developed primarily by definite physiographic conditions of age-long duration. Ethnic traits persist through generations of new influences. This fact is of vital importance to teachers in the management of individual cases.

2. The development of a race must be from within. A civilization imposed from without is usually harmful, often destructive, and always undesirable. This face is the keynote to all that should be attempted by way of educating alien races.

3. Normal schools and other institutions for the training of teachers should give a prominent place to anthropological sciences.

4. A rational educational policy for the various primitive races now under our care must be based on specific scientific knowledge of racial mind and character. This suggests a wide extension of the functions of the Bureau of American Ethnology and the establishment of ethno-educational experiment stations.

5. Our national educational interests have been greatly increased and complicated by the acquisition of new races. The system of distributing these interests among unrelated departments is wasteful and inefficient and calls for the organization of an executive Department of Education.

NOTES

1. "A Study of Tusayan Ritual," *Smithsonian Report*, 1895.
2. W. H. Hailmann, *Education of the Indian*, Monographs on Education in the United States, no. 19. Italics added.
3. *Report of the Philippine Commission*, 1903, pt. 3, p. 694.

3 / Education, Conformity, and Cultural Change

Franz Boas

We have discussed before the causes that make for cultural stability and found that automatic actions based on the habits of early childhood are most stable. The firmer the habits that are instilled into the child, the less they are subject to reasoning, the stronger is their emotional appeal. If we wish to educate children to unreasoned mass action, we must cultivate set habits of action and thought. If we wish to educate them to intellectual and emotional freedom, care must be taken that no unreasoned action takes such habitual hold upon them that a serious struggle is involved in the attempt to cast it off.

The customary forms of thought of primitive tribes show us clearly how an individual who is hemmed in on all sides by automatic reactions may believe himself to be free. The Eskimo present an excellent example of these conditions. In their social life they are exceedingly individualistic. The social group has so little cohesion that we have hardly the right to speak of tribes. A number of families come together and live in the same village, but there is nothing to prevent any one of them from living and settling at another place with other families of his acquaintance. In fact, during a period of a lifetime the families constituting an Eskimo village are shifting about; and while they generally return after many years to the places where their relatives live, the family may have belonged to a great many different communities. There is no authority vested in any individual, no chieftancy, and no method by which orders, if they were given, could be enforced. In short, so far as human relations are concerned, we have a condition of almost absolute anarchy. We might, therefore, say that every single person is entirely free, within the limits of his own mental ability and physical competency, to determine his own mode of life and his own mode of thinking.

Nevertheless it is easily seen that there are innumerable restrictions determining his behavior. The Eskimo boy learns how to handle the knife, how to use bow and arrow, how to hunt, how to build a house; the girl learns how to sew and mend clothing and how to cook; and during all their lives they apply the methods learned in childhood. New inventions are rare and the whole industrial life of the people runs in traditional channels.

What is true of their industrial activities is no less true of their thoughts. Certain religious ideas have been transmitted to them, notions of right and wrong, amusements and enjoyment of certain types of art. Any deviation from these is not likely to occur. At the same time, and since all alien forms of behavior are unknown to them, it never enters into their minds that any different way of thinking and acting would be possible, and they consider themselves as perfectly free in regard to all their actions.

Based on our wider and different experience we know that the industrial problems of the Eskimo might be solved in a great many other ways and that their religious traditions and social customs might be quite different from what they are. From the outside, objective point of view we see clearly the restrictions that bind the individual who considers himself free.

It is not difficult to see that the same conditions prevail among ourselves. Families and schools which assiduously cultivate the tenets of a religious faith and of a religious ceremonial and surround them with an emotional halo raise, on the whole, a generation that follows the same path. The Catholicism of Italy, the Protestantism of Scandinavia and Germany, the Mahometanism of Turkey, the orthodox Judaism, are intelligible only on the basis of a lack of freedom of thought due to the strength of the automatic reaction to impressions received in early childhood that exclude all new viewpoints. In the majority of individuals who grow up under these conditions a new, distinct viewpoint is not brought out with sufficient vigor to make it clear that theirs is not freely chosen, but imposed upon them; and, *if* strange ideas are presented, the emotional appeal of the thoughts that are part of their nature is sufficient to make any rationalization of the habitual attitude acceptable, except to those of strong intellect and character. To say the least, the cultivation of formal religious attitudes in family and school makes difficult religious freedom.

What is true of religion is equally true of subservience to any other type of social behavior. Only to a limited extent can the distribution of political parties be understood by economic considerations. Often party affiliation is bred in the young in the same way as denominational allegiance.

With the weakening of the impressions of youthful instruction and familiarity with many varying forms develops the freedom of choice. The weakening of the valuation of the dogma and the spread of scientific information has resulted in the loss of cohesion of the Protestant churches.

The methods of education chosen depend upon our ideals. The imperialistic state that strives for power and mass action wants citizens who are one in thought, one in being swayed by the same symbols. Democracy demands individual freedom of the fetters of social symbols. Our public schools are hardly conscious of the conflict of these ideas. They instill automatic reactions to symbols by means of patriotic ceremonial, in many cases by indirect religious appeal and too often through the automatic reactions to the behavior of the teacher that is imitated. At the same time they are supposed to develop mind and character of the individual child. No wonder that they create conflicts in the minds of the young, conflicts between the automatic attitudes that are carefully nursed and the teachings that are to contribute to individual freedom.

It may well be questioned whether the crises that are so characteristic of adolescent life in our civilization and that educators assume to be organically determined are not due in part to these conflicts, in part to the artificial sexual restraints demanded by our society. We are altogether too readily inclined to ascribe to physiological causes those difficulties that are brought about by cultural interference with the physiological demands of the body. It is necessary that the crises and struggles that are characteristic of individual life in our society be investigated in societies in which our restraints do not exist while others may be present, before we assume all too readily that these are inherent in "human nature."

The serious mental struggle induced by the conflict between instinctive reaction and traditional social ethics is illustrated by a case of suicide among the Eskimo. A family had lost a child in the fall and according to custom the old fur clothing had to be thrown away. Skins were scarce that year and a second death in the family would have led to disaster to all its members. This induced the old, feeble grandmother, a woman whom I knew well, to wander away one night and to expose herself, in a rock niche, to death by freezing, away from the family who thus would not have been contaminated by contact with a corpse. However, she was missed, found, and brought back. She escaped a second time and died before she was found.

Another case is presented by the Chuckchee of Siberia. They believe that every person will live in the future life in the same condition in which he finds himself at the time of death. As a consequence an old man who begins to be decrepit wishes to die, so as to avoid life as a cripple in the endless future; and it becomes the duty of his son to kill him. The son believes in the righteousness of his father's request, but at the same time feels the filial love for his father, and a conflict of duties arises between filial love and the traditional customs of the tribe. Generally the customary behavior is obeyed, but not without severe struggles.

An instructive example of the absence of our difficulties in the life of adolescents and the occurrence of others is found in the studies of Dr. Margaret Mead on the adolescents of Samoa. With the freedom of sexual life, the absence of a large number of conflicting ideals, and the emphasis upon forms that to us are irrelevant, the adolescent crisis disappears, while new difficulties originate at a later period when complexities of married life develop. A similar example is presented in the life of one of our southwestern Indian tribes, the Zuni, among whom, according to Dr. Ruth L. Bunzel, the suppression of ambition, the desire to be like one's neighbor and to avoid all prominence are cultivated. They lead to a peculiar impersonal attitude and to such an extent of formalism that individual crises are all but suppressed.

We do not know enough about these questions, but our anthropological knowledge justifies the most serious doubts regarding the physiological determination of many of the crises that characterize individual life in our civilization. A thorough study of analogous situations in foreign cultures will do much to clear up this problem which is of fundamental importance for the theory of education.

It is a question whether the doubts that beset the individual in such a period are beneficial or a hindrance. The seriousness of the struggle is certainly undesirable and an easier transition will be facilitated by lessening the intensity of attachment to the situation against which he is led to rebel.

The lack of freedom in our behavior is not confined to the uneducated, it prevails in the thoughts and actions of all classes of society.

When we attempt to form our opinions in an intelligent manner, we are inclined to accept the judgment of those who by their education and occupation are compelled to deal with the questions at issue. We assume that their views must be rational and based on an intelligent understanding of the problems. The foundation of this belief is the tacit assumption that they have special knowledge and that they are free to form perfectly rational opinions. However, it is easy to see that there is no social group in existence in which such freedom prevails.

The behavior in somewhat complex primitive societies in which there is a distinction between different social classes, throws an interesting light upon these conditions. An instance is presented by the Indians of British Columbia, among whom a sharp distinction is made between people of noble birth and common people. In this case the traditional behavior of the two classes shows considerable differences. The social tradition that regulates the life of the nobility is somewhat analogous to the social tradition in our society. A great deal of stress is laid upon strict observance of convention and upon display, and nobody can maintain his position in high society without an adequate amount of ostentation and without strict regard for conventional conduct. These requirements are so fundamental that an overbearing conceit and a contempt for the common people become social requirements of an important chief. The contrast between the social proprieties for the nobility and those for the common people is very striking. Of the common people are expected humbleness, mercy, and all those qualities that we consider amiable and humane.

Similar observations may be made in all those cases in which, by a complex tradition, a social class is set off from the mass of the people. The chiefs of the Polynesian Islands, the kings of Africa, the medicine men of many countries, present examples in which the line of conduct and thought of a social group is strongly modified by their segregation from the mass of the people. They form closed societies. On the whole, in societies of this type, the mass of the people consider as their ideal those actions which we should characterize as humane; not by any means that all their actions conform to humane conduct, but their valuation of men shows that the fundamental altruistic principles which we recognize are recognized by them too. Not so with the privileged classes. In place of the general humane interest the class interest predominates; and while it cannot be claimed that their conduct, individually, is selfish, it is always so shaped that the interest of the class to which a person belongs prevails over the interest of society as a whole. If it is necessary to secure rank and to enhance the standing of the family by killing off a number of enemies, there is no hesitation felt in taking life. If the standards of the class require that its members should not perform menial occupations but should devote themselves to art or learning, then all the members of the class will vie with one another in the attainment of these achievements. It is for this reason that every segregated class is much more strongly influenced by special traditional ideas than is the rest of the people; not that the multitude is free to think rationally and that its behavior is not determined by tradition; but the tradition is not so specific, not so strictly determined in its range, as in the case of the segregated classes. For this reason it is often found that the restriction of freedom of thought by convention is greater in what we might call the educated classes than in the mass of the people.

I believe this observation is of great importance when we try to understand conditions in our own society. Its bearing upon the problem of the psychological significance of nationalism will at once be apparent; for the nation is also a segregated class, a closed society, albeit segregated according to other principles; and the characteristic feature of nationalism is that its social standards are considered as more fundamental than those that are general and human, or rather that the members of each nation like to assume that their ideals are or should be the true ideals of mankind. The late President Wilson once gave expression to this misconception when he said that, if we—Americans—hold ideals for ourselves, we should also hold them for others, referring in that case particularly to Mexico. At the same time it illustrates clearly that we should make a fundamental mistake if we should confound class selfishness and individual selfishness; for we find the most splendid examples of unselfish devotion to the interests of the nation, heroism that has been rightly praised for thousands of years as the highest virtue, and it is difficult to realize that nevertheless the whole history of mankind points in the direction of a human ideal as opposed to a national ideal. And indeed may we not continue to admire the self-sacrifice of a great mind, even if we transcend to ideals that were not his, and that perhaps, owing to the time and place in which he lived, could not be his?

Our observation has also another important application. The industrial and economic development of modern times has brought about a differentiation within our population that has never been equaled in any primitive society. The occupations of the various parts of a modern European or American population differ enormously; so much so that in many cases it is almost impossible for people speaking the same language to understand one another when they talk about their daily work. The ideas with which the scientist, the artist, the tradesman, the businessman, the laborer operate are so distinctive that they have only a few fundamental elements in common. Here it may again be observed that those occupations which are intellectually or emotionally most highly specialized require the longest training, and training always means an infusion of historically transmitted ideas. It is therefore not surprising that the thought of what we call the educated classes is controlled essentially by those ideals which have been transmitted to us by past generations. These ideals are always highly specialized, and include the ethical tendencies, the aesthetic inclinations, the intellectuality, and the expression of volition of past times. After long continued education according to these standards their control may find expression in a dominant tone which determines the whole mode of thought and which, for the very reason that it has come to be ingrained into our whole mentality, never rises into our consciousness.

In those cases in which our reaction is more conscious, it is either positive or negative. Our thoughts may be based on a high valuation of the past, or they may be in revolt against it.

When we bear this in mind we may understand the characteristics of the behavior of the intellectuals. It is a mistake to assume that their mentality is, on the average, appreciably higher than that of the rest of the people. Perhaps a greater number of independent minds find their way into this group than into some other group of individuals who are moderately well-to-do; but their average mentality is surely in no way superior to that of the workingmen, who by the conditions of their youth have been compelled to subsist on the produce of their manual labor. In both groups mediocrity prevails; unusually strong and unusually weak individuals are the exceptions. For this reason the strength of character and intellect that is required for vigorous thought on matters in which intense sentiments are involved is not commonly found—either among the intellectuals or in any other part of the population. This condition, combined with the thoroughness with which the intellectuals have imbibed the traditions of the past, makes the majority of them in all nations conventional. It has the effect that their thoughts are based on tradition, and that the range of their vision is liable to be limited.

There are of course strong minds among the intellectuals who rise above the conventionalism of their class, and attain that freedom that is the reward of a courageous search for truth, along whatever path it may lead.

In contrast to the intellectuals, the masses in our modern city populations are less subject to the influence of traditional teaching. Many children are torn away from school before it can make an indelible impression upon their minds and they may never have known the strength of the conservative influence of a home in which parents and children live a common life. The more heterogeneous the society in which they live, and the more the constituent groups are free from historic influences; or the more they represent different historic traditions, the less strongly will they be attached to the past.

This does not preclude the possibility of the formation of small, self-centered, closed societies—gangs—among the uneducated, that equal primitive man in the intensity of their group feeling and in the disregard of the rights of the outsider. On account of their segregation they no longer belong to the masses.

It would be an exaggeration if we should extend the view just expressed over all aspects of human life. I am speaking here only of those fundamental concepts of right and wrong that develop in the segregated classes and in the masses. In a society in which beliefs are transmitted with great intensity the impossibility of treating calmly the views and actions of the heretic is shared by both groups. When, through the progress of scientific thought, the foundations of dogmatic belief are shaken among the intellectuals and not among the masses, we find the conditions reversed and greater freedom of traditional forms of thought among the intellectuals—at least in so far as the current dogma is involved. It would also be an exaggeration to claim that the masses can sense the right way of attaining the realization of their ideals, for these must be found by painful experience and by the application of knowledge. However, neither of these restrictions touches our main contention; namely, that the desires of the masses are in a wider sense human than those of the classes.

It is therefore not surprising that the masses of the people, whose attachment to the past is comparatively slight, respond more quickly and more energetically to the urgent demands of the hour than the educated classes, and that the ethical ideals of the best among them are human ideals, not those of a segregated class. For this reason I should always be more inclined to accept, in regard to fundamental human problems, the judgment of the masses rather than the judgment of the intellectuals, which is much more certain to be warped by unconscious control of traditional ideas. I do not mean to say that the judgment of the masses would be acceptable in regard to every problem of human life, because there are many which, by their technical nature, are beyond their understanding; nor do I believe that the details of the right solution of a problem can always be found by the masses; but I feel strongly that the problem itself, as felt by them, and the ideal that they want to see realized, is a safer guide for our conduct than the ideal of the intellectual group that stand under the ban of an historical tradition that dulls their feeling for the needs of the day.

One word more, in regard to what might be a fatal misunderstanding of my meaning. If I decry unthinking obedience to the ideals of our forefathers, I am far from believing that it will ever be possible, or that it will even be desirable, to cast away the past and to begin anew on a purely intellectual basis. Those who think that this can be accomplished do not, I believe, understand human nature aright. Our very wishes for changes are based on criticism of the past, and would take another direction if the conditions under which we live were of a different nature. We are building up our new ideals by utilizing the work of our ancestors, even where we condemn it, and so it will be in the future. Whatever our generation may achieve will attain in course of time that venerable aspect that will lay in chains the minds of our successors, and it will require new efforts to free a future generation of the shackles that we are forging. When we once recognize this process, we must see that it is our task not only to free ourselves of traditional prejudice, but also to search in the heritage of the past for what is useful and right, and to endeavor to free the mind of future generations so that they may not cling to our mistakes, but may be ready to correct them.

4 / Native Education and Culture Contact
Bronislaw Malinowski

THE CULTURAL SETTING OF THE TECHNICAL PROCESS IN EDUCATION

Education is bigger than schooling. In every society, however simple or complex, the child has to acquire not only skills and ideas, he has also to be taught the moral values, the social attitudes, the religious beliefs of his community. The integral process of education in every society consists in the formation of mind, character and a sense of citizenship. This process exists at the lowest levels of development, among the Bushmen, Australian aborigines, or Firelanders, as well as in Chicago, Cape Town, or London. In the more highly differentiated societies we also find schooling, in which the child learns from professional teachers such skills as reading and writing, such wisdom as comes from knowledge of history, the scriptures, or natural philosophy. In no community, however highly differentiated, does the school alone teach future citizenship. The earliest molding of mind and character must be given at home. The influence of playmates may be incalculable for good or evil. Apprenticeship to a particular craft or profession, as well as apprenticeship to life, is not given at school, but in actual contact with the future work to be done.

The rift between school and home, between schematized teaching on the one hand and the influences of street and playground, of workshop or professional group, on the other, has become a problem in our own society, and a grave one. When a few centuries ago the school was the anteroom to the monastery, when only scholars were taught or trained scholastically, the difficulties did not exist. Even a generation or two ago in England, when public school and old university had the definite purpose of developing the youth into a gentleman or making him degenerate into a don, the problem was not so urgent. But under our modern strenuous conditions we feel that the discrepancy between what is specifically taught and what would be needed in future life becomes a serious danger. A great deal of what is done in school and in university has become mere waste of time, if not worse. The New Education Fellowship is an organized attempt to deal with these problems in our own civilization.

The difficulties and dangers, however, increase immensely when education is given by a highly differentiated, industrially advanced culture, such as that of Europe, to peoples living in the simple tribal conditions of Africa. Here, schooling is mechanically thrust into a culture where education has gone on for ages without the institution of professional schooling. Here also the rift between school and home, between training and the influences of tribal life, must remain even more profound. For here the schooling given is based entirely on systems developed in the Western European civilization. Yet schooling of unblushingly European type, which even to us has now become almost obsolete, has been pressed upon native races all the world over by missionaries and enthusiastic educationists, by governments, and by economic enterprise.

And here, perhaps, is a topic on which the anthropologist has something to say. His very subject-matter, "culture," in its relation to "race," has been completely left out of account. He has to lay down a number of simple truths which are often mistaken for truisms—especially by those who ignore them—but which ought to be adopted definitely as working principles in all interracial relations.

Culture, that is, the body of material appliances, types of social grouping, customs, beliefs and moral values, is a reality which must be taken into consideration by every one who frames an educational policy. Culture determines the personality of individuals; culture is correlated with tribal beliefs, ideas, and values. It is deeply entrenched in the social organization of the people and firmly rooted in their environmental pursuits. To educate a primitive community out of its culture and to make it adopt integrally that of a much more highly differentiated society is a gigantic task. It cannot be done in a haphazard manner, piecemeal, by combining pressure and persuasion, and working without aim, plan or the knowledge of all the implications. Yet, if we were to study the theory and practice of education as given by one race to another in any part of the world, in India or Africa, in Malaya or Oceania, we should find there a universal assumption "that what we feel necessary and right must be the best for the African," or any other native.

Mr. Dougall is quite right when he tells us that

> very few Europeans can stop to observe, far less to study, the effects of the changes in the Africans themselves. Education . . . becomes simply the communication of knowledge or the imparting of skill, which, so we feel, must bring Africa to its desired haven.[1]

As a matter of fact, since education is a by-product of each culture, and since it is adjusted to the requirements of each culture, it is clear that by imposing a new and extraneous type of schooling we not only give but we also take away. What we take away is their knowledge of their own tribal tradition, of their own moral values, and even of their own practical skills. This point has been brought out very well by Mrs. A. W. Hoernlé, who shows how extraneous schooling inadequately imparted must lead to the disintegration of a primitive society, because it estranges a number of individuals from the traditions still controlling the rest of the tribe.[2] How to obviate or at least to minimize this danger the anthropologist is called upon to advise. For, as Mrs. Hoernlé insists, it is his duty "to study native social organization as a living functioning whole."

In the problem of native education by Europeans there arises another difficulty; this time not so much connected with the native society itself, but with the attitude of the "superior race." European schooling does take away the birthright of the native child, that is, his own tradition and his own place in his tribal life. But does it instead endow him with the charter of citizenship in our own civilization and society? And here we find that the white community in South Africa is not prepared to give a native, however educated and intelligent, that place to which he is entitled by his training. Race prejudices, laws and attitudes connected with the color-bar principle, strong antagonism against that social and personal intercourse which ultimately must lead to race mixture, exclude the educated Bantu, Negro, Hindu, or Malay from taking his full share in the benefits which should go with accomplishment in the Western education. In other words, education as the manufacture of qualified, skilled or professionally trained men and women is a process of supply and demand. To create a supply of colored people educated and skilled, and at the same time to curtail by legal and social action any demand for them, leads to a very dangerous situation. And here comes in what Professor Clarke has so aptly described as "the double mind in African education."

> Administrators, missionaries, teachers may be competent, disinterested and genuinely expert. But it is not they who create the medium of social ideas, race prejudices, economic interests and political passions in and through which they have to work.

He then proceeds to prove that while we believe with one half of our mind in fraternity, Christian ideals, democracy, and liberty, the other half refuses to apply these ideals:

> . . . it is characteristic of the self-deceiving double-mindedness which afflicts western man to-day that he can assert, with every appearance of fervency, a real fraternal sentiment for the "black brother," without intending at all the liberty and equality which are the basis of it.[3]

Or, to put it in slightly different terms, the onslaught of white civilization on native cultures is carried out by two columns, the column of goodwill toward the African and the column of "good sense"—or the column of "good gain" for the European, as some like to call it, if perhaps not quite fairly. The first are prepared to give the native unstintingly our knowledge and our Christianity, our love of sport, and our predilection for cotton and linen. The others, while realizing that the educated African may be useful as laborer, clerk, or assistant, soon become aware that he also grows into a dangerous competitor. Hence he must not be given too much scope even to carry out useful work; he certainly must be given the minimum remuneration and the most restricted opportunities; he cannot be granted political influence; he must be limited even as to the territory which he occupies, the land which he owns and the sites on which he is allowed to live. In all this the white community is not moved by any malice or racial viciousness but too often, alas! by the force of sheer economic necessity.

At the same time we must never forget that to educate a man is to raise not only his knowledge and skills, but also his hopes and his ambitions, his claims for full citizenship, and the sense of his own personal dignity. Hence with an inexorable determinism education implies better conditions of life. It may be ungenerous to stint the native of education. It is, perhaps, necessary to deprive him of land and independence and to limit his opportunities. But it is unquestionably dangerous to expend all our generosity in giving him a goodly measure of education, only to deprive him of the fruits thereof by the force of laws and political discrimination.

It certainly would be unfair to impute any predatory motives either to the early settlers in North America, or to the Dutch pioneers in South Africa, or the earliest colonists in Australia or New Zealand. But those who for generations were born and bred on non-European continents, who have to make their livelihood there and nowhere else, cannot be blamed or treated as intruders. At the same time there is this profound clash of economic interests and, indeed, there is the same struggle for space, expansion, and opportunities as, one might almost say, exists in the organic world. Tragedy is not the clash of right with wrong, but of right with right, and I feel that though it is not the duty of the anthropologist to be pro-native in the usual, rhetorical sense of the word, he is under the obligation, not only of presenting the native point of view, but also of showing its extreme relevancy to the well-being of Europeans in the long run. In history, when tragedy reaches a certain point, it comes near to being the forerunner of catastrophe.

It is neither the privilege nor the duty of the student of anthropology to draw any political conclusions, but it is his task to survey the facts and show their significance. As regards South African politics, of course, I shall say nothing. But the problem is certainly not in any way limited to South Africa. It is the dominant problem of the world at large today. It exists in the United States, in the extreme Orient, everywhere in Africa north of the Zambezi, in India, and indeed, in a slightly different form, also in Europe. The anthropologist, therefore, may be excused in his conviction that an entirely academic and dispassionate approach to this world problem may be of some use, even when it is propounded by one whose outlook is not limited to a special region, however important this might be.

THE THREE PHASES OF EDUCATION: BIRTHRIGHT, MOLDING, AND CHARTER OF CITIZENSHIP

We have described the sociological nature of education as a process of supply and demand; we have also spoken of the three phases: birthright, molding of personality, and the charter of citizenship. The two conceptions coincide, for the molding, whether it be by the nonspecialized tribal agencies or through schooling, does not start with raw material. In this education differs from the industrial process of manufacture. A human being is born with a biological endowment and also with his social destiny largely defined. He has this birthright determined partly by biological heredity, partly by cultural inheritance. Supply, of course, corresponds to what we have termed "molding," that is, the manufacture of the social personality with which a man takes up his citizenship. The charter is that demand for a trained individual, or the place which society is prepared to give him in its body politic.

Let us first discuss birthright. On its biological side it consists in innate endowment. A child is born musical or intelligent, artistically gifted or technically clever; or else it early shows deficiencies in either of these respects. To train him for what he has no aptitude is useless. When it comes, however, to education from one culture to another, we have to compare not individual differences but the average aptitudes of one type of humanity as against another. What we call race is a variety of the human species which is distinguished by a number of physical characteristics. One race probably also differs, however slightly, from others in mental endowment.

It is relatively easy to describe the physical characteristics. It is extremely difficult to define and compare innate mental capacities of different races. Attempts have been made now and again to settle the matter by some physical test. Even quite recently a few hundred skulls have been measured in some part of Africa for their volume, and an elaborate argument based on this thoroughly inadequate assessment was made concerning the spiritual possibilities of a whole race. Such abortive applications of a pseudo-scientific approach would be laughable, were it not that they are used by political elements in a highly irresponsible manner. It is therefore important that every sane anthropologist should protest against such bastard misapplications of science to problems where the only scientific verdict is *ignoramus ignorabimus*.

For it must be emphatically stated that we know nothing and probably shall never know anything about the relation between the structure of the brain and mental processes, still less about the size of brain in relation to intellectual capacity. To take the brute volume of the skull and to make it an index of the spiritual value of a people involves more logical and empirical errors than there are words to express the fallacy. You can measure simple cubic capacity and express its volume in the metric system, but a yardstick to measure human intelligence or character has not yet been invented. Unless there should be devised some measure of empirical calculation, that is, unless the whole problem of psycho-physical parallelism be solved, the time devoted to skull measurement, brain weighing and similar amusements is wasted, that is, as far as any discussion of the innate capacities of one human race as against another is concerned.

But, if we cannot physically measure spiritual values, is there no cultural approach to the assessment of racial ability? I think that if we ever come to define the abilities of an individual, a group, a social stratum or a race, it will be only by assessing their cultural achievements. "By their fruits ye shall know them." Here again it is very easy to fall into a variety of errors. Nothing is simpler than to point out that at the time of the discovery of North America the Indians were less highly civilized than the Spaniards, the West African Negroes at a lower level of culture than the Portuguese, or the Bantu less advanced than the British. But the fact that a certain race is not at a given moment in history occupying the front rank of progress does not yet mean that it is inherently inferior to the others. Civilization began probably in the valley of the Nile, probably some six thousand years before the birth of Christ. Of these eight thousand years there was a long period in which the Egyptians, that is, Africans of a Hamitic stock, led the world. There was a time when the highest development of culture was to be found among the yellow races. There were long periods before the birth of Christ and later on in the early Middle Ages when Semites were the most civilized people in the world. There has been a long time when Mediterranean races of mixed blood were dominant. Finally, in the last five hundred years, the "Nordics" have been dominant—one-sixteenth of the period of which we have a fairly clear knowledge. Members of the same race upon whom we now look down would have turned away with contempt from our ancestors. Who can know what will happen in the future? But the clear lesson of the past is that cultural potentialities and latent capacity must not be confused with fully developed achievement at any period of history.

Thus the test of integral achievement in culture is too complicated and tenuous to be used in any way as a scientific argument for innate abilities of race. What about intelligence tests? Here again the most important point to be remembered is that every system of intelligence tests is only valid if set within a definite cultural medium. Tests devised to suit children in the slums of Chicago will fail when applied to young bushmen of the Kalahari and vice versa. The very low scale which some European immigrants achieved in the intelligence tests of the American army—my own countrymen (Poles) came below the Negroes—is due to the fact that tests valid for one culture do not apply to members of another even if they belong to the same race. So that here again we have nothing to go upon.

The anthropologist cannot sufficiently often insist on the fact that his science does not allow him to grade humanity into races inferior and superior, incapable of survival and capable of intellectual development. Of course, when a small section of humanity was exterminated by another we can say that it was not able to survive. This is true of the Tasmanians and of the Southeastern Australians and of one or two North American tribes. Such a statement is positive but tautological. The African race, however, is certainly not going to be wiped out; indeed, it shows signs of developing strongly in the New World as well as in its own home. The birthright, that is, the innate capacities of the Africans and the limits of these, has not yet been explored.

And here comes the really crucial point of the whole argument: academic discussions as to the exact boundaries of the possibilities of development of the African in higher mathematics, logic, astronomy, music, and painting are entirely beside the point. No one suggests that the Bantu should receive fully the same educational system as do the English, the German, or the Swedes. The question is really whether the average African is capable of receiving European elementary training and whether he will respond well to the training which he receives now. Now on this question there can be no two answers. The average Bantu can reach the level of the fifth, sixth, or seventh form quite as well as the average European. The second question is whether the African, through technical or intellectual education, is capable of becoming a skilled artisan, an industrial foreman, or a clerk. Here again there is overwhelming evidence that the better the education, the better the product and that from all practical points of view the product is perfectly satisfactory. In this we must always remember that when you pay an African clerk £3 per month for exactly the same services as those for which you pay an Indian £10 and a European £30, the three will not be able to work equally well.

Thus, as regards the physical birthright of the African child, this probably requires further intelligent study, not by skull measurement but by education experts well trained in anthropology. All evidence, however, points to the conclusion that the African child responds as well to the same type of schooling as the European.

I have enlarged somewhat on this question because, adding insult to injury, we have not only taken the African's cultural birthright, but we are also trying to take away his character in the matter of a biological birthright. It is his cultural birthright, however, which more directly interests us in this context. I have already indicated that a new type of schooling is not merely an addition but that it takes away something. A new set of ideas, a new system of values, new ways and new manners must clash with the old order, and it is in this old order that the African tribesman found his place.

What is this fact of cultural birthright? In every race and every society a man is born to a certain status within his community. Anthropology teaches that there are patrilineal societies in which the son succeeds to the father and matrilineal tribes where he steps into the shoes of his maternal uncle. Descent—that is, the fact to which side he is linked—succession or inheritance may follow either the sword or the distaff, but by the very fact of birth a child is given something more than his soul and body. And in every case education links up with the initial sociological endowment.

Now, there is no doubt that when any part of the world is colonized the birthright of the native is profoundly affected. The new rules often improve the lot of some, but they invariably worsen the conditions of the whole community. The Europeans have often freed slaves, but they have deprived the whole tribe of its full measure of liberty. And now in every part of Africa the child is born no more to a world of freedom where the integral territory belongs to him and his people, where he can choose among the careers which, though limited, were well adapted to his cultural interests and racial aptitudes. He lives in a world which is politically subject, economically dependent, culturally spoon-fed and molded by another race and another civilization. A considerable portion of his tribal lands has been alienated, the political independence of the whole society modified, his traditional law, his economic pursuits, his religious ideas questioned.

The young African of today has to make a living, and in this he has to tread a difficult and uncharted path. He stands in a no-man's land between two worlds, to neither of which he fully and completely belongs. In short, his cultural birthright has been taken from him, and instead of it what have we given him?

And here we come directly to the process of schooling or molding. Most of those in the European community who are the real friends of the African have only one answer: education has made us what we are, so let us give the African more education, better education, higher education, and we shall equip him with the same weapons for conquering his place in the world as we have. To quote an outstanding example: the Economic Commission, unable for political reasons to recognize that more land should be given to the natives and better economic opportunities granted to them, urges more education and better education, and an energetic onslaught on the native tribal system and native "superstitions."[4]

If we were to run mentally over the various efforts to help the African and assess the monies spent from Europe on his improvement, we should find everywhere the familiar belief that education is a panacea which can work by itself. The Jeanes schools, the Phelps-Stokes inquiries, all the schooling done by the missions work on the principle that education is the royal road to achievement. In looking through the excellent recent book *Western Civilization and the Natives of South Africa* (edited by I. Schapera), I find that practically every article in the joint production contains as its positive advice some scheme of fuller or better education. With all this naturally every one must be in full agreement. But the point here made is that education can never stand alone. You educate a man or woman not merely to be more efficient, to be morally and intellectually superior, but also to have greater demands—spiritual, social, and economic. Education combined with opportunities is the greatest patrimony of a civilized man or woman of whatever race or color he or she might be. But for every pound spent on native education there ought to be at least ten pounds spent on the improvement of native conditions of life.

EDUCATION ON AFRICAN OR EUROPEAN LINES?

This brings us directly to the second element, in a way the most important; that is, the special technique used in molding the mind and character of a child. For it is here that the invading civilization can exercise its influence directly on a native community. And can do it for good or for evil. We are now perhaps aware that, since the process of education is determined by the character of the culture in which the individuals live, it is not an entirely simple matter to apply European schooling to children who will have to live under conditions profoundly different from those in Europe. The early enthusiasm with which the carriers of a superior civilization and higher morality approached the question leaves us now cold and skeptical. Another slogan has found its way into discussions: "development of the African on African lines." But what exactly this means is not so easy to assess, more difficult in fact than the old slogan that the more European education we give, the more we benefit the African.

Let me dwell a little more fully on the meaning of the two slogans. I shall formulate it in a way in which it was put before me at a time when I was mostly interested myself in the antiquarian side of anthropology and had not thought out the problems of our changing world and the relation of races and cultures. Discussing the matter of African education with one of the extreme exponents of equality and goodwill in racial questions, I asked: "What sort of education would be the best for the African child?" My friend took up the question rather sharply and retorted: "What education do you give to your own children? What is best for them is good enough for the Africans." Reflecting on this, I had on balance to reject it as completely inadequate. First of all, having had at that time to choose schools for my own children, I found that it was not so easy to find what was best for them even in our own civilization, for we also are changing, and changing rapidly. Our old type of schooling seems completely out of tune with the world of tomorrow. But also I felt that it was not much good educating an African child without all the expectations, hopes, and claims which we can promise to our own children. The African child when he grows up will be sent back to his tribe or compelled to work on mine or plantation, or live in a native location or township. His life task is different, his economic power of earning depends on different qualities. He is never remunerated according to its intrinsic value. The social expectations and claims which our education in good manners, social ways, and amenities gives to our children will always be an unfulfilled dream in his case.

I was driven back rather radically to the other ideal or slogan. For the African there must be an African education. But here obviously we are immediately faced by two facts. First of all, education in the widest sense—that is, the influence of home, playmates, elders, and tribal tradition—can be much better given by the natives' own educational agencies. The second fact, however, is, that the African needs today something more than being taught in the ways and lore of his own community, tribal or detribalized. His place is, as we know already, not in his own society only but in two worlds or between two worlds. And here again it is not so much that he needs us as that we need him. The native has to work for Europeans, serve Europeans, adjust himself to certain administrative rulings, be judged by a mixture of European and native law, and remain constantly in touch with people who practice an alien religion and belief in a non-African set of values.

The clear distinction which we made at the beginning between schooling and education suggests the only possible practical solution. African education has to proceed on two fronts. The native has to receive schooling which will prepare him for his contacts and cooperation with the European section of society. He has to be taught subjects and skills which will make him as valuable as possible to his white employers and thus secure him the best possible economic and social situation. At the same time, this schooling should be carried out in a manner which would produce the minimum of disintegration and which would keep him still in harmony with his own group.

There is nothing new in this suggestion. It has been framed and reframed several times before. Let me mention only the program drawn up by the Advisory Committee on Education in the Colonies. It is recognized in this program as elsewhere that the school cannot be an isolated factor in a people's development and that knowledge of tribal traditions and tribal methods of life is essential to an intelligent policy. A new attempt is being made in the Swaziland Protectorate to incorporate certain principles of African education into European schooling. It is an application to educational matters of the principle of indirect rule in politics. It implies no great practical difficulties.

The present conditions are almost the reverse of what ought to be the ideal. European schooling is carried out under the dominance of lofty and unselfish ideals which, however, are often dangerous because of their complete disharmony with real conditions. On the other hand, the African influences, what still remains of sound and extremely valuable educational technique of indigenous character, have been so undermined and discredited by various forces and agencies that they have become almost completely inoperative.

Let me substantiate this indictment, however briefly. What is the character of European schooling as given today all over Africa? The first answer to be given, of course, is that it cannot be defined in its full extent by one sentence. Let me first, therefore, limit myself to the British colonies. There the outstanding fact is that perhaps 90 percent, if not more, of the actual schooling is in the hands of missions. The funds are supplied, however, largely by the colonial governments concerned; that is, ultimately they come from native taxation. The native is, in short, made to pay for the education which he receives but over which he has no control whatever. Missionary teaching has historically grown up as a process which had nothing to do with the problems or the aims of education as laid down here; one might almost say, nothing to do with education as a cultural process for the worldly benefit of the people educated. For missionary teaching was at first essentially an adjunct of the work of evangelization.

And here we come to the vast difference between the work of the Roman Catholic missions, with its strong nonworldly bias; the work of the Dutch Reformed

Church mission of South Africa, which combines high ideals of Christianity with a strong color prejudice; the work of such bodies as the Universities' Mission which almost completely profess and even practice the enlightened anthropological outlook; or the Livingstonia mission which in a shrewd way fulfills a great many of the natives' essential requirements. But to the missionary the main end is to save a soul, to produce a good Christian. To some (fortunately now in the minority), in order to achieve this it is necessary to shake the native somewhat rudely out of his heathen superstitions. There is no sarcasm in this last sentence, nor is there, I am convinced, any exaggeration. After all, if the missionary and the anthropologist could, as matters stand, see eye to eye, they would not have much to learn from one another. As it is, the future of their cooperation must involve a greater sympathy on both sides and, incidentally, a reform of anthropological methods and outlook from the old antiquarian point of view to a much greater interest in the psychological and cultural difficulties of the changing native.

Since I definitely disclaim any competence to deal with the technicalities of schooling, I shall not enter into the actual organization of present-day European teaching in Africa. Perhaps the most important instrument of book training is the school in the bush, and about this institution, its workings and its character, very little is known. It is easy to criticize the somewhat mechanical way in which the three Rs, Bible stories, songs with European melodies, and queerly translated European texts are being imparted. I have several times seen bush-school proceedings, but not knowing the vernacular I can, of course, say very little. The impression one receives and which is confirmed by those who can follow the actual teaching is of a somewhat disconcerting nature; in the schools I saw there was little discipline and interest visible; the children seemed to amuse themselves on their own, while the teacher performed at the other end. I may have been unfortunate in the schools visited.

The recent attempt to produce textbooks adapted to African local needs and to choose really useful elementary subjects shows how greatly it is felt that the bush school has failed to fulfill the functions of real training. It would be better, perhaps, if I quoted here the words of one who, while convinced of the value of education, and of Christian education at that, has yet a sense of reality and a great knowledge of the conditions in East Africa—which also obtain farther south.

> It is a common criticism of our educational policy in Africa that education, from the African point of view, has come to mean unrelated information, the acquiring of literary skill and languages, but that it has had singularly little influence on the life of the masses of the people. It has not resulted, as we hoped, in the adoption of improved habits in elementary matters of food and clothing, the care of babies and the practice of agriculture by the communities round the school. Schools have been isolated centres of "learning" rather than centres of training for a life of action. Their influence has been strangely confined to the individuals who have there learned to read, write or do sums in arithmetic. To them the tools of learning have been primarily decorative or profitable to themselves rather than practical and useful in their familiar social background.[5]

I do not think there is much to be added to this sober and measured appreciation. Dougall does not want, any more than I do myself, to indulge in cheap criticisms at the expense of a system which, however defective, must command our admiration and respect. But its difficulties are considerable. At the beginning of the process by which the schools came into being there was no intelligently framed objective, nor yet a carefully laid down plan. Even as it stands, however, Dougall's statement is perhaps a little optimistic. Not many of the products of the bush school have acquired "literary skill and languages," and few of them can "do sums in arithmetic" or even read and write in later life. And then what is the use of reading and writing in a dialect which is spoken at the outside by ten thousand people, in which a literature does not exist, in which letters are not written because simpler means of communication are sufficient? A few scholars retain the capacity for reading the Bible, but even that apparently in a somewhat mechanical way.

The Jeanes school movement, of which Dougall is one of the pioneers in Africa, has made a very energetic and effective attempt to remedy this state of affairs. Practically everything which has been and is being done by the supporters of this movement could be endorsed without any hesitation. The Jeanes policy is still far from dominating the whole educational system. Dougall is quite right in describing the ideas which he advocates as "revolutionary to African teachers and parents of the type who send their children to school."

One of the worst results of the old type of schooling and of the older educational influences was to create "strongly entrenched opinions favouring the present type of education," opinions which have taken root among the Christianized section of the African community itself. This really is the stronghold of the worst by-products of the old schooling. The African church elders, with whom the missionaries have now seriously to reckon, are the legacy of the less discriminating and far less intelligent missionary policies, above all of the strong tendency to discredit all things genuinely African. They and the minority group of narrow-minded and unimaginative white missionaries still retain what might be called the benighted heathen complex. They are unable to regard the ordinary amusements of the African, his dances, his beer drinking, even his tribal markets and public festivities, as anything but evil.

One of the symptoms which shocked me in my brief but extensive survey of Africa from Sudan to Swaziland was the fact that everywhere there existed this profound rift between the Christian and non-Christian section of every tribe. At a dance there would be a group of people standing aside, looking on with keen interest and yet contemptuous, with envy and yet with a show of superiority—these were the Christians. At a funeral there would be two groups—one singing the old traditional songs, the other hymns, very often simultaneously, with strange counterpoint effects. In some parts of Africa even on the marketplace you can distinguish the group of Christians from that of the heathen. This deep belief that only European ways of thinking, of clothing themselves, of playing games, of buying and selling goods, are right, and that all things African are of inferior quality, is one of the most destructive and undermining influences in Africa.

On the social side it means that a modernized African child develops a contempt for his African parents. Now whatever might be said of schooling, there is one effect which it should not produce, and that is to destroy the foundation of all morals and future social vitures by undermining the foundations of the home. As regards political influence and the value of citizenship, the extraordinary fascination which European things have exercised over the native often leads to a serious undermining of the chief's authority. This can be observed clearly in such tribes as the Swazi, where the present Paramount Chief, himself an enlightened African combining a sound appreciation of European values with a love of his own national tradition, has taken action, and successful action at that, in demanding that the national schooling of Swaziland should support his influence and not work against it. I have been able to observe, however, almost wherever I went, that the influence of the "modernization" works against any attempt at reestablishing native authorities and enlisting their effective cooperation with European officials. Those who talk about "segregation" and want to attach a positive meaning to that term must realize that unless some sort of political scope is given to the African he will not be satisfied with anything less than equal political rights with the white settlers.

Even when it comes to beer and dancing, to entertainments and festivities, we take away elements which cannot be replaced by anything else, and yet without which human beings are never quite happy. A missionary who comes over to Africa may sometimes do so out of sheer disgust with the conditions at home. He has found that Christianity as practiced among ourselves in Europe has failed, during the great war and after, in international morals, politics, and in social or economic life. He sees that at present in Europe and America Christianity is in the arena of public life a relatively unimportant issue compared with class war, industrial reform, and the struggle between fascism and communism and democracy. He envisages a land where Christianity may start with the clean slate of newly converted souls, and following his passionate desire to realize the Christian ideal in its pristine purity, he inflicts on the African this ideal, forgetting completely that it is unfair, as well as unwise, to demand of others what we ourselves have not succeeded in achieving. Since African dances may contain "immoral elements," dancing is forbidden; since indulgence in alcohol can do no good and may do harm, native beer is proscribed. Some missions, the early American missionaries in Natal, forbade smoking. A generation later a new relay of young American missionaries arrived pipe in mouth and pockets bulging with Lucky Strikes, Camels, and Chesterfields. A real war of principle ensued, and I am afraid My Lady Nicotine won the day. Some natives were bewildered, others contemptuous, all essentially unsettled: one of the most intelligent Africans I have ever had the pleasure of meeting told me about the influence of that one incident on his mind and on those of his fellow-students—it was devastating.

This is but an extreme illustration of what happens in European contact with natives in Africa and beyond. The superhuman ideals suitable perhaps for the saints of early days—ideals of purity, continence, contempt for dancing and pleasures of the flesh—were preached by the earlier missionaries and are even today preached brazenly as the very essence of Christianity. Then comes the other column of the European army of colonization, drinking and swearing, gambling and smoking, also at times transgressing in word or deed some of the other commandments, with complete disregard for anything that the missionary has to say. This is a well-known story and need not be repeated here. But the remedy lies, I think, not in disciplining the white settlers, traders, or even officials to a puritanic mode of living. This is impossible. The remedy lies in adopting a much more moderate, if not hedonistic, attitude toward beer and song, toward dances and public gatherings, toward markets and social festivities. The truth of the matter is that the early missionary was frightened of the dances without ever coming near them. He believed, for reasons which need not be given here but which were spurious, that all dancing must lead to fornication.[6] This is as untrue and wrong about African dancing and beer drinking as it is partly true about modern cocktail parties and that degeneration of dancing which we practice in our own ballrooms.

But to return to our point, the infection of the native with contempt for all things African has been encouraged rather than combated by the earlier missionaries and by the less enlightened of those now at work. It has taken particularly deep root with African church elders and with educated or semieducated natives. It still dominates everything that is happening in Africa. To avoid misunderstandings I do not for one moment impute that the missions are exclusively or have been mainly responsible for this phenomenon. The African admires the European and despises his own civilization primarily because in matters economic and political he has been made to feel his own weakness and inferiority compared with the ruthless power and irresistible pervasiveness of European might. What I want to say is that a good deal of earlier schooling and of the by-products of early education and the influence of the missions has acted very much in tune with the schemes and interests of the trader and the planter, of the recruiter and the tax collector, instead of combating the disintegrating influence of these latter.

So much for the school in the bush. Of course, some of the higher institutions, some of the central schools or technical colleges, would demand special consideration. Insofar as they train Africans to fulfill advanced tasks well, those of government clerk and of skilled foreman; insofar as they develop better agriculturalists and African teachers or missionaries, they escape any criticism which could be leveled at them. But even here the prevailing tendency is to estrange the African from his tribal culture, to develop in him claims and desires which his future salary and status will never satisfy, and very often to prepare him only partly for his contact with Europeans.

In what way can European schooling combined with wider educational influences assist the native? I have said already that in my opinion education must definitely proceed on two fronts. Since a great many of his future dealings will bring him constantly in contact with Europeans, let us first analyze in what way the native must acquire some elements of the invading culture. In this perhaps the first matter of importance would be some provision for the teaching of a language which would serve as a convenient medium of communication between European and native. Here I cannot enter into the perennial controversy between the sponsors of the vernacular, English, or some local lingua franca such as Swahili, Hausa, or Arabic. I understand that there were suggestions seriously framed of introducing Esperanto, Ido, and even Latin—the last suggestion came, needless to say, from a product of Oxford Greats. The only point which I want to make here is that a great many political, practical, and even sectarian considerations have been allowed to control the problem. But the point which matters is what is best for the natives from the point of view of their European careers. And here I think that the overwhelming force of all arguments would be in favor of teaching the European language of the government as a subject and teaching it in the vernacular.

This conclusion ought to have some weight when promulgated by an anthropologist. For English or French or Portuguese is bound to be in many ways a leveling and disintegrating factor. But since we have to give the Africans our schooling, since schooling receives its only justification in preparing them for cooperation with us, it surely is nothing short of preposterous to deprive them of the best instrument by which they can, on the one hand, master their new environment and, on the other, become most useful in practically every capacity in which they are employed by Europeans. Again, speaking as a product of culture contact myself, I should like to repeat that the teaching of English should be given in the vernacular, that is, by tribesmen who know English well. Those who maintain that good English knowledge is too difficult and that instruction in English cannot be given by African low-grade teachers are either not informed or not sincere in their arguments. Members of simple cultures—"savages" as we call them—are good practical linguists. Speaking as a Pole, on behalf of the African, I again can put my own experience as a "savage" from Eastern Europe side by side with the Kikuyu, Chagga, or Bechwana. If the imparting of good English were compulsory in all the normal schools and training colleges in (British) Africa, the teachers produced by such schools could perfectly well give elementary grounding in English in every bush school. It is a matter of policy and principle and not of practical difficulty.[7]

Writing and reading, instead of being anomalies, would then become really useful pursuits. Of course, here immediately come objections of the political and economic nature. While we all profess a deep belief in education, we are yet aware of its potential dangers. This is a serious point. At the same time I think that sooner or later we shall have to aim at developing intelligent judgment in the Africans and trust them to use their judgment in choosing between extremist propaganda and the legitimate advancement of their own tribal rights. Cooperation, and not coercion and passive obedience, must be the policy of the future.

As regards arithmetic, technical training, and such elements of natural history as can be given, I have little to add, except that here, as everywhere else, the tendency ought to be to translate such elementary knowledge as is developed in our own communities into its African counterpart. There is a great deal in the matter of elementary hygiene, principles of household economics or very elementary book-keeping, questions of food and household duties which could well be incorporated in the curriculum, even as the Jeanes system does today.

One subject matter I would like definitely to include in the elements of African teaching, and that by no means facetiously. I mean something which could be described as an inverted anthropology of European customs and manners, superstitions and beliefs, for the use of the African. There is an extraordinary amount of double-barreled falsehood obtaining in this matter. The European, especially the government official and the missionary, but also the settler, the trader, and even the workingman, is at pains to uphold the prestige and the dignity of the white race. Some of them are doing it in a well-balanced way, safeguarding their dignity and respecting that of the African. Others achieve merely a caricature. But the African has not been slow to develop his own theories concerning the virtues and pretenses, the habits and foibles of the European. An extremely interesting document could be drawn up from really competent research into the picture which the African has made of Boer and Briton, of gentleman and "poor white." Every intelligent European who has lived under conditions of race contact knows that while the master will boast of the wholehearted devotion, and indeed admiration, of his servants and employees, these latter seldom live up to the high ideal of trust and simple reverence and fidelity. Discussing various questions with my informants in East and South Africa I was struck by the fact that having once broken down their shyness I was able to obtain from them a most depressingly lurid picture of the European's character. Pomposities and pretensions, clandestine lapses in conjugal fidelity, or scrupulous honesty were registered, noted, and expatiated upon to me at great length, with name, date, and place. There seems to exist a live tradition of ruthlessly malicious gossip about white residents in every part of Africa.

Considering this, it might be wise to explain to the natives carefully, and without either criticism or hypocrisy, the interests, aims, and duties of various European functionaries and entrepreneurs. It would be also useful to give rudiments of European law, of its working and administration, and a general idea about the wider world to which the Africans now really belong. Such knowledge would naturally have to be imparted with a great deal of skill and tact, and will differ from one part of the country to another. But that a direct and careful interpretation should be given of some of the elements of Western culture, as well as the sociology of its carriers, is in my opinion incontrovertible.

In short, I believe that the European education given to the African ought to be directed so as to give him the maximum preparation for contact with the white community. He ought to have some knowledge of his rights and claims, as also of his duties and liabilities. It ought also to give him a clear idea from the outset of his own artificially imposed disabilities, so as not to develop in him the hope that through education he can become the white man's "brother" and his economic and political equal.

And with all this, such schooling as we give him should never militate against his respect for his own tribal dignity and racial characteristics. And this brings us to the question of how the slogan of "educating the African on African lines" can be interpreted so as to give it some substance, rather than to make it a caricature of itself.

EDUCATION ON AFRICAN LINES

We have dismissed the principle of "educating the African on African lines," insofar as the African does also need frankly European schooling. But this does not mean that he should be brought up through a process of gradual estrangement from things African. This has been said already. The African, because of the European attitude toward him, has to live among people of his own color. Whether after his term of service in white man's employment he returns to his tribe and continues to live in a semiuprooted state on farms or in a native township, his social medium will still be African, tribal or "detribalized." The word "detribalization" is one of those blanket expressions used to obscure the issue, so it will be better to say a word about it. The African, even the highly educated Bantu of South Africa, still prefers to *lobola* his wife; still adheres to his own language, with all the cultural and intellectual attitudes which this implies; still behaves in matters legal, sentimental, and personal according to the old Bantu kinship code. I have had in my class several men, young and mature, of African extraction, and I have found that they and their class have not completely adopted the European social and cultural ways, but have had to preserve a twofold attitude. Even I as a Pole have not adopted the English ways after thirty years of life in this country, but continue with a twofold social personality. The vast mass of Africans still live in an African world, from which they have to emerge but partly and occasionally.[8]

But if it be true that through all the changes the African is still a participant in his own culture, then we must make an attempt to understand what has remained African and why it has remained so. The best way to do it is through the assessment of the old African moral values, social attitudes, and cultural peculiarities. Because, let us realize, whatever has survived from the old African heritage has survived through this wider process implicit in education, which has very little to do with schooling. This process must be studied so that we can appreciate its value and and its vices; see what we ought to preserve of it, where we have to act and where we have to abstain. For, even from a few telling and dramatic examples it could be shown that wherever African customs have been unintelligently and wantonly interfered with, grave consequences have followed.

There is no custom, perhaps, which at first sight would seem so unambiguously objectionable as that generally called "female circumcision." It is practiced in two areas, one in Kenya and the other in Tanganyika. In the first-named, missions and educational agencies have fought against it. In the other, it has been allowed to continue unmolested. In the first the ruthless suppression of the custom has led to strong native resistance and a great deal of political trouble. Incidentally, it has developed among the natives a passionate adherence to the custom. Round the Kilimanjaro the German missionaries as well as the Roman Catholics wisely abstained from any interference with this practice. In consequence, there is no agitation and no strong feeling about cliterodectomy among the natives and the custom shows signs of gradual and peaceful extinction. Initiation ceremonies have been ruthlessly prohibited by one or two governments, as for instance in Portuguese East Africa; they are being incorporated into Christian training by the Universities' Mission in Tanganyika Territory. Here also there is no doubt at all which policy is the wiser and produces better results. It also shows that not infrequently the missions take a more enlightened and sympathetic attitude toward native customs than the government. Native marriage law, of which the bride price is an essential element, has been forcibly abolished in some parts of Africa. It had to be everywhere reinstated and given full legal recognition. Wherever *lobola* and native marriage law have been left alone we find none of the serious disturbances of native domestic life and even of morality which follow any tampering with it.

These instances show that the correct application of full anthropological knowledge by missions or governments is always amply rewarded. The moral is that now, when through the development in modern anthropological technique in field work we can fairly easily learn all there is to be learned about natives and their culture, there is no excuse for committing blunders or continuing in them.

Functional anthropology teaches that education must exist in every culture, because everywhere the continuance of tradition has to be preserved by being handed on from one generation to another. In simple cultures there is no schooling; education takes place partly in the domestic milieu through the personal influence of the parents on the children. Everywhere, however, there are some agencies, customs, initiation ceremonies, and even social groups more specially connected with training. Again, apprenticeship to technical tasks can either be accomplished through parents or nearest kindred, or given by skilled specialists, or else by the very playmates of the child. These factors combine in such a variety of ways that the anthropologist cannot remain satisfied with a mere enumeration. He has to study the problem afresh in every tribe. Even if we were to confine our attention to Bantu Africa, we should find surprising diversities. Among the Thonga the child has to leave its own parents and move either to its paternal or maternal grandparents. These give him a good deal of the earliest training. Among the Bemba the child at a somewhat later stage goes to the maternal grandparents. Among most of the Ngoni-speaking tribes the child remains at home. In some tribes the boy at about six years of age becomes almost completely emancipated from any control of elders and is incorporated into a little independent community of his contemporaries. These groups exercise independent economic functions, usually connected with herding, have their own rules of conduct and a new educational technique with apprenticeship to the pursuit and to communal life. In some tribes there is a long and rigorous system of age-grades, with initiations and severe discipline, as well as startling, almost shocking, liberties. There, general education as well as technical training and instruction in tribal lore is given. Such are the Masai and most of the Ngoni tribes, though here, perhaps, the system was introduced in an exaggerated form by the great conqueror Shaga (Chaka).

In short, anthropological field work ought to study in every tribe the system of education. What modern anthropology has added to the older approach is the functional point of view. By this is meant a study of the effects on the formation of mind and character, of the domestic milieu, of playmates and associates, of initiation rites and age groups, rather than a mere descriptive account of these institutions. The older, formal approach was dominated by the idea that where there is no specific schooling there is no education. On the one hand, wherever there was a formal resemblance of an institution to a school, it was immediately credited with an exclusively educational function. Thus some writers exaggerated the educational character of initiation rites and described them as "tribal schools." In reality, however, primitive institutions show a variety of facets and functions, and the real difficulty in the analysis of primitive culture consists in disentangling the various influences according to their function rather than their form.

Let us examine some phases of Bantu education from this point of view. Every child at the beginning of its life is subject to the influence of the family in the narrow sense of the word, that is, the group consisting of the father, mother, and the child's brothers and sisters. The influence of this group ceases at weaning in some tribes, where the child is removed to another household. Can it therefore be neglected? Obviously not. Even if we do not go the whole length of some modern psychologists, we have to admit that the very early molding of habits, development of bodily faculties, and last but not least, the learning of language, remain the dominant influence in later life. Language consists not only of words, but also of the ideas which the words denote, and behind them lie the first germs of the whole tribal system of social relations, morality, and even religion. When the child remains with its parents and brothers and sisters till the beginning of its independent life, that is, up till the age of seven or eight, he learns a great deal more. He is instructed in good manners of eating and personal cleanliness, of address and respectful and proper conduct; he is taught how to use his hands, how to form his speech, how to behave ethically as well as correctly. The impressions of these early years are indelible. The attitude toward the father and mother, toward brother and sister, are the starting point of all later social relations. I shall take one or two examples from one special tribe, the Chagga, not only because I have spent more time among them than anywhere else in Africa, but also because we have some excellent accounts already published, and finally because I have before me an article soon to be published in the *Journal of the Royal Anthropological Institute* by one of my pupils, Mr. Raum, who himself has grown up in close contact with this tribe.[9]

Take the simplest and most elementary matter of human life: food and eating. Among the Chagga the mother holds the dominant position, not only because she contributes to a large degree to the provision of the food, but also because she controls the stores. The children receive the food first and the mother hands them over the platter without reserving anything for herself. But she expects each of her children to leave over a portion for her and, later on, when they are more responsible, she insists that this is done with due consideration for her claims. Also this is often the occasion for the development of the earliest ethical attitudes in the children. The weaker and younger must get a fair share of food; the older must not only acquiesce but must be active in this. The obedient child with good manners obtains his reward by receiving the better share.

Now those who know the tribal life of the Bantu and who understand human nature in general realize the importance of food in the formation of social attitudes.[10] Not only Pavlov's dogs were conditioned into all types of behavior by the use of a raw piece of steak. Human beings are very largely "conditioned" by food and sex, and food attitudes and sex attitudes are naturally formed within the family. The earliest tabus among the Chagga are also taught by the mother. Familiarities between children of opposite sex who are not marriageable are early eliminated by sarcasm, persuasion, gentle handling, or a rough rebuke.

Family life and the teaching of the most important principles of behavior are but two facets of the same reality. The obligations and duties of kinship, the tribal solidarity of which it is the foundation, the principles of ancestor worship, are inculcated in the family and through the ordinary life of the family. In this the child has to live through certain elementary experiences and acquire a correct use of kinship terms.

In this intimate personal education, the parents and elders teach a lesson which is not made ad hoc, but which is an all-pervading reality in which both parents and children move. The children learn by example as well as by precept; they learn things which they can see and touch.

And here it cannot be sufficiently emphasized that a missionary or a European teacher must not approach the whole problem of training the young in Africa without realizing that he does not deal with a clean sheet or with an infinitely plastic material. He must become aware that he is faced with a living, complex, and powerful reality to which he must conform, and he must not try to force it into his foreign and artificial scheme.

If we were to follow the life history of a typical Bantu, we should find that the boy gradually has to take up his serious life work through apprenticeship to his father or his maternal uncle, his grandfather, or a playground of contemporaries. Very often imitative games gradually pass into serious work. Invariably the manual skills are acquired side by side with a growing recognition of one's duties toward parents and kindred, toward the chief or the tribal elders. When young boys spend some time in a small community of their own, discipline is often imparted by the old and excellent method of thrashing the younger by the older. In such groups a very early sense of citizenship is developed. When children play or roam the jungle or the veldt, they also learn the tribal lore in natural history, always with direct reference to practical activities.

Girls early assist their mothers in looking after younger children. They go with small pots to the waterhole, where they listen to feminine gossip, acquire feminine ways and vanities, and learn tribal lore. At home they assist in looking after the younger brothers and sisters, sweep the hut, and prepare food or stamp corn. Both sexes are constant spectators in the tribal life of elders and acquire early a good deal of diffused folklore; dancing and public ceremonies at first fascinate them and excite their imitative interests; then rouse their curiosity; explanation is asked for and given as to their meaning; and finally, the children are drawn into them.[11]

Volumes could be written and have been written about one phase of African education: I mean, of course, initiation ceremonies and age-grades. I shall only make one or two points in conjunction with this, referring the reader once more to Mrs. Hoernlé's article, to the excellent contribution by the Bishop of Masasi, and to the graphic descriptions of Junod and Gutmann, of Smith and Dale, and Miss Earthy. Miss Earthy and, following her, Mrs. Hoernlé have emphasized the value of initiation ceremonies among the Valenge and Vachopi; at such ceremonies a good deal of tribal lore is imparted, some knowledge of the physiology of sex, rules about the upbringing of children, and the duties between husband and wife. But there is one aspect which has not been brought out and which has been discovered by Dr. Richards in her field work among the Bemba. In that tribe, the leader of the girls at initiation, the *Nacimbusa* as she is called, not merely exercises some authority during the ceremony, but also, later in life, remains an adviser in personal, sexual, or matrimonial matters. Whenever any difficulty arises, the Bantu girl does not need to go to the psychoanalyst, consulting psychologist, or social worker. She goes to the *Nacimbusa*, who advises her and her husband, arbitrates, at times even pronounces judgment. The whole system, therefore, has a permanent value, not merely in the knowledge and training imparted during initiation, but in creating a really practical institution afterward which makes for conjugal stability.[12]

Today, under European influence, marriage is contracted in what to the African is an illegal manner. The abolition or weakening of bride-price guarantees has undermined the effective economic and legal sanctions. Girls are not given any training in matters of personal and domestic conduct. Their natural helpmates and advisers are taken from them. Small wonder that modern marriage in Africa, though nominally often Christian or legal, is a very much inferior institution to the ancient one.

Another point concerning initiation ceremonies, which perhaps is not sufficiently appreciated by the layman, is that the age-grade is another group in which a number of duties, solidarities, and responsibilities are developed and maintained; these once lost cannot be easily recovered. Men, as well as women, who have been initiated together, have mutual loyalties to maintain, practical principles to carry out, and systems of economic cooperation which are invaluable. Where chieftainship is developed, the heir-apparent is usually initiated with a large group of his future subjects, who eventually will form his special bodyguard, or at least owe him special loyalty. The attempt of an enlightened African chief[13] to incorporate the age-grade system into the national training of the Swazi has already been mentioned.

Again, in ancestor worship, there is a spiritual value with enormous moral potentialities, deeply rooted in family life and in the social structure of the whole tribe. In my opinion, Christianity ought to conserve the reverence for father and mother which is at the core of ancestor worship, rather than to destroy it, since it develops domestic virtues and contributes toward healthy and strong family sentiments.

It might be urged by a critic that I have rather emphasized such aspects of African culture as family life, age-grades, or chieftainship, which would naturally be less contested—and so I have. Cannibalism and witchcraft, slavery and mutilations, trial by ordeal or the blooding of spears, I have not discussed. The reason for that is not that I would agree with the wholesale moral condemnation of one and all of these. On the part of Europeans this is mere cant. The small-scale African wars, with all their cruelty and destruction, were not half as barbarous as are our modern European military escapades. The great war claimed some 20 million victims and disorganized a few score nations.

A good case could be made out for African slavery (though not for European and Arab slave raiding in Africa), as compared with the modern systems of organized and forced labor to which we have submitted the African. For this labor is forced

insofar as our method of rigid taxation and the destruction of the natural foundations of his economic livelihood leave him no choice but to sell his work without
the economic and legal safeguards of ordinary hired labor. But, although I have to
put this briefly on record—it is the anthropologist's duty to state the facts of comparative cultural assessment plainly—all this type of argument is irrelevant from any
practical point of view. Witchcraft, cannibalism, African slavery, and warfare are
dead issues, and certainly no sane man, even if he be an anthropologist, would ad-
vocate seminars for sorcerers, refresher courses for culinary cannibalism, or practical
teaching in poison ordeal or witch smelling.

CONCLUSIONS

The motifs which have been running throughout this article and the points which
have emerged can now be briefly summarized:

1. Education is bigger than schooling.
2. We are supplying the schooling somewhat artificially; for full education
the African child has still to rely on his social and cultural milieu.
3. European schooling if divorced from the African background contributes toward the breakdown of tribal life and cultural continuity.
4. African education is not dead, even in "detribalized" areas; it lives in
family life, in the structure of kinship and community, in the special setting
of native economic pursuits, old and new.
5. European schooling and African education have to be harmonized and
carried on simultaneously, with conscious direction and adjustment. The alternative is conflict within the individual and chaos in the community.
6. The focusing of this adjustment lies in respect for African values and an
equipment to meet the impact with European civilization, as well as cooperation with the European community. Education must proceed on these two
fronts simultaneously.
7. The addition of European schooling, as part of our culture impact, raises
the African above his own standard of living; it develops his ambitions and
needs, economic, political and cultural. To pour all the money, energy, and
zeal into schooling and "developing," without any wherewithal to satisfy the
resulting claims, is the royal road to a social catastrophe.

We have started a process which cannot now be checked. The Africans are on the
move. They will not return to the old groove of tribal life, though they will not
abandon all their heritage rapidly and completely for some time to come. Their
capacities and desires have been awakened. They need more land than we have left
them, more economic opportunities than we have opened up for them, and greater
political autonomy. There must take place a revision of the color-bar policy; sooner
or later better conditions in towns and more breathing space in the reserves will
have to be given. These are the cornerstones of a sound educational policy.

These conclusions obviously do not refer to South Africa alone or specially. The
contact of race is a worldwide problem and its implications cannot be discussed
with regard to one part of the world alone. At the same time, what happens in
South Africa affects the events north of the Zambezi, arouses political passions in
the West Indies, and in the United States and begins to attract the interest of one or
two armed and organized powers who have taken upon themselves the leadership of
the colored races as against the white. If in the present essay I have succeeded in
placing education within its wider context, however inadequately, I have to this extent accomplished my task.

NOTES

1. Quoted from "School Education and Native Life" by J. W. C. Dougall, in *Africa* (III: 49). I shall not refer to the older books on African education; they are well known and a glance at them will show that most of the problems discussed in the present essay have been largely neglected in them. Only recently, and in connection with the activities of the International Institute of African Languages and Cultures, have the problems here discussed been taken up. In what follows I shall have more to quote from Dougall's article, from an article on "The Native Conception of Education in Africa" by Mrs. Hoernlé (*Africa*, IV: 145 ff.), and from an essay on "The Double Mind in African Education" by Professor F. Clarke (*Africa*, V: 158 ff.). My present contribution is perhaps nothing more than a synthesis of what these writers had to say. That a distinguished anthropologist well acquainted with South African tribal life, a practical educationist working in East Africa, and one of the leading authorities in the theory of education, with upwards of twenty years of experience in South Africa, were moved almost simultaneously to attack the cultural setting of the problem, which at the same time had been occupying my attention, is significant of the need for its clear statement. Cf. also the excellent book *The Re-Making of Man in Africa* by J. H. Oldham and B. D. Gibson.
2. "If we wish to understand and to help these African peoples, it is essential that we should learn to look at their culture and their world with their eyes, in order that we may know the basis of the faith by which they live, otherwise we run a grave risk of inadvertently destroying the foundations of social organization and belief, which make life not only tolerable but possible at all" (*Africa*, IV: 145).
3. Clarke, *Africa*.
4. See *Report of Native Economic Commission*, 1930–32 (U. G. 22, 1932), para. 14. At the very beginning, italicized by the editors, it reads: "The native economic question is therefore how best the native population can be led onward step by step in an orderly march to civilization." I beg to differ there. The native economic question is how the native can live on an insufficiency of land, on *artificially cut wages* and without any capital whatever which he can devote to the development of his land and the purchase of his working tools. In paras. 20 to 30 entitled jointly "The tribal background of the problem," all the defects of the native social organization are pointed out, with the obvious implication that they are responsible for the low economic status of the natives. In paras. 31 and 32 ancestor worship is submitted to a somewhat similar criticism. Finally, in para. 31, we have a general indictment: "The system is generally opposed to progress, is reactionary, stagnant." In para. 76 it is added: "It would be idle to blame the Native for all this." Yet there is this implication running right throughout the whole report. There is no doubt whatever that the tribal system as it now exists among the Bantu is not one adapted to modern intensive agriculture or industry. At the same time it must be emphasized that on a couple of acres, with no capital for improvement, with no possibilities for marketing, the greatest agricultural expert could do nothing more than starve or semistarve. The present writer fully acknowledges that for political reasons the Economic Commission could do nothing else but recommend the only thing which at present can be recommended, that is, spiritual advancement of the natives. But not being politically bound himself, the present writer also feels that you cannot educate any one to live on two ounces of bread per day if he needs sixteen.
5. Dougall, *Africa*, III: 51.
6. Compare also the article "The Christian Approach to Non-Christian Customs" by the Rt. Rev. W. V. Lucas, Bishop of Masasi, in *Essays Catholic and Missionary*, ed. E. R. Morgan (1928), especially pp. 124–28. Here the story of the changing attitude of missionaries toward heathen customs is sincerely and dramatically told. I quote the author's summary from p. 116: "At first ignorantly indulgent. Pastoral care brings knowledge of evil. . . . First discovery produces the reaction of wholesale condemnation, but such zeal is not according to knowledge. . . . Damage is greatest when a party of revolt arises amongst converts. Conversions hindered by such a party. . . . Strange customs are not necessarily bad. Conservation to be aimed at, consistently with Christian holiness." I should like to add that the whole article, and indeed the whole book, is of the greatest value as a charter for the possible future cooperation between missionary and anthropologist.

7. English would of course have to be replaced by Afrikaans wherever this latter is spoken by the majority of Europeans. The French and Belgians have already adopted the policy here advocated in their colonies.
8. Cf. the contribution of Mrs. Hoernlé to the South African conference on education; also her article in *Africa*, vol. IV, and the memoirs by Mrs. Hellman and Mrs. Krige in vols. VIII and IX. Consult also some of the references under the word "detribalization" in the index of *Western Civilization and the Natives of South Africa*, ed. I. Schapera. In looking through the volumes of *Bantu Studies*, *Africa*, and of the *Journal of the African Society*, the reader will be convinced readily that detribalization in the sense that the African has completely lost touch with his African institutions is a figment.
9. Cf. B. Gutmann, *Das Recht der Dschagga* and *Die Stammeslehren der Dschagga*; and also C. Dundas, *Kilimanjaro and its People*.
10. Compare *Hunger and Work in a Savage Tribe* by A. I. Richards, 1932, an excellent study of the sociology of nutrition with special reference to Bantu cultures.
11. Compare also Mrs. Hoernlé, and I. Schapera's article on "Old Bantu Culture" in *Western Civilization and the Natives of South Africa* (pp. 20-22). I have drawn on these sources, as well as on Raum's manuscript and the book by Dr. A. I. Richards.
12. I am indebted to Dr. Richards for allowing me to use this information which I obtained from her during my month's stay among the tribe; I was also able to follow it up there with several native informants.
13. It may be well perhaps to quote the memorable words of Sobhuza II, Paramount Chief of the Swazi nation, in his memorandum on the subject presented to the European administration. Criticizing the purely European educational system, he says: "It causes the Swazi scholar to despise Swazi institutions and his indigenous culture." He then points out that it is a mistake "to treat Africans as Europeans, without first trying to discover what it was that produced good qualities in their own system of education, and without considering how they might be expected to react to a system of education so foreign to their culture." He suggests that the "better course would appear to be to use their own culture as a foundation and erect the superstructure of European education upon it, and so bring out what is best in both, bringing the Africans to world civilization as true Africans." An enlightened friend of the African, the Bishop of Masasi, also in advocating the incorporation of initiation ceremonies into Christian training writes: "Indeed, it cannot be too strongly emphasized that the ceremonies and beliefs of peoples of lowly culture are so closely bound up with economic and social factors of various kinds that the ill-considered destructions of its ritual and beliefs may involve vital wounds to the whole social structure" (*Essays Catholic*, p. 129).

5 / Primitive Education
Margaret Mead

Primitive education, the process by which preliterate peoples induct children into the cultural tradition of the tribe, is characterized by a very great variety of theories and practices. Different societies select diverse customs for explicit emphasis. The Manus of Admiralty Island give definite early training in the respect for property; Samoans neglect to give any such specific instruction to their children, yet adult Samoans like adult Manus habitually respect property and property rights. Etiquette may be taught very early, as among the Omaha Indians and the Samoans, or the children may be given unbridled license for years, as among the Manus, yet in all three societies the adults observe the customary rules of etiquette. The Manus spend a great deal of time in teaching small children to make correct physical adjustments; the Samoans leave these same adjustments to the casual care of slightly older children and to the processes of imitation. The Kaffirs of South Africa and the Manus do not demand social responsibility from their children until they reach or pass puberty, while the Cheyennes and the Omahas treated the smallest child as an inefficient but nevertheless responsible member of society. A people may select a single technical skill to be taught by social and religious elaboration, as did the Maori in the case of weaving and the Fijians in the case of the art of war, or they may permit their young people to acquire these same arts through play and casual imitation of adult activity, as in the making of mats in Samoa or in the case of the art of spear throwing among the Manus. The importance of the child's role in the community and the consequent attention which is lavished upon him may wax or wane with age: among the Manus young children of two or three are considered of paramount importance and the developing individual is accorded less and less general recognition until after the first few years of married life; in Samoa status and age are positively correlated. The standard set and the progress made by children may be determined by an indivdual standard, as among the Manus and apparently also among the Plains Indians, or by a group standard, in which a child is expected to approximate only to the average of its age group, as in Samoa. Differentiated behavior for the two sexes may be insisted upon at a very early age or not until puberty, and it may be of different sorts. There may be similar games but sex segregation, as in Samoa; or no sex segregation but an early differentiation of types of play, as among the Manus; or the children's group may be regarded as a unit in society, as in the children's camp of the Plains Indians or the Kaffir children's play communities, which had their own rules and regulations.

Adults are guided by varying conceptions of the child, who may be regarded as an adult in miniature, moved by the same motives which actuate his elders, as among the Plains Indians, or as an unaccountable and irritating creature to be deceived, threatened, and intimidated, as among the Kaffirs. There is also a wide variety in the self-consciousness with which the society views any of the processes of education. Among the Manus each child learns to swim by playing with slightly older children and in the same way he learns to beat a slit drum, to throw a spear or shoot a bow and arrow; the elders applaud informally but take no formal part. In Samoa the small child's debut on the dance floor is carefully stylized. The Plains Indians were notable for the degree of conscious instruction which was given children through legends and long moral homilies; among the Omaha a father began to train his young sons into a mystical receptivity to the supernatural at a very early age. Similarly, a Dobuan child is taught magic from his earliest years and is also required to plant and till a small garden plot of his own. The Manus children never receive any formal instruction in religion, magic, and the arts; physical proficiency, automatic respect for property, and intense prudery are instilled more by chastisement and communicated effect than by any formal appeal to reason.

Methods by which the points that the society has selected for emphasis are enforced upon recalcitrant children also vary widely. The Zuñi Indians fiercely deprecate parental corporal punishment but subject the child to the far more nerveracking experience of being whipped by the masked scare dancers. The Samoans have adopted the disciplinary technique of punishing not the culprit but the next oldest child, who is viewed as being responsible for the younger child's good behavior. The Manus punish a child before the age of three for infractions of the rules of physical training and respect for property but then permit the child to gain the upper hand and control the parents through sulking and threatened withdrawal of emotional allegiance—the parents reserving as a weapon the sense of shame which has been instilled into the young children and which can later be invoked to enforce tabus and social conformity. Attitudes toward the pace at which the child should acquire its cultural tradition and attempt to participate in adult activity also vary from the Samoan deprecation of all precocity to the gentleness and care with which the older men among the Cheyenne protect a child member of a war party against the teasing of the young men.

In spite of the greater frankness which characterizes much of primitive life there is wide divergence in attitudes toward sex knowledge and sex behavior. Seemliness is enjoined upon children in Samoa and in the Trobriands as the standard of sex behavior; Dobuan children are permitted a license in speech which would be a matter of insult if spoken by an adult; Manus children are denied the slightest approach to sex play. Manus parents make every effort to prevent their children from witnessing sex activity, while Samoan children make a game of spying upon lovers. In Samoa the youngest child is permitted to witness childbirth, but the Kaffirs felt constrained to lie in answer to children's questions about the facts of pregnancy and birth.

The role of the parents, the grandparents, and the older siblings is very differently conventionalized among different peoples. In many parts of Melanesia the father's role is that of an affectionate and indulgent nurse, which may be further elaborated by the contrast between the gentleness of the father and the sternness of the mother's brother, who in matrilineal societies assumes disciplinary authority. Among the Kru, however, a strong development of patriliny casts the father in a stern role from earliest childhood. Among the Omaha Indians the moral and disciplinary role was taken over by the grandparents; the parents apparently remained the subjects of active identification, so that a split between moral discipline and affectionate identification may have occurred. In matrilocal residence a child may find refuge from too much teasing in the arms of the husbands of his mother's sisters, as among the Zuñi Indians. The strong emphasis upon the fostering role of the father for young children of both sexes among the Manus results in the mother's taking a secondary role, which later complicates her daughter's satisfactory identification with her own sex. Rank within the household may have a strong influence upon the child's development, as in Samoa, where association between men of rank and young children is socially forbidden. The extension of the biological family to include in a close residential unit some dozen to two dozen relatives results in a child's always having brothers and sisters of various ages and makes the sibling relationship a dynamic one educationally. The opposite condition found in Dobu, where each small biological family lives by itself and the child is continuously with its parents, prevents the sibling relationship from any important functioning.

The degree to which the supernatural is invoked as a disciplinary measure also varies arbitrarily. The Kaffirs invoked monsters in whom they do not themselves believe in order to intimidate the children; the Manus rely more upon scare stories of land devils than upon the ancestral spirits in fear of which the community of adult Manus lives; the Dobuans early instill into their children a lively fear of the sorcery of members of other villages and this same fear is a powerful social deterrent in adult life.

Because initiation and puberty rites are conspicuous and lend themselves easily to description, there has been an overemphasis upon their educational significance. Puberty rites are characteristics not of all primitive societies but of some cultural areas in which particular and usually contiguous or related social groups have selected the period of puberty for social, economic, religious, or educational elaboration. Initiation ceremonies for boys and girls are also found to have definite geographic distributions. Where either puberty or initiation rites occur, these ceremonies may have an explicit educational reference, as among the Koko Papuans, where consecutive religious training is given to the segregated boys; or they may be merely the admission of the initiate into some secret of adult life. Puberty ceremonials for girls may be oriented to their future success and moral and social achievement, as among the Thompson Indians, where the girl performs symbolic acts which are believed to encourage her magically and practically in various desirable moral traits; or they may be oriented to a protection of the community of the girl from maleficent supernatural influences, as in various parts of California; or they may be definitely directed toward beautifying the girl, as among the Gilbert Islands and in East Africa. In the Gilbert Islands the nubile girl must remain in a hut which is shrouded from light in order to beautify her complexion, making any industrial pursuit impossible; but moral and legendary exhortation is given her by some elderly female relative. On the other hand, there are many cases, as among the Dobuans, where there is no social recognition of puberty for educational or any other purpose. Puberty only becomes a crisis if the society has so conventionalized it; it is not necessary to tide an individual over the period of physiological puberty nor the period of social acceptance into the adult group unless that adult group has first phrased either one or both of these universal experiences as some sort of dangerous ordeal.

Definite social institutions designed primarily or at least in part for the instruction of the young are the exception rather than the rule in primitive society. They do not correlate with the amount of esoteric lore to be learned or the difficulty and intricacy of any technique which is to be handed down from specialists in one generation to novitiates in the next but are special developments. The formal training given the priestly novitiate in the Whare Wananga, the sacred college of the Maori, observed all the customary fomalities of instruction such as common residence, a teaching class, examinations, and graduation—although these were muffled in magical practices which cloud the analogy. Among the Zuñi, on the other hand, where there is apparently far more ritual to be memorized, no such institution is developed. A similar contrast is found between instruction in the art of housebuilding in Samoa and among the Indians of the northwest coast of America. Housebuilding in Samoa although not remarkably complicated was in the hands of a definitely recognized group of craftsmen, and apprenticeship to this group and recognition by it were necessary before an individual could become an accepted housebuilder. No such institution is found on the northwest coast, although there more elaborate houses are constructed. In Polynesia the emphasis upon payment for magical or traditional information is lacking; in North America payment between the novice and the master is strongly conventionalized. Where hereditary professions are found in a stratified society, such as in Africa with its smith's group or in India, the problem of technical education receives a special emphasis. The lack of correlation between the formality of training and the complexity of tradition no longer obtains when the tradition becomes as complex as that of ancient Mexico or Peru.

Primitive education, whatever its methods, whatever the age at which formal training is given, regardless of who the teacher is or what disciplinary means are employed, is from a superficial angle uniformly successful. In all cases the tradition of the society is absorbed by the young. As primitive education does not aim at improvement or at innovation, the standards which modern educational philosophers set up cannot be applied to it. Although divergent societies seem to attain objectively similar results, more detailed studies of primitive education, using as criteria the special consequences to the individual rather than the general results for the society as a whole, may provide data showing differential results. The varying ages at which different social attitudes and habits are instilled may be found to be a decisive factor in the peaceful adjustment of the individual to the demands of his society. Whether respect for property is made an automatic response, as among the Manus, or is enforced by fear of sorcery, as in Dobu, or by the fear of vendetta, as in Ifugao, may make a significant difference. The relative degree to which affection, fear, or shame are utilized as socializing techniques may also be found to have important reverberations in the individual personality. The institutions of social control in any society may be found to be in some measure necessitated by or at least responsive to the type of training which is given the children, to the sex, age, and relationship of the teacher, to the age of the child, and to the techniques of training which are employed.

Striking contrasts are found when primitive education is compared with education in modern society. Modern education is a formal institution integrated with economic and political institutions, a fact which tends to obscure the essential similarity in all societies of the purpose of a total educational process, which may be defined as the assimilation of each individual to a cultural tradition. The great accumulation of knowledge and techniques in a society with a written tradition, a huge population, and extensive division of labor makes the educational process impinge differentially upon members of the growing generation. The heterogeneity of contemporary culture also results in propagandist groups developing educational institutions of their own. Although modern man like primitive man cannot teach his children anything which some adults in the culture have not already mastered, it is possible to change so radically the proportions among those who learn different aspects of the accumulated tradition that profound quantitative changes may be wrought in society. It is for this reason that primitive education appears to be much more static than does education in our modern civilization.

REFERENCES

Chinnery, E. W. P., and Beaver, W. N. "Notes on the Initiation Ceremonies of the Koko, Papua." *Royal Anthropological Institute of Great Britain and Ireland Journal* 45 (1915): 69–79.

Fortune, R. F. *Sorcerers of Dobu* (London, 1931).

Gennep, Arnold van. *Les rites de passage* (Paris, 1909).

Grimble, Arthur. "From Birth to Death in the Gilbert Island." *Royal Anthropological Institue Journal* 51 (1921): 25–54.

Grinnell, G. B. *The Cheyenne Indians*, 2 vols. (New Haven, 1923).

Hambly, W. D. *Origins of Education among Primitive Peoples* (London, 1926).

Hovey, E. O. "Child-life among the Smith Sound Eskimos." *Natural History* 18 (1918): 361–71.

Kidd, Dudley. *Savage Childhood* (London, 1906).

Malinowski, Bronislaw. *Sex and Repression in Savage Society* (London, 1927) and *The Sexual Life of Savages in Northwestern Melanesia* (London, 1929).

Mead, Margaret. *Coming of Age in Samoa* (New York, 1928) and *Growing Up in New Guinea* (New York, 1930).

Miller, N. *The Child in Primitive Society* (London, 1928), chs. vii–x.

Ploss, Heinrich. *Das Kind in Brauch und Sitte der Völker*, 2 vols. (3rd ed. by B. K. Renz, Leipsic, 1911–12).

Van Waters, M. "The Adolescent Girl among Primitive Peoples." *Journal of Religious Psychology* 6 (1913): 375–421, and 7 (1914–15): 75–120.

Part III

The Relation of Anthropology to Education

6 / An Anthropological Framework for Studying Education

Thomas J. La Belle

Cultural anthropology is perhaps the most recent of the social sciences to concern itself with the field of education. Although educators have for some time been concerned with the influence of society and culture on the goals and content of educational programs, until recently the anthropologist has not been active in the analysis of educational phenomena or in educational decision making. Instead, educators have been forced to rely upon ethnographies which often have little apparent relevance to their more applied interests.

With the increased attention given to subcultural groups in the United States during the 1960s, however, the two fields began to merge. Scholars soon realized the contributions which could be gained from systematic investigations of schools and their relationship to these minority populations. Thus in 1968 members of the American Anthropology Association formed the Council on Anthropology and Education in order to create a group of individuals concerned with the application of anthropological concepts and methods to the study of the educational process. In addition, departments of education and anthropology respectively began to offer courses and programs for the training of educational anthropologists.

Although much confusion exists about how the two fields can best unify efforts, there is common interest in the educational process, in what learners do as they adapt to certain environments, and what is done to and for learners with respect to specific educational goals.

This process is viewed in terms of cultural learnings as individuals and institutions adhere to one or more sociocultural traditions. The educational anthropologist investigates the orientation of transmitter and learner as well as the content and method of the transmission to test for continuity and discontinuity within and between cultural groups. My purpose here is to offer a cultural perspective on the school and the teaching-learning process.

ENCULTURATION AND SCHOOLING

Many individuals, including educators, are guilty of a somewhat narrow conception of education. We have been accustomed to viewing education as an institutional outcome, something which results from attending a school. Thus experiences which occur outside of school become, in terms of sociocultural expectations, nonsanctioned learnings. These out-of-school learning experiences occur most often without credit or recognition even though educators know them to have tremendous impact on in-school and out-of-school behavior. Anthropologists, on the other hand, reverse this outlook. They have viewed education as being synonymous with enculturation or the process by which an individual learns his own culture—a conception more adequate for simple rather than complex societies because the homogeneity of the former supports only one cultural tradition.

Through the analysis of the patterns of behavior instilled in early childhood, anthropologists have assumed that one can understand much of the adult behavior of a particular cultural group.[1] Until recently anthropologists have not had occasion to view the school as an aspect of this enculturation process. One of the reasons for this somewhat curious omission may be related to a perception of the school as a societal institution which reflects the wider social and cultural influences and is assumed to reinforce the externally sanctioned customs. Although this is true, there ı reason to believe that the school establishes a discontinuous relationship with society,[2] first because it may not meet with society's stated expectations by failing to instill widely held values and attitudes, and second, because it is discontinuous with the population it serves. As some have suggested, the school is designed to make lawyers out of farm boys and patriots out of immigrants. Such a discontinuity exists most often when the school is in the hands of a dominant culture and the population it serves is not in accord with that pattern.

Schools as the locus for culturally sanctioned learning are associated with much of this discontinuity for learners. Although a young person is physically mature in his teens, in the United States his level of cultural maturity is viewed as insufficient for full participation in the society. Schools assume the function of providing recognized learnings which enable the young person to eventually adjust to and be creative in the greater culture. Compulsory schooling, therefore, extends the period of adolescence, or the "crisis" period (as North Americans tend to perceive it). Compulsory schooling, however, is not manifested solely in the laws which fix minimum age for school leaving, but also in the social importance placed on increasing levels of school attainment. The sociocultural press encourages youngsters from grammer school through high school to "go to college."

As an example, assume that a male in the United States graduates from high school at the age of eighteen, enters the military service, and upon discharge, goes to college. He spends a minimum of four years receiving his degree and decides to become a schoolteacher. He is twenty-four or twenty-five. He completes an additional year of course work for his state teaching certificate and finds that in order to compete with teachers who presently hold positions he must secure a Master of Arts degree. After an additional year behind a school desk, he celebrates his twenty-seventh birthday and begins his search for a teaching position. He has used more than one-third of his life, mostly in school, in preparation for his first opportunity to assume responsibility outside of school.

The responsibilities he has had prior to assuming the role of teacher have been minimal: a few part-time jobs to see him through the extended period financially and some structured decisions regarding which courses to take to fulfill requirements. Above all he has learned to become dependent upon others and, through this, has acquired great skill in following instructions. Although there are many variations on how a person makes it through extended adolescence, the outcome is much the same. The period is marked by crisis; the individual may not only have thought that during at least the last ten years of his life he was physically mature, but also might have been confident of his ability to make substantive contributions to the society. Such cases may indicate a society which places great faith in institutional schooling and which is ready to cope with the insurrections which are indirectly supported through such a system.

Educational anthropologists are concerned with the process by which children become adults and the cultural definition of adulthood. Not all cultures view the process of maturation as we do. Adolescence might not be recognized at all, as was shown by Margaret Mead's investigations in Samoa. Institutional schooling, as is the case with literacy, may play a part in the demarcation of particular stages of development within cultures.

> In preliterate cultures, knowledge is sought by pupils as a guide to their inevitable life roles. The child always is in close physical contact with the matured activity that he is merely learning. By contrast, in literate cultures, the very phenomena of literacy permits a separation between the learning and the doing. The school itself, and what the pupil is learning in it, are physically separate from adult application of the learning. One result is the child's failure to feel an immediate relevance in the relation between what is being taught him now and what this has to do with the rest of his life.[3]

Educators are slow to note that institutional schooling fosters discontinuity and alters conceptions of child growth and development, and the school continues to be viewed narrowly as the panacea for answering present and future societal problems. Our orientation apparently assumes that a world characterized by crisis can be changed by placing more and more individuals in schools.

THE "TOUSLED-HEAD" PHENOMENON

There are other social and cultural reasons for keeping people in school. As George A. Pettitt remarks:

> Many non-educational agencies are not at all unhappy with the school system because it gives them a scapegoat to blame for sociocultural ailments. The United States Department of Labor has consistently maintained that unemployment occurs because the most elaborate school system in the world is not elaborate enough. Organized labor is relieved of responsibility for restrictions on apprenticeships in skilled trades and is free to fight for higher minimum wage laws because of the growing acquiescence in the idea that all young people are better off in school. Industrial and business management, which must compete with the world on the basis of quality, production efficiency, and cost, prefers not to be bothered with inexperienced juveniles for whom minimum wage laws make no reasonable differential, whose ages must be doubly checked for compliance with school attendance laws, whose employment involves added paper work with governmental and union supervisors of apprenticeships, and whose hours and working conditions must be watched to avoid infraction of child labor laws. In addition, there is no special provision for juveniles in unemployment insurance, social security, pension plans, or health and other fringe benefit payments. This situation results from well-intentioned cultural elaborations promoted by public servants looking for popular causes to serve and private volunteers looking for worthy purposes to push. Unfortunately, neither category of culture-makers can appreciate the problems created in some of the tousled heads they are trying to save.[4]

The "tousled-head" phenomenon is evidence of an adult-centered world and is partly a result of the contradictory values which are set in front of a young person attempting to cope with his environment through adherence to an established orientation. The continuity in simple, as opposed to complex, societies is greater because the child's work and play are integrated into the total society. In American schools, however, the teacher often emphasizes one thing, such as creativity or individuality, yet makes an evaluation on the basis of an external source, for example when a primary student is asked to trace a cardboard figure of a clown rather than to draw or paint one.[5] Such activities, however, may be seen as both hypocritical and paradoxical by students. For example, learning the importance of the content of the constitution is one experience, but participation in student government is another, perhaps more important and lasting. Yet in school such student activities are often so tightly monitored by and dependent upon the approval of adults that the experience does not fulfill the ideal; it instead highlights the double standard upon which our wider sociocultural process depends.

The conflicts of cooperation versus competition, equality versus segregation, success in work versus social consciousness and sociability, independence versus obedience, and puritan morality versus situational ethics are only a few of the values which confront the American youngster as he attempts to learn appropriate culturally sanctioned behavior. Although such conflicts are most likely inevitable in a complex culture, the role of the school in coping with them is not yet clear. The youngster's peers provide sustenance for one set of value orientations, but the school and its referent culture are confused over which values to champion and under what conditions these values should be promoted. Thus the youngster may find solace with his peers and may work to promote continuity between opposing orientations. It is not that he rejects completely the values set out by the older generation; he cannot. Instead, he seeks to establish an integrative, noncontra- dictory thread to give coherence to such values. The school, in both the recognized and unrecognized learning experiences to which it acts as catalyst, is able to build upon this worthy effort by fostering consistency in such experiences.

THE SCHOOL AS LOCUS FOR CULTURAL LEARNING

All of the teaching and learning which occurs inside and outside of the school is related to one or more cultural traditions. Each activity can be explained rationally or nonrationally by the actors if they are queried about why they behave as they do, although such explanations may be no more than "we have always done it that way." The educational anthropologist views the planned and unplanned activities in which individuals engage from the perspective of an outsider in an attempt to ferret out the meaning they have for the participants.

As an example, schools show considerable dependence upon ritual and ceremony in the normal round of activities characterizing a school day.[6] From the lining up at classroom doors and raising of hands for permission to relieve oneself to the pep rally and graduation ceremony, such rites provide cohesion and structure to the institution yet are unrelated to the achievement of pragmatic ends. They enable participants to predict behavior patterns of others under similar circumstances. In part they form the recognized learning activities which transpire in the school.

The educational anthropologist identifies these recognized activities by interview- ing the participants, reviewing the curricular materials, and recording the daily activities of the transmitters and learners. The activities may be planned, in that they are sanctioned because they lead to a premeditated change in behavior, or they may be unplanned, in that they may inadvertently give rise to unintended behavior change. For example, the student council might be thought of as a recognized activity which is designed to foster in students behavior characteristic of legislators participating in a democratic decision-making process. Thus the experience is planned to manifest specific outcomes in learners. As mentioned earlier, however, the learners may find that the legislation they are asked to pass on is insignificant, or that the decisions made within the council are vetoed by the administration. Thus the recognized activity promotes covert behavior change in the form of nega- tive attitudes toward the council, the school, or the process. Recognized activities, therefore, can be analyzed in terms of anticipated and unanticipated outcomes.

Unrecognized learning activities also occur under the direction of the school. The school is tied to a referent culture, one from which it derives its norms and values and by which it justifies its activities. Value orientations form the basis for individual and societal needs and include our conceptions of time, space, innate human nature, causality, acceptable human activity, and the way in which men interact with each other.[7] Values indicate the ideals and goals of a culture and provide a population with rules to judge right from wrong and good from bad. Associated with these values, yet seldom mentioned, is the observation that much of everyone's behavior is based on habit, and is, therefore, unconscious and acquired over prolonged periods of time. These unconscious activities are often viewed as constants in the school and are, therefore, referred to here as unrecognized since they are rarely analyzed for their impact on learners. The gestures and forms of salutation we employ and our styles of walking and talking are some of the numerous activities which go unrecognized. These habitual acts provide us with a predictable pattern of behavior and they are the activities which give the population its unique life style. During crisis periods, when danger is perceived, or when we are deprived of essentials to carry on habitual acts, we may question these behaviors. Thus the student strike or the ethnic group picketing the school board may give rise to increased questioning of our normal activities.

In the school unrecognized learnings form a part of what Philip Jackson has called the "hidden curriculum," which he suggests requires as much mastery by students as the planned curriculum.

> Consider, as an instance, the common teaching practice of giving a student credit for trying. What do teachers mean when they say a student tries to do his work? They mean, in essence, that he complies with the procedural expectations of the institution. He does his homework (though incorrectly), he raises his hand during class discussion (though he usually comes up with the wrong answer), he keeps his nose in his book during free study period (though he doesn't turn the page very often). He is, in other words, a "model" student, though not necessarily a good one.[8]

Jackson implies that much of what goes on in classrooms may be expected activity but is not recognized as part of the stated curriculum sanctioned by the school. Jules Henry also has referred to these unrecognized learnings.

> A classroom can be compared to a communications system, for certainly there is a flow of messages between teacher (transmitter) and pupils (receivers) and among the pupils, contacts are made and broken, messages can be sent at a certain rate of speed only, and so on. But there is also another interesting characteristic of communications systems that is applicable to classrooms, and that is their inherent tendency to generate *noise*. . . . In a classroom lesson on arithmetic, for example, such *noise* would range all the way from the competitiveness of the students, the quality of the teacher's voice ("I remember exactly how she sounded when she told me to sit down") to the shuffling of the children's feet. The striking thing about the child is that along with his arithmetic—his "messages about arithmetic"—he learns all the *noise* in the system also. . . . It is this that brings it about that an objective observer cannot tell which is being learned in any lesson, the *noise* or the formal subject matter. But—and mark this well—it is *not* primarily the message (let us say, the arithmetic or the spelling) that constitutes the most important subject matter to be learned, but the *noise!* The

most significant cultural learnings—primarily the cultural drives—are communicated as "noise."[9]

Such observations suggest that what students really learn in schools is not the recognized curriculum; instead they learn from the way in which the schooling process is habitually conducted. They learn to be dependent, competitive, and obedient—goals which few curriculum specialists would sanction, yet goals which would be recognized by anyone who has thought about his school career as essential for survival.

Although we now have the technology and expertise to ensure the mastery of certain concepts by learners, we would be naive to view the objectives of a lesson, whether it be by teaching machine or by student contract, to be the only outcome of the process itself. Thus the unconscious messages transmitted as a result of the machine or the contract, or for that matter as a result of any human activity, must be acknowledged and evaluated from the perspective of the receiver as well as the transmitter. The educational anthropologist is concerned with investigating this sociocultural process across cultural boundaries from these two perspectives.

Both the recognized (planned and unplanned) and the unrecognized activities are important culturally because they may be directed to culture-specific or nonculture-specific ends when viewed in relation to the orientations of the learner (see table). For example, when the Anglo teacher begins teaching in a culturally different community, he becomes an agent of cultural diffusion. He utilizes his own cultural

	Culture-Specific to the Learner	Nonculture-Specific to the Learner
Recognized Planned Activities		
Recognized Unplanned Activities		
Unrecognized Activities		

tradition as a guide to promote changes in a new culture. In some respects the cultural traditions of teacher and learner are in conflict. In other words, what the teacher provides may not already be part of the students' community heritage. The outcome is cultural change by the teacher rather than reinforcement of the learner's referent culture.

Textbooks and other instructional materials can be an example of recognized unplanned activities which lead to nonculture-specific ends for the learner. In some social studies texts the Mexican-American is not only made out to be the descendent of aggressors and criminals as a result of the Alamo, but must read or see capsule portraits of himself as a lazy, fatalistic, and present-oriented individual whose only concerns are fiestas and *mañana*. One can only hypothesize the impact of such content on the self-fulfillment of a Mexican-American child, let alone the impact such sterotypes have for the Anglo child. The educational anthropologist wishes to view the impact on the group as a whole and may ask whether the self-fulfilling prophecy[10] is valid for an entire ethnic group.

LACK OF RECOGNITION

The Anglo teacher who interacts with a group of Anglo students will find great congruence in cultural background and consequently will reinforce the traditions of the learners. The teacher must recognize, however, even in this case, that some of the experiences in which teacher and learners engage are not those to which the teacher would adhere if the teacher realized that the messages transmitted were the result of adherence to habit rather than of conscious intent. I am suggesting that teachers take cognizance of the amount of behavior in classrooms which would not be sanctioned if that behavior was described for the teacher and the teacher knew that the result of such message transmission was either tangential or even antithetical to his stated goals. In the cross-cultural situation even the consciously planned activities are not scrutinized for their cultural loadings and can thus terminate in conflict and the cultural alienation of the learner.

The ways, for example, in which the teacher responds to student behavior, the often subtle distinctions made between the sexes, the nature of the classroom control mechanisms, the topics and issues chosen for classroom study, the schedule of activities in terms of the amount of time devoted to particular aspects of the school day, the spatial organization of the classrooms, and the rewards and punishments meted out are only a few of the activities which are culturally loaded and which, through habitual acts on the part of educators, transmit messages which reinforce certain student behavior and discourage others. Such daily activities tend to be characteristic of particular cultural groups, and thus are more widespread than phenomena resulting from individual personality types or social class groupings.

Dumont and Wax, in an article on the Cherokee Indians in northeastern Oklahoma, support this position. Most of the schools attended by these tribal Cherokee children are staffed with educators ethnically and linguistically different from the students they teach.

> Such classrooms may be denominated as "cross-cultural," although the ingredients contributed by each party seem to be weighted against the Indian pupils. The nature and layout of the school campus, the structure and spatial divisions of the school buildings, the very chairs and their array, all these are products of the greater society and its culture— indeed, they may at first glance seem so conventional that they fail to register with the academic observer the significance of their presence within a cross-cultural transaction. Equally conventional, and almost more difficult to apprehend as significant is the temporal structure: the school day; and the school calendar. The spatial and temporal grid by which the lives of the Indian pupils are organized is foreign to their native traditions, manifesting as it does the symbolic structure of the society which has encompassed them.[11]

Thus the organization and structure of an institution are evidence of cultural influences which prove alienating to a different ethnic population. The recognized schooling process in this case is directed toward nonculture-specific ends in terms of the orientation of the school administration when viewed in relation to the cultural background of the students.

The teacher in the classroom often evidences behavior which is based upon her expectations of appropriate human activity. One such expectation relates to social organization. For example, the teacher may view the nuclear family as the only stable family social organization in that it provides a child with siblings, father, and mother, all of whom reside within one dwelling. The teacher will also recognize that divorce and separation may negatively affect the child's personal and social development if it occurs after the basic nuclear pattern has been instituted. The teacher may not, however, realize that the matrifocal, or mother-headed family, if purposefully instituted by some ethnic groups, may be as stable as the nuclear type given the nature of the adaptations required for survival by those groups. The word "stable" then becomes exceedingly value laden since textbooks, classroom discussions, telephone calls to the home, and participation in some school activities are oriented toward the existence of a father in long-term residence.

Although more examples could be cited, the thrust of the argument should be clear. Schools do not promote cultural continuity for all students. Instead schools are just as likely to promote cultural change and force youngsters to cope with conflict in basic value orientations between the family and the wider society. Teachers must, therefore, take note of the nature of their habitual behavior and begin to analyze it for the effects it has on all of the students in the school. Forcing oneself to stand back from the school environment to discover those orientations which inhibit communication and are most likely to prove damaging seems to be the most valuable first step in such an analysis. This leads us to a discussion of the importance of culture in viewing the relationship between the school and its referent community and in viewing the school and classroom as sociocultural systems.

THE CULTURE CONCEPT

The culture concept forms the basis for the field of anthropology and inevitably permeates the field of educational anthropology. Culture encompasses the wide variety of customs and forms of social life characteristic of human behavior. Education, on the other hand, is the process through which cultures perpetuate and attempt to change themselves; it is concerned with the transmission, conservation, extension, and reconstruction of culture.

In order to understand how educational anthropologists use culture to view educational phenomena, it is necessary first to note the somewhat arbitrary use of the concept of anthropologists. Traditionally the culture concept has been applied to fit the ethnographer's operationally defined social group. In other words, the anthropologist draws arbitrary boundaries around a specific target population. This cultural system is then described as a relatively self-sufficient entity in which the decision-making capacity is inherent and the group's membership is controlled.[12] Some have suggested that there were never many truly isolated populations studied by anthropologists, since most populations have some contact with other groups. Anthropological boundaries are, therefore, tenuous and artificial; they are drawn in order to delineate in some way the traits which distinguish a particular community from others.[13] As will be shown later, the educational anthropologist is faced with a similar task as he views the school and classroom; the same arbitrary boundaries must be drawn.

In pluralistic societies such as the United States ethnic groups exist side by side with each other as well as with the dominant Anglo majority. As in other societies, religious, economic, political, and educational institutions transcend these specific minority cultures and exist irrespective of the specific settlement patterns of a minority group. As is the case with the school, these institutions reflect the dominant culture and are often called on to act as mechanisms for cultural integration. For example, some highland Indian populations of Latin America were absorbed into the greater or larger Hispanic tradition as a result of the Spanish conquest. Today, when studying such Indian populations, one needs to define which traditions have been imposed through dominant institutions. As an example, the rural Latin American village usually has a Catholic church which draws the Indians into a particular nation as well as into a wider world community.

The educational anthropologist studies how the assimilation is achieved through the school. Although the school is the main focus of school-community studies, it is assessed in terms of its incorporation into the society. Political and religious behavior, family life, peer mechanisms, language, economic pursuits, health practices, and social-class phenomena are viewed as part of the school's aims and daily operation.

Published school-community case studies now number about twenty and are available for Canada,[14] British Columbia,[15] Japan,[16] and Germany,[17] among others. The investigator in these situations is not attempting to suggest how the school should meet such problems; instead he is trying to describe what actually happens in schools.

The most successful investigations demand that the ethnographer live in the community and work with the school personnel as he describes day-to-day routine and conducts in-depth interviews with participants. We are currently studying the relationship between lower socioeconomic status families and one public and one private school in a Mexican border city. The early results indicate that the availability of schools is an important contribution factor to urbanization. The school, however, apparently does little to relate its existence to fulfilling student or community needs. The more than 60 percent dropout rate which occurs during the first three years of primary school attests to this lack of attention. By visiting homes and classrooms and by accompanying students, teachers, and parents in their daily activities, I and my colleagues hope to provide some insight into why Mexican migrants view the school positively yet dropouts are no numerous, and what the relationship is between life style and the curriculum and instruction encountered at school.

Such studies are more than statistical profiles. They also encompass more than attitudinal questionnaires. The school and its community are viewed as a cultural process, a system in operation. Educators then use such information to provide more concrete and relevant learning experiences for students. The school-community study becomes the base line for changes within the school. The school administrator and classroom teacher in the United States would most likely find such investigations valuable in designing curricula.

The educational anthropologist may apply the culture concept to a study of the school and classroom as sociocultural systems. It is recognized that the school cannot be viewed as a culture in and of itself since it draws external rules and norms, ideals, and values from the community of which it is a part.[18] Yet because of social class, racial caste, or ethnic differences few American communities are sufficiently homogeneous to warrant being considered complete cultural units. Rather, such communities are part of a wider sociocultural entity. Therefore, the investigator in a school which serves a multiple subcultural population must address himself to the various subcultural referent groups which come together in the institution. He studies the cultural backgrounds of students and staff and then looks at the compatibility between these populations and the experiences and goals established as part of the schooling process.

Although schools are inextricably bound to the external society and mirror that sociocultural influence, it is often difficult to identify the referent culture to which such schools are tied.[19] It is well known, however, that in cultural traits such referent populations may differ considerably from what is expected in the school and thereby widen rather than narrow the incongruity between the school and the population it serves.

The school and its primary unit, the classroom, are the locus for this cultural interaction and it is here that the educational anthropologist can pursue further ethnographic research. In addition, such analyses are appropriate irrespective of the classroom's function as a cultural interface. One of the major concerns of curriculum specialists is their lack of knowledge concerning what actually goes on in classrooms. Thus the educational anthropologist as participant-observer may aid in the development of curricular theory through cross-cultural research.

THE CLASSROOM AS SOCIOCULTURAL SYSTEM

One approach to classroom ethnography is to treat the classroom as a sociocultural system in which small groups of people are engaged in habitual activities leading to the achievement of specific goals. One anthropologist, Alan Beals, feels that any group of people who come together for a purpose can be considered a sociocultural system even though they may disband after such interactions. Airplane flight crews and children's play groups are among the units which Beals has analyzed in this way.

> When a set of people form a cultural system, a distinction is made between the things that belong to that group and the things that do not belong. Within the cultural system are the things (material culture), the people (society), the tradition (culture), and the activities that belong. Outside are the things, people, traditions, and activities that do not belong. A single game of seed, like a single funeral, can be considered to be an example of a particular process. Process is merely cultural system written small. Put another way, a cultural system is the sum total of all the processes, happenings, or activities in which a given set or several sets of people habitually engage. A process or a cultural system exists only when activities are taking place.[20]

It is possible that students and teachers engaged in goal oriented behavior can be analyzed as a subcultural system which meets the criteria established by Beals: the classroom contains people, material objects, a system in operation, and a tradition established over time. Students and teacher come together in a classroom to achieve goals. They use certain materials such as paper, pencils, desks, and blackboards to achieve these goals. The system revolves around teaching and learning through teacher- or student-designated experiences which are expected to enable children to achieve the desired ends. The tradition evolves or develops as a result of student and teacher coming together regularly in an attempt to fulfill the purposes of the system. Such a tradition includes expected behavior patterns based on the values and attitudes of the members and provides the group with a predictable set of circumstances which will be in operation each time the group meets and carries on activities.

The classroom so defined is an arbitrary entity much as ethnic groups or minority subcultures are often arbitrary designations. For analytic purposes, however, such entities must be separated and analyzed as units in order to predict and explain classroom behavior.

Depending upon age and grade the classroom can be an extremely complex entity which encompasses numerous simultaneous activities. In some ways, however, these separate activities form a mosaic which can be used for comparative purposes within and across socioeconomic status and ethnic groups. Numerous studies are currently under way in which the educational anthropologist uses his participant-observer methodology to view the classroom, or in some cases the entire school, from an ethnographic perspective.[21]

Philip Jackson has shown the "interpersonal interchanges" between a single teacher and her students in one elementary classroom can reach one thousand per day. Thus the seemingly organized, relatively quiet classroom which greets the visitor is in actuality a place of intense activity. Yet the quantification of such behavior is only one aspect of the classroom environment which interests the educational anthropologist.

> School is a place where tests are failed and passed, where amusing things happen, where new insights are stumbled upon, and skills acquired. But it is also a place in which people sit, and listen, and wait, and raise their hands, and pass out paper, and stand in line, and sharpen pencils. School is where we encounter both friends and foes, where imagination is unleashed and misunderstanding brought to ground. But it is also a place in which yawns are stifled and initials scratched on desktops, where milk money is collected and recess lines are formed. Both aspects of school life, the celebrated and the unnoticed, are

familiar to all of us, but the latter, if only because of its characteristic neglect, seems to deserve more attention than it has received to date from those who are interested in education.[22]

One method of studying what goes on in schools is to follow teachers and school principals while they engage in their normal behavior. One very recent study which exemplifies the participant-observer technique viewed the daily patterns of an elementary school principal.[23] As a participant-observer, the ethnographer, over an extended period, described the many roles of the administrator during his daily activities. In addition, this same educational anthropologist observed the way in which applicants for a principalship position were interviewed and evaluated during a series of meetings of a review committee. This particular study supplied insight into the actual means by which individuals were evaluated as opposed to published criteria.

Our primary interest in pursuing such microethnographic[24] investigations rests with the area which Alan Beals calls "tradition." We are assuming that classrooms differ according to this multidimensional variable and that they do so in relation to wider cultural influences which evidence themselves in classrooms through the people who participate in the learning process. As in any cultural or subcultural system, classroom behavior must be predictable within definable limits so that teaching and learning may occur. When students enter the classroom at the beginning of the semester, they await the arrival of the teacher who will provide, either on her own or in concert with them, the ground rules for classroom operation. Some teachers do so gradually, whereas others may immediately present specific guidelines or rules which set minimum standards. Furthermore, no matter what the teacher does consciously, the unconscious transmission of rules and norms in response to certain stimuli occurs regularly and often has more impact on students than the preplanned verbal or nonverbal behavior. I alluded to this earlier by suggesting that students learn to be dependent upon teachers in order to achieve school success. Such behavior often lies in opposition to the verbal commitment to provide flexibility enabling each student to progress at his own rate of speed.

As an example, we are presently studying how classroom behavior is justified and controlled by teachers and students and whether such behavior is derived from the class and school subculture or from outside the school.[25] In observing three- and four-year-old children, we have found that teachers at several private schools concentrate more on justifying the control of classroom behavior by establishing themselves as providers and enforcers of organization and efficiency that on enforcing and transmitting external social norms and values. Thus the tradition of administrative organization for efficient operations appears to begin early in the child's school experience. The teachers create a situation in which class activities center on directions by the teacher and obedience by students. Therefore, students spend the majority of class time learning appropriate classroom behavior which may or may not relate to externally sanctioned behavior. For example, hand raising, use of books and toys, and sitting and standing at appropriate times and places received much more attention from teachers than external norms such as respecting others, taking turns, and honesty. Based on our small sample such activity appears to transcend teacher personality.

This dependency on the teacher makes self-directed learning, if it ever occurs at later stages, a new phenomenon for students, and often frustrating for them and their teachers. The secondary school or university teacher who encourages students to choose their own topics for research often finds students unable to make such decisions; nothing apparently interests them. Instead they wish to know what they can do to receive a particular grade. Undoubtedly teachers at all levels take too much initiative, which results, as Margaret Mead suggests, in a system which emphasizes teaching rather than learning.[26]

CULTURE CONFLICT AND THE APPLIED EDUCATIONAL ANTHROPOLOGIST

In addition to descriptive studies of schools and communities and studies of class-rooms and schools as sociocultural systems, the applied educational anthropologist uses the culture concept to aid schools in achieving more relevant schooling. In recent years there has been increased interest in analyzing ethnic groups in order to design curricular and instructional changes which would be more congruent with their life patterns. The anthropologist's contribution lies in analyzing data on the ethnic group and then designing culturally relevant schooling experiences to move the population toward achieving specific goals.

The educational anthropologist would suggest that schooling objectives must be approached within the cultural orientations of the target population. In other words, objectives in and of themselves have little merit unless one views the target population's values, perceptions, cognitive processes, and language with respect to these goals. For example, to say that all children should have a specific reading vocabulary at the end of a school year says nothing about how one choses the words to be learned, how the instructional materials relate to the life style of a given ethnic group, or how the teaching-learning process should be altered to take into account cultural difference.

Paulo Freire suggests that literacy training should be centered around a dialogue about meaningful situations in the life of the learners. Freire attempts to isolate a minimal core vocabulary regarding actual situations in which the learners have participated. The words are chosen through informal conversations with the learners in order to isolate words which include the basic sounds of the language, which will move from simple to complex letters and sounds, and which awaken in the learner a consciousness about social, cultural, and political reality. The learners are not, therefore, subjected to trite and inconsequential experiences through stories centering on how to make "Spot" run.[27]

Although many educators concur verbally with the principle of cultural relevance, culturally relevant schooling seldom occurs. Teaching materials and methods continue to be imposed by the dominant group. Textbooks designed to teach Mexican-American youngsters to read, for example, may come from Puerto Rico, where Spanish is the language but where values and attitudes, as well as vocabulary, are at variance with the Mexican-American culture.

Such incongruities can be found with American Indian groups who attend schools operated by non-Indians. As an example, it is known that the Hopi Indians value cooperation and sharing.

> Sharing is an adaptive pattern since Amerindians often inhabit difficult environments. In a desert culture, such as the Hopi, "no one gets ahead unless we all get ahead. The threat of death from thirst and starvation hangs over all of us." The same attitude no doubt carries over into the school, where one Hopi student will be unlikely to raise his hand before another one, since he has always been taught not to excel.[28]

As a result, one might find that Hopi students talk to each other during written classroom examinations. An anthropologist working with Hopi youngsters might attempt to devise instructional materials appropriate to group activities, thus reinforcing such behavior patters common to these Indian communities.

The school is a natural laboratory for the study of cultural change. Accultura-tion, as a slow process of change in two or more cultures, occurs daily in class-rooms across the country as teachers and students hold varying degrees of com-mitment to a given cultural tradition.[29] Schools which are currently experiencing forced integration provide an excellent opportunity to view cultural change in progress and thereby provide insight into other forms of integration, such as housing and employment. Change, however, is not a one-way process; it is as important to view the impact of culture contact on the majority as on the minority culture. This has almost been forgotten in the rush to turn the "disadvantaged" into the "advantaged."[30]

In studying a southwestern city, the following process was found: first a Spanish-American family moves from the northern part of the state where the land is no longer fertile to a large city into a predominantly lower-class Mexican-American community. With very good fortune, five or ten years later a move is made across town into a middle-class area, or the children of that original family make such a move, and their offspring begin attending a predominantly middle-class or lower-middle-class Anglo school.

At the school the child is in what might be termed a conflict situation for cultural identification. His family abandons traits which might label it Mexican or Spanish, and the child finds it difficult to make the language and cultural leap. For example, there may be instances in which such children will ask to be dismissed from taking lunch in the cafeteria to avoid eating enchiladas or tacos and being labeled Mexican. This phase invariably passes, with the permanent impact unknown. In time such families often reverse their stand and become intensely proud of their heritage and such overt cultural items as food, music, and dress.

LANGUAGE

Cross-cultural problem areas like those just mentioned are not limited to the United States and are often complicated by the existence of other languages. In the developing nations of Latin America, for example, educational planners are faced with integrating numerous culturally and linguistically different populations. Schooling is often called upon to achieve this end. Guatemala, for example, is characterized by approximately five major linguistic codes and over two hundred dialects among a population of less than five million. It is not feasible to develop each major language for national and international affairs; therefore, the task becomes one of promoting literacy in a second language while retaining the first. Yet language does not exist in a vacuum; it is closely related to a given environment and cultural tradition.[31]

It can be assumed that a given population will have words for material objects as well as social concepts and that this vocabulary in some ways structures the universe for the population. The nation that is characterized by the existence of two or more languages finds that each language serves distinct functions for the user. One set of behavior patterns is supported and expressed through one language and another set through another. The languages are often separated in accordance with their usage; one may be used in school and the other may be used at home and in the neighborhood. The same distinctions may be made within a single language which is characterized by several dialects. Language has a strong impact on perception and conception. The Navajo Indians, for example, divide the color spectrum differently than we do.[32] Abruptly divorcing an individual from this language is likely, therefore, to cut him off from his traditional life style and his unique perception of the world.

In schools in which the majority of the staff represent cultural and linguistic background which differ from those of the students, it is likely that the students will rely upon support from those who are closest in background to themselves. Thus Spanish-speaking children in the Southwest are likely to turn to Spanish-speaking cooks in the cafeteria when anxious about something rather than to an Anglo teacher.[33] Children who are prevented from speaking their native language at school are cut off from their own culture. Because the truly bilingual person by definition must also be bicultural, second-language programs must be combined with culture and area studies at all levels of schooling. Bilingual programs which fail to recognize this interrelationship are most likely doomed to leave in their wake culturally alienated youngsters who mature in a conflict state, confortable with neither their native nor their second language.

CONCEPTUAL STYLES

In addition to being concerned with value orientations and language, the educational anthropologist also recognizes the importance of cognition and conceptual style in the learning process. This topic, which might best be categorized as cognitive anthropology, concerns itself with learning styles and the influence of language, culture, and environment on the aptitude of given populations. Although such studies are few in number, it has been shown that there are environments which support different methods of knowing. A given cultural tradition may or may not lend itself to the learning of concepts and skills of another culture, without relevant curricular and methodological approaches.

The imposition of a Western technological orientation on the study of mathematics in Liberia was investigated by Gay and Cole.[34] They experimented with Kpelle students as well as with control groups from the United States. They found that the Kpelle could judge more accurately the number of cups of rice in a bowl than could the Americans. Another experiment asked that the same populations sort a number of cards. The task was to sort the cards consecutively into three categories according to various symbols. The Americans experienced few problems yet the Kpelle found great difficulty in sorting the cards even once. Such simple experiments indicate the influence of culture on the performance of cognitive and psychomotoric tasks. The Americans failed to make a simple numerical judgment and the Kpelle failed to make a simple sorting judgment.

Such experiments make questionable the universality of cognitive structures. Rosalie Cohen has analyzed two conceptual styles which emerged from a series of research studies in the United States. One is referred to as "analytic," and the other is called "relational." According to Cohen, our schools require, through intelligence and achievement tests, increasingly sophisticated analytic cognitive skills rather than relational skills, yet both are characteristic of a segment of the school population. Both have been found to be independent of native ability. These conceptual styles were associated with formal and informal primary group socialization patterns. The child who demonstrated a relational approach to reality organization was characterized by shared-function environments common in families of lower socioeconomic status, whereas the child who demonstrated an analytic approach to reality organization was characterized by more formal primary-group participation common in middle-class families. Thus the analytic rule set for the organization of sense data is embedded in the formal school organization where teaching and learning take place. For example, Cohen remarks that:

> ... the analytic mode of abstraction presumes a system of linear components. Similar linear components are found in the perception of time as a continuum or in a linear projection of social space, and they underlie the notion of multiple causality. This linear component does not appear among polar-relational children on tests of cognitive style, in their characteristic language style, nor in the ordering of authority or responsibility in shared-function social groups. Certain common values and beliefs follow from such a common component. For instance, without the assumption of linearity such notions as social mobility, the value of money, improving one's performance, getting ahead, infinity, or hierarchies of any type, all of which presume the linear extension of

critical elements, do not have meaning for the relational child. In essence, the requirements for formal abstraction and extraction of components to produce linear continua are not logically possible within the relational rule set.[35]

Although much attention has been given to the amount of information a culturally different child is able to exhibit, the research just cited poses questions regarding the nature of the organization of sense data rather than of the substance or information component of that data.

In other words, the quantity of information possessed by a population is only one aspect of cultural difference; the other, or conceptual style, is of at least equal importance in terms of designing and planning the curriculum and instructional process. Both the Gay and Cole and the Cohen studies may lead toward the development of varied approaches to the creation of specialized learning environments in terms of school organization, curricula, and teaching methods. As Cohen suggests, the development of "procedures for more valid measurement of learning potential and the development of more appropriate learning methods and settings are dependent upon the abandonment of assumptions that there is a single method for knowing."[36]

In conclusion, I have attempted to point out those areas in which I feel the educational anthropologists are most active and the kinds of insights a cultural perspective on the school might contribute to a greater understanding of the teaching-learning process: first, with regard to enculturation and schooling; second, with the school as locus for cultural learning; third, the culture concept; and fourth, culture conflict and the applied educational anthropologist. It should be obvious that these are overlapping rather than separate areas.

Because we are all products of at least one cultural tradition, our behavior manifests certain expectancies which we anticipate in others. The teacher expects that others will behave within reasonable limits established by cultural traditions. When the behavior of others falls outside of these tolerable boundaries, our response may be consternation, frustration, or anger. Alternatively our response may show sympathy, patience, and consolation.

Neither end aids the teacher in the classroom who may have to cope with cultural difference on a day-to-day basis. Instead the teacher must systematically investigate the cultural background of her students in order to comprehend the impact such a background has on the way in which the child perceives the world and is accustomed to learning and being taught. On the basis of such investigations the school and the teacher can promote continuity for the child and increase the likelihood that recognized and unrecognized activities will transmit the intended messages to the learner.

NOTES

1. See, for example, Beatrice B. Whiting, ed., *Six Cultures, Studies of Childrearing* (New York: John Wiley, 1963). Also, Margaret Mead and Martha Wolfenstein, *Childhood in Contemporary Cultures* (Chicago: University of Chicago Press, 1955).
2. George F. Kneller, *Educational Anthropology, An Introduction* (New York: John Wiley, 1964).
3. Henry G. Burger, *Ethnopedagogy: A Manual in Cultural Sensitivity, with Techniques for Improving Cross-Cultural Teaching by Fitting Ethnic Patterns* (Albuquerque, N.M.: Southwestern Cooperative Educational Laboratory, 1968), p. 88.
4. George A. Pettitt, *Prisoners of Culture* (New York: Charles Scribner's Sons, 1970), p. 133.

5. See, for example, Dorothy Lee, *Freedom and Culture* (Englewood Cliffs, N.J.: Prentice-Hall, 1959).

6. Jacquetta Hill Burnett, "Ceremony, Rites, and Economy in the Student System of an American High School," *Human Organization* 28, no. 1 (Spring 1969): 1-10.

7. Florence Kluckhohn and Fred L. Strodbeck, *Variations in Value Orientations* (Evanston, Ill.: Row, Peterson, 1961).

8. Philip W. Jackson, *Life in Classrooms* (New York: Holt, Rinehart and Winston, 1968), p. 34.

9. Jules Henry, *Culture Against Man* (New York: Vintage Books, 1963), p. 289.

10. Robert Rosenthal and Lenore Jacobson, *Pygmalion in the Classroom: Teacher Expectation and Pupils' Intellectual Development* (New York: Holt, Rinehart and Winston, 1968).

11. Robert V. Dumont, Jr., and Murray L. Wax, "Cherokee Society and the Intercultural Classroom," *Human Organization* 28, no. 3 (Fall 1969): 219.

12. Alan R. Beals et al. *Culture in Process* (New York: Holt, Rinehart and Winston, 1967).

13. Ibid.

14. Richard A. King, *The School at Mopass: A Problem of Identity* (New York: Holt, Rinehart and Winston, 1967).

15. Harry F. Wolcott, *A Kwakiutl Village and School* (New York: Holt, Rinehart and Winston, 1967).

16. John Singleton, *Nichu: A Japanese School* (New York: Holt, Rinehart and Winston, 1967).

17. Richard Warren, *Education in Rebhausen: A German Village* (New York: Holt, Rinehart and Winston, 1967).

18. See, for example, Jacquetta Hill Burnett, "Culture of the School: A Construct for Research and Explanation in Education" (paper presented at the American Educational Research Association, Minneapolis, 1969). Also, Peter S. Sindell, "Anthropological Approaches to the Study of Education," *Review of Educational Research* 39 (December 1969).

19. Burnett, "Culture of the School."

20. Beals, *Culture in Process*, p. 9.

21. See, for example, Louis M. Smith and William Geoffrey, *The Complexities of an Urban Classroom: An Analysis Toward a General Theory of Teaching* (New York: Holt, Rinehart and Winston, 1968). Also, G. Alexander Moore, *Realities of the Urban Classroom; Observations in Elementary Schools* (Garden City, N.Y.: Doubleday, 1967).

22. Jackson, *Life in Classrooms*, p. 4.

23. Harry F. Wolcott, "The Elementary School Principal: Notes from a Field Study" (Center for Advanced Study of Educational Administration, University of Oregon, 1969). Mimeographed.

24. Louis M. Smith, "The Microethnography of the Classroom," *Psychology in the Schools* 4, no. 3 (1967): 216-21.

25. Thomas J. La Belle and Val Rust, "Control Mechanisms and Their Justification in Pre-School Classrooms," *Small Group Behavior* 4, no. 1 (Feb. 1973).

26. Margaret Mead, "Our Educational Emphasis in Primitive Perspective," *American Journal of Sociology* 38 (May 1943).

27. Thomas Sanders, "The Paulo Freire Method," American Universities Field Staff, Fieldstaff Reports: West Coast South American Series 15, no. 1 (1968).

28. Burger, *Ethnopedagogy*, p. 135.

29. See, for example, Jacquetta Hill Burnett, "Event Analysis in the Microethnography of Urban Classrooms" (Paper presented in the annual meeting of the American Anthropological Association, November 1968). Mimeographed.

30. Thomas J. La Belle, "What's Deprived About Being Different?" *Elementary School Journal* 72, no. 1 (October 1971).

31. Thomas J. La Belle, "Schooling in Cultural Perspective," in Peter T. Furst and Karen B. Reed, eds., *Stranger in Our Midst* (Los Angeles: Latin American Center, University of California, 1970).

32. Paule Henle, "Language, Thought, and Culture," in Peter Hammond, ed., *Cultural and Social Anthropology Readings* (New York: Macmillan, 1964).

33. Burger, *Ethnopedagogy*, p. 64.

34. John Gay and Michael Cole, *The New Mathematics in an Old Culture: A Study of Learning Among the Kpelle of Liberia* (New York: Holt, Rinehart and Winston, 1967).

35. Rosalie Cohen, "Conceptual Styles, Culture Conflict, and Nonverbal Tests of Intelligence," *American Anthropologist* 71, no. 5 (October 1969): 839.

36. Ibid., p. 843.

7 / Education and Anthropology: Areas of Common Concern

Solon Kimball

Any appraisal of the relation between anthropology and education should first specify the areas of common concern. From the anthropological perspective, the most inclusive concept is the transmission of culture (Kimball, 1966) which encompasses not only what is taught and learned, but also the organization, pattern, and processes of education in their social and cultural settings. Professional educators usually would agree that the transmission of culture also is their major concern; but they would then insist that, as practitioners, their orientation is primarily programmatic. They would say that their job is to know what to do and how to do it, although some might add that they could use assistance in developing new understanding of their problems and in learning how changes in current practices could produce improved results.

The sharpest differentiation between educator and anthropologist is likely to appear in the perspective, definition, and solution of educational problems. Teachers, school administrators, and other educational specialists are primarily trained for and engaged in activities subsumed under instruction. In contrast, the anthropologist, proceeding from the perspective of his discipline, seeks to describe the social system and cultural behavior within the educational institution and to place it in the context of the community. By ordering this accumulated knowledge, the anthropologist may suggest modifications in organization or procedures that will increase the effectiveness of the educational system. When he works with educators, he functions primarily as a consultant and refrains from direct intervention in the responsibility of those trained to operate the system, the professional educators. Anthropologists who have worked in applied anthropology are aware of the connection between preliminary, traditional field research on a problem, and the preparation of innovative proposals based upon the findings of this research. They also are aware that they must resist becoming practitioners since this responsibility belongs to those whose training, experience, and aptitudes have prepared them for this role.

I should draw attention to another fundamental distinction between educators and anthropologists, since they may view such specific problems as those of school dropouts, underachievement, or discipline from quite different perspectives. The cross-cultural and holistic perspective of the anthropologist permits him to interpret the data from specific research in a wider context than the educator who usually is concerned with one specific situation. Furthermore, some aspects of behavior which educators may ignore, treat casually, or even be unaware of, such as informal groupings or induction of new personnel or students, may strike the anthropologist as of major significance. In particular, the anthropologist's perspective gives him a strategic view of the relationships among schools, the educative process, and the community. His knowledge of cultural continuity and comparative analysis also should prove advantageous in understanding cultural change.

These differences in outlook and procedure need to be examined in the context of purposes and their associated values, although it is difficult for me to phrase or specify them, except in the most general terms. Let us assume that American anthropologists and educators are equally committed to the principles of democracy. Although no attempt will be made to enumerate these principles in any detail nor to assess the congruency between ideal and practice, for illustrative purposes, I shall mention representative government, cultural pluralism, equality of opportunity, and protection of individual dignity. The immediate problem is of another kind:

to examine the extent to which democratic tenets influence the American anthropologist, first, in his analyses of the school system operation either as implicit or explicit assumptions, and, second, in the solutions he recommends for an educational problem. Can we, as anthropologists, claim some deeper and more universal insights about human nature, culture, and social groupings than those implicit in the democratic creed and, if so, do these contribute to a dilemma by contradicting the validity of some goals which we readily accept?

Presumably, few educators need to be confronted with the doubts which I suggest face anthropologists. Although thoughtful educators are distressed by the gap between ideal and practice, the pressure of daily responsibility leads many to do their job without a sufficient understanding or questioning of the system and makes them largely insensitive to its inconsistencies. For example, the once prevalent belief that the United States was free of social class was supported by contrasting the United States to Europe where a hereditary aristocracy barred the advance of the capable and ambitious. It was believed that in the land of the free any man could rise to great heights, as had Lincoln, Edison, and Ford. When the community studies of the early 1930s began to provide evidence for the existence of social-class distinctions in the United States, some labeled both studies and researchers as un-American. Later, Warner, Havighurst, and Loeb in *Who Shall Be Educated?* (1944), showed how children of different social levels were differentially treated in the schools. Subsequent studies in Chicago by students of Everett Hughes and in Detroit by Patricia Sexton (1961) confirmed the disadvantages that children of the working class faced through unequal distribution of educational resources and personnel.

The assumption that equitable distribution of resources ensures equal educational opportunities or results is, of course, fallacious. Class biases appear in subtle and unconscious ways, even among those who profess ardent support of democratic equality. In Spindler's 1959 research, the teacher so stereotyped class behavior that he was unaware of the differences between his rating of students and their actual performances. Jules Henry (1963) has shown the subtle and automatic rewards and punishments which teachers mete out to those students who conform to, or violate, their class-oriented sense of proper behavior. Ruth Landes (1965) reported that Mexican-American students in California rejected certain aspects of schooling which threatened their cultural identity. Thus, boys who took part in athletic programs were accused by their peers of becoming "Anglicized," and cultural values of Mexican girls were violated by what they considered the immodest exposure they suffered when they were required to shower in open stalls in physical education classes. Landes further reported that when these ethnic-based behaviors were understood by the teachers and efforts were openly made to accommodate to them, much of the unwittingly created tension disappeared. Perhaps stress generated by violations of class identity might also disappear given the same treatment, although traditionally subcultural variations expressed in social class have not been accorded the same dignity and respect sometimes given autonomous cultures.

In other words, the American acceptance of cultural pluralism and the anthropological value of respecting cultural autonomy are fairly well in accord. But the problem gets sticky when we view social class as a subcultural variant while adhering to a relatively uniform educational approach expressing only middle-class values. In the extension of middle-class values in education, we witness an attempt to bring children of the lower class into the orbit of middle-class behavior. Many attempts are made to justify this procedure, but this might also be construed as an example of social class, or cultural imperialism. The recent spot announcements on television which urge continued education, predicting a dismal future for the unheeding, are obviously intended to reach working-class youth and, regardless of the validity of the exhortation, those who respond to the message serve middle-class values.[1]

It is generally accepted that the schools which serve the slums of the big cities are relatively unsuccessful in their educational efforts when judged by, and compared with, middle-class standards.[2] One problem that plagues educators in slum sections is the inability to keep older children enrolled in school. There are several ways in which this high dropout rate may be interpreted. The school program may be so inept and the school environment so punishing that they may contribute to the high attrition rate. Perhaps those who withdraw or are rejected represent the intellectually marginal. Perhaps they withdraw because they equate a given age with adulthood and see school as only for children. Or perhaps all three ideas possess some validity as explanations of the situation, although educators are less likely to look to the social and cultural setting for explanations than to purely pedagogical ones.

From time to time some educators have had the temerity to suggest special curricula for the so-called culturally disadvantaged, but such propositions are repugnant in a democracy unless they carry a magical label such as "enrichment." Even these labels can be political dynamite. Nevertheless, differential schooling already is in effect. The "track" system is justified on the basis of vocational interests and aptitudes, while in reality it divides students on the basis of class background. A further separation appears with the special treatment accorded the mentally retarded and the emotionally disturbed, most of whom are recruited from the poorer classes, as exemplified in the "600" schools in New York City.

This brief excursion into aspects of social class and education is primarily intended to show some of the complications facing both educators and anthropologists in a society where practices and ideals are not, and cannot be, in accord, and where the complexities of a culturally diverse society create conflicting values.

If the problems confronting educators seem difficult, those facing anthropologists who attempt to analyze the educational system and to work with educators seem even greater. For example, should the degree of objectivity maintained when observing initiation ceremonies among Australian aborigines be any different from that maintained when observing a school monitor system, where students selected for their size use force to punish other students who have violated school rules? Is not the principle of cultural congruency demonstrated by the discovery that physical prowess is the basis for a pattern of dominance and submission among the same students outside the school? What should be the basis for intervention in either case? As anthropologists, we have not been overly sympathetic with missionary or governmental suppression of native custom. Is it possible that we have a double set of values when confronted by behavior we label offensive in our own culture? Instead of protesting the danger of going native, should we not recognize that we are already one with the natives when we make judgmental evaluations based on their values? If our perspective and method are to be useful to American education, we must learn to keep our analysis free of culture bias to the same degree demanded in our work elsewhere. Otherwise we had better steer clear of advocating educational reform since its practitioners are far more competent than we are in their spheres.

Perhaps the distinctive role and contribution of the anthropologist in the field of education can be further clarified if we examine some specific area of research. Consideration of the informal group system of a high school student body can well serve this purpose. These groups are not areas of great concern to either school administrator or teacher, and I know of no books on school organization or curriculum, excepting those written by sociologists, which even mention the subject. From such evidence I think we are justified in concluding that educators do not consider informal grouping among students, or its absence, to be of any great relevance to the educative process. Some years ago, student peer group choices were explored when sociometrics made quite a splash; however, the interest continued for only a brief period. Like so many other innovations, the mechanics of determining student preference and rejection were adopted to serve the needs of teachers and administrators, but the flesh and blood of theory and the therapeutic goals of the method were never assimilated. Actually, small group theory in anthropology is genetically unrelated to sociometrics, although the techniques of the latter have some utility.

Three major reasons manifest the importance of informal or small group studies. First, we know that in many societies much of what a child learns is acquired from his peer group. Where education is institutionalized under the control of adults, the official knowledge of textbook and lecture must contend with the unofficial and possible contradictory lore which children teach each other. Furthermore, knowledge and experience always are assimilated through a perceptual screen which includes the criteria for discrimination and evaluation.

The relationship between the student's informal system and that of the community and of the institutional structure of the school provides the second reason for the importance of small group studies. Hollingshead's 1949 study in Elmtown, for example, shows that the high school clique system reproduces the parental status and value systems. There are many intriguing problems in this area, such as the relationship between student and teacher cliques and the evaluations which each group makes of the other; it is obvious that we need several studies to provide us with comparative data. Research on the school has not yet established the correspondences between formal and informal systems, but the results of studies in hospitals, factories, and prisons have demonstrated such relationships.

A final reason for the importance of small group studies is covered by such rubrics as morale, organizational health, job satisfaction, and productivity. Other ways of describing these phenomena include participation and involvement, organization and communication, or executive function. Here again we must turn to industrial research to provide us with the clues to what we might expect to find. Mayo's 1933 report on the consequences of changed conditions in the textile plant upon worker behavior seem particularly relevant. In this plant, it will be remembered, the general malaise which afflicted all workers gradually disappeared as they were brought into a meaningful relationship to their environment. Arensberg's 1951 analysis of numerous such studies supports the same conclusion. A vitally important area of study is the extent and the ways in which student peer groups mediate a meaningful and participant relationship between students and the school environment.

The student system is much more than informal grouping as Gordon (1957), Coleman (1961), and Burnett (1964) have told us in their major studies of high schools. It also includes the extracurricular programs organized around student government, athletic, literary, dramatic, musical, and club activities. Events associated with these activities are highly visible and involve varying degrees of faculty assistance and control and parental participation. Extracurricular activities provide a meeting ground between school and community that is not provided in any other fashion. In addition to being viewed as an extension of the academic program, these activities represent the varied social and cultural interests of the community and, as such, serve as a training ground for them. This, however, is not the perspective emphasized by educators. Although they are well aware of this phase of school life, with some misgivings I may add, they are more concerned with program and supervision than they are with the social and cultural implications. This narrow emphasis of the educator provides the anthropologist with the opportunity, even the responsibility, to bring the systematic approach of social science analysis to this aspect of the educational system. Here the anthropologist can exercise his competency in describing the relationship between social structure and culture pattern in an institutional and community setting.

Thus, the student system is a social science problem with relevance for education, while its programmatic aspects remain the responsibility of professional educators. With this distinction, we can avoid distorting our results through culture bias. For example, the discovery that lower-class children opt for adult values and behavior at earlier ages than do middle-class children is a consequential scientific finding for educators who are programmatically concerned about dropouts. As applied anthropologists, however, we also have the right to evaluate or recommend procedures designed to change the situation in one or another direction. The ethics involved in offering such advisements have already been clearly stated by the Society for Applied Anthropology (1963–64) and need not be elaborated here.

In order to broaden the scope of this inquiry, I will designate divisions for grouping specific problems of education, and discuss relevant anthropological theory for each of them.

There are six major areas which are broadly inclusive of the enterprise of education. These are (1) training of school personnel, (2) organization and management of schools, (3) the specification of curriculum and preparation of materials, (4) pedagogical practices, (5) the relations between school and community, and (6) philosophy of education. In no sense should these categories be considered mutually exclusive units for study. Obviously, the activities of a teacher and students in a classroom have relevance for all these, but for research purposes these items, singly or in combination, must be viewed as primarily topical. Although this does not invalidate them as appropriate research subjects, we should try to find some alternative or complementary arrangement, some frame of reference, which provides a more insightful conceptualization and serves the goals of social science as well as those of education. To do so we must turn to anthropology.

Anthropology utilizes an inductive, empirical, natural history method through which it seeks to describe the structure, pattern, and process of human behavior. It shares with other sciences the ordering of data as systems which reflect the qualities and relationships of individual items in their activities. From anthropological operations and from the results of analysis, we theorize about the connections between patterns of behavior and the forms of human grouping in stable or changing environments. We have developed theoretical formulations for many aspects of behavior. The problem here is to decide which of these areas of theory are most appropriate to educational research.

Earlier I suggested that the transmission of culture, inclusive of developing cognitive capacities and technical skills, should be the primary objective of an educational system. But the strict application of such a view would neglect the implicit, and often intended, socialization and growth of affective, evaluative capabilities, to say nothing of the purely physiological aspects. Obviously, all of these must be considered in framing research. Other ingredients in the teaching-learning process include the institutional setting, the traditional practices of school and classroom, and the relationships with other institutions in a specific community environment. Together, these items suggest four areas of applicable theory: learning theory, culture theory, theory of organization, and theory of change.

Learning theory, thus far, has not been a major concern to anthropologists. Wallace (1962) has been interested in this problem and has called attention to the contrast between stimulus-cue-response and cognitive learning. In an earlier period, Mead, Hallowell, Linton, Kardiner, and others produced useful and exciting studies of child-rearing practices which helped us understand how personality is formed in a cultural environment. Their theory, however, borrowed mainly from psychoanalysis, gave much greater emphasis to psychomotor and affective learning and behavior than to cognitive or intellectual learning. Among both anthropologists and psychologists, the implicit acceptance of the stimulus-response paradigm and of the conditioned reflex as basic neurological processes may help to explain the neglect of the distinctly human, symbolic aspects of behavior, and the processes of their acquisition. If the study of culture transmission is to be truly comprehensive, it also must be concerned with the cognitive, symbolic structure, the cultural behavior, and the social groupings within which learning occurs.

The realization of such an objective requires that we broaden our area of inquiry

considerably beyond the traditional description of child-rearing practices and specification of personality formation. We must look for the congruencies between
culture pattern, social grouping, and the logics of mythology and language and
their relationships to the cognitive screen through which experience is received
and organized.

Once this objective has been realized, we are in a better position to seek solutions
to some perplexing problems, such as defining the relationships between psychomotor, affective, and cognitive learning. What consequences will ensue in the results
we obtain if we shift from treating directed learning as stages in development to
focusing on transition or, alternatively, to viewing learning as pattern embellishment
and expansion? Can we establish cultural levels of cognitive complexity and relate
these to culture and community? It seems to me that learning theory based on
solutions to these problems is directly applicable to curriculum materials and
pedagogy, as well as to teacher training and the philosophy of education. Actually,
the inductive, natural history approach contains a powerful learning tool and implicit
learning theory.

Culture theory, in contrast, has general applicability for all aspects of education.
In particular, those understandings of continuity and persistence and of pattern and
congruency will be useful in tracing the origin and development of custom and in
explaining their function. Education has much to learn from specific research
utilizing the time and space formulations of Hall (1961) and the studies of body
socialization and movement by Birdwhistell (1952). In international and cross-
cultural education, many of the difficulties accompanying attempts to transfer
educational systems from one culture to another without taking into account the
distinctive culture patterns of the recipient culture could be alleviated or eliminated
if these anthropological concepts were available.

Theory of organization has particular relevance for the training of administrators,
for school organization and management, and for relations between school and
community. Studies in industry can contribute both method and theory to this
area of interest which is shared with some sociologists and social psychologists.
The contributions of many individuals in these several fields are worthy of close
study, specifically Arensberg, Richardson, Whyte, Hughes, Becker, Rossi, Sanders,
and Sayles. Atwood (1964) has already demonstrated the utility of interaction
theory in school organization. One significant question, of course, is the extent to
which custodial or supervisory practice facilitates or impedes the learning process.
When we examine the dimensions of school and community relations, we encounter
a much broader and less clearly defined area, but the technique of event analysis
should help to place schools in the institutional setting of the community.

Theory to deal with problems of educational innovation and change comes from
anthropology's long-standing interest in culture growth and spread, and from its
more recent concern with the forms of human groupings and their dynamics, as
well as with the relationship between culture and community. Anthropology's
natural history approach leads us to the processes of transformation, either those
affecting the individual as they may be observed in rites of passage, or those of
group and community as seen in stress or in the stabilizing rites of intensification.
From this perspective, we seek to understand the process of group formation, modification, or dissolution, as well as what happens with individual induction or expul-
sion. The notable accomplishments of applied anthropology in the theory and procedure of innovation and change should give us confidence that the principles and
procedures we have already tested also are applicable to educational problems and
processes.

These, then, are the areas of anthropological research competence and theoretical
concern which seem to have special relevance for education. The insistence upon
framing problems in social science terms does not negate the importance of problems

as they are seen and described by educators. It is our task, however, to translate these into research problems where our theory and techniques can apply. Also, the perspective and inductive methodology characteristic of our discipline can make additional and unanticipated contributions.[3]

NOTES

1. A strict application of this interpretation would view schooling for middle-class children as a form of age-status imperialism.
2. Whether educational programs are any more or any less effective than other social betterment efforts in these areas is a moot point.
3. Although I have given no attention to the introduction of anthropology as subject matter in school curricula, this omission is not an oversight. In my opinion, it is not the content of class materials, as much as the manner in which they are organized and presented, that is important. If materials about the American Indian are taught in the traditional fashion, it is history and nothing more.

REFERENCES

Arensberg, C. M. "Behavior and Organization." In *Industrial Studies. Social Psychology at the Crossroads*, edited by John H. Rohrer et al. New York: Harper & Brothers, 1951.

Atwood, M. "Small-Scale Administrative Change: Resistance to the Introduction of a High School Guidance Program." In *Innovation in Education*, edited by Matthew B. Mills. New York: Teachers College Press, 1964.

Birdwhistell, R. L. *Introduction to Kinesics*. Washington, D.C.: Department of State, Foreign Service Institute, 1952.

Burnett, J. H. "A Participant Observation Study of a Sociocultural Sub-System of the Students in a Small Rural High School." Unpublished Ph.D. dissertation. Columbia University, 1964.

Coleman, J. S. *The Adolescent Society: The Social Life of the Teenager and Its Impact on Education*. Glencoe, Ill.: Free Press, 1961.

Gordon, W. *The Social System of the High School*. Glencoe, Ill.: Free Press, 1957.

Hall, E. T. *The Silent Language*. Greenwich, Conn.: Premier Book, 1961.

Henry, J. "Attitude Organization in Elementary School Classrooms." In *Education and Culture*, edited by George D. Spindler. New York: Holt, Rinehart and Winston, 1963.

Hollingshead, A. B. *Elmtown's Youth*. New York: Wilcy, 1949.

Kimball, S. T. *The Transmission of Culture. The Body of Knowledge Unique to the Profession of Education*. Washington, D.C.: Pi Lambda Theta, 1966. Pp. 45-70.

Landes, R. *Culture in American Education*. New York: Wiley, 1965.

Mayo, E. *The Human Problems of an Industrial Civilization*. New York: Macmillan, 1933.

Sexton, P. C. *Education and Income*. New York: Viking Press, 1961.

Society for Applied Anthropology. "Statement on Ethics of the Society for Applied Anthropology." *Human Organization* 22 (1963-64).

Spindler, G. *The Transmission of American Culture*. Cambridge, Mass.: Harvard University Press, 1959.

Wallace, A. "Culture and Cognition." *Science* 135 (1962): 351-57.

Warner, W. L., R. Havighurst, and M. Loeb. *Who Shall Be Educated?* New York: Harper & Brothers, 1944.

8 / An Anthropological View of Urban Education

G. Alexander Moore, Jr.

Anthropologists have come late, compared to other social scientists, as commentators on the institution of U.S. education. Although our coming is welcomed by educators—partly as a perfunctory response to the doctrine that education needs many voices expressing many points of view—the legitimacy of anthropological commentary is not at all self-evident. There is, of course, our basic contribution, made as well to mankind and to science. That contribution is knowledge of pan-human cultures and societies, now entering the curriculum in the "new social studies." It is an important contribution, but one that will not be discussed here. Rather, I will comment on the changing business of U.S. education as another proper object of anthropological curiosity. That business consists of one particular social institution demanding an ethnographic, or natural science, description and explanation of its own.

Ethnography, or the description of human groups, is the first-order anthropological activity. Its accomplishment is as legitimate in modern Western society as in any primitive one. Only strategic priorities have kept anthropologists so concerned with non-Western tribal peoples. Our mission through the first half of the twentieth century has been to reach and to describe tribal peoples, or their remnants, before they disappeared. Although that mission is by no means ended, its urgency is no longer felt so earnestly.

Now there is a new ethnography of America and of American schools, still in its barest beginnings. Full descriptions of American schools do not exist, though considerable ethnographic efforts have been undertaken by Henry (1963), Wax (1964), Atwood (1960), and Eddy (1967). Nor do we have enough data to go on fully to the second order of anthropological business; the controlled comparison of human institutions from different cultures. Our records are replete with accounts of child rearing among tribesman and peasants, but we lack ethnographic descriptions of complex urban school systems in other modern, technological societies. Comparative illumination so far has come from the contrast between modern urban school systems and their immediate rural predecessors, as Kimball and McClellan (1936: 183–215) have done in a very fruitful inquiry. The comments offered, then, will of necessity come from that first descriptive effort and from the comparisons of ourselves with our immediate forerunners.

I propose to use some anthropological weapons in a minor skirmish against the conceptual problems posed by urban education. My first sally will concern the nature of today's metropolis, where I will use the comparative work by Kimball and McClellan, who hold that today's educational system is the "antithesis" worked out against the Main Street town's one-room schoolhouse, the "thesis" of yesteryear. Second, I will comment on the intellect of today's agrarian migrant to the city—viewed by others as a question of "cultural deprivation"—in relation to our extreme, but flexible, class structure. Third, I will conceive of the urban school system as just one of many bureaucratic corporations, whose ideological self-conception may be at variance with its actual functions.

A COMPARATIVE VIEW OF AMERICAN COMMUNITIES OVER TIME: MODERN METROPOLIS VS. MAIN STREET TOWN

The theory of community is one of social science's most powerful tools today. The mutual concern of anthropology and sociology with the human group, as cultural pattern for the first, and as social system for the second, converges in the study of communities. Conrad Arensberg was the first to recognize this convergence, which he states succinctly by saying that the community is the locus of culture, the place where it emerged or originated, and where it is elaborated and continually transmitted from one generation to another (Arensberg 1961),[1] Arensberg has worked out a theory of community broad enough to include the urban form, even the modern metropolis, within the range of all human communities, all the way out to include the hunting band. For students of Western society the importance of Arensberg's concept is that it obliges us to grasp—as we hope to do later in this—the enormous modern metropolis as a single whole. This newly dominant community form will be contrasted with the rural counterparts that formerly held sway in American society and culture.

The midwestern Main Street towns were the most singularly American community form in a rural America before 1920. They had emerged as the preeminent form after the Civil War. The southern counties were ruined. The New England townships were being emptied by crop failures and the lure of the seaports and of the West. Midwestern Republicans controlled Congress. Our plain states had developed the world's richest commercial agriculture, its crops exported by the railroads. They had also developed schools in every town.

An anthropologist sees the problem of any institution as an evolutionary one. In primitive and agrarian societies education, or as some call it, "socialization," was carried out by the whole community. This was so even in those literate societies that had separate entitites called "schools." In the Main Street towns, that old little red, one-room schoolhouse performed functions that were largely peripheral to the adult life the pupil was to lead. Indeed his schooling was hardly necessary. The three Rs could have been learned just as well at home, from one's father or mother, or some other adult tutor. The rest of the curriculum was largely a collection of irrelevancies: bits and pieces of Western culture, often classical, taught with little coherence, and, least of all, likely to encourage future learning or research of any sort. From the pupil's point of view it really didn't matter. One learned what one needed to know just by growing up among peers and elders in one's community. They taught you how to make good. One could be a success in the community quite in spite of the schoolmarm.[2] Indeed, it was even possible to achieve enormous national success without having been successful at schooling. Commodore Vanderbilt, for example, reached the pinnacles of wealth and fame while remaining a functional illiterate. He could sign his name. Others did the rest for him.

But in today's urban and highly technological world schooling is no longer peripheral but central. There is no such thing as a successful illiterate in today's cities. Even gangsters and labor leaders, people who traditionally rise from lowly backgrounds, if, for quite opposite purposes, need complex skills to direct the big organizations they command.

Socialization in today's city is, then, factored out. It, literally, cannot be inculcated by the family and peer group alone, as it once could be. Moreover, that business of socialization has come to be performed, not by the individual practitioner serving diverse clients at once—the schoolmarm of one-room days—but by a vast bureaucratic establishment that seeks to serve vast numbers of diverse clients at once, by dividing them into age and ability groupings.

The answer to the new central function of education lies in the vast demographic transformation that the western world is undergoing. We have ceased to be a nation of small towns. The process has picked up speed since the 1930's, and indeed it is seen abroad, where, in some places, the urban revolution has been more rapid.

For today's city person, life seems to be reaching the most extreme impersonality that mankind has ever known. Much of life is carried on in public places, amid people who are often strangers, and certainly not the lifelong associates of a quasi-familial nature that any hometown fellow once was. Only one's kin and friends belong to the private world of the household. Homes, even bachelor apartments, today form havens of personality for the conduct of one's "private life," which may have very little to do with the public world of work.

In old hometown America the distinction between private and public worlds hardly existed. One's private life—of family, home, and church—was public knowledge. One's public life of occupation, trade, or profession was likewise little separated, if at all, from the home and the circle of kin and lifelong friends. One's identity was one piece.

To maneuver in an impersonal world, a great deal of impersonal knowledge is needed. That is the business of education. Indeed, one cannot know today's urban world just by growing up within it, without the help of formal schooling. The experience of the home is too limited to partake of all the meaning a big city offers. Even the homes of our professional people, highly educated and lively as they may be, cannot hope to present all the knowledge and variegated experience of the rich curriculum of the schools that typically serve such persons.

That is not to say that anthropologists do not discern a wholeness to the modern metropolis. That wholeness may be overlaid by so many confusing patterns of residence, occupation, social class, and ethnicity that it is all but impossible to see. Yet we hold that big cities are communities like any other. According to Arensberg's theory, all communities define themselves as such by possessing common centers of assemblage and dispersal. There all city folk, regardless of family background, religion, wealth, or any other recognized differences, may join together in a common identity as city folk. Such places may be largely symbolic and ritual in nature.

It would seem that in today's metropolis the only center of assemblage and dispersal in space, which meets this requirement of bringing together all city folk as *city folk*, is the sports stadium. To be a "real" metropolis a city must have a stadium. Cities reaching "big league" status, like Atlanta and Houston, have lately spent enormous sums on stadia. Older cities such as Boston, Saint Louis, and New York have felt obliged to build new ones. By doing so the newer cities present a new definition of themselves, and permit their citizens to participate in that new definition. Likewise in the older great cities, citizens throng to the new playing fields to affirm their citizenship, in the place best suited for that affirmation.

But a city's ceremonial unity does not simplify its underlying complexity, it simply focuses that complexity. Consider the degree of impersonal trust and knowledge it takes a city person to get to a municipal stadium. The urbanite may go completely alone, but he must deal with a number of strangers with confidence: bus drivers, ticket sellers, and fellow rooters. He may never have met the players, but most fans have read or heard great quantities of facts about them. The game itself is highly organized and specialized. The players are workers of considerable skill, both native and trained, and they work for corporations that are efficient and rationalized, in short, special though rather small bureaucracies, with an intensive technology of their own.

Developed personal skills and impersonal knowledge are the necessary equipment for survival in today's metropolis. They are necessary as the old biological given, once thought to be one's only necessity for a free life, an able body. Even the able-bodied man who lacks skills and knowledge may not find a job in the bureaucratic corporations of today's public world. He may be forced back into public welfare and hence into servility.[3]

The social meaning of our urban school system can only be understood through its special functions for vast cities characterized by giant bureaucratic corporations. That function is to separate the growing individual out of the private world of family and to recruit him into the public world of work. This function is not that which schoolmen would usually call the purpose of education, and therefore perhaps we should call it a "latent" function; but empirically it is by far the most important one.[4] A more clearly manifest function would be the transmission of knowledge. The schools may store some knowledge, but this function is more specifically relegated to libraries. The schools also may generate new knowledge through research, but this is emphatically not a characteristic of urban school systems. Rather, that function is carried out by the universities and the research centers. In the cities, then, the first job of the schools is to move people.

The Rural Migrant: The Formerly Oppressed or the Culturally Deprived?

All urban corporations, whether marketing and manufacturing firms seeking labor or schools forced to take an entire age group or welfare and police agencies with "undesirable" clients, have difficulty working with large numbers of clients who do not understand the ways of an organized, impersonal life. The corporate bureaucrats may mistake ignorance for stupidity, and the supposedly stupid, once scorned, may retreat further into ignorance, never learning the ins and outs of the organizations that face them. Nonetheless, generation after generation of rural immigrants has had to adapt itself to urban vastnesses. But today this problem is reaching unprecedented dimensions. The numbers of agrarian migrants are just as great, but they reach cities that are far more vast and impersonal than the cities that received migrants in the nineteenth century. Moreover, the world of work is more impersonal, vast, specialized, and technological than it was a century ago. Because of the technological revolution in the countryside, the agrarian unskilled continue to flow to the cities in unabated torrents. Indeed, it is particularly the marginal farmers who come, having been the tenants, the sharecroppers, and the migrant fieldhands. Ethnically they are no longer foreigners from Europe, as were the first great waves of immigrants. Instead Negroes, Appalachian poor whites, and Spanish-speakers from the Southwest and Puerto Rico crowd into our central cities. Since they already are American citizens, assimilation is not a simple ideal to be held up to them.

These new urban poor do not fare well in our cities. They have trouble finding employment and keeping it. In short, the public world does not welcome them. Much of the attention they have received concentrates on deficiencies imputed to the migrants themselves, not to their situation. Thus, attention focuses on their supposed stupidity, not their justifiable ignorance. These deficiencies have been catalogued.[5] Let us take up these imputed deficiencies one by one and comment on them, seeing the unemployed as also the newly urbanized.

First, there is "impaired intellectual functioning." In general, this means that the urban poor score low on intelligence tests. However, there has been enough literature now on the subject for all of us to know that low IQ scores do not necessarily reflect innate intelligence, but merely poor preparation for the tests. If migrants have had little schooling, and that quite meager, in their native states, it is unfair to expect that their IQ scores should compare with those of established citizenry in urban centers.[6]

Second come "deficient conceptual abilities. . . . Lower-status persons . . . are poor at handling abstractions, relationships, and categories." Once again we detect the results of poor schooling elsewhere.

Third are "inadequate verbal skills. . . . Reading and writing abilities are defective, and general linguistic retardation is common." This can be taken to mean that we are dealing with a population that speaks a rural dialect, far removed from the standard literary English spoken in the big cities. For example, in rural Mississippi counties the planter not only understood, but could speak the dialect of his Negro fieldhands. There was no need for reading or writing, or even well-ordered and connected sentences, expressed in a wide vocabulary, at least not in the world of work. Such oral literature as might exist in such counties stands the migrants in little stead in the big cities, save perhaps for those few who become blues singers.

Fourth, there is "cognitive restriction. The cognitive process of lower-status persons is relatively unstructured. Ideas of what the outside world is like are garbled and hazy." This simply means that the persons we are talking about have little knowledge, that is, "cognition." In particular they know little geography, least of all of urban areas, and find it difficult to get about.

Fifth, there is "defective self-esteem and low self-esteem. . . . The self system of lower-status persons tends to be unintegrated and characterized by poor ego controls. Their self-concepts are only minimally shaped by social structure." They "commonly suffer from a severe degree of low self-esteem." Here again we are talking about the marginal, depressed labor force of an agrarian society. For such persons, moving through an ever more successful career, preferably linked with business or science, was never even remotely realistic. Low self-esteem, on the other hand, was quite realistic in a social system that emphasized humility and "knowing one's place."

Sixth, there is "limited role repertory. . . . Lower-status persons appear restricted in their ability to take the role of the other. Complex role playing may be beyond the capacities of lower-status persons in view of their lack of subtleties in role-playing and difficulties in shifting perspectives." This simply means that most of our fieldhands have not been trained for many jobs, nor given the idea that they might advance above the level of unskilled labor.

Seventh, we have "minimai motivation. The conditions of life of lower-status persons make planning and concern for the future unrealistic. They are preoccupied with the struggle to obtain basic necessities of life." Indeed a constant day-to-day struggle with staying alive makes a concern with saving, studying, or other austere means to self-advancement quite unrealistic.

In conclusion we see that these so-called deficiences are to be understood as the natural attributes of an agrarian people who were marginal to begin with, even in the countryside. In this their provenience is instructive. The dominant American middle class has, in large measure, been shaped by the pioneer experience of the Main Street towns, or, earlier, by the Puritan experiments in the New England townships. Both community forms were permeated with an egalitarian ethic. Such inequality as there was could be mitigated by personal ties or be fled from by migration to the West. The new migrant in the cities, by contrast, comes from southern counties or Puerto Rican *municipios*, where class divisions are openly recognized and even violently enforced. Instead of staying in his place, the poor migrant is now expected to rise above it. He has changed not only his residence, but his entire cultural milieu.

If a people in the city display these same "deficiencies," even in the second generation, in large scale, then both they and all other observers have cause for alarm. Our cities, particularly New York, have absorbed waves of such immigrants before. The second and third generations have proved more urbane, at least in having skills necessary for the urban job structure. The evidence of New York, where each immigrant group that entered the city in the nineteenth century has left the ranks of unskilled labor, would seem to support this contention. That is, each second generation does not have to become doctors and lawyers en masse, but simply employable.

There is good indication, however, that the urban schools are turning out large numbers of persons, the children of today's immigrants, who are only slightly less unemployable than their parents. There is the startling fact that IQ scores go down the longer the children stay in slum schools. There is the tremendously high drop-out rate. And last and worst, there is the tremendously large number of unemployed youths in all our big city slums.[7] One has a suspicion that the schools treat these clients just as any other impersonal corporation treats them. Just as the others find them unemployable, so the schools find them unteachable. They were unprepared for urban living before they reached the school system, just as their parents needed those skills before reaching the city.

In contrast to the slum children are the educational careers of the real urbanites: the middle-class children who shall, indeed, inherit the metropolis, even though most of them grow up in its suburbs.

The goal of separating children from their families and providing them with a springboard for careers in the public world is one which is enthusiastically espoused by middle-class, urban parents. They share the American values on hard work and mastery over nature. They see the school system as a way to a career that is itself an avenue to achieving or realizing those values. Any middle-class urban or suburban residential district in America is filled with parents who themselves are achieving these careers in our great corporations. Given our present economic structure, these parents are not accumulating private fortunes. Therefore, the best they can pass on to their children is an opportunity to share in these same career structures.

Since many middle-class parents have left their native backgrounds—whether central cities or American towns—to come to the suburbs or inner-city, silk-stocking district, their most intense private world centers on their households, occupied by single nuclear families of parents and children together. They have left the relatives and lifelong friends of the past. Therefore it is precisely for these people that separation from their children, so necessary for the career structure they want, is extremely difficult emotionally. Four years of college away from home provide the means of separating children from parents with a minimum of strain. That is one of the most important functions of college for our middle classes. It is no accident that these parents are intensely interested in their children's education, for their own education was paramount to them. Since they value knowledge, particularly scientific knowledge, they take a personal interest in the curriculum. Perhaps in no other culture in the world does one find educated and cultured parents expecting to learn from their children. Today's changing curriculum, even though it lags behind the knowledge explosion, nonetheless provides the opportunity for children to instruct parents.[8]

The Schools as Bureaucratic Corporations: Ideological Captives

One of anthropology's central concepts is bureaucracy, originally defined by Max Weber as that form of social organization that maximizes efficiency in administration. Bureaucracy means the specialization of labor, according to function, into bureaus, with recruitment, after proper training, into specific jobs in a career ladder. This definition implies ever increasing rationality within the course of human evolution, which to Weber meant the factoring out of functions. One may judge rationality, or efficiency, in terms of any of Weber's criteria for defining bureaucracy. Each one becomes an axis of rationality, so to speak.[9] Weber assumes that the march of human history is toward the fulfillment of these criteria.

History has proved Weber right beyond his wildest dreams fifty years ago. Moreover, modern history has webbed the old Roman legal device of the corporation to the bureaucratic form. A corporation is simply a legal fiction granting an association of persons the right and privileges of one person. They become, for certain purposes, legally one. By replacing their members, corporations may live on indefinitely and hold property forever. Today many such private corporations are great bureaucracies, whose form was borrowed straight from the political sphere for private, usually economic, ends.

In America the double form—the bureaucratic corporation, the private bureaucracy—has come to dominate our entire society as never before. We find corporations in trade, finance, and industry, where we would expect to find them. But they have also spread to education, medicine, religion, and agriculture. Even the traditionally decentralized Protestant churches, such as the Congregationalists, have their secretariats occupying huge office buildings and attending to many tasks. Within the traditionally bureaucratic and hierarchical churches, such as the Roman Catholic, the process is, of course, carried much further. In agriculture the individual farmer survives, even though he directs a much bigger enterprise than formerly, but he finds he must sell to larger corporations, which process and market his goods through the chain stores. It is no accident, then, that when observers go to the contemporary schools, they expect to find bureaucratic corporations.[10]

Urban schools are most successful in their suburban versions, where they serve the parents who themselves dominate the entire public world of the corporation. Here the schools manifestly do separate children from the homes, which willingly become empty nests. Here the schools do recruit, via college, the offspring into the world of work, which the recruits will eventually run. The schools manifestly do transmit knowledge, and they are manifestly responsive to the creation of new knowledge by the constant endeavor to revise the curriculum.

In contrast, in the inner city the immigrant peoples do not understand, let alone share the value on a career. Indeed, the teachers in the inner city, who can often be classed as "upper working class," both in origin and job behavior, do not necessarily share these values. For most of them teaching is a job, often treated just as if it were industrial labor. For all too few, it is a means of self-improvement and continuous instruction of the sort we find among true professionals. The inner-city schools are great bureaucracies, with an ideology that explains to themselves what they are doing, while at the same time obscuring much of the real activity in which they engage.

This ideology is but the repetition of the same doctrines that, at one time or another, have held sway in the suburban schools. The difference is that in the latter places the clientele is attuned to these doctrines, and ever vigilant that means do not become ends in themselves. The inner-city clientele does not exercise such vigilance, and in its absence old doctrines become routine ideology.

Let us look at the components of that ideology. First, there is the logic of hierarchy and specialization. This means that children must be grouped so as to be instructed easily. The grouping is according to age and ability. There is an unexamined proposition that children of like age are of like ability. So children are split up into groups defined by their having been born in the same calendar year. If these groups are large enough, they will be split further according to "ability" usually as reflected on standardized tests. Until recently schoolmen believed that IQ tests reflected innate ability. Many still do, unfortunately.

Second, there is the ideology of efficiency. In part this reflects the natural conditions of any bureaucratic organization. But the larger, and more deceptive part, stems from an inappropriate analogy with the factory. Raymond Callahan has documented how the languages of efficiency in the schools was borrowed from time-unit studies of industrial efficiency.[11] This language was borrowed as rhetoric, without precise investigation as to the aptness of the analogy. Essentially the idea has meant that schools have come to look like factories, in that small numbers of teachers administer large numbers of pupils. In this, they are like the foremen of industrial shops, while their supervisors and principals act as management. The foremen of our factories simply enact the policy laid down to them by the management, and supervise an industrial process whereby the actions of men are carefully coordinated with the activities of machines, all according to an engineered blueprint carefully worked out in advance. So too do teachers simply administer prepackaged learning. The idea here is that a good lesson plan, just like a good industrial blueprint, can be largely left to itself once it is set up, that is, it can be self-taught. The logic of efficiency is also the logic of clock time. Learning can be measured in the amounts of time it takes groups of individuals, classified according to their age, to learn it. Thus children simply move through a twelve-year process whereby the appropriate packages are presented to them at the appropriate level.

This ideology has been extremely attractive to administrators. From it they get the best of two worlds. They can present themselves to city schoolboards, often comprised of businessmen, as efficient businessmen. On the other hand to their teachers they present themselves as wise superteachers, helping the ordinary teachers by giving them their curricula ahead of time. In truth, they are neither businessmen nor teachers, but public administrators. In such a situation we find that the teachers themselves are managed just as much as the pupils.

The factory model was superimposed upon an earlier administrative one: the Lancaster system. This was a method devised in England in the early nineteenth century to propagate literacy to large numbers of persons at a time. One teacher could administer lessons to hundreds of pupils by means of pupil monitors, who went over the lessons lock-step with their assigned groups of pupils. Here the organizational analogy is clearly the military, the corporate bureaucracy that antedates the factory. What educators did was to graft a time and motion study method, intended to synchronize man's movements with those of machines, to an essentially military model. Teachers have replaced the monitors, but they are no less managed than the pupils. Again by military analogy, teachers are on a level with sergeants in the army. Both are analogous to foremen in factories.

Now this "factory model" has never worked perfectly even back in the days, such as the 1930s, when the urban poor were composed of more tractable populations than today, and when the knowledge level had not reached its present proportions. There were always large groups of students who did not absorb the learning presented to them. This inconvenient fact could be explained away in terms of the pupil's own deficiency. His low IQ was expressed, of course, with a number. With the advent of the new immigrant populations, these groups are much larger. Moreover the psychologists have taught us to be skeptical of IQ. Educators, however, have found another, no less convenient, means of explaining the failure of pupils to learn in terms of the pupil's own deficiency. This is the current ideology of cultural deprivation. By this ideology children are thought to reach the school with all the deficiencies of the urban unemployed[12] catalogued above.

Elizabeth Eddy's descriptive, but highly ordered, account of slum schools has shown that, instead of finding new strategies for teaching the "culturally deprived," the schools continue to lump them and treat them just as they did the older group of mentally deprived. The schools do so in the track system, whereby children are placed in classes based first on age and second on ability. Those children who are placed in the bottom classes are often regarded as unteachable and such classes become custodial. Such classes may be composed of people who cannot speak English, who score low on tests, or who have been for years in school without learning to read. Their ranks are joined by pupils who are notorious troublemakers in other classes. Experienced teachers soon learn to avoid such classes. If such teachers have proved themselves in a school, they expect a reward from the principal in the assignment of good, or high-ranking classes. Consequently inexperienced, and even marginal teachers, are often those who have to confront the most difficult classes in our urban schools.

Moreover, as both Eddy and I have documented, the slum schools seldom succeed in assimilating the children, at least during school hours, to the body style that they will need if they are to move before future employers with urbane confidence.[13] On the contrary, at worst the schools require a very rigid, quasi-militaristic style, which is of use only to its own organizational ends. It is a way of marching everyone through the day without incident. It is not unusual for slum schools in Harlem, for example, to have teachers meet their small charges at the gate in the morning and march them into the classes when the bell rings. Students often march to one class or another, and movement through the halls during class time, virtually prohibited, is even more rigidly controlled. Behavior in the classroom is no less rigidly patterned. Students are expected to sit up straight and tall, with a minimum of movement not directly connected with their studies. The implicit idea being that such a posture is "educational" and allows the young mind to receive the learning that is being presented to it.

In the worst classes, this stance, as indeed every other item of the prepackaged blueprint, breaks down. Some teachers become relaxed and unrestrained with their charges, allowing them to dance at certain times of the day, for example, while paying really very little attention to the lesson plan. Other teachers go through the lesson plans almost by ritual recitation while engaging in a running battle with their pupils.

Only in the model classes do the children go beyond the adoption of a military stance to something like an urbane, confident one. The model classes are composed of those very few children who are performing on tests at grade level. That is, these children can recite or demonstrate the same amount of knowledge in the same amount of time as the majority of children their age throughout the nation. It is not surprising, however, that when Eddy examined the actual conduct of these classes, she found that the required information was somehow being passed along in lessons that stressed a presentable appearance and graceful manners.

An Organizational Analogy for Urban Schools

I can offer no blueprint. My only prescription is a selfish one: more ethnographies of urban schools. However, I can make a cautious practical suggestion and also some speculations.

The practical suggestion concerns the proper organizational analogy for the schools. Factories typically employ what James Thompson calls a "long-linked" technology. Perhaps the real technical model for schools is his "intensive technology," typified by hospitals. There specific tasks cannot be forecast in advance but the hospital must keep many experts on call. Their expertise comes into play in varying combinations, according to the task at hand. An intensive technology is a custom technology. In short, the schools need to look at other, more flexible organizational models (Thompson, 1967).

Now to the broader perspective, which also has to do with management, but at the highest levels. Solon Kimball and James McClellan, in *Education and the New America* (1963: 259–304), note that the current dynamism of American civilization comes from a peculiar organization within our great corporations. That is the task force. Here groups of people of every sort are thrown together with the expectation that they must solve a problem. In our defense establishment and in our business establishment the criteria of success are very simple. Famous task forces include the Manhattan Project, which perfected the atomic bomb, and the recent force that retrieved our H-bomb off the coast of Spain at Palomares.

It would seem likely that only by evolving this kind of task force approach, of very richly constituted committees, will our schools begin to solve their problems in curriculum and instruction. Only by setting aside the overrigid, hierarchical organization of nineteenth-century armies and factories will our urban school corporations enter the late twentieth century. To do so our schools are also going to need much greater resources than their present fragmented tax base allows. Inner-city schools typically rely on a tax base representing only part of the metropolitan area they serve. Perhaps federal funds will make up this deficiency. Our great corporations do put enormous resources at the disposal of their task forces. This is particularly true of the military establishment, but private industry commands great resources as well (especially when the federal government helps). Indeed, everywhere in the world of organizations, earlier, very rigid, hierarchical, bureaucratic structures seem to be outdated.

SUMMARY

Let us summarize our anthropological observations. The school systems in our citites have come to resemble the other major institutions of our society. They are corporate in nature, bureaucratic in form. They perform manifest or explicit functions long reserved for schools in the West. But their latent or unconscious function—that of separating children from their families and launching them as adults into an impersonal public world, also composed of bureaucratic corporations—has now become central. This function assumes more importance than the old one of transmitting knowledge precisely, because of the magnitude and complexity of the metropolis. Today's urbanite needs a schooling that no home can impart, unlike the farm boy of old. But the modern school corporation finds a heretofore insuperable problem in the newly urban population that have not grasped this newly central fact: that the home can no longer be the main educational force. The problem is all the greater since the successful urban populations have faced it unawares, and have grasped the importance of schooling in other terms.

To solve that problem it must be grasped in explicitly social terms, and then the full technical, academic, and organizational resources of our society must be brought to bear upon it in a flexible manner, as exemplified in the highly skilled task force in industry. Hopefully, such action will lead to an urban civilization including every one of its citizens in meaningful participation in its sciences and arts, and where none will be the unransomed hostage to an agrarian past.

NOTES

1. Reprinted as a chapter in Conrad Arensberg and Solon T. Kimball (1965).
2. See the section "The Meaning of Schooling in Agrarian America," Kimball and McClellan (1963: 90-95).
3. It is Lewis A. Coser's (1965) idea that the poor are best defined, cross-culturally but particularly today, as those who accept public charity. Such acceptance implies both humiliation and servility. For evidence that the able-bodied often cannot get employment in today's cities even when they want it, see Ben B. Seligman (1967).
4. For this definition of the function of urban education, as well as the all-important distinction between private and public worlds, I am indebted to Kimball and McClellan (1963).
5. Orville R. Gursslin and Jack L. Roach (1964). The issues are also quoted and discussed by Elizabeth M. Eddy (1967: 53-57).
6. Joan I. Roberts reviews and discusses the question before presenting a number of articles on the subject. See her "Introduction: Cognitive Factors and Environment" (1967: 17-28).
7. See Kenneth B. Clark's (1965: 34-41) discussion of the difficulties of getting Harlem youth employed. Presumably he found Harlem educated youth no less unemployable than those educated elsewhere, though he doesn't make the distinction. In any case, a major part of his Haryou proposal was to provide an agency to get all Harlem youths employment.
8. Elizabeth M. Eddy (1967: 11-44) treats this question broadly in her chapter "Family and School in the New Metropolis."
9. Max Weber (1946). Most sociologists have treated Weber's formulation in terms of contemporary examples. The evolutionary discussion that follows was suggested by the lectures of Conrad Arensberg at Columbia University.
10. For the best discussion I know of the bureaucratic corporation see the chapter "The Corporate Society and Education," in Kimball and McClellan (1963: 183-215).

11. Raymond E. Callahan (1962). For a critique of the concept of efficiency, even as applied to industry, see Daniel Bell's essay "Work and its Discontents: The Cult of Efficiency in America."
12. Clark (1965: 125-133) examines the birth of this ideology in detail.
13. Alexander Moore (1967: 48-79); Elizabeth M. Eddy (1967: 90-130). The discussion of educational science and the administered blueprint above are all drawn from Eddy's book.

REFERENCES

Arensberg, Conrad. "The Community as Object and as Sample." *American Anthropologist* 63 (April 1961): 341-53.

Arensberg, Conrad, and Kimball, Solon T. *Culture and Community*. New York: Harcourt, Brace & World, 1965.

Atwood, Mark. "An Anthropological Approach to Administrative Change: The Introduction of a Guidance Program to a High School. Ph.D. dissertation, Columbia University, 1963.

Callahan, Raymond E. *Education and the Cult of Efficiency*. Chicago: University of Chicago Press, 1962.

Clark, Kenneth B. *Dark Ghetto: Dilemmas of Social Power*. New York: Harper & Row, 1965.

Coser, Lewis A. "The Sociology of Poverty: To the Memory of George Simmel." *Social Problems* 13 (Fall 1965): 140-148.

Eddy, Elizabeth M. *Walk the White Line: A Profile of Urban Education*. New York: Anchor Books, 1967.

Gursslin, Orville R., and Roach, Jack L. "Some Issues in Training the Unemployed." *Social Problems* 12 (Summer 1964): 91-93.

Henry, Jules. *Culture Against Man*. New York: Random House, 1963.

Kimball, Solon T., and McClellan, James E., Jr. *Education and the New America*. New York: Random House, 1963.

Moore, Alexander. *Realities of the Urban Classroom: Observations in Elementary Schools*. New York: Anchor Books, 1967.

Roberts, Joan I. *School Children in the Urban Slum: Readings in Social Science Research*. New York: Free Press, 1967.

Seligman, Ben B. "Automation and the Work Force." In *The Guaranteed Income: Next Step in Socioeconomic Evolution*, edited by Robert Theobald. New York: Anchor Books, 1967.

Thompson, James. *Organizations in Action*. New York: McGraw-Hill, 1967.

Wax, Murray L. "Formal Education in an American Indian Community." *Social Problems* 2 (Spring 1964): supplement.

Weber, Max. *Essays in Sociology*, translated by H. H. Gerth and C. W. Mills. New York: Oxford University Press, 1946.

9 / A Cross-Cultural Outline of Education

Jules Henry

INTRODUCTION

The names of many anthropologists have become associated with the cross-cultural study of education. Pettitt (1946), Raum (1940), Mead (1939), and Spiro (1958) have devoted entire volumes to the subject. A short but enlightening work is that of Fortes on the *Social and Psychological Aspects of Education in Taleland*

(1938). Volume 48 of the *American Journal of Sociology* (1943) contains several papers by anthropologists on education. A few anthropological monographs contain sections on education, though others make reference to the subject merely in passing. Recently, a review of problems in education appeared as a collaborative work of anthropologists and educators (Spindler 1955).

In surveying these publications, it seemed that it might be useful if a general outline of the educational process could be provided for the anthropological field worker. With such an outline, the scientist would not need to rely solely on his creative imagination and on works that are often incomplete and focused on particularistic interests, for he would have available also a methodological tool that might help increase the scope of his observations.

As industrial cultures become more and more the target of anthropological interest, anthropologists will sooner or later have to study their educational systems too, so that an outline of education for anthropologists should take account not only of pre-literate culture but of industrial society also.

Much material that one might wish to see included in an outline of education is concerned largely with personality, with physiological pathways to enculturation, and with the conditioning of the very young child while feeding, eliminating, or, in general, in close physical contact with his family. The present outline, however, deals primarily, though not exclusively, with children about six years of age and older, and concentrates on the formal, conscious aspects of education. Furthermore, since the outline and text are concerned solely with education as a social process, no attention is given to knowledge the child acquires while alone.

Education can be looked at from the standpoint of the adult educator and from that of the child who is learning. The adult generally wants to do something to the child, and sees education as a process through which the child should become what the adult wants him to be. From the position of the child, however, education is also finding a way to certainty: the child wants to know what he should do about everything, and how he should do it, and he looks to the adult—to the educational process—to help him. This outline and text take account only of the first view.

Origins of the Outline

While the outline derives in part from the work of others and in part from my own field experience in nonindustrial cultures, much of it has grown out of research on cultural factors in learning that was begun seven years ago at Washington University. Several hundred protocols of direct observation of American classrooms have been collected by me and my students, and it was the analysis of these observations that made necessary the bulky (but by no means complete!) outline. The research continues (Henry 1955a, 1955b, 1957a, 1957b, 1959).

The records collected during this research are factual, relatively unscreened process notes of what the observer saw. The major selective factor was the observer's concentration on teacher-pupil interaction.

Some Theoretical Problems

Humans must learn much more than other animals, and the evolution of *Homo sapiens* has been characterized by a great expansion of his dependence on learning and of his capacity to learn. This has been accompanied by an increase in the number of teaching devices. For these reasons the outline contains a partial inventory of the materials humans must learn and of teaching methods.

Although in the past thirty years or so the dependence of lower animals on learning has become apparent, due particularly to the work of the comparative psychologists, learning in *Homo sapiens* differs from that in other animals in some striking ways. Among these are the following: (1) In man, learning is dominated by symbolic processes. (2) In man, the motivational organizers of learning are more variable—that is to say, much less subject to innate determinants than in subhuman species. (3) There are apparently, in man, no innate limits on learning: the outer limits of the capacity of human beings to learn have not yet been discovered. (4) A striking feature of man is the extent to which his learning is polyphasic (Henry 1955a), that is, affected by a strong innate tendency to learn more than one thing at a time. While it is true, as Pavlov (1928) has shown, that animals also learn more than one thing at a time, polyphasic learning is much more extensive in man.

The combination in *Homo sapiens* of genetic variability, absence of obvious, biologically determined limits on learning, and great capacity for polyphasic learning has brought it about that the social processes of learning have become extremely complex, and therefore require long-sustained and meticulous observation and recording by the researcher. The net, but by no means final, result of an effort to catalogue the actual—as distinguished from laboratory—learning *events* in human children is a long and complicated outline like the one offered here. When, to this, we add the dimension of cultural variability, the catalogue becomes even more impressive. It then becomes clear that the education of humans cannot be understood through conceptually reducing the entire process to a simple reward reinforcement system (Miller and Dollard 1941).

The paradoxical aspect of human education is that in spite of the overshadowing tendency of human learning to variability and expansion, educational procedures have regularly taken as a model the innate release mechanism postulated by ethology (Tinbergen 1951). That is to say, it would appear that human societies have tried repeatedly to accomplish in their members a completely predictable response system. The model, though not the reality, of the educated human, is the mass tendency of an American audience to rise to its feet whenever it hears the national anthem: the response is predictable and almost automatic. Teachers in American elementary schools rely heavily on the culturally determined and learned tendency of children to raise their hands whenever the teacher wants the answer to a question; Pilagá mothers depend on the learned tendency of their children to recoil from the village boundaries or to duck into their houses whenever an adult shouts the term "sorcerer." The processes whereby these tendencies to respond predictably to single or complex symbols are internalized in the child form the matrix of education everywhere. The outline, particularly the sections on teaching methods (II) and on conduct control (IX), attempts to take account of these processes.

Thus, as one peruses the outline, one cannot but be struck by the fact that what it represents, in part, is a measure of the extent to which human learning has departed from that of lower animals. Stated another way, if one wished to obtain an answer to the question, "How does human learning differ from animals?" a first step might be to examine this outline, for here, quite apart from the general theoretical points raised, the mere catalogue of the dimensions of human education serves to place human learning on an entirely different plane from that of even the higher primates.

Further theoretical issues will be discussed in explaining the categories contained in the outline.

EXPLANATION OF THE OUTLINE

The outline contains twelve major sections, each divided into many subsections. Only those subsections the titles of which do not seem self-explanatory will be discussed. I have tried to present here both an explanation of the outline and a theoretical orientation to problems of education in its cross-cultural aspects. I have attempted also to raise theoretical issues of anthropological relevance insofar as they relate to matters impinging on education. For this reason the paper, in addition to being a set of explanatory notes, is also a collection of miniature theoretical essays.

A Cross-Cultural Outline of Education
I. On what does the educational process focus?
- 1. Environment (other than human)
    - 1. Flora
    - 2. Fauna
    - 3. Climate
    - 4. Geographical features
    - 5. Anthropomorphized flora
    - 6. Anthropomorphized fauna
    - 7. Anthropomorphized or zoomorphized machines
    - 8. Anthropomorphized or zoomorphized natural phenomena other than flora or fauna (winds, rivers, mountains, etc.)
    - 9. Space
    - 10. Time
    - 11. Motion
    - 12. Space-time motion
    - 13. The world view of the culture
        - 1. Isolate-static
        - 2. Communicate-changing
            - 1. Engulfing
        - 3. Hostile or pacific
            - 1. Hostile
            - 2. Pacific
            - 3. Selectively hostile or pacific
        - 4. Geographical position of places studied
            - 1. Near: own town, state or province, village, tribe
            - 2. Near-distant: other states or provinces, nation in general; other villages or tribes
            - 3. Distant: other lands
        - 5. Temporal position
            - 1. Immediate
            - 2. Contemporary
            - 3. Near past
            - 4. Distant past
            - 5. Mythological past
    - 14. Clothing
    - 15. Food
    - 16. Transportation and communication
- 2a. Values
    - 1. Good and bad: moral rules
    - 2. Work, success, failure
    - 3. Being on time
    - 4. Culture
    - 5. Proper dress
    - 6. Strength, activity, power
    - 7. Beating the game
    - 8. Politeness, tact
    - 9. Cooperation, helpfulness, togetherness
    - 10. Patriotism
    - 11. Cleanliness, orderliness
    - 12. Thrift, saving, don't waste
    - 13. Parents are good
    - 14. Prettiness, beauty
    - 15. Love
    - 16. Mother, motherhood

17. Happiness
18. Competitiveness
19. Equality
20. Novelty, excitement
21. Pride
22. Knowledge as value
23. The "beautiful person"
24. Private property
25. Democracy
26. Family
27. Responsibility
28. Generosity, doing more than required, noncommercialism
29. The state
30. Deference
31. Enlightened self-interest
32. Independence, toughness
33. Physical intactness
34. Sense of emergency
35. Constancy
36. Solicitude for others, kindness
37. Composure under stress
38. Courage
39. Knowledge as means to an end
40. Compromise
41. Fun, relaxation
42. Friends, friendship, faithfulness
43. Fairness
44. Flattery, empty praise
45. Honor (integrity), personal autonomy
46. Self-restraint
47. Trying hard, don't give up
48. Fame, ambition
49. Honesty
50. Prestige
51. Niceness, likeableness
52. Respect for authority
53. Excitement
54. Gentleness, nonviolence
55. Speed, alertness
56. Sacredness, etc., of parents
57. Flexibility
58. Modesty
59. Tolerance
60. Freedom
61. Peace
62. Progress
63. Wealth
64. U.S.A.
65. Loyalty
66. Money, greed, etc., are corrupting
67. Smartness, cleverness, thinking
68. Profit
69. Size

2b. Value conflict
3. Institutions

      1. Social structure
      2. Religion
      3. Economic system
  4. Technology, machines
  5. Reading, writing, and arithmetic
  6. Social manipulation
      1. Recognition-seeking behavior
      2. Manipulation of others
      3. Manipulation of self
  7. Responsibility
  8. How to compete
  9. How to take care of others
10. Use of the mind
      1. How to think
      2. Disjunction
          1. When to disjoin
          2. How to disjoin
          3. From what to disjoin
      3. Concentration
          1. Interest stimulation defining purpose; motivation
          2. Force
          3. Shutting out external stimuli
          4. Visualization
          5. Focused retention
      4. Preparation of the mind
      5. "Mental discipline"
11. Body parts or functions
      1. The voice
      2. The sphincters
      3. Care of the body (like getting enough rest)
      4. Posture
      5. How to relax
      6. The mouth
12. Art
13. History
14. Some other facts about which information is communicated
      1. About systems of rewards and punishments
      2. About what the culture promises its members
      3. About permitted and forbidden activities
      4. About how to get pleasure and avoid pain
      5. About whom to love and whom to hate
      6. How to handle frustration
      7. The difference between the real and the manifest (this refers to situations in which an effort is deliberately made to enable the child to see "behind" the obvious)
      8. About death
      9. About sex relations
      10. About race, class, or ethnic differences
15a. Instruction in identifiable adult tasks
15b. Teaching about adult tasks
16. Scientific abstractions
17. Science (general)
18. Routine procedures
19. Childish handiwork
20. Cultural stereotypes

    21. Warfare and associated activities
    22. Safety
    23. Songs, music
    24. Mythology
    25. The object system
    26. Games
    27. Cultural fictions

II. How is the information communicated (teaching methods)?
    1. By imitation
    2. By setting an example
    3. By instruction in schools, ceremonials, or other formal institutions
    4. By use of punishments
    5. By use of rewards
    6. Problem solving
    7. Guided recall
    8. Giving the child tasks to perform beyond his immediate capacity
       1. Jamming the machine
    9. Mechanical devices
    10. By kinesthetic association
    11. By experiment
       1. By teacher
       2. By pupil
    12. By doing
    13. By symbolic association
    14. By dramatization
    15. By games or other play
    16a. By threats
    16b. By trials
    17. By irrelevant association
    18. By relevant association
    19. Through art
       1. Graphic
       2. Music, general
       3. Songs
       4. Literature (stories, myths, tales, etc.)
    20. By stating the opposite of the truth ("Water's a solid, isn't it?"); writing antonyms
    21. By holding up adult ideals
    22. Acting in undifferentiated unison
    23. Physical force
    24. By positive or negative assertion
    25. Repetition
    26. By specifically relating information to the child's own body, bodily function, or experience
    27a. Through ego-inflation
    27b. Through ego-deflation
    28. Through use of humor
    29. By telling
    30. By watching
    31. By listening
    32. Question and answer
       1. Teacher question, pupil answer
       2. Pupil question, teacher answer
    33. Holding up class, ethnic, national, or religious ideals
    34. By doing something on his own

35a. By repeating the child's error to him
35b. By repeating the child's correct answer
36. By accusing
37. By following a model
    1. Human
    2. Nonhuman
38. By comparison
39. By filling in a missing part
40. By associative naming (e.g., a book mentions gingham as a material, and teacher asks students if they can name other materials)
41. By identifying an object (like going to the board and underlining "a noun" in a sentence)
42a. By group discussion
42b. By class discussion
43. Physical manipulation
    1. Bodily manipulation
    2. Bodily mutilation and other physical stresses
44. Rote memory
45. By working together with a student (as when teacher and student work together to make a battery, or as when teacher and student go over reference books together)
46. Through special exhibits
47. By having children read substantive materials (e.g., reading the chemistry lesson in the reader)
48. By putting the child on his mettle ("Now let's see how well you can read")
49. Through group projects
50. By giving procedural instructions
51. By demanding proof
52. Through reports by students
53. By pairing (e.g., one child gives a word and calls on another child to give a sentence with the word; one child gives the state and another gives the capital)
54. By asking for volunteers
55. Through isolating the subject

III. Who educates?
  1. Males or females?
  2. Relatives or others?
  3. On which age group does the burden of education fall?
    1. Peers
      1. Boy
      2. Girl
    2. Older children
      1. Male
      2. Female
    3. Adolescents
      1. Male
      2. Female
    4. Adults
      1. Male or female
      2. Younger or older
      3. Married or unmarried
    5. Others
  4. Is education by "successful" people?
  5. What rewards accrue to the educator?

        1. Enhanced status

        2. Material rewards

        3. Emotional satisfactions

  6. Are there education specialists?

  7. Does the educator wear distinctive dress or other insignia?

  8. Is the educator of the same or of a different social group from that of the person being educated? (national, racial, class, etc.)

IV. How does the person being educated participate? (What is his attitude?)

    1. Accepting

    2. Rejecting, resistive

    3. Bored, indifferent

    4. Defiant

    5. Inattentive

    6. Social closeness of teacher and child

    7. Social distance of teacher and child

    8. Finds the process painful?

    9. Finds the process gratifying?

10a. Competitively

10b. Cooperatively

11a. With inappropriate laughter

11b. Ridiculing peers

  12. Laughter at humor of peers or teacher

  13. Overt docility

  14. Eagerly

        1. Facial expression

        2. Hand raising

        3. Talking out

        4. Heightened bodily tonus

  15. Through making independent decisions and suggestions

  16. Asks for clarification, direction, etc.

  17. Through spontaneous contributions or other demonstrations not precisely within the context of the lesson

  18. Through spontaneous contributions within the context of the lesson

  19. Attentively

  20. Spontaneously humorous

  21. Spontaneously expressive

  22. Approaches teacher physically

  23. Mobile—free

  24. Immobile—constricted

  25. Through performing special assigned tasks

26a. Hostile to peers

26b. Protective of peers

  27. Diversion to peers

  28. Anxiously

  29. Disjoined hand-raising

  30. By whispering to teacher

  31. Laughs at peers

  32. Corrects teacher

33a. Disruptively

33b. Critically

  34. By carping criticism

  35. By praising work of peers

  36. Dishonesty, cheating, lying, etc.

  37. Attempts to maintain order

  38. Guiltily

39. With sense of inadequacy
40. With sense of adequacy
41. By copying from peers
42. Attempts to control the class
43. No response
44. Uses teacher's last name
45. Uses teacher's first name
46. Calls out to teacher
47. Uses kinship term
48. By public performance

V. How does the educator participate? (What is his attitude?)
  1. Eagerly
    1. Facial expression
    2. Bodily movement
    3. Tone of voice
    4. Heightened bodily tonus
  2. Bored, uninterested, etc.
  3. Embarrassed
 4a. Dominative
 4b. Integrative
  5. Insecure
  6. Politely
  7. Enjoys correct response
  8. Resents incorrect response
  9. Can't tell
 10. Seeks physical contact with person being educated
 11. Acceptance of blame
 12. Putting decisions up to the children
 13. Discouraging
 14. Encouraging
 15. Hostile, ridiculing, sarcastic, belittling
 16. Relatively mobile
 17. Relatively immobile
 18. Personalizing
    1. Use of request sentence with name
    2. Use of name only
    3. Use of hand-name technique
    4. Use of equalizing, leveling term like "comrade"
 19. Depersonalizing
    1. Use of class seating plan for recitation in succession
    2. Use of "next" or some such impersonal device
    3. Use of "you" instead of name
    4. Pointing, nodding, looking
 20. Irritable
 21. Accepts approach
 22. Repels approach
 23. Accepting of child's spontaneous expressions
 24. Rejecting of child's spontaneous expressions
 25. Humorous
 26. Handles anxiety, hostility, discomfort, etc.
 27. Acts and/or talks as if child's self-image is fragile
 28. Acts and/or talks as if child's self-image is irrelevant
 29. Defends child against peers
 30. Responds to nonverbal cue other than handraising
 31. Excessively polite

    32. Keeps word
    33. Fails to keep word
    34. Praises and rewards realistically
    35. Praises and rewards indiscriminately
    36. Critical (does not point out good things in student's work)
    37. Does not reward correct answer or good performance
    38. Does not punish incorrect answer or poor performance
    39. Acknowledges own error
    40. Uses affectional terms like "honey" or "dear"
    41. Awakens anticipation ("Now we are going to get some nice new books")
    42. The inclusive plural

VI. Are some things taught to some and not to others?
    1. Do different age groups learn different things?
    2. Do the sexes learn different things?
    3. Are different groups taught different things?

VII. Discontinuities in the educational process
    1. Discontinuities between age periods
        1. In regard to techniques
        2. In regard to values
    2. How do all of these apply between the sexes?
        1. Are discontinuities different for boys and girls?
        2. The secrecy of initiation rites

VIII. What limits the quantity and quality of information a child receives from a teacher?
    1. Methods of teaching
    2. Available time
    3. Quality of equipment
    4. Distance from the object
    5. Ignorance or error of teacher
    6. Stereotyping of the object
    7. Failure of teacher to correct pupil's mistakes
    8. Failure of teacher to indicate whether the pupil's answers are right or wrong
    9. Failure of teacher to respond to a question
    10. General vagueness or fumbling of the teacher

IX. What forms of conduct control (discipline) are used?
    1. Relaxed
    2. Tight
    3. Sense of propriety
    4. Affectivity
    5. Reprimand
        1. Direct
        2. Gentle
        3. Mixed ("We like for you to have an opinion but it is childish for you to shout out your numbers like that")
        4. Impersonal ("Some of you are holding us up")
    6. Ridicule
    7. Exhortation ("How can I teach you if you keep making so much noise?")
    8. Command
    9. Command question or request
    10. "We" technique
    11. Instilling guilt
    12. Cessation of activity
    13. Group sanction

14. Threat
15. Putting the child on his mettle
16. Nonverbal signal
17. Reward
18. Promise of reward
19. Special strategems
20. Awakening fear
21. Using a higher power
    1. Human
    2. Nonhuman
22. Exclusion
23. Punishment
24. Encourages peer-group control
X. What is the relation between the intent and the results of education?
    1. Relatively high correlation between intention and results
    2. Relatively low correlation between intention and results
XI. What self-conceptions seem reinforced?
    1. Ego-forming factors
        1. Syntonic: praise, support, status inflation
            1. Grandiose self-conception
        2. Dystonic: blame, shame, guilt, fright, exclusion, depersonalization
XII. How long does the process of formal education last?

I. On What Does the Educational Process Focus?

The first step in a discussion of the educational process must be to make a reasonably complete catalogue of what is taught. The outline is an attempt to do this, from the point of view of what an observer can rather readily see with the naked eye. The theoretical point in this section is that, in humans, behavior is everywhere organized relative to a specific universe that is culturally determined, and that, accordingly, we need to know for each such universe what subject matter education includes. On the other hand, since, in each culture, an effort is made to exclude perceptions not relevant to its universe, education is also a process of exclusion (see I:10:2).

I:1. Environment (Other than Human)

In this section are catalogued factors in the natural nonhuman environment, in the broadest sense, and no attention is given to their "inner meaning." However, it does appear relevant to point out that, whereas a primitive child's knowledge of the flora and fauna in his environment generally has direct survival relevance, this natural world of flora, fauna, and even weather is largely peripheral to the life of the child in industrial cultures.

I:1:5. Anthropomorphized Flora; I:1:6. Anthropomorphized Fauna;
I:1:7. Anthropomorphized or Zoomorphized Machines;
I:1:8. Anthropomorphized or Zoomorphized Natural Phenomena Other than
Flora or Fauna (Winds, Rivers, Mountains, etc.)

One of the principal functions of anthropomorphized animals is to serve as a medium for the transmission of values. The *Panchatantra* of India is an excellent example of this from a literate culture. In the life of young children in industrial cultures, this function overshadows the real aspects of animals. Everywhere, flora and other nonanimal natural phenomena function less in this way.

The use of anthropomorphized and zoomorphized machines as vehicles for general ideas is well illustrated in M. Ilin's *The Story of the Great Plan*. Written to acquaint Soviet boys and girls twelve to fourteen years old with the Five Year Plan launched in 1928, it appeared in English under the title *New Russia's Primer*

(1931). Ilin makes vivid and poetic use of anthropomorphized and zoomorphized machines and natural phenomena to communicate to children a breathless, value-laden excitement about the Great Plan. Some examples will illustrate the point:

> There is a giant excavator. It has only one arm, but this arm is twenty meters in length. In its hand it holds a shovel. . . . The scoop cuts into the ground with teeth made of forged steel and is filled with earth. . . . The giant excavator turns to the left in a circle, as a soldier at a drill. (Ilin 1931: 30-31)

> Wind, water, coal, wood, may not be alive, but they can be forced to work. They can be compelled to turn the wheels of machines. In Baku the wind flaps the wings of a windmill. . . . (Ilin 1931: 33)

> Our mountains and plains are well supplied with rivers. These rivers could give us 65 million horse-power of electrical energy. But to compel them to work for us is not so easy. Man must fight the river, as the animal-tamer tames wild beasts. If he becomes careless only for a moment, he will make a mistake and the beast will spring upon him and tear him to pieces. (Ilin 1931: 35-36)

It would appear that the function of this kind of writing is to bring the children closer to the machines and the land in order to adapt the children to the requirements of the economic effort.

I:1:12. Space-Time-Motion

An example of teaching materials involving simultaneous consideration of space, time, and motion is the statement that, "It takes a plane, traveling X miles an hour, Y hours to get from B to C."

I:1:13. The World View of the Culture

I:1:13:1. *Isolate-Static*. A culture with an "isolate-static" world view sees itself as isolated from the rest of the world, fixed in respect to its spatial orientation on the earth's surface, and static in regard to change. This is typical of the *Gemeinschaft* type of society.

I:1:13:2. *Communicate-Changing*. A culture with a "communicate-changing" world view is in communication with the surrounding world, is expansive in regard to its orientation on the earth's surface, and dynamic in regard to change. This is a world outlook in which the members of the society see themselves in contact with the rest of the world and are oriented toward change. The attitude is characteristic of the *Gesellschaft*.

I:1:13:2:1. *Engulfing*. The culture with an "engulfing" world view is one that views itself as conquering and swallowing up other cultures. This would characterize the Nazi world view (Childs 1938: 107 et seq.) and the Inca world view.

I:1:13:3. *Hostile or Pacific*

I:1:13:3:3. *Selectively Hostile or Pacific*. Some groups divide the world into friend and foe, and attempt to instill in children hostility toward foes and acceptance toward friends. The Kaingáng, however (Henry 1941), have no friends outside the narrow group of the extended family, and view themselves as surrounded by enemies. Something similar seems to characterize the Sirionó (Holmberg 1950), but particularly with respect to the band.

I:1:13:5. *Temporal Position*

I:1:13:5:5. *Mythological Past.* Subject matter from the mythological past is a category delineated from the point of view of the ethnographer, since, as some peoples see it, there is no separation between the real and the mythological past. For example, there are many people nowadays to whom the biblical story of Jonah who, swallowed by a whale, lived inside it, may still be true. The distinction made by the ethnographer is one of convenience, and he can always explain the native attitude.

1:2a. Values

In the course of the research, no less than sixty-nine values were tabulated. This is partly because "value" was construed to mean any normative idea or sentiment, in Radcliffe-Brown's sense, that serves as an organizer of culturally standardized behavior. Thus honesty (I:2:49) has been listed as a value, but so have dishonesty, deception, and chicanery (I:2a:7) because they too are normative organizers, as among the Alor and Chagga (Du Bois 1944: 64, 65, 66; Raum 1940: 210, 211). Values are dealt with here without reference to what should be, but rather with reference to what is expressed in the ongoing life of the culture.

A focus on values in the study of educational processes has implications not only for understanding the organization of behavior, but also for understanding poly-phasic learning, since education, the fundamental organizing process, occurs always in a context of values, and teachers are usually teaching values by implication, regardless of the immediate subject matter. When, for example, a Pilagá mother tells her baby to give his food to a relative (Henry and Boggs 1952), the baby's behavior is being organized with respect to a particular group of people at the same time that he is learning it is good to give food away. In the example quoted above from *New Russia's Primer*, the values of challenge, mastery, bigness, man-over nature (F. Kluckhohn 1951), compulsion, struggle, danger, vigilance, and mechanization all appear in a text acquainting the children with the Five Year Plan and what must be done to effect it.

Values may be openly asserted, such as, "It is good to work hard"; be expressed indirectly, as in the *Primer* (Ilin 1931); or be conveyed in a situation, such as in the East European Jewish *shtetl* where children had to work hard at their studies all day long in the *kheder*, early elementary school (Zborowski and Herzog 1952: 89), with no appeal to "fun in learning." Of Ilin's book, one may say that it "breathes an ideology." Soviet education (Counts and Lodge 1947) is very sensitive to values, and, to judge from Counts and Lodge's book, faces squarely any problems connected with them. This is true also of *kibbutz* education in Israel (Spiro 1958: 250). Meanwhile, there is always the question of the relation between ideology and results, and this ought to be studied in all educational systems. In this connection, one difficulty is that a teacher's own unconscious behavior may contradict the values he is attempting to teach; another is that the educational system may attempt to emphasize contradictory values (see I:2b).

I:2a:23. The "Beautiful Person"

The "beautiful person" refers to an ideal best described in the literature for traditional China and the Jewish *shtetl*. The following from Zborowski and Herzog (1952: 81) expresses the idea. Speaking of the *talmid khokhem*, the "wise student and scholar," they say:

> He is not even expected to know the value of money, but it is taken for granted that the keenness of his mind, sharpened by lifelong study, will allow him to penetrate the most complicated business.
>
> A talmid khokhem, a wise scholar, is easily recognizable in the streets of the shtetl. He walks slowly, sedately, absorbed in his thoughts. His speech is calm, rich in quotations from the Bible or the Talmud, allusive and laconic— his words "are counted like pearls." He is greeted first by other members of the community, in deference to his high position. Not only the poor but also the wealthy greet him first, if they are less learned than he. . . .
>
> A learned man seldom laughs aloud. Excessive laughter, like any sort of

excess, is considered the mark of an amorets [boor]. . . . The talmid khokhem must indicate his dignity and sophistication by his behavior and his
appearance.

The shtetl ideal of male beauty again reflects the high value set on learning.
A man with *hadras ponim*, a distinguished, beautiful face, ideally has a long
beard—symbol of age and therefore of wisdom. His forehead is high, indicating well-developed mentality; his complexion is pale, revealing long hours
spent over books. Thick eyebrows showing penetration jut out over deep-set,
semiclosed eyes, indicating weariness from constant poring over texts—eyes
that shine and sparkle as soon as an intellectual problem is discussed. Very
important are the pale, delicate hands, evidence that the owner has devoted
his life to exercise of the mind rather than of the body.

The relevance of such a value to this study is that it anchors moral and behavioral
ideology to a fixed image, which serves as a guide to the organization of general cultural behavior. For students of social organization and disorganization—for the
understanding of problems of anomie—it is important to examine the difference in
functioning between societies that have such guides and those that do not. A problem of contemporary society is that it has no beautiful people—only beautiful
actresses.

I:6 Social Manipulation

The teaching of social manipulation looms large in all cultures but is given relatively little attention in anthropological monographs or in writings on education.
"Social Manipulation" includes all techniques for getting along with other people
and for using people as instruments for survival, social mobility, and so on. Training in "being nice to people," in smiling, in ingratiation, etc., fall under this I:6.
Outstanding among techniques of recognition seeking (I:6:1) in American schools
is, of course, the raised hand. "Manipulation of Self" (I:6:3) refers to training in
how to handle one's self: role taking, and self-restraint in social situations, fall in
this category.

I:10. Use of the Mind

I:10:1. How to Think

Nowadays, in America, there is much talk about teaching children to think. In five
years of observation in American schools, however, we have found very little behavior that tends in this direction, and, therefore, this category is not expanded in
the outline (in contrast, for example, to I:10:3). Thinking would seem to involve
an analytical process of some kind and also a process of synthesis. Almost none of
this takes place in elementary school (though we have found it occasionally), and
little more even in high school science courses.[1] Our research has not discovered
in primitive societies emphasis on teaching children to think.

I:10:2. Disjunction

The category "Disjunction" refers to situations in which the child becomes a nonparticipant, or in which the environment behaves in one way and the child *with-
draws* instead of behaving in the expected manner. The American child who keeps
his hand raised in the air regardless of what is taking place in the classroom is typical. In general, this category refers to all those situations in which the child with-
draws mentally from the environment. This is the "It-does-not-concern-me" effect, or the "I-dismiss-it-from-my-mind" effect.

Training in disjunction occurs at every level in American schools, and most of it
occurs without conscious effort by the adult. Rather, the adult, notably the classroom teacher, is constantly concerned to prevent disjunction. Nevertheless, lessons
in subjects in which children are not interested, for example, are lessons in disjunction, for the children become detached from the subject matter, and, in an effort

to escape from boredom may cast about—through daydreaming, drawing, or readying a forbidden book under the desk—for some way of escaping from the situation. Since the child discovers that one or another of these techniques is psychologically rewarding, he tends to revert to it whenever the uninteresting subject matter comes up, and, in this way, becomes educated in disjunction. The child who keeps his hand up in class even though he does not know what is going on—as evidenced by his confusion if the teacher calls on him—is one who disjoins from the subject matter but remains in touch with the social requirements of the situation. The capacity to dismiss things from one's mind—to "filter out" unwanted stimuli—is an important capacity in a complex culture like that of the United States where one is always in danger of being inundated by stimuli. The process of disjunction, in the sense intended here, is not described in the literature for nonindustrial civilizations, though it did occur in traditional China (Yang 1945: 145, 147; Williams 1849: 434) and in the East European Jewish *shtetl* schools (Zborowski and Herzog 1952: 88, 104).

Dismissing a thing from the mind is one aspect of the general process of filtering. At the beginning of section I, it was remarked that all cultures organize behavior with respect to their own culturally selected portion of the universe. This must mean that education attempts to exclude from perception (filter out) all aspects of the surroundings not included in the culturally delimited universe. We know, in a systematic way, practically nothing about how adults train children to exclude from perception everything that does not belong in the culturally standardized perceptual universe.

The narrowing of the perceptual field is accomplished in part through emphasizing only certain things during education. By this process, nothing that is not emphasized will be learned by the child. Meanwhile, since humans are inveterate polyphasic learners (Henry 1955a), the process is never completely effective, and the resultant educational failure must be one of the sources of sociocultural conflict and change. We may speculate that very stable cultures have perfected, or nearly perfected, the process of narrowing the child's perceptual field—of training the child to dismiss from his mind anything not selected for his perceptions by the culture.

In section II we will consider in more detail this process of narrowing the perceptual field.

I:10:3. Concentration

I:10:3:2. *Force.* The use of force to compel students to concentrate is described by Zborowski and Herzog (1952: 89-104) for the East European Jewish *shtetl* culture where children in the *kheder*, the earliest years of school, were struck by the teacher if their attention wandered.

I:10:3:5. *Focused Retention.* "Focused Retention" refers to efforts to achieve concentration on the part of the child by obliging him to focus on textual materials. Thus, in reading in elementary schools, the children, through being required to answer questions about stories, learn to fix their minds on the details of the text.

I:16. Scientific Abstractions;
I:17. Science (General)

The difference between "Scientific Abstractions" and "Science (General)" may be exemplified as follows. In the former, instruction is given in the nature of electricity, while in the latter, the child is taught how to make a battery. In the former, a student in biology is taught that the cell is the basic building block of all organisms, while in the latter, he is told the structure of the cell.

I:18. Routine Procedures

"Routine Procedures" has to do with actions such as distributing books, collecting papers on which the children have done their lessons, and so on.

I:19. Childish Handiwork

Making valentines, matlike holders for pots, etc.—all those time-killing activities that help fill the day in many American elementary schools—fall into the category of "Childish Handiwork." On the other hand, one ought not to include here the making of seed necklaces, flower chains, etc., that are *used* by the children in their games (Gorer 1938: 308-9; Chaudhuri 1951: 21). Rather, where such activity is taught by adults, one ought to delineate a separate, appropriate category, such as "how to make toys or game-relevant objects."

I:25. The Object System

In all societies material culture is part of a complex of interpersonal relations, values, beliefs, and patterns of spatial arrangements. For example, in American culture a stove is made, owned, sold, and bought as private property. As part of the American system of values, however, it not only expresses the value of private ownership, but, by its quality and form, expresses a standard of living, which is also held as a value. Furthermore, children and adult males are generally aloof from stoves, and although this is changing, it is on the whole still true that in American homes most of the time it is women who operate the stove. Again, stoves are sold not only in terms of their beauty and cost, but also in terms of their capacity to heat rapidly, which thereby gives expression to the value of speed. Finally, in regard to patterns of spatial arrangement, stoves are almost always kept in the kitchen, sometimes in the living room—if the living room is in a modern, compact apartment, where the kitchen may be separated from the living room merely by a difference in furnishings, including the stove—and never in a bedroom. The complex of associations that attaches to objects of material culture is here called the "Object System," and it is one of the principal foci of education in all societies. Mead says of Manus children (1939: 32-33):

> . . . In Manus where property is sacred and one wails for lost property as for the dead, respect for property is taught children from their earliest years. Before they can walk they are rebuked and chastised for touching anything which does not belong to them. . . . The slightest breakage is punished without mercy. Once a canoe from another village anchored near one of the small islands. Three little eight-year-old girls climbed on the deserted canoe and knocked a pot into the sea, where it struck a stone and broke. All night the village rang with drum calls and angry speeches, accusing, deprecating, apologizing for the damage done and denouncing careless children. The fathers made speeches of angry shame and described how roundly they had beaten the young criminals. The children's companions, far from admiring a daring crime, drew away from them in haughty disapproval and mocked them in chorus.

It can be seen from these examples that the object system is the broader system within which an economic system (I:3:3) may fit: "Economic System" refers to patterns of production, distribution, and consumption of objects, while "Object System" refers to objects in all their aspects. When a child in an American elementary school is taught to collect books and *put them in the closet*, the knowledge that books belong in a closet is knowledge about the object system, while the relevance of that knowledge to the economic system is rather remote.

I:27. Cultural Fictions

A "cultural fiction" is an idea known by at least one group in the culture to be untrue. There comes a time in the life of a person in such a culture when he learns that the idea is a fiction. For example, the Chagga fiction that men do not defecate is revealed as untrue to Chagga boys at initiation (Raum 1940: 248); and the Hopi fiction that the dancing figures in the plaza are gods is revealed as a fiction also at initiation (Eggan 1956). Thus learning a cultural fiction refers to the revelation of the fictional nature of an idea.

It is not always clear what the function of the revelation itself is. In Hopi (Eggan 1956), the revelation seems to precipitate a reorganization of the personality in the effort to manage the overwhelmingly shocking realization of the deception that has been worked on one, and to accelerate (1) a turning away from childish ways, (2) a turning toward adulthood, and (3) a turning inward of the personality toward self-examination and criticism. While (1) and (2) seem to be present in Chagga also, there is no evidence of (3). Rather, there appears the development of an extreme insecurity of men with respect to women, and a concomitant hostility. On the other hand, it may be, also, that the men's awareness that psychologically they are frauds may be an added incentive to them to attempt to validate themselves as genuine warriors and workers.

Hopi and Chagga practice represent formalizations of the widespread use of fictions for the achievement of various cultural goals. Actually, fictions seem to have dysfunctional effects in the long run: even the Hopi case, so sympathetically described by Eggan, seems to have had long-run dysfunctional effects in residual hostility and oppressive guilt.

II. How is the Information Communicated (Teaching Methods)?

Pettitt (1946: 40 et seq.) has emphasized the importance of knowing exactly what techniques adults use to teach children. This section is devoted to the elucidation of the problem of specificity in reporting such data. The following quotations illustrate certain excellences and certain shortcomings:

> Eskimo mothers begin exercising the arms of young infants in the motions of paddling. . . . (Pettitt 1946: 43)

> Freuchen illustrates the eagerness of Eskimo parents to encourage hunting pursuits by young children. A three-year-old boy, Megusak, happened to sight a distant polar bear before anyone else saw it. He was praised mightily, and when the bear was killed a spear was put into his hands so that he could give it a poke, whereupon they praised him more. (Pettitt 1946: 43)

> When [a Manus boy] is about a year old, he has learned to grasp his mother firmly about the throat, so that he can ride in safety, poised on the back of her neck. She has carried him up and down the long house, dodged under low-hanging shelves, and climbed up and down the rickety ladders which lead from house floor down to the landing verandah. The decisive angry gesture with which he was reseated on his mother's neck whenever his grip tended to slacken has taught him to be alert and sure-handed. (Mead 1939: 23)

The description of the Eskimo mother exercising her infant in the motions of paddling could hardly be more specific, except to state more precisely how the baby's hands were held and, perhaps, whether the mother sang a song, and so on. The second example is strikingly specific. What is lacking is some statement to the effect that the child was *told* to poke the bear. The example from Manus would be better if we were told how the child learned to grasp its mother about the throat. On the other hand, the observation that the mother reseats the baby on her neck with a "decisive angry gesture" is the kind of specificity needed to clarify the learning process.

In contrast, the following is vague:

> By the time a boy is 3 years of age he is already pulling on some kind of bow, and with his companions he spends many hours shooting his weapons at any non-human target that strikes his fancy . . . and when his marksmanship is perfected he is encouraged to stalk woodpeckers and other birds that light on branches near the house.
> . . . the boy gradually learns when, where and how to track and stalk game. His father allows him to take easy shots, so as to reinforce his interest in hunting. . . . During all this time, of course, he is also learning to make bows and arrows. . . . (Holmberg 1950: 378)

The reason the description is vague is because we are not told how the boy is taught to pull "on some kind of bow," how his marksmanship comes to improve, how the boy is "encouraged to stalk woodpeckers," or how he learns to track game or make bows and arrows.

The purpose of section II is to raise in all its complexity the question of the specificity of teaching methods.

II:1. By Imitation

In his chapter on "Imitation versus Stimulated Learning," Pettitt attacks the uncritical use of the term "imitation," pointing out that most of what has been called imitation is really "directed practice" (Pettitt 1946: 44) under the stimulation and guidance of adults. He reserves the term "imitation" for learning experiences in which the child *spontaneously* copies a human model. Pettitt also provides a host of examples of child learning that are accounted for under separate headings in the outline accompanying this paper. Molecular analysis of the educational process makes the category "imitation" a residual one in which may be placed all examples of copying that do not fall into *other* categories in this section, most specifically:

II: 2. By setting an example
12. By doing
15. By games or other play
30. By telling
31. By watching
32. By listening
37. By following a model
1. Human
2. Nonhuman

II:3. By Instruction in Schools, Ceremonials, or Other Formal Institutions

The ceremonial initiation is a common device for educating children in primitive cultures. The Murngin (Warner 1937) and Chagga (Raum 1940) are good examples. Schools, that is, relatively permanent buildings especially dedicated to education, are not familiar outside of the literate civilizations. In undeveloped forms of education in the literate cultures, teachers' homes have been used (Zborowski and Herzog 1952: 89; Bayne-Powell 1939: 57, 61). Poor Arabs in Egypt have built simple schools (*maktab*) for instruction in the Koran (Ammar 1954: 206). The use of buildings for systematic instruction, whether a teacher's home or a separate school building, seems to be associated with literacy, occupational specialization, and target-seeking learning; instruction through ceremonials appears to occur in societies where more diffuse learning patterns are institutionalized (Henry 1955a), together with highly structured personal communities (Henry 1958). Ceremonial education seems to bring together two things: the responsibility of the broader kin group and the communication of knowledge.

In *The West African "Bush" School*, Watkins (1943) describes aboriginal schools for boys and girls, conducted by secret societies and lasting from about two to eight years. The schools are isolated from the ongoing life of the tribe, and the buildings are destroyed when the session is over. There are separate schools for boys and girls. "No one except members of the society is permitted entrance to the [school] area." Among the Vai,

> The principal official of the school is the *dá zò*. . . . "the leader who stands at the mouth or head," who is endowed with wisdom and mystic power in a superlative degree. He has a majestic status in the society [see III], is respected by the chief and elders of the tribe, and is honored with intense devotion by the youth of the land. (pp. 668-69)

Among the Kpelle,

> The grandmaster, *namu*, is, of course, a human being and is known as such by the members. At the same time he has attributes which raise him above the merely human. (p. 669)

In these schools,

> The boys are divided into groups according to their ages and aptitudes and receive instruction in all the arts, crafts, and lore of native life. . . . The first instruction involves a series of tests in order to determine individual differences, interests, and ambitions. . . .
>
> All this training is tested out in the laboratory of "bush" school life. For example, instruction in warfare is accompanied by actual mock battles and skirmishes. . . .
>
> Life in the secret society is a complete *rite de passage* from the helplessness and irresponsibilities of childhood to citizenship in a world of adults. Thus a youth acquires a new name in the *beli*, according to his rank in the group and his achievements. . . . Entrance to the society is a symbolic death for the young, who must be reborn before returning to the family and kin. Those who die from the strenuous life are considered simply not to have been reborn, and their mothers are expected not to weep or grieve for them. (pp. 670-71)

Here, then, is an entire area of the preliterate world where there are schools similar in many ways to those of the literate world. It is hard to believe that these schools are not a combination of native initiation rituals and the white man's idea of a school.

II:4. By Use of Punishments;
II:5. By Use of Rewards

In the *Ethica Nicomachea* (1172a: 20), Aristotle says of pleasure that "it is thought to be most intimately connected with our human nature, which is the reason why in educating the young we steer them by the rudders of pleasure and pain." Since these are used consciously in education by all societies, it would seem that their use must reflect that "psychic unity" of mankind of which anthropologists speak. II:4 ("By Use of Punishments") does not refer merely to the use of pain as an accompaniment to learning (see II:16b) but to the use of punishment as a means of redirecting deviant behavior. Similarly, II:5 ("By Use of Rewards") refers to recognition of accomplishment, as when, for example, adults in American society express to the child pleasure at his mastery of language, walking, or going to the toilet instead of wetting. When the Chagga (Raum 1940: 135) tie little bells to a baby's ankles to "give him pleasure in stamping his feet so that he may become steady on his legs," this is not reward in the sense implied here. But if the mother hails the child's efforts to walk with articulate joy, that is reward in the sense implied here.

One of the most interesting problems in education is the shift that takes place from reward for conformity to mere punishment for nonconformity as the child grows older; and the gradual dropping out of rewards as the child's competence comes to be taken for granted. One might hypothesize, for example, that the American middle-class child who, let us say, is praised every time he passes a "dry night," might feel disappointed when his dryness is taken for granted. On the other hand, he might feel insulted, once dryness has been achieved, if he is still praised for something that any child of his age ought to be able to do. The problem may be summed up as follows: when a child has been rewarded for his childish accomplishments, how does he feel when these sources of recognition come to an end, especially when he is then punished for his lapses?

II:6. Problem Solving

"Problem Solving" refers not to answering a question in arithmetic or filling in a missing word in a sentence, but to analytico-synthetic processes that bear on the logic of a situation. It is closely related to the idea of decision making. For example, there is a story in an American fourth-year reader (Gray et al. 1956) in which a man and a boy are in a rowboat on the water when a fog comes up. The boy knows the coast, but the man does not. The man asks the boy to let him row, and the boy, just "to be polite," lets him, even though there is grave danger from rocks. Here a *problem* would be: "Did Andy do the right thing in letting the man row?"

II:7. Guided Recall

"Guided Recall" refers to the nearly universal procedure in American elementary and even high schools whereby the pupil is guided by the teacher in recalling to mind the specific content of a lesson. With reference to the example in II:6 above, guided recall would involve asking questions such as the following: "Where were they?" ("Out in a boat.") "What happened?" ("A fog came up.") "Why was it dangerous?" ("Because of the rocks.") In guided recall, problem-solving opportunities in the lesson are not exploited.

II:8. Giving the Child Tasks to Perform Beyond His Immediate Capacity

II:8:1. Jamming the Machine

Fortes says of education in Taleland that "a child is never forced beyond its capacity" (1938: 13). In American schoolrooms, on the other hand, in spite of the ideology of "readiness,"[2] one observes a constant urging of children, sometimes to the limits of their capacity, toward a culturally determined standard of mastery. The result of this is that the learning "machine" sometimes becomes "jammed," and a child may, at that moment, be completely unable to perform. The following is an example from a fifth-grade class (Henry 1955: 202):

> The child at the board stares at $2/3$ minus $2/3$. There is a faint titter, snicker,[3] giggle or something. . . . as the child stares, nonplussed by the problem. The teacher goes up to her and demonstrates with a measuring cup: "If we have $2/3$ of a cup here, and we pour it out, what is left?" The child remains baffled, and the teacher says it again, seeming to try to force her presentation of

the problem on the child in such a way as to cut out the distracting influence of the class, which is eager to be helpful. Child finally says, "Nothing," and the teacher says, "*That's right.*"

In these contemporary schoolrooms, the child who says "I can't" is urged until he can. As I read Fortes, I would interpret him to mean that, given a situation like the above, the Tale would let the child be, and try again a month or a year later. On the other hand, the Chagga (Raum 1940) would appear to be much more determined than the Tale in their resolve to bring the child up as quickly as possible to a level of performance. The "blackboard paralysis" we have seen above is a biosocial phenomenon that can occur only when there is a critical moment in the educational process at which massive pressures are brought to bear on a child to get him to perform an incompletely mastered task within a narrowly limited time. These are the conditions for what is here called "jamming the machine."

II:10. By Kinesthetic Association

By "Kinesthetic Association" is meant the accompaniment of learning by gross muscular movement. Thus a Murngin boy (Warner 1937) who executes a large number of ceremonial movements while he is learning the tribal traditions during initiation may tend to remember the traditions well because they have become associated to a complex series of physical maneuvers. In the same way, a child in an American elementary school who paints a picture of some African scene when he is learning the geography of Africa may tend to remember his lesson well because the gross physical movements involved in painting become associated with the lesson. Finally, the child who goes through the *movements* of a play he enacts in connection with a lesson on Africa may tend to remember Africa not only because of the actual contents of the play but also because he has "gone through" Africa with his body!

II:12 By Doing

"By Doing" refers only to education in which the child learns a life role by performing that role—for example, when a child learns to farm by cultivating the soil, or to fish by fishing. This contrasts with learning something *about* farming by reading on the life of a farmer. It does not include learning arithmetic by doing arithmetic, or learning reading by reading, etc.

II:13. By Symbolic Association

The display of totemic emblems (Warner 1937: 345) in an Australian initiation is education in basic tribal ideas concerning religion and social structure through symbolic association. The emblem is a symbol with which the boy associates the religious and sociostructural ideas. When a teacher in an American school draws a picture of a shamrock on the blackboard while she is talking about Saint Patrick's Day, this also is education through symbolic association. Another example is education of the Chinese boy in his ancestral traditions through showing him the clan books (Chiang 1952: 9).

II:14. By Dramatization

Any act in which children dramatize a cultural fact is education through "dramatization," whether it be ritual enactment in a ceremonial, or secular acting out of a story, as fourth-grade American children might act out the story of "The Golden Pears" (Gray et al. 1956).

II:16b. By Trials

The use of physical trials or endurance tests as part of the educational process has had a wide vogue. Pettitt (1946) has documented this usage for the North

American Indians. Raum (1940: 205–8) says that at about twelve years of age Chagga boys are taught "endurance and diligence" with the hoe, and that,

> when the boy gets tired, he is threatened or beaten. The father scorns to take refreshment to him; this makes the boy's trial the more excruciating. Girls who hoe with their mothers are occasionally given something to nibble.
> [In learning how to plant bananas, the boy] sometimes has to carry a heavy plant for several miles, and begins to weep or ask permission to set his load down. His father tells him to bear up.

These excerpts from Raum illustrate not only II:16b but also the use of physical force (II:23), and the use of threats (II:16a), in education.

The following from India illustrates another, apparently idiosyncratic, trial (Chaudhuri 1951: 43):

> contracted a life-long dislike for a most estimable relative of mine by being told that he was such a conscientious student that he never used the mosquito net, lest left in peace by the mosquitoes he might over-indulge himself in sleep, and also that before examinations he tied his legs with a rope to the beam so that, not being able to lie flat and in comfort on his bed, he might be cogitating his books in a state of half wakefulness.

II:17. By Irrelevant Association;
II:18. By Relevant Association

There is an American game called "spelling baseball" for which the children in a classroom are divided into two teams. The teacher gives each child in turn a word to spell, and, if it is spelled correctly, the child is credited with "a hit" and goes to "first base." His next teammate is given a word, and, if the teammate is correct, he goes to first base and the first child moves to second base—and so on, until the team gets a "run." Each misspelled word is an "out." In this game, the competition runs high, and the children are nervously alert. Yet it is education through irrelevant association, because there is no connection between spelling and baseball: a perfectly illiterate man might make an excellent ballplayer. On the other hand, a game of "cafeteria," in which the children play at being in a cafeteria, and having to spend money and figure the bill while making payment with toy money to a child appointed as cashier, is education through relevant association, because it is necessary to know how to count in order to buy in a real cafeteria, or in order to manage one. The American educational process does not reveal many examples of education by irrelevant association, and our research has not uncovered any at all from other cultures.

II:19. Through Art

Education *through* art is not education *in* art.[4] Education through art is the issue here: it has to do with the use of artistic endeavor to facilitate the learning process. When children are being taught about Africa, and have an art period in which they draw or paint pictures of Africa, this is education through art; when they are having a lesson on "Ireland and her neighbors," and sing songs from those countries, this too is education through art, for songs are an art form. Obviously, education through art can be considered from another point of view, i.e., the educating of children through the use of artistic creations by others, such as plays or paintings. A good example is the play of Bali (Belo 1949), which is at once artistic and educational. The Balinese plays are also entertaining. The American analogue, but on a much, much lower level almost wholly lacking in artistry, would be the preprocessed television cartoons that are used in some educational systems for teaching purposes. In this latter case, however, we are really dealing rather with II:9, education through the use of mechanical devices, rather than with education through art.

II:24. By Positive or Negative Assertion

Asking leading questions such as, "We like rhyming words, don't we?" or making statements such as, "The illustrations are very clever," which the child is not expected to challenge, is what is implied by "positive or negative assertion." It would appear that what the teacher is aiming at by such verbalizations is student acquiescence-through-affirmation—a kind of acceptance-through-head-nodding. The *intent* of such verbalizations can be grasped if one tries to imagine any child saying, "No, teacher, I hate rhyming words," or, "But really, teacher, I think the illustrations are terrible."

II:26. By Specifically Relating Information to the Child's Own Body, Bodily Function, or Experience

Teachers in American elementary schools make broad use of the method of specifically relating information to the child's own body, bodily function, or experience. A reading lesson about pets will call forth from the teacher the question, "Do any of you have pets?" A lesson on the functions of the body will lead the teacher to ask, "What happens when you run?" ("We get out of breath.") Sprio (1958: 258) says of education in the *kibbutz:*

> The teacher generally attempts to make the subject meaningful in terms of the child's own experiences and his immediate (physical or temporal) environment. In a fourth-grade art lesson, for example, the objects cast in plaster-of-Paris were animals and flowers with which the children were immediately familiar; in seeking for a subject for a drawing class shortly before the advent of Passover, the teacher suggested that the children draw a Passover scene. . . .
>
> But the teacher attempts to relate the materials not only to the child's immediate experiences, but to his deepest interests as well. In a second-grade lesson in arithmetic, for example, the exercises in addition and subtraction were concerned with the winning and losing of marbles—an activity in which almost all the children were temporarily absorbed.

This subject is discussed further in section VII.

II:27a. Through Ego-Inflation

The method of "ego-inflation" aims specifically at the child's conception of himself. A procedure, such as praise, for example, that enhances a child's opinion of himself or makes him feel appreciated, falls in this category. II:27a *can* differ from II:5 in that the latter can be mere recognition of a lesson well learned, as in the case of an American child who is permitted to use the family car when he has learned how to drive. II:27a, on the other hand, is aimed *specifically* at improving a child's opinion of himself. II:27a and II:5 may coincide in the same act, as in praise, for example.

II:27b. Through Ego-Deflation

A procedure, such as humiliation, for example, that diminishes the child's opinion of himself, falls in this category "Ego-Deflation."

II:30. By Watching

Probably all education involves some watching, but this category II:30 attempts to capture that learning situation which is construed largely as one in which the learner learns primarily by watching. Thus Chiang says (1952: 58):

> I do not remember that I ever had any proper lessons in painting from my father. He told me to watch him as closely as possible. . . . I remember that after watching my father painting a few times I thought I knew just how to

paint, but when I actually began I found I was mistaken! . . . I asked my
father to help, but he only smiled and told me to watch him again.

Fortes has the following to say about the Tale (1938: 13):

> Rapid learning or the acquisition of a new skill is explained by *u mar nini
> pam*, "he has eyes remarkably," that is, he is very sharp. A friend of mine
> who was a cap-maker told me how he learnt his craft, as a youth, from a
> Dagban by carefully watching him at work. When he was young, he ex-
> plained, he had "very good eyes." This conception of cleverness is intelligible
> in a society where learning by looking and copying is the commonest manner
> of achieving dexterity both in crafts and in the everyday manual activities.

It is hard to find any conscious human learning that does not include all three
processes of listening, watching, and doing. Yet, it seems that cultures may differ
in the degree to which one or the other is stressed, and in the degree to which one
or the other is stressed in learning different *things*. Contemporary cultures, of
course, have substituted reading for much of listening, and even of watching, since
written directions accompanied by diagrams can replace watching. On the other
hand, the American stress on "learning by doing" suggests an "action" approach to
education. It seems possible that, while learning by doing may lead to an early
mastery of, let us say, agricultural techniques, it may lead to a premature sense of
mastery in painting, with consequent poor production. Belo and McPhee (Mead
and Wolfenstein 1954) have given us exciting materials on children's painting and
music in Bali, but no description of the actual learning process. One of the puzzling
problems in education is the exciting quality of children's painting and its disappearance in later life. What happens to all the budding artists? Why do they
abandon their art altogether, or discard its most original dimensions—as in Bali,
for example? One factor is suggested here: that children who learn by doing develop a premature sense of mastery, and that later comparison of their own work
with that of a mature adult artist leads to destructive self-criticism. In offering this
hypothesis I am not unaware of the importance of institutional supports for art.
What place does a creative artist have in industrial culture, anyway? And what
scope is there for originality in Bali? The answer in both cases is, *little*.

II:31. By Listening

A great deal of learning involves listening, but this category II:31 applies only to
learning situations that are *defined* as listening ones. Thus Fortes quotes a Tale
man as follows (1938: 12):

> "If he listens will he not know, will he not acquire wisdom?" When children
> are very small. . . . they know nothing about religious things. "They learn
> little by little. When we go to the shrine they accompany us and listen to
> what we say. Will they not [thus] get to know it? . . . Whatever I do [my
> son] also sits and listens. Will he not get to know it thus?"

II:32. Question and Answer

The "question and answer" method is so common in American culture that it is
not easy for Americans to imagine another in which the child is expected, not to
ask questions, but to learn by passively watching, listening, or copying. Yet, we
have seen that the Chinese stress watching (see also II:37) and that the Tale stress
watching and listening. Among the Pilagá, the educational process includes a further interesting characteristic: Pilagá children learn a great deal simply by making
incorrect statements that adults correct. For example, a child will point to an
insect and give its name, and, if the name is incorrect, the adult will correct it.

II:34. By Doing Something on His Own

A child is said to be "doing something on his own" when, for example, after he has asked, "What makes clouds?" he follows an instruction to find the answer himself by going to an encyclopedia and other books on the subject. This category also covers the case of the Lepcha child who is given his own animals and plot of land to take care of (Gorer 1938: 108, 307).

II:36. By Accusing

"Young ears don't listen. Can't you look after your cattle properly, you good-for-nothings, you things-with-sunken-eyes . . ." is one example, from Tale, of educating through accusation (Fortes 1938: 14). It is also II:27b, education through ego-deflation.

II:37. By Following a Model

When a teacher plays a song, or the first note of it, on a musical instrument, and children try to follow it, singing, this is following a nonhuman model (II:37:2). But when the teacher beats time with her arm for the children, this is following a human model (II:37:1). Again, when the teacher writes on a blackboard and the children try to copy her writing, this is following a human model. Any instance of a child's attempt to follow this kind of direction is considered to belong in II:37. In Pettitt's language, it is "directed practice."

II:38. By Comparison

The category "By Comparison" has to do with those cases in which a child is educated through asking him to compare two or more objects, such as two lines of unequal length, or three colors like yellow, orange, and chartreuse.

II:39. By Filling in a Missing Part

Teaching "by filling in a missing part" is carried out by, for example, showing a child a book on language skills containing sentences with missing words, and requiring him to fill in the missing words.

II:43. Physical Manipulation

II:43:1. Bodily Manipulation

Mead and Bateson (1942) afforded an example of "Bodily Manipulation" in describing how children learn to dance in Bali: the child's body is against that of the instructor, and the two move in unison, the child learning how to dance partly through making his own movements coalesce with the instructor's.

Gorer (1938: 305) says the following of the Lepcha:

> Children are taught work techniques by being instructed to copy their elders, by verbal admonition, or by having their arms held while they are put through the appropriate gestures.

II:43:2. Bodily Mutilation and Other Physical Stresses

Bodily mutilation as an educational technique is common enough in primitive societies, and includes the piercing of lips and ears, removal of teeth, scarification, circumcision, subincision, and clitterodectomy. It would appear that man early made the discovery that, within limits, learning would be most strongly reinforced in the presence of anxiety, hence the inclusion of bodily mutilation in many tribal rituals in which fundamental tribal lore is taught to young men or women. The relation between mutilation and learning has many complexities, as can be seen, e.g., from the following about the Chagga (Raum 1940: 311):

That the parental generation regards circumcision, not only as a test, but as an opportunity for cumulative punishment appears from the fact that any notorious mischief-monger is submitted to a severe trial. His circumcision is attended by those of his elders who bear a grudge against him. When the operator has made the preliminary incision, he is told to stop. Someone steps on the victim's big toe to find out whether he squirms and to beat him if he does. He is told to sing a song without hesitating or trembling. After some other boys have been circumcised, the operator is allowed to continue on the culprit, but before he is finished he is told: "Leave him for another while!" Only after a lengthy interval is the operation completed. In some cases a boy is under the knife for an hour or longer. The report of this torture is spread among the uncircumcised and stupefies them with terror. In consequence they willingly obey and honor their elders. . . .

Here the Chagga have contrived that circumcision shall be an *anticipated* threat, so that the ensuing anxiety may provide a motivation for learning. Circumcision, a physical stress, is accompanied by emotional stress.

The Chagga case opens up the general problem of the introduction of stress into the educational process. Pettitt (1946: 89) has the following to say about the functions of stress in the education of some North American Indians:

The point to be made is that in the vision quest [a major educational experience] . . . . the objective was. . . . to produce an independent, self-confident, and self-reliant personality, buoyed up by an inner conviction of his ability to meet any and all situations. . . . The painful ordeals . . . strengthened his character, and supplied him with experience in withstanding physical suffering, which was . . . important in giving him self-assurance. . . .

Pettitt, abstracting from Teit's numerous publications on the Thompson River Indians of British Columbia, describes the Thompson River Indian boy's vision quest as follows (1946: 87–88):

. . . When a boy's dreams became propitious . . . his vision quest began in earnest. As a ceremonial beginning, he was required to run, with bow and arrows in his hands, until bathed in perspiration and on the point of exhaustion, when he was made to plunge in cold water. This was repeated four times a day for four days . . . Although his first four days were consumed in running and bathing, the first four nights were given to dancing, singing, and praying, with little or no sleep, around a fire on some near-by mountain peak. . . .

Having acted out the prologue, the boy then began work in earnest. He went on lonely pilgrimages into the mountains, staying away from home and eating nothing for from four to eight days on end. It was a common practise to schedule these pilgrimages in winter, so that the boy would not be tempted by berries and roots. During these vigils the boy usually took nothing with him but a fire drill and a sleeping mat. He intensified the effect of his fasting by taking herbal concoctions with a purgative action, and by poking long twigs down his throat until he vomited. . . . The boy continued this exhausting regime until he had a dream of some animal or bird which would be his protector through life. . . .

Pettitt summarizes also (1946: 101) some of Stern's material on the Lumi Indians of the Pacific Northwest of North America:

The first objective of training is to give the boy confidence and make him fearless. He is sent out on dark stormy nights to perform trumped-up errands, such as fetching a bow or some other article from a friend or relative living at some distance . . . The status of childhood is made uncomfortable by depriving him of the best foods, discriminating against him, making him bathe in cold water, morning and night. At the slightest breach of this discipline, which he knows will end when he proves his manhood, his father becomes enraged, and may throw burning bark in his face. As he grows older the rigor of his regime increases. He is instructed to rub his body with cedar bark to toughen his muscles. His father tests his stamina from time to time by cutting gashes in his body, starting with the more calloused parts and working up to the more tender. He is stimulated to greater efforts by the warning that he will turn into a girl unless he watches out. In fact, these warnings are often taken so seriously that a boy rubs his breasts with sand until they bleed, or smashes the nipples between rocks to stop a fancied over-development.

Finally, he is ready to make his quest. He goes to some secluded spot and seeks by his endurance to out-strip all other boys of whom he has heard, thereby winning the favor of the supernaturals. . . . If rocks assume strange shapes in the darkness, he must stand his ground, in fact run toward them and grapple with them . . . The boy may stay away from his village for a year or even four years. . . . through living alone he builds up a sense of self-sufficiency.

Thus, through isolation (see II:55) and the self-imposition of various austerities, the boy made himself physically and emotionally capable of withstanding pain, hunger, and thirst in later life. What happened, in addition, was an orientation of the personality away from childish things, a hardening of determination, and, most importantly, a consolidation of the culturally requisite conceptions of the world—in Radcliffe-Brown's terminology, a crystallization of the "collective sentiments."

Among the Tiwi of North Australia, physical and emotional stresses are combined in the educational process in a different way. There, initiation is taken over by persons who are strangers to the boy. This in itself is frightening to him, but, in addition, the way in which the strangers appear on the scene is terrifying. Hart describes this vividly (1955: 134–35):

Among the Tiwi of North Australia, one can see the traumatic nature of the initiation period in very clear form, and part of the trauma lies in the sudden switch of personnel with whom the youth has to associate. A boy reaches thirteen or fourteen or so, and the physiological signs of puberty begin to appear. Nothing happens, possibly for many months. Then suddenly, one day toward evening when the people are gathering around their campfires for the main meal of the day after coming in from their day's hunting and food-gathering, a group of three or four heavily armed and taciturn strangers appear in camp. In full war regalia they walk in silence to the camp of the boy and say curtly to the household: "We have come for So-and-So." Immediately pandemonium breaks loose. The mother and the rest of the older women begin to howl and wail. The father rushes for his spears. The boy himself, panic-stricken, tries to hide, the younger children begin to cry, and the household dogs begin to bark. . . .

The father's rush for his spears . . . is make-believe. . . . With the father immobilized the child clings to his mother, but the inexorable strangers soon tear him (literally) from his mother's arms . . . and, still as grimly as they came, bear him off into the night. No society could symbolize more dramatically that initiation necessitates the forcible taking away of the boy from the bosom of his family, his village, his neighbors, his intimates, his friends.

While Hart needlessly generalizes the use of force, and overestimates the extent to which in other parts of the primitive world education is shifted at puberty from intimates to strangers, the fright of the boys and the mock battle staged by their fathers are described by Warner (1958: 261), with variations, also for the Murngin, another Australian tribe. The point is that the initiation begins with massive fright stimuli which are repeated at strategic moments during the ceremony (see, for example, Warner 1958: 282). Presumably their function is to force a reorientation of the boys' personalities.

It has been pointed out that education always involves a narrowing of the perceptual field to the universe selected by the culture. It has also been suggested that narrowing occurs partly through emphasizing only that cultural universe. But the important question then is: How is that cultural universe emphasized? Some answers to this question have been suggested in section II. For example, punishment for straying from cultural norms, and reward for consistently practicing them, are obvious devices for narrowing the perceptual field to the desired universe.

It would appear from the primitive North American, Australian, and Chagga data, that the massive application of pain to, and provocation of anxiety and other stresses in, primitive boys during periods of great solemnity, would serve, in general, to narrow the perceptual sphere. The Chagga technique of making circumcision an implied threat (II:16a) is a good example of a special use of anxiety for this purpose: any indulgence before initiation in behaviors not sanctioned by the elders might result in torture at initiation.

In American public schools there are no physical stresses comparable to those experienced by the Chagga, by the North American Indians, or by the Australians. Emotional stresses are, nevertheless, constantly operative in American classrooms. Outstanding, of course, is the ever-present fear of failure, which tends to make the student accept almost any idea. There are, in addition, more specific techniques for fixing cultural configurations in the student's mind, like teaching by holding up adult ideals (II:21), by having the children act in undifferentiated unison (II:22), and by using positive or negative assertion ((I:24). For example, if the child has held up before him certain adult ideals as he acts in undifferentiated unison with a group of his peers, the emotional impact will reinforce commitment to the culture. The method of positive or negative assertion, II:24, is a kind of implied threat, which seems to say, "If you do not like [whatever the teacher wants you to like], you probably have something wrong with you; so you had better learn to like it." With respect to using ego-inflation (II:27a) or ego-deflation (II:27b), it seems likely that since a cultural experience that enhances the self-image will be rewarding, such an experience will serve to anchor the components of that experience in the child's personality; while, on the other hand, ridicule or contempt accompanying failure may make the child struggle hard to succeed. Of course, the experience may have the opposite effect, thereby laying the basis for culture conflict and change. This is true also of II:4, using punishment.

Before closing this section, it is necessary to indicate that there seem to be some physical stresses accompanying education, especially in literate cultures, which tend to act in an inhibitory way on some aspects of learning, perhaps while reinforcing others. For example, long hours spent sitting in one spot might render students antagonistic to subject matter but teach them self-control. This suggests that the imposition of such physical restrictions during education would be a screening device through which only the culturally most desirable persons could pass, i.e., those who could combine attention to subject matter with self-control. Thus all the rules of order in school, to the degree that they govern physical behavior, are, along with the curriculum, mechanisms for separating the children into good learners and poor ones.

As one glances over this list of educational methods that is section II, one cannot but be struck by their mere number. The reason for the number is that since humans have no innate techniques of adaptation to the environment, including culture, they have to learn them. The problem for *Homo sapiens* was twofold, for not only was the *acquisition* of knowledge through learning essential to his adaptation, but he had also to devise *methods* of teaching what he knew to his offspring. Thus a further problem arose out of his necessity for devising different methods for teaching different bodies of knowledge. The result was a lengthening list of teaching methods as knowledge increased.

The length of the list raises a general question as to the relation between number of methods and level of cultural complexity. Some answer to this question has been attempted (Henry 1955a: 199–202), and the suggestion made that, as the number of cultural items to be learned increases, the number of teaching methods increases also, but that the time expended to educate about each item probably fluctuates too (see section XII, below). Actually, what we seem to have in contemporary American culture, as compared with primitive societies, is a greater number of teaching methods, less time allotted to each subject taught, but an enormous amount of time spent in formal instruction. Meanwhile, the American child is repeatedly placed in the position of having his "machine jammed" (II:8:1). Jamming the machine is so characteristic of contemporary culture because, given the enormous amount of learning expected of a child, there has not been sufficient improvement in teaching methods, even though the catalogue of them seems extensive. Modern man's inventiveness of cultural content appears to have outstripped his ingenuity in devising methods to communicate that content. Students whose failure compels them to drop out of school or curtail their schooling are thus, in part, casualties of cultural lag—of the failure of teaching methods to keep pace with content.

III. Who Educates?

III:1. Males or Females?
The revolutionary change in the United States from male to female teachers occurred in the 1860s during and after the Civil War. Even before this, American women had been breaking the socioeconomic taboos that blocked their entrance into the labor force, but with the increased use of women workers by the government and the rapid expansion of American industry after the war, with consequent more lucrative opportunities available to men, women began to flock into the educational system (Calhoun [1945] II:359–61). At the same time, the curriculum became a "common gender" curriculum—not "masculine" or "feminine." That is to say, the American public school curriculum became more and more shaped to fit the requirements of both males and females rather than of males only. Thus there is a relationship in the United States between the development of a common-gender curriculum and the lack of sexual specialization in teaching: though most elementary school teachers in America are females, males are very much desired and they are heavily represented in high schools and colleges.

III:2. Relatives or Others?
Another feature of preliterate education has been the concentration within the kin group of responsibility for educating the young (Fortes 1938: 5). The child's mother's brother and father's sister (Pettitt 1946: 15–24) have often assumed this responsibility. Meanwhile, there appears to be a systematic relationship between the content of education at any given moment and the kin category, or categories, that assumes responsibility for it (Henry 1955a: 191–92). One of the commonest is the responsibility of the same-sex parent for training in occupational techniques, and the responsibility of the wider kin group for training in morality. In contemporary America, neither schools nor parents are required by law to teach morality, though the social conscience still expects parents to assume this responsibility. Occupational training, on the other hand, has been handed over to nonkin agencies, the reverse of the more ancient cultural pattern.

III:3. On Which Age Group Does the Burden of Education Fall?

III:3:1. Peers

Many references to peer education are scattered through Fortes' penetrating study (1938). In this respect, Chagga boys emphasize masculinity (Raum 1940: 241). Egyptian boys are sensitive to standards of "maturity," and are bitterly scornful of a boy whose behavior does not come up to his age level (Ammar 1954: 128). But the educational responsibilities that children's peer groups had in preliterate and peasant cultures have tended to diminish with the emergence of the common-gender curriculum, the approximation of male and female roles, and the handing over of occupational training to nonkin.

Peer education seems most prominent at all cultural levels in the area of conformity to cultural standards. In preliterate and peasant societies, the peer group is a major force against delinquency. In contemporary society, the peer group seems split on this issue; it is a major support of rebellion against parents (and hence of the cultural standards they represent), while, at the same time, it does use its power to assist conformity to accepted adult standards of morality (Hollingshead 1949). It would seem that this capacity to take rebellion as a standard of conformity to peer-group mores is related to the fact that *in the long run* children in contemporary culture will not, as in many peasant and preliterate cultures, receive their economic foundation in life from their parents.

III:4. Is Education by "Successful" People?
III:5. What Rewards Accrue to the Educator?

The categories "Is Education by 'Successful' People?" and "What Rewards Accrue to the Educator?" are closely related. For example, Williams ([1849] I:426) says of Chinese teachers that they are "unsuccessful students or candidates for literary degrees" but that, nevertheless, "When a boy comes to school in the morning he bows first before the tablet of Confucius, as an act of worship, and then salutes his teacher. . . ." For the teacher taught the sacred writings of Confucius and his disciples. Chiang (1952: 79–82) tells about the reverence with which his teacher was treated and the absolute authority over the children granted him by parents. Thus there has been no necessary connection between success, as measured by worldly standards, and the *deference* accorded a teacher (III:5:1, 3). In the *shtetl* (Zborowski and Herzog 1952: 89) the *melamed*, the teacher of the youngest children, was looked down upon as a man who, because "he has fallen into his profession because he has failed elsewhere," is driven to sell what should be given freely, i.e., learning. Nevertheless, his word was law in the school, and there was no appeal to parents from his cruelty. In eighteenth-century Germany (Bruford 1935: 247–50), teachers were of low status and were often treated like servants. In nineteenth-century England (Bayne-Powell 1939: 69), the outstanding requirement in schoolmasters was "humility," and they were "despised." In Egypt, on the other hand, the Sheikhs were accorded great deference, a function of the fact that "they are the perpetuators of the Holy Book" (Ammar 1954: 211). From all of this, four factors seem to emerge. (1) There is no necessary connection between the success of a teacher according to worldly standards and the deference granted to him. (2) There is no necessary connection between the deference granted a teacher and the authority he, compared with parents, wields over children. (3) There seems to be a connection between the sacredness of knowledge and the deference accorded a teacher in the community as a whole. (4) Europe and the United States have a recorded history of low esteem for schoolteachers.

In the light of the foregoing, we can obtain some understanding of the reason for the poor pay received by American teachers. The low esteem in which teachers have been traditionally held in the United States continues today (Kahl 1957: 73), and low esteem is usually accompanied by low pay. It is further suggested that the reason for the disdain of teachers in the detachment of American education from the "sacred" (Durkheim 1947), i.e., the lack of any deeply felt social consciousness of the aims of education.

III:8. Is the Educator of the Same or of a Different Social Group from That of the Person Being Educated?

The issue of coincidence or lack of coincidence between the social group of the educator and of the educated of course vigorously confronts anthropology in situations of acculturation, but, since it constitutes a chapter by itself in the history of education, it will be barely touched on here. Malinowski (1943: 649-65) has discussed the issue with insight and feeling in connection with Africa, pointing out that missionary education "undermined and destroyed" the native culture, while holding out a promise of equality with Europeans that was, however, not kept. Thompson (1943: 720) says that a committee appointed to inquire into British educational policy in Ceylon found that the policy there had done nothing more than produce

> a class of shallow, conceited, half-educated youths who have learned nothing but to look back with contempt upon the conditions in which they were born and from which they conceive that their education has raised them, and who desert the ranks of the industrious classes to become idle, discontented hangers-on of the courts and the Public Offices.

In the United States, arbitrary efforts to educate Indians along lines laid down by the federal government's Office of Indian Affairs had for many years an inglorious outcome. Macgregor (1946), concentrating on the disastrous consequences for Dakota Indian children, emphasizes (1946: 134-37): (1) the children's fright at encountering large numbers of strange children in the government boarding schools maintained for Indians; (2) fear, by these noncompetitive Indian children, of the competitive situation created by the white schoolteachers; (3) fear of white teachers because whites had always been looked upon as enemies of the Indian; (4) severity of school discipline as contrasted with the more permissive atmosphere of Indian family life; (5) linguistic difficulties, so that many children could not even understand "the teacher's simplest directions." As a consequence, many children "refuse to enter into competition, withdraw from activities, and sometimes become unwilling to make any response." Children would withdraw into themselves or run away from school. They were often overwhelmed with shame when they could not win in a given situation. Leighton and Kluckhohn (1948) discuss similar conditions in Navaho schools.

Study of these and similar situations, and Hollingshead's study (1949) of the relation between social class and education in a small American city, document the fact that a controlling social group, whether it be whites over Negroes (Warner, Havighurst, and Loeb 1944), whites over Indians (Macgregor 1946), a colonial power over its colonial peoples (Malinowski 1943; Thompson 1943), or the higher classes over the lower (Hollingshead 1949), tends to organize the educational system so as to strengthen and maintain its own position.

The works of anthropologists tend to stress the repressive and destructive effects on the subordinate group of education by the dominant group. Malinowski (1943), however, though giving the white man's education of the African little quarter, mentions that missionary education did start the African on the way toward dealing with the new civilization. Sometimes subordinate peoples exposed to modern education have extracted benefits from it, ranging from increased capacity to earn a living in the modern milieu, to the ability to engineer and sustain a social revolution, as in contemporary Africa. Leonard and Loomis (1941) have shown that while education of Spanish-Americans by Spanish-American teachers in New Mexico accomplished little because of the teacher's poor training. Spanish-American boys enrolled in Civilian Conservation Corps and National Youth Administration camps run by non-Spanish-Americans emerged well trained in reading, writing, and other academic skills and returned to their native towns with enhanced status.

IV. How Does the Person Being Educated Participate? (What is His Attitude?)

All the following attitudes of children toward education are known exclusively from literate cultures: "rejecting; resistive" (IV:2), "bored; indifferent" (IV:3), "defiant" (IV:4), "inattentive" (IV:5), "diversion to peers" (IV:27), "disruptively" (IV:33). These seem to stem most generally from the child's failure to feel an immediacy in the relation between what is being taught him in school and the rest of his life. Studies of education in preliterate cultures emphasize that knowledge is *sought* as a guide to an inevitable life role. This contrasts, as Mead (1943) has pointed out, with literate cultures, where the child is subjected to compulsory education but may not see its relevance to his future role as an adult, or to his immediate life outside of school. More concretely, in nonliterate cultures the child is always in close physical contact with the matured activity that he is merely learning. In literate cultures, the school itself, and what he is learning in it, are physically separate from adult *application* of the learning: offices and other places where writing and arithmetic are *used* are separate from the school where the child is learning how to read and add.

Spiro was struck by the apparent boredom, indifference, and inattention, of many children in the kibbutz high school (1958: 296-97):

> Taking a random sample of twenty-four observational protocols, we rated the students' apparent interest on a simple interested-disinterested dichotomy. Lively group participation, careful attention, intelligent questions, and so on, were taken as indications of interest, while such statements in the protocols as: "The children looked bored and sleepy"; "They daydream, doodle, play with objects in their desks . . ."; "The children are apathetic and listless; they do not participate in the discussion. They look bored. At least three heads on the desks"; . . . [etc.] were taken as indications of disinterest. On the basis of these simple criteria, fifteen of the twenty-four sessions were judged to elicit the students' interest, and nine were rated as sessions in which they were disinterested or bored.

It seems likely that in the kibbutz this behavior stems from the same factors as in other literate cultures.

IV:6. Social Closeness of Teacher and Child;
IV:7. Social Distance of Teacher and Child

Spiro (1958: 263) ascribes "informality" in the kibbutz primary school largely to the lack of "social distance" between teacher and children: the children know the teacher personally, and see her in many roles outside of school. "Social closeness" is thus viewed in terms of long-standing continuous interaction. But the term may be used also to describe less permanent interaction situations, as in American classrooms, where the children see the teacher only during class periods. In the American classroom, social distance may be gauged in terms of certain kinds of behavior peculiar to the classroom, that is, the following categories in section IV:

IV: 15. Through making independent decisions and suggestions
    17. Through spontaneous contributions or other demonstrations not precisely within the context of the lesson

18. Through spontaneous contributions within the context of the lesson
20. Spontaneously humorous
21. Spontaneously expressive
22. Approaches teacher physically
23. Mobile—free
32. Corrects teacher
45. Uses teacher's first name
46. Calls out to teacher

That is to say, the extent to which children make independent decisions and offer suggestions to an adult mentor regarding the conduct of a lesson or other activity, the level of general mobility or of approach to the teacher's person, and the frequency with which children call out to the teacher and use his first name (rare in American culture outside the nursery school) all bear upon social distance. This term refers to a bundle of behaviors that are related to how secure, relaxed, and accepted children seem to feel in a teacher's presence, and he in theirs.

Since the children's behavior occurs in interaction with the teacher, it is necessary at this point to consider the relevance of these categories in section IV to certain categories in section V. In section V—"How Does the Educator Participate? (What Is His Attitude?)"—the categories most relevant to the problem of social distance would appear to be:

4b. Integrative
7. Enjoys correct response
10. Seeks physical contact with person being educated
11. Acceptance of blame
14. Encouraging
16. Relatively mobile
18. Personalizing
21. Accepts approach
23. Accepting of child's spontaneous expressions
25. Humorous
26. Handles anxiety, hostility, discomfort, etc.
27. Acts and/or talks as if child's self-image is fragile
29. Defends child against peers
30. Responds to nonverbal cue other than hand raising

That is to say, when American *children* display behaviors indicating their feeling of social closeness to the teacher, the American teacher will probably be found to be "integrative." He will show pleasure at correct responses, occasionally pat a child, be encouraging, move about the room, make frequent use of the children's names, let them come close to him, accept outbursts of joy, sorrow, or anxiety, deal appropriately with emotional problems as they arise, be sensitive to the children's feelings, defend a child who comes under verbal or physical attack by another child, and be perceptive enough to cues emanating from the children so that he will respond to frowns, smiles, tenseness, etc.—in other words, not wait for a question or a raised hand before responding. Thus social closeness can be expressed as a pattern of classroom behaviors quite apart from whether the children see the teacher after class periods.

Spiro describes kibbutz behaviors that in American schools would also indicate closeness (1958: 264):

> Students leave the classroom at will—to get a drink, to go to the toilet, or for any reason which they deem important. Similarly, they may leave their desks without permission—to get supplies from the cabinet, to sharpen a pencil, and so on.

They may talk among themselves [IV:27] both during oral lessons and while working privately at their desks; some hum or sing to themselves while writing or studying.

A second expression of informality is readiness of the children to criticize the teacher when they feel he is wrong.

Students . . . address their teachers by their first names and the latter address their students as chaverim, "comrades."

The kibbutz is much more tolerant of random behavior than the American classrooms studied:

A final expression of classroom informality is the poor discipline . . . particularly in the second through fourth grades in the primary school, and the eighth through tenth grades in the high school—and which often results in utter chaos. (Spiro 1958: 264)

Such behavior would be considered "disruptive" (IV: 33a) in most American classrooms, though Henry (1959) has described occasional approval of it in suburban schools. Spiro (1958: 263) feels that this extreme informality is due to lack of social distance between teacher and child; yet, though in primitive cultures the social distance between teacher and pupil is, with certain exceptions (Watkins 1943), very small, I have not found in primitive culture such generalized random behavior *when the children are receiving systematic instruction in cultural skills*. The most general explanation of the occurrence of random behavior is that adults permit it—if, indeed, they do not encourage it—by failure, as in the kibbutz and in some American suburban schools, to establish a clear locus of authority. Both in the United States and in the kibbutz, this is an expression of a special interpretation of democracy. On the other hand in the suburban American schools studied by Henry (1959), the chaos itself seems to be a value: random behavior is believed to be creative behavior. Finally, it is likely that lack of unity in the social sphere makes its contribution to unruliness, for when children do not see the relevance to their life roles of what they are doing, boredom and inattention (IV:3, 5) may ensue.

IV:11a. With Inappropriate Laughter

"Inappropriate Laughter" signifies laughter that occurs in a context not socially defined as humorous, or laughter that is not part of a formal sanction pattern. The following from an American fifth-grade schoolroom is illustrative:

The child at the board stares at $\frac{2}{3}$ minus $\frac{2}{3}$. There is a faint titter, snicker, giggle or something . . . as the child stares, nonplussed by the problem.

Also illustrative is the following from a spelling lesson in a fourth-grade class:

The child writing "Thursday" on the board stops to think after the first letter, and the children snicker. He stops after another letter. More snickers.

At the same time, it is not quite correct to say that failure is not "socially defined" as humorous *by the children*; or that, for children in American society, laughter at failure is not part of the *children's* formal sanction pattern. Since it occurs so frequently among children in our research, it must be assumed to be a sanction within the children's group, and, therefore, to be inappropriate only from the adult point of view. This does not mean that adults in American society do *not* take pleasure in other people's failure (Henry 1957a).

IV:11b. Ridiculing Peers

Ridicule is closely related to laughter as a social sanction against those who fail to come up to cultural demands. Pettitt says ridicule is "world-wide in distribution" (1946: 50), and makes the important observation (1946: 53) that in primitive North America "ridicule follows and supplements praise rather than vice versa. Praise is more frequently used at all age levels, and the ratio of praise to ridicule is relatively greatest at the younger ages." The materials from contemporary American public grade schools do not parallel those from primitive North America. Our records show that, in American primary public schools, children do praise one another's work, but that ridicule, as expressed in spontaneous tittering, is more frequent. On the other hand, it is rare to find in these schools a ridiculing *teacher*, or one who laughs at the failure of one of her students.

The impression one derives from the literature on both literate and nonliterate cultures is that ridicule is more common with the peer group than across age lines, and that it is less common for a younger person to use it toward an older person than the reverse. This latter is understandable since the younger is more often the subordinate both in learning situations and with respect to the sanction system.

Among the numerous penetrating insights in Pettitt's work is his observation that ridicule did not occur in a random way among the Indians of North America. He says that "the right to ridicule with impunity was generally limited," and that there was usually a "privileged" group of ridiculers (like certain relatives) for every person (1946: 50-52). Thus ridicule, probably because of its damage to the self-image and its great potential for generating hostility, was strictly controlled. There is no doubt that the importance of controlling ridicule was a brilliant psychological discovery by primitive man, and one wonders, therefore, why, once he had made that one, he did not go on to further triumphs. Speaking impressionistically again, it seems that they did, but that we need another Pettitt to comb the literature to find them, for these discoveries occurred in a scattered, unsystematized way, some in one tribe, some in another.

IV:13. Overt Docility

Ammar says of education in Egypt (1954: 127):

> The keynote to the educational process is the eagerness of the adults to create a docile attitude in their children and thus make them acquire filial piety.
> The children readily accept the authority of their seniors, whether in work or play, and they endeavor to avoid their anger.

This is *not* the type of docility to which IV:13 refers. Henry (1955b) describes "overt docility" as a child's renunciation of his own ideas in order to please the teacher. Two examples from a fourth-grade class in an American public school will illustrate the point:

> During the art lesson Mrs. Mintner holds up a picture and says, "Isn't Bobby getting a nice effect of moss and trees?" The children utter ecstatic Ohs and Ahs.

> The children have just finished reading the story of *The Sun, Moon, and Stars Clock* (Savery 1942) and Mrs. Mintner asks them, "What was the highest point of interest, the climax?" The children tell her what they think it is. The teacher is aiming to get from them what she thinks it is, but the children give everything else but the answer she wants. At last Tom says, "When they capture the thieves," and Mrs. Mintner asks, "How many agree with Tom?" A great flurry of hands goes up.

IV:29. Disjoined Hand Raising

"Disjoined Hand Raising" has been discussed at some length under I:10:2 ("Use of the Mind: Disjunction"). The "disjoined hand" is the hand that is kept raised for no objective reason: the teacher has asked no question, nor created any other situation that calls for hand raising, but the child's hand is up because he is detached from the situation and does not know what is going on.

IV:34. By Carping Criticism

Henry (1957a) has discussed the phenomenon of "Carping Criticism" in public elementary school classrooms. Carping criticism ignores the virtues in a work and concentrates destructively on petty details. For example, when a student reads to the class a little story he has composed, his classmates may ignore the good things in the story and pick out insignificant items to devalue. Often this occurs as a miscarriage of the idea that children should be taught to think "critically," the teacher herself inadvertently starting criticism of this kind (see V:36).

Carping criticism does not appear to occur in kibbutz schools:

> ... The emphasis on group criticism can potentially engender competitive, if not hostile feelings among the children. Frequently, for example, the children read their essays aloud, and the others are then asked to comment. Only infrequently could we detect any hostility in the criticisms of the students, and often the evaluations were filled with praise. (Spiro 1958: 261)

IV:37. Attempts to Maintain Order

In some suburban schools in the United States, where the ideology of permissiveness has penetrated deeply so that the classroom becomes very noisy, the tolerance limits for disorder are at times passed for some children, and they spontaneously "Shush!" (i.e., to quiet) their peers. This exemplifies what is meant by "Attempts to Maintain Order," and raises the interesting problem of the tolerance of different children for disorder. In the language of communications theory, the question would be, "How much noise can different persons tolerate in the communications system before the messages coming to them become completely blurred?" The problem of motivation is also involved here, for some children might not care how much noise there is in the system because they are not interested in the messages anyway. From the standpoint of the teacher, the issue would seem to be, "How much noise can a child tolerate in the communications system before messages are lost to him or before he feels incapable of competing with the noise?" These problems have been taken up by Henry (1955a).

IV:42. Attempts to Control the Class

The category "Attempts to Control the Class" differs from "Attempts to Maintain Order" (IV:37) in that its referent is not the teacher but the child. The focus is not on a teacher's efforts to maintain order, but rather on one child's efforts to get other children in the educational situation to do what he wants them to do. An example from a fourth-grade class in singing will illustrate the point:

> The children are singing songs from Ireland and her neighbors. . . . While the children are singing some of them hunt in the index of the song book, find a song belonging to one of the countries, and then raise their hands before the previous song is finished, in order that they may choose the next song to be sung. The index gives the national origin of each song.

When, in this situation, the teacher calls on a child whose hand is raised and accepts his selection of a song, the child has controlled the other children, because they have to sing his song. This category differs also from III:3:I, "Peer-Group Responsibility for Education," because in the latter we are concerned only with whether or not instruction is given by the peer group, whereas in IV:42 we are interested in whether or not a child attempts to impose his will on a learning group.

V. How Does the Educator Participate? (What is His Attitude?)

V:1. Eagerly

No anthropologist has ever asked whether adults in nonliterate societies enjoy teaching. This must be because instructing the young in the tribal ways is as natural as breathing: the adults have a vital interest in the children they teach, and they often seem to have even a broader interest in the tribal existence as a whole. While Dubois (1944) and Raum (1940) give some evidence to show that children outside of Western culture can be reluctant to learn what they are supposed to learn, the overall impression gained from reading the literature on nonliterate cultures is that children appear to want to learn tribal ways, and that adults take the children's role as learners, and their own as educators, for granted. But this is only impression, for anthropology has not explored systematically the problem of the eagerness of the primitive teacher to teach, or, indeed, of the primitive child to learn.

In contemporary culture, teachers have no kinship or other compelling motivations for eagerness in their work, and there arises in the study of classroom learning the problem of discovering whether such a teacher enjoys his occupation and whether he demonstrates it in class. It is suggested that observations focused on the subcategories under V:1 in the outline, and on the following group of categories indicating social closeness, would cast light on this matter:

V: 4b. Integrative
    7. Enjoys correct response
   10. Seeks physical contact with person being educated
   16. Relatively mobile
   18. Personalizing
   21. Accepts approach
   22. Repels approach
   25. Humorous
   26. Handles anxiety, hostility, discomfort, etc.
   27. Acts and/or talks as if child's self-image is fragile
   30. Responds to nonverbal cue other than hand raising

V:11. Acceptance of Blame

The category "Acceptance of Blame" would seem to apply more to literate than to nonliterate cultures, and is particularly relevant in the kind of "democratic" classroom atmosphere peculiar to the United States. The category would cover a situation where something goes wrong in the conduct of the lesson, the children tell the teacher it is his fault, and he accepts the blame.

V:12. Putting Decisions up to the Children

Spiro (1958: 264) describes decision making in the kibbutz school as follows:

> The teacher, furthermore, generally consults with his students, rather than informing them of decisions he had made independently. Even in the Grammar School, for example, the teacher chooses a project only after consultation with the class. It is true that she presents them with the suggestions from which a project is to be chosen, but the final choice rests on the decision of the class. An even more "democratic" procedure is adopted with respect to the writing of essays for which the children themselves suggest the topics.

In this type of situation where the teacher puts decisions up to the children, there is always the problem of whether such action by the teacher is democratic or pseudo-democratic. In pseudo-democratic action, the teacher, by suggestion or by limitation of the area of selection, can actually bind the act of choice while making it appear that it has been free. Henry (1959) has described such a situation in one American elementary school where a teacher said his children themselves set up the behavior rules, but where, actually, they did so under his direction, so that the rules were in the end what he wanted them to be. Placing decision making in the hands of the children is not characteristic of American public elementary schools. Even cases of pseudo-democracy, such as that described by Henry, would appear to be infrequent.

V:18. Personalizing; V:19. Depersonalizing

The categories "Personalizing" and "Depersonalizing" refer largely to the way teachers call on students in class. It has struck our observers that teachers who impress them as being aloof from the children frequently will not use the children's names in calling on them, but, rather, use some impersonal device such as those listed in the outline under V:19. Nevertheless, this is far from being an established correlation: some teachers who appear to be bitterly hostile to their students make frequent use of their personal names, while others who seem much closer to the students use the techniques listed under V:19. The following, from an eighth-grade class in the United States, provides an example of a hostile teacher who generally uses the children's names:

> Cyril reads. He stumbles and mispronounces the word con'-tent. After three attempts he pronounces it con-tent'. Teacher says, "Cyril, do you or don't you know what you're reading?" She emphasizes "do you" or "don't you" as she gives Cyril a sharp look. "Are you making up words to suit yourself?" Cyril looks at the teacher, smiles, then lowers his head, and reads on. He comes across a sentence stating that "Interest is our first important point," but he reads it, "Interest is one of our most important point." The teacher raises her voice as she looks at Cyril directly, and says, "Don't add words that are not there. Alright, Jerry, you read for us." Jerry reads softly and rapidly, and the teacher says, sternly, "Open your mouth." As she says this she opens her own mouth in order to say each word distinctly. Jerry stumbles over the word cumulatively but pronounces it correctly. . . .

> A boy reads smoothly. He has no trouble in pronouncing the word pinioned. The teacher interrupts him to ask, "What do we mean when we say pinioned?" The boy says, "tied down," and the teacher asks, "Are you sure?" The boy shrugs his shoulders and smiles as he slowly writes the word on a piece of paper in a half disinterested manner. The teacher says, "That's why we don't understand what we read. What's the use of copying the word and looking up the meaning later. It is now that you need the meaning, to give the story some sense." She looks around the room and calls on Antoinette who had her head down on her open book. "Antoinette, you tell us all about it, since you know so much; (pause) or is it that you are too tired or too old to look?"

It is to be observed that though this teacher calls the children by name, she is hostile, ridiculing, sarcastic, and belittling (V:15) and, also, that she resents an incorrect response (V:8). She is also irritable (V:20), discouraging (V:13), and acts as if the child's self-image is irrelevant (V:28). Further, it would appear that the process is painful to the children (IV:8), and that their frequent stumbling is evidence of anxiety (IV:28), feelings of inadequacy (IV:39), and machine jamming (II: 8:1).

The following provides an example of a nonhostile teacher who, nevertheless, often does not use the children's names. The observations were made in a sixth-grade American classroom:

> The teacher says, "Mike, how is your eye?" and Mike replies, "Fine today."
> The teacher says to the class, "First I'd like to talk to you about some work
> in vocabulary that you handed in and on which you made some mistakes."
> She goes to the board and writes the words our, are and or. She now says,
> "Let's have some sentences; first with are." She points to a girl at the front
> of the room, and the girl makes up a sentence, "Are you going too?" Teacher
> says, "Yes. Another." She points to a boy, who makes up the following
> sentence, "Tom and John are going to town or for a ride." The teacher says,
> "Good. I'm glad you used or in there too." She points to a girl, who says,
> "I or Jim are going to the show." The teacher says, "How did you say that?
> Which did you put first?" The child says, "I or . . . Oh! Jim or I are going to
> the show." The teacher says, "O.K., that's better. You all seem to know
> how to use them right today."

We may notice here that this teacher shows solicitude for a child's sore eye (V:4b), that she is polite (V:6) in phrasing her requests to the students, and that she rewards correct responses (V:34, II:5) and seems to take pleasure in them (V:7). To anticipate discussion a little, this teacher attempts to be "ego-syntonic" (XI:1:1).

V:21. Accepts Approach; V:22. Repels Approach

Children in American schools, especially in the lower grades, often attempt to be near the teacher. Categories V:21 and V:22 are meant to take account of whether or not the teacher accepts this.

V:23. Accepting of Child's Spontaneous Expressions

The following, observed also in the sixth-grade class used as an illustration under V:18 and V:19, illustrates the category "Accepting of Child's Spontaneous Expression." The children have been answering questions about a story they have read, and they are to be graded on the number of correct answers; the teacher is about to tell them the grading system:

> "Now I'll tell you the bad news," she says. Several of the children moan and
> groan, and the teacher says. "It's not so bad. Take off 16 for each one
> wrong." The children moan some more. . . . The teacher says, "If you have
> one wrong your score is 84, two wrong, you have 68, etc." (She continues
> with the scores.) A girl says, "Why don't you give us 2 points if we get 68 so
> we will have above failing?" The teacher smiles and says, "If you miss six
> you get zero." A girl says, "Ouch, that hurts. I hope no one gets that," and
> the teacher says, smiling, "I do too."

The spontaneous expressions of the children all stem from their anxiety about the outcome of the grading, and the teacher accepts these expressions. Of course, not all spontaneous expressions stem from anxiety; some are merely opinions elicited by the lesson or observations about things in general (IV:17, 18). In this teacher's acceptance of the spontaneous expressions of the children, there is also a manifestation of V:26, her ability to handle their anxiety without becoming annoyed and repressive. Obviously the categories in the outline are not mutually exclusive.

V:29. Defends Child against Peers

The category "Defends Child against Peers" was developed to take account of situations in which the teacher defends a child, not so much from physical attack, but against verbal attacks, which are the major expression of internal aggression in children's classrooms in the United States (Henry 1957a). The following example of a teacher's so defending a child is from observations made in a fifth-grade classroom. As one child after another stands up before the class and reads a little story he has written, the other children, reinforced by the teacher's critical attitude (V:36), proceed to demolish his work with trivial, carping criticism (IV:34). In spite of the fact that the teacher, with a mistaken notion of what critical thinking is all about, consistently fails to praise the children's work (V:36), she does, very occasionally, defend a child against his carping critics:

> Harriet says that in Mae's story of "Custard the Lion" Mae said " 'most bravest animal' and that isn't very good English." The teacher then says, "No it isn't, but sometimes in stories for little children they say things like that. . . ." Victor reads a story called "The Unknown Guest." . . . The teacher asks the class, "Are there any words that give you the mood of the story?" Barbara says, "He could have made the sentences a little better. . . . [After a long carpingly critical discussion of Victor's story by the children] the teacher says, "We still haven't decided about the short sentences—perhaps they make the story more spooky and mysterious."

V:34. Praises and Rewards Realistically;
V:35. Praises and Rewards Indiscriminately

The categories "Praises and Rewards Realistically" and "Praises and Rewards Indiscriminately" must be considered in connection with V:27, the teacher "Acts and/or Talks as if Child's Self-Image Is Fragile," for the cause of indiscriminate praise in American schools is, in considerable part, fear of hurting a child's feelings. Thus, at a polar extreme from the teacher who never praises, but is only silent or critical, is the teacher who says everything is good. Such a teacher would, in a so-called art lesson, praise all the paintings as "fine," "beautiful," and so on. While V:35 is related to V:27, it is related also to VIII:5, "Ignorance or Error of Teacher," as a limiting factor in learning, for most elementary school teachers do not know how to teach art. Since they know so little about teaching art, and possibly about art, their failure to praise or criticize with discrimination is understandable. Meanwhile, children with talent might be discouraged by hearing everything praised, whether it was actually good, bad, or indifferent. Thus indiscriminate praise becomes inadvertent discouragement.

V:42. The Inclusive Plural

"The Inclusive Plural" refers to a practice, widespread among teachers at all levels in the United States, of including themselves in statements and instructions meant only for their students. Thus a teacher, referring to the students' unfamiliarity with the use of quotation marks, says, "We haven't learned to use them yet." It seems that the function of this "we" is to diminish the status gap between pupil and teacher.

A preliminary survey of education in nonliterate societies yields the impression that the following attitudes are found among teachers there as well as in American culture:

V: 4a. Dominative
   4b. Integrative[5]
   7. Enjoys correct response
  13. Discouraging
  14. Encouraging
  15. Hostile, ridiculing, sarcastic, belittling
  20. Irritable

27. Acts and/or talks as if child's self-image is fragile
28. Acts and/or talks as if child's self-image is irrelevant
34. Praises and rewards realistically
38. Does not punish incorrect answer or poor performance

Other attitudes enumerated under this section V may be present in nonliterate societies also, but relevant information is still so scant that one must hope that future studies will be more sensitive to this field of research.

VI. Are Some Things Taught to Some and Not to Others?

The question, "Are some things taught to some people and not to others?" raises the issue of the apportionment of the contents of a culture among its members. For, if some things are, for example, taught to girls, and others to boys, it can only be because when the young people are mature men and women they will be responsible for different things in the culture. One obvious difference between men and women with respect to apportionment is in the work men and women do, and from this has arisen the classic conception of the sexual division of labor. However, not only labor but everything else in a culture is apportioned, hence the educational process provides for much more than the division of labor. Further, it varies not only with sex but also with age, social class, and other categories of persons, for each one of these carries a different part of the cultural baggage.

As a matter of fact, the concept of apportionment implies also the broad issue of the philosophical ideas that lie behind it and ultimately determine the educational process. If the pivotal problem in a culture is man's relation to God, then religious instruction will play an important role in the education of all. But if, as in the Eastern European *shtetl* culture, the pathway to God is the prerogative of males (Zborowski and Herzog 1952), then males alone will receive formal religious instruction.

All cultures have, in addition to a general conception of man's relation to the world, some ideas about the inherent nature of children, and such ideas affect education. For example, since both nineteenth-century Calvinists (Sunley 1954: 159) and twentieth-century Lepchas (Gorer 1938: 305) thought children were born bad, their educational processes focused on eradicating the badness. In the same way, status systems are typically buttressed by ideas, and education is shaped to fit those ideas. One of the most widespread status differentiations is between men and women. Since in the Chinese, Hebrew, and Indo-European traditions men have stood for intellect and strength, and women for emotion and weakness, the cultural baggage has been apportioned accordingly, and the educational process has differed for boys and girls.

Data is abundant in the area of differential education by sex, for the sexual division of culture has, throughout human history, been one of the most obvious and dramatic aspects of apportionment. In the West, it has been a matter for controversy. The issue pivots on a central contradiction, namely, that culture has striven *both* to unite and to separate the sexes, at the same time, thus *their unity was sought through dividing them*. The line of division was at the separation of functions, and it was this line that was *also the line of unity*, for those functions were complementary. As long as men and women do different things they need each other, and this need adds to the ties of matrimony and children. A Sirionó man without a woman cannot hunt, because she makes the string for his bow (Holmberg 1950: 14)!

So, though it is correct to say that men and women are taught different things because they have different things to do, the fundamental point is that they *must* have different things to do. From this stems the pressure to keep their educational areas separate.

In the ensuing paragraphs, stress will be placed on status differences as expressed in education, but it must be borne in mind that at the base of such status differences there is always a philosophy of the differences between persons, which itself is everywhere subject to the inexorable law of apportionment.

VI:1. Do Different Age Groups Learn Different Things?

All societies have recognized that children of different ages are capable of learning different things, although they may differ in opinion with respect to the specific age at which children are capable of learning some one thing. For example, though *shtetl* children (Zborowski and Herzog 1952: 89) start to learn to read and write at the age of three, Americans think this is premature and "pushing" the child. On the other hand, in early eighteenth-century America, "Boys entered Boston Latin School as young as six and a half. They often began Latin much younger," and three-year-olds were taught to read Latin as well as English (Calhoun [1945] I:110). Williams says of China that during the Middle Kingdom boys seven years old were taught to count and name the cardinal points.

> At eight, they must be taught to wait for their superiors, and prefer others to themselves. At ten, the boys must be sent abroad to private tutors, and there remain day and night, studying writing and arithmetic, wearing plain apparel, learning to demean themselves in a manner becoming their age, and acting with sincerity and purpose. At thirteen, they must attend to music and poetry; at fifteen they must practise archery and charioteering. At the age of twenty, they are in due form to be admitted to the rank of manhood, and learn additional rules of propriety, be faithful in the performance of filial and fraternal duties, and though they possess extensive knowledge, must not offer to teach others. (Williams [1849] 1:423–24)

On the whole, anthropological monographs have not dealt in detail with the ages at which children learn particular things. Among the few authors who do discuss age differences at some length are Raum (1940) and Ammar (1954). Ammar has provided a thorough timetable for Egyptian children, and though it deals with the tasks they perform rather than the tasks they learn, it may be safely assumed, I think, that the time gap between doing and learning is not great. Since he has worked it out so carefully, and since anthropology is in need of similar tables, it may be worthwhile to present here (table 8.1) his table for children from ages three to seven (Ammar 1954: 30–31).

There is, of course, a great difference between a record of what children are doing and a record of what they are learning, for the record of learning involves a study of precisely how the adult makes known his wishes and transfers his knowledge to the child, and/or how the child learns what the adult wishes are and absorbs the necessary knowledge. Hence table 8.1 is merely a good start.

To return to education in early eighteenth-century Boston, it would seem that such education has to be understood as one phase of a total emphasis on early growing up. That was a culture in which boys "became men at sixteen, paid taxes and served in the militia" (Calhoun [1945] I:110). With respect to the *shtetl*, the emphasis on early reading and writing of Hebrew can be understood in terms of cultural survival depending on reverence for, if not knowledge of, the Hebrew classics. In general, the age at which education in a given skill begins may be seen as a function of the total organization of the culture, including ideas about children.

At this point one may generalize and say that what children are taught at a particular time in their lives is determined by the following factors: (1) what there is to learn; (2) the objective physical and intellectual maturity of the child, as well as the members of the culture are able to perceive it; (3) the attitude toward children —which, of course, may seriously modify the cultural perception of (2); and (4) the

TABLE 8.1

BOYS	GIRLS
No serious tasks are expected till the age of five, whereupon they are required to work as messengers fetching goods from the shop, or running errands for their parents, uncles, etc. . . . fetching and taking things from and to other homes. Children (between five and seven) are considered to be the best messengers, especially for invitations or for asking help from neighbors, and borrowing from them, being less embarrassed, less inquisitive, and only repeating faithfully what is told to them.	Care of infants is one of the girl's main tasks at all ages, and starts as early as five, when she takes her younger sibling outside for play, or attends to him while mother is doing some domestic task.
In the absence of older sisters he takes care of his younger brother or sister.	Runs errands like boys, especially for her mother or aunt, e.g., fetching fire, bringing food or other things that need to be hidden with the dangling parts of her head cloth.
Toward the end of this period he goes to the field with his older siblings, or with his father, riding behind him on donkey back or balanced in one of the camel's panniers.	Accompanies mother to the well or to the Nile with her small pot or tin, carried on her head and supported by her lifted arms.
Helps in carrying grass to the animals, scaring birds from the field, filling waterpots from the canal; ties or unties the cow, donkey, and camel for his father or older brother.	Helps mother in bringing fuel to the oven or the fire, consisting of millet stems, tree branches, dry animal dung, etc.
On the whole for him this is a stage of observation without allotted specific responsibilities. As the villagers put it, this is the period for children "to be moistened with earth."	Makes her own loaf with the last bit of dough which she eats after it is baked. This is a means of her initiation to domestic tasks by being "moistened with dough," and a reminder that "kneading and baking" are one of the most important jobs for a girl.

major goals of the culture—which may be "prestige through head-hunting," "accumulation of capital," "maintenance of *shtetl* culture against the gentiles," "social mobility," and so on.

VI:2. Do the Sexes Learn Different Things?

While published materials lack specificity with respect to differences in education according to age, they are rich in reports of differences in education according to sex. A few examples will suffice. The first is from contemporary Egypt (Ammar 1954: 207–8):

> All the Kuttabs, except the aided one, are confined to boys. Only recently have some girls begun to attend the aided Kuttab. . . . In fact, throughout the history of Moslem Egypt the keenness on teaching girls the Koran has never been so strong as in the case of boys. MacDonald mentioned, however, that there are records of learned women who had finished a Kuttab course and proceeded to a higher educational course in either al-Azhar or the College Mosques (Madrasah); but their numbers were very small in comparison.

Of England in the eighteenth century Bayne-Powell says (1939: 106, 23):

> The majority of the girls of the upper classes did not go to school at all.
> Parents considered it a waste of money to pay for an expensive education,
> when a governess or waiting gentlewoman could teach them at home for
> £20 a year all they needed to learn. It was thought, too, as Swift complained,
> that a "humour of reading books, excepting those of devotion or house-
> wifery, is apt to turn a woman's brain . . . that all affectation of knowledge,
> beyond what is merely domestic, renders them vain, conceited, and pretend-
> ing," and that "a girl will have all the impertinence of a pedant without the
> knowledge."

> [Girls] were carefully taught how to enter and leave a room, how to get into
> a carriage, how to hand a cup of tea.
>   The curtsy was an elaborate affair of many gradations, scarcely perceptible
> in some cases, and in others a fine reverence to the very ground. It was con-
> stantly performed, even children curtsied ceremoniously to each other when
> they met.

In eighteenth-century Germany, it was "particularly difficult for women [of the
aristocracy] to cultivate their minds" (Bruford 1935: 65) because of the danger of
putting ignorant men to shame. (See VI:3.)
  The Dutch both in New Netherlands and in Europe seem to have constituted in
the literate world a marked exception to the rule that women should not have an
education that made demands on the intellect or trespassed on the prerogatives of
men:

> The women of the Dutch Netherlands in the sixteenth and seventeeth cen-
> turies were more highly educated, better protected by the laws, and more
> prominent in station than any of their contemporaries. On the woman's judg-
> ment, prudence, foresight, everything hinged. (Calhoun (1945) I:48)

Calhoun says that foreigners disapproved of the Dutch woman's "ascendancy," and
adds, "In New Netherlands both sexes received education and that men and women
were more equal than later under English fashion" ([1945] I:167). With the exception of the Dutch settlements, early education in the United States followed
closely the widespread European pattern of confining female education to domestic
tasks, writing, and "social skills." In conversation with me, Dietrich Gerhardt has
suggested that the attention given to the education of upper-class Dutch women
may have been related to the important role they played in commerce, even including holding partnerships in mercantile establishments.

VI:3. Are Different Groups Taught Different Things?

The problem of class differences in education in the United States is well known
from the work of Hollingshead (1949) and of Warner, Havighurst, and Loeb (1944).
These authors describe the ways in which lower-class children in small cities are excluded from educational opportunities that would put them on the "social ele-
vator." Fortes, describing education in Tale society, emphasizes that the uniformity in education there is due to absence of social stratification, but also shows
that, as soon as any status factor enters the society, it is taken account of by the
educational process (1938: 9-10). In Samoa the *taupo*, or village princess, receives
an education quite different from that of other girls (Mead [1939] Part 1:78-79).
  Since in Western civilization variously privileged types of instruction were un-
equally apportioned according to economic level and social class, it would be well
go give consideration to some data on the subject. In eighteenth-century Germany

(Bruford 1935: 67, 68, 71), the nobility were ignorant, and the cultivated bourgeoisie were the intellectual leaders. "Almost all [the aristocracy] considered it beneath the dignity of a nobleman to desire any genuine scholarship." In the second half of the same century, however, the nobility began "to follow in the footsteps of the bourgeoisie," although it was still important for their sons to learn dancing, fencing, and riding, along with modern languages. The curricula in the boarding schools for sons of the nobility, therefore, were a mixture of the social arts, including cards, chess, and music, along with subjects like arithmetic, history and geography, and "perhaps some snippets of natural science, the 'curiosities' of botany, anatomy, physics and chemistry." A little ethics and law were also included, along with meat carving! Bruford ends his discussion by stating that, "The proper study of mankind was how to please the great."

It is clear that regularly in Western civilization some class has looked with contempt on enlightenment: knowledge in all areas has had to fight to come into existence and to survive. The history of education in England (Bayne-Powell 1939: 11) and Germany (Bruford 1935) shows, also, that enlightenment by no means always flowed from the higher to the lower classes. It would appear that as the feudal system in Europe began to disintegrate, the bourgeoisie played an important role in forcing new knowledge upon a reluctant nobility and church (Pirenne 1937: 123-24). In the history of Western civilization new knowledge was a threat to traditional status relationships, whether between classes or between sexes, and fear of this threat remains. For this reason a prime effort in Western civilization has been to tame new knowledge and direct it in such a way that it would strengthen the traditional social structure rather than unhinge it.

From the preceding there emerges the interesting fact that the absorption of new knowledge implies a change in the existing social structure. From this generality we may now proceed to some interesting refinements.

Let any increment in knowledge be represented by k. Then, in an infinite universe, the sum of all possible k is $K = \infty$. If we assume no limit to what mankind can learn, it follows that social structures will go through an infinite number of changes, if, in the course of an infinite history, mankind absorbs all possible knowledge. Of course, man, as Spinoza has taught us, is finite, so he cannot know everything, and hence not all possible social structures will be experienced. It is also unlikely that mankind will be around forever! But, if we assume that a great deal of knowledge will yet be absorbed by cultures, it follows that we have very many social structures ahead of us.

Now k is not a simple quantitative function; it has also a quality, which derives from its consequences for social structure. Some ks are low in social-structure relevance, others high. For example, it is of little social-structure relevance if somebody discovers a new color for a lipstick, but if someone discovers a new basis for understanding human behavior (e.g., Freud), this has great social-structure relevance. It is clear therefore, that we must always multiply k (increment in knowledge) by some variable factor α[6] (which stands for "social-structure relevance"), and that a (adaptation) is a function of the number of k multiplied by their corresponding α. Where $\alpha > 0$, we get $a = f(\alpha k)$. This is a *general sociological law of knowledge and social change*. It states that social change is a function of new knowledge and the social-structure-relevance of that knowledge. (We know, of course, that social structure changes for reasons other than merely new knowledge. The model expresses only the relation of change to knowledge.)

Now, we know that different status groups in a society may exclude each other from knowledge to which each group considers it has proprietary rights. Traditional India is an excellent example of a society structured in this way. In an open system, however, anyone may, theoretically, know anything there is to know.

If a closed system is inundated with knowledge (i.e., k increases greatly), it will eventually fall apart, for the magnitude of the required adaptation (a) will destroy the old system. On the other hand, an open-class system inundated with knowledge allows scholarship and economic exploit to create new status groups to manipulate the new knowledge. Expressing these statements as hypotheses, we may say that (1) knowledge circulates among social-status groups more readily in open social-status systems than in closed social-status systems, and (2) new intellectual horizons are revealed more readily in open social-status systems than in closed social-status systems. The evolutionary, as well as the thermodynamic, implications of these hypotheses are obvious, viz., "Nature hates closed status systems" because they are "counter-evolutionary" in that biologic systems must absorb energy from outside the system (Von Bertalanffy 1950).

VII. Discontinuities in the Educational Process

Benedict (1938) applied the concept "discontinuity" to that type of cultural experience in which there is a sharp break between child and adult roles. In *Coming of Age in Samoa*, Mead (1928) had discussed the problem of abrupt differences between child and adult education. Both writers urge that discontinuities create conflict and tension.

In most cultures, knowledge appropriate to one sex appears to vary primarily with age (i.e., time), and hence, all things being equal, the more that people of the same sex approximate each other in age, the more equal their knowledge. There are cultures, however, where all things are not equal, but where a specific *exclusion factor* creates a massive difference between two persons of almost equal age. Such a factor might be, for example, the withholding of certain kinds of information from a boy who has not yet passed through an initiation ceremony. In such a case there might be a crucial difference in knowledge (i.e., a discontinuity) between two boys separated by a relatively small age difference. Thus once an exclusion factor is introduced into the educational process, the learning curve can take almost any course, and a discontinuity can arise even between persons adjacent in age.

The theoretical issue in discontinuity in education does not pivot on *any* items of knowledge, but on *critical* items. In the United States it is of little significance that at twelve years of age Mary does not know the history of the Balkan Wars though her mother does. But it is of critical significance that Mary does not understand menstruation though her mother does. The issue in the study of discontinuities in education, then, is to discover whether there are critical areas of knowledge from which children are deliberately excluded by adults.

Meanwhile it is necessary to take account of the fact that the exclusion factor is often inefficient in operation, so that critical items do get to the child either in whole or in part, or in a distorted form. Though Benedict says that adults in our culture *view* the child as "sexless," the *child* is not sexless; and he manages to find out a great deal about sex, and engage in sexual experimentation, in spite of adults. This leads to the interesting conclusion that knowledge drags role performance after it. In less vivid language, a person possessing knowledge will tend to put it to use even in the face of social sanctions against such behavior. This might be called "the law of the forbidden fruit," i.e., forbidden knowledge will be put to use when the resultant rewards exceed the punishments, or when the culprit feels he can evade the consequences of breaking the law.

When the exclusion factor affects whole groups of adults, we get differentiation in the social structure. It would appear, therefore, that the exclusion factor has social-structure relevance. We infer from this that the persistence of exclusion must have as its function the prevention of social change. Armed with this inference, we may return now to the world of the child, to inquire whether the exclusion of children from certain areas of knowledge is not for the purpose of preventing social change. It seems likely, for example, that keeping knowledge of sexuality from children in American culture has served to maintain the old authoritarian family structure in which the children remained unmarried until they fought their way to independence. Among the Chagga, ignorance on the part of young women that men really do defecate is related to male prestige. Among the Hopi, keeping children in ignorance of the fact that the *kachina* dancers are men, not gods, helps maintain the moral sanction system.

When a child is excluded from knowing *all* about something of which he knows part, he tends to imagine the rest, provided he is interested. Since adults tend to fill the gap in the child's knowledge with stories, in lieu of the truth, it often becomes difficult to tell what the child has spontaneously imagined, and what he has been told in stories by adults. There is this danger inherent in educational systems containing discontinuities, that they foster distorting fantasies in children, and oblige adults to lie or to maintain a silence that perplexes the child and breeds distrust. The Manus, in the Admiralty Islands, seem to constitute an exception to this, for, Mead tells us (1939: pt. 2), the children contemptuously thrust the adult world from them.

Today the nursery tales that formerly were told to children to explain the world they did not know have given way to television programs which pour *their* tales into the minds of children. That is to say, young children, knowing little about what adult jobs really are, fill their fantasy world with mass-produced distortions. The following examples from interviews with nursery school children illustrate the point. The interviews were carried out by Mrs. William Gomberg.

> *Frankie:* He wants to be like the Lone Ranger[7] when he grows up, or like any cowboy. Cowboys are all good and their only occupation is to kill bad guys, ride horseback "real good" and fire a gun very well.

> *Robson:* I don't like the Indians, they are naughty, they go where they are not supposed to. . . . I like the Lone Ranger, he shoots some cowboys; some cowboys aren't good. [Why?] Cause they were bad; they were riding and they were dead, and then they were bleeding, and that means you are dead, and when you're dead that means you are bad and you then fall down. Death is bad; you bleed and bleeding is bad. . . . He would like to be big like Lone Ranger and shoot the bad people.

> *Netti:* Superman[7] didn't come, he was far away in Brazil where I was a baby. He's real. . . . He and Mighty Mouse,[7] they're real, Oh yes; he's not make-believe, I know. I got a picture of him and he loves me and he kisses me and he gives me things, like a sewing machine and beer and candy and toys. Oh yes, he came to my house and brought it to me, I saw him. No, not on TV. I see him on TV, but this was different; he came to my house and kissed me.

> *Roger:* I see Lone Ranger on TV sometimes. I like him and cowboys but they shoot people and then people have to go to the hospital. They are always mad at people cause they always shoot and they don't like each other and that's why they shoot. People shoot but they shouldn't do that, it's wrong to shoot one another. I don't like to watch anything else. I ask my mother all the time, why do they have to shoot one another and she tells me they get very mad. I don't know if they are good people or bad people. They must be bad people if they have to shoot one another, don't you think so? My mother thinks so too.

> *Michael* [He says of the program "Calling all cars"]: That's the police car calling. That means to come out and fight the bad guys. Police are good guys and they have to fight the bad people. [He seemed disgusted at my lack of knowledge, and threw his hands out, saying, "Don't you know nothing?"]

While in cultures characterized by unity of the social sphere (Fortes 1938) the play aspects of socialization tend to relate directly to the realities of future adult roles, in American society they become deeply enmeshed in mass-produced fantasies. The above interviews are responses by children who act out in their play the characters they mention in their interviews. Thus there enters into the children's play, not the make-believe or practice dimensions of a genuine adult world, but commercial distortions of the world based on *adult* fantasies. The point is that the children's play becomes saturated with their *own* fantasy versions of adult fantasies, thus "compounding a felony." The groundwork for this is laid by the discontinuity in education.

Since discontinuity, true exclusion of children from adult knowledge, creates conflict and distortion, one might think that the phenomenon is rare. Yet, it is rather common the world over. Possibly one of the most "popular" discontinuities in primitive education occurs in the realm of ceremonial, religion and magic, and such discontinuity is often broken at initiation. As we have noted above (I:28), it would appear that the function of this discontinuity and the abrupt breaking of it is to effect reorganization and reorientation of the personality. The following is an illustration from the life of one Hopi:

> I had a great surprise. They were not spirits, but human beings. I had recognized nearly every one of them and felt very unhappy because I had been told all my life that the Kachinas were gods. I was especially shocked and angry when I saw my uncles, fathers, and own clan brothers dancing as kachinas . . . [but] my fathers and uncles showed me ancestral masks and explained that long ago the kachinas had come regularly to Oraibi and danced in the plaza. They explained that since the people had become so wicked . . . the kachinas had stopped coming and sent their spirits to enter the masks on dance days . . . I though of the flogging and the initiation as a turning point in my life, and I felt ready at last to listen to my elders and live right. (Simmons 1942: 84-87)

We have one similar example from the Chagga:

> Before circumcision I was very much annoyed at being called *iseka* by those already circumcised and even by women. I was told that I would not be able to bear the pain, and that if I frowned or moved even my big toe even a little I would be beaten. A song would be composed about my cowardice, and my chances of being married spoiled. For these reasons I was very much afraid lest I should fail to stand the excruciating pains that make you a man. I had half a mind to shirk circumcision, but realized it was better to be mutilated than to be ridiculed and despised. At the time of the circumcision itself I was neither elated nor disappointed. My body felt as if benumbed, but presently I felt a pain the like of which I had not suffered before. At once a great joy welled up in me at having passed the test of pain without disgracing myself. This joy was increased by the congratulations of my relatives and their words of comfort and admiration. After my recovery I felt proud to be a man whom nobody dared to call "hobbledehoy." (Raum 1940: 310)

The phenomena of reorientation and reorganization accompanying the rupture of a discontinuity lead to the necessity for evaluating discontinuity in other than purely conflict terms. In view of the Hopi and Chagga evidence, it appears necessary to consider the possibility of a new dynamism's entering life through the burdens placed upon the personality by the need to overcome the shock of new knowledge.

VIII. What Limits the Quantity and Quality of Information a Child Receives from a Teacher?

This section is not concerned with the question "What makes men blind?"—which alone would require a book to answer. Rather, it is confined to the question "When a teacher has before him a child to whom he must communicate a definite body of information, what limits the quantity and quality of the information the child receives from him?"

Before taking up in detail the ten categories in this section, it might be interesting to ask, "Are there differences between American and nonliterate cultures with respect to any of those categories?" For example, is it possible to say that the methods used to teach a skill in some nonliterate culture, whether hunting, fishing, agriculture, dancing, or ceremonial, limit the proficiency with which that knowledge or skill is mastered (VIII:1)? If there are differences among Tikopia men in fishing skill, are these differences due to the way the various men were taught, or to differences in the men themselves? Firth (1936) raises this question, but, on the whole, information on the subject is lacking from nonliterate cultures. Information is lacking also for the categories:

> VIII: 7. Failure of teacher to correct pupil's mistakes
> 8. Failure of teacher to indicate whether the pupil's answers are right or wrong
> 9. Failure of teacher to respond to a question
> 10. General vagueness or fumbling of the teacher

None of the following considerations seems to affect the educational process in nonliterate cultures:

> VIII: 2. Available time
> 3. Quality of equipment
> 4. Distance from the object
> 5. Ignorance or error of teacher

That is, there seems to be no time pressure; equipment seems to be adequate; the object of instruction—the land, the bow, the fishnet—is always available; the teachers seem always to know their subject matter. On the other hand, there seems to be a great deal of hostile stereotyping (VIII:6): members of other villages may be witches or "constipated," as among the Pilagá; or, more commonly, members of other tribes are considered nonhuman, and their customs absurd.

In American culture, by contrast, a pupil is limited in what he may learn from his teacher by the fact that the teacher often rushes through the lessons, lacks adequate equipment, teaches about things that are often remote from him and from the pupil either in space or time or both, and teaches subjects in which he himself is weak in knowledge. When we realize that categories VIII:7-9 set still further limits on what children in American culture may learn, it becomes abundantly clear that it is more difficult for a child to learn in this culture than in nonliterate cultures.

The complexity of classroom experience in contemporary American culture is such that the quotations which follow will reveal several limiting factors to be operating at the same time. The first examples are taken from a sixth-grade elementary school class. The students are having an arithmetic lesson. The recorder was Amanda Chura.

> *Teacher:* Monitors, are you ready yet? They shake their heads, no. Two children go to the teacher's desk to talk to her.

> *Teacher:* Alright, girls, you have no time to waste. Now *I'm* waiting. Hurry!

Some of the children have been working problems on the board. Gloria drops her ruler, looks at AC, puts hand to mouth, looks guilty. . . .

1:16 P.M.

Teacher: Alright, monitors, collect the noonday problems. Alright, first class ready. Alright, let's take out our graphs that we worked on this morning. Alright, hurry up. You take too long on these problems. It should only take you about five minutes.

Teacher: Now let's take out the graphs that you drew. Now when we looked at our graphs before—what other words do you know that end in g-r-a-p-h? David?

David: Telegraph.

Teacher: Ray?

Ray: Phonograph.

Teacher: Richard?

Richard: Paragraph.

Teacher: Yes; and what about photograph? A photograph is a picture; it carries a message to our eyes. A telegraph carries a message.

The teacher's asking for words ending in -graph was accompanied by eager waving of hands by the children.

Teacher: Who would get a lot of use out of these graphs, Larry?

Larry: The business bureaus.

Teacher: That's right. The businessman could just look at a graph and he could read something from it.

The first thing to be noted here is the emphasis on shortage of time, and that it is not to be wasted. American children work almost constantly under the lash of time. The second point of interest is the teacher's ignorance. Words ending in "-graph" are given her by the students, and she suggests that the morpheme indicates "message." It is possible that the significance of the similarity among "graph," "photograph," and "telegraph" may have been grasped by the students along with the (erroneous!) idea that they all "mean" message. Where in his picture, however, would the wondering child fit "phonograph," and, especially, "paragraph"? The teacher avoids the problem by not responding to the waving hands of the children. Third, note her lack of concreteness about businessmen's use of graphs.

The lesson now turns to review of the problems of perimeters.

Teacher: We'll do a little reviewing of measuring by feet, inches and yards. That measure is called linear—it is along a line. What could you measure by feet and inches? Roy?

Roy: A swimming pool.

Teacher: A swimming pool? No, I don't think so. . . .

Teacher: I want you to make up six problems and work them: two with perimeter, two with square measure, and two with cubic measure. Right now we will make up a few examples.

1:45

David raises his hand practically right away.

Teacher: David?

David starts.

Teacher: Wait a minute, I can't hear you. You talk too low anyway. Now stand up nice and straight.

David: A farmer had a field 30 by 40 feet. He bought another of the same size. What are the dimensions of both together?

Teacher: Now you don't mean dimensions, do you? You already gave us that.

David: I mean perimeter.

Teacher: Alright, now repeat the problem.

David repeats.

Teacher: You'll have to tell if it's the right answer or not. I'm not in on this one.

(AC notes: The way she said it made it appear to me that she didn't understand the problem or else couldn't figure it out.)

David calls on Arthur and Arthur answers 280.

Teacher: Yes. Now let's have another one: don't make it too hard. Make it so we can all work it in our heads. Now make up a problem for square measure. Make it easy enough. Save the hard ones for your written problems.

Obviously there are three possible solutions to David's problem, depending on whether the fields are separate, contiguous on their long sides, or contiguous on their short sides, and the teacher was not able to solve it.

This was followed by another "hard" problem, and the teacher said, "Alright, we won't give the answer, but we'll tell how to work it right now." The teacher then became irritated and issued a flurry of commands. At 2:00 P.M. the observer recorded: "Teacher still sits there staring at them with that mean look." The sudden burst of irritation suggests that she was upset by the problems.

At this point it is useful to remark on some limiting factors that are not listed in the outline but are apparent in the above examples. It has been noted that the teacher introduced into the discussion of graphing a consideration of the meaning of the morpheme "graph." In so doing, she distracted the children from the immediate subject matter. We might call this an instance of irrelevant introduction of polyphasic learning (Henry 1955a). It might not have been so bad if the teacher had given an adequate explanation of the meaning of the morpheme, but, instead, she merely generated confusion about it. Thus, the irrelevance interfered with learning in two ways: it interrupted the learning of graphs, and was itself erroneous.

The teacher's command to David to stand up straight while he was reciting belongs in this same general category of irrelevant introduction of polyphasic learning. Of what importance to arithmetic is it that David stand up straight while he presents his problem?

A second limiting factor is listed in the outline as V:5, insecurity of teacher. In the above example, the teacher's insecurity further muddied the waters of knowledge.

We turn now to a classroom in which, according to the system used in some American cities, bright students are taught together with slow students who are a year ahead of the bright ones in grade. The lesson is on geography, the recorder is Ella Brown, the teacher is a man, and the students are a combination of the grades sixth-high and seventh-low. As in the example above, the children are very eager.

Teacher: Look at page 206. Where would you find Portugal?

Several children give the boundaries of Portugal and the countries that lie nearest it. All the children were talking at once.

Teacher: Now find Switzerland. Where is Switzerland, Essie?

Essie: Kind of north of Italy.

Teacher: Alright. Now where is Denmark?

A girl says, Sticking out into the North Sea.

Teacher: Genevieve Wells, What is Denmark, that Switzerland and Portugal are not?

Genevieve: A seaport.

Teacher: Oh, no! (*Disappointedly*) Lisbon is one of the largest seaports in the world.

Children answer. It's a peninsula.

Teacher: That's right. What is a peninsula? He calls on several children who do not give the right answer. Then he calls on Bob, Susan, Phillip. Melvin's hand is waving among others. Teacher calls on him.

Melvin: A peninsula is a piece of land surrounded on three sides by water.

Teacher (very enthusiastically): Yes, that's right; a peninsula! A peninsula is a piece of land surrounded on three sides by water. What do these three countries [Portugal, Switzerland, Denmark] have in common?

Linda and Melvin have their hands up.

Teacher: Linda.

Linda: They're small.

Teacher: Yes, they're all small. Now look at the picture on page 215. What are the women doing? The children look at the picture and a girl answers that they are drawing water.

Teacher: Yes. In many of these countries there is no plumbing. Why do you think they have no plumbing? Several hands are up. Teacher calls on Essie.

Essie: It's too expensive.

Teacher: Yes, it's too expensive.

Linda's hand is up. Teacher calls on her by name.

Linda: It's a backward country.

Teacher: Yes, it's a backward country.

The picture shows a number of women with earthenware vessels drawing water from a well that seems to be in a central place.

Let us discuss in order the points raised by this lesson. (1) The teacher, by failing to adequately correct Genevieve (VIII:7), permits her and the rest of the students to remain confused about the difference between a port and a country. (2) Considering the distance of these children from Europe (VIII:4) and their general provincialness, it is important to correct such a misconception, even though it might seem on the surface that the misconception is merely inadvertent. (3) Generation upon generation of American children have been enthusiastically taught by teachers that a peninsula is a body of land surrounded on three sides by water. One wonders: (a) what is the reason for the enthusiasm over *this* relatively unimportant fact, and (b) of what importance is it to know what a peninsula is? Emphasis on one relatively insignificant item such as this tends to make it stand out, and exercises a limiting effect on the learning of more important data. This plays a role in narrowing the perceptual field. (4) Since Portugal, Denmark, and Switzerland are grouped together as small, the child's conception of them becomes stereotypic (VIII:6), thus obscuring the great differences among them. This kind of teaching lays the groundwork for a stereotyped world divided into large (important, significant, prestigeful) countries, and small (insignificant) ones. (5) Protugal, Switzerland, and Denmark are grouped together as backward and lacking plumbing. Here we deal not only with stereotyping but also with ignorance on the part of the teacher (VIII:5). All these elements of a learning situation have profound influence on the child's conception of the rest of the world, even to influencing his later voting behavior and his attitude toward war and peace. Further, we must remember that this teacher probably thinks and believes as he is teaching the children to think and believe, and that *he* votes and has ideas on the "international situation" too!

These teaching failures, considered together, are related to the following features of American culture: (1) the vast size of the available body of knowledge; (2) the absence of the teacher's role performance of the specific knowledge he is required to impart; (3) the low status of teachers; (4) the remoteness of the consequences of teaching failure; (5) the orientation of the total system; (6) the obsolescence of knowledge.

1. In societies inundated with knowledge, like contemporary industrial societies, we encounter such enormous differences in knowledge among individuals that many may be unaware of even the existence of whole bodies of knowledge. This is absolutely different from nonliterate cultures, where, although some people may not know some of the things there are to know, everyone knows what knowledge exists. As knowledge increases in any *culture*, ignorance tends to increase in *individuals*, for these come to know less and less of the total available information. The quip that "a college professor is a person who knows less and less about more and more," applies to everyone in contemporary culture, and especially to school-teachers since they are expected to teach many subjects.

2. In section VII, on discontinuities, it was stated that knowledge drags role performance after it. It would follow that, in the *absence* of role performance, there is no knowledge: a man who has never taught would, ordinarily, not know how to teach (although he might know something about teaching). This same reasoning applies to teachers who have no role involvement in the *subject matters* they teach. That is, they cannot be said to really have knowledge of those subject matters. For example, anthropologists would not ordinarily tend to make mistakes about the geography of areas on which they specialize, for their role performance enforces knowledge of those areas; but elementary school teachers who have never been to Europe, or worked in a travel agency or an importing or exporting company, might have but the haziest notions of the geography of Europe. A drafts-man or a surveyor would be expected to be able to calculate a periphery rapidly and correctly, for his role performance requires this. But a teacher is role involved only in teaching; he knows about peripheries only at second hand, and therefore is not unlikely to make mistakes in calculating them. In stark contrast with contemporary industrial societies, teachers in all nonliterate cultures are role involved in what they teach: archery is taught to the children by accomplished hunters, agriculture by husbandmen, religion by men and women who practice what they preach (whether it be good or evil!), and so on.

3. Since most elementary school teachers teach the same limited number of subjects year in and year out, one might conjecture that they ought to know those subjects very well. But this cannot be expected unless they are given satisfying incentives in money or prestige. Since they are given neither incentive in American culture, teachers tend to stay at the lowest level of performance that is acceptable to their administrations.

4. In nonliterate cultures, the consequences of an adult's failure to properly teach culturally requisite skills would be immediately felt. For example, the boy who was inadequately taught to hunt would be an unsuccessful hunter, with the result that both he and his kin-group teacher would suffer hunger. In contemporary American culture, the involvement of the teacher with his students is more remote. There are probably teachers who do experience student failure in terms of concern about the student's life chances, but, for the most part, American culture does not encourage such concern, and it certainly does not make the teacher suffer so directly for want of it. A teacher's standing may depend in some degree on his pupils' achievements, but this does not imply personal involvement in his students' *welfare*, and the lack of deep involvement permits him to remain at a minimal level of efficiency. Firth's remarks on education in Tikopia (1936: 148) underscore the relationship between personal involvement and expertness in teaching, and also bring out a further fact, the importance to the teacher of his student's gratitude:

> The training of a boy . . . is often due to the interest of one of his mother's brothers in him. If this man is an expert in any branch of knowledge he will probably see to it that his nephew receives some of the results of his experience. If he is a noted canoe-voyager and fisherman he will pass on his store of

information in the finer points of his craft to the lad: especially will he show him the location of fishing-banks, a prized set of data not possessed by all fishermen. In dirges composed to the memory of mother's brothers reference is not infrequently made to this sort of assistance. A grandfather may take a great interest in a child's upbringing and may provide him with traditional lore, names of family ancestors and their history, tales of ancient fights and immigrations. . . . The transmission of details of family ritual and more esoteric information concerning the family religious life is essentially the role of the father, and not infrequently does the head of the house lament the fact of his own comparative ignorance due to his father's early death.

5. The orientation of the total educational system is an important factor at the root of teaching failure. For example, in the United States there is a sharp division between those who think that the primary function of a teacher is to facilitate a child's emotional adjustment, and those who think that the teacher's main function is to teach subject matter. In nonliterate societies, education does not face this problem. While it is obvious that this and similar dilemmas arise because man is groping toward a new adaptation, it is also clear that they are related to the complicated role involvement of the American teacher. That is, constantly teaching subject matters of which his knowledge is imperfect, he reaches, in his anguish, toward a subject matter in which he can imagine himself to have some broad competence. Alas, it is only too clear that he does not even have expertise in "adjustment" (Henry 1955b, 1957b)!

6. The dictionary definition of *obsolete* is "gone out of use." In this sense, almost no knowledge becomes obsolete in a literate culture with an interest in history: knowledge of alchemy and of the building of pyramids and battering rams still has a use in the history of science. Whether for historical or other reasons, it is difficult to dis-use knowledge in a culture with written records. Nevertheless, there is a sense in which knowledge does go out of use even in a literate culture: it becomes obsolescent if there is no role attached to it.

Since the next examples I give are derived from elementary school classes in ancient history, I shall discuss the obsolescence of knowledge, and its relation to social role, in the context of ancient and nearly forgotten things. Nowadays, there are still people who know the ancient art of throwing the discus and can teach it, but, since we no longer hold the polytheistic beliefs of the ancient world from which the art comes, there are no priestesses of Athena among us, and the knowledge of how to be a priestess to Athena is dead. What little remains of the knowledge associated with the roles of priestess and oracle is well known only to ancient historians, i.e., to persons who specialize in knowledge of archaic roles and the associated knowledge. Parenthetically, the fact that little of the technical knowledge that went along with these roles is available today testifies to the validity of the generalization that knowledge and role are indissolubly linked.

Let us now picture the sixth-grade teacher who is supposed to teach the history of ancient Greece. She suffers from all the five disabilities listed above, she has never been to Europe, and, above and beyond these, she is obliged to teach about a civilization most of the roles of which have disappeared. Let us look at excerpts from the record of the performance of such a teacher and her pupils. The observations were made by Amanda Chura:

> *Teacher:* We've been reading about this parade in Greece to honor Athena. Why did they honor her?
>   Pat says she gave wisdom.
> *Teacher:* What else?
>   Norma thinks she symbolized something.

Teacher: The Greeks had beliefs. What do we call them today?
Child: Myths.
Teacher: And these are read by children today. What Greek building have we read about? I should say temple. Someone says, Parthenon.
   The teacher now talks about carved stone with animals or figures and these are raised.
Teacher: What do we call this?
Child: Bal-relief.
Teacher: It looks like bas- but it's really bal-.

Teacher: The Oracle of Delphi represented Apollo. There was a woman there to answer questions, but Apollo was not a woman. Today people go to places where they make you believe that the dead speak. I don't know how real this oracle was.

Teacher: Let's look at the map. It is in the book. I see a lot of people haven't even bothered to turn the page. Come on now.
   Teacher names Olympia and other places.
Teacher: Start reading, Sharon.

   Darius is not paying a bit of attention, but is looking to the back of the room. Antoinette is talking to her neighbor.
   Teacher explains what is meant by foreign birth. If a male is not born in Greece but in a foreign country he is not eligible to compete in the Olympic games. . . . Somebody says that the Olympic Festival is like the Muny Opera (i.e., the St. Louis Municipal Summer Opera where musical comedies like *Oklahoma* and *Guys and Dolls* are performed).
Teacher: Well, yes, but just a little.

Teacher: What great difference was there between the purposes of Athena and Sparta, Pat?
Pat: Athens was a city of beauty and Sparta a city of war.
Teacher: I agree with the Athens part but not with Sparta. David?
David: Spartans were trained to be soldiers while Athenians were interested in their city.
Teacher: Yes, a good answer. (She repeats it.) We can go to college and take subjects just about art and music. Of course we have to take English and Language, but we can major in art. Why have the stories of the battles of Marathon and Thermopylae been told through the ages?
Child: Because they fought so bravely.
Teacher: Yes, because they fought so bravely. In our country we have a similar example in Remember the Alamo. [In 1836 a group of Texans, defending the fortress Alamo against Mexican troops, was destroyed. For many years the cry "Remember the Alamo" was the rallying cry of those Texans who fought against Mexico for independence.]

Since the teacher is dealing with a social system the roles of which have disappeared, she attempts to make the subject matter live by using bad analogies from contemporary roles: the Oracle at Delphi is likened to a vague "place where they make you believe that the dead speak," and the Olympic competition is compared by teacher and a student to a musical-comedy performance. Since all ancient Athenians and Spartans have disappeared, the teacher and students accept the empty cliché that, "Spartans were trained to be soldiers while Athenians were interested in their city." Thus the fact that the knowledge about ancient Greece has become obsolescent, in the sense intended here, leads teacher and students into ignorance. Further revealed in the excerpts is the guided recall (II:7) method of instruction, according to which students are required to remember separate "facts" but receive no integrated picture of ancient Hellenic life and thought. This, too, is a limitation on learning, and, in this connection, it is relevant to note the instances of inattention by students (Darius and Antoinette).

IX. What Forms of Conduct Control (Discipline) are Used?

In this section I distinguish between order and discipline. "Order" is defined here as a state in which a person is oriented toward social goals, while "discipline," in the sense intended here, refers to methods used to prevent disruptive behavior. An orderly person is essentially a thinking person highly motivated toward social goals; while, in the present context, a disciplined individual is one who is merely controlled in his outward conduct. Discipline *can* work in the service of order, and often does, but not always. For example, a child sitting quietly in his seat in class may detest the work. Thus he is outwardly disciplined but is, in the present definition, disorderly, for he is not oriented toward the social goal, i.e., the lesson. On the other hand, a child oriented toward social goals could not be undisciplined, because disruptive behavior is generally antithetical to social goals.

Order and discipline, or, rather, order versus discipline, is an ancient issue in Western culture. In the winter of 431 B.C., in the course of delivering the panegyric at a public funeral for war casualties, the Athenian Pericles compared the Lacedaemonians with the Athenians as follows:

> In education, again, we leave it to our opponents to cultivate manliness by a laborious training from their tender years upward, while we, with our undisciplined life, are as ready as they to face every reasonable danger. . . . The fact that we preserve a military spirit by a life of ease instead of deliberate hardship and by a natural rather than an artificial courage gives us a double advantage. We are not compelled to anticipate the rigors of war, yet we face them, when they come, as courageously as those who are in perpetual training. (Toynbee 1953: 39, quoting Thucydides)

This was the attitude of men who lived by laws "whose moral sanction is so strong that there is no need for them to be written" (Toynbee 1953: 39, quoting Thucydides).

Pericles' speech shows that the issue of order versus discipline was joined more than 2,000 years ago. It is still with us today. Something of this nature must have been in the minds of the Russian educators P. Yesipov and N. K. Goncharov, when they formulated the following (Counts and Lodge 1947: 94, 96, 97):

> An extremely important component part of moral education is the education of children in conscious discipline. Without discipline and habits of organization one cannot study, one cannot work. But it is not merely a question of ensuring the *discipline* of pupils during the school years. Before the teacher stands a much deeper task: the cultivation in children of a *state of discipline* as a high quality of communist morality and one of the most important traits of character. The development of this quality in children is linked with the task of preparing future citizens of the Soviet state who will act from a sense of public duty and will possess a feeling of responsibility before the socialist Motherland. . . .
>
> A state of discipline cannot bear merely an outer character. The qualities [of discipline] require an inner condition. Conscious discipline cannot rest on a foundation of fear. . . . It is important that our pupils desire and strive

to become disciplined, not because of external pressure but because of their own voluntary promptings. It is important that their own active disciplinary powers function and that they have an inner harmony with discipline and a desire to achieve it. Such discipline leads inevitably to self-discipline. . . .

The basic conditions for the cultivation of conscious and firm discipline in pupils are clearly outlined in a recent decree of the People's Commissariat of Education of the RSFSR: "The discipline of pupils is nurtured by the general practice and the whole content of the work of the school: skillful teaching of school subjects, strict regimen for the entire school life, unwavering observation by each pupil of the 'Rules for School Children,' firm organization of the children's collective, and rational use of measures of rewards and punishments. The leading role in this work belongs to the teacher."

In the thinking of Pericles and the Russian educators, it would appear, discipline is an ideal inner state, a moral principle, a trait of character. This is what is meant here by "order."

When we turn now to the more specific problems of education, we discover that the need to exercise conduct controls over the child during instruction in formal skills arise almost exclusively in literate cultures, and it is the difficulties arising in connection with this need that are the concern of the present section.

Since schoolchildren of all ages in the United States tend to be unruly, much of a teacher's energy goes into the effort to maintain conduct controls, for an undisciplined class cannot learn a subject matter, i.e., it is oriented away from the social goals by its disruptive behavior. Thus an undisciplined class falls naturally into disorder. The ability to maintain discipline in a classroom seems to consist of the following components: (1) the specific techniques available to the teacher for the purpose; (2) the attitudes of the teacher (V); (3) the characteristics of the students (covered in part in section IV); and (4) the teacher's manipulation of the instruction itself (much of this is included in section II, but some is found in section V also). To these we might add (5) the attitude of the culture toward knowledge; and (6) the nature of the cultural ideals. These, however, would affect order largely through the person of the teacher in interaction with the students.

In the extracts from observations of American classrooms we will see that the techniques employed to exert conduct control are rarely used with a moral implication, or with the implication by the teacher that some deeply felt social ideal is being violated. Rather, the reason the student is commanded, threatened, or reprimanded in connection with walking around, talking to his neighbor, or daydreaming, is simply because it interferes with work, or because it offends the teacher. From studying disciplinary mechanisms year after year in American classrooms, one derives the pervasive impression that discipline has become detached from a socially significant moral base.

In the outline, twenty techniques for maintaining discipline have been listed. A finer coding might discriminate further, and separate listing of all the idiosyncratic devices grouped under 19, "Special Strategems," would expand the list even more. The list as it stands, however, is adequate for the present purpose of illustrating techniques used for conduct control in one contemporary industrialized culture, the United States.

Not all American teachers use the same techniques, and even widely used techniques, like 8 ("command") and 5 ("reprimand"), are employed more frequently by some teachers than by others. Furthermore, teachers using 8 and 5 may use them in qualitatively different ways: some teachers may be sarcastic in their reprimands, and some may be gentler than others in issuing commands. Always it must be borne in mind that the image of a teacher as a disciplinarian is tempered by other things—especially by V ("What Is His Attitude?"). For example, a strict disciplinarian might also joke with his students and permit them to argue or joke with him. Thus, study of IX alone, and study of IX in association with V, IV ("What Is the Attitude of the Student?"), and II ("What Are the Teaching Methods?") suggest a great variety of discipline-maintaining patterns, each peculiar to different types of teachers, and to different types of students: first graders as compared with fourth graders, high school students as compared with elementary school students; incipient delinquents as compared with more conforming children, and so on.

Illustration of the categories in this section on discipline requires considerable fragmentation of the data, thus each category that is discussed will be listed according to the number it bears in the outline, and each illustration will be followed by the code letter of the observer and the year of the observation. Protocols have been selected only for the years 1957, 1958, and 1959.

IX:3. Sense of Property
The children in this fifth grade class are about to be the audience for another class which is going to show off the Easter bonnets they have made. The teacher says to her children: if we're going to be an audience we have to be very, very polite. Just admire them. (LaB. 4/12/57)

This observation also embodies IX:10 ("'We' Technique") and IX:15 ("Putting the Child on His Mettle").

Teacher: Wait a minute, Gertie; someone is very rude behind you—someone very nice too. (D. 4/11/57)

This observation also embodies IX:11 ("Instilling Guilt") and IX:12 ("Cessation of Activity").

The students are seventh and eighth graders. The teacher had to step out of the room for a moment and it became a bit noisy. When the teacher returned he said: in a calm, soft, conversational tone to the very still class, I am disappointed at some people's manners. I am talking to someone out here in the hall and you people are talking and mumbling and having fun when there is plenty of work to do. (Va. 4/24/59)

This observation also embodies IX:11 ("Instilling Guilt").

In this first grade class the children are having a reading lesson. The word *sailboat* has come up, some children have failed to identify it in the reader, others are eagerly waving their hands, and some in the front seats are leaning forward and shaking their hands for attention. The teacher, in an annoyed voice, says, How would you like it if I did that to you? (C. 5/11/59)

This observation also embodies IX:5:4 ("Impersonal Reprimand") and IX:11 ("Instilling Guilt").
It will be noted that, if any morality is at issue in these observations, it is the morality of decorum. Observation Va. 4/24/59 seems to imply that disorder both violates decorum and also interferes with work.

IX:4. Affectivity
The category "Affectivity" has been explored at length by Henry (1959). The essential point is that the teacher attempts to keep the children under control by making himself a love object to them, and awakening in them both a fear of loss of love should they do anything to offend him, and a sense of guilt when they have offended him. One example, taken from a reading lesson in Mrs. Thorndyke's third-grade class (the children are about 8-9 years old), will illustrate this point.

The observer is Henry. On this day, the children are asking each other questions about the story, instead of being asked questions by the teacher. There are 25 children in the class, but the group to be described is made up of the dozen or so best readers, who sit facing each other on two rows of chairs in the front of the room. At 10:27 A.M. Mrs. Thorndyke is standing behind one of the rows:

> She pats Alfred to restrain him and he shows a slight tendency to withdraw. There is a loud burst of noise. Mrs. Thorndyke's hand is on Alfred and he seems to wish to get out. Now her hand is on Arty, who makes no move. Teacher pats and strokes Matty who also makes no move to withdraw. Now Teacher is standing behind Arty, lightly passing here finger-tips over his neck. She goes back to Arty, puts a hand on Alfred to restrain him. He makes withdrawal signs. Alfred and Arty are now interlocking *their* hands in the air and Alfred is talking to Arty. 10:32 Teacher stops behind Otto to restrain him. Her hands are on his cheeks; his tongue goes in the direction of his right cheek and pushes it out as he closes his eyes. When Mrs. Thorndyke withdraws her hands, his eyes pop open as if he had suddenly awakened. Mary, who previously was holding onto Mrs. Thorndyke as the teacher stroked the child's arm, has now slumped in her seat. Teacher goes to her, puts her arms around her and pulls her back. Mary takes Teacher's hand. Alfred is talking and Mrs. Thorndyke pats and strokes him. He does not withdraw this time. Alfred is now talking to Arty and Teacher is stroking Alfred. Again he does not withdraw. Now Alfred caresses Otto and Arty caresses Alfred. 10:38 Malcolm asks questions now and all the children say his questions have been asked. Mrs. Thorndyke says, "My only objection to that question is that it can be answered by either yes or no." She strokes Matty. All this time the questions are being asked and there is great excitement among the children. Sherry asks questions and Teacher says, "We've gone over that." She strokes Matty and he does not resist. She touches Mary flutteringly with her finger tips.
>
> Now Mrs. Thorndyke terminates the lesson, and the papers with the questions are collected. Suddenly she becomes very grave and silent. She later told me that Mary had answered a snippity "no" to something Teacher had said. Now Mrs. Thorndyke says, *"My, I'm terribly disappointed."* There is absolute silence, and Mrs. Thorndyke says, "Matty, you're excused to go to your seat." She later told me it was because he's a general all-round talker and wouldn't quiet down. Matty goes to his seat looking very unhappy, his lips compressed. The room is silent now.
>
> Now Group 2, the poorer readers, occupies the seats deserted by Group 1. Teacher seems very tired now, and goes through the lesson mechanically. Her voice is weak and she leans against the blackboard. Time, approximately 10:50.

IX:9. Command Question or Request

"Let's sit down please." This example also illustrates IX:10 ("'We' Technique"), for the teacher uses the first person plural although the command-request is intended for the pupils only.

IX:12. Cessation of Activity

Teacher says, Bill and Joe, would you like to leave the room? She is silent for a long time. (McK. 4/9/57)

This example also embodies IX:14 ("Threat").

> There is an increase in noise and teacher says, Just a moment, Mary. Teacher looks briefly at two boys who are talking, and then back at Mary. Begin again, Mary. (Pe. 3/10/58)

This example also embodies IX:16 ("Nonverbal Signal"), for a look is a non-verbal signal.

> Teacher says, Wait, we can't hear because someone is talking. Several children had been talking but they quieted when she spoke. (Pa. 3/17/58)

> The children are noisy again. Teacher says, Wait a minute. I don't want any more noise or moving around in the room. We'll wait until everything is quiet. This is a school and everything is going to be quiet. (Ik. 4/18/58)

This example also embodies IX:5:4 ("Impersonal Reprimand"), IX:8 ("Command"), and IX:10 ("'We' Technique").

IX:13. Group Sanction
The following example is from a class of fourteen-year-old unruly delinquent and near-delinquent children:

> (The students are rehearsing a play. The teacher, Sa, is his own recorder. The record reads:) I notice Herb goofing[8] around while waiting for his cue, and I say Hold it, everyone, Herb is putting on his own little show. Let's take time out to watch him. Herb says, Aw, I'm not doin' nuttin'. Ben says, Yeah, he goofs around all the time until it's time to act and then who clams up[9] and acts stupid? Bob (the class bully) says, Let's get him. Bob goes to attack Herb, and the teacher says, Bob, we don't need that stuff, Herb will straighten up, won't you, Herb? Herb says, Aw, I ain't bothering nobody and I know my part. (Sa. 4/28/58)

This example also embodies IX:24 ("Encourages Peer-Group Control").

Some teachers have been observed to encourage peer-group control in a more systematic and open way. When a child does something of which such a teacher disapproves, he may call upon the other students to "try" the culprit and punish him (Henry 1957a, 1959).

IX:15. Putting the Child on His Mettle
To put a person "on his mettle" is to convey to him that the situation he faces is a challenge. When a teacher, in order to keep his pupils quiet, says, "You are on your honor" (Sa. 3/??58), he is simply telling them that their ability to maintain discipline is a challenge to their "honor."

IX:19. Special Stratagems
Some teachers develop purely idiosyncratic stratagems for maintaining discipline, but these stratagems are interesting because any one of them might some day become relatively institutionalized. For example, the use of affectivity, excessive politeness, and turning the maintenance of discipline over to the students, now characteristic of some suburban schoolteachers in the United States (Henry 1959), are relatively new developments in disciplinary techniques for grammar school children, but will probably become more generalized in American culture in the future.

IX:21. Using a Higher Power
Sometimes responsibility for discipline is shifted by the person who is disciplining the child to some higher authority, human or nonhuman. In the latter event, it might be a god or goblin who, it is claimed, will punish the child for misbehavior. In American schools, the higher power is generally the (very human) principal or vice-principal. Thus:

The teacher looks at the class disapprovingly, pauses, and says, Just a minute. This girl right here. Leave now. The best place for you is the principal's office. The girl leaves the room. (Pa. 3/17/58)

IX:22. Exclusion

"Exclusion" is most commonly effected by sending the misbehaving child out of the room temporarily. Of course, this is also IX:23 ("Punishment"). An occasional teacher develops an idiosyncratic form of exclusion, such as the following:

Teacher looks up and catches Katy over by her neighbor. Teacher says, Will you come over here please, and she points to the floor on the left side of her desk. Katy comes over and sits down on the floor next to the teacher's desk. (Se. 5/7/57)

Again, this is IX:23. But the incident is coded also as IX:22 because Katy is subjected to a kind of exclusion in being separated from the rest of the class.

The multiplicity of techniques used by teachers to maintain discipline in American schools is related to the severity of the disciplinary problem; the severity of the disciplinary problem is related to the fact that the children are not interested in being educated; the children are not interested in being educated because of the lack of unity between education and the rest of the social sphere. It may also be that the children lack interest because the social goals are uninspiring even when they can be clearly perceived—and who can clearly perceive them? In that case there would be little impetus to that kind of order of which Pericles spoke in his panegyric, and hence the children would fall into disorder, which is the root of the problem of discipline.

X: What Is the Relation between the Intent and the Results of Education?[10]

Implied in the teacher-pupil relationship is that the teacher teaches something, let us say science, and that the pupil learns it. However, the teacher not only gives instruction in a subject matter but also does many other things—like being sweet or sarcastic, telling the child to stand up straight and take his hands out of his pockets, or giving a pat on the back. Thus the child may not only "learn science," but at the same time also learn to hate the sarcastic teacher or to love the benign one, to loathe standing up straight, to enjoy being patted on the back, etc., etc. A general theory of unintended learning should take account of this variety of things the teacher does as he teaches. At the same time it should try to include also his intent or purpose. Since, as the teacher practices his art, he has an intention, all teaching activity is a logical product of these intentions and what the teacher actually does. This formulation seems general enough to cover all cases of social learning. We may note in passing that all intentions are capable of translation into action—though some of them may never be so translated.

It is rarely true that a teacher has only one intention. Nowadays, most American elementary school teachers seem to have a variety of them: they not only want to teach subject matter, but in addition they may want their students to be good citizens, to work hard, to live comfortably, to love their parents and the teacher, to be orderly, to have spiritual values, and so on. Accordingly, such teachers express this variety of intentions in a great variety of behaviors, which may or may not be logically related to their subject matter. We cannot predict the total consequences of this on a relatively responsive and plastic child. Even after the most careful observation and analysis of all of a teacher's actions and inferred intentions, much of what is learned by the pupil in the classroom remains, by and large, indeterminate. This fact need not, however, deter us from the attempt to study it. Of course, the more a teacher is trained to limit his intentions and his actions, the greater is the predictability of the consequences of his teaching.

To this point, we have been examining classroom learning with the teacher as the center of analytic focus. However, the pupils' potentialities for response to the teacher are central to analysis both of the relation between the intentions and actions of the teacher, on the one hand, and of what the student learns, on the other. For example, it is crucial to the understanding of a spelling competition that we be aware of the pupils' potentiality for response to a competitive situation, for, if the overwhelming majority of the children are not already competitive *children*, the spelling competition will fail. Again, we can comprehend a teacher's telling her pupils not to paint with dark colors because they indicate unhappiness, only if we assume that both teacher and students feel that unhappiness is somehow culturally unacceptable (Henry 1955a).

Such considerations enable us to draw the conclusion that *for the actions and intentions of the teacher there are, in all cultures, complementary responses and response tendencies in the pupils.* The complementary *response* can occur only if the teacher is able to mobilize the students' latent, culturally determined attitudes, but this he should be able to do because he is a product of the same culture as his students and should know intuitively their social character. The complementary *response* is therefore the response the teacher wants. Complementary *attitudes*, on the other hand, are latent, culturally standardized, tendencies to *give* the culturally acceptable response under the proper circumstances, e.g., a teacher's demand for the response.

Though complementarity exists when the pupil responds to the teacher as desired, e.g., he competes with his fellows when directed to do so as in a spelling competition, some children who *participate* actively might nevertheless *react* inwardly to the spelling competition *antithetically*, i.e., with anxiety and tendencies to withdraw. Thus, while it is probable that in the usual social learning situation most of the attitudes of the children would be complementary, some could be covertly antithetical. Many might be neither complementary nor antithetical, but, rather, "indeterminate."

As an approximate definition of the term "indeterminate" let us say that an indeterminate attitudinal response is one not readily predictable from knowledge of the structure of the learning situation alone. If we ask, "Not readily predictable by whom?" the answer is (*a*) by the organizer of the lesson being taught; and (*b*) by the person who hears only a formal account of the lesson without being present at it. Indeterminate and antithetical responses are covert metaresponses—they *go along with* the lesson, but are features that the teacher, perhaps, would rather not have there. To illustrate, there follows material on a game of "spelling baseball" in a fourth-grade class observed by Henry (1955a).

Children form a line along the back of the room. There is to be "spelling baseball," and they have lined up to be chosen. There is much noise, but teacher quiets them. Teacher has selected one boy and one girl and sent them to front of room to choose their sides. As the boy and girl pick children to form their teams, each child chosen takes a seat in orderly succession around the room. Apparently they know the game well. . . . Now Tom, who has not yet been chosen, tries to call attention to himself, in order to be chosen. Dick shifts his position more in direct line of vision of the choosers so that he may be chosen. Jane, Tom and Dick, and one girl whose name Observer does not know, are the last to be chosen. . . . Teacher now has to remind choosers that Dick and Jane have not been chosen. . . . Teacher gives out words for children to spell, and they write them on the board. (Each word is a "pitched ball," and each correctly spelled word is a "base hit." The children move from "base to base" as their teammates spell the words correctly.) With some of the words the teacher gives a little phrase: "Tongue—watch your tongue; don't let it say things that aren't kind; butcher—the butcher is a good friend to have; dozen—12 of many things—knee—get down on your knee; pocket—keep your hands out of your pocket, and anybody else's. No talking!" Teacher says, "Three outs," and children say, "Oh, oh!" . . . "Outs" seem to increase in frequency as each side gets near the children chosen last. . . . Children have great difficulty spelling August. As children make mistakes those in seats say, "No." Teacher says, "Man on third." As child at board stops and thinks, teacher says, "There's a time limit; you can't take too long, honey." At last, after many children fail on August, a child gets it right, and returns grinning with pleasure to her seat. . . . (Observer notes: Motivational level in this game seems terrific. They all seem to watch the board, know what's right or wrong, and seem quite keyed up. No lagging in moving from base to base.). . . . Child who is now writing Thursday stops to think after first letter, and children snicker. Stops after another letter. More snickers. Gets word wrong. . . . (Frequent signs of joy from the children when their side is right).

In the above, we may note the following as probable indeterminate responses: (1) anxiety and feelings of depreciation in the children chosen last by the captains; (2) feelings of self-depreciation and hostility in the students subject to snickers; and (3) anxieties aroused by the teacher's random phrases, "get down on your knee," and "keep your hands out of your pockets and anybody else's." None of these responses could have been foreseen from a simple description of the game.

The next example is from a fifth-grade arithmetic lesson (Henry 1957a: 123):

Boris had trouble reducing 12/16 to lowest terms, and could get only as far as 6/8. There was much excitement among the students who were watching him at the board. The teacher asked him quietly if that was as far as he could reduce it. She suggested he "think." There was much heaving up and down from the other children, all frantic to correct him. Boris looked pretty unhappy. The teacher was patient, quiet, ignoring the other students while concentrating with look and voice on Boris. . . . At last, when Boris is unable to solve the problem the teacher turns to the class and says, Well, who can tell Boris what the number is? There is forest of hands and the teacher calls on Peggy who says that 4 should be divided into both the numerator and denominator.

It is obvious that Boris' failure made it possible for Peggy to succeed, and, since the excited handwaving of the children indicates that they wanted to exploit Boris's predicament to succeed where he was failing, it appears that at least some of these children were learning to hope (covertly) for the failure of fellow students. Having been reinforced in this way during long years of schooling, the "I-hope-he-fails" attitude is common enough in the American character. It is an indeterminate, covert learning. If some teachers knew their students were learning to hope for the failure of fellow students they would be horrified—provided they believed it was happening, since they certainly had no *intention* of teaching children to feel this way.

Many children have Boris's experience frequently during their school years, and possibly acquire a variety of indeterminate learnings over the long run. For example, they might learn hostility toward all successful children, fear of facing an audience, and hostility toward teachers, especially females (since most elementary school teachers are females).

In addition to complementary, antithetical, and indeterminate responses there is still another *meta*response, which I have called *pseudo*-complementary (Henry 1955b). This is the response in which children, *without conviction*, give the teacher what they perceive she wants, and by so doing appear to be learning something they are not. In these circumstances, the lessons that are really learned are how to be docile—to give the teacher what she wants—and the importance of docility. This is not the same phenomenon as head-nodding in college, in rhythm to a professor's lecture, while inwardly denying the truth of everything he says. The latter is a feeble voice inwardly affirming autonomy, while *pseudo*-complementarity is real abandonment of it.

In sum, what a child learns (i.e., what responses are reinforced) is a result of the teacher's actions and intentions and of the child's own tendencies to respond. Out of the interplay between these grow complementary, *pseudo*-complementary, antithetical, and indeterminate responses on the part of the child. At any given time, any of the last three may be unintended by the teacher, and the only way for an observer to take account of them is by making an inventory of the response universe. Even then, the observer is still somewhat in the position of a man surveying space with a very small telescope: he can see some things and make shrewd guesses about others, but he also misses a great deal. However in the absence of observation or inventory of the classroom response universe, we might imagine that all responses were complementary—that nothing happens in a classroom except the children's answers to the teacher's questions. A theory of social and unintended learning must include antithetical, indeterminate, and *pseudo*-complementary responses, and must anticipate them methodologically by an inventory of the response universe.

XI. What Self-Conceptions Seem Reinforced?

A teacher cannot avoid contributing to a student's self-conception, for human beings are self-concept-forming animals whose self-conceptions are in process of formation at every stage of learning. Among factors contributing to the formation of the self-conception are:

II. How is the information communicated (teaching methods)?
   27a. Through ego-inflation
   27b. Through ego-deflation
IV. How does the person being educated participate? (What is his attitude?)
   11b. Ridiculing peers
   26a. Hostile to peers
   34. By carping criticism
   35. By praising work of peers
V. How does the educator participate? (What is his attitude?)
   13. Discouraging
   14. Encouraging
   15. Hostile, ridiculing, sarcastic, belittling
   18. Personalizing
   19. Depersonalizing
   23. Accepting of child's spontaneous expressions
   24. Rejecting of child's spontaneous expressions
   27. Acts and/or talks as if child's self-image is fragile
   28. Acts and/or talks as if child's self-image is irrelevant
   34. Praises and rewards realistically
   36. Critical (does not point out good things in student's work)
IX. What forms of discipline are used?

Of course, much of the conception of the self is formed during an early period of nurture within the family, but that early period is beyond the scope of this paper. Thus this section is confined to the question, "What are the results, for the conception of the self, of the behavior listed in sections II, IV, V, and IX?"

For anthropology, the importance of self-conceptions resides in the fact that they tend to be fairly uniform throughout each culture, and that social intercourse pivots on them. Thus the potlatch relationship between Kwakiutl chiefs is based on their recognition of each other's expansive self-conception (Benedict 1946); and supreme conformity to peer-group norms among American teenagers stems from their sense of personal inadequacy (Remmers and Radler 1957, especially tables on pp. 80–85). Our conclusion, similar to one derived in the preceding section, is that in all cultures there must be an institutionalized self-conception complementary to the cultural goals. This conclusion seems obvious enough, for it would certainly be disruptive if, in a culture like Hopi, where social life depends on severe subordination of individual drive to group goals, people learned a grandiose, individualized self-conception. A striking example of the relation between a poor self-conception and cultural goals is given by Mead (1939: pt. II) for Manus. After describing the free, generous, unfettered, and independent life of the male children, she points out that this must be abandoned, and the adolescent boy's spirit broken, at marriage, in order that he may take a position at the bottom of adult society and start to learn the workings of the economic system. Gradually, then, he will work his way up to economic strength. Mead says ([1939] pt. 2: 208–209):

> On all sides he must go humbly. He is poor, he has no home; *he is an ignoramous*. . . . He enters an era of social eclipse. He cannot raise his voice in a quarrel, he who as a small boy has told the old men in the village to hold their noise. Then he was a gay and privileged child, now he is the least and most despised of adults.
>
> All about him he sees two types of older men, those who have mastered the economic system, become independent of their financial backers, gone into the gift exchange for themselves, and those who have slumped and who are still dependent nonentities, tyrannised over by their younger brothers, forced to fish nightly to keep their families in food. Those who have succeeded have done so by hard dealing, close-fisted methods, stinginess, saving, ruthlessness. If he would be like them, he must give up the good-natured ways of his boyhood. . . . So the independence of his youth goes down before the shame of poverty. [Thus the young married men are] meek, abashed, sulky, skulking about the back doors of their rich relations' houses. [Italics supplied.]

Thus, in Mead's analysis, the debased self-conception provides the compensating dynamic of striving, so necessary for learning and succeeding in the Manus socioeconomic system.

On the other hand, the physical rigors and trials (see II:16b, 43:2) imposed on boys by many of the North American Indian tribes served to create a self-conception in which self-assurance and independence were conspicuous elements. Such self-conceptions were complementary to the daring and independence of action demanded by a rigorous life.

XII. How Long Does the Process of Formal Instruction Last?

It is very clear that one has to learn much more in American culture than in, say, Kaingáng culture (Henry 1941). Therefore, the time spent being educated must be greater in cultures with elaborate technologies and ideologies than in those with simple ones. Indeed, the period of education might have had to be prolonged indefinitely in highly elaborated cultures, where there is so much to learn. However, this problem has been solved in all the great civilizations by apportionment of different activities to different social groups. Correlatively, status rank has been assigned to the latter in terms of the former. Coinciding with this, there has been, of necessity, a proportionate relationship between social status and the time spent in getting educated: persons of higher status tend to spend more time being educated than persons of lower status, and persons who are mobile upward spend more time in educating themselves than those who are not mobile upward.

Interestingly enough, these generalizations seem to hold even at relatively primitive levels of culture where there is little differentiation into structural classes or castes. A boy in any primitive society has to learn adult male subsistence techniques, and he often has to learn ceremonial too. If he wants to become a shaman or priest, he has to learn the techniques and ideologies of that occupation. The point of stating such truisms here is that *time* is expended to achieve a *change of status* which is regularly, but not always, a *rise* in status. In other words, commonly, though not universally, the higher one wishes to be in social status, the more time one has to spend educating oneself. We have already referred above to Pettitt's analysis of the relation between education and the exercise of supernatural functions in primitive North America (1946: 108 et seq.). Here it is only necessary to underscore that his material shows (1) the frequent correspondence between status change, for example advancing in the priesthood or in a secret society, and the length of time spent in being educated, and (2) the direct proportion between time spent in learning about the supernatural and the *elaboration* of priestly and related function.

It seems likely that in all educational systems, literate as well as nonliterate, some assumptions must be made about *pace*. In Samoa nobody must learn too fast (Mead [1939] pt. I: 33, 35), while in Taleland rapid learning is admired (Fortes 1938: 13). The pace at which education is conducted is, of course, related to the cultural dictate about how much of a life-span should be given to education. But a great deal of further research is necessary in cultures other than our own on the matter of pace and its relation to total cultural configurations.

SUMMARY AND CONCLUSIONS: SOME ANCIENT AND ABIDING CHARACTERISTICS OF HUMAN EDUCATION*

1. Use of reward stimuli to learning: primarily praise, appreciation, and status elevation.

2. Use of pain stimuli to learning: ridicule, accusation, physical pain, physical confinement (restriction of movement).

3. Use of role occupant as role instructor (teaching of archery by archers, of agriculture by farmers, of warfare by warriors, of mathematics by practitioners of mathematics, of carpentry by carpenters, etc.) This has undergone radical change since the emergence of modern mass education.

4. In high civilizations: low status of teachers, unless they teach sacred matters.

5. In high civilizations: a correlation between (*a*) love of knowledge for its òwn sake, with (*b*) status of teachers, and with (*c*) the interest of students in learning.

6. Confinement of creativity to gifted individuals (creativity never a mass phenomenon).

7. Absence of the assumption of a natural impulse to learn. (This does not mean that children are not everywhere naturally investigative, but there is no evidence that children will not lose interest in learning when it requires work.)

8. Congruence of status change with education, coupled with definite marks of adult recognition of status change.

9. Unity of the social sphere, including education, in nonliterate cultures outside the stream of industrialization.

The main point deriving from this cross-cultural study of education is that *Homo sapiens* learned long ago that there is no such thing as "natural maturation" in a social sense, and that the central problem for human beings is the adaptation of each new generation to culture. This includes learning the techniques for survival each particular culture has found reliable.

*Commentary is not reprinted here.

It would appear that, on the whole, adult *Homo sapiens* has rarely taken it for granted that children could or would just naturally learn by spontaneous imitation. At the same time, the children of *Homo sapiens* have not assumed that they would just naturally grow into adulthood. Rather, children have always been aware that they have to validate their status as adults by learning adult techniques from older teachers. It follows that *Homo sapiens* has been born on a kind of status machine—a status escalator or a status treadmill, depending on the culture—from which there has rarely been any socially acceptable escape. Thus, throughout his historic course, *Homo sapiens* has been a "status seeker," and the pathway he has had to follow, by compulsion, has been education. Furthermore, he has always had to rely on those superior to him in knowledge and social status to enable him to raise his own status. On the other hand, it is not clear that adults have always assumed that children would naturally wish to be adult. Over and over again, the data shows that children have had to be urged up the status ladder by rewards, punishments, and other even more complex devices. From the point of view of the adults this is absolutely necessary, for otherwise the children would remain dependent and disgracefully deviant in other ways. From the standpoint of the child, he must climb the status ladder or suffer the consequences of dependence and deviance. It is likely, meanwhile, that this compulsion and the inner conflict involved leave a lasting impression on the child, so that as a mature adult these memories can provide a fertile soil for social change, for if conditions arise that seem to provide an opportunity to eliminate the sources of the pains of childhood growth, adults may be happy to take advantage of the situation and push for change, often, perhaps, not knowing the real sources of their readiness.

Also deriving from this study is an insight into the enormous effort that *Homo sapiens* has put into narrowing the perceptual sphere of the individual. To this end he has employed ridicule, praise, torture, admonition, etc., etc., with all the ingenuity his great brain has been able to devise. Thus, though *Homo sapiens* has been also *Homo inquisitor*—man the curious, the inquirer—he has always worried that his careful arrangement of cultural patterns would be destroyed if he *learned without limit*.

Finally, protecting himself from *inundation by stimuli, Homo sapiens* has erected the categories of his languages and his culture patterns. Of course, in the long run these intellectual walls crumble because of the inherently variable mental constitution of *Homo sapines*, because many devices he uses for narrowing the perceptual sphere are unrewarding and self-defeating, because of the polyphasic nature of human learning, and because of the indeterminate factors that are always present in human learning. Thus, the dialectic of man's effort to understand the universe has always decreed that he should be alternately pulled forward by what has made him *Homo inquisitor* and held back by the fear that if he knew too much he would destroy himself, i.e., his culture. So it is that though language has been an instrument with which man might cleave open the universe and peer within, it has also been an iron matrix that bound his brain to ancient modes of thought. And thus it is that though man has poured what he knows into his culture patterns, they have also frozen round him and held him fast.

NOTES

1. In the United States the first eight years of school are called elementary school, grammar school, or the primary grades. They are for children from six to fourteen years of age. The next four years are called high or secondary school. After completion of high school the individual is ready for college.
2. The educational theory according to which all curricula should be carefully planned so that a student enters on each new subject matter and each advance in an old subject matter in terms of graduated steps that prepare him ("ready" him) for the change.

3. To *snicker* is to laugh in a sly, partly stiffled manner.
4. Most art lessons in American public schools are not lessons in art, for the reason that most teachers do not know how to teach art. The curriculum may produce art *periods*, during which the children paint or draw or cut out so-called "abstractions," but the periods are usually not art *lessons*. The art periods in many school systems are merely minutes during which the children engage in some manual exercise prescribed by a routinized municipal curriculum. During such moments, the children may make valentines, puppets, tiny woven mats to hold pots, etc., according to prescribed rules. Many teachers see the art period merely as a relaxation for the children, and only two of the regular teachers in our sample of several dozen seemed even to try to give any instruction in art at all.
5. Actually V:4a and 4b are very complex. H. H. Anderson (Anderson and Brewer 1945, 1946; Anderson, Brewer, and Reed 1946) has made the fundamental contribution to the elucidation of this problem.
6. Alpha will vary with every bit of knowledge, for each bit has different social-structure relevance. For example, alpha will have one *value* for a new lipstick color and a different one for a new theory of interpersonal relations. Thus the value of alpha is always purely empirical.
7. The Lone Ranger, Superman, and Mighty Mouse are characters in television shows. The Lone Ranger appears in cowboy pictures. He wears a mask, rides a wonderful horse called "Silver," is accompanied by a faithful Indian companion, and always does good, defeating the "bad guys," the evil men. Superman can fly through the air, hold mountains in the palm of his hand, and withstand most lethal weapons. In everyday life he is a newspaper reporter, Clark Kent, but when he dons his magic clothing he becomes Superman. Mighty Mouse is a Superman-like mouse.
8. To *goof* is to fail or to do nothing. "I goofed off" means "I did nothing when I was supposed to be busy." "I goofed" means "I failed" or "I made a mistake."
9. To *clam up* means to become silent, i.e., to shut tight like a clam.
10. Previous publications on this problem are: Henry 1955a, 1955b, 1957a, 1957b, Rabin 1959; Spindler 1959.

BIBLIOGRAPHY

American Journal of Sociology 48 (1943): entire issue.

Ammar, H. *Growing Up in an Egyptian Village*. London: Routledge & Kegan Paul, 1954.

Anderson, H. H., and Brewer, H. M. *Studies of Teachers' Classroom Personalities*. Vol. 1. Stanford: Stanford University Press, 1945.

Anderson, H. H., and Brewer, J. *Studies of Teachers' Classroom Personalities*. Vol. 2. Stanford: Stanford University Press, 1946.

Anderson, H. H., Brewer, J., and Reed, M. F. *Studies of Teachers' Classroom Personalities*. Vol. 3. Stanford: Stanford University Press, 1946.

Aristotle. *The Works of Aristotle Translated into English*. Vol. 9. Oxford: Clarendon Press, 1925.

Bayne-Powell, R. *The English Child in the Eighteenth Century*. New York: E. P. Dutton, 1939.

Belo, J. *Bali: Rangda and Barong*. New York: J. J. Augustin, 1949.

Belo, J. "Balinese Children's Drawings." In *Childhood in Contemporary Cultures*, pp. 52-69. Chicago: University of Chicago Press, 1954.

Benedict, R. "Continuities and Discontinuities in Cultural Conditioning." *Psychiatry* (1938): 161-67.

Benedict, R. *Patterns of Culture*. New York: Pelican Books, 1946.

Bertalanffy, L. von "The Theory of Open Systems in Physics and Biology." *Science* 111 (1950): 23.

Bruford, W. H. *Germany in the Eighteenth Century*. Cambridge: Cambridge University Press, 1935.

Calhoun, A. W. *A Social History of the American Family*. New York: Barnes & Noble, 1945.

Chaudhuri, N. C. *The Autobiography of an Unknown Indian*. New York: Macmillan, 1951.

Chiang, Y. *A Chinese Childhood*. New York: John Day, 1952.

Childs, H. L. *The Nazi Primer*. New York: Harper & Bros, 1938.

Counts, G., and Lodge, N. P. *I Want to Be Like Stalin*. New York: John Day, 1947.

Dennis, W. *The Hopi Child*. New York: Appleton-Century, 1940.

Durkheim, E. *Elementary Forms of the Religious Life*. Glencoe, Ill.: Free Press, 1947.

Eggan, D. "Instruction and Affect in Hopi Cultural Continuity." *Southwestern Journal of Anthropology* 12 (1956): 358–65.

Du Bois, C. *The People of Alor*. Minneapolis: University of Minnesota Press, 1944.

Elwin, V. *The Baiga*. London: John Murray, 1939.

Firth, R. *We, the Tikopia*. New York: American Book Co., 1936.

Fortes, M. *Social and Psychological Aspects of Education in Taleland*. Oxford: Oxford University Press, 1938.

Freud, S. *A General Introduction to Psychoanalysis*. New York: Perma Books, 1955.

Fuchs, S. *The Children of Hari*. Vienna: Verlag Herold, 1950.

Gorer, G. *Himalayan Village*. London: Michael Joseph, 1938.

Gray, W. S., Monroe, M., Artley, A. S., and Arbuthnot, M. H. *More Streets and Roads*. Chicago: Scott, Foresman, 1956.

Hart, C. W. M. "Contrasts between Prepubertal and Postpubertal Education." In *Education and Anthropology*, G. Spindler, pp. 127–45. Stanford: Stanford University Press, 1955.

Henry, J. *Jungle People*. New York: J. J. Augustin, 1941.

Henry, J., and Boggs, J. W. "Child Rearing Culture, and the Natural World. *Psychiatry* 15 (1952): 261–71.

Henry, J. "Culture, Education, and Communications Theory." In *Education and Anthropology*, edited by G. Spindler, pp. 188–207. Stanford: Stanford University Press, 1955a.

Henry, J. "Docility, or Giving Teacher What She Wants." *Journal of Social Issues* 11 (1955b): 33–41.

Henry, J. "Attitude Organization in Elementary School Classrooms." *American Journal of Orthopsychiatry* 27 (1957a): 117–33.

Henry, J. "Working Paper on Creativity." *Harvard Education Review* 27 (1957b): 148–55.

Henry, J. "The Personal Community and Its Invariant Properties." *American Anthropologist* 60 (1958): 827–31.

Henry, J. "The Problem of Spontaneity, Initiative and Creativity in Suburban Classrooms." *American Journal of Orthopsychiatry* 29 (1959): 266–79.

Hollingshead, A. B. *Elmtown's Youth*. New York: John Wiley, 1949.

Holmberg, A. R. *Nomads of the Long Bow*. Smithsonian Institution, Institute of Social Anthropology, Publication No. 10. Washington, D.C.: Government Printing Office, 1950.

Hutton, J. H. *Caste in India*. Cambridge: Cambridge University Press, 1946.

Ilin, M. *New Russia's Primer*. Boston and New York: Houghton Mifflin, 1931.

Kahl, J. *The American Class Structure*. New York: Rinehart, 1957.

Kluckhohn, F. "Dominant and Variant Cultural Value Orientations." *Social Welfare Forum* (1951): 97–113.

Leighton, D., and Kluckhohn, C. *Children of the People*. Cambridge: Harvard University Press, 1948.

Leonard, O., and Loomis, G. P. *Culture of a Contemporary Rural Community: El Cerrito, New Mexico*. Department of Agriculture, Bureau of Agricultural Economics Rural Life Studies No. 1. Washington, D.C.: Government Printing Office, 1941.

Macgregor, G. *Warriors Without Weapons*. Chicago: University of Chicago Press, 1946.

Malinowski, B. "The Pan-African Problem of Culture Contact." *American Journal of Sociology* 48 (1943): 649–65.

Matthay, T. *The Act of Touch*. New York: Longmans, Green, 1903.

Mead, M. *Coming of Age in Samoa*. New York: Mentor Books, 1928.

Mead, M. *From the South Seas*. New York: William Morrow, 1939.

Mead, M. "Our Educational Emphasis in Primitive Perspective." *American Journal of Sociology* 48 (1943): 633–39.

Mead, M., and Bateson, G. *Balinese Character*. New York: Academy of Sciences, 1942.

Mead, M., and Wolfenstein, M. *Childhood in Contemporary Cultures*. Chicago: University of Chicago Press, 1954.

Miller, N., and Dollard, J. *Social Learning and Imitation*. New Haven: Yale University Press, 1941.

Pavlov, I. P. *Lectures on Conditioned Reflexes.* New York: International Publishers, 1928.

Pettitt, G. A. *Primitive Education in North America.* Berkeley: University of California Press, 1946.

Pirenne, H. *Economic and Social History of Medieval Europe.* New York: Harcourt Brace, 1937.

Rabin, B. "Teacher Use of Directive Language." *Educational Leadership* 17 (1959): 31–34.

Radcliffe-Brown, A. R. *The Andaman Islanders.* Glencoe, Ill.: Free Press, 1948.

Raum, O. F. *Chagga Childhood.* Oxford: Oxford University Press, 1940.

Remmers, H. H., and Radler, D. H. *The American Teenager.* Indianapolis and New York: Bobbs-Merrill, 1957.

Savery, C. *Luck and Pluck.* Boston: D. C. Heath, 1942.

Simmons, L. W. *Sun Chief: The Autobiography of a Hopi Indian.* New Haven: Yale University Press, 1942.

Simpson, G. G. *The Meaning of Evolution.* New York: Mentor Books, 1951.

Social Welfare Forum. *Social Welfare Forum.* New York: Columbia University Press, 1951.

Spindler, G., ed. *Education and Anthropology.* Stanford: Stanford University Press, 1955.

Spindler, G. *The Transmission of American Culture.* Cambridge: Harvard University Press, 1959.

Spiro, M. *Children of the Kibbutz.* Cambridge: Harvard University Press, 1958.

Sunley, R. "Early Nineteenth-Century American Literature on Child Hearing." In *Childhood in Contemporary Cultures,* pp. 150–67. Chicago: University of Chicago Press, 1954.

Thompson, E. T. "Comparative Education in Colonial Areas, with Special Reference to Plantation and Mission Frontiers." *American Journal of Sociology* 48 (1943): 710–21.

Tinbergen, N. *The study of Instinct.* Oxford: Clarendon Press, 1951.

Toynbee, A. J. *Greek Civilization and Character.* New York: Mentor Books, 1953.

Warner, W. L. *A Black Civilization.* New York: Harpers, 1937.

Warner, W. L., Havighurst, R. J., and Loeb, M. R. *Who Shall Be Educated?* New York: Harpers, 1937.

Watkins, M. H. "The West African 'Bush' school." *American Journal of Sociology* 48 (1943): 666–75.

Whiting, J. *Becoming a Kwoma.* New Haven: Yale University Press, 1941.

Williams, S. W. *The Middle Kingdom.* Vol. 1, 3rd ed. New York: John Wiley, 1849.

Yang, M. C. *A Chinese Village.* New York: Columbia University Press, 1945.

Zborowski, M., and Herzog, E. *Life Is with People.* New York: International Universities Press, 1952.

10 / The Socialization of Juveniles in Primate and Foraging Societies: Implications for Contemporary Education

John D. Herzog

Five years ago, at the meeting CAE members now refer to as the "Miami Conference," Sherwood L. Washburn presented what was (for me) a very frustrating paper in which he attempted to connect recent thinking in primatology with the somewhat "applied" concerns of the anthropologists and educationists there assembled. (The essay ultimately appeared in the Wax et al. volume [1971] that includes most of the papers of the Conference.) The paper was frustrating mostly because of what Washburn did *not* say. Confronted with a friendly yet sophisticated audience, all of whom were expressly interested in education, he restricted his extrapolations about modern man to one brief remark: "Studies of nonhuman primates suggest that it is the preschool years that are most important educationally, that the process of education should be fun, and that adult life should be understandable to the child" (1971, p. 96).

Since 1968, convinced that there was more than this to learn from socialization studies in primatology and ethology of possible application to modern education, I have read, listened, and talked in a kind of haphazard but continuous effort to inform myself and to arrive at more detailed yet tentative generalizations than Washburn cared to utter at that time. In the intervening years also, the study of hunters and gatherers gained momentum and theoretical recognition, and I broadened my focus to include this area. I want to make clear that I am not a primatologist or ethnographer of foraging peoples. I am a psychological and educational anthropologist with field experience in Kenya, Barbados, and the United States, and with a career-long commitment to the analysis of education from the perspectives of anthropology.

Last winter, when Elizabeth Eddy asked me to participate in this symposium, I resolved to be a little foolhardy and to use the opportunity to put together what I thought I had learned about childhood among the monkeys, the apes, and foraging man, and also to try out some speculations about the implications of this knowledge for the understanding and reform of contemporary man's strategies for dealing with his children and adolescents. I hope this paper is an initial contribution to the building of a model of learning and development in humans that takes into full account what we know of "man-the-primate" and of the child-rearing practices he used during the period of his foraging adaptation, which he followed during 99 percent of his existence on earth.

My present interest is restricted to generalizations that can be made about the life of *juveniles* in foraging and primate societies; in other words, to the regimens of immature individuals who have begun the process of independent exploration of their physical and social worlds. Concerning mother-infant interactions and the mother-infant bond, several excellent reviews have been written (Blurton-Jones 1972, Bowlby 1969, Rheingold 1963) on primates and on humans in technological society. The study of infancy and maternal behavior in foraging societies has only recently begun (Konner 1972).

To my great relief, Washburn recently published a second paper, "Primate Field Studies and Social Science" (Nader and Maretzki 1973), in which he states directly certain ideas about education that are very close to my own conclusions but which, coming from Washburn, should be more palatable to those who prefer their primatology or extrapolations therefrom from a primatologist. Let me then quote the heart of Washburn's more recent comments on education:

> A view of traditional European educational practices from the vantage point of the primatologist suggests that the school system is based on a series of traditional mistakes. . . . To the student of monkey behavior, schools seem grounded in ignorance of the kind of being they are trying to teach. The view of the human beings as a particular kind of primate makes the schools seem strange and leads to the conclusion that human customs are not necessarily efficient, necessary, or useful in the way that they are supposed to be. Educational institutions cannot be designed effectively without regard for the biology of human beings. . . . Through a profound misunderstanding of the nature of primate biology, the schools reduce the most intelligent primate to a bored and alienated creature. (1973, p. 131)

These are strong words, derived (it is important to note) not from the fulminations of radical school reformers, but from field studies of apes and men. They are based on three straightforward principles or assumptions:

1. As the result of the process of adaptation, the members of a species have special capabilities to learn—early, quickly, and easily—those behaviors which have been critical for the survival of their species during its evolution.

2. Modern man, although considerably more "open" or "plastic" than other animals, most efficiently learns behaviors earlier important to his survivals as a foraging animal according to timetables and under conditions of acquisition specifically calibrated for *Homo sapiens*.

3. Man's peculiar learning characteristics evolved during a foraging mode of subsistence in which all men lived until less than 10,000 years ago; consequently, we can learn a great deal about the parameters of learning for modern children and youth by observing juveniles in hunting and gathering societies, as well as in the societies of lower primates.

At this point, from my incomplete review of the literature, I want to propose seven generalizations about the learning and development of juveniles in primate and foraging societies that seem to me to have validity for young *Homo sapiens* in technological society as well. I offer them here unsupported by authenticating empirical data, but believe that each will stand up to systematic interspecies and cross-cultural analysis. I also note that none is original with me, although the compilation into a list is. I contend that the seven generalizations are a partial description of maximally efficient learning circumstances for modern children and adolescents, although this opinion is contrary to most current educational practices and is unsupported by objective studies.

First, numerous studies demonstrate the enormous strategic significance of *early experience* for the course of later development. Such effects are more clearly established for nonhuman primates (e.g., Harlow 1962) than for humans (e.g., Bloom 1964; as mentioned earlier, the study of infants in foraging societies has scarcely begun). Strictly speaking, the most influential periods of "early experience" occur prior to the juvenile years, but even after the symbiotic mother-infant relationship has loosened, the rule of "the earlier the impact, the more profound the effect" seems to hold true.

Second, studies of primates especially (e.g., Washburn and Hamburg 1965) underscore the *critical function of play* as perhaps the major channel through which juveniles acquire information about their physical environment, familiarize themselves with the social structure and conventions of their group, and test and improve their motor skills. It is conceptually difficult for most modern persons to take children's play seriously, but ethologists and ethnographers agree that the young of all primate species are highly motivated to play, invest enormous amounts of energies in it, and grow up socially or physically retarded if deprived of opportunities to engage in it. The children of most hunting and gathering groups typically have few subsistence responsibilities, and thus spend most of their time in rough-and-tumble and imitative activities, in addition to watching the affairs of adults. By means of such enterprises, they appear to acquire adequate understanding of the behaviors expected of them and of others in their culture.

Third, in the societies of both foraging humans and of other primates, the *social group and the geographic niche it occupies* are the juvenile's actual learning environment (cf. Washburn and Hamburg 1965, p. 613). He may investigate virtually all sectors and crannies; he is allowed to observe or participate in all, or almost all, of the activities of the adults in his group. It is easy to underestimate the richness of opportunities for learning in, for example, the young Bushman's social and physical environment. The dialect group of 500 or more members, not the camp of 50 or

100, comprises for him a fluid social world certainly no less variegated than the social "surround" of the average suburban child in our own society, and the physical stimuli contained in several hundred square miles of veldt are not prima facie inferior to those present in the typical bedroom community backyard. There is a direct connection, I believe, between the "openness" to children of the societies we are examining and the effectiveness of play as a vehicle of socialization. Without the accessibility enjoyed by the young, their play would become rootless and unbeguiling to them and to the outside observer.

Fourth, the really influential socializers in primate and foraging societies after infancy are the juvenile's *peers and slightly older playmates* (e.g., Mason 1965, p. 540). In interaction with other children, not with adults, the youngster develops his physical abilities, acquires facility with the signals or language of his group, and explores the physical environment. Slightly older playmates rarely act as caretakers or tutors; more often, they serve as models and exemplars of competent behavior which the younger child can easily and realistically emulate.

Fifth, the juvenile period of *freedom from responsibility* and of the need for self-support is unusually long in man (16 years), chimpanzees (8 years), and presumably other apes (Washburn 1973, p. 131), compared to other animals. During these years of maturation, juveniles spend their time in the literally "serious business" of play. Prolongation of the juvenile period creates those conditions in which learning from peers and near-peers becomes a major vehicle of socialization, for even in a small band the juvenile almost inevitably participates in a play group composed of other juveniles of greatly differing ages.

Sixth, much learning in primates occurs rapidly, in an all-at-once form, as the result of fortuitous or arranged *intense emotional experiences*. "Fears in particular must be quickly learned, if the animals are to survive," Washburn points out (1973, p. 128). A young creature must learn speedily which shapes in the night are dangerous or he may never be privileged to learn anything else. Similarly, brief but tension-filled skirmishes with age mates may communicate important information about relative positions in the forthcoming dominance hierarchy. Man is especially able to stimulate and focus emotions in ceremonies such as initiation rites, thus rendering participants maximally receptive to messages about their culture incorporated in the rituals.

Finally, in both foraging and subhuman primate societies there is *relative little teaching* (i.e., direct and deliberate tuition) of the younger members by mature individuals. This circumstance is probably the corollary of the preceding six characteristics, but it deserves emphasis considering how "natural" the notion of overt instruction appears to us. Even hunters and gatherers with plenty of time left over from the subsistence quest (such as Bushmen and Northwest Coast Indians) seldom sit their young down to give them lessons. Schools, and even systematic instruction of children by their parents, are devices of humans living in more recently invented subsistence systems.

Quite clearly, the lives of juveniles in foraging and primate societies contrast dramatically with conditions of existence for children and youth in the technological world. With us, the "preschool years" up to age five or six are generally considered to be inconsequential and uninteresting, as implied in the term we use to refer to them. "Play" is conceived as the opposite of "work" or meaningful activity, and few parents or schools count their children's playful involvements as significant socialization experiences. All children and almost all teen-agers are systematically discouraged and prevented from exploring the settings and activities of the adult world. Schools and the other institutionalized settings of childhood are among the most successful agencies of segregation anywhere devised by man. Within schools and other institutions established for juveniles, the inmates are carefully stratified by age, and most forms of collaboration in learning among them are prohibited as "cheating." Further, many parents are alarmed by and actively suppress mixed-age play groups. Our adolescents experience a period of dependency and formal lack of responsibility at least 25 percent longer than that in foraging societies, yet are simultaneously deprived of contact with the adult world and thus of devising related "play" activities that could enliven and enrich these extra years. We eschew emotion-arousing experiences for our young, providing instead controlled, repetitive days inside drab classrooms or equally "safe" suburban backyards. And in partial consequence of the foregoing, we resort to *teaching* as the preferred mode of intervention into the lives of our children and youth. The contrasts could not be more extreme!

The critical tone of the preceding should not be accepted too readily. Schools and the basic norms of education will not be changed by a sneer. Indeed, it is by no means certain that our system of education is as perverse as I have implied. Many educationists and academicians—even anthropologists!—classify schools among the most precious adornments of Western civilization. Sociologists consider schools to be essential boot camps for prospective citizens of a technological society characterized by extreme specialization and routinization of occupational roles (e.g., Dreeben 1968). Michael Cole, my colleague in this symposium, and Sylvia Scribner very recently summarized evidence indicating that schooled children become competent in the manipulation of symbol systems useful in solving problems "out of context," whereas unschooled children do not (Scribner and Cole 1973).

Yet important questions remain. *Why* have we departed so thoroughly from the basic socialization procedures of our not-so-remote ancestors? For how much longer are we likely to need to employ techniques apparently foreign to the propensities of the species? Is it possible to conceive of a system of education that conforms to the model of human learning preliminarily sketched in this paper, but that also develops in children the powers of reasoning and abstract thinking toward which the present system so clumsily strives? Let me close with a few speculations on these questions.

Schools as we know them are institutions alien to the "normal" ways of learning of the human juvenile, yet they have proliferated like Triffids across the industrialized world. The work of Aries and his associates (1962) notwithstanding, social and cultural historians have not yet taken up the challenge of explaining why this expansion occurred, or of showing why a medieval vocational training program for priests and scribes became an invariant feature of industrial society. Why was the incarceration of children and the emasculation of adolescents such a necessary proceeding, and why do we consider it so inevitable even today? I want to suggest two pieces of a possible answer.

First, industrial society as it took shape in the eighteenth and nineteenth centuries was a dangerous place in a double sense. It was dangerous for children to wander about in exploring and observing; and children themselves were threats to the smooth functioning and physical facilities of both industry and increasingly complex and cluttered homes. Children and teen-agers are still dangerous in this second sense today, as I expect we shall rediscover traumatically this winter if the fuel shortage forces schools to close. In short, the technological mode requires relatively cheap and safe places in which to warehouse juveniles. Until recently, schools have discharged this function rather well.

Second, full participation in industrial life requires the mastery of certain cognitive skills such as reading, writing, and calculating, regardless of what the earliest capitalists thought, and the acquisition of normally rare behavior traits such as punctuality, docility, and reliability, which the first captains early recognized (cf. Katz 1968). In a society in which few persons were literate and only a similar number possessed the personal attributes required in the new factories and offices, a vigorous social action program was needed. Expansion of primary education proved for some time to be that sort of program. (That schools might also disseminate habits of mind useful in more general kinds of problem solving was not noticed until much later.) Thus, for two or three hundred years in the West, and more recently in the "developing" countries of the world, schools functioned to transform people who came to them with minds and attitudes unsuited for life in technological society. We must now ask ourselves—and thousands of middle-class adolescents are already pressing the point—whether the continuing effort at transformation is any longer a vital social necessity.

Today, in the vast middle-class reaches of this affluent country and in much of Europe as well, many (but not all) of the preconditions that brought forth the response of schooling no longer prevail. Most dramatically, middle-class Europe and America are almost 100 percent literate, in numbers as well as letters. Under these conditions, it seems reasonable to suppose that children or teen-agers might be able to "pick up" skills such as reading and adding through observation, mimicry, and self-initiated practice, much as the children of foragers acquire equally complex skills of tracking, weaving, dancing, or knowledge of complex mythology. In a society where all members practice a skill, when full adult status is not accorded without evidence of minimal acquisition of it, the motivation for learning is very strong. I wonder, too, if in our reading and arithmetic classrooms, we actually "teach" these subjects or whether we really force the pliable majority of the children to attain a limited proficiency so that the teacher will get off their backs. Many of the recalcitrant minority remain functional illiterates, of course. Would this happen to them if they were introduced to reading with due regard for the "biology of human beings"?

It must also be noted that in the nineteenth century and for most of the present one, the hordes of young people who flocked to school had some notion, often dim and confused but positively motivating nonetheless, of a new way of life for which the drudgery and irrelevancies of schooling would qualify them. This sense of purpose can still be felt, almost palpably, in the schools of developing countries— without really understanding what it entails, the youngsters strive for the transformation that schooling brings. In middle-class sectors of the Western world, circumstances are quite the reverse. These children are virtually literate when they come to school, cosmopolitan thanks to television, and at least strongly disposed to an analytic frame of mind as a result of exposure to the "hidden curriculum" of the middle-class household. Yet they lack (and they know it) a realistic picture of the adult world in which they will ultimately practice the skills and attitudes they have learned. Segregation of the young was intended as a device of mutual protection, but it has become so perfect an instrument that it threatens to disrupt the whole process of socialization.

I don't like to hear or read papers that end with an exhortation to a presumably convinced audience to "reexamine their assumptions," or words to that effect, and I won't end this one that way. In fact, I suspect that our system of education is already changing in ways that will make it be much more closely attuned to man's primate nature than is the present system, and that radical reforms are inevitable within the next ten or twenty years. Anthropologists may be able to assist (through sophisticated interpretation of the changes) in making the shift smoother and more rational, but it will occur whether we participate or not.

The basic reasons why a return to more "normal" ways is likely are two that have already been mentioned—near 100 percent literacy in large sectors of Western society, and the counterproductivity of our current segregation of the young; and one reason not mentioned—general rejection of the notion that "docility" is an appropriate goal for contemporary education. The educational system is already responding to these changed circumstances in various ways of which three seem most important and interrelated, though they are not always perceived as connected:

Open education, particularly in preschools and the elementary grades. Open education grows out of an explicit philosophy of the child that leads to the creation in the classroom of circumstances very similar to those observed in foraging societies.

Open education would be very difficult to practice in an industrialized society in which literacy was not widespread and available for children to "discover." The amazingly rapid spread of open education in suburbia during the past decade is in large part the result of the growing homogeneity of population in these towns, especially along the dimension of literacy.

Schools-without-walls, especially at the secondary and college levels. Under this rubric I mean to collect phenomena such as NIE's career education, cooperative education, work-study programs, college furloughing, internships, deferred admission, and other formal arrangements that get students out of school and into the real world and then back to school again. Also included are less thoroughgoing shifts into the sphere of adults such as community service for credit and courses taught wholly or partially in the "field." All these operations tend to break down the walls of segregation, and they are much more common and popular with students than most adults not close to the high schools and colleges realize.

"Technologized education," a term under which I group thrusts such as computer-assisted instruction, self-paced instruction, performance-based teaching, the contract system, and other efforts to rationalize and speed up the processes of acquiring traditional school subjects. When these techniques attain full momentum in the school program, both elementary and secondary, the effects will be that (1) students will master the so-called essentials much more rapidly and thoroughly than they now do; (b) much instruction will have moved out of the classroom into the community because mastery criteria will specify performance in "real" settings, not in the schoolhouse. The impact of this revolution on present practices of segregation is likely to be greater than that of open education or schools-without-walls, in my view, largely because it will be so unexpected.

There is one remaining obstacle to the "normalizing" of the educational system around which I see no ready pathway. This is the fact that the physical and social environment in which our children (and we) live is still an incredibly dangerous one; on this issue many of the new programs may temporarily flounder. However, the environment-as-a-problem has at last seized the attention of many thoughtful persons, and with patience and imagination we may be able to reconstruct our homes and our communities in a more humane mold. When that occurs, we will have approximated the sort of personal security enjoyed by our ancestors 10,000 years ago and more, and our children once again will be able to learn like the primate juveniles they are.

REFERENCES

Aries, P. *Centuries of Childhood*. New York: Knopf, 1962.

Bloom, B. *Stability and Change in Human Characteristics*. New York: Wiley, 1961.

Burton Jones, N. G. "Comparative Aspects of Mother-Child Contact." In N. G. Burton Jones, ed., *Ethnological Studies of Child Behavior*. Cambridge: Cambridge University Press, 1972.

Bowlby, J. *Attachment and Loss*. Vol. I: *Attachment*. London: Hogarth, 1969.

Harlow, H. "The Heterosexual Affectional System in Monkeys." *American Psychologist* 17, no. 1 (1962).

Katz, M. *The Irony of Early School Reform*. Cambridge, Mass.: Harvard University Press, 1968.

Konner, M. "Infancy among the Kalahari Desert San," Ms. prepared for Burg Wartenstein Symposium No. 57, June 1973.

Mason, W. A. "The Social Development of Monkeys and Apes." In I. DeVore, ed., *Primate Behavior*. New York: Holt, Rinehart and Winston, 1965.

Rheingold, H., ed., *Maternal Behavior in Mammals*. New York: Wiley, 1963.

Scribner, S., and Cole, M. "Cognitive Consequences of Formal and Informal Education." *Science* 182, no. 553 (1973).

Washburn, S. L. "On the Importance of the Study of Primate Behavior for Anthropologists." In M. Wax, S. Diamond, and F. Gearing, eds., *Anthropological Perspectives on Education.* New York: Basic Books, 1971.

——. "Primate Field Studies and Social Science." In L. Nader and T. Maretzki, eds., "Cultural Illness and Health," *Anthropological Studies* 9 (1973).

——, and Hamburg, D. A. "The Implications of Primate Research." In I. DeVore, ed., *Primate Behavior.* New York: Holt, Rinehart and Winston, 1965.

11 / From Omnibus to Linkages: Cultural Transmission Models

George D. Spindler

In the brief compass of this paper I will try to describe how I have looked for theoretical models that would help me and my students in the analysis of cultural transmission—the educational process broadly conceived. The search began in the 1950s when I started teaching anthropology courses that were intended to be relevant to educators.

The purpose of theoretical models, as I understand it, is to provide coherent statements of relationships concerning some phenomena that will generate questions and hypotheses leading to further exploration and eventually to the discard or modification of the model. The model tentatively explains how something works.

We began with what could be called an "omnibus model." We simply wanted to know what to look for in the cross-cultural study of education. Jules Henry's *Cross Cultural Outline of Education* (1960) is the logical culmination of this approach. His outline is directly concerned with cultural transmission and it contains some interesting statements of relationships and functions; for example, "One of the principal functions of anthropomorphized animals is to serve as a medium for the transmission of values" (p. 273). Generally speaking, however, guides of this kind call attention to phenomena but do not clarify the relationships between them.

Next was the socialization and enculturation model. Definition of these terms is fruitless in this context. The two concepts intergrade but emphasize different aspects of the whole process of becoming human. The contributors to this approach would include nearly every anthropologist who has written on culture and personality. As is particularly clear in the *Field Guide for the Study of Socialization*, developed by John Whiting and his associates (1966), this model is very broad. Its very breadth discourages all but the most energetic from focusing upon manageable relationships.

Nobuo Shimahara discusses some of the problems involved in using an enculturation model (1970). He is concerned with whether enculturation can include the innovative and creative aspects of cultural and personal development as well as the more static processes involved in the transmission of the cultural status quo. He also points out that the concept has been used inconsistently because it has had no articulate definition, excepting that provided in Herskovits' original statement (1947, p. 40ff.). Shimahara's article and the replies to it in "Current Anthropology," though very interesting, support my opinion that this model is also more orienting than definitive. It helps us to know what to look for, but it does not help us very much to explain what we find. By "explain" I mean that one is able to use words or formulae to express how some aspects of a system works, using bounded, operationally defined variables.

Our dissatisfactions, particularly in the context of seminars, about cultural transmission and its consequences considered cross-culturally led us to develop a *cultural compression* and *discontinuity* model. Ruth Benedict's early work on cultural discontinuity (1938), a statement by Calverton (1931) on cultural compulsives, van Gennep's (1960) and others' analyses of rites of passage, and Steve Hart's discussion (1955) of pre- and postpubertal education were particularly influential. This model was an attempt to narrow the scope of concerns. It was also a reaction to the Whiting and Child, Kardiner and Linton (Kardiner 1945) emphasis on certain biocultural promontories in infancy and early childhood, such as weaning, toilet training, the control of aggression and sex, and so forth. I felt, with Steve Hart, that there was too much emphasis on the early years of childhood and not enough on the middle and later years. In fact, when one examines the evidence proffered by Whiting and Child (1953), one is struck by the fact that, in most societies in their sample, infants and young children are treated mildly and supportively. Though there are culture-linked variations in this treatment, the variability does not seem sufficient to account for either major characterlogical variation or major variations in what Kardiner has called the "secondary institutions," such as law, religion, and political structure. What I wanted to do was to put the whole life cycle into some frame of reference that would permit us to talk about relevant processes beyond the early years of child training.

In my seminars at Stanford we analyzed most of the cultures for which there was adequate ethnographic description. We attempted to draw up fairly precise statements, accompanied by diagrams of cultural compression and decompression, that would succinctly describe at what points in the life cycle the individual experienced a narrowing of cultural alternatives. Rites of passage at preadolescence and adolescence are characteristic of the cultural compression model. One enters a phase of life where one is able to do certain things one couldn't do before, but only certain things and in only certain sanctioned ways. We found that cultural "decompression" also occurred at various points throughout the life cycle, most notably at old age but not infrequently at earlier points in the life trajectory. We found it possible to draw up diagrams expressive of cultural compression and decompression throughout the life cycle for a large number of societies and from these to consolidate several major types. I do not have time to go into these types. They raise some interesting questions about the relationship between the learning experience of the individual and the type of cultural system in which it occurs.

Our basic problem was that we were dealing with such massive variables that we could exert little control over them. I do find the model still useful, however, as a descriptive frame of reference. The cultural compression model is referred to in my chapter on cultural transmission in *Culture in Process* (Beals et al. 1973).

There are other major problems with the cultural compression-decompression-discontinuity model. Grossly put, it is too cultural. It does not give us a direct route into involvements with the development of cognitive structures or, for that matter, into any aspect of psychological adaptation. It is true that we can ask what reactions compressed people have and how these reactions are expressed in alternative cultural forms such as revolutions, juvenile delinquency, and pathogenic personality development, as well as complacent adjustment, but these concerns are not a part of the model. The model works best with a steady state system where there are specific channels—ideally only one for each sex—throughout the life cycle. The model does, I believe, have some capacity for useful predictions of responses to the exigencies of culture change or modernization, since I believe that cultural commitment is partly a product of the cultural compression-discontinuity sequence and cultural commitment is a significant factor in resistance to change or appropriation of it. This is also a matter beyond the scope of this brief paper.

As man responds to the confrontations and disjunctions implied by terms like urbanization and modernization, he becomes protean (see Linton 1968). He is released from traditional cultural compulsives and is able to transform himself. All models of cultural transmission that are immutably linked with established cultural forms therefore become obsolete unless we are interested in cultural persistence, and indeed this may be a worthy object of attention.

What is most important, however, is that man under the conditions described by terms like acculturation, urbanization, and modernization can, in fact must, make choices between different courses of action and different goals. A steady state model does not provide for this freedom and its consequences. In a steady state system decisions are made in a symbolic-cognitive field where limits are clearly defined and the compressive-decompressive sequences of an individual's life have led him or her to an acceptance, in fact often to a committed defense, of these limits. Under conditions of transformative change such as those characterizing most of the world's population at present, decisions are made in an open symbolic-cognitive field where limits are rarely clearly defined excepting on a political-ideological basis that may be culturally spurious. It is true that segmentalized "cultural compressions" may occur in specialized occupational routes such as becoming an anthropologist, a university professor, a researcher, a social science analyst, a pimp, a lawyer, a dentist, a businessman, or a longshoreman. Segmentalized compressions also occur as one becomes a member of current peer groups such as communes, experiments in group marriage, ski clubs, or the Airstream Trailer Association. There are, however, so many of these segmentalized cultural compressions and their results are so transitory that the model is immediately strained beyond its capacity.

Our thinking has gone in other directions recently (in this case "our" means Louise Spindler and me). In our fieldwork with the Menomini of Wisconsin and then with the Blood Indians of Canada, we early developed a multiple acculturative adaptation model. It was apparent to us that our communities were not homogeneous and consisted of people in varying degrees of groupness whose strategies of adaptation to the confrontation with white-man culture were different from each other, but exhibited some regularities cross-culturally. We were interested from the start in our research in understanding the complex relationships between how people perceive and respond to the world about them and their manifest socio-cultural adaptations (such as type of residence, clothing, speech, group affiliations, occupations, etc.). We began this task by using the Rorschach projective technique, autobiographic interviews and life histories, various types of interviews and, of course, participant observation, as well as sociocultural index schedules. I could get quite involved with the vicissitudes and rewards of this work, but will have to bypass all of it only to say that, although we felt and still do feel that the Rorschach gave us very valuable information on perceptual structure, cognitive process, and emotional response we would not have got by other means, we were missing the boat just when we wanted to get on board. That is, the Rorschach did not give us much direct information about how the individual perceives social reality and rationalizes his perceptions and the alternative courses of action and value contained within that perceived reality—and this was one of the major objects of our research. Expressive autobiographic interviews (L. Spindler 1963), life histories, interviews, and observational data did, of course, give us relevant information, but these types of data are very hard to code systematically and they are so emic that it is very difficult to do any cross-cultural comparison.

We therefore devised a new technique we have called the Instrumental Activities Inventory (IAI) which we used first with the Blood, then with Cree adolescents at Mistassini (Quebec), and finally in studies of cultural transmission in two rapidly urbanizing German villages. The interested reader can pursue the matter further in the references cited. I will concentrate at this point on the instrumental model, which makes the Instrumental Activities Inventory work. Perhaps I should say first that neither the inventory nor the theoretical model emerged in their entirety with a blinding flash of insight. In fact, we started with the inventory and developed the model afterward. We were responding to a perceived need in a field research situation. We knew what it was we wanted to find out but were not exactly sure why. The inventory and the model remain very close to the phenomena with which we are concerned. It is also true that we started with a technique and model that grew directly out of our concerns with psychocultural adaptation and not with my concern with cultural transmission. It was not until I faced the problem of trying to understand what was happening in a small German *Grundschule* in a transforming urbanizing German village that I saw the utility of the instrumental model and technique for the study of cultural transmission. As I came to understand certain relationships better, however, it became apparent to me that, indeed, cultural transmission and what we have called cultural change or acculturation are intimately linked. Cultures as systems really change only when they are transmitted differently to new members or within peer groups. Conversely, any stabilization of cultural forms, however temporary, must be a function of cultural transmission, even though strictly among peers rather than from older to younger people.

The IAI itself consists of a number of ethnographically accurate line drawings depicting various activities that, within the perceptual field of the respondent, lead to certain goals that in turn are expressive of certain life styles. The technique is therefore *emic* in that the respondent's perceptions of specific activities and linkages between activities and goals are pertinent only to a given situation. The technique is *etic* in that the phenomena, "instrumental activities," are universal and the categories into which they fall are similar across cultures. Some activities have to do with subsistence, other with recreation, social control, housing, personal appearance, group behavior, and the like. Even the relevant aspects of cultural change and urbanization tend to be cross-culturally regular.

In the culture change and urbanization situations in which we have worked with the technique and the model behind it, the line drawings have included representations of instrumental choices that are clearly related to the new culture or to the urban complex, and others that are representative of a traditional way of life, whatever it may be. The drawings are not like the Thematic Apperception Test or any other projective technique where a certain degree of ambiguity is a part of the stimulus. IAI drawings must be precise, accurate, and clear. They must represent in the most direct manner possible the actual instrumental choices available to the individual or that appear to him to be available. We can go no further with the description of the technique here. I will touch very briefly upon some results after the instrumental model is explained.

The broad premises and concepts included in the theoretical model can be stated as follows: we assume that a cultural system operates so long as acceptable behaviors usually produce predictable and desirable results, and unacceptable behaviors produce predictable and undesirable results. These behaviors are instrumental to goals, such as states of being or possessions, associated with desired life styles. The relationship between activities and goals can be termed an *instrumental linkage*. Instrumental linkages are systematized and interrelated, and constitute the core of any cultural system. Cultural belief systems help support the credibility of these linkages. Educational institutions and processes maintain them. Children are taught what the linkages are, how they work, and why some are better than others in schools, churches, initiation ceremonies, and families. They are also taught why some linkages function for them as individuals in certain relationships and others do not, and why everyone cannot make the same instrumental choices. The result of this cultural transmission in the individual is a cognitive structure that is a kind of working model of the culture system. This working model permits the individual to maintain control of his life space so long as the established instrumental relationships within the system continue to function.

Cognitive control as socially relevant is therefore the ability of the individual to maintain a working model in his mind of potentially productive instrumental linkages and their organization. *Identity*, which may be considered a precondition to cognitive control, is a cathexis with certain instrumental linkages that are central to one's presentation of self in the context of one's life style. Identities tend to persist but are also situationally adaptive. This model, as we have said, is formed in the mind by cultural transmission. During rapid culture change or urbanization, established instrumental linkages are challenged by new information, behavior models, and belief systems, and their credibility is therefore weakened. Alternative linkages are recognized, acquire credibility, and become operable. This process constitutes for us a key focus in the study of the psychology of cultural change and urbanization, and the processes of cultural transmission within this framework. In using this model one may be concerned with either the culture system processes that result in new instrumental linkages or with the perception, selection, and cognitive ordering of alternative linkages by individuals.

The results produced by administration of the IAI to Blood Indians and Mistassini Cree teen-agers, and to German schoolchildren, their parents and teachers, are complex and have been analyzed elsewhere. I will comment only briefly on the results obtained with the German school sample.

The purpose in administering the IAI and using this backup model was to determine how the school as a cultural transmitting agency affected the children's cognitive management of instrumental choices when the cultural system within which these choices could function was transforming in the course of rapid urbanization. Specific questions were generated, which are reported in another publication (Spindler 1974). One of the major questions was: does the culture transmitted by the school constrain instrumental choices children make of urban lifestyles and the means to them? In order to answer this question it is necessary to study the instrumental linkages being transmitted in the school and how they were transmitted. Data provided by participant observation, interviews with teachers, children, and parents, and the analysis of curricular materials were used as the basis for this ethnography. The IAI was used to elicit data on the effect of this cultural transmission. It should be emphasized that utilization of the technique and the model made it possible to employ the same data-gathering device for a large sample of children in two schools as well as a sample of their parents and their teachers. It was therefore possible to compare the cognitive organization of instrumental linkages among the three groups most relevant to the cultural transmission process in this situation.

The most significant conclusions for our purposes are: (1) that the linkages the school transmitted were more traditional than urban in orientation; (2) this orientation results in an idealized identification with the land, village, and the *Weingartner* (vintner) instrumental relationships; (3) where instrumental choices are not governed by pragmatic realities, children make choices relevant to this idealized identification; (4) when, however, the pragmatics of adaptation to an urban environment appear to be a significant consideration, instrumentalities relevant to the urban environment are perceived and chosen most frequently.

Apparently the transmission of a traditionally oriented culture by the school does not constrain instrumental choices by the schoolchildren, particularly at the point where in mid-adolescence they are about to enter adult roles and life styles. More positively, it provides the basis for an idealized identity centering on the traditional linkages that seem to have performed a balancing function in the adaptation to transformative urbanization. The cognitive organization of the majority of the children in our sample is therefore composed of three parts: (1) the idealized identity—village and Weingartner—with supporting values such as independence, quiet, fresh air, friendliness, love of nature, and the like; (2) the pragmatic instrumental preference system—modern house, white-collar work—together with supporting values such as comfort, regular income and hours, security, and cleaner work; and (3) the romanticized instrumental preferences—traditional church, wine grape harvest, traditional house structures, and so forth—with supporting values such as beauty, freedom, and symbolic representation of the past. The majority of the children appear to maintain cognitive control over these three potentially conflicting dimensions. Pragmatism has priority in critical areas of choice but an idealized or romanticized identity provides a security base. The use of the technique and the model therefore permitted us to see how these children managed to maintain cognitive control in a changing milieu and what role the school played as a culture transmitting agency, and these were our purposes.

The instrumental model and technique (I find it impossible to separate the technique from the model) therefore serves the purposes of a useful, working, theoretical model at the middle level. It told us what to look at, something of what to look for, generated questions and hypotheses, indicated ways in which they could be tested, and allowed us to work in different cultural situations with the same model and essentially the same procedures, therefore making our results potentially comparable at the same time that we elicited relevant in-depth emic data.

POSTSCRIPT

Like most of the rest of us interested in theories and models of cultural transmission, I have been studying with great interest the products of the *Project in the Ethnography in Education* at the Department of Anthropology, SUNY-Buffalo, directed by Fred Gearing. I have read his brief paper in the *CAE Newsletter* titled "Where We Are and Where We Might Go: Steps Toward a General Theory of Cultural Transmission" (1973), and Working Paper No. 5: "A General Cultural Theory of Education" by Gearing and his associates. Though I find some of what is said difficult to understand, I believe that they are on the right track. They are concerned with such matters as agenda and premises that are prior to the interaction within any given setting; they pay specific attention to transactions in the form of encounters in which transmission may occur; and they are concerned with cognitive structuring of both the process and the results of cultural transmission. The theory has in it, as I understand it, means for linking ideational with social process, and I think this is absolutely essential for any working theory of cultural transmission. To me, however, the instrumental model that I have briefly sketched above focuses upon an area that is left a bit cloudy in theirs. The instrumental model calls attention to a specific and manifest area of perception, choice, and behavior. It focuses directly on the central problem—how choices are made and what they are made about, with what kind of cognitive (read "cultural" for certain purposes) organization, and allows us to ask how these processes are affected by selected features of the cultural transmission process in any given situation. What the instrumental model lacks is a more sophisticated statement of the processes of cognitive organization and cognitive control, and a more explicit conceptual ordering of the encounters that make possible the transmission of information, skill, knowledge, and the like, in what we have called the cultural transmission process. I do not offer the instrumental model as competitive with anything. I do think that a marriage, or possibly just an alliance, between these two models, one of them middle level and the other one a grand theory, might be productive (I hesitate to say pregnant with possibilities).

BIBLIOGRAPHY

Beals, Alan R. *Culture in Process*. New York: Holt, Rinehart and Winston, 1967.

Benedict, R. F. "Continuities and Discontinuities in Cultural Conditioning." Psychiatry 161, no. 1 (1938).

Calverton, V. F. "Modern Anthropology and the Theory of Cultural Compulsives." In *The Making of Modern Man*, edited by V. Calverton. New York, 1931.

Gearing, F. O. "Where We Are and Where We Might Go: Steps Toward a General Theory of Cultural Transmission." IV CAE Newsletter 1, 1973.

——, et al. "Working Paper No. 5: Outline: A General Cultural Theory of Education." SUNY-Buffalo, 1973.

Hart, C. W. M. "Contrasts Between Prepubertal and Postpubertal Education." In *Education and Anthropology*, edited by G. Spindler. Stanford University Press, 1955. Reprinted in *Education and Culture: Anthropological Approaches*, edited by G. Spindler. New York: Holt, Rinehart and Winston, 1963.

Henry, J. "A Cross-cultural Outline of Education." *Current Anthropology* 267, no. 1 (1960).

Herskovits, M. J. *Man and His Works*. New York: Knopf, 1947.

Kardiner, A. *The Psychological Frontiers of Society*. New York: Columbia University Press, 1945.

Lifton, R. "Protean Man." *Partisan Review* 15 (Spring 1968).

Shimahara, N. "Enculturation—A Reconsideration." *Current Anthropology* 143, no. 11 (1970).

Spindler, G. D. *Burgbach: Urbanization and Identity in a German Village*. New York: Holt, Rinehart and Winston, 1973.

——. "Schooling in Schonhausen: A Study of Cultural Transmission and Instrumental Adaptation in an Urbanizing German Village." In *Education and Cultural Process: Toward an Anthropology of Education*, edited by G. Spindler. New York: Holt, Rinehart and Winston, 1974.

——, and Spindler, L. S. "The Instrumental Activities Inventory: A Technique for the Study of the Psychology of Acculturation." *Southwestern Journal of Anthropology* 1 (1965).

Spindler, L. S. "Menomini Women and Culture Change." *American Anthropological Association Memoir* 64:1:2 (1962).

Van Gennep, A. *The Rites of Passage*, translated by M. Vizedom and G. Caffee. Chicago: University of Chicago Press, 1960.

Whiting, J. W.; Child, I. L.; and Lambert, W. W. *Field Guide for a Study of Socialization*. New York: Wiley, 1966.

——, and Child, I. L. *Child Training and Personality: A Cross-Cultural Study*. New Haven: Yale University Press, 1953.

Williams, T. R. *Introduction to Socialization: Human Culture Transmitted*. St. Louis: C. V. Mosby, 1972.

12 / Steps Toward A General Theory of Cultural Transmission

Frederick O. Gearing

KEY TERMS

Two pivotal notions permit us to envisage the outlines of a general theory of cultural transmission. Hopefully, these notions will, through use, acquire sufficient precisions and elegance that we soon can without embarrassment call them concepts. The notions are *transaction* and *equivalence*. The cultural system of any society or group consists of an array of diverse but interlocking equivalences of meaning which have been variously transacted in the course of recurrent encounters of each member of the group with some others (Wallace); cultural transmission consists of such transactions of equivalences in certain encounters, principally of nonadults with adults and each other.

These notions, as used here, are purely interpsychic in nature.

Equivalence

The notion of equivalence suggests that the two parties in any encounter bring to that encounter their cognitively mapped prior experience, that their respective mappings will in part be drawn upon, that the two mappings will reveal in those germane parts various degrees and kinds of fit and ill-fit, and that the mappings and their fit typically change in the course of an encounter or series of encounters. Thus the notion of equivalence causes the researcher to inquire as to realms of *content* of each cognitive map and as to kinds of *fit* between any two maps.

The contents of cognitive mappings include at least four realms which may in these early stages of investigation be analytically separated, all four of which presumably are drawn upon in any encounter. First, parties bring some sense of *setting*, some mapping of categories of situation which defines for each of them the particular encounter as to its kind. The grab-bag of named events as employed in any community (coffee break, PTA meeting, basketball game) is such a mapping at one level. Of greater research interest are the groupings of such events into larger categories. Men in sectors of this society evidently perceive sundry activities to fall into categories of "work" or "play"; domains roughly similar to work and play may or may not be present in other cultural systems. Similarly, there may be, variously in many societies, discoverable domains perceived by actors as those roughly suggested by the words sacred and profane, or domains of ritual as against something else—not ritual (note Turner and ethologists on ritualization, and Jacquetta Burnett's study of high school ritual).

Second, parties bring to an encounter some mapped sense of the nature of the world about them, human and nonhuman. This includes perceptions as to the categories into which things fall and perceptions as to logics, i.e., the ways such parts are connected, the two together constituting the unreflecting *natural sciences*, as it were, of the two parties. Hallowell's Ojibwa studies as to the Ojibwa domain "person" is a dramatic case in point, and learning about such mappings as to categories is of course one central task which has been addressed over the last twenty years by ethnoscience and other forms of cognitive anthropology. Inquiry into mappings as to the logics, the connections among things, is in non-Western contexts not nearly as extensive, but Michael Cole and his colleagues have recently made most encouraging reports.

Third, parties bring mappings as to a crucial subset of the above, the ways men generally are sorted into categories of social *identity* and how such categories are connected in role relationships, of differential power and the like. Inquiry into these mappings constitutes of course one of the best established research traditions in anthropology, the study of social structure as behavioral code or idiom, for example ranging in time from the work of Evans-Pritchard in 1940, to that of Ward Goodenough today.

Finally, each party brings to any encounter a mapping of a fourth realm, quite different from the above three, a mapping as to an implied *agenda*, an expectation as to how the encounter promises or threatens to unfold. The parties' senses of agenda are closely related to the other named realms. The settings work and play, for example, imply quite different agendas; different elements in those natural sciences, as whether germane aspects of the environs are somehow affectable (war is hell) or not affectable (the earth is round), imply different agendas; the mappings of identity and role imply agendas quite directly. All these, however, typically define options among which the parties can and must choose. What this fourth dimension adds at the outset of an encounter is the anticipated positioning of self, each party in respect to the other, for the encounter. Goffman's extraordinary work over the last twenty-five years has principally dealt with this dimension of cognitive mapping. Agenda is the dimension of personal operationalization: What do I want? How important is that to me? What does he want and how badly? What are his options? My opinions?

The notion of equivalence adds a dimension to cognitive studies; it additionally raises, and pivotally, the question of *fit* as between the mappings brought by the two parties to the encounter. Wallace has held that a cultural system tends less to generate identity of perception and more to organize diversity of similar and dissimilar perceptions; this seems a useful assumption in respect to small and stable societies, and it is self-evident truth in respect to large and fast-changing societies. Thus, there is the question of cognitive equivalence and nonequivalence, in the sense of the degrees of similarity as between perceptions of two or more parties. There is also functional equivalence, where two parties adequately predict each other's behavior, perhaps on the basis of very dissimilar maps.

Transaction

All of the above four dimensions of cognitive mappings are brought to an encounter by each party, and those two mappings may or may not be equivalent, cognitively and functionally. Of course these are all subject to change during an encounter or series of encounters. The notion of transaction calls to attention the interpsychic processes by which cognitive mappings may change in the course of an encounter or series of encounters. Thus the notion focuses attention on the *forms* of communication, the *kind* of cognitive change and on the *direction* of that change. Perhaps the most readily discoverable indicators of cognitive change lie in the cognitive realm earlier termed agenda.

The processes of communication in transactions seem well but incompletely described by models developed in communication theory, e.g., Shannon's as reported by Pierce in *Scientific American*: an information source, conveying a message to a transmitter, translating that into a transmitted signal, which moves through a channel, becomes a received signal, is translated into a message, and reaches a destination; this confounded by noise which enters the above channel. Congruent with that, readily identified alternative *forms* of transaction as between men in an encounter can be described and are often described in ethnography: verbal and non-verbal interchange between peers as in conversation; interchange whereby one party watches another and perhaps intimates; other verbal and nonverbal interchange between nonpeers as with instruction; no doubt several other alternative forms.

Cognitive change involves, of course, changes in each of the four realms of mappings, as earlier named. But changes in those realms vary as to *kind*, may entail the exchange of a total boundary system for another, or the creation of boundaries where none existed, or the elaboration or "fleshing out" of an existing boundary system, or combinations of these. The last, elaboration, is what Fortes reported as the process by which Tallensi children learn their kinship system (they learn a "schema" and, bit by bit into their adult years, learn the details.) Probably, in the context of cultural transmission, the three kinds of change occur in characteristic frequencies, least to most frequent as listed. Analogously, changes occur in the mapping of logics, the perceived possibilities of connection among parts. This (seen as intrapsychic, not interpsychic process) is the focus of Piagetian studies of levels of cognitions, and is also seen in cross-cultural contexts in the work of Cole and his colleagues. Following Piaget, the exchange of one logic for another does occur in cultural transmission (as when an adult tries to comprehend a new realm of phenomena using only formal logical language, but it is abortive if it does), the addition of new logics is pivotally entailed from infancy into adolescence, and fleshing out is lifelong.

In the course of any encounter, whenever maps change, they change in a direction. The two cognitive mappings may become more similar; in that case, the perceptions of one of the parties may move principally toward that of the other with little or no reciprocal movement. Or cognitive mappings may diverge, as with schizmogenesis (Bateson), and here too one party's mapping may change much while the other changes little. In studies of cultural transmission, the matter of direction is of course critical.

But the heart of transaction, the aspect which looms theoretically significant and pragmatically important is not yet in evidence. "Agenda" names the ways by which parties to an encounter or series of encounters position themselves, and how, in course, they transact and retransact that positioning.

The notion of agenda reveals the inadequacy of the communication model taken alone, for the communication model does not bring into focus the multiplicity of messages evidently present in any encounter. The notion of agenda does precisely this. A verbal interchange among peers may be such that each party seriously wants to understand the other, call that a "conversation"; or it may be a "debate" wherein it is useful to willfully misunderstand; the difference lies in the way the parties position themselves in respect to one another. Of course, parties may come to an encounter with like or unlike mappings in this regard, and each or both may remap once or several times in the course of transaction during one or several encounters. Similarly, one party, after watching another some while, may identify and imitate, or he may mock; or an instructor may spoon-feed and dictate, or he may enter into joint inquiry. Such positioning efforts are not "noise"; these efforts constitute one of the messages, and are often the principal message, whatever the interchange may be nominally about.

The impressive, fine-grained analysis of filmed behavior, such as that of Birdwhistel, Condon, and Fred Erickson, seems principally to fix upon these phenomena. Literature of theoretical importance which here bears most directly is both extensive and disparate. For example only: Goffman's work; Bateson culture as cybernetics.

A simple pair of models seems dependably to sort otherwise imponderably complex phenomena into handleable simplicity. In this model (1.): one party to an encounter, A, transacts with a second party, B; they imagine two critical audiences,

1.

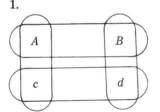

each constituted of one party or many, physically present or not, c and d. The encounter of A with B may be about almost anything, and it is necessarily some exchange drawing upon and perhaps affecting their perceptions of setting and natural science and organization. But whatever that content, A is also actively about defining who he is vis-à-vis B and who those audiences are in relation to them; the encounter is a complex and shifting series of negotiations—assertions and counter assertions—as to who are "we" and who "they." By this first model A has only two fundamental options: he and B are "we," in opposition to c and d who are "they"; or he and c are "we," and B and d are "they." B of course has the parallel options.

2.

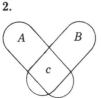

Alternatively, the second model (2.): A transacts with B and they compete for allegiance with a single audience, c, which is one party or many, physically present or not.

The presumption is strong that, in any encounter or series of encounters, each party moves among all these options, in synchrony and out with each other.

In the course of such positioning and repositioning, parties to an encounter selectively preempt other aspects of the transaction in the service of this negotiation. For example, if B asserts that war is hell, A's response is probably more related to efforts to position himself than to the nature of war, or hell for that matter. On the other hand, if B says the earth is round, presumably A has only the option of continuing that conversation or changing the subject, but his choice will probably reflect the same efforts to position himself. Still further, if B by implication, suggests that the encounter falls into the category "work," (for example by alluding to an attribute of that category, entailed obligations perhaps) possible A will not even catch the assertion, the categories being relatively "deep." This is to say, the ongoing transaction as to agenda powerfully but selectively affects the course of transactions in those other realms.

The research implication seems evident: the most difficult and probably the key dimension of transaction to watch, with the finest grained analysis possible, is the transaction of equivalences and the failures of transaction of equivalence in respect to agenda. The key questions become two: Do A and B settle upon some stable way to define their relationships of alliance and apposition in respect to one another and their critical audiences, and if so how? And, what other aspects of their cognitive mappings have they put into the service of this negotiation and this resolution, and how?

A wit once epitomized by chance some of the complexity of the notion of equivalence. Writing (some few years back) about the U.S. Communist party's ideological need of the FBI and writing about the FBI's reverse need of the Communist party, he called J. Edgar Hoover and Gus Hall the Yin and Yang of American politics. That is a system of equivalence of a kind.

A disclaimer: boundaries. There is no mention of boundaries in the sense that no attempt is made to respond to the question: So you want to study cultural transmission; by what abstract criteria do you select some events and put others aside? The history of economic anthropology and political anthropology is suggestive. Those fields struggled with class concepts which would so sort events, finally shifted to analytic concepts which focussed on selected aspects of any and all events. Transaction and equivalence are now notions and hopefully will be concepts—analytic concepts. In respect to any and all two-party events, these concepts do not select, they analytically focus.

However, boundaries are a problem, since one cannot look everywhere at once. At the very least, establishing such boundaries is a nuts-and-bolts logistic problem. The implication is that one wisely leaves it at that—and copes.

Additionally, one needs, especially at early stages of research, some orienting ideas. Anthropologists can do no better than fall back upon our knowledge of human biological evolution and human cultural history. As Washburn has said, the human brain is an adaptive organ and, through processes of natural selection it, like other animal brains, has taken neurological shape so that human organisms learn (read transact) easily and surely in respect to those things men need to know in order to survive. Learning a language is surely a transactional process, and it is virtually impossible to prevent a normal child from learning whatever language or languages are being spoken around him. But the human brain came to that neurological shape about 35,000 years ago when all men lived in very small groups. Thus the human brain, presumably, can readily transact equivalences of meaning in respect to those things necessary for survival in a hunting band, and presumably transacts more tortuously and riskfully other things newly required for survival and effective behavior in urban-centered national and international social systems. Washburn says that the unaided human brain copes readily with things nearby in space, things proximate in time, and things few in number, and that constructions used in coping are usually simple, and we may surely add, anthropocentric.

This is to say, hosts of orienting ideas which will suggest foci of cultural transmission interest can be generated by reexaminations of human life in very small communities as against human life in very large communities, thereby to identify presumably easy transactions and other transactions presumably more riskful, empirically to investigate in any cultural transmission system some sampling of both.

A final implication: "culture." It has been implied but must be said: the notions of transaction and equivalence make untenable some familiar phrases: "a culture," "a subculture," "cross-cultural" (in the usual sense that some situations are and some aren't one of these). Those are reifications which variously distort depending on the degree to which the communities are small or large, stable or fast changing, isolated or not. In all human situations one has, speaking more precisely, cultural systems constituted by complex networks of transacted equivalences and not yet transacted nonequivalences. Twin brothers who have lived twenty years in the same household have transacted a lot of equivalence and have but rare need to transact more. Chagnon, looking up at that first day into the green-snotty noses of armed and threatening Yanomamo, enjoyed very little equivalence and had yet to transact a lot. The two instances are different in degree, not kind.

A GENERAL THEORY?

A future general theory of cultural transmission is at least thinkable: It would entail mapping many societies as to their patterns of encounter (i.e., as to occasions for transaction) who with whom, would entail identifying types of "before" equivalence states types of transactional processes, types of "after" equivalence states, in short, these taken together, a mapping of societies as to their characteristic transactional careers. A general theory would then consist of a series of predictive propositions as to occasions for, content of, relative riskfulness of, communication processes during, and outcomes of transactions—the cumulative results being the systems of equivalences which constitute the cultures at issue. But the apparent core of such a future general theory of cultural transmission would deal with agenda, would be a series of predictive propositions as to what types of recommendations as to positioning are sent, by whom to whom; how these are received and negotiated; how some cultural "information" is preempted into the services of these negotiations, some not. Such a general theory would tell us how transmission selectively occurs and how, from these internal forces, cultural systems endure and change.

A theory which is thinkable is not necessarily do-able. Some research beginnings, actual and potential, are suggested in the section to follow.

RESEARCH ACTIVITIES, THEIR RELATIONSHIPS

The following six research and research-related activities, with which the Project in Ethnography in Education is variously involved or potentially so, taken together, seem to lead toward a general theory of cultural transmission. The first four are listed in what is emphatically not a chronological order: each one complements and variously assists others, but all can usefully go forward together. The last two follow chronologically, since they do presuppose specific areas of progress in the others.

Cognitive Probes: Sampling Along a Learning Career Axis

In the manner of ethnoscience and other cognitive anthropological research it is possible to elicit from a series of parties folk taxonomies and the like. But unlike most such studies, one interested in cultural transmission selects these parties so as to form analytic pairs, and one seeks to measure the degrees of equivalence (similarity and difference) in such pairs of cognitive maps. This roughly describes Allan Tindall's study of Utes and Mormons as they perceive and participate in basketball. Add a sampling along a learning career axis and it describes Tom Carroll's projected study of the categories "work" and "play" in the mappings of teachers and pupils, the latter chosen at selected points in the usual school career; he thus will derive inferentially a sequence of transactions toward equivalence in respect to the cognitive domains under examination. Basic methodological know-how is reasonably well established. However, this strategy implies prior knowledge or fortunate hunch of two kinds: as to the significance of the selected cognitive features for cultural transmission generally in the society at hand, and as to the time, place, and sequence of the encounters critical to that learning.

The Analysis of Transaction-in-Progress

The direct examination of transactions-in-progress implies some mechanical recording (i.e., video tape or film) so as to permit many fine-grained reexaminations of the behaviors entailed. Direct examination can and probably must proceed simultaneously in contrived experimental settings and in natural settings.

For experimental settings, "culture machines" (e.g., the elaborated seal hunt game which requires players to transact a set of role relationships and beliefs and through further transactions to pass these on to subsequent generations) permit a start. The advantages of these contrived settings is, of course, that, through manipulating the conditions and terms, one can selectively bring various dimensions of otherwise impossibly complex phenomena into play. And that done, one can watch for various behavioral indications (including speech of course) of equivalence and nonequivalence and, separately, probe (in the manner of section one, above) into the cognitive mappings of the parties; each measure, observation and probe, serves as a reality check against and perhaps sharpens the other.

In parallel examination of naturally occurring transaction, one loses much power of manipulation, but perhaps finds the phenomena more saliently meaningful in virtue of the possible real-life seriousness of the matters at issue in the transaction. It is evident that, should one know on the basis of studies such as those described in section one above approximately when and where transactional work is getting done, one knows better what scene he wants to record and examine.

The linked Frank and Hughes studies plus Carroll's study (above) in part fall in this realm. The work over the past twenty years of Birdwhistel and Condon, and more recently Erickson, provide excellent foundation for such transactional analysis.

Procedurally, it appears necessary, in respect to both contrived and naturally occurring transactions, at least at this early stage of investigation, for the observer to assume a series of "as if" instances. One takes the stance, for example, that in the course of a transaction all the behavior has solely to do with agenda and devises a series of examinations (e.g., different forms of verbal interchange, as questionings, responding, etc. viewed one at a time, then nonverbal interchanges) so as to read the whole as a complex negotiation among the parties as to positioning. Then one takes a contrasting stance, as if all the behaviors were solely directed to communicating mappings as between the parties (e.g., as attempts of each party to explicate his own map to himself, to convey it to others, to read their maps, etc., one focus at a time, and in respect to selected matters of setting, natural science, organization, one at a time). Such examinations move, of course, from relatively amorphous casting-about to systematic coding, as understanding permits. Such examinations always include both observation and eliciting probes.

Ethnographic Stock-Taking

It is timely and seems possible to attempt a resynthesis of ethnographies of cultural transmission now in hand, using the set of notions earlier outlined. The anthropological literature on cultural transmission (whether one includes or excludes studies of personality formation in early childhood) is quite vast and of course conceptually disarticulated in large measure. That literature does admit of translation in some serious measure, and when that is done it will surely be evident that in fact anthropologists not only have a lot of information bearing on cultural transmission cross-culturally, but understand a great deal more as well. We will attempt this collectively over the next six months, in the form of a *Current Anthropology* review article.

Creating an Encounter Matrix

The two research activities above have pointed to studies of single cultural systems. The resynthesis of literature will perhaps draw diverse information into a common conceptual framework, and that will invite cross-cultural comparison and no doubt even suggest cross-cultural regularities. But a general theory of cultural transmission will require broad comparison of more rigorous nature. Naroll and others use the term hologeistic, meaning analysis on the basis of an adequate sample of known human societies. An encounter matrix, as will be described, will be useful in the single-society studies. But such a matrix seems virtually a prerequisite for hologeistic studies. Thus it newly introduces the key problem of comparative analysis and is the logical context to introduce that problem, the matter of emics and etics.

The encounter matrix in question is a purposefully simplistic, computerized storage and retrieval system of sociometric information having the following two features:

> 1. The matrix has three dimensions and is so designed that "cells" are created for any thinkably dyadic encounter in any social system, each cell defined by the age, sex, and social stratum of each of the two parties to the encounter; probably some 300 cells are implied, possibly many more.
>
> 2. Additionally, the matrix is so designed that estimates can be entered as to the frequency of encounters of each kind, relative to all other kinds, and as to the relative frequency, within each kind, of (a) encounters where both parties are from the same household, or that not being so, from the same local community (village, functioning neighborhood, etc.) or residually, from a wider, bureaucratically organized system but from the same language or dialect community, or that wider system and from contrasting language communities; *and* (b) encounters where the parties are under strong obligation or weak obligation to enter and sustain such encounters.

It should be noted that the matrix itself and the above information to be entered are empty of transactional content. That is, the matrix reveals only that encounters of specified kinds occur in estimated relative frequencies. The presumption is, of course, that, coming together, the parties communicate in some discoverable manner about some discoverable thing or things and achieve or fail to achieve equivalences of some discoverable kind. But the matrix as here described does not contain and cannot reveal these matters; it merely maps the stage upon which transaction occurs.

Such a matrix is necessarily organized by etic categories (of age, sex, social stratification), and the information to be entered is necessarily reduced to etic categories (as to group membership, obligation). Following Goodenough, etic language should be derived inductively from emic languages. That is, the pivotal criterion for a system of etic categories is that it contain the discriminations which mark the emic boundaries as perceived by each cultural group under comparative study; the etic system describes each emic system and violates none of them.

The obverse, by Goodenough's standard, is that one does *not* set out to generate at the outset a universally applicable etic system; one starts from an array of selected societies and attempts to find or create an etic system which works, by that standard, for them; any later addition to the array requires reexamination of the etic system as to its adequacy in describing the emic system newly brought under examination.

The selection of an initial sample of societies is guided by technical standards now well established through some three decades of broadly comparative work (Murdock, Naroll, and many others); by those standards the HRAF Quality Control sample of nonliterate, nonurban societies provides an optimum initial pool. From that, some societies can readily be selected with an eye to two criteria: that the selected societies represent the full range of social complexity within that pool, and that the ethnographic literature on the selected societies be relatively rich in data bearing on cultural transmission. Finally, a few literate urban societies not in the pool must be added, including the United States.

The matrix requires a system of etic categories embracing the three dimensions; it is probable that others have already largely done that work; here the task is to examine etic categories others have devised, access those as to their adequacy in respect to the selected societies by Goodenough's standard, and adopt and modify as indicated.

Similarly, the earlier-named frequency estimates to be entered in the matrix require etic systems meeting the same standard which discriminate as between paired parties in any encounter (same or different household, local community, wider bureaucratic system cum language community). Of these probably only the linguistic community dimension remains to be done; recent research in sociolinguistics, especially the ethnography of communication (Cazden et al.) probably makes possible the inductive generation of these etic categories. An etic system in respect to obligation must be derived, probably from scratch.

The encounter matrix is a system for storing and retrieving information. The three decades of anthropological experience in such research strongly indicate that such systems are best created in the course of doing actual research. This is to say, some set of appropriate hypotheses must be devised, and in the course of testing these the matrix will be created. Of course, the hypotheses must be of interest and possible significance in their own right. Several dozen which compare societies in relevant terms are surely evident, among them: several hypotheses which treat contrasting levels of social complexity or contrasting modes of subsistence as independent variables, and which predict as dependent variables characteristic densities of encounter; e.g., of nonadults in contrasting relative frequencies with adults of grandparental generation, compared to adults of parental generation, compared to other nonadults; or of nonadults with the above subdivided as to same social stratum or other social strata; etc.

The crux, of course, is how readily the ethnographic literature will yield up the required information. Pragmatically, this means whether a reader can identify from direct or indirect evidence those 300 or more kinds of encounters earlier mentioned (the cells) and derive the named frequency estimates both among the cells and within each cell; more, whether two readers can independently do so with adequate measures of agreement.

The main purposes to be served by such an encounter matrix are three:

1. From the information stored by such a matrix on any society, a researcher can generate an encounter profile of that society, i.e., a gross mapping of densities of (presumptive) transaction; such patterns of density can be read as they vary along a life career axis, can be read for males in contrast to females, for persons of high strata in contrast to others low, etc. It should be noted: in general, but not in all particular instances, areas of high encounter density are likely to be areas of low transactional activity; nonequivalence, and transactional work, is more likely in new or infrequent encounters. Such a profile will help reduce gross sampling error, overgeneralization, and perhaps other forms of ethnographic error.

2. Analogously, such mappings will probably permit the generation of typologies of societies according to their encounter profiles; such comparative sorting will help in the selection of societies for original ethnographic research

and in establishing priorities for analysis of extant literature. Such typologies additionally will invite the generation of hypotheses for hologeistic tests.

3. Finally, such a matrix can serve as the basis for organizing a data archive of information about transaction itself, as that information, through translation from extant bodies of ethnographic information and through new research, becomes available.

Indirect Mapping of Cultural Transmission Systems

On the basis of a series of probe studies (see p. 188) in respect to some one cultural system and with a completed encounter profile for that system, it should be possible economically to map a system of equivalences which together constitute the scrutinized aspects of the cultural system of the community or society in question. From the probe studies the researcher must derive various shorthand indices of the cognitive mappings at issue, and from the encounter profile he must plot areas of relative transactional density; with the two he can with some precision map the patterns of equivalence and nonequivalence through the population at a hypothetical moment in time.

The same information, organized along a life career axis (variously as between male and female, social class, etc., according to the nature of the society in question) becomes an indirect mapping of the cultural transmission system, revealing patterns of convergence and divergence through time as among cognitive maps. "Indirect," because transactions themselves have not been attended, only the presumptively resulting equivalences. It should be possible to make determinations as follows, principally four:

First, with an eye to the major sortings employed in the society in question (i.e., rich and poor, black and white, etc.), a determination as to the de facto *gatekeeping* function of the transmission system taken as a whole; that is, one treats the mapped cultural transmission system as "cause" and the resulting economic or political placement of that adult population as "effect."

Second, a parallel determination of that aspect of gatekeeping which selectively *recruits* the participants to those encounters which are critical in cultural transmission—i.e., the educators and their charges, plus other adults with power whom the educators critically encounter.

Third, the examination of the forms of *testing* and credentialing (i.e., both test and the testing behaviors) in the society in question, as measurements of equivalences in respect to each of the four dimensions of equivalence described earlier (not only the dimension nominally being tested). In complex societies probably the equivalences being tested for are between the potential teacher (or whomever) being tested, and others at and near centers of economic and political power.

Fourth, an examination of gatekeeping, recruiting and testing cumulatively, as forces of cultural persistence and, as facts may dictate, change.

Hologeistic Analysis

Analyses as those suggested on page 189 being completed for any array of cultural systems, those data would in part already be in a condition which permits comparison; and when completed for a sufficient array, hologeistic comparison. The implied tasks of such hologeistic study are large, but no unusual methodological difficulties are evident. Etic systems for newly added facets are entailed in all four of the suggested analyses; but with the possible exception of the third-named, testing, the inductive generation of those etics do not seem from this remote vantage difficult. This is to say, a very large array of hypotheses as to cross-cultural regularities (in respect to gatekeeping, recruitment of educators, testing, and cultural persistence) would seem to admit of very early hologeistic analysis. Walter Precourt's current study of initiations in tribal societies and chiefdoms is a good case in point.

Indeed a good number, roughly fitting into this realm (most have intrapsychic "middle terms") have been completed over the last twenty years.

In contrast, effective hologeistic analysis is more remote in respect to transaction processes per se. These, of course, are the culminating studied toward which all others lead. These await a good deal of inquiry in the general manner of section two above, await, that is, the time when transaction processes yield to analysis in one cultural system, then another and another. There will then remain the task, clear in principal but doubtlessly very difficult in the doing, inductively to derive, from emic systems of categories and from emic systems of logics, adequate etic systems, following Goodenough's standard. One would not reasonably expect much return from these culminating efforts in this decade.

REFERENCES

Bateson, Gregory. *The Naven* (first printed in 1956). Stanford: Stanford University Press, 1958.

Birdwhistel, Ray L. *Introduction to Kinesics*. Louisville: University of Louisville Press, 1952.

Burnett, Jacquetta. "Ceremony, Rites, and Economy in the Student System of An American High School." *Human Organization* 28, no. 1 (Spring, 1969): 1–10.

Carroll, Tom. "A Probe of the Formation, Use, and Intersection of Adult and Child Activity Categories." M.D. dissertation, State University of New York at Buffalo, in progress.

Cazden, Courtney B.; John, Vera P.; and Hymes, Dell, eds. *Functions of Language in the Classroom*. New York: Teachers College Press, 1972.

Chagnon, Napoleon A. *Yanomamo, the Fierce People*. New York: Holt, Rinehart, and Winston, 1968.

Cole, Michael, et al. *The Cultural Context of Learning and Thinking*. New York: Basic Books, 1971.

Condon, William. "Film as a Microscope for the Study of Behavior." Paper read at the 71st Annual Meeting of the American Anthropological Association, Toronto, Canada, December, 1972.

Erickson, Frederick David. "Talking to the Man." Paper read at the 71st Annual Meeting of the American Anthropological Association, Toronto, Canada, December, 1972.

Evans-Pritchard, E. E. *The Nuer*. New York: Oxford University Press, 1940.

Fortes, Meyer. "Social and Psychological Aspects of Education in Taleland" (first printed in 1938). In John Middleton, *From Child to Adult*. New York: Natural History Press, 1970.

Frank, Frederick P. "Ethnographic Procedures for Collecting Base Line Data on Role Retransactions between Educational Administrators and Their Staffs." Ph.D. dissertation, State University of New York at Buffalo, in progress.

Goffman, Erwin. *The Presentation of Self in Everyday Life*. Garden City, N.Y.: Anchor, 1959.

Goodenough, Ward. *Description and Generalization in Anthropology*. Chicago: Aldine, 1970.

Hallowell, A. I. *Culture and Experience*. Pittsburgh: University of Pennsylvania Press, 1955.

Hughes, Wayne D. "An Examination of the Effects on Individuals of Constructing and Testing a Schedule for Systematic Observation." Ph.D. dissertation, State University of New York at Buffalo, in progress.

Murdock, George Peter. "Cross-Cultural Sampling." *Ethnology* 2 (1963).

Naroll, Raoul. "Data Quality Control in Cross-Cultural Surveys." In Raoul Naroll and Ronald Cohen, eds., *A Handbook of Method in Cultural Anthropology*. New York: Natural History Press, 1970.

Pierce, John R. "Communication." *Scientific American* 227 (September 1972).

Precourt, Walter. "A Hologeistic Study of Explicit and Hidden Curriculum in Initiations in Tribal Societies and Chiefdoms." Paper presented at a conference of the East-West Center, Honolulu, January 29–February 4, 1973.

Tindall, B. Allan. "The Psycho-cultural Orientation of Anglo and Ute Indian Boys in an Integrated High School." Ph.D. dissertation, University of California, Berkeley, in progress.

Turner, Victor W. "Forms of Symbolic Action: Introduction." Proceedings of the Annual Spring Meeting, American Ethnological Society, University of Washington, 1969.

Wallace, Anthony. *Culture and Personality.* 2nd ed. New York: Random House, 1970.

Washburn, Sherwood. "A View of the Evolution of Human Behavior." Paper read at the 71st Annual Meeting of the American Anthropological Association, Toronto, Canada, December, 1972.

13 / A Cultural Theory of Education

Frederick O. Gearing

In any contemporary community, every man and woman, and every boy and girl, move daily into and out of at least two smaller worlds. One of these consists of household and neighborhood and club and so on; within any contemporary community of any size there are many such localized worlds which contrast and, where contrasts in ethnicity and economic class are involved, perhaps contrast markedly. The second world is a network of bureaucratically organized business and government, which world in part unfolds in the same geographic space and in part draws persons daily outside that space; this network reaches around the earth and is remarkably homogeneous. Paul Bohannon has called all this the two-story system of contemporary life.

The life career of a man or woman consists of movements through two or more of these worlds; more particularly, a life career unfolds as he or she becomes a participant in first one, then the others, of the events which together constitute life in these worlds. These life careers are not random: within any localized world, boys and men move through those worlds differently than girls and women; there is little movement between localized worlds; men from some localized worlds move into the upper echelons of the bureaucratically organized world, while men from other localized worlds do not; and so on.

In empirical fact, each regularly occurring event is itself an education system; the events which together constitute the life of some localized world or some sector of that wider world are together the education systems of those worlds. Any person who is to become a participant in any recurring event enters as a newcomer and later becomes an old hand. What transpires in between—the face-to-face interchanges which transform the newcomer into an old hand—may look like instruction or may more resemble on-the-job training, but is, in whatever form, education.

In the contemporary world, in short, every person gets many educations. As his worlds and the events which constitute those worlds vary, so do the processes which transform him from newcomer into old hand in one event then another, in one of his worlds and then in the other. Further, the fact that life careers are patterned suggests that there are somehow involved matters of fit and ill-fit as among these worlds and their respective education systems.

From all this it would follow that the contemporary world being what it is, one cannot adequately comprehend the operations of any one education system in a community unless one comprehends as well the operations of the variety of education systems which coexist and may compete. For an obvious example, the behaviors which regularly occur in the places called schools and colleges are most imperfectly comprehensible unless one also comprehends, as coexisting education system, households and neighborhoods (from which the students come), jails and asylums (into which some may alternatively move), and the factories and enterprises and government agencies (into which most will move). Such arrays of coexisting education systems, of course, contrast in form and content each with the others.

In short, a comparative theory of education is necessary. A comparative theory of education is an array of concepts and operations which permit analyses of the full variety of extant education systems. This theory of education is a comparative theory; it permits analysis in common terms of much of that variety and has potential, we believe, for analysis of all of that full variety.

Any theory of education necessarily deals with information. By the formulation of this comparative theory we assume, in effect, that knowing about only some of that information—knowing where some items of information "go" and where not—is worth the effort. The theory seeks to deal with most of the information which is used in the normal course of events by most of the people in a community. More specifically, "most of the people" means that large number who (if there were a measure for intelligence and if the measure were tallied as IQ is tallied) would score between 80 and 120, and who are established members of the community in question. Similarly, "most of the information" means those items of information used by those persons in some modest or high frequency. Finally, "used" means actually displayed in some naturally occurring and recurrent interchange; note well that this last leaves to one side any determinations as to whether a person who regularly does not display an item *could* do so.

This theory moves from three methodological assumptions, each of which does some violence to received wisdom. The reader, simply to comprehend, must temporarily suspend disbelief.

First: all information is property. That is, any item of information can appropriately be displayed by some parties, not by others, according to the social identities of the parties. Put otherwise, all displays of information are role behaviors; thus, any display carries two principal messages, one the manifest content of the utterance or enactment, the other a tacit message about who is making the display with whom. There is one qualification, in pragmatic effect though not in principle: if there be, within the bounded community under analysis, items of information displayed by each with all, those items are not propertylike within that community (but would be found to be propertylike in some more inclusive community).

Second: education proceeds through the elimination of inappropriate displays. Put otherwise, displays of information would occur randomly through any population in the absence of constraints. But information is property (above), is displayed selectively, not randomly. The empirical task is to identify the constraints which so reduce randomness, the processes through which inappropriate displays are eliminated.

Third: by the terms of this theory, the irreducible atoms of analysis are not individuals but dyads. Dyads are, in empirical fact, real; dyads form, they assume describable attributes, they behave vis-à-vis other dyads, they dissolve. In face-to-face interchange, any utterance or enactment is, in empirical fact, a joint product of the two parties to a dyad or the several parties to a set of dyads. Individuals and their psyches are also real and may be knowable, but that reality and that knowledge are, by the terms of this theory, put (temporarily) to one side. The constraints which reduce randomness are, thus, dyads and systems of dyads. This is a cultural theory of education, informed by a radically *inter*psychic conception of cultural analysis.

OUTLINE OF THE THEORY: OVERVIEW

We seek to describe, in outline, a cultural theory of education. To this purpose we imagine an investigation which is improbably ambitious. This imagined investigation would address a contemporary community of some size and complexity; for example, a neighborhood which is ethnically heterogeneous and mixed in terms of economic class. The investigation would seek to describe the community's total education structure, which is to say the full array of regularly recurring face-to-face interchanges through which all salient items from the community's full pool of cognitively organized information is regularly distributed and redistributed among the members of the community across the generations.

Such an ambitious investigation would require a team at work over some duration. For our current descriptive purpose, we imagine three principal investigators: one a student of social organization, the second a student of cognitive organization (both of these working principally at a community-wide macro level), and the third, for whom no established label exists, working principally at the micro level of face-to-face transaction. The imagined period of investigation would be two years, the three kinds of investigation proceeding simultaneously, variously intersecting at most points.

The final product of such an investigation would be a description of the community as patterns of life career; these patterns described as functions of the education structure; the education structure described as a surface structure and infrastructure; these two structures described as reciprocally constraining each other, the education structure thereby being under continuing reconstruction. Throughout such a description, three analytically separable patterns of constraint to display of information enter pivotally, a pattern of "paced exchange," a pattern of "selective exchange," and a pattern of "proforma exchange," as will be defined in course.

OUTLINE OF THE THEORY: OPERATIONS

The improbably ambitious investigation which for descriptive purposes we imagine, entails an array of operations. The sequence of operations as described below moves from macro to micro and back to macro levels. However, macro-level investigations of social organization and of cognitive organization, and micro-level investigations of transaction are variously foreground and background each to the other, and in that sense are interwoven in all operations. The several operations which follow thus form a set, not always or principally a series in the sequence here described.

1. The investigators, through an array of analyses at the macro level, *describe the community as recurrent patterns of life career*. These analyses follow the reasonably well established methods of ethnography involving direct observation and the help of community members as informants. The operations are three:

1.1 The investigators explicitly *identify the community*. A community is a population which includes both sexes and all ages, all these persons in some pattern of systematic interaction with one another and with others outside the community, a cradle-to-grave but not self-contained social system. Identifying the community means defining its members.

1.2 The investigators *draw an ethnographic portrait* of the community. An ethnographic portrait seeks to describe all the recurrent activities of all the members of the community including those activities in which any member of the community joins regularly with others outside the community. Such an inclusively holistic portrait is, of course, approached through judicious sampling of persons and events, and it is only approached, never achieved.

1.3 The investigators redescribe the community as *recurrent patterns of life career*. Analysis describes an array of contrasting patterns of life career which tend to recur, as these may vary according to sex, economic class, ethnicity, and according to the division of labor in economic, political, religious realms, and according to other such attributes of community life.

2. The investigators, through a set of operations at principally the micro level of face-to-face transaction, select an adequate sample of events and, taking the events one at a time, *describe each selected event as a protocol.* An event is a face-to-face encounter which recurs and which, because it recurs, is routinized. To describe certain features of such a routine is to describe the event as a protocol. Most germane events involve less than fifty people. These operations require direct observation and the help of participants as informants, and additionally they require film or video records of several occurrences of the events. The operations are five:

2.1 Over a series of occurrences of any event, every participant forms, in principle, a dyadic relation with each fellow participant. Out of this array of dyads, the investigators select some adequate samples of dyads and *describe the event as a system of dyadic dances,* through a set of three determinations, as follows. First, each participant is identified as an old hand, that is, a long-established and well-versed participant in the event; or is identified as a recent newcomer (note that a newcomer apprentice becomes an old hand apprentice in a relatively brief period); or as something in between. Taking only those parties who are well established and those who are recent newcomers, the investigators array these in their various permutations as two kinds of dyad—old hand with old hand, and old hand with newcomer (leaving aside dyads between pairs of newcomers). Second, the investigators, principally through viewing film or video recordings, examine each of these dyads over a sufficient number of interchanges to make determinations as to the recurrent patterns of attention and inattention evidenced, and as to the recurrent patterns of leading-following evidenced. The array of dyads are then sorted according to the two dimensions. Three, the set of dyadic dances are summarized as a system of dances, in some variant of the following schematic form:

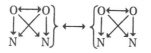

where: O = old hand; N = newcomer; solid lines indicate a high or moderate level of attentiveness, broken line indicates a low level or marked inattention; ↑ indicates the direction of leading, either reciprocal or one-directional; brackets indicate subgroup membership.

2.2 Attending for the moment only those dyads between old hand and old hand, the investigators redescribe the event as a *system of constraints to displays of information.* This operation entails three sub-operations, and a fourth confirming operation, as follows:

2.2.1. The investigators assemble and classify an adequate sample of items of information observed to have been displayed in some frequency in the course of the event. This sample corpus represents the *pool of information* which is variously drawn upon and displayed by the parties, one with the other, as they participate in the event. An item of information is the whole utterance or the whole interchange of utterances as bounded by topic shifts. The items of information are sorted into two types and so listed: first, items of *knowledge,* made up of clustered bits of information wherein the connections which join the bits (e.g., cause-and-effect, class inclusion, etc.) are explicitly named in the display, or where such connections, not being named, are by the parties readily nameable. Contrasting with these are items which are *premises,* made up of similarly connected cluster but where the connections are not named and not readily nameable. There may remain items where connections are indeterminant.

2.2.2. A *matrix is drawn* with two axes. The vertical axis treats social identities. The investigators compile an aggregate list of terms of reference and address, variously used by parties in the event, which terms ascribe social identities, including analogous but less standardized verbal glosses. These terms and glosses are analytically dissolved into component attributes of social identity (categories of age, of sex, of intelligence, etc.); these are joined in pairs, each attribute with every other which logically contrasts. These contrasting pairs of attributes are sorted into three types: those pairs of attributes between which the sole contrast is categories of age and any other pairs of attributes between which in virtual certainty mobility will occur or might plausibly and with full propriety occur, as this is perceived by the parties; a second type, those pairs of attributes between which the sole contrast is categories of sex and any other pairs between which, like these, in virtual certainty mobility will not and ought not occur, as perceived by the parties; and a third type consisting of pairs of attributes where the attributes themselves or mobility between the attributes is viewed discrepantly by different involved parties or are otherwise problematic, as often between smart and dumb (in whatever phrasing). The attributes of social identity, so sorted and listed, constitute the vertical axis of the matrix.

The second, horizontal axis of the matrix consists of three patterns of display of items of information where, in dyadic interchange between some pair of named parties, some item is regularly not displayed by the first of the two parties, but may be displayed by the second; conversely, where some item is regularly not displayed by the second, but may be displayed by the first; and where some item is regularly not displayed by either of the two named parties.

2.2.3. The two axes form a series of cells, mapping each pair of contrasting attributes by each pattern of display. The investigators select items of information from the compiled pool of information (2.2.1.) and, by the above matrix, *map constraints to displays* of each selected item. That is, the investigators map regular *absences* of display, mapping first an adequate sample of items of knowledge, then separately an adequate sample of items of cultural premise, entering notations as to each item of information in the appropriate cells. The investigators observe, in the course of the event, fully public displays (involving all dyads simultaneously), semi-public displays (involving some few dyads), and may observe private displays between the two parties to a single dyad. By noting the contrasting patterns of display in the three contexts and through the help of participants as informants, the investigators seek to infer: (1) among the identity attributes that parties to a dyad could be enacting, which pair of attributes are they saliently enacting; and (2) which pattern of constraint would apply if the interchange were private. The investigators thereby map the selected items of information according to these two inferences.

2.2.4. The investigators seek confirmation of the above mapping; going back to the mode of description of the event as a system of dances, they note the *incidence of stumbles* in the dance. Insofar as inappropriate displays occur, stumbles should occur. Notations of the incidence of such stumbles are added on the matrix; in these dyads, old hand with old hand, the incidence would be low (in the absence of social change underway).

2.3 Shifting now to the dyads between an old hand and a newcomer, the investigators redescribe the event as a *rite of passage* whereby newcomers become old hands.

2.3.1. The transformations of newcomers into old hands are traced by noting the *decrease in inappropriate displays* as inappropriateness was revealed above (2.2.3.). On copies of the same matrix, notations are entered in each cell of the decreasing incidence of inappropriate displays, items of knowledge and premises separately.

2.3.2. Analogously, the *decrease in the incidence of stumbles* is recorded.

2.4 The investigators *identify contrasts in three patterns of constraint*. The three categories of paired identities (2.2.2.) isolate three patterns of exchange, to which we now give names. The patterns of constraint which occur in interchanges where contrasting attributes vary solely by age and by attributes like age (where future mobility in respect to the attributes is deemed certain) constitute a type called a pattern of *paced exchange*, paced in the sense that an item of information which is the property of the older party will, later if not now, become the property of the younger (and items now the property of the younger will later cease to be so). The patterns of constraint which occur in interchanges where contrasting attributes vary by sex and by attributes like sex (where mobility is deemed in virtual certainty never to occur) constitute a second type, a pattern of *selective exchange*, selective in the sense that an item which is the property of one but not the other remains so permanently. Where, between pairs of attributes, mobility is problematic, that is, where the attributes themselves are disputed, or the matter of mobility between the attributes is disputed, *and* where dispute has become an impasse, a third type occurs, a pattern of *proforma exchange* which is basically a pattern of parallel coexistence. In earlier versions of these theoretical efforts, the first two types of patterns were described as two forms of a pattern then called "stable exchange."

The following suggests the nature of these three patterns of constraint and may, in empirical investigation, be treated as hypotheses; other such hypotheses will suggest themselves.

(a) The *relative magnitude of constraints* in dyads between old hands seen as the relative numbers of items of information whose display would be inappropriate in dyads where each pattern of exchange prevails.

	all information	knowledge	premises
paced exchange	++	++	0
selective exchange	+	+	0
proforma exchange	++++++	+++	+++

Most of the constraints will be in the form wherein one party displays the item but the counterpart regularly does not.

(b) The *rate of decrease in frequency of stumbles and inappropriate displays* in dyads between newcomers and old hands where each pattern of display prevails.

	frequencies of stumbles or inappropriate displays				
	early ⟵			⟶ late	
paced exchange	hi	hi	lo	0	0
selective exchange	hi	hi	lo	0	0
proforma exchange	hi	lo	lo	lo	0

2.5 The investigators proceed to a second event, repeating these analyses, and to a third, and so on to a description of an adequate *sample* of events as protocols. In the contemporary world, we said, every person lives in two kinds of social systems, daily moving into and out of events which make up one or more localized worlds and a wider world. An adequate sample of events must include events which are parts of such localized systems singly and in some combinations, other events which are parts of such wider networks, and still others which are parts of both in some interpenetrating mix. In the improbably ambitious event that the study seeks to describe the total education structure of the community, an adequate sample would include events from the various realms of work and play and worship which are together the life of that community, and events involving old and young, male and female, rich and poor, and so on. The net product is an adequate array of events, described as protocols.

It is evident that, as selected events are described as protocols and in part as by-products of those analyses, the initial description of the community as patterns of life career (1.3.) will have been elaborated and modified.

3. The investigators, through analyses at principally the macro-, community-wide level, *describe patterns of life career as functions of the education structure*. The theory at this writing is but little elaborated, at this macro level.

3.1. The array of events described at the micro level as protocols cumulatively *describe the equivalence structure and the transaction structure*. The equivalence structure is surface structure, the transaction structure is infrastructure; the two structures reciprocally constrain one another and together describe the education structure. Many events having been described, that aspect of each protocol which describes patterns of constraint operating between old hands cumulatively describes the community as an equivalence structure, a mapping of information as property, selectively distributed according to the social identities of the members of the community and in use by them. That aspect of the protocols which describes the transitions of newcomers into old hands cumulatively describes the community as transaction structure, a mapping of an array of rites of passage wherein inappropriate displays are eliminated. It is broadly evident that the equivalence structure constrains the transaction structure, principally in virtue of the fact that old hands lead and newcomers follow; it is also broadly evident that the transaction structure perpetually recreates and thereby constrains the equivalence structure.

3.2. The investigators, drawing on the existing description of the community as patterns of life career, *redescribe the community as a system of life career constraints*; that is, as a mapping of the boundaries which saliently reduce randomness in movement. In most contemporary communities, these more salient constraints coincide with the boundaries which separate those localized cultures which are organized by ethnicity and economic class; coincide with regularities of pattern whereby members of some localized cultures penetrate the upper levels of the wider network, others not; and coincide with sex roles (as this as it would generally appear).

3.3. The above description of life career constraints (3.2.) allows the investigators to predict where patterns of proforma exchange will occur (and where patterns of both selective exchange and paced exchange will occur). The above descriptions of the community as equivalence structure and transaction structure (3.1.) allow the investigators to confirm that these patterns of exchange do occur and to see what education work is done at those junctures and how that work continues to be done, other things being equal.

3.4. It is probable that events usefully aggregate into classes, thus the education work done in those classes of event can be aggregated analogously. It is evident that in some bureaucratically organized events, the principal purpose is instructional (one thinks of jails, asylums, churches, the military, and, of course, schools and colleges), instructional in the sense that the items of information displayed there are mixed, some being items of idle information presumptively useful at some later time in some other context, but some items, dealing with the organization of the event itself, being immediately useful. It is evident that these events contrast with other bureaucratically organized events wherein the principal purpose is the work of the world (one thinks of business enterprises, government). In the instructional events there are relatively few old hands and, at those junctures in time when there are newcomers, many newcomers; here the old hands have status and power and keep both, irrespective of the fact that the newcomers become old hands; here the career of a student or other such client is a whole series of little rites of passage, steps and plateaus of quite a short duration. The latter class of event contrasts in all the named respects. Still further, events not bureaucratically organized (one thinks of households, teams, clubs) may form another class, contrasting with both the above. These three classes of event, with their contrasting classes of education work, invite a series of three subtheories, but the operations entailed cannot, at this writing, be described. Other such classes may be evident.

Social Change

When one describes an event or a community as an education structure, certain raw phenomena are selectively lifted out; these are aggregated in some set of categories, and the categories are joined and apposed in some fashion. This theory is one such description. One may redescribe the same event or community as a political and economic structure. The first description as education structure necessarily describes the acquisition and display of information. The second necessarily describes the concentration and deploying of power.

It would seem to follow that the origins of social changes, those behaviors which put processes of social change in motion, are best identified through description of an event or community as political and economic structure, not through description as education structure. It would also seem to follow that a description of an event or community as education structure most directly and unambiguously reveals whether the social changes in question are being assimilated into the existing organization of community life or whether that organization itself is irreversibly changing. Probably, all social change involves new items of information and new kinds of persons. If new items of information and new kinds of persons are being assimilated into preexisting classes of information and person, and if the patterns of appropriate display of those classes of information by those classes of person remain unchanged, the organization of community life is not changing. Conversely, if the emergence of new classes of information or new classes of person is evident, or if a new pattern of appropriate display of the preexisting classes of information by the preexisting classes of person is evident, then the organization of community life is changing: the social changes are systemic.

By the terms of this theory, social changes are reflected when any of the three named patterns of exchange are opened for renegotiation by the parties; this is evidenced by an increased incidence of stumbles in the interchanges between old hands.

Two parallel sets of pattern in negotiation career are, by implication of the theory's terms, suggested and invited empirical attention. First, a pattern of paced exchange (where identities contrast by age) may give way to an episode of renegotiation marked by stumbles and thence back to a pattern of paced exchange, modified from the original or not, as the case may be; or similarly a pattern of selective exchange (whose identities contrast by sex), thence renegotiation, then back to selective exchange. In the human experience very generally, it would seem that renegotiations occur more frequently where patterns of paced exchange prevail, but that episodes of renegotiation are longer, the negotiation more troublesome, where patterns of selective exchange prevail. The second pattern in negotiation is where, out of an episode of renegotiation, there emerges, not the earlier pattern of paced or selective exchange, but the parties instead settle into a pattern of proforma exchange. In the human experience very generally, it would appear that this happens increasingly as social systems become increasingly large and complex.

All three patterns of exchange do education work, but especially in the context of analysis of social change, patterns of proforma exchange are pivotal. That pattern emerges in situations of impasse as to identities and roles. Where that pattern has come to prevail, parties tune each other out; they coexist. To speak somewhat figuratively, it is rather easy in complex social systems to settle into a pattern of proforma exchange, and quite difficult to negotiate a way out.

Recent domestic experience provides numerous instances of massive social change: the space effort, the world of television, desegregating schools. The question is whether these social changes are systemic, whether these very real changes are being assimilated to preexisting organization, or whether that organization is itself changing. Our strong intuition is that the changes are not systemic, but it is a matter for empirical investigation. And in contrast to this, unplanned and unwanted, its origins not convincingly identified, there would strongly appear to be a sea change which is systemic—the steadily increasing incidence of patterns of proforma exchange; this, too, is a matter for empirical investigation, plus intervention.

Cognitive Organization and Process

All information is, in Bateson's phrasing, "news about difference." To a thermostat, the drop in room temperature as it passes a selected point is news. In human communication, much information (quite possibly, all information) is news about contrasts between categories, i.e., contrasts between classes of things, classes of persons, classes of actions and feelings, and contrasts as well between classes of connection (cause-and-effect, inclusion and exclusion, and the like) between any of these. And in human communication, most of these categories are contrived, culturally given.

This cultural theory of education deals, among other things, with the rates by which inappropriate displays are eliminated, as newcomers move toward becoming old hands. A display may be inappropriate solely because the parties are not privileged to that display: grown-ups displaying children information, for an obvious example. We here leave this aspect of inappropriateness to one side. A display may be inappropriate in that, while the parties are privileged to engage in the display, the display is simply "wrong," as "2 + 2 = 5" is wrong. That inappropriate display may soon get eliminated (leaving "2 + 2 = 4" to reign alone). But "2 apples and 2 giraffes are 4" may be appropriate or inappropriate, sense or nonsense, depending on whether the ideas "set" and "number" are what the display was about. Set and number are, of course, labels for systems of categories. Less schoolish examples abound: an anthropologist who tries to enact a cultural premise in the field is (almost inevitably) wrong, in the sense that he is almost but not quite right.

This theory seeks to treat the elimination of, among other things, errors that form of inappropriateness. That purpose conspicuously raises two questions: What, in terms of cognitive organization, are the salient differences between one cluster of information and another, as such differences affect, among other things, the rate at which errors are eliminated? And what, in terms of cognitive process, are displays (by dyads!) in virtue of which errors get eliminated at all? We can only suggest the possible directions the answers will take.

The cognitive organization of clusters of information would seem to vary as to complexity of the sets of interconnected categories, as to whether the categories are digital or typological in form, and as to the presence or absence of verbal labels for the categories and connections. Information may, by these terms, be located in a field as follows:

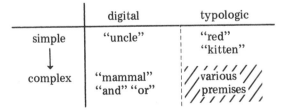

	digital	typologic
simple ↓ complex	"uncle"	"red" "kitten"
	"mammal" "and" "or"	various premises

The contrast between digital and typological categories has been treated by E. Heider: a class is digital in form where it is marked by a set of attributes such that an item does or does not have each attribute and, if all attributes are present, the item is a member of that class; a class is typologic in form where a prototypic example stands for the class and items are members of the class insofar as they approximate the prototype. The shaded area in the above field would seem to locate the kind of information we have called cultural premises, i.e., those quite complex clusters of information which have no verbal labels and, though regularly enacted, cannot readily be verbally characterized by the actors. In general, it would appear that the rate of decrease of inappropriate displays is slower as one moves from left to right and from top to bottom in the above field. Hypotheses which would elaborate and confirm that general intuition may suggest themselves to the reader.

In terms of cognitive process, what are displays? Thomas Carrol (in studies from which report in this issue derives) is seeking to adapt the Piagetian concepts of assimilation and accommodation. For Piaget, these are processes which occur inside psyches: new information is stimulus—if the person's prior cognitive map is able to receive the stimulus, that is assimilation; if not, the cognitive map may be altered and, if so, that is accommodation.

Perhaps, on the basis of three assumptions, the concepts can be adapted so as to usefully make assimilation and accommodation attributes of dyads. These assumptions are: (1) two parties to a dyad never perceive identically (or, if they do is unknowable to an observer); (2) the two parties will, nevertheless, assume they are perceiving identically if they possibly can; (3) when they cannot, the recognized fact of ill-fit in their perceptions is jointly enacted by them. Thus, where the categories entailed in a display can be imagined by the parties to be alike, the reciprocal information display is assimilation (i.e., in Piaget's intrapsychic terms, any new information is being assimilated into preexisting maps by one or both parties). And, where the categories entailed cannot be imagined by the parties to be alike, the reciprocal information display is not assimilation and may be accommodation (i.e., in Piaget's intrapsychic terms, the cognitive maps of one or both parties are changing so as to admit the new information).

Such an adaptation and development of cognitive process, reapplied congruently with the interpsychic conceptualization of this cultural theory, seems possible. Such a development would infringe on the theory pervasively, as perhaps will be suggested by the following metaphor, intended here merely as a heuristic:

assimilation: accommodation ::enactment: negotiation ::leading: following ::proforma exchange: paced and selective exchange ::social stability: social change.

Glossary: Analytic Terms

At micro levels of analysis

Dyad: An event may be described as a set of dyads. A dyad describes the totality of face-to-face interchange between any two specific individuals, the relationship they negotiate, enact, and perhaps renegotiate, recurrently in the course of their encounters on the occasions of some recurring event. In principle, in any many-party encounter, each participant forms a dyad with every other party. What the parties exchange is described as information; in face-to-face interchange communication occurs simultaneously through linguistic, paralinguistic, proxemic, and kinesic channels. A dyad is analytically dissolved into two aspects, displays and dances.

Display: A display is a description of the manifest content of any interchange, a verbal interchange or an enactment with or without verbal commentary. In face-to-face interchange, a display is thoroughly reciprocal, a property of the dyad or set of dyads. A display may be appropriate (figuratively, information offered while sought and sought while offered), or inappropriate.

Dance: A dance is a description of messaging, parallel to displays. Dances centrally involve synchronies between parties (as where the voice of the speaker establishes a beat for the overtalk and nonverbal behaviors of his listener or listeners); through synchronies and other signals dances additionally involve patterns of turn-taking, facing formations, patterns of attention and inattention, and of implicit leading and following. As a display may be appropriate or inappropriate, analogously a dance may unfold smoothly or be marked by stumbles.

Identity attributes: A dyad is analytically dissolved, as well, as some cluster of attributes of social identity. These attributes are the categories of sex, of age, of kinship, of social and economic strata, of ethnicity, and so on, as these are found to be enacted in the course of a recurring event. In face-to-face interchange, parties exercise options as to which attributes they will deem salient, options such that individual A, in interchange with B, may be "we" in apposition to some C (physically present or not), *and* at another moment, A with C are "we" in apposition to B; it is presumptive that, over an interchange of some duration, all such options will be exercised, but some more saliently than others.

At middle levels of analysis

Protocol: A protocol is two descriptions of an event as certain features of a routine. A protocol describes the event, first, as routines in interchanges among well-established participants (old hands), describes recurring patterns of display and dance as these covary with contrasting pairs of identity attributes.

At macro levels of analysis

Equivalence structure: Descriptions of an adequate sample of events as routines among old hands (above) constitute a description of a community as an equivalence structure, a pool of information selectively distributed and in use.

Transaction structure: Parallel descriptions of routines between old hands and newcomers (above) constitute a description of a community as a transaction structure, a systemic array of rites of passage whereby persons through their life careers recurrently become newcomers, then old hands.

Education structure: The equivalence structure, as surface structure, and the transaction structure, as infra structure, in a relationship of reciprocal constraint, together describe the community as an education structure.

None of the three studies described below address in its entirety the cultural theory of education, above. Each, however, directly articulates with the theory at various junctures.

Tindall's study examines how Ute Indian and Mormon Anglo high schoolers form and play games of pick-up basketball, in school and out. Such games are, of course, regularly occurring events, as that term has been used in these pages, and such events are themselves describable as small education systems whereby, at some point, each participant has entered as a newcomer and in time has become an old hand. (In the study itself, only one person is seen in this transition, the new high school gym teacher, plus Tindall himself.) Among many kinds of information presumptively entailed, Tindall focuses on certain cultural premises bearing on how men exercise control over other men. It emerges that Utes and Mormons entertain contrasting premises, as we may have supposed, but it also emerges that, as the theory would predict, Utes and Mormons vis-à-vis one another have settled into a pattern of proforma exchange, parallel coexistence, so that groups of Ute players regularly enact the Ute premise and only that, and groups of Mormon players the Mormon premise and only that. Whether Utes *could* enact, if they wished, the Mormon premise (or Mormons could enact the Ute premise) is moot. That members of each group regularly do not is evident. The propertylike nature of these items of information is clear, and in effect members of each group, in engaging in displays of these messages, are displaying simultaneous messages about their respective ethnic identities.

Smith's study deals with a rather different kind of recurring event, teacher meetings in a Montessori school. The participants are a head teacher and two apprentice teachers. The latter are newcomers in course toward becoming old hands. The pattern of exchange appears to be of the type called paced. The information entailed is knowledge, and is unusually complex in nature: what kinds of causes are appropriately to be ascribed for "our" behaviors (where "we" are teachers) and for "their" behaviors (where "they" are students)? Inappropriate displays by these newcomers do occur; quite probably the incidence of these is decreasing over time, but at this point in Smith's work, that matter has not yet been systematically reviewed. Additionally, Smith briefly looks at the pattern of appropriate displays functionally: why this pattern in this context? And he sees the pattern serving to create and sustain for the teaching staff a posture of control while avoiding blame, which certainly serves and may be necessary, that this professional group perform their difficult professional task.

Carrol's ethno-semantic report traces some wider implications of a study in which he examined the events which are the school days of children and their teachers, kindergarten through fifth grade in a suburban school. The study probes into the realm of cognitive process, one of the largely unexplored aspects of this cultural theory of education. He, like Tindall, is dealing with premises here, by what criteria in an activity deemed "work" (as against play and other such domains); and he, like Smith, is dealing with the pattern of exchange called paced. In contexts of this pattern of exchange and in respect to premises as complex and elusive as those here in focus, questions as to who is newcomer, who old hand, become confounded. Carroll's study, because it explicitly breaks new ground, best underscores a fact that the reader should not lose throughout all these pages: This cultural theory of education is far from "finished." We do have the conceit that we are gaining.

14 / Another Route to a General Theory of Cultural Transmission: A Systems Model

Marion L. Dobbert

BASIC ASSUMPTIONS

Fred Gearing, in his February 1973 CAE Newsletter article "Where We Are and Where We Might Go: Steps Toward a General Theory of Cultural Transmission," singled out some important aspects of contemporary science which might contribute toward the formulation of a general theory of cultural transmission. In my mind, two of the central ideas identified by Gearing—"transaction" and information theory—are indeed important. It seems equally likely to me that in these two aspects of contemporary social science we will find the beginning steps for our general theory.

Most social scientists will agree in principle with Gearing's statement that a culture is built up out of the transactions between the members of a society and between members and their environments over time; that transactions, both with persons and with an environment, imply an exchange of information; and that transaction and information exchange imply the buildup and maintenance of a system. The Gearing model and the systems model proposed herein are in substantial agreement upon these fundamental points. At this point, however, the two theories diverge by focusing upon different aspects of information exchange. Gearing's focus is interpersonal and his research strategies center upon two-by-two interactions and upon the characteristics of information exchange in dyadic and triadic relationships. He achieves a cultural view of information exchange and transmission through a network analysis procedure.[1]

The inference that I draw from the ideas inherent in the notions of transaction and in information theory have led me in a somewhat different direction. The theoretical formulation of cultural transmission proposed below is not posed, however, as a rival to Gearing's formulation, but as a complementary theory dealing with cultural transmission at a different level.

CULTURE AND INFORMATION

Gearing proposes a theory of cultural transmission. Yet he backs away from the idea of culture (dismissing the notion as a reification) and turns to something more concrete—the study of individuals involved in information transactions. The purpose of Gearing's study is to determine the nature of the individual's cognitive maps and to determine how such maps are built, modified, and transmitted. Gearing thus treats culture as immanent. His argument that the relationship between Napoleon Chagnon and a Yanomamo, and the relationship between that Yanomamo and his twin brother, are not qualitatively different demonstrates his view. Gearing states that both dyadic relationships are transactional, one merely has a longer history and therefore the transactions have greater equivalence. Thus Gearing implies that numerous transactions *add up* to a culture, as the term "culture" is ordinarily used. We use the term culture, then, in Gearing's view as a convenience to demarcate the thin places in essentially indivisible transactional networks.

I cannot agree with Gearing that culture is immanent and that the actions, interactions, and understandings of individuals add up to a culture. My own studies of a Quaker group that has survived for over 140 years while transacting constantly and heavily with the non-Quakers surrounding them in the contexts of farm work, school, Grange, WCTU, and even of marriage (up to two-thirds of a generation married non-Quakers) have convinced me that there is more to culture than transaction. Within the anthropological tradition the notion of culture as superorganic, though exaggerated, emphasizes the transcending aspects of the undefined phenomenon which we label culture. Traditionally also, British social anthropology from Malinowski onward has emphasized a notion of social structure in which structure was considered more than the sum of individual interactions. The conceptual anthropology of Boas and his students also recognized culture as transcendant.

I do not raise these points in order to argue them in detail; rather, I raise them to suggest that the idea that culture transcends personal interaction is a formidable part of the anthropological intuition. However, meticulous scientists such as Gearing have not been satisfied with fuzzy notions about the superorganic, structure or culture, and because these notions have not been rigorously defined they have rejected the idea of culture. Nevertheless, Gearing has thrown the baby out with the bath water. Thus, what he defines in his article is a transaction theory of information sharing processes rather than a theory of cultural transmission. All the study in the world of individual cognitive maps and of dyadic or triadic transactions (or million person television-mediated transactions) will not lead us to a general theory of cultural transmission—if, indeed, anthropological intuition has been correct and the transcending something called culture can be defined scientifically.

Since it is my intention to propose a theory of cultural transmission, I must certainly begin (at the least) by approaching a scientific, operational definition of culture.[2] Such a definition can be approached through the use of key concepts from the General System Theory (von Bertalanffy 1968). One such concept is the relativity concept: systems always consist of parts in relation; however, the parts and relations identified exist only in the context defined by the researcher. Gearing has defined the systems for transactions of equivalences. The systems Gearing describes have parts—human beings—joined in the relation of transaction. Culture, however, is a higher level system and the systems that Gearing describes are subsystems of culture or parts of culture. To define culture, we may turn to the study of genetics and evolution for a definitional model which will suggest ways of dealing with the integration of several complex levels of subsystems.

The Darwinian notion of evolution as developed in modern science is based upon the idea that a genetic system built up of chemical elements, genes (i.e., the parts), is a mapping of an environment (relation). Genes are seen, then, as a symbolic replication of an environment, just as a road map or topographic map may be replications of that same environment, though in different terms. Were we to study evolution following a scheme equivalent to Gearing's dyadic transactional approach, we would proceed to study the chemical make-up of the individual genes (their equivalent of his cognitive mappings) and look at their interactions with each other in the production of the organism. Clearly we would learn nothing about evolution. To study evolution, we would have to turn to a study of the way the whole set of genes maps the entire environment. We would also have to study the way in which the environment, which includes for any individual gene all other genes, is replicated in the genetic *system*. This suggests that we study not dyadic transaction, but the whole system of meaning-transactions of which dyadic transactions are only small parts, if we wish to study *cultural* transmission.

It is at this point that we return to systems theory, specifically to information theory within that context. Although information theory does model the process of communication, when placed in the context of system theory it takes on a broader aspect which is of greater interest for a discussion of enculturation. In the systems context, information is used to explain the nature of organization and to answer the question of how organization qua organization is maintained in a system through the importation of information. For example, in the physical system of an animal, the method of maintaining organization (i.e., life) is evident—food which is energy is imported and incorporated. The situation in a nonphysical system is analogous: the nonphysical system imports and incorporates information and thus maintains structure. The importance of this analogue is seen in the fact that information is defined mathematically by an expression which is isomorphic to the expression of the formula for negative entropy in thermodynamics (von Bertalanffy 1968).

A second concept from information theory is of equal importance to an operational definition of culture: the communication of information does not imply replication; rather, it implies symbolic correspondence. This is clearly seen in an examination of the relationship of correspondence between genetic systems and environments. This correspondence can also be accounted for at the cultural level. The following definition of culture takes account of the notion of correspondence, of the importance of information as an organizer, and of the need to consider levels as discussed above.

> Culture is a system for mapping information from an environment. This information is stored in shared conceptual patterns, in patterns for social interaction and in patterns for getting a living.[3]

Just as a genetic system may be considered a map of an environment since an existing system has, by definition, taken account of an environment and adapted to it to a successful degree, so may a cultural system be considered a successful map. I have earlier illustrated this concept (Dobbert 1971) by showing how Teton-Dakota religious beliefs; band, encampment, and tribal structures; and individual and group food-gathering patterns mapped information from the pre-European environment, and how, through making use of the information stored in the three patterns designated, the Dakota adapted to early reservation conditions.[4]

TOWARD A GENERAL THEORY

A theory of cultural transmission based upon the above definition of culture and informed by the same theoretical considerations would have to explain how the adaptive information system historically connected with any one society might be passed on. Or, to state it another way, a model of culture transmission which assumes that culture is a symbolic map of an environment must show how information stored in structure may be transmitted between generations in a society. In order to avoid the danger of reification, the model will have to consist of two parts on two separate levels. The one part will represent humans who store information in their brains, and the other part will represent culture which stores information in structures or patterns corresponding to the environment. At this first level, then, the systems models will look like this.

Diagram 1

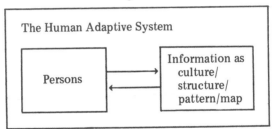

The boxes represent the two subsystems. The arrows represent the transmission of information, so that the variety in one subsystem constrains the variety in the other. In other words, because persons exist, act, believe, and choose, culture cannot be made up of all possible patterns. Rather, it is limited by the options selected by the persons. Similarly, because patterns exist historically and are transmitted in shared behaviors, or patterns, the possible varieties of acts, beliefs, and choices are also limited—the persons are constrained in their behaviors.

It is clear from this diagram, then, that the process of cultural transmission is a process in which individuals come to store the pattern information in their brains and thus come to act in ways that are reasonably complementary, thereby perpetuating the patterns. It will also become clear that the patterns in themselves (as stored in the persons making up the society) perform the task of transmission, which is to say that they are self-transmitting (at least according to the logic of the diagram). Or, to state it another way, it is the learner's exposure to the whole of culture that results in cultural transmission. This can be demonstrated in an expanded version of the above diagram. Diagram 2 depicts the essential aspects of a theory of cultural transmission which is intergenerational, nonreductionist, materialistic, and interactionist.[5] Two major assumptions of the theory are also evident in the diagram, but should be stated for purposes of clarity. The first is that culture is patterned probabilistically; cultural patterns are stochastic organizations of information. This makes the model non-deterministic with respect to single learners, thus allowing for individuality. The second assumption is that a learner learns an entire pattern and not just a response, a technique, or a state.

The model states the general theory of cultural transmission in the following way: (1) The learner is an individual person at a given age possessing certain abilities for action (box 1.1). (2) The age of the learner limits him/her to certain cultural

Diagram 2

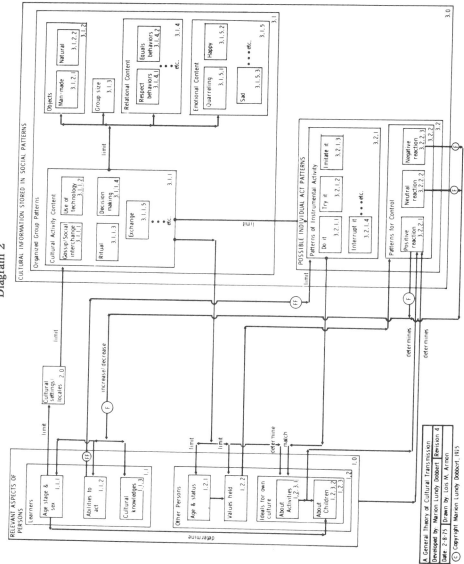

locales. An infant, for example, would in many cultures be limited to household settings, or a boy to masculine settings (box 1.1.1). (3) A setting (2.0) defines possible activities. A household ritual would be different from a village ritual. (4) Each cultural activity has four appropriate aspects (3.1.2, 3.1.3, 3.1.4, 3.1.5) which the learner has chosen along with the activity and learns along with them. In a household setting for making beer among the Ngoni, a girl also learns about beer pots, grain, and fire (objects, 3.1.2), learns that this is a small group activity (group size, 3.1.3), learns that respectful behavior toward seniors is the proper mode (relational, 3.1.4), and learns that this is a time for happy joking (3.1.5) (Read, 1960). (5) The nature of the activity (3.1.1) limits the kind of personnel (1.2.1), and limits the range of values and ideals applicable (1.2.2 and 1.2.3.1). However, the model shows that personnel, values, and ideals are a part of the situation. In the beer-making situation, the personnel are grown women, never men. Values about social interaction and pride in work apply, but never values about warfare. An ideal picture of peaceable cooperation also applies in the Ngoni case. (6) The nature of the activity (3.1.1) allows the child to pick only certain types of acts (3.2.1). For example, a child at an American rodeo does not have the option of riding a bull. Returning to the Ngoni example, let us assume that a young boy and a young girl both try to join the activity (3.1.1) and stir the beer (3.2.1).

(7) The ideal picture of the activity (1.2.3.1) does not preclude this act chosen by the children. (8) However, another factor comes into play—the appropriateness of the act for the child (1.2.3.2). The women present will react to the children on the basis of sex appropriateness (1.2.3.2 + 1.1.1). (9) They will also react on the basis of relevant values (1.2.2). Let us say that the grandmother (1.2.1) reacts to the small boy (1.2.3.2 + 1.1.1) on the basis of sex-appropriate behavior values (1.2.2). Grandmothers have very great importance in Ngoni life and so do sex-related values. Thus, the negative reaction (3.2.2.3) will be very strong and will decrease strongly the boy's likelihood of picking that action in that setting (1.1.1 + 1.1.2 + 3.2.1), and will also decrease his likelihood of picking that setting again (1.1.1 + 2.0). The little girl, however, was noticed by a young woman of the household, a person of lower status (1.2.1) and was praised (3.2.2.1) for being willing to work, a value of less importance (1.2.2) than the sex-appropriateness value. The low-level positive response (3.2.2.1) will increase in a small amount the girl's likelihood of choosing that action (1.1.2 + 3.2.1) or that setting (1.1.1 + 2.0) again.

(10) The girl, unlike the boy, has participated in a culturally appropriate pattern for her. Thus, the cultural pattern consisting of an activity, objects, appropriate group size, specific relations, an emotional content, a set of persons, and relevant values and ideals becomes part of her knowledge (1.1.3). The model weights the strength of the knowledge (loop from 1.2 to 3.2.2 and 1.1). As she grows older and chooses it more often, the weight of the knowledge will grow, although as the model provides it will not be absolutely consistent. Sometimes the women will be quarreling; sometimes they will judge her performance by other values or, as she gets older, by a different standard. Further, since the model is probabilistic, it allows for contradiction such as is found in real human culture.

POTENTIAL OF THE SYSTEMS MODEL

What use can be made of this type of cultural transmission theory?[6] At the most basic level, the model provides a guide for gathering cultural transmission data. Because it stems from a different perspective, an ethnographer using it will look for different materials than would an ethnographer using the Henry (1960), Hilger (1960), or Whiting (1966) outlines. At this level we are currently testing the model by reorganizing published cultural transmission data gathered by other workers. Through work with these materials the subcategories for data-gathering of greater specificity than those illustrated in Diagram 2 are being developed. Material gathered with the refined model will then be put to two uses.

The first use of the model will require a coding of cultural patterns from a number of societies. We hope to compare the similarity and dissimilarity of these patterns over a large number of societies. The second use of the model will be to set up a computerized cultural transmission simulation. By using the model to process a large number of children and then examining the cultural knowledges of that group of children as adults, we can compare pattern changes inter-generationally. In theory, the model should produce slight changes through the actions of chance for every generation, even if the environment stays the same. When the model proves workable, we will introduce known historical changes which affect cultural patterns, such as the introduction of schools. Then, using a culture for which historical data is available, we will attempt to reproduce the known change through simulation.

At this point we will come to the most potentially exciting aspect of the work. We will deliberately alter aspects of the cultural pattern in order to study the possible effects of the alteration and to answer questions such as "Does a minor change in control patterns like a change from physical to verbal reinforcement produce a future generation which is different?" "Do value changes produce important differences, technology changes?" "How large a change is required to seriously alter the future generation's patterns?" These questions can be explored across the types of societies identified in step two of the work. The simulation will also test the validity of the typology constructed, since truly differing systems should react in distinct ways to similar change inputs. These two aspects of the work, the measure of similarity and the computer simulations, are being done in conjunction with other University of Minnesota faculty.

Needless to say, we do not expect to complete this research program in the near future.

NOTES

1. This is how I have interpreted his work as presented orally in his symposium, "Explorations in a General Cultural Theory of Education," at the 1973 AAA-CAE meetings, and in his informal discussion session at the 1974 meetings.
2. We have, of course, a superabundance of descriptive definitions. Another one would add nothing of interest. The proposed definition, however, is operational and, therefore, manipulable and potentially useful.
3. In this definition, the word "pattern" is equivalent in meaning to "subsystem." See Young 1969 for a slightly different use of this idea.
4. It would be useful at this point to demonstrate fully the utility of such a definition of culture. That, however, is impossible in context of the current discussion. For further clarification of this point, the reader is referred to the article cited.
5. Philosophically, the notion of culture employed is probably best described as modified realistic.
6. We do not pretend that the theory as modeled in this paper has reached a satisfactory state. It is lacking in two respects: (a) We have been unable to satisfactorily account for all the aspects of culture which seem relevant. In this model, for example, accurate account of social institutions such as the Ngoni boys' dorms is not achieved. (b) We have not made all our subsystem aspects of the model correspond to our information-based theory. The psychological tone of a number of the subsystems indicates this. Nevertheless, the model and the theory have both grown during the past two years and now appear to be approaching a functional, operational state.

REFERENCES

Dobbert, M. L. "General Systems Theory and Change." 3:4 *General Systems Bulletin* 1971.

Gearing, F. O. "Where We Are and Where We Might Go: Steps Toward a General Theory of Cultural Transmission." IV:1 *CAE Quarterly* 1, 1973.

————. "Explorations in a General Cultural Theory of Education." AAA Symposium, New Orleans, 1973.

Henry, J. "Cross-Cultural Outline of Education." I:4 *Current Anthropology* 267, 1960.

Hilger, I. "Field Guide to the Ethnological Study of Child Life." New Haven CT: Human Relations Area Files, 1960.

Read, M. *Children of Their Fathers.* New York: Holt, Rinehart and Winston, 1960.

von Bertalanffy, L. *General System Theory.* Braziller, 1968.

Whiting, J. W. N. *Field Guide for a Study of Socialization.* New York: Wiley, 1966.

Young, T. R. "A Survey of General Systems Theory." IX *General Systems* 61ff, 1969.

————. "Social Stratification and Modern Systems Theory." 14 *General Systems* 113ff, 1969.

15 / Controls, Paradigms, and Designs: Critical Elements in the Understanding of Cultural Dynamics

Arthur M. Harkins

In February 1960, the Rand Corporation released a paper, "On the Epistemology of the Inexact Sciences," written by Olaf Helmer and Nicholas Rescher (Helmer 1960). This now well-known paper cautioned the "inexact" sciences against emulation of the physical sciences, and urged an approach that we may conveniently label sociocultural design. This approach would convert the activities of the social sciences away from emulation and in the direction of research which would stress new forms of information flow and feedback among persons participating in sociocultural design experiments. While others have chided the social sciences for their slavish copying of textbook natural science activities, none, perhaps, has been so effective in their constructive criticisms as have been Fred L. Polak and Wendell Bell (Bell 1971)

Wendell Bell and James Mau believe that effective control should be the first hallmark of knowledge. Calling for the exercise of control over the generation of predictions, Bell and Mau follow the lead of Bertrand de Jouvenel and others in admitting there are no future facts; instead, the future we desire must be manipulated into being. The role of prediction therefore loses its (rhetorical?) preeminence in social science and plays second fiddle to the larger directive of real (not simply experimental) control of the variables. The roles of both speculation and "creative imagination" in the control function are paramount, according to Bell and Mau. For a new social science to emerge, Bell has suggested (after Kuhn) that epistemological changes must occur within which the routines of science may produce new results. He labels the six "stages" of such scientific development (1) paradigmatic pluralism, (2) emergence of a unified paradigm, (3) normal science, (4) the beginning of doubt, (5) the scientific revolution, and (6) the new reigning paradigm—normal science again. In the epilogue to the *Sociology of the Future*, Bell outlines the primary features of "purposing" social science, a science of manipulation, design, and control (but a science that leaves room for creative imagination).

Starting from acceptance of the positions above, this paper attempts to demonstrate the importance of control in the quasi-experimental design of alternative sociocultural and educational futures. It begins with several assumptions derived from a divergent viewpoint on the epistemology of the social sciences.

SOME BASIC ASSUMPTIONS

Assumption One: Cultures are *purposing cybernetic systems* controlling themselves and being controlled through information flow.

Assumption Two: Humans are the product of culture; culture is the product of humans. Thus, *"humanism" may legitimately refer to anything and everything about culture and behavior falling within the self-or-other-protective interests of any person or human collective.*

Assumption Three: Culture is subject to design and redesign through a variety of methods.

TRANSITIONAL ASSUMPTIONS (THEORY TO OPERATIONS)

Cultures as purposing cybernetic systems exhibit comparatively greater or lesser "automation" in particular institutions. People or other systems may be viewed in a similar way. To "progress" (become more complex and "survival fit" through provision of alternative paradigms among which to choose), cultures and other systems must automate and deautomate functions within *flexible* paradigms. Flexible paradigms (scientific theory, myths, supernatural thought, etc.) guide automation and deautomation. In our present circumstances, increasing pluralism significantly complicates the information environment at the meta level. Epistemologically, the environment is becoming more complex.

"Technology" refers to the *relationships between means and ends*. It has hardware (biotechnology, laser technology, human body technology) and software (nonmaterial) aspects. It is present (inferred) in every system (solar, simian, human). "Paradigmatology" refers to the manipulation of world view parameters. All software operates to control behavior. The critical question is: What software for whose behavior to what ends and with what implications?

"Power" is the ability to commit resources and to decommit them with minimal "loss" and maximal "gain." Power authorizes and deauthorizes. It plans and replans, designs and redesigns. Some power extends to paradigm control (elites), and has a synergetic effect on gains in many parts of the environment. Some power extends to controls which give only localized reactive "gains" (philosophy of "poor but happy").

Attempts to enhance alternatives for concrete choice involve the use of sociocultural technology. Sociocultural technology in practice becomes a "problem" when paradigms generating past/present/future "realities," desirable and undesirable, do not match up. In our type of society, the critical problem mentioned earlier becomes critical *problems* as more people become manipulatively, visibly, and widely involved in the cybernetic functions. Software/hardware developments are emerging to "deal with" conflicting stasis and change, but themselves will enter into complex feedback relationships, often of indeterminate dimensions and implications.

For many purposes, but not for all, we may assume that the "future is now." Following from Saint Augustine, who pointed out that all past, present, and future events can be observed only in the existential now, we can see how alternative interpretations of the past or of alternative futures can actually lead to pluralization of the present—the development of "alternative presents." Conventional interpretations of the "separate" times of past, present, and future also have their place.

ALTERNATIVE HUMANISTIC PARADIGMS

Following the initial basic assumptions, three operational, interactive views of humanism may be identified, each of which treats perceived situations of abundance and scarcity of physical and cultural resources in different but related ways. A design approach to the various modes of using any one or a combination of the three types of humanism may be envisioned. Such a design approach makes possible a directly operational approach to the core assumptions. For purposes of educational design, the three types of humanism constitute distinct but interrelated "settings" for purposeful change in, theoretically, any direction, including the expansion of educational pluralism.

Type I: Local Humanism. Heavily operational emphasis upon loyalty, support for, and responsibility to self, kin, community, nation, allies. A basic consideration in the moral structure (values) of this type of humanism is the "ethic of scarcity," or the concept of "limited good"—the conviction that there are not enough of certain key resources to go around, that some will lose while others will win in the competition for such scarce resources. Prone to privacy and secrecy outside the "in group."

Type II: Cosmoscentric Humanism. Heavily verbal emphasis upon certain purportedly global or universal metaphors, myths, and secular or sacred philosophies, which offer some or all men essentially rhetorical opportunities or fates, usually under "all things being equal" types of qualifiers. May be based upon an "ethic of abundance," but usually in an afterlife or a life to come after rebirth. The "ethic of scarcity" tends to pervade much of the worldly circumstances in which forms of cosmoscentric humanism are expressed. Prone to privacy and secrecy when operating in Type I, but more open and often proselytizing when operating in Type II.

Type III: Noetic (Intellectual) Humanism. Heavy emphasis upon the "ethic of abundance," as opposed to the "ethic of scarcity." Information- and feedback-oriented humanism which assumes that "knowledge is power" and that all individuals should have maximum opportunity for personalized access to and feedback into all information banks of concern to them. An active, process and exploration type of humanism which acts to cut across both local and cosmoscentric levels of humanism, respecting few or no barriers in the generation, transmission, storage, and usage of information of any type. The approach to "abundance" as opposed to "scarcity" is first informational, under the assumption that physical abundance depends upon maximum appropriate cultural abundance. No privacy and secrecy unless constrained by considerations in Types I or II.

SOCIOCULTURAL/EDUCATIONAL SCENARIO DEVELOPMENT

Alternative futures in the design of sociocultural systems may be made on a comparative basis following from the assumptions and design approaches outlined above. One operationally meaningful approach to this task seems to lie in the preparation of those alternative scenario sets deriving from the three interactive types of humanism and their "logical" output of scenario ranges:

Humanism Types

		I		II		III	
		I	1	II	2A	III	3B
	I	I	"pure"	I		I	
		I	1A	II	2	III	3A
	II	II		II	"pure"	II	
		I	1B	II	2B	III	3
	III	III		III		III	"pure"

(row label, left side, rotated: Humanism Types)

From the matrix, which acts to generate nine theoretical varieties of interaction for the three "pure" types of humanism we have discussed, three "ideal-typical" scenarios of sociocultural and educational futures may be generated. These scenarios are heuristic or paradigmatic. They do not represent "plans," but offer an opportunity to assess present conditions and alternative futures in society and education against other hypothetical potentials. They are useful for the broader-gauge thinking which must precede effective normative (deductive) planning. The scenarios also offer an opportunity to employ sociocultural and educational images in conjunction with the design process, in order to provide for constant comparisons between our workaday activities and our images of alternative futures. The scenarios are purposely "pure" in the sense that they represent a "logical" over-emphasis of their particular virtues. The scenarios are purposely "futurized" because of the probable importance of certain hardware technological development areas over the coming years. Much hardware may be considered "neutral" and transferrable from one scenario to another. "Mixed" scenarios may be generated out of the combinations of characteristics suggested by the other six cells in the matrix. All the scenarios that follow were developed with technical-industrial societies and with continua from past/present to futurizing sociocultural and educational processes in mind.

SCENARIO ONE: THE (IDEALIZED) FIXED KNOWLEDGE SYSTEM

Social Stability

No search for solutions because officially there are no problems. Individual and society are officially regarded as one. Personality and social status/role are regarded as isomorphic (identical). Unwanted diversity is dangerous and unnecessary. Negative feedback loops are everywhere, from the law through gossip and superego (conscience). Official goals are set by hierarchical subordinates who operate deductively after considering limited types and amounts of information. People who are not "approved" tend to be viewed as incompetent to assist in planning processes. Suspicion is generated by every potential or actual change in the status of individuals and groups, because the system operates on a hyper-developed scaricty ethic. Change of status suggests a threatening realignment of these scarce resources. Loyalty is paramount, and severe penalties as well as desirable rewards are readily produced for the loyal and the disloyal. Anxiety pervades the system, fear has been experienced by all, and terror is never very far away. Official concern for the past and future is in terms of the problem-solving demands of the present, but mediated through the needs of hierarchical superordinates to survive and to enhance their own careers. Examples of the effects of the Peter and Paul Principles abound in the highest decision-making and planning circles.

Education

Great concern for "an" appropriate curriculum for each "level" of the highly controlled educational system. Curricula are geared to the maintenance of preferred assumptions about religion, economics, politics, life style, and values. What is done "in school" is supposed to be directly useful "outside" the school in "real life." This means that the fixed system spends a great proportion of its resources preparing people for activities which might have been productive in the past or in the rapidly altering present, but not many emerging futures. Graduates of the schools are not seen to work in different futures, because all officially imaginable futures are merely extensions of the present, requiring but relatively minor modifications in the "capabilities" of graduates. Other institutions in the fixed system tend to support this point of view, so that the formal education system is never "out of step"; it is viewed by outsiders as "prudently" and "responsibly" preparing persons for the (largely fictional) future. As the larger system may refer to itself as "Mother Russia," so the local school, a part of the whole, may refer to itself as a "family" of teachers and learners, or as a "tribe" (Synanon). People are seen as things to be processed by the education system, which also processes ideas as things, particularly when there is some suspicion that they may be subversive. Official ideology is not placed in the same category as ideas, so that indoctrination without critical assessment is rampant. This type of system becomes stupid because it has rendered itself incapable of learning, and therefore incapable of teaching, in a great many areas. Its parochialism, fear of change and newness, and constant narrow preoccupation with "costs," force it into an acceptance of its own epistemological inadequacies. Because of this, its insecurities tend to increase as a function of inadvertent self-awareness of incompetencies in critical areas. It is a system which must affirm its own incapacities to learn, and it often does so while performing acts of psychic or physical violence for the "good" of all concerned.

Hardware (*Nelson 1973*)

A television or radio is located in each room of each private home, recreation area, and public service facility; these receivers are capable of two-way interchange with both auditory and visual capabilities. These receivers can be turned on or off at the discretion of the state, allowing the state to monitor the behavior and speech of each resident without their knowledge.

Receivers with the same capabilities are built into street and yard lamps, which exist in every yard and street, at close intervals throughout the state.

Satellites with close-range viewing capabilities are continuously recording the quantity and quality of all resources throughout the world. The satellites also provide the state another check on its citizens through a combination of photographs and printouts from instruments recording pattern disturbances of any kind.

Machines, robots, and computers perform all tasks formerly done by humans, freeing them for leisure activities. The governing elite is the exception.

Advanced communication technology and simulation devices have reduced travel and interpersonal contact. Large crowds are outlawed by the state.

A wired world allows the state instant contact with any point at any time, on earth or any of its colonies. This network includes satellite and microwave transmission, light "pipes," and cables.

Mini-biocomputers are installed in each individual at infancy, eliminating any chance of harmful environmental influence. All individual perception is interpreted by uniform knowledge base.

A pleasure button is also installed at birth, which can be pressed by the individual for an instant thrill (Nelson 1973, pp. 5-6).

SCENARIO TWO: THE (IDEALIZED) RHETORICAL, LIMITED LEARNING OPPORTUNITY SYSTEM

Social Stability

"Democratic," meaning that some will always suffer at the hands of the majority, no matter who the majority may be. Constant public search for problems in order to "smooth out" the sailing of the social ship. Emphasis upon order and good housekeeping. Limited allowance for the participation of citizens in various types of official information inputs and decision making. Scarcity ethic abounds, but is modified by obvious gains in the well-being of many persons. One problem is that many persons in the system are convinced they will never "have" anything until they have as much as the most privileged; hence, the *limited* opportunity system. Many types of gains in the system, unless "equally" distributed within very narrow time frames, create a sense of relative deprivation on the part of the have-nots. This problem tends to lead to the support of an ethic which stresses hard work and prudence leading to "reasonable" rewards in this life, and to extraordinary rewards in the afterlife. As the afterlife is part of the functional belief system of many persons, the mythic approach "works" to keep within limits the aspirations of persons who might otherwise become disenchanted to the point of social action. Hence, the *rhetorical* opportunity system. The rhetorical, limited opportunity system also controls opportunity perception through the management of eliptical political language and posturings, usually to the accompaniment of familiar but manipulative "down-home" styles.

Education

Concern for a "Christian" or a "human relations" rhetorical base for school process and curriculum, since these catchwords signal deferred gratification in the face of the powerful "givens" associated with social class structure, religion, belief in the afterlife, sex roles, programmed limited self-awareness, extrapolated life chance expectancies, and the like. The predominance of the work ethic predisposes most persons associated with formal education to look upon educational "output" in terms of employability factors—career education concerns, not educational career concerns. Scarcity ethic promotes anxiety over retaining teaching jobs, even though the information/computer technologies cause increasing pressures for automation of many or most white-collar functions (and functionaries) in education. Fear is expressed over the "creeping" influence of CAI (computer-assisted instruction), modular curriculum formats which reduce redundant teacher activities, broadcast television or CATV education, and so forth.

Teachers and publishers alike "know" that too easy dissemination of their wares may make them obsolete before personal success or survival deadlines are met; college professors in schools of education assist by making knowledge "cost" in such ways as will trickle downward the "payments" for such knowledge. The key word for the rhetorical, limited opportunity system is, indeed, "cost," measured in fiscal terms on the social surface, but in institutional and personal terms when the eyes and ears of the public are out of range. Lip service is paid to "innovation" and "risk-taking," but most functionaries know that this is rhetoric intended to pacify the usually small proportion of vocal publics seriously concerned with educational reforms. Educational success is measured in terms of those variables which will publicly support the apparent merits of the formal system, casting doubt or blame upon "nonachievers" whose performances do not reflect well upon the *a priori* claims of the system to have isolated the most crucial variables of educational success. The rhetorical, limited opportunity system is especially pernicious because it gives the *impression* of being open to any and all kinds of new (or old) information when, in many cases, it has "learned" to promote such a "liberal" façade in order to enhance its own survivability. The system produces the seeds of its own torment through the accidental by-product of truly knowledgeable critics/persons and groups who have learned enough from the system to comparatively analyze and critique it, and who have at least the partial support of a social milieu prone to band-waggoning on social crusades. The system also produces its own relief, generally, through coopting many of the critics into a search for their own educational legitimation through the very system they seek to change. The iconic referent for the rhetorical, limited opportunity system is the smile of reason . . . of enlightened cynicism.

Hardware (Nelson 1973)

Two-way interactive, broad-band communication system connecting every point on the globe with any other and to all space colonies. Each home has its own communication terminal which includes: (1) interactive, multi-channeled cable television; (2) picture-phone; (3) computer-computer, man-computer, computer-man communication; (4) combination of keyboards, light pens, printers and electronic logic and storage; (5) videotape porta-pak; (6) quad-sound unit including receivers, tape deck, speakers and turntable.

Satellite surveillance of earth to access resources at hand for equitable distribution and planning purposes. This surveillance would guarantee the success of every crop for ameliorative measures could be taken when needed. It would also eliminate any illegal weaponry by its electromagnetic wave-detection devices. The only weaponry allowed would be under the aegis of the world organization, for emergency use only.

Personal book size computers alloted to each individual, programmed to his specifications.

Local resource centers include: (1) voice-programmed central data computers accessible through home terminal unit through a multitude of modes including light pens, television receivers, various combinations of keyboards and printers; (2) simulation devices; (3) holograms; (4) completely equipped science and engineering laboratories; (5) theaters of different- types; (6) musical instruments and sound reproduction equipment; (7) completely equipped artist-craft workshops (Nelson 1973, pp. 11–12).

SCENARIO THREE: THE (IDEALIZED) OPEN INFORMATION SYSTEM

Social Stability

Based upon the on-faith assumption that the more knowledge people possess, the better off they will be, at least in the long run. Social system constraints are seen to be a function of the choices of a maximally enlightened, genuinely wealthy citizenry, governing itself through a rational dialogue unimpeded by vulgar concerns for status, fixed roles, the limitations of democracy, or other common problems. Although some are more equal than others because their choices of participation style put them temporarily apart, every action may be observed and analyzed through a ubiquitous public information system which operates to protect citizens against specialists. The open information system reduces secrecy—and privacy— to a minimum. It is assumed that those who govern themselves best are those who are victimized least by ignorance and stupidity. Multiple, interactive levels of information flow virtually guarantees that no person or group can carry out private acts for longer than bare minimum of time, for one of the features of the system consists of a random polling of human settings, including the most intimate, with transmission of what is occurring to as many as millions of other citizens. Based upon the extreme likelihood that not even the most private act can be shielded against observation, people act openly, within a comparatively small number of proscriptions, on their impulses, needs, and values. The good person is the person who attempts to hide nothing; gradations from good to bad are measured in terms of amounts of "dishonesty" as indicated by attempts at concealment. Within the ideological framework of the open information system many epistemologies reside and flourish. It is assumed that variations in life style accompanying epistemological pluralism are an indication of the system's vitality and survivability.

Education

Education in the open information system is everywhere and nowhere. The entire system is based upon the notion that more information from more sources feeding into more and more people—who may respond to that information—is an inherent good, and a sufficient base upon which to build an entire society. The system already has developed CAI, satellite transmission systems, parental tutorial cadres, international travel, sleep learning, emotion transmission, and early childhood-to-grave experiences which constantly challenge the individual to greater heights of intellectual and collective diversity and sophistication. It is expected that people will live by what they know—that intellectual diversity will alter epistemologies and that this will lead to life style changes. A concern of the system is to develop telepathy—the direct connection of all members of the system on a real time, brain-to-brain basis—without the necessity for speech. Another important goal of the system is to extend its less exotic communication links to as many non-system people as possible on this world and nearby others where humans already reside. An adjunct of both these goals is the search for intelligence from distant star systems and in earth's own seas, in order to further the sophistication of internal and external dialogue among the system's citizens. Perhpas the greatest efforts, though, are extended in two areas of difficult research and development activity—the enhancement of human intelligence through genetic engineering, and the creation of electronic devices with intelligence at least equal to the best of human capacities. Many members of the system dream of the day when hyper-intelligent humans may interact with artificial intelligences (AI) of human making, but enjoying social equality with the makers. All of these activities and many more are undertaken with the assumption that all knowledge is good, but that extreme care must be taken to monitor constantly how the knowledge is employed in the everyday affairs of the system.

Hardware (Coles et al 1974)

Automated Inquiry System. An automatic information retrieval system, using a man/machine dialogue to determine user needs, which can search its data base to present the user with specific information or "facts," rather than references to other sources.

Automated Intelligence System. General augmenter of human intelligence, capable of automatically monitoring ongoing streams of input data, coordinating facts, and making logical inferences to obtain insights and alert the human as appropriate.

Talking Typewriter. Voice typewriter, capable of converting spoken natural language into typewritten form in essentially real time, with an error rate equal to a human's.

Automatic Language Translator. Language translating device capable of high-quality translation of text in one foreign language to another (both technical and commercial material).

Automatic Identification System. System for automatically determining a person's identity by recognizing his voice, fingerprints, face, and the like.

Machine/Animal Symbiont. Tapping the brain of a living animal such as a bird or a rat, to obtain preprocessed sensory inputs (visual, auditory, olfactory, etc.) to augment the capabilities of a mechanical device.

Computer Psychiatrist. A system in which the patient's written or verbal input is sufficiently understood that the system can legitimately counsel and advise the user for commonly encountered problems.

Computer Arbiter. A system in which adversaries enter their mutual complaints and the interactive system uses a data base of precedents and value rules to deliver either advice or a verdict.

General Factotum. A robot servant, capable of smooth verbal interchange and versatile perception and manipulative activity in a household environment.

Creation and Valuation System. Capable of creative work in such areas as music, art (painting, sculpture, architecture), literature (essays, novels, poetry), and mathematics, and able to evaluate the work of humans (Coles et al., 1974, p. 6).

REFERENCES

Bell, W., and Mau, J., eds. *The Sociology of the Future.* New York: Russell Sage, 1971.

Coles, L. S., et al. "Forecasting and Assessing the Impact of Artificial Intelligence on Society." Paper presented to the IEEE, March 1974.

Helmer, O., and Rescher, N. *On the Epistemology of the Inexact Sciences.* Santa Monica: Rand, 1960.

Nelson, A. *Cultural Futures and World Information Systems.* Minneapolis: Office for Applied Social Science and the Future, University of Minnesota, 1973.

SUGGESTED READING

Conference Board Inc., eds. "Information Technology: Some Critical Implications for Decision Makers." New York, 1972.

Gearing, F. O. "Where We Are and Where We Might Go: Steps Toward a General Theory of Cultural Transmission." IV: 1 *CAE Newsletter* 1, August 1973.

Harking, A. M.; Joseph, E.; Shafer, J.; and Nelson, A. "Pluralism, Participation and Choice in a Wired World." In *World Information Systems and Citizen Participation.* Minneapolis: Office for Applied Social Science and the Future, University of Minnesota, 1972.

———, and Maruyama, M. "Rules for Anthropologists I: The Future is Now." IV: 2 *CAE Newsletter* 27, November 1973.

Hawkins, D. "The Nature of Purpose." In Foerster et al., eds., *Purposive Systems.* New York: Spartan, n.d.

Irvine, D. J. "Specifications for an Educational System by the Future." *Phi Delta Kappan*, February 1972.

Jones, J. C. "The Total Future." IV: 2 *Futures*, 1972.

Joseph, E. C. *The Science of Futurology.* Minneapolis: Sperry-Univac, 1971.

Maruyama, M. "Toward a Cultural Futurology." In AAA pre-conference volume, *Cultural Futurology Symposium*, University of Minnesota, 1970.

———. "Symbiotization of Cultural Heterogeneity." In AAA pre-conference volume, *Cultural Futurology Symposium*, University of Minnesota, 1970.

———. "A New Logical Model for Futures Research." V: 5 *Futures* 435, 1973.

———. "Hierarchists, Individualists and Mutualists: Three Paradigms Among Planners." VI: 2 *Futures*, April 1974.

Miller, P. A. "Major Implications for Education of Prospective Changes in Society." In Morphet and Ryan, eds., *Designing Education for the Future.* New York: Citation, 1967.

Parker, E. B., and Dunn, D. A. "Information Technology: Its Social Potential." V *Science* 176, June 1972.

Reiser, O. *Cosmic Humanism.* Cambridge, Mass.: Schenkman, 1966.

Shane, H. G. "Future-Planning as a Means of Shaping Educational Change." In NSSE *70th Yearbook*, Chicago, 1971.
Spindler, G. D. "From Omnibus to Linkages: Cultural Transmission Models." V : 1 *CAE Quarterly* 1, February 1974.

16 / On the Analog between Culture Acquisition and Ethnographic Method

Jacquetta Hill Burnett

Although the boundaries of the domain of anthropology of education are variously set and are as yet by no means conventionalized, the domain is more or less generally agreed to have to do with culture transmission and culture acquisition. Gearing's (1973) recent article in the *Quarterly* was addressed specifically to the problem of a theory of culture transmission. By some peculiar semantics in the anthropologist's use of the term, culture transmission always also in part entails culture acquisition. I am not here concerned with this peculiar semantic, however, but rather with culture acquisition and ethnographic method.

Recently I have been engaged in a project concerned with culture acquisition and have noticed in the literature of anthropology an intriguing habit of reasoning about ethnographic methodology on the basis of analogy with culture acquisition. Usually the analog, specifically or by implication, refers to acquisition by children, although ages are not usually spelled out. Admittedly this analog is used most frequently in discussions of discovery procedures for ethnography conceived of as producing a theory or guide to how a culture works, a guide that enables one to act appropriately in a society or to predict when an observed action or behavioral pattern will be thought to be appropriate by members of the society in that culture. Put in other words, these are discovery and formulation procedures that produce a conceptual device or model that distinguishes between allowable behavior sequences that are not allowed. "Common wisdom" about children's acquisition of culture is often used in discussions about methodological questions concerning such ethnographies.

Spradely, in his introductory chapter to *Culture and Cognition*, puts the parallel as follows:

> The task for the anthropologist studying culture and cognition is much the same as for every child: by *inference* and *instruction* he seeks to acquire a comprehensive knowledge of both tacit and explicit culture rules. These, taken as a guide for behavior, should enable him to act appropriately in the society he studies. (1972, p. 22)

The idea that symbolic communication, or instruction broadly conceived, and inference are employed by social scientists to learn a culture as well as by the child undergoing socialization underlies the analogy between method and acquisition.

Thus, anthropologists interested in culture acquisition, and cognitive anthropologists in their discussion of methodology, are discussing and working on problems of mutual interest and theoretical significance.

Although Goodenough does not use the analogy directly, he suggests that there is between the ethnographer and the child a parallel concern with a fundamental theoretical question: the relationship of the individual to culture. He insists that part of our difficulty with ambiguities when we talk of a society's culture is our "failure to stick with the implications of the idea that culture is learned" (1971, p. 18). As soon as learning is taken seriously as part of the definition of culture, then one must deal with processes or manifestations of mind, with the products of learning: concepts, definitions, beliefs, preferences, principles, rules, or standards. Thus, says Goodenough:

> If culture is learned, the problem of method is the problem of how scientists learn culture in order to be able to describe them. The relation of the individual to culture is, therefore, crucial to method and theory in cultural anthropology. (1971, p. 20)

And culture acquisition by infant, child, or adult, insofar as it involves the development of "equivalence" or sharedness is fundamentally involved with the relation of the individual to culture.

As noted, the parallel between ethnographic method and culture acquisition rests in part on a particular way of defining the goals of an ethnography; to wit, the goal of an ethnography, *or* a valid description of a culture as something learned, is an account or model or system of statements that predicts whether or not any particular action will be accepted by those who know the culture as conforming to their standards of conduct. In more holistic terms, an ethnography of a community's culture is a model that:

(a) encodes and decodes the behavior of the community's members and makes it as predictable and understandable to the ethnographer as it is to them;

(b) if used as a guide for the ethnographer's own behavior, it makes his conduct as intelligible to each of the members (in terms of their models of their community's culture) as is the behavior of most of their fellows.

Culture acquisition can be easily conceived to involve the same process, although it may at any one time be less "holistic" and less explicit than the ethnographer's model.

Yet we must be cautious and subtle about this. The final product of the discovery procedures—an ethnographic model—is presented step by step as logically as possible. That logical ordering, however, may not recapitulate the ontogeny of learning. Thus, the logical ordering presented by the ethnographer may not present the steps by which people learn a culture or by which children arrive at an understanding of how their culture works. The parallel between culture acquisition and ethnography probably lies in the discovery procedures and processes more than with form of the final product. Then, if we reverse the direction of reasoning, the ethnography that presents a "self" conscious account of an ethnographer's discovery of how a culture works may be of great value to our understanding of how culture is acquired.

The suggestion that we reverse the analogy should have no logical problems to offer. After all, what is an analog model but "some material object, system, or process designed to reproduce as faithfully as possible in some new medium the *structure* or web of relationships in an original" (Black 1968)? One uses an analogy with something better known to think about something less well known. I am simply suggesting that we may know our own minds better than the minds of others so that, as ethnographers learning a culture, we may be able to reason from processes happening to us to develop better understanding, new insight, useful hunches and speculations about culture acquisition processes in others.

Having clarified the basis for some mutual benefits between studies of culture acquisition and ethnographic methodology, we find in recent arguments about methodology some problems for the use of methodology as the analog of acquisition. These problems arise in discussions of the locus of culture codes, or culture models, and the relevance or irrelevance of discovery procedures for judging ethnographic models. In some ways the connection between discovery procedures and culture acquisition rests on the assumption that the ethnographer's account, his model, represents a description of what goes on in the minds of native users of that culture code. It is easy to begin to talk as if one were actively working out rules that are in the heads of native users of the culture, rules that one discovers through appropriate methodological procedures.

Burling's answer (1969) to this "locus of rules" question is that in practice it does not matter whether you think the model is an invention of the ethnographer to account for behavior, or is a set of rules in the natives' heads, so long as the model works; i.e., so long as the ethnographer's system of rules accounts for or "predicts" back to the known data, as well as "predicts" or generates new data that are not contained in the original body of information from which the ethnographer worked. Nevertheless, the general reasonableness of an ethnographer's setting out to construct a "model" is argued by Burling, in part from an analogy with the acquisition of the ability to use language appropriately, a process which entails extra-linguistic as well as linguistic variables. Thus, in regard to semantic analysis, Burling says:

> Since speakers can learn to use words appropriately, it hardly seems unreasonable to attempt to construct a formal statement that will duplicate a speaker's ability. (1970, p. 42)

Burling, following Chomsky, even has some unsettling suggestions for ethnographic discovery procedures as well. We can put the question as follows: Should the ethnographer rely mainly on eliciting statements about behavior from his informants in order to construct his model of the culture; or, like the linguist who relies mainly on utterances, should he rely entirely on examples of behavior, i.e., on the behavioral description of events from which he constructs "accounting rules" (X behaves as if he is following rule Y)? Burling concludes that either or both will do, so long as the rules work; in other words, so long as they account for data observed and predict new data. And so far as discovery procedures themselves do not qualify or disqualify the final product they are unimportant.

But even in this argument Burling himself engages in reasoning from culture acquisition to research procedures in order to help justify eliciting statements about behavior from informants.

> To the extent that a child requires a verbal context and verbal instruction to learn his own culture, an anthropologist would seem to be forced to rely upon similar sorts of verbal description. (1969)

Thus, even with a position as extreme as Burling's with respect to the "locus of rules" and irrelevance of the way the ethnographer produces his model of how a culture works, culture acquisition and ethnographic method have much in common.

Yet with this one might think a careful account of discovery procedures is superfluous. Not entirely, it seems, for Burling himself gives two reasons to believe some procedural rules do work better than others, and some questions require for answers a careful methodological account of how the ethnographer discovers how a culture works. In his discussion of referential and verbal definitions, Burling suggests that, heuristically, to study meaning one must begin with referential definition, but can then proceed to verbal definition. The context for offering this suggestion is his commentary on the fact that, although linguists have ignored nonlinguistic factors in their investigation of language, most anthropologists have ignored the possibility of defining some words by other words and have confined their attention largely to relating them directly to the world of sensory experience. The relationship between referential and verbal definition suggests something about the way anyone learns to use the terms of a language appropriately.

> One is forced to conclude that *left* and *right* cannot possibly be defined except by appealing to a context outside of language. Surely that is the way children learn these terms. We point to their left eye or their right hand and we tell them in which direction they are turning. (Burling, 1970, p. 70)

In his argument for fair attention to both referential and verbal definition, Burling concludes that while both logical and ontogenetic associations between terms and observable phenomena must come first, once some minimum set of terms and operations have been learned we are able to use these terms to define a vocabulary of larger and larger proportions. Continuing to use the analogy of acquisition of meaning by children in his argument, he says:

> Most children probably have little direct experience with God, but they learn what *God* means and they can learn the meaning of London and Paris without ever visiting those cities. (Burling 1970, p. 71)

So, too, the anthropologist who sets out to develop a model of how terms are used by a given group should well begin, as he usually has been doing, with associations between terms and observable phenomena, but he should also build into such a model the process of using referentially defined terms to define other terms. So, rules of discovery procedure are *not* entirely irrelevant.

Finally, there is still the important and interesting question of how closely the explicit rules of a people correspond to the rules of the ethnologist. That question can never be dealt with in clear fashion unless the explicit rules that are formulated and articulated by the people themselves are *first* clearly differentiated from those rules that the ethnologist constructs. So, again, there is reason to keep careful logs of one's discovery procedures in order to keep the source of the rules separate. And ethnographers' logs will include descriptions of how models are produced and will thus be useful to students of culture acquisition.

At this point a caution is in order with respect to the limits of the analogy we are discussing. Those concerned with the early stages of ontogenetic development in the infant and the child may be quite dissatisfied with drawing the analogy at all. Thus it is appropriate to ask where in the life cycle, and with respect to what culture acquisition situations, the analogy is most appropriate. It is fair to point out, however, that when anthropologists use culture acquisition as an analog for the anthropologist's learning a culture in order to describe it, they appear to usually have children in mind and they usually do not bother to specify to what stage of ontogenetic development they are referring. Yet, if we are to use the ethnographer's experience in learning a culture to help clarify culture acquisition, it is desirable to ask what the ethnographer's experience is most like:

(a) the child learning a culture for the first time?
(b) adult socialization into a new role?
(c) child or adult acculturation?

The classic scenario of the ethnographer is an adult, already well versed in at least one culture code and system, going into a different social group with a very distinctive, very contrastive second culture and setting out to learn and describe that second culture code. For an anthropologist studying subcultures and subvarieties of his own culture, this scenario is somewhat different and is very much like the second acquisition situation mentioned above. But for purposes of the present discussion let's consider the first scenario.

The circumstances of the first scenario really may not be very much like the child who is acquiring a first culture while undergoing ontogenetic developmental processes. Certainly the discoveries concerning the ontogenesis of grammar, such as the generalization that the semantic relations which a child can express *and interpret* in speech are limited by his level of cognitive development, places early childhood learning and the ethnographer's learning into very different cause-effect contexts (Slobin, quoted in Brukman 1973). Moreover, if such concepts as learning-to-learn or deutero-learning have any validity, an ethnographer may go about his learning in a very different way than the child who is learning-to-learn in culturally different ways (Bateson 1970). Yet these limitations may hold true mainly for infancy and early childhood, for it seems most anthropologists would agree there are important characteristics in common between middle or later childhood and the ethnographer's culture learning processes.

The ethnographer may be more like the older child or adult undergoing the socialization into a new status at a distinctively new phase in the life cycle; or, in a complex culture, entering into the culture of a new group that is a subculture of the same culture system. Depending on the similarity or difference between this subculture and the individual's primary or "mother" culture, his culture acquisition is more or less analogous to the ethnographer's problem. On further thought, it seems the situation that is most like the ethnographer's is that of older childhood or the adult who has migrated to a new social setting and is undergoing acculturation in that situation. Thus method in ethnography can be used in closest analogy with adult acquisition of a second culture, and may most effectively assist in our understanding of and reasoning about second culture acquisition.

We have been exploring the claim that participant observation and the production of an ethnography also produces data and insights for the field of educational anthropology, specifically for better understanding of culture acquisition. That is, on every occasion on which an anthropologist undertakes to do an ethnography, he is producing potential data for the field of educational anthropology. If my arguments have been persuasive, then there are several suggestions to be derived from the discussion.

Perhaps the least profound is the comforting thought that the present financial depression in research funds need not thwart the rapid development of data, analysis, and theorizing in this area since, by the arguments marshalled here, every piece of ethnographic research that is financed by anybody is a potential contribution to the data and the study of the processes of culture acquisition.

A second important implication of this argument is that introspection, an important tool in research on cognition, may serve inquiry in our field as it has served linquistics. We should not neglect the potential of introspection or intuition in the study of culture acquisition, for it has served linguistics very well as Brukman has recently noted (1973):

> As we are all quite aware, many of the generalizations about language that have been proposed in recent years have been based on deep intuitions about the nature of certain kinds of utterances. These intuitions Bever has quite rightly labeled a kind of speech event which takes the form of having intuitions about language. (p. 50)

Many questions in cognitive socialization require the resources of "self-aware native actors." Brukman suggests that in order to study how children learn their culture, and more specifically the key process of language socialization, we must not only collect more data on children's talk in natural settings but also must take great risks in the interpretation of that data. I am suggesting that the ethnographer's own experience in attempting to learn a culture from the inside as a native actor can be used to guide those risky interpretations. In brief, the production of an ethnography, if one consciously notices and conscientiously records the process by which one discovers how a culture works, gives some insight into how a child is enculturated, more insight into how a youth or adult is socialized, and a great deal of insight into how an adult is acculturated into a second culture.

In this discussion I have emphasized recent uses of the parallel between learning culture and anthropological method, but over ten years ago Kimball (1960) proposed that some kinds of child learning and the natural history emphasis of anthropological methodology had much in common. Later, he suggested that it be used to teach the young (1965). That is an insight that deserves further attention, and it is an example of the kind of problem that deliberate exploration of the parallel between culture acquisition and anthropological method will allow us to pursue to some new and significant level of understanding.

Finally, with respect to the analog between culture acquisition and ethnographic method, I think many of the important theoretical issues now being discussed in connection with methodology are fundamental issues in the theory of culture transmission and acquisition. The question of equivalence and sharedness among persons with the same culture is the same problem as the cognitive status of the ethnographer's model and its psychological reality or equivalence with the natives' models. We have much to learn from, and should find ourselves contributing to, the theory of method in anthropology.

REFERENCES

Bateson, G. "Social Planning and the Concept of Deutero-Learning." In G. Bateson, ed., *Steps to An Ecology of Mind*. New York: Ballantine, 1972. P. 159.

Black, M. *Models and Metaphors: Studies in Language and Philosophy*. Ithaca, N.Y.: Cornell University Press, 1962.

Brukman, J. "Language and Socialization: Child Culture and the Ethnographer's Task." In S. Kimball and J. Burnett, eds., *Learning and Culture: Proceedings of the 1972 Annual Spring Meeting of AES*. Seattle: University of Washington Press, 1973. P. 43.

Burling, R. "Linguistics and Ethnographic Description." 71 *AA* 817, 1969.

Burling, R. *Man's Many Voices: Language in Its Cultural Context*. New York: Holt, Rinehart and Winston, 1970.

Gearing, F. O. "Where We Are and Where We Might Go: Steps Toward a General Theory of Cultural Transmission." 4 *CAE Newsletter* 1, 1973.

Goodenough, W. *Culture, Language and Society*. Reading, Mass.: Addison-Wesley, 1971.

Kimball, S. T. "Darwin and the Future of Education." 25 *Educational Forum*, 59, 1960.

Kimball, S. T. "Anthropology and Teacher Training." In D. B. Gowin and C. Richardson, eds., *Five Fields and Teacher Education*. Ithaca, N.Y.: Cornell University Press, 1965.

Slobin, D. I. "Suggested Universals in the Ontogenesis of Grammar." Working Paper No. 32, Language Behavior Laboratory. Berkeley: University of California (quoted in Brukman) 1970.

Spradely, J. "Foundations of Cultural Knowledge." In J. Spradely, ed., *Culture and Cognition*. San Francisco: Chandler, 1972.

Part IV

Anthropological Methods of Studying Education

17 / Methods of Study

William Whyte

ON THE EVOLUTION OF *STREET CORNER SOCIETY*

In the years since completing *Street Corner Society* I have several times sought to teach students the research methods needed for field studies of communities or organizations. Like other instructors in this field, I have been severely handicapped by the paucity of reading matter that I can assign to students.

There are now many good published studies of communities or organizations, but generally the published report gives little attention to the actual process whereby the research was carried out. There have also been some useful statements on methods of research, but, with a few exceptions, they place the discussion entirely on a logical-intellectual basis. They fail to note that the researcher, like his informants, is a social animal. He has a role to play, and he has his own personality needs that must be met in some degree if he is to function successfully. Where the researcher operates out of a university, just going into the field for a few hours at a time, he can keep his personal social life separate from field activity. His problem of role is not quite so complicated. If, on the other hand, the researcher is living for an extended period in the community he is studying, his personal life is inextricably mixed with his research. A real explanation, then, of how the research was done necessarily involves a rather personal account of how the researcher lived during the period of study.

This account of living in the community may help also to explain the process of analysis of the data. The ideas that we have in research are only in part a logical product growing out of a careful weighing of evidence. We do not generally think problems through in a straight line. Often we have the experience of being immersed in a mass of confusing data. We study the data carefully, bringing all our powers of logical analysis to bear upon them. We come up with an idea or two. But still the data do not fall in any coherent pattern. Then we go on living with the data—and with the people—until perhaps some chance occurrence casts a totally different light upon the data, and we begin to see a pattern that we have not seen before. This pattern is not purely an artistic creation. Once we think we see it, we must reexamine our notes and perhaps set out to gather new data in order to determine whether the pattern adequately represents the life we are observing or is simply a product of our imagination. Logic, then, plays an important part. But I am convinced that the actual evolution of research ideas does not take place in accord with the formal statements we read on research methods. The ideas grow up in part out of our immersion in the data and out of the whole process of living. Since so much of this process of analysis proceeds on the unconscious level, I am sure that we can never present a full account of it. However, an account of the way the research was done may help to explain how the pattern *of Street Corner Society* gradually emerged.

I am not suggesting that my approach to *Street Corner Society* should be followed by other researchers. To some extent my approach must be unique to myself, to the particular situation, and to the state of knowledge existing when I began research. On the other hand, there must be some common elements of the field research process. Only as we accumulate a series of accounts of how research was actually done will we be able to go beyond the logical-intellectual picture and learn to describe the actual research process. What follows, then, is simply one contribution toward that end.

Planning the Study

As soon as I had found my slum district, I set about planning my study. It was not enough for me at the time to plan for myself alone. I had begun reading in the sociological literature and thinking along the lines of the Lynds' *Middletown*. Gradually I came to think of myself as a sociologist or a social anthropologist instead of an economist. I found that, while slums had been given much attention in the sociological literature, there existed no real community study of such a district. So I set out to organize a community study for Cornerville. This was clearly a big job. My early outline of the study pointed to special researches in the history of the district, in economics (living standards, housing, marketing, distribution, and employment), politics (the structure of the political organization and its relation to the rackets and the police), patterns of education and recreation, the church, public health, and—of all things—social attitudes. Obviously, this was more than a one-man job, so I designed it for about ten men.

With this project statement in hand I approached L. J. Henderson, an eminent biochemist who was secretary of the Society of Fellows.

We spent an hour together, and I came away with my plans very much in a state of flux. As I wrote to a friend at this time: "Henderson poured cold water on the mammoth beginning, told me that I should not cast such grandiose plans when I had done hardly any work in the field myself. It would be much sounder to get in the field and try to build up a staff slowly as I went along. If I should get a ten-man project going by fall, the responsibility for the direction and co-ordination of it would inevitably fall upon me, since I would have started it. How could I direct ten people in a field that was unfamiliar to me? Henderson said that, if I did manage to get a ten-man project going, it would be the ruination of me, he thought. Now, the way he put all this it sounded quite sensible and reasonable."

This last sentence must have been written after I had had time to recover from the interview, because I remember it as being a crushing experience. I suppose good advice is just as hard to take as poor advice, and yet in a very short time I realized that Henderson was right, and I abandoned the grandiose plan I had made. Since people who offer painful but good advice so seldom get any thanks for it, I shall always be glad that I went to see Henderson again shortly before his death and told him that I had come to feel that he had been absolutely right.

While I abandoned the ten-man project, I was reluctant to come down to earth altogether. It seemed to me that, in view of the magnitude of the task I was undertaking, I must have at least one collaborator, and I began to cast about for means of getting a college friend of mine to join me in the field. There followed through the winter of 1936–37 several revisions of my outline of the community study and numerous interviews with Harvard professors who might help me to get the necessary backing.

As I read over these various research outlines, it seems to me that the most impressive thing about them is their remoteness from the actual study I carried on. As I went along, the outlines became gradually more sociological, so that I wound up this phase planning to devote major emphasis to a sort of sociometric study of the friendship patterns of people. I would start with one family and ask them who their friends were and who the people were that they were more or less hostile to. Then I would go to these friends and get the list of their friends and learn in the process something of their activities together. In this way, I was to chart the social structure of at least some of the community. Even this, of course, I did not do, for I came to find that you could examine social structure directly through observing people in action.

When, a year later in the fall of 1937, John Howard, also a Harvard junior fellow, changed his field from physical chemistry to sociology, I invited him to join me in the Cornerville study. We worked together for two years, with Howard particularly concentrating on one of the churches and its Holy Name Society. The discussions between us helped immensely in clarifying my ideas. But only a few months after I had begun Cornerville field work, I had completely abandoned the thought of building up Cornerville staff. I suppose that I found Cornerville life so interesting and rewarding that I no longer felt a need to think in large-scale terms.

Although I was completely at sea in planning the study, at least I had valuable help in developing the field research methods which were eventually to lead to a study plan as well as to the data here reported.

It is hard to realize now how rapid has been the development of sociological and anthropological studies of communities and organizations since 1936, when I began my work in Cornerville. At that time nothing had yet been published on W. Lloyd Warner's "Yankee City" study. I had read the Lynds' *Middletown* and Carolyn Ware's *Greenwich Village* with interest and profit, and yet I began to realize, more and more as I went along, that I was not making a community study along those lines. Much of the other sociological literature then available tended to look upon communities in terms of social problems so that the community as an organized social system simply did not exist.

I spent my first summer following the launching of the study in reading some of the writings of Durkheim and Pareto's *The Mind and Society* (for a seminar with L. J. Henderson, which I was to take in the fall of 1937). I had a feeling that these writings were helpful but still only in a general way. Then I began reading in the social anthropological literature, beginning with Malinowski, and this seemed closer to what I wanted to do even though the researchers were studying primitive tribes and I was in the middle of a great city district.

If there was then little to guide me in the literature, I needed that much more urgently to have the help of people more skilled and experienced than I in the work I was undertaking. Here I was extraordinarily fortunate in meeting Conrad M. Arensberg at the very outset of my Harvard appointment. He also was a junior fellow, so that we naturally saw much of each other. After having worked for some months with W. Lloyd Warner in the Yankee City study, he had gone with Solon Kimball to make a study of a small community in Ireland. When I met him, he had just returned from this field trip and was beginning to write up his data. With Eliot Chapple, he was also in the process of working out a new approach to the analysis of social organization. The two men had been casting about together for ways of establishing such social research on a more scientific basis. Going over the Yankee City data and the Irish study, also, they had set up five different theoretical schemes. One after the other each of the first four schemes fell to the ground under their own searching criticism or under the prods of Henderson or Elton Mayo or others whom they consulted. At last they began to develop a theory of interaction. They felt that, whatever else might be subjective in social research, one could establish objectively the pattern of interaction among people: how often A contacts B, how long they spend together, who originates action when A, B, and C are together, and so on. Careful observation of such interpersonal events might then provide reliable data upon the social organization of a community. At least this was the assumption. Since the theory grew out of research already done, it was natural that these previous studies did not contain as much of the quantitative data as the theory would have required. So it seemed that I might be one of the first to take the theory out into the field.

Arensberg and I had endless discussions of the theory, and in some of these Eliot Chapple participated. At first it seemed very confusing to me—I am not sure I have it all clear yet—but I had a growing feeling that here was something solid that I could build upon.

Arensberg also worked with me on field research methods, emphasizing the importance of observing people in action and getting down a detailed report of actual behavior completely divorced from moral judgments. In my second semester at Harvard, I took a course given by Arensberg and Chapple concerning social anthropological community studies. While this was helpful, I owed much more to the long personal conversations I had with Arensberg throughout the Cornerville research, particularly in its early stages.

In the fall of 1937 I took a small seminar with Elton Mayo. This involved particularly readings from the works of Pierre Janet, and it included also some practice in interviewing psychoneurotics in an Eastern City hospital. This experience was too brief to carry me beyond the amateur stage, but it was helpful in developing my interviewing methods.

L. J. Henderson provided a less specific but nevertheless pervasive influence in the development of my methods and theories. As chairman of the Society of Fellows, he presided over our Monday-night dinners like a patriarch in his own household. Even though the group included A. Lawrence Lowell, Alfred North Whitehead, John Livingston Lowes, Samuel Eliot Morrison, and Arthur Darby Nock, it was Henderson who was easily the most imposing figure for the junior fellows. He seemed particularly to enjoy baiting the young social scientists. He took me on at my first Monday-night dinner and undertook to show me that all my ideas about society were based upon softheaded sentimentality. While I often resented Henderson's sharp criticisms, I was all the more determined to make my field research stand up against anything he could say.

First Efforts

When I began my work, I had had no training in sociology or anthropology. I thought of myself as an economist and naturally looked first toward the matters that we had taken up in economics courses, such as economics of slum housing. At the time I was sitting in on a course in slums and housing in the Sociology Department at Harvard. As a term project I took on a study of one block in Cornerville. To legitimize this effort, I got in touch with a private agency that concerned itself in housing matters and offered to turn over to them the results of my survey. With that backing, I began knocking on doors, looking into flats, and talking to the tenants about the living conditions. This brought me into contact with Cornerville people, but it would be hard now to devise a more inappropriate way of beginning a study such as I was eventually to make. I felt ill at ease at this intrusion, and I am sure so did the people. I wound up the block study as rapidly as I could and wrote it off as a total loss as far as gaining a real entry into the district.

Shortly thereafter I made another false start—if so tentative an effort may even be called a start. At the time I was completely baffled at the problem of finding my way into the district. Cornerville was right before me and yet so far away. I could walk freely up and down its streets, and I had even made my way into some of the flats, and yet I was still a stranger in a world completely unknown to me.

At this time I met a young economics instructor at Harvard who impressed me with his self-assurance and his knowledge of Eastern City. He had once been attached to a settlement house, and he talked glibly about his associations with the tough young men and women of the district. He also described how he would occasionally drop in on some drinking place in the area and strike up an acquaintance with a girl, buy her a drink, and then encourage her to tell him her life story. He claimed that the women so encountered were appreciative of this opportunity and that it involved no further obligation.

This approach seemed at least as plausible as anything I had been able to think of. I resolved to try it out. I picked on the Regal Hotel, which was on the edge of Cornerville. With some trepidation I climbed the stairs to the bar and entertainment area and looked around. There I encountered a situation for which my adviser had not prepared me. There were women present all right, but none of them was alone. Some were there in couples, and there were two or three pairs of women together. I pondered this situation briefly. I had little confidence in my skill at picking up one female, and it seemed inadvisable to tackle two at the same time. Still, I was determined not to admit defeat without a struggle. I looked around me again and now noticed a threesome: one man and two women. It occurred to me that here was a maldistribution of females which I might be able to rectify. I approached the group and opened with something like this: "Pardon me. Would you mind if I joined you?" There was a moment of silence while the man stared at me. He then offered to throw me downstairs. I assured him that this would not be necessary and demonstrated as much by walking right out of there without any assistance.

I subsequently learned that hardly anyone from Cornerville ever went into the Regal Hotel. If my efforts there had been crowned with success, they would no doubt have led somewhere but certainly not to Cornerville.

For my next effort I sought out the local settlement houses. They were open to the public. You could walk right into them, and—though I would not have phrased it this way at the time—they were manned by middle-class people like myself. I realized even then that to study Cornerville I would have to go well beyond the settlement house, but perhaps the social workers could help me to get started.

As I look back on it now, the settlement house also seems a very unpromising place from which to begin such a study. If I had it to do over again, I would probably make my first approach through a local politician or perhaps through the Catholic church, although I am not myself Catholic. John Howard, who worked with me later, made his entry very successfully through the church, and he, too, was not a Catholic—although his wife was.

However that may be, the settlement house proved the right place for me at this time, for it was here that I met Doc. I had talked to a number of the social workers about my plans and hopes to get acquainted with the people and study the district. They listened with varying degrees of interest. If they had suggestions to make, I have forgotten them now except for one. Somehow, in spite of the vagueness of my own explanations, the head of girls' work in the Norton Street House understood what I needed. She began describing Doc to me. He was, she said, a very intelligent and talented person who had at one time been fairly active in the house but had dropped out, so that he hardly ever came in any more. Perhaps he could understand what I wanted, and he must have the contacts that I needed. She said she frequently encountered him as she walked to and from the house and sometimes stopped to chat with him. If I wished, she would make an appointment for me to see him in the house one evening. This at last seemed right. I jumped at the chance. As I came into the district that evening, it was with a feeling that here I had my big chance to get started. Somehow Doc must accept me and be willing to work with me.

In a sense, my study began on the evening of February 4, 1937, when the social worker called me in to meet Doc. She showed us into her office and then left so that we could talk. Doc waited quietly for me to begin, as he sank down into a chair. I found him a man of medium height and spare build. His hair was a light brown, quite a contrast to the more typical black Italian hair. It was thinning around the temples. His cheeks were sunken. HIs eyes were a light blue and seemed to have a penetrating gaze.

I began by asking him if the social worker had told him about what I was trying to do.

"No, she just told me that you wanted to meet me and that I should like to meet you."

Then I went into a long explanation which, unfortunately, I omitted from my notes. As I remember it, I said that I had been interested in congested city districts in my college study but had felt very remote from them. I hoped to study the problems in such a district. I felt I could do very little as an outsider. Only if I could get to know the people and learn their problems first hand would I be able to gain the understanding I needed.

Doc heard me out without any change of expression, so that I had no way of predicting his reaction. When I was finished, he asked: "Do you want to see the high life or the low life?"

"I want to see all that I can. I want to get as complete a picture of the community as possible."

"Well, any nights you want to see anything, I'll take you around. I can take you to the joints—gambling joints—I can take you around to the street corners. Just remember that you're my friend. That's all they need to know. I know these places, and, if I tell them that you're my friend, nobody will bother you. You just tell me what you want to see, and we'll arrange it."

The proposal was so perfect that I was at a loss for a moment as to how to respond to it. We talked a while longer, as I sought to get some pointers as to how I should behave in his company. He warned me that I might have to take the risk of getting arrested in a raid on a gambling joint but added that this was not serious. I only had to give a false name and then would get bailed out by the man that ran the place, paying only a five-dollar fine. I agreed to take this chance. I asked him whether I should gamble with the others in the gambling joints. He said it was unnecessary and, for a greenhorn like myself, very inadvisable.

At last I was able to express my appreciation. "You know, the first steps of getting to know a community are the hardest. I could see things going with you that I wouldn't see for years otherwise."

"That's right. You tell me what you want to see, and we'll arrange it. When you want some information, I'll ask for it, and you listen. When you want to find out their philosophy of life, I'll start an argument and get it for you. If there's something else you want to get, I'll stage an act for you. Not a scrap, you know, but just tell me what you want, and I'll get it for you."

"That's swell. I couldn't ask for anything better. Now I'm going to try to fit in all right, but if at any time you see I'm getting off on the wrong foot, I want you to tell me about it."

"Now we're being too dramatic. You won't have any trouble. You come in as my friend. When you come in like that, at first everybody will treat you with respect. You can take a lot of liberties, and nobody will kick. After a while when they get to know you they will treat you like anybody else—you know, they say familiarity breeds contempt. But you'll never have any trouble. There's just one thing to watch out for. Don't spring [treat] people. Don't be too free with your money."

"You mean they'll think I'm a sucker?"

"Yes, and you don't want to buy your way in."

We talked a little about how and when we might get together. Then he asked me a question. "You want to write something about this?"

"Yes, eventually."

"Do you want to change things?"

"Well—yes. I don't see how anybody could come down here where it is so crowded, people haven't got any money or any work to do, and not want to have some things changed. But I think a fellow should do the thing he is best fitted for. I don't want to be a reformer, and I'm not cut out to be a politician. I just want to understand these things as best I can and write them up, and if that has any influence. . . . "

"I think you can change things that way. Mostly that is the way things are changed, by writing about them."

That was our beginning. At the time I found it hard to believe that I could move in as easily as Doc had said with his sponsorship. But that indeed was the way it turned out.

While I was taking my first steps with Doc, I was also finding a place to live in Cornerville. My fellowship provided a very comfortable bedroom, living room, and bath at Harvard. I had been attempting to commute from these quarters to my Cornerville study. Technically that was possible, but socially I became more and more convinced that it was impossible. I realized that I would always be a stranger to the community if I did not live there. Then, also, I found myself having difficulty putting in the time that I knew was required to establish close relations in Cornerville. Life in Cornerville did not proceed on the basis of formal appointments. To meet people, to get to know them, to fit into their activities, required spending time with them—a lot of time day after day. Commuting to Cornerville, you might come in on a particular afternoon and evening only to discover that the people you intended to see did not happen to be around at the time. Or, even if you did see them, you might find the time passing entirely uneventfully. You might just be standing around with people whose only occupation was talking or walking about to try to keep themselves from being bored.

On several afternoons and evenings at Harvard, I found myself considering a trip to Cornerville and then rationalizing my way out of it. How did I know I would find the people whom I meant to see? Even if I did so, how could I be sure that I would learn anything today? Instead of going off on a wild-goose chase to Cornerville, I could profitably spend my time reading books and articles to fill in my woeful ignorance of sociology and social anthropology. Then, too, I had to admit that I felt more comfortable among these familiar surroundings than I did wandering around Cornerville and spending time with people in whose presence I felt distinctly uncomfortable at first.

When I found myself rationalizing in this way, I realized that I would have to make the break. Only if I lived in Cornerville would I ever be able to understand it and be accepted by it. Finding a place, however, was not easy. In such an overcrowded district a spare room was practically nonexistent. I might have been able to take a room in the Norton Street Settlement House, but I realized that I must do better than this if possible.

I got my best lead from the editor of a weekly English-language newspaper published for the Italian-American colony. I had talked to him before about my study and had found him sympathetic. Now I came to ask him for help in finding a room. He directed me to the Martinis, a family that operated a small restaurant. I went there for lunch and later consulted the son of the family. He was sympathetic but said that they had no place for any additional person. Still, I liked the place and enjoyed the food. I came back several times just to eat. On one occasion I met the editor, and he invited me to his table. At first he asked me some searching questions about my study: what I was after, what my connection with Harvard was, what they had expected to get out of this, and so on. After I had answered him in a manner that I unfortunately failed to record in my notes, he told me that he was satisfied and, in fact, had already spoken in my behalf to people who were suspicious that I might be coming in to "criticize our people."

We discussed my rooming problem again. I mentioned the possibility of living at the Norton Street House. He nodded but added: "It would be much better if you could be in a family. You would pick up the language much quicker, and you would get to know the people. But you want a nice family, an educated family. You don't want to get in with any low types. You want a real good family."

At this he turned to the son of the family with whom I had spoken and asked: "Can't you make some place for Mr. Whyte in the house here?"

Al Martini paused a moment and then said: "Maybe we can fix it up. I'll talk to Mama again."

So he did talk to Mama again, and they did find a place. In fact, he turned over to me his own room and moved in to share a double bed with the son of the cook. I protested mildly at this imposition, but everything had been decided—except for the money. They did not know what to charge me, and I did not know what to offer. Finally, after some fencing, I offered fifteen dollars a month, and they settled for twelve.

The room was simple but adequate to my purposes. It was not heated, but, when I began to type my notes there, I got myself a small oil burner. There was no bathtub in the house, but I had to go out to Harvard now and then anyway, so I used the facilities of the great university (the room of my friend Henry Guerlac) for an occasional tub or shower.

Physically, the place was livable, and it provided me with more than just a physical base. I had been with the Martinis for only a week when I discovered that I was much more than a roomer to them. I had been taking many of my meals in the restaurant and sometimes stopping in to chat with the family before I went to bed at night. Then one afternoon I was out at Harvard and found myself coming down with a bad cold. Since I still had my Harvard room, it seemed the sensible thing to do to stay overnight there. I did not think to tell the Martinis of my plan.

The next day when I was back in the restaurant for lunch, Al Martini greeted me warmly and then said that they had all been worried when I did not come home the night before. Mama had stayed up until two o'clock waiting for me. As I was just a young stranger in the city, she could visualize all sorts of things happening to me. Al told me that Mama had come to look upon me as one of the family. I was free to come and go as I pleased, but she wouldn't worry so much if she knew of my plans.

I was very touched by this plea and resolved thereafter to be as good a son as I could to the Martinis.

At first I communicated with Mama and Papa primarily in smiles and gestures. Papa knew no English at all, and Mama's knowledge was limited to one sentence which she would use when some of the young boys on the street were making noise below her window when she was trying to get her afternoon nap. She would then poke her head out of the window and shout: "Goddam-sonumabitcha! Geroutahere!"

Some weeks earlier, in anticipation of moving into the district, I had begun working on the Italian language myself with the aid of a Linguaphone. One morning now Papa Martini came by when I was talking to the phonograph record. He listened for a few moments in the hall trying to make sense out of this peculiar conversation. Then he burst in upon me with fascinated exclamations. We sat down together while I demonstrated the machine and the method to him. After that he delighted in working with me, and I called him my language professor. In a short time we reached a stage where I could carry on simple conversations, and, thanks to the Linguaphone and Papa Martini, the Italian that came out apparently sounded authentic. He liked to try to pass me off to his friends as *paesano mio*—a man from his own home town in Italy. When I was careful to keep my remarks within the limits of my vocabulary, I could sometimes pass as an immigrant from the village of Viareggio in the province of Tuscany.

Since my research developed so that I was concentrating almost exclusively upon the younger, English-speaking generation, my knowledge of Italian proved unnecessary for research purposes. Nevertheless, I feel certain that it was important in establishing my social position in Cornerville—even with that younger generation. There were schoolteachers and social workers who had worked in Cornerville for as much as twenty years and yet had made no effort to learn Italian. My effort to learn the language probably did more to establish the sincerity of my interest in the people than anything I could have told them of myself and my work. How could a researcher be planning to "criticize our people" if he went to the lengths of learning the language? With language comes understanding, and surely it is easier to criticize people if you do not understand them.

My days with the Martinis would pass in this manner. I would get up in the morning around nine o'clock and go out to breakfast. Al Martini told me I could have breakfast in the restaurant, but, for all my desire to fit in, I never could take their breakfast of coffee with milk and a crust of bread.

After breakfast, I returned to my room and spent the rest of the morning, or most of it, typing up my notes regarding the previous day's events. I had lunch in the restaurant and then set out for the street corner. Usually I was back for dinner in the restaurant and then out again for the evening.

Usually I came home again between eleven and twelve o'clock, at a time when the restaurant was empty except perhaps for a few family friends. Then I might join Papa in the kitchen to talk as I helped him dry the dishes, or pull up a chair into a family conversation around one of the tables next to the kitchen. There I had a glass of wine to sip, and I could sit back and mostly listen but occasionally try out my growing Italian on them.

The pattern was different on Sunday, when the restaurant was closed at two o'clock, and Al's two brothers and his sister and the wives, husband, and children would come in for a big Sunday dinner. They insisted that I eat with them at this time and as a member of the family, not paying for my meal. It was always more than I could eat, but it was delicious, and I washed it down with two tumblers of Zinfandel wine. Whatever strain there had been in my work in the preceding week would pass away now as I ate and drank and then went to my room for an afternoon nap of an hour or two that brought me back completely refreshed and ready to set forth again for the corners of Cornerville.

Though I made several useful contacts in the restaurant or through the family, it was not for this that the Martinis were important to me. There is a strain to doing such field work. The strain is greatest when you are a stranger and are constantly wondering whether people are going to accept you. But, much as you enjoy your work, as long as you are observing and interviewing, you have a role to play, and you are not completely relaxed. It was a wonderful feeling at the end of a day's work to be able to come home to relax and enjoy myself with the family. Probably it would have been impossible for me to carry on such a concentrated study of Cornerville if I had not had such a home from which to go out and to which I might return.

Beginning with Doc

I can still remember my first outing with Doc. We met one evening at the Norton Street House and set out from there to a gambling place a couple of blocks away. I followed Doc anxiously down the long, dark hallway at the back of a tenement building. I was not worried about the possibility of a police raid. I was thinking about how I would fit in and be accepted. The door opened into a small kitchen almost bare of furnishings and with the paint peeling off the walls. As soon as we went in the door, I took off my hat and began looking around for a place to hang it. There was no place. I looked around, and here I learned my first lesson in participant observation in Cornerville: Don't take off your hat in the house—at least not when you are among men. It may be permissible, but certainly not required, to take your hat off when women are around.

Doc introduced me as "my friend Bill" to Chichi, who ran the place, and to Chichi's friends and customers. I stayed there with Doc part of the time in the kitchen, where several men would sit around and talk, and part of the time in the other room watching the crap game.

There was talk about gambling, horse races, sex, and other matters. Mostly I just listened and tried to act friendly and interested. We had wine and coffee with anisette in it, with the fellows chipping in to pay for the refreshments. (Doc would not let me pay my share on this first occasion.) As Doc had predicted, no one asked me about myself, but he told me later that, when I went to the toilet, there was an excited burst of conversation in Italian and that he had to assure them that I was not a G-man. He said he told them flatly that I was a friend of his, and they agreed to let it go at that.

We went several more times together to Chichi's gambling joint, and then the time came when I dared to go in alone. When I was greeted in a natural and friendly manner, I felt that I was now beginning to find a place for myself in Cornerville.

When Doc did not go off to the gambling joint, he spent his time hanging around Norton Street, and I began hanging with him. At first, Norton Street meant only a place to wait until I could go somewhere else. Gradually, as I got to know the men better, I found myself becoming one of the Norton Street gang.

Then the Italian Community Club was formed in the Norton Street Settlement, and Doc was invited to be a member. Doc maneuvered to get me into the club, and I was glad to join, as I could see that it represented something distinctly different from the corner gangs I was meeting.

As I began to meet the men of Cornerville, I also met a few of the girls. One girl I took to a church dance. The next morning the fellows on the street corner were asking me: "How's your steady girl?" This brought me up short. I learned that going to the girl's house was something that you just did not do unless you hoped to marry her. Fortunately, the girl and her family knew that I did not know the local customs, so they did not assume that I was thus committed. However, this was a useful warning. After this time, even though I found some Cornerville girls exceedingly attractive, I never went out with them except on a group basis, and I did not make any more home visits either.

As I went along, I found that life in Cornerville was not nearly so interesting and pleasant for the girls as it was for the men. A young man had complete freedom to wander and hang around. The girls could not hang on street corners. They had to divide their time between their own homes, the homes of girl friends and relatives, and a job, if they had one. Many of them had a dream that went like this: some young man, from outside of Cornerville, with a little money, a good job, and a good education would come and woo them and take them out of the district. I could hardly afford to fill this role.

Training in Participant Observation

The spring of 1937 provided me with an intensive course in participant observation. I was learning how to conduct myself, and I learned from various groups but particularly from the Nortons.

As I began hanging about Cornerville, I found that I needed an explanation for myself and for my study. As long as I was with Doc and vouched for by him, no one asked me who I was or what I was doing. When I circulated in other groups or even among the Nortons without him, it was obvious that they were curious about me.

I began with a rather elaborate explanation. I was studying the social history of Cornerville—but I had a new angle. Instead of working from the past up to the present, I was seeking to get a thorough knowledge of present conditions and then work from present to past. I was quite pleased with this explanation at the time, but nobody else seemed to care for it. I gave the explanation on only two occasions, and each time, when I had finished, there was an awkward silence. No one, myself included, knew what to say.

While this explanation had at least the virtue of covering everything that I might eventually want to do in the district, it was apparently too involved to mean anything to Cornerville people.

I soon found that people were developing their own explanation about me: I was writing a book about Cornerville. This might seem entirely too vague an explanation, and yet it sufficed. I found that my acceptance in the district depended on the personal relationships I developed far more than upon any explanations I might give. Whether it was a good thing to write a book about Cornerville depended entirely on people's opinions of me personally. If I was all right, then my project was all right; if I was no good, then no amount of explanation could convince them that the book was a good idea.

Of course people did not satisfy their curiosity about me simply by questions that they addressed to me directly. They turned to Doc, for example, and asked him about me. Doc then answered the questions and provided any reassurance that was needed.

I learned early in my Cornerville period the crucial importance of having the support of the key individuals in any groups or organizations I was studying. Instead of trying to explain myself to everyone, I found I was providing far more information about myself and my study to leaders such as Doc than I volunteered to the average corner boy. I always tried to give the impression that I was willing and eager to tell just as much about my study as anyone wished to know, but it was only with group leaders that I made a particular effort to provide really full information.

My relationship with Doc changed rapidly in this early Cornerville period. At first he was simply a key informant—and also my sponsor. As we spent more time together, I ceased to treat him as a passive informant. I discussed with him quite frankly what I was trying to do, what problems were puzzling me, and so on. Much of our time was spent in this discussion of ideas and observations, so that Doc became, in a very real sense, a collaborator in the research.

This full awareness of the nature of my study stimulated Doc to look for and point out to me the sorts of observations that I was interested in. Often when I picked him up at the flat where he lived with his sister and brother-in-law, he said to me: "Bill you should have been around last night. You would have been interested in this." And then he would go on to tell me what had happened. Such accounts were always interesting and relevant to my study.

Doc found this experience of working with me interesting and enjoyable, and yet the relationship had its drawbacks. He once commented: "You've slowed me up plenty since you've been down here. Now, when I do something, I have to think what Bill Whyte would want to know about it and how I can explain it. Before, I used to do things by instinct."

However, Doc did not seem to consider this a serious handicap. Actually, without any training he was such a perceptive observer that it only needed a little stimulus to help him to make explicit much of the dynamics of the social organization of Cornerville. Some of the interpretations I have made are his more than mine, although it is now impossible to disentangle them.

While I worked more closely with Doc than with any other individual, I always sought out the leader in whatever group I was studying. I wanted not only sponsorship from him but also more active collaboration with the study. Since these leaders had the sort of position in the community that enabled them to observe much better than the followers what was going on and since they were in general more skillful observers than the followers, I found that I had much to learn from a more active collaboration with them.

In my interviewing methods I had been instructed not to argue with people or pass moral judgments upon them. This fell in with my own inclinations. I was glad to accept the people and to be accepted by them. However, this attitude did not come out so much in interviewing, for I did little formal interviewing. I sought to show this interested acceptance of the people and the community in my everyday participation.

I learned to take part in the street corner discussions on baseball and sex. This required no special training, since the topics seemed to be matters of almost universal interest. I was not able to participate so actively in discussions of horse racing. I did begin to follow the races in a rather general and amateur way. I am sure it would have paid me to devote more study to the *Morning Telegraph* and other racing sheets, but my knowledge of baseball at least ensured that I would not be left out of the street corner conversations.

While I avoided expressing opinions on sensitive topics, I found that arguing on some matters was simply part of the social pattern and that one could hardly participate without joining in the argument. I often found myself involved in heated but good-natured arguments about the relative merits of certain major-league ball players and managers. Whenever a girl or a group of girls would walk down the street, the fellows on the corner would make mental notes and later would discuss their evaluations of the females. These evaluations would run largely in terms of shape, and here I was glad to argue that Mary had a better "build" than Anna, or vice versa. Of course, if any of the men on the corner happened to be personally attached to Mary or Anna, no searching comments would be made, and I, too, would avoid this topic.

Sometimes I wondered whether just hanging on the street corner was an active enough process to be dignified by the term "research." Perhaps I should be asking these men questions. However, one has to learn when to question and when not to question as well as what questions to ask.

I learned this lesson one night in the early months when I was with Doc in Chichi's gambling joint. A man from another part of the city was regaling us with a tale of the organization of gambling activity. I had been told that he had once been a very big gambling operator, and he talked knowingly about many interesting matters. He did most of the talking, but the others asked questions and threw in comments, so at length I began to feel that I must say something in order to be part of the group. I said: "I suppose the cops were all paid off?"

The gambler's jaw dropped. He glared at me. Then he denied vehemently that any policemen had been paid off and immediately switched the conversation to another subject. For the rest of that evening I felt very uncomfortable.

The next day Doc explained the lesson of the previous evening. "Go easy on that 'who,' 'what,' 'why,' 'when,' 'where' stuff, Bill. You ask those questions, and people will clam up on you. If people accept you, you can just hang around, and you'll learn the answers in the long run without even having to ask the questions."

I found that this was true. As I sat and listened, I learned the answers to questions that I would not even have had the sense to ask if I had been getting my information solely on an interviewing basis. I did not abandon questioning altogether, of course. I simply learned to judge the sensitiveness of the question and my relationship to the people so that I only asked a question in a sensitive area when I was sure that my relationship to the people involved was very solid.

When I had established my position on the street corner, the data simply came to me without very active efforts on my part. It was only now and then, when I was concerned with a particular problem and felt I needed more information from a certain individual, that I would seek an opportunity to get the man alone and carry on a more formal interview.

At first I concentrated upon fitting into Cornerville, but a little later I had to face the question of how far I was to immerse myself in the life of the district. I bumped into that problem one evening as I was walking down the street with the Nortons. Trying to enter into the spirit of the small talk, I cut loose with a string of obscenities and profanity. The walk came to a momentary halt as they all stopped to look at me in surprise. Doc shook his head and said: "Bill, you're not supposed to talk like that. That doesn't sound like you."

I tried to explain that I was only using terms that were common on the street corner. Doc insisted, however, that I was different and that they wanted me to be that way.

This lesson went far beyond the use of obscenity and profanity. I learned that people did not expect me to be just like them; in fact, they were interested and pleased to find me different, just so long as I took a friendly interest in them. Therefore, I abandoned my efforts at complete immersion. My behavior was nevertheless affected by street corner life. When John Howard first came down from Harvard to join me in the Cornerville study, he noticed at once that I talked in Cornerville in a manner far different from that which I used at Harvard. This was not a matter of the use of profanity or obscenity, nor did I affect the use of ungrammatical expressions. I talked in the way that seemed natural to me, but what was natural in Cornerville was different from what was natural at Harvard. In Cornerville, I found myself putting much more animation into my speech, dropping terminal g's, and using gestures much more actively. (There was also, of course, the difference in the vocabulary that I used. When I was most deeply involved in Cornerville, I found myself rather tongue-tied in my visits to Harvard. I simply could not keep up with the discussions of international relations, of the nature of science, and so on, in which I had once been more or less at home.)

As I became accepted by the Nortons and by several other groups, I tried to make myself pleasant enough so that people would be glad to have me around. And, at the same time, I tried to avoid influencing the group, because I wanted to study the situation as unaffected by my presence as possible. Thus, throughout my Cornerville stay, I avoided accepting office or leadership positions in any of the groups with a single exception. At one time I was nominated as secretary of the Italian Community Club. My first impulse was to decline the nomination, but then I reflected that the secretary's job is normally considered simply a matter of dirty work—writing the minutes and handling the correspondence. I accepted and found that I could write a very full account of the progress of the meeting as it went on under the pretext of keeping notes for the minutes.

While I sought to avoid influencing individuals or groups, I tried to be helpful in the way a friend is expected to help in Cornerville. When one of the boys had to go downtown on an errand and wanted company, I went along with him. When somebody was trying to get a job and had to write a letter about himself, I helped him to compose it, and so on. This sort of behavior presented no problem, but, when it came to the matter of handling money, it was not at all clear just how I should behave. Of course, I sought to spend money on my friends just as they did on me. But what about lending money? It is expected in such a district that a man will help out his friends whenever he can, and often the help needed is financial. I lent money on several occasions, but I always felt uneasy about it. Naturally, a man appreciates it at the time you lend him the money, but how does he feel later when the time has come to pay, and he is not able to do so? Perhaps he is embarrassed and tries to avoid your company. On such occasions I tried to reassure the individual and tell him that I knew he did not have it just then and that I was not worried about it. Or I even told him to forget about the debt altogether. But that did not wipe it off the books; the uneasiness remained. I learned that it is possible to do a favor for a friend and cause a strain in the relationship in the process.

I know no easy solution to this problem. I am sure there will be times when the researcher would be extremely ill advised to refuse to make a personal loan. On the other hand, I am convinced that, whatever his financial resources, he should not look for opportunities to lend money and should avoid doing so whenever he gracefully can.

If the researcher is trying to fit into more than one group, his field work becomes more complicated. There may be times when the groups come into conflict with each other, and he will be expected to take a stand. There was a time in the spring of 1937 when the boys arranged a bowling match between the Nortons and the Italian Community Club. Doc bowled for the Nortons, of course. Fortunately, my bowling at this time had not advanced to a point where I was in demand for either team, and I was able to sit on the sidelines. From there I tried to applaud impartially the good shots of both teams, although I am afraid it was evident that I was getting more enthusiasm into my cheers for the Nortons.

When I was with members of the Italian Community Club, I did not feel at all called upon to defend the corner boys against disparaging remarks. However, there was one awkward occasion when I was with the corner boys and one of the college boys stopped to talk with me. In the course of the discussion he said: "Bill, these fellows wouldn't understand what I mean, but I am sure that you understand my point." There I thought I had to say something. I told him that he greatly underestimated the boys and that college men were not the only smart ones.

While the remark fitted in with my natural inclinations, I am sure it was justified from a strictly practical standpoint. My answer did not shake the feelings of superiority of the college boy, nor did it disrupt our personal relationship. On the other hand, as soon as he left, it became evident how deeply the corner boys felt about his statement. They spent some time giving explosive expressions to their opinion of him, and then they told me that I was different and that they appreciated it and that I knew much more than this fellow and yet I did not show it.

My first spring in Cornerville served to establish for me a firm position in the life of the district. I had only been there several weeks when Doc said to me: "You're just as much of a fixture around this street corner as that lamppost." Perhaps the greatest event signalizing my acceptance on Norton Street was the baseball game that Mike Giovanni organized against the group of Norton Street boys in their late teens. It was the old men who had won glorious victories in the past against the rising youngsters. Mike assigned me to a regular position on the team, not a key position perhaps (I was stationed in right field), but at least I was there. When it was my turn to bat in the last half of the ninth inning, the score was tied, there were two outs, and the bases were loaded. As I reached down to pick up my bat, I heard some of the fellows suggesting to Mike that he ought to put in a pinch-hitter. Mike answered them in a loud voice that must have been meant for me: "No, I've got confidence in Bill Whyte. He'll come through in the clutch." So, with Mike's confidence to buck me up, I went up there, missed two swings, and then banged a hard grounder through the hole between second and short. At least that is where they told me it went. I was so busy getting down to first base that I did not know afterward whether I had reached there on an error or a base hit.

That night, when we went down for coffee, Danny presented me with a ring for being a regular fellow and a pretty good ball player. I was particularly impressed by the ring, for it had been made by hand. Danny had started with a clear amber die discarded from his crap game and over long hours had used his lighted cigarette to burn a hold through it and to round the corners so that it came out a heart shape on top. I assured the fellows that I would always treasure the ring.

Perhaps I should add that my game-winning base hit made the score 18-17, so it is evident that I was not the only one who had been hitting the ball. Still, it was a wonderful feeling to come through when they were counting on me, and it made me feel still more that I belonged on Norton Street.

As I gathered my early research data, I had to decide how I was to organize the written notes. In the very early stage of exploration, I simply put all the notes, in chronological order, in a single folder. As I was to go on to study a number of different groups and problems, it was obvious that this was no solution at all.

I had to subdivide the notes. There seemed to be two main possibilities. I could organize the notes topically, with folders for politics, rackets, the church, the family, and so on. Or I could organize the notes in terms of the groups on which they were based, which would mean having folders on the Nortons, the Italian Community Club, and so on. Without really thinking the problem through, I began filing material on the group basis, reasoning that I could later redivide it on a topical basis when I had a better knowledge of what the relevant topics should be.

As the material in the folders piled up, I came to realize that the organization of notes by social groups fitted in with the way in which my study was developing. For example, we have a college-boy member of the Italian Community Club saying: "These racketeers give our district a bad name. They should really be cleaned out of here." And we have a member of the Nortons saying: "These racketeers are really all right. When you need help, they'll give it to you. The legitimate businessman—he won't even give you the time of day." Should these quotes be filed under "Racketeers, attitudes toward"? If so, they would only show that there are conflicting attitudes toward racketeers in Cornerville. Only a questionnaire (which is hardly feasible for such a topic) would show the distribution of attitudes in the district. Furthermore, how important would it be to know how many people felt one way or another on this topic? It seemed to me of much greater scientific interest to be able to relate the attitude to the *group* in which the individual participated. This shows why two individuals could be expected to have quite different attitudes on a given topic.

As time went on, even the notes in one folder grew beyond the point where my memory would allow me to locate any given item rapidly. Then I devised a rudimentary indexing system: a page in three columns containing, for each interview or observation report, the date, the person or people interviewed or observed, and a brief summary of the interview or observation record. Such an index would cover from three to eight pages. When it came time to review the notes or to write from them, a five- to ten-minute perusal of the index was enough to give me a reasonably full picture of what I had and of where any given item could be located. . . .

Back on Norton Street

As I became more active once again on Norton Street, the local world began to look different. The world I was observing was in a process of change. I saw some of the members of the Italian Community Club establishing contacts with the upper world of Yankee control as I followed them to All-American Night at the Women's Republican Club. I saw the stresses and strains within the Nortons growing out of contacts with the Aphrodite Club and the Italian Community Club. I watched Doc, completely without scientific detachment, as he prepared for his doomed effort to run for public office.

Then in April 1938, one Saturday night I stumbled upon one of the most exciting research experiences in Cornerville. It was the night when the Nortons were to bowl for the prize money; the biggest bowling night of the whole season. I recall standing on the corner with the boys while they discussed the coming contest. I listened to Doc, Mike, and Danny making their predictions as to the order in which the men would finish. At first, this made no particular impression upon me, as my own unexpressed predictions were exactly along the same lines. Then, as the men joked and argued, I suddenly began to question and take a new look at the whole situation. I was convinced that Doc, Mike, and Danny were basically correct in their predictions, and yet why should the scores approximate the structure of the gang? Were these top men simply better natural athletes than the rest? That made no sense, for here was Frank Bonnelli, who was a good enough athlete to win the promise of a tryout with a major-league baseball team. Why should not Frank outdo us all at the bowling alley? Then I remembered the baseball game we had had a year earlier against the younger crowd on Norton Street. I could see the man who was by common consent the best baseball player of us all striking out with long, graceful swings and letting the grounders bounce through his legs. And then I remembered that neither I nor anyone else seemed to have been surprised at Frank's performance in this game. Even Frank himself was not surprised, as he explained: "I can't seem to play ball when I'm playing with fellows I know like that bunch."

I went down to the alleys that night fascinated and just a bit awed by what I was about to witness. Here was the social structure in action right on the bowling alleys. It held the individual members in their places—and I along with them. I did not stop to reason then that, as a close friend of Doc, Danny, and Mike, I held a position close to the top of the gang and therefore should be expected to excel on this great occasion. I simply felt myself buoyed up by the situation. I felt my friends were for me, had confidence in me, wanted me to bowl well. As my turn came and I stepped up to bowl, I felt supremely confident that I was going to hit the pins that I was aiming at. I have never felt quite that way before—or since. Here at the bowling alley I was experiencing subjectively the impact of the group structure upon the individual. It was a strange feeling, as if something larger than myself was controlling the ball as I went through my swing and released it toward the pins.

When it was all over, I looked at the scores of all the other men. I was still somewhat bemused by my own experience, and now I was excited to discover that the men had actually finished in the predicted order with only two exceptions that could readily be explained in terms of the group structure.

As I later thought over the bowling-alley contest, two things stood out in my mind. In the first place, I was convinced that now I had something important: the relationship between individual performance and group structure, even though at this time I still did not see how such observation would fit in with the overall pattern of the Cornerville study. I believed then (and still believe now) that this sort of relationship may be observed in other group activities everywhere. As an avid baseball fan, I had often been puzzled by the records of some athletes who seemed to be able to hit and throw and field with superb technical qualifications and yet were unable to make the major-league teams. I had also been puzzled by cases where men who had played well at one time suddenly failed badly, whereas other men seemed to make tremendous improvements that could not be explained simply on the basis of increasing experience. I suspect that a systematic study of the social structure of a baseball team, for example, will explain some of these otherwise mysterious phenomena. The other point that impressed me involved field research methods. Here I had the scores of the men on that final night at the bowling alleys. This one set of figures was certainly important, for it represented the performance of the men in the event that they all looked upon the climax of the year. However, this same group had been bowling every Saturday night for many months, and some of the members had bowled on other nights in between. It would have been a ridiculously simple task for me to have kept a record for every string bowled by every man on every Saturday night of that season and on such other evenings as I bowled with the men. This would have produced a set of statistics that would have been the envy of some of my highly quantitative friends. I kept no record of these scores, because at this time I saw no point to it. I had been looking upon Saturday night at the bowling alleys as simply recreation for myself and my friends. I found myself enjoying the bowling so much that now and then I felt a bit guilty about neglecting my research. I was bowling with the men in order to establish a social position that would enable me to interview them and observe important things. But what were these important things. Only after I passed up this statistical gold mine did I suddenly realize that the behavior of the men in the regular bowling-alley sessions was the perfect example of what I should be observing. Instead of bowling in order to be able to observe something else, I should have been bowling in order to observe bowling. I learned then that the day-to-day routine activities of these men constituted the basic data of my study.

Replanning the Research

The late spring and summer of 1938 brought some important changes into my research.

On May 28, I was married to Kathleen King, and three weeks later we returned to Cornerville together. Kathleen had visited me at the restaurant and had met some of my friends. Even as a married man, I did not want to move out of the district, and Kathleen, fortunately, was eager to move in. This presented problems, because, while we were not asking for everything, we did hope to find an apartment with a toilet and bathtub inside it. We looked at various gloomy possibilities until at last we found a building that was being remodeled on Shelby Street. Some of my Norton Street friends warned us against the neighborhood, saying that the place was full of Sicilians who were a very cut-throat crowd. Still, the apartment had the bathtub and toilet and was clean and relatively airy. It had no central heating, but we could be reasonably comfortable with the kitchen stove.

Now that we were two, we could enter into new types of social activities, and Kathleen could learn to know some of the women as I had become acquainted with the men. However, these new directions of social activity were something for the future. My problem now was to find where I was and where I was going. This was a period of stocktaking.

In describing my Cornerville study, I have often said I was eighteen months in the field before I knew where my research was going. In a sense, this is literally true. I began with the general idea of making a community study. I felt that I had to establish myself as a participant observer in order to make such a study. In the early months in Cornerville I went through the process that sociologist Robert Johnson has described in his own field work. I began as a nonparticipating observer. As I became accepted into the community, I found myself becoming almost a nonobserving participant. I got the feel of life in Cornerville, but that meant that I got to take for granted the same things that my Cornerville friends took for granted. I was immersed in it, but I could as yet make little sense out of it. I had a feeling that I was doing something important, but I had yet to explain to myself what it was.

Fortunately, at this point I faced a very practical problem. My three-year fellowship would run out in the summer of 1939. The fellowship could be renewed for a period up to three years. Applications for renewal were due in the early spring of 1939.

I was enjoying Cornerville, and I felt that I was getting somewhere, yet at the same time I felt that I needed at least three more years. I realized that so far I had little to show for the time I had spent. When I submitted my application for renewal, I must also submit some evidence that I had acquitted myself well in the first three-year period. I would have to write something. I had several months in which to do the writing, but the task at first appalled me. I sat down to ask myself what it was in Cornerville upon which I had reasonably good data. Was there anything ready to be written up? I pondered this and talked it over with Kathleen and with John Howard, who was working with me in the district.

Still thinking in terms of a community study, I recognized that I knew very little about family life in Cornerville, and my data were very thin upon the church, although John Howard was beginning to work on this area. I had been living with the restaurant family in a room that overlooked the corner where T. S., the most prominent Cornerville racketeer, sometimes was seen with his followers. I had looked down upon the group many times from my window, and yet I had never met the men. Racketeering was of obvious importance in the district, yet all I knew about it was the gossip I picked up from men who were only a little closer to it than I. I had much more information regarding political life and organization, but even here I felt that there were so many gaps that I could not yet put the pieces together.

If these larger areas were yet to be filled in, what on earth did I have to present? As I thumbed through the various folders, it was obvious that the Norton and Community Club folders were fatter than the rest. If I knew anything about Cornerville, I must know it about the Nortons and the Italian Community Club. Perhaps, if I wrote up these two stories, I would begin to see some pattern in what I was doing in Cornerville.

As I wrote the case studies of the Nortons and of the Italian Community, a pattern for my research gradually emerged in my mind.

I realized at last that I was not writing a community study in the usual sense of that term. The reader who examines *Middletown* will note that it is written about people in general in that community. Individuals or groups do not figure in the story except as they illustrate the points that the authors are making (the sequel, *Middletown in Transition*, presents one exception to this description with a chapter on the leading family of the community). The reader will further note that *Middletown* is organized in terms of such topics as getting a living, making a home, training the young, and using leisure.

The Lynds accomplished admirably the task they set out to accomplish. I simply came to realize that my task was different. I was dealing with particular individuals and with particular groups.

I realized also that there was another difference that I had stumbled upon. I had assumed that a sociological study should present a description and analysis of a community at one particular point in time, supported of course by some historical background. I now came to realize that *time* itself was one of the key elements in my study. I was observing, describing, and analyzing groups as they evolved and changed through time. It seemed to me that I could explain much more effectively the behavior of men when I observed them over time than would have been the case if I had got them at one point in time. In other words, I was taking a moving picture instead of a still photograph.

But, if this was a study of particular individuals and there were more than twenty thousand people in the district, how could I say anything significant about Cornerville on this individual and group basis? I came to realize that I could only do so if I saw individuals and groups in terms of their positions in the social structure. I also must assume that, whatever the individual and group differences were, there were basic similarities to be found. Thus I would not have to study every corner gang in order to make meaningful statements about corner gangs in Cornerville. A study of one corner gang was not enough, to be sure, but, if an examination of several more showed up the uniformities that I expected to find, then this part of the task became manageable.

On the Italian Community Club, I felt that I needed no additional data. There were few enough college men in Cornerville at the time, so that this one group represented a large sample of people in this category. It also seemed to me that they represented significant points in the social structure and in the social mobility process. There would certainly be others like them coming along after they had left the district, even as the Sunset Dramatic Club had gone before them. Furthermore, examination of their activities showed up important links with Republican politics and with the settlement house.

I now began to see the connection between my political study and the case study of the corner gang. The politician did not seek to influence separate individuals in Cornerville, consciously or unconsciously he sought out group leaders. So it was men like Doc who were the connecting links between their groups and the larger political organization. I could now begin writing my study by examining particular groups in detail, and then I could go on to relate them to the larger structures of the community. With this pattern in mind, I came to realize that I had much more data on politics than I had thought.

There were still important gaps in my study. My knowledge of the role of the church in the community was fragmentary, and this I hoped to fill in. I had done no systematic work upon the family. On the one hand, it seemed inconceivable that one could write a study of Cornerville without discussing the family; yet, at the same time, I was at a loss as to how to proceed in tying family studies into the organization of the book as it was emerging in my mind. I must confess also that for quite unscientific reasons I have always found politics, rackets, and gangs more interesting than the basic unit of human society.

The gap that worried me most was in the area of the rackets and the police. I had a general knowledge of how the rackets functioned, but nothing to compare with the detailed interpersonal data I had upon the corner gang. As my book was evolving, it seemed to me that this was the gap that simply must be filled, although at the time I had no idea how I would get the inside picture that was necessary.

I finished the writing of my first two case studies and submitted them in support of my application for a renewal of the fellowship. Some weeks later I received my answer. The fellowship had been renewed for one year instead of the three for which I had been hoping. At first, I was bitterly disappointed. As I was just beginning to get my bearings, I did not see how it would be possible to finish an adequate study in the eighteen months that then remained.

I am now inclined to believe that this one year cut-off was a very good thing for me and my research. In a sense, the study of a community or an organization has no logical end point. The more you learn, the more you see that there is to learn. If I had had three years instead of one, my study would have taken longer to complete. Perhaps it might have been a better study. On the other hand, when I knew I had just eighteen months to go, I had to settle down and think through my plans more thoroughly and push ahead with the research and writing much more purposefully.

Again the Corner Gang

The most important steps I took in broadening my study of street corner gangs grew out of Doc's recreation center project, although at first I had some other interests in mind. It began with one of my periodic efforts to get Doc a job. When I heard that the Cornerville House had finally been successful in getting its grant to open three store-front recreation centers, I sought to persuade Mr. Smith, the director, to man them with local men who, like Doc, were leaders in their groups. I found that he had planned to man them with social workers trained in group work. When I realized that it was hopeless to get him to select three local men, I tried to urge at least Doc upon him. I could see that Mr. Smith was tempted by the idea and afraid of it at the same time. When I brought Doc in to meet him, I found that I lost ground instead of gaining it, for, as Doc told me later, he had got a dizzy spell there in the settlement-house office, and he had been in no condition to make a favorable personal impression. If Doc and I had figured out correctly the underlying causes for his dizzy spells, then a steady job and the money that would enable him to resume his customary pattern of social activity would cure these neurotic symptoms. On the other hand, I could hardly explain this to Mr. Smith. I was afraid that it appeared that I was simply trying to do a favor for a friend. As my last effort in this direction, I turned over to Mr. Smith a copy of my case study of the Nortons—and asked him please to keep it confidential, since I was not ready to publish.

This made the difference. Mr. Smith agreed to hire Doc.

As the preliminary activities of setting up the recreation centers got under way, I began to worry about my confident predictions of Doc's success. In the preliminary meetings to discuss plans for the centers, Doc was passive and apparently apathetic. Nevertheless, almost from the moment that Doc's center opened, it became apparent that it was to be a success.

On one of my early visits to Doc's center, he introduced me to Sam Franco, who was to play a far more important part in my study than brief mentions of him in the book indicate. Doc met Sam the night his center opened. Sam's gang was hanging around outside of the center looking the place over. Sam came in as the emissary of his group—a move which immediately identified him as the leader to Doc. The two men discussed the center briefly, and then Sam went out and brought his gang in. By the second night of the center, Sam had become Doc's lieutenant in its administration. Doc knew a few people in this part of the district, but Sam knew everybody.

Doc knew that I was trying to extend my corner gang study, and he suggested that Sam might be the man to help me. Doc had already learned that Sam had been keeping a scrapbook with newspaper accounts of Cornerville activities and some personal material on his own group.

I invited Sam and his scrapbook up to our apartment. There I learned that Sam had got started on his scrapbook after an experience on a National Youth Administration Project, where he had been working for a man who was writing a study of the problems of youth in this region. The scrapbook was completely miscellaneous and undirected, but it did have one part that particularly interested me. Sam had a section for his own gang with one page for each member. At the top of the page was a line drawing (from memory) of the individual, and then he wrote in such points as age, address, education, job, and ambition. (Usually he had written "none" opposite the heading "ambition.")

My task was now to persuade Sam that, while it was fine to look upon these men as individuals, it was even better to look upon them in terms of their relations with each other. I had only begun my explanation when Sam got the point and accepted it with enthusiasm. Of course, this was the sort of thing he knew; he had so taken it for granted that it had not occurred to him how important it might be. From this point on until the end of my study Sam Franco was my research assistant. I even managed to get Harvard to pay a hundred dollars for his services.

We began with an analysis of Sam's own gang, the Millers. We also looked at other gangs that came into Doc's recreation center. Here we had the great advantage of having two sharp observers checking each other on the same groups. I was reassured to find that they were in complete agreement on the top-leadership structure of every gang—with one exception. This one exception did trouble me until the explanation presented itself.

I had spent part of one afternoon listening to Doc and Sam argue over the leadership of one gang. Doc claimed that Carl was the man; Sam argued that it was Tommy. Each man presented incidents that he had observed in support of his point of view. The following morning Sam rushed up to my house with this bulletin: "You know what happened last night? Carl and Tommy nearly had it out. They got into a big argument, and now the gang is split into two parts with some of them going with Carl and the rest going with Tommy." So their conflicting views turned out to be an accurate representation of what was taking place in the gang.

As I worked on these other gang studies, I assumed that I had finished my research on the Nortons. Still, I kept in close touch with Doc, and, just for recreation, I continued to bowl with the remnants of the Nortons on some Saturday nights.

With my attention directed elsewhere, I failed to see what was happening among the Nortons right before my eyes. I knew Long John was not bowling as he had in previous years, and I also knew that he was not as close to Doc, Danny, and Mike as he had been. I had noticed that, when Long John was on Norton Street, the followers badgered him more aggressively than they ever had before. I must have assumed some connection among these phenomena, and yet I did not make much of the situation until Doc came to me and told me of Long John's psychological difficulties.

It was as if this information set off a flash bulb in my head. Suddenly all the pieces of the puzzle fell together. The previous season, I had stumbled upon the relationship between position in the group and performance at the bowling alleys. I now saw the three-way connection between group position, performance, and mental health. And not only for Long John. Doc's dizzy spells seemed to have precisely the same explanation.

We could put it more generally in this way. The individual becomes accustomed to a certain pattern of interaction. If this pattern is subject to a drastic change, then the individual can be expected to experience mental health difficulties. That is a very crude statement. Much further research would be needed before we could determine the degree of change necessary, the possibilities of compensating with interactions in other social areas, and so on. But here at least was one way of tying together human relations and psychological adjustment.

Furthermore, here was an opportunity to experiment in therapy. If my diagnosis was correct, then the line of treatment was clear: reestablish something like Long John's preexisting pattern of interaction, and the neurotic symptoms should disappear. This was the first real opportunity to test my conclusions on group structure. I embraced it with real enthusiasm.

Convinced as I was of the outcome that should follow, I must confess that I was somewhat awestruck when, under Doc's skillfully executed therapy program, Long John not only lost his neurotic symptoms but also closed out the season by winning the prize money in the final bowling contest. Of course, this victory was not necessary to establish the soundness of the diagnosis. It would have been enough for Long John to have reestablished himself *among* the top bowlers. His five-dollar prize was just a nice bonus for interaction theory.

18 / The Methodology of Participant Observation

Severyn T. Bruyn

In the search for meaning and understanding in human relationships a significant number of sociologist in the classical tradition, as well as in contemporary research, have recognized the importance of participant observation in methodology. The place of this technique in the methodology of social sciences has yet to be thoroughly examined. It still remains a questionable technique for some social scientists largely because it raises some of the most fundamental questions about epistemology and challenges the traditions of science.

This article proposes to confront these questions and challenges in the light of larger perspectives involved in the pursuit of knowledge. To accomplish this purpose we shall review the conclusions of past researchers regarding the social role of the participant observer, then examine questions of epistemology, the challenges the role presents to the scientific perspectives and standards of research, and finally the potential that exists for developing new perspectives for research.

THE SOCIAL ROLE

Certain summary statements can be made regarding the role of the participant observer on the basis of research findings already reported. This should serve to orient our analysis of the methodological foundations of this approach.

1. The participant observer shares in the life activities and sentiments of people in face-to-face relationships.

Florence Kluckhohn has thus succinctly described the role as: "conscious and systematic sharing, in so far as circumstances permit, in the life activities, and on occasion, in the interests and affects of a group of persons."[1]

While the traditional role of the scientist is that of a neutral observer who remains unmoved and unchanged in his examination of phenomena, the role of the participant observer requires sharing the sentiments of people in social situations, and thus he himself is changed as well as changing to some degree the situation in which he is a participant. However, researchers have found that although he becomes changed through his participation, it is important that part of him remain unchanged and detached. Although "sharing" the experience, he is not entirely of it.

2. The role of the participant observer requires both detachment and personal involvement.

In a research report by Morris and Charlotte Schwartz, the involvement of the researcher is recognized and qualified:

> The issue is not whether he will become emotionally involved, but rather the nature of the involvement. The involvement, whether it is closer to one end of the continuum (sympathetic identification) or the other end (projective distortion), is very little a function of an observer's role. Rather, it is primarily a function of his experience, awareness, and personality constellation and the way these become integrated with a particular situation. . . . Sympathetic identification includes emphatic communication and imaginative participation in the life of the observed through identification and role taking. In this type of involvement the observer is both detached and affectively participating; he feels no need to moralize or judge the interaction; his attitude is one of interested curiosity and mater-of-fact inquiry directed toward understanding the observed.[2]

In seeking to share something of the experience of the observed the researcher must not only become personally involved, he must also acquire the role which can function within the culture of the observed. There is no standard role which he can assume, but the requirements for the selection of the role are evident.

3. The researcher acquires a social role which is determined by the requirements of the research design and the framework of the culture.

Some of the types of roles which researchers have considered include: general and specific, active and passive, complementary, and others designated but not fully described. In the Schwartz report on field observation in a mental hospital they note:

> The role of the participant observer may either be formal or informal, concealed or revealed; the observer may spend a great deal of time or very little time in the research situation; the participant observer may be an integral part of the social structure or largely peripheral to it.[3]

Active and passive roles are selected for description in their report.

Florence Kluckhohn makes the distinction between general, specific, and complementary roles. In her study of a Mexican village she took the role of a local storekeeper (a role complementary to her customers) and thus came to understand reflectively the lives of the villagers. Her role as a housewife she conceived as a general role similar to that of most women in the village. Other examples of general roles (i.e. identical with a significant portion of persons studied) would be the researcher's role as prisoner in studying prison socialization,[4] or the role of an air force recruit which a researcher undertook in studying a military program.[5]

4. The scientific interests of the participant observer are interdependent with the cultural framework of the people being studied.

In his scientific role the participant observer is seeking to apprehend, register, interpret, and conceptualize the social facts and meanings which he finds in a prescribed area of study. He is interested in the people as they are, not as he thinks they ought to be from some standard of his own; he is interested in the uniformities of their culture, in their existent, predictable state of being. To achieve these ends he finds his cultural role an indispensable part of the process.

He finds that only by coming to know people personally can he achieve his scientific aims. In his cultural role he becomes involved, but his procedures, his hypotheses, his experimental design, his social role remain objectively recorded. They are not so rigidly fixed that they cannot be changed. As with all experimental work if he finds that any one of these elements is not broadly enough conceived to encompass the data, he refocuses, reformulates his project in whatever way he finds advisable. He assumes he can do this without ignoring the interests of the people he is observing or the standards of his own research.

The scientific role and the cultural role of the researcher are interdependent and complementary.[6] The personal lives of the people he is studying are of great importance to him in both roles. It may be assumed that without this primary interest in them as persons in his active role as participant observer his study and findings become subject to distortion. His skills in reporting his findings objectively and the means he takes to insure this are also of primary interest to him. He assumes that one dimension makes the other possible. (He also assumes that no wholly "neutral" relation can exist in personal relations; such attempts often result in being impersonal, which is in effect becoming personal in a negative way.) He believes that valuing his subjects as persons increases the likelihood that he will come to understand them in their true state. The two roles not only coexist and complement one another, in some ways they can be seen as two reflections of the same social process as the researcher becomes a natural part of the life of the people he studies.

5. The social role of the researcher is a natural part of the cultural life of the observed.

The role of the researcher coincides with the role of the observed in the sense that both reflect the basic social process necessary to live in society. In his description of scientific methodology Cooley has stated:

The human mind participates in social process in a way that it does not in any other processes. It is itself a sample, a phrase, of those processes, and is capable, under favorable circumstances, of so far identifying itself with the general movement of a group as to achieve a remarkably just anticipation of what the group will do. Prediction of this sort is largely intuitive rather than intellectual.[7]

The elements that go into participant observer research are a reflection of the universal process of role taking in socialization from childhood through adulthood. In his description of a self, G. H. Meade describes the fundamental character of learning as role taking whose end is the complete self which "reflects the unity and structure of the social process as a whole."[8] Without disregarding the tensions and disharmonies inherent in the social process (which Meade neglected to explore), the aim of the participant observer is to take part in the socialization process just as the other participants do, to the point where his own inner experience can reflect the unity and structure of the whole.

The participant observer has usually been conceived as one who is an outsider and seeks to take part in a culture unlike his own. It is now apparent that the elements that go to comprise the participant observer technique *are fundamental to the social act* (in the Meadean sense) and therefore are to some degree a part of all social research. This explains why a discussion of participant observation must go to the heart of general methodology in the social sciences. The role of the participant observer is in process of refinement, out of the natural social process, just as the role of the physical scientist was refined out of the natural experiments made by ordinary people interested in the world about them.

EPISTEMOLOGICAL BACKGROUNDS

A. Naturalism and Idealism

The technique of any researcher evolves from philosophic traditions and is founded in certain epistemological beliefs about the origin of knowledge. Broadly speaking, two major traditions lying behind the development of the social sciences are naturalism and idealism. Both philosophies have undergone considerable change and development since their modern origin in the seventeenth century.

The formulator of the modern variant of naturalism (having had earlier roots) was Thomas Hobbes, who conceived all of nature as basically materialistic. He believed that all men's actions, thoughts, and feelings could be reduced to their true state as small particles of matter in motion. A later naturalistic interpretation can be illustrated in Jeremy Bentham's official philosophy that all man's actions could be determined and understood on the basis of weighing (literally as would a physicist) the gains and losses people felt existed between pleasureful and painful consequences. A still later development was seen in Karl Marx who raised the particle theory of Hobbes and the physiological theory of Bentham to a broader base in economic determinism. The changing economic forces became the mechanism through which all of culture was determined. Still later, neopositivists broadened the position further to include man's *general behavior* (not simply economic) as the foundation for understanding and predicting man's actions. Throughout this development however, the deterministic-mechanistic image of man was retained and it was assumed that all behavioral phenomena could be quantified.[9] The foundations of modern science have been built from this philosophy.

The modern expression of idealism took form with Berkeley, an English clergyman, who radically held that the external world had no real existence outside of the mental processes themselves. It was clear to him that physical properties could not be known outside the mind, therefore the mind itself was the source of all knowledge. Later developments such as German idealism (as in Kant and Hegel) accepted physical reality but insisted on the supremacy of the mind as a source and creator of knowledge. A still more recent variety, called personal idealism, focuses upon personality as the source of knowledge.

The modern conceptions of idealism base the source of knowledge in experience itself with its many dimensions. Thus, it has broadened to a position which, while emphasizing the importance of certain qualities of the mind to produce knowledge independent of external factors, does not ignore their place in the experience of man. In various ways modern approaches to these early divergent philosophies are interpenetrating as philosophy continues to explore the foundation upon which sciences can build systems of knowledge.[10]

B. The Empirical, Rational, and Intuitive Sources

Empiricism[11] and rationalism are epistemological traditions which have grown to be commonly accepted among social scientists. In various ways they have both been associated with previously described philosophies. Empiricism, however, in the narrower usage (associated only with building knowledge from sense data) has largely been associated with naturalism. Rationalism assumes that knowledge may be found or created through the association and dissociation of concepts, that truth may be revealed in the structure of thought. The dispute about which of these sources is more important is no longer serious; it is widely recognized that while different research activities emphasize one or the other, in all experience there is a common interplay, and both are basic to the development of scientific knowledge.

The intuitive capacity of the mind however has been less accepted as a legitimate source of scientific knowledge. Nevertheless, the participant observer finds it an important part of his work. Without ignoring the rational process or the importance of his record of sense observations, he must recognize an additional source—the nonrational, nonsensible, affective experience of the observed, as reflected in his own experience. He assumes that there exists in human feelings a capacity to reveal knowledge which is independent (as well as interdependent with) the rational-empirical sources of knowledge.

The veracity or proof of this position is no more possible outside of itself than is the proof of the rational or empirical traditions outside themselves. These are the initial assumptions that must be made about the nature of knowledge. However, the necessity for persuasion or validation remains for social scientists and usually develops through a combination of trusted traditions bearing witness to its own value to the human enterprise. For example, one important justifying authority in science today is pragmatism whose major test would be a method's capacity to void knowledge which stands the test of time. Another would be its demonstrated ability to predict or anticipate human action. The participant observer technique has already begun to demonstrate this productiveness, but this should increase still further as the technique becomes increasingly utilized and procedures for its application systematically developed.

In order to clarify and underline the importance of this intuitive epistemological position for the observer, it is necessary to examine in some detail the kinds of data which researchers encounter in their efforts to understand human relationships.

SCIENTIFIC DATA

Social scientific data are symbolic in the sense that all culture is symbolic. A brief view of the basic types of symbols existing in culture should provide a closer look at the subject matter (and the conceptual tools) of the participant observer.

The Sign

George Herbert Meade, Ernst Cassirer, Suzanne Langer, Talcott Parsons, Leslie White, and many others have made an important distinction between sign and the symbol which marks the beginning of culture. A sign is any human expression which communicates a message to another in a particularized situation in which the parties are involved. Examples would be the gesture to wave good-bye, or to verbalize "go," or "come here," or to cry for help. The sign is an early development in communication expressed (as Meade illustrates) in the bark of the wolf to the pack or the cluck of a hen to the chickens.[12] The development of language has been traced from the original cry of an organism (sign of need) to a call (a sign expressed to specific individuals) to the world and the differentiation of sentence structures.[13] Anthropologically the graphic expression of this development can be seen from pictographs (illustrations of specific events or things) to ideograms (pictorial symbol of an idea) to phonetic expressions (symbols representing speech sounds). Symbols always stand in place of something or referent. Words may be understood as symbols insofar as they stand for that which is apprehended and are understood by people without making reference to a particular object in their immediate environment. The symbol involves a capacity to abstract and recall; their references become removed from the immediate environment.

Denotative Symbols

The denotative symbol begins where the sign leaves off. These symbols *stand for* observable objects such as chairs or tables. Initially they were in the form of signs directing attention to particular objects, such as the moon, the sun, or Fido the dog. But soon a broader image becomes necessary to communicate not simply the uniqueness of a particular object, but the meaning of objects of a similar nature. The elementary processes of abstraction enter into forming the symbol.

The process is more complex than it would seem to indicate. To know the idea of a table requires considerable previous learning at the tactile or sense reactive level. That is the learner must have had a sense of surface, an impression of solidity, of dimension, etc., before the elements can come together to form something new, a general image, which has a central figure and peripheral possibilities of form which allows judgement as to whether different objects meet primary or secondary requirements.

Denotative symbols are the data with which the strict empiricist is primarily concerned. He is interested in defining operationally the visible world about him. He does this to maintain precision and clarity in his work. However, there is considerably more complexity and indefiniteness than technicians would always admit. A simple reference to a piece of furniture like a sofa has such diverse reflections in our language as davenport, settee, couch, divan, dais, ottoman, daybed, etc., all having their own central images overlapping to some extent. In fact, like the active participant observer, he must make certain inferences that the references he makes are the same among different researchers, *on the basis of verbal agreement.*

Abstract Symbols

As degrees of generality continue to be formulated, the image becomes entirely removed from visibility in the outside world. A symbolic fundament is built out of common experience parts of which (ideas, concepts) begin serving as the source of reference in themselves. For example, the idea of "society" is a highly abstract symbol around which focuses much of sociological theory. Its level of generality is clearly higher than any of its constituent parts, such as "institution," and still more removed from a more denotative component, the "primary group." The theorist assumes, like the operationalist, that there is something common about symbolic development in people which allows agreement in meaning, and if standard procedures are followed, knowledge can be developed at each level of inquiry.

Levy-Bruhl once claimed that primitives could not abstract, that they were prelogical and tended to participate personally in the objects about them without the capacity to differentiate themselves from the inanimate objects. This unconditional description of primitive mentality has since been qualified by recognizing at least an elementary logic in all human culture. The primitive does distinguish between subject and object, but he refuses to believe that "all reality lies in our external perception of it. There is an internal side and there are effects, constraints, from subject to object and from object to subject."[14] The primitive's failure to develop his logic, to deny the existence of beings in inanimate objects, has been a major basis for the claim to civilized man's superiority. However, in civilized man's efforts to overcome the indistinctiveness and emotional projections of the primitive life, he has become subject to error in denying the other reality, the "sensuous forms" (as Cassirer would describe it aesthetically) of the inner perspective as a source of truth.

Northrop makes the distinction between the theoretic component (highly developed in Western civilization) and the aesthetic component (developed in the East). It is difficult he says, for the Western man to realize or understand Eastern culture because of his irresponsible habit of abstracting everything from experiences. It is difficult for him to appreciate and know a thing for what it is, to know it emotionally, to empathize with it, and consider this an end in itself.[15] As William James would have said, it involves the difference between knowledge about a thing and knowledge of it. The Western scientist is quite capable of developing the former, but quite unprepared to understand the latter.

Emotive Symbols

Like the denotative symbol, "emotive" symbols begin as signs. The origin, however, is to inner needs and feelings rather than indications of external objects. Expressions of pain or surprise, or the child's call for "mommy" are such signs.

In secondary levels of learning these signs, the cry, or call, become emotional conditions which are understood without reference to specific persons. Just as the image of the chair persists through time in the mind of the learner, similarly the emotion of pride or anger takes on a persistence, is talked about, conveyed to others, has a life of its own independent of immediate needs. Thus the tribe develops a feeling of loyalty over a period of time. Ceremonial dancers cultivate religious devotion. The significant feature of the emotive symbol lies in its capacity to persist through time and be shared. It may be evoked by an outside reference; just as the sight of a chair may evoke the idea of one, so the sight of an enemy may evoke the fear or anger; but the inner condition develops an independence which is transmitted among participants and retained over a period of time.

Charles Cooley describes how our language has already given us the data by the mere fact that man has needed to record these states of being:

> Under the leading of words we interpret our observation, both external and introspective, according to patterns that have been found helpful by our predecessors. When we have come to use understandingly such words as "kindly," "resolute," "proud," "humble," "angry," "fearful," "lonesome," "sad," and the like, words recalling motions of the mind as well as the body, it shows that we have not only kept a record of our inner life, but have worked up the data into definite conceptions which we can pass on to others by the aid of the common symbol.[16]

Symbols of Sentiment

Emotive symbols move into another stage in which (like abstract symbols) it is not possible to refer to an immediate external cause or reference. Such may be called spiritual symbols or symbols of sentiment representing the spirit of man which has become more deeply set in experience, less moved by outside stimuli, having its own level and pace of development. The expressions of modern man which indicate such conditions, types of anxiety, suffering, joy, are not altogether unknown to primitive man. However, like abstract forms, these symbols are less developed and encountered less frequently.[17]

The primitive's emotional experiences are more particularized in the sense of pain or pleasure, and have some real, if not imaginary, reference to a cause he considers outside himself. Creative suffering perceived as an end in itself, the inner peace in the culture of the mystics, the Buddhistic state of Nirvana, the persistent anxiety of the mobile man in mass society, persists through the daily emotional reactions and changing external stimuli. They vary in their independence from or dependence upon the emotional and physiological needs of the individual and his place in society. Like conceptual development, these symbols (and the conditions they represent) grow more from the association of other like symbols of the inner life than the emotive or denotative symbols to which they are ultimately connected.[18]

Ideological and Substantive Symbols

As these various symbols combine with each other and with the human need for purpose and direction, we can designate other variations on these basic themes. Combinations of emotive and abstract symbols create ideological symbols such as "communism" or "Christianity." Adding denotative references, we find substantive symbols such as the flag or the cross, which represent considerable rational development and deeply felt human interests.

The position of the symbol in the culture of the observed is fundamental to the interpretation made by the participant observer. Robert Redfield describes the various ways an observer may approach this problem by illustrating his efforts to comprehend the inner world of the Mayan villagers of Chan Kom. One approach came to him as several of the villagers traveled with him to the sea coast and expressed amazement at how people could live without maize. Then he began to see the vital position of this symbol in the village life:

> So I began to form another way of conceiving parts as related to one another in a system of activity and thought. This third system is neither chainlike or maplike. It is radial: maize is a center and other things are grouped around it, connected to it in different ways, some by a series of useful activities, some by connections of symbolic significance. The mind goes out from maize to agriculture, from maize to social life, from maize to religion. Maize is always the center of things.[19]

The participant observer must comprehend all these basic symbolic forms as he may find them in his area of study. He recognizes that by his acquaintanceship with symbols of sentiment and emotion in a particular setting he is more likely to adequately conceptualize the meaning and significance of events in the lives of those he is observing.

BASIC PERSPECTIVES

Any description of the basic perspectives of men in the pursuit of knowledge necessarily includes only selective abstractions of what in reality merges in varying degrees according to the type of research. Such descriptive statements, in the tradition of the Weberian ideal type, are formulated for the purpose of gaining some further insight into the nature of the participant observer process of research.

Different types of research have indicated two basic perspectives, an inner and outer. The latter assumes that the study of man's *behavior* or conduct is adequate to produce knowledge about social life. The inner perspective assumes that understanding can only be achieved by actively participating in the life of the observed and gaining insight by means of introspection. There is no disjunction between these perspectives in reality because all research involves something of both. However, as one comes to analyze them and the types of research that tend to associate with them, other perspectives reveal themselves as important to understand.

Determinism and Cultural Freedom

As the participant observer enters into the common life of those whom he is studying, he must act within a cultural framework which recognizes a measure of personal freedom, to which responsibility and obligations are attached. The amount and kind of free choice that is recognized varies from culture to culture and such differences become a part of the social role of the researcher.

The frame of reference of freedom which the participant observer assumes would seem to challenge the perspective of scientific determinism which research has inherited from the natural sciences. The dilemma must be resolved at the working level where the participant observer accepts the definition of freedom perceived by his fellow participants, yet also comes to perceive the determining factors in their background.

Social sciences still utilize the perspective of determinism as the basis for interpreting social life; some scientists hold to it as the only correct perspective possible.[20] There should be no need for conflict between the determinism of science and the culture of the observed. There is a rational basis for the researcher to genuinely understand and accept the concept of cultural freedom.

The research design arising from scientific determinism does not generally account for the fact that all factors or variables are to some extent determinants or causes in themselves. Which is cause and which effect depends upon the perspective of the observer. In the cultural framework, the participant observer simply enters into the inner perspective of the determinant, in this case the people themselves, and sees them as determining (causing) the effects about them. From their perspective of personal responsibility and free will, it is legitimately assumed that freedom exists to the extent that knowledge about and power over existential conditions is demonstrable. The two perspectives coexist, have validity, and actually depend upon the position one takes to his subject.

The Causal and Telic Principles

The participant observer seeks to know and become part of the purposes and interests of people. He assumes that all people have aims and that they have some latent or manifest knowledge about means to achieve these aims. The importance of understanding the purposive aspects of social phenomena has been stressed from Durkheim to modern functionalism, but the importance of this perspective to the participant observer requires that it be restated.

Without ignoring causality, in fact being quite aware of causes and effects, he nevertheless comes to act toward people and react toward events within a purposive framework which comes to infuse and pervade his descriptions. The interest and valuations of people become a central pivot around which he guides his conduct and interprets all the social setting in which he works.

Analysis and Synthesis

As the participant observer records, interprets, and explains social phenomena, he analyzes it; he takes apart the events and looks at them separately. However, there are two important ways in which contrasting features must be noted by the participant observer. First, he seeks to find some identity with the observed without analyzing them. Analysis at certain stages may prove to be a barrier to his understanding. The researcher seeks a certain kind of communion with the observed and in any efforts to comment descriptively about the situation keeps himself outside it.

There is no place for either rational or emotional comments at the point of intuitive contact. Cooley stresses this point with regard to reflective emotions:

Sympathy in the sense of compassion is a specific emotion or sentiment, and has nothing necessarily in common with sympathy in the sense of communion. It might be thought, perhaps, that compassion was one form of sharing feeling; but this appears not to be the case. The sharing of painful feeling may precede and cause compassion, but is not the same with it. When I feel sorry for a man in disgrace, it is, no doubt, in most cases, because I have imaginatively partaken of his humiliation; but my compassion for him is not the thing that is shared, but is something additional, a comment on the shared feeling. I may imagine how a suffering man feels—sympathize with him in that sense—and be moved not to pity but to disgust, contempt, or perhaps admiration. Our feeling makes all sorts of comments on the imagined feeling of others.[21]

Secondly, the tendency of the participant observer is to seek the essence of the life of the observed, to sum up, to find a central unifying principle. The documents of many anthropologists are evidence of this inclination. Ruth Benedict's descriptions of the two Indian cultures as Apollonian and Dionysian and Opler's culture themes are cases in point.

Of course there are limitations in stressing either mode of interpretation without some reference to the other. The difficulties in synthetic descriptions lay in the tendency to oversimplify (and thereby misunderstand) the nature of the culture. The difficulties of analysis lay in the failure to see the whole, and thereby the significance of the parts. All researchers inescapably apply both modes but the conditions under which they work cause one or the other to be emphasized.

Types of Concepts: Operational and Sensitizing

All scientific research involves the conceptualization of data. The types of concepts employed differ with the kinds of research design. The operational concept is most frequently used in quantitative research. It is defined as a statement of the specific procedures or operations used to identify and measure a phenomenon under study. Another kind of concept more frequently used in research has been described by Herbert Blumer as the "sensitizing concept." Blummer raises the question of how these concepts can be formulated and communicated. He notes that, rather than by formal definitions, "It is accomplished instead by exposition which yields a meaningful picture, abetted by apt illustrations which enable one to grasp the reference in terms of one's own experience."[22]

This statement describes the character of much of participant observer research.

Contrary to the opinion of some operationalists, sensitizing concepts are not all necessarily on the road to becoming definitive, as though they were ideal. Such a position would deny the reality which they represent. By operationalizing a concept, one changes its meaning. Although it is true that all data are subject to measurement, it is also true that when this is done the distinctive character and meaning of the data is lost. Defining an emotion or sentiment, for example, as that which is measured by certain visceral responses, cannot convey the true meaning of that feeling. Sensitizing concepts, therefore, have a right to their own existence without changing their expression by way of enumeration.

Merging Reality

Anyone accustomed to the discipline of research knows that the types listed in table 18.1 are only abstractions of what in reality tends to merge together in various ways. The ways in which this dichotomy of perspectives (illustrated in table 18.1) does not fit reality is as important to understand as the abstraction itself.

A complete statement of how these divergent perspectives have crossed in history and in the configuration of actual research projects would involve a lengthy disser-

Table 18.1

	INNER PERSPECTIVE	OUTER PERSPECTIVE
Epistemological background	Idealism Intuitive imagination	Natural materialism Logical empiricism
Explanatory principle	Teleology	Causality
Acting framework	Cultural freedom	Scientific determinism
Methods and techniques	Participant observation Personal documents	Statistics
Aims	Sensitive understanding of human values, institutions; anticipation of new directions	Adequate measurement and prediction of human behavior
Mode of study	Synthetic emphasis	Analytic emphasis
Concepts	Sensitizing	Operational

tation. However, a few basic points will illustrate the crossings: 1. The participant observer is sometimes a part of a larger quantitative study and may enumerate his data to contribute solely to the larger quantitative study. 2. A functional (telic) analysis of social phenomena may very well also be quantitative in nature. 3. The history of idealism as an epistemological theory has also included theories of determinism. 4. Sociological analysis need not be cast in a deterministic framework.[23] 5. The participant observer (as has been noted) is aided by his senses and reason as well as by intuition; the logical empiricist is aided by intuition.[24] 6. Max Weber's concept of bureaucracy involved a process of synthesis (putting together of significant elements) as well as analysis, as does most of theoretical work.

With these and other exceptions which could be noted, the ideal type still stands on the basis of the emphasis which is given to each perspective. That is, the use of the participant observer to simply quantify data, while useful in some cases, is not the general role he assumes; while quantitative methods are used in functional analysis, the functional interpretations must be made on the basis of participant observation which characterizes the work of researchers who study their own culture[25]; while at times idealism has included deterministic perspectives, its emphasis in history has been on freedom; while the rational-empirical-intuitive capacities are interdependent, one or another is more evident in different research designs; much of highly abstract theoretical formulation involves intuitive observation.[26]

SCIENTIFIC STANDARDS

The standards of objectivity, control, reliability, and validity are still important concerns for the participant observer. These guides to research require reexamination in the light of what they mean today.

Objectivity

Objectivity is an ideal, a state which is always in process of becoming. It is never fully achieved by any investigator in any final sense. It is a condition of reporting without prejudice, but it need not be a report without feeling or sentiment. There are two ways in which the participant observer assumes that feeling and objectivity may coexist.

First, it is possible for the investigator to have a feeling of respect for his subjects and remain open and unprejudiced in apprehending and reporting about their way of life. Second, it is possible for the sentiments of people being studied to be conveyed in the report without prejudicing the accuracy of correctness of the report itself.

Maurice Stein describes a "dramatic theory" developing among some sociological circles which focuses the problem of the participant observer.

> From a dramatic standpoint, the central problem of the community sociologist is to achieve an objective perspective that encompasses the partial perspectives held by various groups in the community in such a fashion as to call attention to hidden processes without losing sight of the meanings of the various partial perspectives. The playwright seeks to present his characters sympathetically without going so far as to allow the sympathy they evoke to swallow the larger meanings that emerge when they are viewed within the context of the entire plot and action of the play. The play suffers as much when the context is allowed to override full presentation of diverse characters.
>
> The playwright seeks a profound balance and it is similar to the balance sought by the community sociologist.
>
> Dramatic sensibility then consists of the capacity to encompass multiple interpretations of a social world with a larger context which distinguishes objective structures without obliterating subjective meanings.[27]

Participant observer methodology broadens the limits of the scientific framework to permit ideas for social and cultural studies which would not ordinarily be entertained.

Reliability and Validity

The participant observer does not need to defend the reliability or validity of his data (in the traditional sense) in certain stages of his work. This point has been sufficiently discussed in the research on personal documents.[28] As research proceeds, however, the accuracy of the denotative references of the subject's statements adds to the objectivity of the research. A description of the connection between the inner and the outer world of the subject is fundamental to a complete report.

The participant observer technique in some ways has already proved itself to be more reliable than other methods available. In the article previously quoted, Florence Kluckhohn describes how the direct interview and the questionnaire create special or unnatural situations. The subject may not know how to respond to formal methods, may unconsciously or purposely err, or may have a faulty memory. In contrast, the participant observer is there in the social setting which the interviewer may be seeking to learn about, and has the opportunity to record what actually happens. He is in a position to evaluate any rationalizations which the subject may make to a questionnaire or a formal interview.

Guides to Adequate Research

Rules which are appropriate for the participant observer to follow in his research are generally applicable to all research. Nevertheless, through practical experience, there is developing a know-how, and a set of principles which guide the observer around the pitfalls which are peculiar to his kind of work. A few of these guides can be summarized in the following directives.

1. *Examine all significant rules existing in counter-position in a circumscribed social setting.*

The inclination of observers is to so identify with a particular segment of the population being studied that their work is hindered or their reporting is obstructed.

Two pitfalls are in evidence here. First, the tendency of "overrapport" in which too close a contact with the observed does not allow an investigation into certain questions without serious breech of the relationship.[29]

Second, the tendency to report sympathetically the plight of the subject under study. For example, studies of the juvenile delinquent in his natural setting have tended in some cases to romanticize his role. Examining only the symbolic meaning of "cop" in the life of the young slum dweller may shut out or overshadow the meaning of "brat" or "cop-killer" for the police officer. The participant observer should include both subject and object in contra-position to convey objectively the social context.

2. Relate the research problem to a larger social context.

In the field of industrial relations the role of the laborer needs not only to be examined with reference to the counter-position of manager, but ideally the two powers need relating to the community and the economic system in the context of the whole society. There are limits to any research problem to be sure, but accurate references to the nature of the larger context adds to the objectivity of the report.

3. Examine and describe the participant observer's own status in the social system.

A participant observer can very well make use of the findings and guides developed in the sociology of knowledge as a bridge from the biases inherent in his social position to a point of objectivity. Merton's paradigm is a good beginning guide.[30]

The stages of his acceptance into the community are vital to the kind of data he will receive.[31] The kind of image which those around him have of him provides a basis for their response to him. By examining and reporting these facts carefully, the research may avoid this easy pitfall.

4. Observe the subjects under contrasting social and isolated settings.

Misconceptions have been avoided and insight added when this directive is followed. Howard Becker reports an experience in studying medical students:

> Thus, students in their clinical years may express deeply "idealistic" sentiments about medicine when alone with the observer, but behave and talk in a very "cynical" way when surrounded by fellow students. An alternative to judging one or the other of these situations as more reliable is to view each datum as valuable in itself, but with respect to different conclusions. In the example above, we might conclude that group norms may not sanction their expressions.[32]

5. Evaluate the information as any personal document.[33]

6. Indicate the proportion or segment of the group which expresses the norms or conduct being recorded.

7. Carefully specify the procedures used so that other investigators may follow and check the findings from the same (and from different) social positions in the setting under study.

8. Examine indexes of distortion in reporting and evaluate the data with reference to them.[34]

NEW PERSPECTIVES

The study of participant observation stimulates new perspectives. Just as the social scientist has consciously transposed and developed his techniques and methodology from the physical and organic sciences, so he may become conscious of the possibilities in other disciplines, including the humanities and the arts. He is far from alone in his pursuit of the meaning and objective character of culture and social conduct. He has a special opportunity to produce new blends, new research which will cast the social scene into a more human (and therefore a more realistic) form.[35]

Given the separate academic disciplines existing in their own right, there is still room for considerable fruitful exchange among them. For example, the fact that the subject matter of the social sciences and literature is so similar makes it unusual that so little attention has been given to studying and comparing the approaches of each. The social scientific descriptions of latent and manifest functions, of social incongruities and dysfunctions in institutional settings, have long been a part of the devices of literary expression.

In the rhetorical allusion, in satire and irony, in the metaphor, the analogy and allegory, in the parable, and many other age-old artistic and literary modes, may be found important instruments of inquiry and analysis, yet unexamined in the methods of sociological studies. The employment of such literary devices need not distort or misrepresent the essential purpose of sociological reporting. As techniques to convey social meaning (derived from empirical studies), they can be as useful and vital as have been the modes of logic or statistical analysis to scientific research.

Such literary devices need not be conceived as masked instruments of ideological or moral doctrine. They should rather be seen as tools of the intellectual craftsman to be used well or badly according to his training and experience. In a rather thorough analysis of the use of allegory in modern literature, Edwin Honig summarizes its instrumental character:

> In one of its aspects allegory is a rhetorical instrument used by strategists of all sorts in their struggle to gain power or to maintain a system of beliefs. (Such usage and the motives lurking behind it have recently had the close study of critics as part of the semantic problem of symbolic action.) In addition to serving the expression of ideological aims, allegory is a fundamental device of hypothetical construction. In this broad way allegory is part of the creative process, observable in all literature generally, where the formulation of vital beliefs seems essential to maximum expressiveness.
>
> The literary allegory does not oppose a realistic account of the universe. Its very power lies in its giving proof to the physical and ethical realities of life objectively conceived.[36]

Some of these literary mechanisms have been built into the structure of language from its very beginning.[37] With language so basic to social life, sociologists are coming to see their fundamental place in their work. Anthropologists have already recognized their importance in the study of primitive society. Robert Redfield describes the necessity of the ethnographer and the sociologist to make use of such devices in making their descriptions of community life.

> In the portraitures accomplished by art, exaggerations, distortions and substitutions of one sort or another play important parts. Caricature and satire are special forms of portraiture. Each describes the whole by overemphasizing something felt to be significantly true of the whole. Metaphor and analogy offer different and parallel images for understanding the whole, as does the parable: a narrative standing for a human something other than itself. And in the more nearly scientific portraiture of communities, metaphors and analo-

gies play a useful part. No one expects Professor Fortes to produce the tangible warp and woof of Tallensi social structure; for the words bring forward a metaphor which helps us to understand Tallensi life, and, indeed, the concept of social structure itself.[38]

There is no longer a necessity to justify the use of these rhetorical figures. The need now is for their study, and more critical use as part of the methodology of the social sciences.

The parable has its own place in the record of man's search for knowledge. It has often been employed by charismatic founders of religious movements in an effort to convey meanings which they believe have not yet been grasped by their followers. The function of the parable is to set a moral or spiritual truth aside from the usual affections of the self so that it can be grasped more objectively or at least on another level of experience. It is usually a short fictitious narrative which is intentionally obscured so that it requires some reflective thought before it is grasped. It is not a device for hidden persuasion; it requires voluntary effort to see the meaning. It functions to establish or verify a new experience, a new understanding of an old principle, or a new state of mind. Students of theology have much to contribute to the sociologist in their studies of this medium of communication. Sociologists can utilize such knowledge in their analysis of the diffusion of the religious movement throughout the society.

Such studies have various applications to the field of sociology. They can increase our understanding of the social character of language; they can cast light on the field of communication and studies of socialization; they can act as an enhancement (as well as a self-corrective)[39] of professional descriptions of social life.

The field of art has its own contributions to make. A study of the state of the aesthetic observer viewing an art object cannot help but add insight into the role of the participant observer as he observes the actors in his social setting. In a provocative discussion of aethetic experience, Cassirer comes to Aristotle's theory of catharsis and interprets how, through tragic poetry, a person takes on new attitudes toward his emotions.

> The soul experiences the emotions of pity and fear, but instead of being disturbed and disquieted by them it is brought to a state of rest and peace. At first sight this would seem to be a contradiction. For what Aristotle looks upon as the effect of tragedy is a synthesis of two moments which in real life, in our practical existence, exclude each other. The highest intensification of our emotional life is thought of as at the same time giving us a sense of repose. We live through all our passions feeling their full ravages and highest intensity. But what we leave behind when passing the threshold of art is the hard pressure, the compulsion of our emotions; and he is able to transfer this mastery to the spectators. In his work we are not swayed and carried away by our emotions. Aesthetic freedom is not the absence of passions, not stoic apathy, but just the contrary. It means that our emotional life acquires its greatest strength, and that in this very strength it changes its form. For here we no longer live in the immediate reality of things but in a world of pure sensuous forms. In this world all our feelings undergo a sort of transubstantiation with respect to their essence and their character. The passions themselves are relieved of their material burden. We feel their form and their life but not their encumbrance. The calmness of the work of art is, paradoxically, a dynamic, not a static calmness.[40]

Cassirer quotes Hamlet in speaking of the function of dramatic art which might as well be interpreted as the function of the participant observer in recording and interpreting his observations of a particular culture.

The purpose of playing, [as Hamlet explains] both at the first and now, was and is, to hold, as 'twere, the mirror up to nature; to show virtues her own feature, scorn her own image, and the very age and body of the time his form and pressure.

But the image of a passion is not the passion itself. The poet represents a passion but does not infect us with this passion. At a Shakespeare play we are not infected with the ambition of Macbeth, with the cruelty of Richard III, or with the jealousy of Othello. We are not at the mercy of these emotions; we look through them; we seem to penetrate into their very nature of essence.... It is not the degree of intensification and illumination which is the measure of the excellence of art.[41]

The cultural organization of people may be viewed in many ways other than its symbolic character, which has been of principle use in this article. It can be viewed as an aesthetic creation and described from the models of art criticism. For example, culture, like any art object, has many dimensions: its material product, its expression, its form, its function in the social order. If the sociologist were to begin by analyzing the *form* which culture assumes, by using a model in art criticism, he would guide his study through the principles of harmony, balance, centrality, and development, and pursue his analysis by way of their derivatives—recurrence, similarity, gradation, variation, hierarchy, and progression, all of which can be aesthetically perceived and reported in an empirical study of a cultural system.[42]

The technique of participant observation is basic to the methodology of the social sciences. It presents real dilemmas for the researcher who identifies his field solely with the physical sciences. In this article the congruities and incongruities of these dilemmas have been sketched and judged in the light of the scholarly pursuit of knowledge. This pursuit is conceived as a creative one in which new techniques, new perspectives are continually being formulated. The methods of the social sciences cannot remain static; in full regard of the standards of research which are its heritage, it must move on in its probe of the character, the drama, and the meaning of human enterprise.

NOTES

1. Florence Kluckhohn, "The Participant-Observer Technique in Small Communities," *American Journal of Sociology* 46 (November 1940): 331.
2. Morris S. Schwartz and Charlotte G. Schwartz, "Problems in Participant Observation," *American Journal of Sociology* 60 (January 1955): 350.
3. Ibid., 344.
4. Hans Reimer, "Socialization in the Prison Community," *American Prison Association Proceedings* (1937): 151-55.
5. Mortimer A. Sullivan, Jr., Stuart A. Queen, and Ralph C. Patrick, Jr., "Participant Observation in a Military Program," *American Sociological Review* 23 (December 1958): 660-67.
6. The problems and conflicts which can arise between these roles (not the subject of discussion here) are reported elsewhere. See William Foote Whyte, *Street Corner Society* (Chicago: University of Chicago Press, 1955), pp. 279-358; Arthur J. Vidich, "Freedom and Responsibility in Research," *Human Organization* 19 (Spring 1960): 3-4.
7. Charles Cooley, *Sociological Theory and Social Research* (New York: Henry Holt, 1930), p. 308.
8. Anselm Strauss, ed., *The Social Psychology of George Herbert Mead* (Chicago: University of Chicago Press, 1956), p. 221.
9. Recent conceptions of naturalism broaden its form to cut across the stream of of Western thought, including some modern strains of idealism. See Vergilus Ferme, "Varieties of Naturalism," in *A History of Philosophical Systems* (New York: Philosophy Library, 1950), pp. 429-40.

10. For a modern system of metaphysics which links the traditions of idealism and naturalism, see D. W. Gotshalk, *Metaphysics in Modern Times* (Chicago: University of Chicago Press, 1940).

11. The term "empiricism" has developed varied meanings which can be described on a continuum from rigidly defined procedures for obtaining sense data with no inferences of a "subjective" kind, to the acquisition of knowledge on the basis of experience, which stands in contrast to the normative or ethical field of knowledge. The usage in this article refers to the former end of the continuum.

12. Strauss, *Mead*, p. 213.

13. G. Revesz, *The Origins and Prehistory of Language* (New York: Longmans Green, 1956).

14. Paul Radin, *The World of Primitive Man* (New York: Henry Schuman, 1953), p. 49.

15. Filmer Stuart Cuckow Northrop, *Meeting of East and the West* (New York: Macmillan, 1946).

16. Cooley, *Sociological Theory*, p. 299.

17. An example of primitive suffering which appears from the report to exist at this level of symbolization may be found in: Knud Rasmussen, *Observations on the Intellectual Culture of the Caribou Eskimo* (Copenhagen, 1930), pp. 52-55. Quoted in Radin, *Primitive Man*, pp. 76-78.

18. This rough classification of symbols could obviously bear further analysis, but remains in this form only to indicate the kinds of cultural data the participant observer must learn to apprehend and interpret.

19. Robert Redfield, *The Little Community* (Chicago: University of Chicago Press, 1955), p. 22.

20. Donald R. Taft, *Criminology* (New York: Macmillan, 1956), pp. 343-46.

21. Cooley, *Sociological Theory*, p. 102 *n*.

22. Herbert Blumer, "What Is Wrong with Social Theory?" *American Sociological Review* 19 (February 1954): 9.

23. McIver's concept of "dynamic assessment" illustrates an effort to overcome the deterministic perspective. Robert M. McIver, *Social Causation* (New York: Ginn, 1942), pp. 292-293.

24. From his logical perspective, any discovery not evident in operational procedure would be defined as "rational processes" operating at the subliminal level of consciousness.

25. Arthur J. Vidich, "Participant Observation and the Collection and Interpretation of Data," *American Journal of Sociology* 60 (January 1955): 385.

26. Contrariwise, participant observation has contributed to the breakdown of Weber's concept into more predictable parts. Alvin W. Gouldner, *Patterns of Industrial Bureaucracy* (New York: Free Press, 1954).

27. Maurice R. Stein, *The Eclipse of Community* (Princeton, N.J.: Princeton University Press, 1960), p. 325.

28. "It should be pointed out, also, that the validity and value of the personal document are not dependent upon its objectivity and veracity. It is not expected that the delinquent will necessarily describe his life situations objectively. On the contrary, it is desired that his story will reflect his own personal attitudes and interpretations, for it is just these personal factors which are so important in the study and treatment of the case. Thus, rationalizations, fabrications, prejudices, exaggerations, are quite as valuable as objective descriptions, provided of course, that these reactions be properly identified and classified." Clifford Shaw, *The Jack-Roller* (Albert Saifer Publications, 1930), pp. 2-3.

29. S. M. Miller, "The Participant Observer and Over-Rapport," *American Sociological Review* 17 (February 1952): 97-99.

30. Robert Merton, *Social Theory and Social Structure* (New York: Free Press, 1949), pp. 217-245.

31. Robert W. James, "A Note on Phases of the Community Role of the Participant-Observer," *American Sociological Review* 26 (June 1961): 446-50.

32. Howard S. Becker, "Problems of Inference and Proof in Participant Observation," *American Sociological Review* 23 (December 1958): 655.

33. Louis Gottschalk, Clyde Kluckhohn, and Robert Angell, *The Use of Personal Documents in History, Anthropology and Sociology* (New York: Social Science Research Council, 1945), pp. 15-27, 38-47.

34. Schwartz and Schwartz, "Participant Observation," p. 347.

35. This does not call for a super-discipline or new eclecticism among the social sciences. Like other disciplines they are circumscribed in their search for knowledge. The physical sciences do not wrestle with purpose in their data; the biological sciences do not reckon with sentiment; art, literature and drama

do not characteristically pursue knowledge systematically, building propositions into a coherent theory of life. The social scientists in their turn do not
search out the uniqueness of an event as an end in itself as does the poet or the
artist. The social scientists cannot derive moral truths out of their studies as
would the theologian or a playwright.

36. Edwin Honig, *Dark Conceit* (Cambridge: Walker-deBerry, 1959), pp. 179–80.
37. Susanne K. Langer, *Philosophy in a New Key* (New York: Mentor Books, 1942), pp. 111–15.
38. Redfield, Little Community, p. 162.
39. It is worthwhile to examine the use of metaphors, similies, a set of images, in any sociological analysis as they affect the total meaning conveyed to the reader. Caroline Spurgeon sets an example by her study of the substructure of Shakespeare's tragedies. By the use of various literary figures the reader is un-wittingly led to conclusions by way of various literary devices. For example, in Hamlet the various images of disease (ulcer, cancer), a motif which suggests that the Prince is not to blame, but the whole state of Denmark is diseased. Carol-ine Spurgeon, *Shakespeare's Imagery and What It Tells Us* (Cambridge, 1935).
40. Ernst Cassirer, *An Essay on Man* (Garden City, N.Y.: Doubleday, 1956), p. 190.
41. Ibid.
42. D. W. Gotshalk, *Art and The Social Order* (Chicago: University of Chicago Press, 1947), p. 114. This text presents a most unusual model for art criticism.

19 / Grounded Theory and Educational Ethnography: A Methodological Analysis and Critique

Louis M. Smith and Paul A. Pohland

This is the second in a pair of papers that deal with the concept of "grounded theory" developed by Glaser and Strauss (1967). In the first (Smith and Pohland 1969a) we made the main focus a review of their book and, secondarily, analyzed their major concepts in the light of our several efforts to use a similar methodology (Connor and Smith 1967; Pohland 1968; Pohland and Gussner 1968; Smith and Brock 1969; Smith and Geoffrey 1968; Smith and Keith 1967, 1970; Smith and Pohland 1969b). In this paper we take a slightly different approach. We wish first of all to present a more explicit account of the methodological strategies we have employed in our part of the CAI evaluation and the rationale of this effort as it re-lates to the Glaser and Strauss position. In this sense, their work provides a spring-board for discussion. Second, we wish to raise some issues that relate in a broad sense to educational research and evaluation as a whole. Third, we would like to present a point of view for classifying field-work methodologies and thus hope-fully clear up some of the confusion that has existed in the area.

The plan of the paper is quite simple. The major divisions are organized around Glaser and Strauss's three main concepts: the nature of grounded theory, theoretical sampling, and the constant comparative method. Around this framework we spin our own web of field-work practices, illustrative material, and, if you will, biases.

One disclaimer, however, before we begin. We do not agree entirely with the con-ceptual stance taken by Glaser and Strauss. These differences we have dealt with elsewhere (Smith and Pohland 1969a). By the same token we take issue with other reviewers who have damned the book indiscriminately (*American Journal of Sociology* 1968; *Book Review Digest* 1968). Our general position is that they have generated some provocative "grounded theory" of their own, and that it is more fruitful as well as charitable to winnow out what is useful than to engage in deprecation.

GROUNDED THEORY AND FIELD-WORK METHODS

The central concept delineated by Glaser and Strauss is that of "grounded theory." Essentially this means generating a theory from data through a process of research. Glaser and Strauss argue that such procedures have decided advantages over the more traditional logico-deductive method of theory development. Briefly, they maintain that "theory based on data can usually not be refuted by more data or replaced by another theory" and that "grounded theory can help to forestall the opportunistic use of theories that have dubious fit and working capacity" (p. 4). In a very basic sense our position is much the same. In our own research we have accented the twin goals of careful description and subsequent development of concepts, hypotheses, and models from the data. Our recently completed Computer Assisted Instruction evaluation project is a case in point. With the exception of in situ "interpretive asides" and some speculative "summary observations and interpretations," our data file is comprised largely of careful descriptive material: field notes recording observations of classroom instruction; observations of children working at the teletypes; conversations and interviews with children, teachers, and administrators; computer printouts; formal documents; and the like. Conceptual development, hypotheses formation, and model building were derived from these sources.

Glaser and Strauss posit four formal properties of grounded theory: fitness, understanding, generality, and control. Of these, fitness, i.e., close correspondence to the realities of the substantive area, is conceived as the "underlying basis" of the theory. This relates to their earlier point that theory based on data usually cannot be replaced by another theory or refuted by acquiring more data. Given "fit," Glaser and Strauss contend that grounded theory "will make sense and be understandable to the people working in the substantive area" (p. 239). It is precisely on this point that we would argue the efficacy of grounded theory and the value of participant observation as an evaluation style. We share Jackson's (1968) position that classroom teachers as a whole reject the theories generated by classical experimental psychologists because of their perceived lack of relevance to the realities of the classroom. It seems to us that it is incumbent upon the profession to narrow the gap between educational theory and practice in terms that are both appropriate and understandable to the practitioner. We would argue in our own modest way that this is precisely what we tried to do in *The Complexities*. There we dealt with the immediate and practical as well as the theoretical. Issues that loom large in the teacher's "real world," such as assignment giving, the nature and purpose of gentleness in pupil-teacher interaction, pacing, banter, the antecedents and consequences of textbook teaching on various aspects of classroom and the larger social structure, and so forth, received considerable attention. As we begin to extend our analysis of the CAI data we hope to do the same. For example, issues such as the competitive and social aspects of a conceptually individualized program emerged as major and unanticipated elements of the program. These are realities in the teacher's world.

As "fit" and "understanding" seem to be conceptually related, so do "generality" and "control." As the "grounded theorist" develops his theory through careful selection of groups, constant comparison, and other techniques we will discuss shortly, caution must be observed in choosing variables which are relevant both for the researcher and the practitioner. Glaser and Strauss write: "The categories should not be so abstract as to lose their sensitizing aspect, but yet must be abstract enough to make his theory a general guide to multi-conditional, ever-changing situations" (p. 242). To the extent that this balance is achieved, the ultimate values of any theory—prediction and control—can be maximized.

In opting for theory development in the "grounded" sense, Glaser and Strauss raise an issue that has plagued the field for decades—the possible conflict between generating and verifying theory. In a sense, this is also the same distinction we have been making in accenting the former rather than the latter. Their treatment of the problems encountered by scholars who wish to develop theory in this "grounded" sense and the more traditional scholars interested in verification has all of the emotional components that we have found in our own work. We are particularly concerned about making this work acceptable to our colleagues because of the problems encountered by students who wish to pursue this style of investigation and, in effect, break with the traditions of the last three or four decades within both educational psychology and educational sociology.

Our personal preferences are to move toward verification in settings where careful controls can be instituted, careful measures developed for significant concepts, and large enough samples of subjects can be obtained. The concept of teacher awareness, generated in Smith and Geoffrey (1968), has received this attention in Smith and Kleine (1969).

In the social science field another major quarrel has existed regarding the importance of qualitative versus quantitative data. Depending on the issues under discussion within the methodology, verification of theory and discovery of theory, the qualitative-quantitative issue can become a "red herring." Because the generation of theory and the use of qualitative data tend to be correlated, they tend to be attacked or supported indiscriminately. Some of the variations on this theme, for instance, the work of Festinger, Riecken, and Schachter, in their book *When Prophecy Fails* (1956), have been treated in our methodological discussions in *The Complexities of an Urban Classroom*. In that analysis we presented qualitative work in a verificational context as the atypical example of the usual use. However, their work does represent an important effort and does indicate possibilities in the use of qualitative data for hypothesis testing. We feel now as we stated then (Smith and Geoffrey 1968), a number of events and problems that might have generated important theory were not raised and discussed by Festinger and his colleagues. In brief, what we are in part arguing is that the qualitative versus quantitative controversy has generated more heat than light. Both approaches yield theoretic advance from their respective points on the continuum.

Such varying conceptions and approaches to field work have led us to a preliminary analysis which we have organized as table 19.1. Four dimensions of field work—descriptive narrative, generation of theory, verification of theory, and quantification—have been placed on a continuum of emphasis from low to high. For illustrative purposes, six examples of field work have been utilized. In doing so, major differences in approach have been isolated. Only Glaser and Strauss deemphasize the descriptive narrative. The generation of theory distributes the research styles. Festinger et al. come in with an intensively developed theory; traditional anthropology is less interested in theory generation. In contrast, Glaser and Strauss and Smith and Pohland strongly accent such efforts. The verification of theory is minimized by us (Smith and Pohland) except for the cumulative efforts of our research. Festinger et al. saw it as their principal target. Regarding quantification, Becker et al. are the only strong adherents. Glaser and Strauss fall midway on the continuum. Becker and his colleagues in psychological ecology accent quantification and verification of propositions and tend to be moderate on theory generation and description.

TABLE 19.1 APPROACHES TO FIELD WORK

	EMPHASIS		
	LOW	MODERATE	HIGH
Descriptive Narrative	Glaser and Strauss	Barker et al.	Smith and Pohland Becker et al. Festinger et al. Anthropologists (e.g., Spindler's culture and education series)
Generation of Theory	Festinger et al. Anthropologists (e.g., Spindler's culture and education series)	Becker et al. Barker et al.	Smith and Pohland Glaser and Strauss
Verification of Theory	Smith and Pohland	Glaser and Strauss Becker et al. Anthropologists (e.g., Spindler's culture and education series)	Festinger et al. Barker et al.
Quantification of Data	Smith and Pohland Festinger et al. Anthropologists (e.g., Spindler's culture and education series)	Glaser and Strauss	Becker et al. Barker et al.

Figure 19.1 presents an alternative model for handling several aspects of such typical dichotomies as field work versus experimental research, generation of theory versus verification of theory, educational research versus education practice, and qualitative versus quantitative research and evaluation. Our clearest implementation of the model in figure 19.1 occurred in "Teacher Awareness: Social Cognition in the Classroom" (Smith and Kleine 1969).

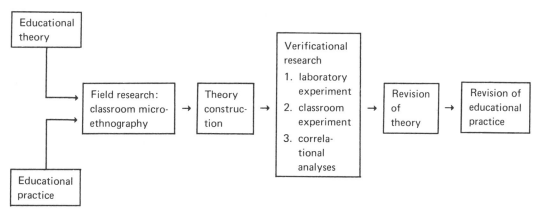

FIGURE 19.1 A Process Model Integrating Educational Research Styles, Educational Practice, and Educational Theory (From Smith and Geoffrey 1968: 249).

GENERATING GROUNDED THEORY

We now move to a discussion of some of the conceptual underpinnings of grounded theory as we understand it and some of the techniques of using the procedure that we have found fruitful in our recent field work.

Emphasis on the Narrative

Most field work places some emphasis on the descriptive account or narrative. Our own preference as nonparticipant observers is to emphasize the narrative strongly.[1] There are several reasons for this. First, it seems to us that a careful, thoroughgoing descriptive account is a prerequisite for grounded theory. Stated somewhat differently, the presence of a carefully documented narrative seems to correlate closely with credibility. We developed some of the descriptive material in *The Complexities* explicitly for this purpose. Second, we have strong feelings and beliefs that the utilization of theory for the solution of practical problems in education is very important. We think this requires a fairly intensive descriptive account, particularly since teachers and educational administrators tend to think in situationally specific terms. One needs to know the context out of which the concepts came and to which they will be referred back. Third, the kind of theory that we have been generating is more of what Glaser and Strauss would call a substantive rather than a formal theory. In this sense it is more closely tied to a particular setting and the requisite description of that setting. Fourth, we take the position that when an investigator begins his work, he does not know the full range of theoretically relevant concepts. In a study such as our CAI project the dynamics of the innovation changed over time, and a concept of theoretic relevance might be only dimly perceived or perceived not at all at the beginning. Again, this suggests the necessity for a detailed descriptive account. Given the choice of an overabundance of data containing much chaff but a potentially dense data base, or a choice of little chaff but a potentially thin data base and a resulting "thin unvalenced theory," we opted for the former. Fifth, and related to the preceding, is the possibility of integrating data obtained from one study with that of other studies. We would simply maintain that the richer the descriptive account of each study, the easier and potentially more fruitful this cumulative effort can become. Sixth, most of the teaching in which we have been involved has been of an applied sort, and the people who finish the training programs go into the kinds of settings that we have been studying. Once again, this provokes a need for a more careful view and descriptive account. Seventh, in working with a number of students and others who have used and/or wanted to learn the method there is often a good bit of anxiety about the way the method works. The descriptive or narrative job, while difficult to write in an interesting and lucid style, is, at least initially, an easier place to begin. Only after one has struggled a bit with the description and begins to see the possibilities of organizing and abstracting from such concrete materials the broader ideas, concepts, hypotheses, and models can one move freely and well.[2]

We have a strong conviction that ultimately all hypotheses and models must be put to careful verification. The usual strategy here becomes the correlational analysis, field study, or even better, the laboratory or field experiment. Additionally, however, the building of a series of interrelated participant observer field studies in which one is basically generating a theory also has, as a side result, the gradual accumulation of propositions that have more than a bit of credibility and that approach the form of principles. We will return to this point later when we talk in more detail about the constant comparative method of qualitative analysis.

Theoretical Sampling

The concept of theoretical sampling as defined by Glaser and Strauss is, in our opinion, their most significant contribution to the methodology of nonparticipant observation. Despite their relegation of this concept to a subordinate position (a rationale for the selection of groups to be studied), we feel that theoretical sampling should be the basic rationale for a more general theory of research strategy or decision-making in the field.

Briefly, theoretical sampling is defined as "the process of data collection for [the purpose of] generating theory whereby the analyst jointly collects, codes, and analyses his data and decides what data to collect next and where to find them, in order to develop his theory as it emerges" (p. 45). We were attracted to this concept because it formalized some things we had stated earlier at an intuitive level, e.g., having enough evidence, enough data in a particular area, and moving into other related problems. In the Kensington setting (Smith and Keith 1967) this involved concerns within different pupil age levels or divisions; independent study division versus transition versus basic skills; issues internal to the school; and external phenomena such as the parent council. In the CAI project theoretical sampling involved the preliminary and basic view of the realities of the way CAI was used in a particular school or in several specific schools, as well as the more general issue of how one goes about introducing and implementing an innovative practice in an established school system. Theoretical sampling concerned also a fundamental issue in continuing the elaboration of a psychological theory of instruction.

A number of subordinate concepts are subsumed under the generic concept of theoretical sampling. Among these are "saturation," "slices of data," and "depth." By "saturation," Glaser and Strauss mean that no additional data are found which contribute to the properties of the categories under consideration. This is a useful but somewhat tricky concept. It assumes that one knows in advance what the key categories are and where the locus of information is. We have not found it quite that easy. In our work in the past and in our future work with CSMP (Comprehensive School Mathematics Program), the broader context for which we would argue is that we begin with an initial array of problems and issues, that is, strategies of teaching, innovation, and so forth. As we work in a particular context or setting we try to exploit that setting for all of the information and all of the ideas that we can find. In a sense, we keep looking until we can generate no more of what we've called in the past "insights" and "interpretive asides." It is at that point that we tend to quit. In this situation our experience has been that beyond the initial focus, the narrative or story line soon carries us into a whole variety of other problems and issues that we had not anticipated in our preliminary entrance to the problem. This is moving from the foreshadowed problems into the scientific issues.

The CAI project was a beautiful example of this. Initially we had conceived the project in terms of the psychology of mathematics teaching. As we began carrying out our observation, however, the exigencies of the situation shifted the focus of investigation to the politics of education, interorganizational issues, the problems of introducing sophisticated twentieth-century technology into an underdeveloped region, and the like. In a very real sense the twin concepts of saturation and flexibility run parallel courses in the field work.

Perhaps here is a further reason for the need for description. When we finally know enough about a particular setting and have described it in detail and there are no more issues coming out, then it is time to quit. Perhaps in this context "really knowing" not only means having it conceptualized but also being able to describe its day to day workings as well as, if not better than, the man who is actually living and working in the setting.

Glaser and Strauss make an important subpoint here as they talk of the joint collection and analysis of data. This gets them involved in memo writing and discussions with their colleagues. We have done little memo writing. More typically we have incorporated our analytical discourses, hunches, and hypotheses within the body of our "summary observations and interpretations."[3] In a sense, each of us is talking to himself rather than formally to his colleague. Yet in another sense, the discourse so recorded serves as an insight-generating memo to his colleague.

All of this raises a fundamental issue of research style. While some investigators may work best alone, we have found it extremely rewarding both personally and substantively to work as a team. We have, for example, found the joint recording of "summary observations and interpretations" most effective in a number of ways. First, it facilitated recall of specific events or details of those events that occurred during the field observation. Second, it provided a built-in check for accuracy of recall. On some occasions we interpreted statements or recalled events differently. These differences were recorded and thus suggested areas that needed further study. Third, and perhaps most important, it facilitated interpretation and hypothesis formation. We found as we listened to each other record, that interpretive asides or hypotheses made by the recorder set off a change of thought that would perhaps never have occurred to either singly. As we then began to exchange insights and interpretations, issues began to emerge in new and more interesting lights. All of this can be considered a variant on Glaser and Strauss's conception of saturation.

A subissue of the preceding, and one that argues for a team approach to field work, is the likelihood that two or more researchers working together bring a diverse set of skills and backgrounds to any given project. Such backgrounds are akin to Malinowski's (1922) foreshadowed problems. As events occur, they become interpreted in the light of the researcher's own unique experiences and frame of reference. As the various perceptions of the same event are exchanged, one gains a broader perspective of the situation than perhaps he would have working alone. In this sense, too, the dangers of the "two realities" as we discussed them in *The Complexities* becomes minimized.

A related issue that again argues strongly for a team effort is the flexibility of roles that is available. Gold (1969) points out that in participant observer methodology, a minimum of four roles can be assumed. He views the methodology as spread out along a continuum for complete observer to complete participant. Intermediate on the continuum are the participant-as-observer and the observer-as-participant. Given multiple investigators, a variety of roles can be played. We experienced the potency of this approach in both our summer school student teaching (Pohland and Gussner 1968) and Washington School (Smith and Geoffrey 1968) studies. In those cases specific "inside-outside" roles were assigned analogous to Gold's complete observer, complete participant roles. In our CAI study our normal role was closer to the complete observer end of the continuum. Yet we found ourselves constantly drawn more into the participant role in the sense of "making the system go." As these occasions occurred we found our individual observations differed significantly. Our combined observations were much more detailed and insightful than those gained individually.

The potency of multiple roles was brought home forcibly in our current involvement with the Comprehensive School Mathematics Program curriculum development project. One of the researchers played the participant-as-observer role in that he attended every session of a two-week workshop and participated actively as a member of the group. A second researcher attended sporadically as the "complete observer." Methodologically this proved fruitful as we gained depth ("saturation") while retaining that freshness of experience that Geer (1964) speaks of as occurring on the first days in the field. Stated another way, we were attacking a common problem from different vantage points. On a more general level we would argue that the criticisms leveled at findings derived from participant observer studies, particularly their "subjective" bias, can be considerably reduced by maximizing multiple roles.

All of this relates neatly into the generic concept of saturation, and, from our point of view, reemphasizes the need for careful description. We feel rather strongly that unless one can tell the practitioner, the person living daily in the situation, exactly what has and what is likely to happen, he may see the relevance of some of your concepts and models and yet argue that they are superficial and do not reflect the totality of life there. Perhaps the additional point we need here lies in the notion of integration and density of the theory. One can not have this, in our judgment, without the intense description of what Glaser and Strauss refer to as the "empirical limits of the data," and what we have referred to previously as the "data base."

Selection of Groups

One of the problems facing the researcher as he makes his first forays into the field is the selection of a group or groups to study. Without a well-conceived rationale a great deal of valuable time may be lost in flitting from setting to setting. Glaser and Strauss neatly resolved this issue by advancing "theoretical purpose and relevance" as the twin criteria for the selection of groups. These criteria were most useful to us as we determined the settings for our CAI study.

To be more specific, we initially had a choice of 9 locations. We also had reason to anticipate the opening of 20 additional stations during the course of the investigation. Obviously, doing any in-depth study in 29 rather widely separated locales (10,000 square miles!) was not feasible. Making a decision about where to concentrate our efforts was critical.

Briefly, the procedure we used was as follows: during late spring of the preexperimental year we toured the region with the assistance of a guide provided by the funding agency. This gave us a chance to "size up" the various locations as it were. Once that had been done, several decisions had to be made. Should we work together or divide the territory between us in some rough fashion? Should we try to divide our resources exclusively between the 9 stations in operation at the beginning of the year and ignore the other 20, or should we so plan the work that all stations would be subject to some intensive observation? Or should we further limit ourselves to one or two schools for the purpose of intensive observation? Ultimately these decisions were made on the Glaser and Strauss conception of theoretical purpose and relevance. Our prior interests in the broad aspects of teacher training suggested that the local university laboratory school should receive considerable attention. It would, presumably, enable us to view a variety of models of arithmetic teaching and student teaching processes. Furthermore, since the computer was located on the campus, we would be at the center of one of the communication networks. Additionally, it was geographically close to several rural, outlying schools which also received the CAI program. Hence, we would be in a position to observe similarities and differences on a number of cultural dimensions, e.g., variance of socioeconomic status, level of aspiration, rural versus urban, isolationism versus cosmopolitanism, and so forth. Given that decision, we searched for other settings which would further serve to maximize similarities and differences and thus generate comparative groups for analytic purposes. Ultimately we located a school where all the math was taught by one teacher; was geographically far removed from the laboratory school and its communication linkages; was less cosmopolitan, and which also was close to a rural school, thus maintaining immediate rural-urban reference points. A third site was also selected. Two considerations precipitated this: (1) we wished to include a nonpublic school in our intensive reference group, and (2) the school was located in the same community as the central office of the funding agency. This gave us access to information that would have been more difficult to obtain otherwise. Once the sites were selected, the other decisions came easily. We split forces as it were, and each of us concentrated in one geographic area. However, we maintained that "fresh viewpoint" by periodically switching vantage points. Again, this emphasizes, as we argued earlier, the potency of a team approach to field work.

A further subissue, highlighting the interrelationship between the descriptive narrative and the genesis of the substantive theory, becomes a factor in the decision about how one parcels out scarce resources. The point we want to make regarding this decision is the tremendous amount of time that it takes to become well enough acquainted with a group of people so that they will talk freely about what they do and how they do it. In this sense, one adds to the direct observing the more informal comments and conversations that one obtains in the course of getting to know the people as they work in the setting. To fathom and probe that source of data carefully takes a tremendous amount of time. As one tries to build an awareness which goes into the descriptive account one communicates this kind of interest and orientation to the people in the setting, and these people then tend to speak more readily about their jobs, problems, and ideas. In the past we have found this to be a very rich source of hypotheses about the nature of teaching. In a sense, it has been built into most of our analyses; for instance, teacher plans and teacher strategies are basic conceptions in our theories of teaching. The relevant data would be less available without the self-reported descriptions.

In short, we are making a point comparable to Glaser and Strauss's conception of slices of data, e.g., "different kinds of data give the analyst different views or vantage points from which to understand a category and to develop its properties" (p. 65). In more general psychology this has been discussed as multitrait and multimethod matrix (Campbell and Fiske 1959). In one of our uses of participant observational techniques, the teacher apprenticeship at City Teachers College (Connor and Smith 1967), we were struck by what a test maker might call the validity of his measures. We observed our apprentices teach a variety of lessons. We talked with them informally about their problems, plans, intentions, and practices in these same lessons. We listened to them talk with each other and with their cooperating teachers about the lessons. And finally, we talked informally with the cooperating teachers, principals, and supervisors about the same events. In most instances we got along very well with the various persons; in some instances we were father confessors who were out of the authority structure, who knew what was going on, who would listen, and who would empathize. This aspect of method has a potency which we are only now coming to appreciate; we think we obtained a valid picture of the apprenticeship. We reflected further on this issue in "Classroom Ethnography and Ecology" (Smith 1969).

We employed an additional research strategy prior to the CAI experimental year. "Strategy" might be a slightly inflated term since at the time we were only partially aware of many latent functional consequences it was to have. Specifically, we attended a two-week teacher workshop on CAI during the summer preceding the opening of school. Our purposes for attending were quite simple: we wished to find out something about the program firsthand and, second, to become somewhat acquainted with the people. As it turned out, our efforts were well rewarded.[4] Our presence in the workshop and the consequent developing of close interpersonal relations with the teachers, technicians, and staff members of the university and funding agency facilitated entry into the classroom during the year. In a sense, we had gained a head start on obtaining those "slices of data" which come one's way as people begin interacting freely and openly. Secondly, our experiences with the program, and particularly the technology, alerted us to problems that might arise during the course of the year. In that sense we moved from the "unanticipated" to the "foreshadowed problems" and toward what Glaser and Strauss refer to later as "theoretical sensitivity" quickly and easily. A third major set of advantages accrued in acquiring early in the field work some conception of the "life style" that pervaded the region. As events piled up, this gave us a frame of reference for later analysis. We absorbed some of the cultural and social milieu within which the experiment was taking place and in which the participants were living out their lives. As we began work on our next project, we capitalized on the workshop experience as an integral part of a more general research strategy.

Comparative Analysis of Groups

An issue that we have touched upon briefly but which we turn our attention to explicitly at this point is what Glaser and Strauss call "the comparative analysis of groups." Briefly, the trust of their argument is that no issue can really be clear until it is presented in the context of other similar and relevant research. For instance, Glaser and Strauss cite the illustrative case of Louis Wirth's study of the Chicago ghetto and their developing a contrast with European ghettos. It is only in such a comparison, or such a contrast, that one really sees the distinctive features of the new.

In our own work we found that we kept turning back to our prior studies. For instance, in the Kensington analysis (Smith and Keith 1967, 1970) and in the City Teachers College (1967) analysis we kept referring back to situations, ideas, and points of view out of *The Complexities* analysis. In a sense we did this intuitively without trying to formalize the potency of what we were doing as a major method in the study of educational groups and educational settings.

The CAI study allowed us to pursue further several interests generated in prior research. For example, the CAI program was a mode of instruction, and we have been involved in numerous other modes of instruction in the Washington School, Kensington, and elsewhere. More specifically, CAI falls into the category of individualized instruction, and the observations made in that program should be of significant value as we analyze the data from our Suburban High School project (Smith and Brock 1969) and the contrasting mode of discovery learning. Furthermore, the CAI data should prove invaluable as we begin work on the CSMP project which also involves individualized instruction as the learning model. Second, CAI was an important educational innovation both conceptually and operationally as a model of research, diffusion, and implementation, and we have been involved both in the past, e.g., Kensington, and in the present, e.g., CAI and CSMP, with innovations in education on a broad scale. Third, intensive observation at the university laboratory school provided a continuity with previous interests in teacher education. The similarities and contrasts with our prior City Teachers College and summer school student teaching studies added new dimensions to our understanding of this aspect of American education. Fourth, the issues of elementary versus secondary education and the comparative kinds of elementary education from the several contexts that we have been involved in also was helpful. Fifth, the children from the Washington School were essentially poor, rural whites who had migrated to the city. Our understanding of those children was appreciably enhanced as we observed first-hand their origins and as we came to appreciate the reasons for the massive outmigration from their place of birth. Sixth, and in a related way, we have dealt briefly but not clearly with problems of school-community relations in several of our studies, but we have not focused upon the interrelationship between the community and the school.

At the Washington School there were the racial issues in the community, and at the Kensington School there were issues in the parents council, a type of PTA, and the way in which the broader institution of the Milford Public Schools affected the Kensington School itself. Our quest for the nature of the milieu and culture of the region and the readings that we've been engaged in, such as the Kluckhohn and Strodtbeck book, *Variations in Value Orientation*, the several accounts of the Elizabethan period in contemporary America, for instance, the Sherman and Henry account of the *Hollow Folk*, the writings of Jesse Stuart, and other recent books, provides part of this as well. In short, we have a number of settings in which we have spent considerable time and which we have been involved in interlocking problems, issues, hypotheses, and middle-range theories. Hopefully, our current CSMP study will build upon and integrate with these.

Theoretical Sensitivity and Insight

A number of important issues are subsumed under Glaser and Strauss's general rubric of "theoretical sensitivity and insight." One of the most significant is the conception of the researcher as a "highly sensitive and systematic agent." Actually, two closely related concepts are involved here: (1) the researcher as a person, including his own cognitive acuity, training, experiences, and ability to comprehend, analyze, synthesize, and evaluate what he observes; and (2) the efficiency and effectiveness of the research techniques he employs in a given study. Both of these become the determinants of the insights that are generated from a given study.

In earlier portions of this paper we implicitly suggested several sources of "insights." One of these was one's own previous research. This ties back into the general proposition of choosing comparative groups for their theoretical purpose and relevance. As one can multiply settings and mine them for variants on a common concept, the emergent theory takes on increased credibility and validity. More formally, one is in a position to defend his theory on the basis of generalizability.

A second source of insights is within the extant literature. As we move into new settings we begin to immerse ourselves in the relevant literature. For instance, when we began the CAI project we reviewed briefly some of the data on CAI. As the innovative aspects became more pronounced we returned to Miles' *Innovation in Education* (1964) and Rogers' *Diffusion of Innovation* (1962). Likewise, as organizational issues came to the fore we redirected our attention to that body of literature as we had in the Kensington study, broadening it to include the inter-organizational literature. As the politics of education became more significant we moved to that source, e.g., Iannaccone's *Politics in Education* (1968); Masters et al. *State Politics and the Public Schools* (1964); Meranto's *The Politics of Federal Aid to Education in 1965* (1967); a search through the *Congressional Record* on the genesis of the Green Amendment, and the like. In so doing, we took a position midway between Malinowski's stance toward knowing a considerable amount of theory before moving into the setting, and Glaser and Strauss's concern that too strict an adherence to existing theory early in the field research may stifle one's own creative powers.

A third source of insight comes through maximizing the experiences of others. This relates back to the previous notion of exhausting different "slices of data." Specifically, we refer here to insights gained by formal and informal contact with a broad range of informants. In the CAI study, for example, our best insights into the magnitude of the competitive and, more broadly, the social aspects of a conceptually individualized program, came from direct conversations with students. Again, our interest in the politics of education in the region stemmed from long informal "bull sessions" with other participants in the summer workshop.

All this leads to a related point, the flexibility needed to move freely and well within a broadly conceived educational research issue. As one is able to discard what Glaser and Strauss in another context refer to as the constraints imposed by "preplanned, routinized, arbitrary criteria" (p. 48), one is able to exploit tangential issues which in their totality shed light on various facets of the central issue. Perhaps this is another reason why we argue strongly for the narrative. As we said earlier, unless one can communicate the totality of the setting, both the "outsiders" and the "natives" have legitimate cause for questioning one's concepts, hypotheses, and theories.

It is clear, however, that there are limits to the extent that one can justifiably allow oneself to be pushed and pulled by emergent issues that are inherently interesting in and of themselves. The danger is that the integrity of the basic research may easily be lost amid a welter of intriguing but peripheral issues. Glaser and Strauss neatly resolve the problem in their discussion of basic ("core") and secondary theoretical categories, "saturation," and termination of data collection. In brief, the emergent theory, the guiding question, defines the category and suggests the temporal limits of data collection. Our recent CAI study again provides illustrative examples of the potency of the interrelated concepts. We were constantly tempted to make major foci of investigation such issues as the nature of the county superintendency; the politics of education as it involved interaction among the national, state, regional, and local governmental agencies; the conflicting needs and values between research and development centers and service agencies. Ultimately we had to decide that such problems were research issues in their own right, and that as "categories" they were "saturated" sufficiently for the main purpose of the investigation. It is ture, of course, that when such a decision is made, one forecloses the possibility of gaining data that might provide new and important insights. This is a risk that is taken. Thus we modify the Glaser and Strauss stand to include termination of data when we are reasonably sure that the major insights have been extracted.

This leads to a final point. Glaser and Strauss maintain reasonably enough that "an insight, whether borrowed or original, is of no use to the theorist unless he converts it from being simply an anecdote to being an element of theory" (p. 255). This rather aptly describes our own procedure. Typically, we seek out the antecedents and consequences of important phenomena. These we build into figural models. The models can be converted in the kind of axiomatic propositional theory suggested by Zetterberg (1965). Our most thorough development of this occurs in chapter 1 of Smith and Geoffrey (1968).

Temporal Aspects

Glaser and Strauss conclude their discussion of theoretical sampling with an analysis of its temporal aspects. Their major point is that the specific nature of generating grounded theory requires a different time sequence than other methodologies. They comment briefly upon the need for "respites for reflection and analysis" of the data already collected; the need to pace the "alternating tempo of his collecting , coding, and analyzing in order to get each task done in appropriate measure, in accordance with the stage of his research and theory development" (p. 72); the temptation to overextend the research in order to "know everything"; the difficulties of anticipating the time needed to complete a study; the extensive and indeterminate amount of time required to work one's self into the significant social systems to the point where information is freely obtained; and the time required to mine the contributing slices of data, e.g., reading in related literature.

Our own experiences coincide with these observations. The nature of our research both intensifies and diminishes these problems. While that may seem a contradiction in terms, it fairly accurately describes the position we find ourselves in. We will speak to each of them in turn.

As we have stated before, we tend to begin with a description and analysis of a position or setting rather than a "problem," e.g., the nature of educational politics. As that descriptive/analytical account achieves depth, subordinate and superordinate issues emerge. These in turn become the foci of additional description and analysis. The points of tangency between the several issues are amenable to the kind of if-then propositional theory we work into our figural models.

Methodologically this seems an important point. Our dissatisfaction with much published educational research leaves us unmoved as it concentrates on the minutia of the enterprise and never grasps the totality of what goes on. In the CAI project as well as in Kensington, we found ourselves in a complex network of organizations, technologies, politics, personalities, and educational issues related to school and classroom functioning as it affected teaching and learning. We feel now as we did then that what is badly needed in education is a set of concepts which will integrate the various elements which are usually, and unfortunately, compartmentalized. We feel a start in that direction was made in *The Complexities* and in Kensington. We hope to move further in that direction with our CAI study. Obviously, this takes a great deal of time, and emphasizes that need for "respites for reflection and analysis" that Glaser and Strauss talk about as well as highlighting the dangers inherent in the "need to know everything." Yet that is both the joy and frustration of doing field research. Perhaps, too, this is also an additional reason for working in teams. While one member takes such a "respite," another can be in the field, and thus the continuity of the enterprise is not lost. Additionally, such a procedure makes it feasible for one member to concentrate on an emergent and potentially significant issue while his colleague concentrates on another. In that sense, the research becomes more manageable and the work load as it is distributed becomes diminished.

THE CONSTANT COMPARATIVE METHOD

For Glaser and Strauss, the constant comparative method lies at the heart of the discovery of grounded theory. We do not totally subscribe to this position for reasons we made clear in an earlier paper (Smith and Pohland 1969a). It is not our purpose here to reiterate those arguments; rather, as has been our procedure thus far, we wish to extract from their discussion concepts which we find useful in our own research.

Essentially, the constant comparative method includes four steps keyed on explicit coding and analysis: (1) comparing incidents applicable to each category, (2) integrating categories and their properties, (3) delimiting the theory, and (4) writing the theory [p. 105]. (We have touched on a number of issues either directly or indirectly already, e.g., step 3, and thus limit ourselves to steps 1 and 2.) Briefly, step one suggests that once the data are gathered, the analyst codes each incident into as many emergent or extant categories as possible. The process is refined in line with "the basic, defining rule": "*while coding an incident for a category, compare it with the previous incidents in the same and different groups coded in the same category*" (p. 106). This procedure is designed to start the analyst thinking about "the full range of types or continua of the category, its dimensions, the conditions under which it is pronounced or minimized, its major consequences, its relation to other categories, and its other properties" (p. 106).

Typically this has not been our practice. In part, explicit coding or not coding is a matter of personal style. We prefer a more free-wheeling free association type of analysis. More seriously, however, we feel that explicit coding, particularly early in the study, tends toward producing a psychological set, a closure to divergent thinking, and, in general, imposes a rigid structure to the research issue prematurely. As we stated earlier, we tend to go into a research situation with a broad array of problems and interests, and see "how it goes" from there. By this we mean seeking relationships with some of the interlocking parts of earlier problems and projects in which we have been involved. "Seeing how it goes" also involves all of the new ideas and issues that occur serendipically as we are in the situation.

For instance, in the CAI project an interest was generated in the politics of education, the unique role of the county school superintendency, and so forth. We find that not coding initially facilitates an openness to diverse stimuli. Additionally, we find that not having an explicit code in mind, similar but widely dispersed events in time and place maintain a fresh quality that is quite striking. For that reason, too, we typically do not read and reread our printed notes during the course of the field work. Consequently, when we do begin the analysis and writing, similar events though separated by several hundred pages of notes stand out boldly. However, intuitively and without complete awareness of what we were doing, we were engaged in much the same process. For example, in our CAI project "systems breakdown" quickly emerged as one of the basic categories. As specific incidents occurred, we found our major category quickly breaking down into relevant subcategories, e.g., programming difficulties, technical difficulties, personnel problems, organizational problems, and the like. These in turn were further refined into sub-categories, e.g., technical difficulties broke down into line trouble, computer break-down, terminal breakdown, and so forth. We found ourselves positing relationships between the various subcategories as well as between categories. Our preference as previously noted has been to go to the antecedents-consequences route. We find that as we draw out the models, the interrelationships become increasingly clear.

Glaser and Strauss propose that two general types of categories emerge: those he has constructed himself, and those that have been abstracted from the language of the research situation. Our own experience confirms this. While we were able to generate a category such as "systems failure" ourselves, it was only in direct conver-sation that the broader category of "line trouble" emerged or the still more refined class of technical difficulties centered on "loading the machine."

The second step in the process is "integrating categories and their properties." Essentially, this shifts the focus of attention from comparing incident with incident to comparing discrete incidents with properties of the category derived from prev-ious incident to incident comparison. Ultimately this procedure is designed to ac-hieve a closer integration of properties internal to a given category and integrate diverse categories into a theoretical whole. This is essentially what we hope to ac-complish as one goal of our CAI study—the integration of categories and their properties into a middle-range theory of instruction. Our attempts to phrase latent variables such as enthusiasm, animism, competitiveness, and sociability in an indi-vidualized instructional system such as CAI represents this synthetic focus. In short, what we are saying is that Glaser and Strauss's constant comparative method as a research style contains numerous concepts which provide operational guides to research. While we disagree on some details, we find their basic conception useful.

CONCLUSION

As we stated in the introduction, we think Glaser and Strauss make a significant contribution to the discussion of field methods. This is particularly true with refer-ence to their extended discussion of theoretical sampling. While they make this a subordinate issue, we see it as a more general and basic research strategy. In retro-spect, and as we attempted to explain through our illustrative material, this was the strategy we have employed in our research. Making this point explicit clarified further what we have been doing. Perhaps if we had been formally trained in sociology or anthropology this would not have had the impact that it did.

In somewhat rambling discourse we have detailed some of our own biases with respect to field research and educational research in general. In a sense, one of the major methodological points we were making is that to a greater degree than usually acknowledged research styles are individualistic. The operational aspects of the constant comparative method are incompatible with our own less structured procedure. We do not imply one is better than another. By the same token, our penchant for team research may be inimicable to others. Yet we found that through a fortuitous combination of interests, personalities, and styles it was both personally and professionally gratifying. To us, the advantages measurably out-weigh the disadvantages.

Much the same can be said about the relative emphasis a researcher puts on the descriptive narrative, the generation and/or verification of theory, and the quan-tification of data. Table 19.1 suggested the range of options available in non-experimental field work. Ideally, perhaps, all four variables should be rated "high." In practice, and for good and valid reasons, this is not done. Our own preferences are, as we stated, to initially produce a thorough descriptive narrative out of which we generate middle-range theories and then in subsequent investigations move toward verification and quantification.

On a more general level, we have remarked on the need for more comprehensive research studies on enduring problems in education. Our involvement in a series of innovative programs suggests that widescale studies are both appropriate and necessary. We feel that one of the things that is badly lacking in much research is a set of integrating concepts that can be incorporated into a theory of innovation. One can without much difficulty find reports and monographs that deal with isolated, compartmentalized aspects of the problem: the administrator and innovation; the curriculum writer and innovation; the classroom teacher and innovation; innovation in substantive areas, e.g., reading, science, mathematics, etc.; the child and innovation; the role of the state department in innovation; and so on. We are not downgrading such studies: no doubt they were necessary as writers began attacking the problem. But we are at the stage now where the individual pieces must be incorporated into some larger mosaic. It seems to us that well-conceived nonparticipant observation studies designed to produce detailed descriptive narratives from which "grounded theory" may be generated is a logical and potentially profitable strategy for accomplishing that goal.

NOTES

1. This is in contrast to Glaser and Strauss who deprecate that effort along with verification. For them it "stifles" the generation of theory (see pp. 28 and 58).
2. One of our chief objections to much anthropological and historical writing and research lies in the fact that anthropologists and the historians often never get beyond trying to straighten out the narrative, that is, "telling the story." This reiteration of daily life in a variety of inaccessible communities frequently does *not* make an interesting account, for us, and often leaves the materials at a very concrete level. In this form the writer can never answer the "so what?" kind of question regarding the purpose of their efforts.
3. These were dictated into a portable recording machine shortly after leaving a school and as we drove to another school or as we went over notes in a motel room later in the evening.
4. In this sense, the parallels with our Kensington summer workshop were brought strikingly to mind (Smith and Keith 1967).

REFERENCES

Barker, R., ed. *The Stream of Behavior.* New York: Appleton-Century-Crofts, 1963.
Barker, R. G. *Ecological Psychology.* Stanford: Stanford University Press, 1968.
Barker, R. G., and Gump, P. V. *Big School, Small School.* Stanford, Calif.: Stanford University Press, 1964.
Barker, R. G., and Wright, H. F. *Midwest and Its Children.* Evanston, Ill.: Row, Peterson, 1954.
Becker, H. et al. *Boys in White.* Chicago: University of Chicago Press, 1961.
Book Review Digest 64 (1968): 123.
Campbell, D. T., and Fiske, D. W. "Convergent and Discriminant Validation by the Multitrait-Multimethod Matrix." *Psychological Bulletin* 56 (1959): 81–105.
Connor, W. H., and Smith, L. M. *Analysis of Patterns of Student Teaching.* Washington, D.C.: U.S. Office of Education, Bureau of Research, Final report 5-8204, 1967.
Festinger, L., Riecken, H., and Schachter, S. *When Prophecy Fails.* New York: Harper Torchbook, 1964.
Geer, B. "First Days in the Field." *Sociologists at Work,* edited by P. Hammond. New York: Basic Books, 1964.
Glaser, B. G., and Strauss, A. L. *The Discovery of Grounded Theory: Strategies for Qualitative Research.* Chicago: Aldine, 1967.
Gold, R. L. "Roles in Sociological Field Observation. In *Issues in Participant Observation,* edited by G. McCall. Reading, Mass.: Addison-Wesley, 1969.
Iannaccone, L. *Politics in Education.* New York: Center for Applied Research in Education, 1968.

Jackson, P. *Life in Classrooms*. New York: Holt, Rinehart and Winston, 1968.

Kluckhohn, F. R., and Strodtbeck, F. L. *Variations in Value Orientations*. Evanston, Ill.: Row, Peterson, 1961.

Loubser, J. "Review of B. G. Glaser and A. Strauss, *The Discovery of Grounded Theory*," *American Journal of Sociology* 73 (1968): 773-74.

Malinowski, B. *The Argonauts of the Western Pacific*. London: Roultedge, 1922.

Masters, N. A. et al. *State Politics and the Public Schools*. New York: Alfred A. Knopf, 1964.

Meranto, P. *The Politics of Federal Aid to Education*. Syracuse, N.Y.: Syracuse University Press, 1967.

Pohland, P. A. "Teacher Effectiveness: A Non-Participant Observer Study." Unpublished seminar paper, Washington University, 1968.

Pohland, P. A., and Gussner, W. *Report on the 1968 Summer School Student Teaching Program*. St. Louis: Graduate Institute of Education, Washington University, 1968.

Rogers, E. M. *Diffusion of Innovations*. New York: Free Press of Glencoe, 1962.

Sherman, M., and Henry, T. R. *Hollow Folk*. New York: Crowell, 1933.

Smith, L. M. "The Micro-Ethnography of the Classroom." *Psychology in the Schools* 4 (1967): 216-21.

Smith, L. M. *Classroom Ethnography and Ecology*. St. Ann, Mo.: CEMREL, 1969.

Smith, L. M., and Brock, J. A. M. *"Go, Bug, Go!": Methodological Issues in Classroom Observational Research*. St. Ann, Mo.: CEMREL, 1969.

Smith, L. M., and Brock, J. A. M. *Teacher Plans and Classroom Interaction*. St. Ann, Mo.: CEMREL, forthcoming.

Smith, L. M., and Geoffrey, W. *The Complexities of an Urban Classroom*. New York: Holt, Rinehart and Winston, 1968.

Smith, L. M., and Keith, P. M. *Social Psychological Aspects of School Building Design*. Washington, D.C.: U.S. Office of Education, Cooperative Research Report #S-223, 1967.

Smith, L. M., and Keith, P. M. "Fantasy and Reality in the Language of the New Technology." *Educational Technology* 8 (1968): 5-9.

Smith, L. M., and Keith, P. M. *Anatomy of Educational Innovation*. New York: John Wiley, 1970.

Smith, L. M., and Kleine, P. F. "Teacher Awareness: Social Cognition in the Classroom." *School Review* (In Press).

Smith, L. M., and Pohland, P. A. *Grounded Theory and Educational Ethnography: A Methodological Analysis and Critique*. St. Ann, Mo.: CEMREL, 1969a.

Smith, L. M., and Pohland, P. A. "Participant Observation of the CAI Program." In *Evaluation of Computer Assisted Instruction Program: Interim Report*, edited by H. Russell. St. Ann, Mo.: CEMREL, 1969b.

Zetterberg, H. L. *On Theory and Verification in Sociology*. New York: Bedminster Press, 1965.

20 / The Ethnography of a Japanese School: Anthropological Field Techniques and Models in the Study of a Complex Organization

John Singleton

How does one justify the intrinsically enjoyable experiences of an extended sojourn in Japan; participating in a school outing to the seashore, visiting farmers in their ancestral homes, drinking sake with teachers in celebration of the end of the school term, or getting to know intimately a lively rural hamlet? Only an anthropologist could label this "work." In spite of the puritanical underpinnings of American academicians, we must admit that the raw data of ethnography can come from just such pleasurable settings. Reports of these experiences were, indeed, some of the basic data of an educational ethnography of one Japanese school, Nichū, and its district (Singleton 1967). The process became painful only when the sojourn was over and the ethnographic report begun. Sifting through the heavy files of journal entries, interview surveys, and supplementary materials a conceptual model was necessary to bring order to an ethnographic description.

The model was then found in a suggestion from Bernard Siegel (1955) that an "acculturation model" could treat the school as a community, that is, as a group of people with common interests and common loyalties, in contact with other communities like teacher training institutions, ethnic and class groups of the local community, the state government, school boards, and the PTA.

It is suggested here that ethnographic approaches to the study of education are important to educators for understanding the social role of schools in modern societies. More importantly for anthropologists, they can contribute to the understanding of socialization, cultural dynamics, and cultural conflict in modern societies.

If educational ethnographies are to demonstrate this anthropological relevance, the ethnographers must begin to treat such educational institutions as schools with the same depth of concern previously accorded to isolated primitive tribes. Not surprisingly, this means, for the researcher, the study of new languages and cultural frames (even in his native society), intensive participant observation in the formal educational organizations, and the application of a holistic point of view to social institutions too often described in narrow and idealistic terms. Warren (1968) has described here the discrepancy between ideology and behavior of teachers in our schools, certainly a factor in the unrealistic descriptions of schools in our society.

Some anthropologists have been seduced by the idea that schools are somehow the most important instruments of enculturation for modern children of school age. They accept the publicly stated intentions of politicians and professional school people without critically examining the continuing and pervasive influence of family, neighborhood, peers, and the national society. For instance, one anthropologist says schoolteachers "are the important links in the transmission of the formal patterns of local culture." Another says, in justification for further studies of the culture of schools, "In our socially and spatially mobile society, the school provides the major continuity in the child's developing efforts at social orientation." That parents, teachers, and citizens so believe is important to us. That such is actually the case can be doubted until the ethnographic reports are in.

In this researcher's Japanese study, one public middle school (grades seven to nine) was chosen for intensive ethnographic study in the context of the community from which it drew its students. Nichū, the school, was chosen because its district contained both urban and rural settings within its boundaries, because the school was unexceptional—if not verifiably typical—and because the teaching staff seemed willing to accept a foreign researcher without fuss.

The researcher moved with his family into a local rural hamlet through the introduction and guarantee of a PTA officer. The PTA officer, a bicycle repairman, had lived more than twenty years as colonist on a Pacific island where the researcher had later spent three years as a teacher. "We worry about opening our poor homes to critical Americans, but I know you are different. Since you lived on Truk, I will help you." Several times during residence in the hamlet, this connection to Truk was instrumental in achieving our goals. Even in arranging for our household goods to be shipped back to the United States at the end of our stay, a man who had soldiered on Truk did the job. Residence, like kinship, leads to important and lasting ties in Japan.

The ethnographic field research model led to several definitions of a participant-observer role in the school and community. Though the original plan had called for formal assumption of a teacher's role, the role of an educational researcher was found to be understandable and eminently respectable with the school's staff. The researcher was assigned the use of a desk in the teachers' room and treated by teachers and principal as a fellow professional. The teachers' room in a Japanese school is the center of teacher activities and communication because all teachers have a desk there. Classrooms are primarily assigned to specific classes, and the teachers rather than the pupils rotate from one class to the next. The researcher's desk was located at the foot of the room and would normally have been assigned to the most junior teacher. It was an ideal location for observation without intrusion during teachers' meetings, informal periods of leisure, and even teacher-student conferences.

Though the researcher did not assume the formal role of teacher among teachers, there were a few occasions of substitute teaching for absent English teachers and a job as adviser to the English-Speaking Club that met once a week. With pupils and parents, however, he was perceived to be a teacher and was addressed as *sensei* (teacher) by them in most settings. Neighbor children would occasionally, in the researcher's home, act in another role as informants on the peer culture of students— but they were easily embarrassed when reminded by others of the researcher's role as "teacher." They could not tell a "teacher" the disrespectful nicknames given to other teachers by the pupils.

Observation extended throughout the program of the school and the activities of people connected with the school. During the study, attention gradually focused on the role of the teacher and his position in the organization. The status of the researcher, the opportunities for informal participant observation, and the fascinating problem of how teachers resolved the various expectations and forces acting upon them in the determination of their organizational roles led to the attention paid to teachers in the final report.

During the school year, systematic observations were made of teacher interaction, classroom instruction, the school's ceremonial and testing cycles, extracurricular pupil activities, parent-related organizations, and teacher activities outside of the school.

CLASSROOM INSTRUCTION

Observation of the regular formal classroom instruction of the school was usually carried out with the advance permission of the teacher concerned, but was apparently sufficiently frequent to calm the anxieties of most teachers and pupils. Special attention was paid to the social studies curriculum, but all subjects and teachers were observed. Classroom observation was most frequent at the beginning of the study. The purpose of the classroom observations was to note teacher characteristics, approaches to specific content of instruction, and general teaching methods, as well as observing the forms of teacher-pupil interaction. In the long run, classroom observation did as much to legitimize the presence of the researcher in the school as to provide significant data. This observation was expected by teachers; requests to attend a teachers' union meeting were not.

THE CEREMONIAL CYCLE

Ceremony occupies a good deal of time in many Japanese settings, and the school was no exception. Recurrent ceremonies of the school included such functions as the weekly school assemblies, the opening and closing of the three school terms during the year, sports-related ceremonies, the induction of new pupils at the beginning of the year, award ceremonies of various kinds, and, most important in any school, the graduation ritual. In addition, there were ceremonies related to PTA activities, teachers, and ceremonial responsibilities of the school officials in settings outside the school. Because a new gymnasium was built for the school during the course of this research, it was possible to observe the ceremonies associated with the building and dedication of a new school building.

THE TESTING CYCLE

Preparation for the entrance examinations of the senior high schools is one of the important functions of the middle school. Therefore, observation of the testing program, which both prepares pupils for the all-important entrance tests as well as furnishing data for the teachers in their guidance of the pupils' high school entrance applications, was important. Preparation for, administration of, and posting of the results of a variety of tests were observed. The ritual of testing and the testing cycle were essentially one part of the ceremonial cycle.

EXTRACURRICULAR ACTIVITIES

Pupils and teachers were engaged in a large variety of extracurricular activities as a part of the school's educational program. Trips, sports events, club activities, home-room activities, and student government organizations were observed as much as possible. It was in following the meetings of the school's student council that the researcher was able, for instance, to watch a pupil revolt in action. Two teachers had written and presented to the council a list of rules entitled "Proper Living for Winter Vacation." Instead of the expected docile discussion of how to implement the rules for vacation behavior, two of the older boys decided to criticize the rules they had been expected to approve as a document "from" the council. Several hours of discussion ensued in which the pupil representatives made it clear that they did not want to agree to the teachers' rather narrow strictures, which had little connection with school or academic responsibilities.

PARENT-RELATED ORGANIZATIONS

The PTA and Sports-Supporters Association were two organizations centered in the school. Other local organizations also related in one way or another to the school. An interlocking directorship in the PTA and the local Shinto Shrine Officials Organization made the latter group one of interest to this study.

Study of the PTA showed that it carried an important fiscal function in supplying the largest part of local operating funds for the school exclusive of teachers salaries. In the traditional manner of local community organization, the PTA relied upon community solidarity to enforce a legally voluntary system of school support through social obligations. Though the ethnographic report described the system of collecting annual family "contributions" to the PTA, the essay must report that the data came from a formal visit to the researcher's home by his community guarantor, the PTA official. Carrying out his duty of systematically approaching each family for their contribution, he started with the most prestigious household and worked his way down the hamlet social ladder. The names and amount contributed were recorded in a book which was then shown to each successive donor. During the formal visit, the book would be produced and the prospective donor would look down the list of contributors making appropriate exclamations about the generosity of his predecessors. He could then calculate the amount expected in order to meet the quota previously alloted to the hamlet. The researcher, not yet fitted into the permanent hamlet family hierarchy, was given more leeway by being the last one approached and, thus, choosing his social standing by the amount donated. Too small a contribution would have been a denial of community membership; too large would have embarrassed one's neighbors. Even a sociologist would have been pleased with the exact measurement of community prestige afforded in this setting, as the researcher looked closely at the PTA donation record book.

TEACHER ACTIVITIES

Both in the school and outside, a number of activities engage the teachers as teachers. In the school, daily teachers' meetings in the morning before school and periodical afternoon meetings of longer duration were observed. Outside the school, teachers' union activities, in-service training programs for teachers, research circle meetings, various professional organizations, and meetings sponsored by the city or prefectural boards of education were attended as often as possible.

Situations of conflict between different groups were especially dramatic in the Japanese context which emphasizes harmony and good feelings between people. The researcher's desk in the teachers' room allowed him to observe the process of conflict and its resolution as the local school board's supervisors attempted to get the teachers to accept an experimental three-year program in morals education. Springing the news on the teachers in a formal teachers' meeting, it took six months and many formal meetings, with an interesting shifting pattern of public leadership among the teachers, before they finally acquiesced in the supervisors' decision. The substance of this conflict was worked out only gradually by the researcher in individual contact with the teachers in a variety of settings. Arguments at the end of a teachers' sake-drinking party, idle conversation on the way to a prefectural teachers' meeting, research planning meetings, and attempts by friendly teachers to explain the silent-resistance tactic employed in formal teachers' meetings all helped the researcher to understand the substance and process of conflict resolution.

TEACHER INTERVIEWS

Toward the end of the study at Nichū, a series of significant and informative interviews took place in a semistructured fashion with all the teachers and administrative staff. The principal, the head teacher, twenty-two teachers, and the school clerk responded favorably to a request for a two-hour private interview at their convenience. Most of the interviews were arranged to fall on the night that the teachers were scheduled for night duty at the school. This night duty included the male teachers who took turns performing the function of a night watchman. The female teachers and a male teacher recovering from tuberculosis were expected to do their watchman's duty on Sundays and holidays during the daylight hours.

An interview schedule was prepared to cover the life history of the teacher and to elicit opinions and underlying attitudes about certain issues currently important in educational disputes at the national level.

Because the interviews generally began at night and took place next to the coal stove on cold winter evenings, the situation was private, relaxed, and informal. Communication had already been well established with most of the teachers and they were accustomed to the note-taking habits of the researcher. Questions were held to a minimum, were frequently made somewhat ambiguous, and teachers were encouraged to expand on any points of personal interest. Quite a few became so expansive that a second and even third interview had to be scheduled to complete the interview questionnaire or to record personal comments of the teachers.

Interview data was particularly valuable in assessing self-perceptions of a teacher's role in a Japanese school. On the basis of these interviews, a classification of teachers' characteristics and role perceptions was made.

Some of the most relevant data in this study for the understanding of personal resolution of cultural conflict in Japan came from the combination of teacher-interview data with previous observations of teacher role behavior in the school. One lively male teacher represented dramatically the problems of resolving the different and conflicting forces which impinge on a Japanese teacher. He had been elected by the teachers, in the year of this study, as the Nichū representative to the city-wide teachers' union executive committee. With extensive prewar teaching experience, he had originally opposed the formation of the Japan Teachers Union (JTU).

> He was opposed on the grounds of what he called "Buddhist philosophical principles." One should not push for himself, but be contented with what he is granted by others. As a teacher, he did not feel that he should fight for better living conditions for teachers at the expense of other groups.
>
> Though he had joined the union, he never felt attracted to its major purposes as a labor union or as an anti-Ministry educational organization. He had accepted the responsibility of being Nichū's union representative with a great deal of reluctance and trepidation.
>
> "When I told one of the other teachers I wanted to get out of the job, he said I should stay and apply the brakes instead."
>
> As the local union representative, he had the responsibility for communicating union information to the teachers. This he did with outward equanimity, though he was personally opposed to most of the activities which he was supposed to be leading for the union among the Nichū teachers. Thus he distributed campaign literature to the teachers on behalf of the JTU candidate for the Diet and organized a postcard mailing from the Nichū teachers to their friends on the candidate's behalf; but he, himself, did not vote in that election. He identified himself with the Liberal-Democratic party. At another time he brought the anti-achievement test petition to Nichū and passed it around for the teachers' signatures, explaining the basis of the unions' concern in this affair. He did not indicate to the teachers his own personal opposition to this struggle, and claims that he did not sign the petition himself. He told the author that all the teachers except the principal and head teacher had signed the petition, though several teachers later denied to the author that they had signed it.
>
> The interesting, and perhaps representative, feature of this man's relationship to the JTU was the way in which he personally rejected the basic principles of the union; yet, when called upon to perform an active role in the furtherance of union concerns, he energetically fulfilled the distasteful personal responsibilities that had been thrust upon him by his fellow teachers.
>
> In somewhat exaggerated form, this man represented the conflicts felt by a majority of the teachers. He also represented the resolution of these conflicts through the fulfillment of his obligations to his fellow teachers in service to the union. He was able to separate his personal feelings from his roles as a Nichū teacher and union member, but he could not shirk his responsibility to his fellow Nichū teachers. Nichū teacher unity was an important value to him. (Singleton, 1967)

PUPIL HOME SURVEY

A systematic survey was carried out with fifty-four ninth-grade pupils. The survey was designed to get background information on a manageable number of pupils, their homes, teachers' impressions of them and their homes, and their parents' opinions about their own children and about postwar Japanese education.

Preliminary arrangements were made for home interviews of the pupils' parents in several ways. An explanation of the researcher's purpose and a request for cooperation was sent out by the school principal to the homes concerned. With this was included a short questionnaire about the pupil and his home which asked for a list of family members in the household, their relationship to each other, birth date, occupation, and educational history. Also included were questions about plans of the pupil after middle-school graduation, the pupil's special interests and activities at the school, and a request for a map of the home's location so that the author might find his way to it.

A second questionnaire on each child was filled out by the appropriate homeroom teacher on school record and achievement test results, his impressions of the pupil's parents, their home and economic level, and the student himself. The latter questionnaires were then used as the basis for a short interview about each pupil with the homeroom teacher in which the questionnaire responses were explained by the teachers and anecdotal material about the pupils and their homes was systematically collected.

Thus prepared, visits were scheduled to each of the fifty-four pupil homes included in the sample. Notices were sent out with the pupils of the approximate time scheduled for the interview with parents. An interview schedule was prepared concerning the family's social and economic situation, history, questions about the pupil in relation to his schoolwork and future plans, and general attitudes of the parents to the school and present-day Japanese education.

Because the interview period coincided with the summer vacation of the school, the pupils concerned participated in a few of the interviews. All but one home was reached and extended cooperation with the interview.

PTA OFFICER INTERVIEWS

To gain some systematic background information on the PTA officers of Nichū and their attitudes toward the public schools, the last survey undertaken in the field research was concerned with the important officers of the PTA organization. An interview schedule was prepared so that it included a few questions about personal background and role in other community organizations than the PTA before giving attitude questions similar to those asked in the teachers' and parents' interviews.

Fifteen interviews were conducted, but two officers, with whom it was impossible to arrange an interview, had to be left out of the survey. They were both hesitant to schedule an interview and seemed uncomfortable about such an idea. One was the mayor's daughter-in-law who had sent one child to a different junior high school than Nichū, while living in the Nichū district, and had no children currently in Nichū. The other was a nervous oil distributor who thought the researcher wanted to test him on his knowledge of education, regardless of reassurances. Having previously asked the author to make a local Rotary Club speech, the latter's avoidance of an interview was somewhat disappointing.

SURVEY OF ALL NINTH-GRADE NICHŪ PUPILS

On completion of the home survey, several questions arose which made it seem desirable to conduct a questionnaire survey of all 297 ninth-grade pupils. Questions included family composition, occupation and education of family members, plans of pupils after middle-school graduation, and out-of-school participation in formal educational programs.

Questionnaires were sent home with the pupils and later collected by the teachers. For those pupils who failed to return the questionnaires, about 10 percent of the group, the information was taken from school and teacher records.

Teachers were asked to supply test results, data about school achievement for each pupil, performance scores on the high school entrance examination, class standing, and actual disposition of the pupils after graduation. From this, exact information about the dispersal of middle-school graduates among the region's high schools and employment in different areas was determined.

SURVEY OF 1962 NICHŪ GRADUATES

To determine the postcompulsory education opportunities open to Nichū graduates, a survey of school records was undertaken by the author to determine what had happened to the graduates of the previous year. Scores were available for the entrance examinations of high school applicants and it was thus possible to trace the records of students who had failed in the exams as well as those who had passed and were admitted to high schools. Pertinent material from the school records relating to academic achievement, intelligence tests, national achievement test scores, absence records, and some anecdotal entries were recorded for 268 graduates and for 7 who failed to graduate.

Entrance examination scores were also recorded for each high school to determine the relative academic rank of the local high schools. Very clear patterns of difference or academic ranking emerged in this examination.

SURVEY OF LOCAL SCHOOLS

Most important to an understanding of the role of the middle school was an understanding of the schools and formal education programs that coexisted with it at lower, equivalent, and higher levels. The two elementary schools located in Nichū District, private and public kindergartens, abacus schools, classes in caligraphy, other middle schools in the city, local public and private high schools, higher education, vocational training programs, and "cram schools" to prepare for high school or college-entrance examinations were all considered important. Kindergartens and elementary schools were observed as a parent with children of the author enrolled as regular pupils in them. Special attention was paid to a survey of all postcompulsory education educational tracks.

COMPARATIVE OBSERVATIONS

To have a basis for comparing the school and its district with a different type of Japanese community, arrangements were made for a shorter community study of a school located in the Tōhoku section. In that area, a smaller middle school serving a purely rural community was chosen for study. The particular convenience of the school chosen was because an anthropologist, Keith Brown, was residing in the district of the school. He was willing to exchange information about the community and the school, as well as to provide an introduction to the school. Four one-week visits were made to the school, in the course of which a survey of twenty-five pupil homes was made, conducted on the same basis as the Nichū survey of pupil homes. Similarly, a quesitonnaire survey was made of all ninth-grade pupils to determine post-middle-school aspirations, out-of-school formal educational experience, family composition, and occupation and education of family members.

The visits to this school also involved participation in both Board of Education-sponsored teachers' meetings and union-sponsored meetings. Educational officials and union leaders were visited and proved very helpful in describing the pattern of relationships existing in their area. Teachers Union–Board of Education relations proved very different from the Nichū area, and added further insight into the different ways which conflict over national policy in Japan is resolved at the local level.

THE ETHNOGRAPHIC REPORT

The structuring of data collected and the analysis of research results in the present study were heavily influenced, as noted earlier, by the models introduced in a short theoretical paper by Bernard Siegel entitled "Models for the Analysis of the Educative Process in American Communities" (1955). His paper suggested several models for the use of educators and anthropologists in their study of American school systems.

Some of the assumptions of his paper, which are also the underlying assumptions of the present study, include:

> 1. There is an educational community which can be conceived of as the *formal* school system—sites and interacting members, stated goals, and the role relations in terms of which the goals are translated into action.
>
> 2. The school is no isolated organization; its operational structure is continually affected by outside environmental forces. It does not set its own goals, nor can it seek to implement them completely independently of other community agencies. The relationship between the educational community and the community as a whole, however, is reciprocal and interacting.
>
> 3. The flow of what is taught is screened, interpreted, and reinterpreted at several levels as a consequence of the carrying networks of role relationships.
>
> 4. We can . . . think of the school system as an organization standing in apposition to other collectivities to which it must adapt, and which in turn it seeks to influence. (Seigel 1955)

Seigel proposed an "acculturation model" of the educative process in which the school is treated as an educational community in contact with other specific communities. The other communities in interaction with the educational community of the school were, he suggested, the academic community of teacher-training institutions, the ethnic groups and class aggregates of the local community from which the school draws its pupils, and the organizations of the state government, the school board, and the PTA.

It was called an acculturation model because of the emphasis on changes resulting from the interaction of quasi-autonomous communities.

The importance of this acculturation model is that it leads one to examine each of the communities involved, once they are identified, and to their interrelationships. Because the model is based on the concept of acculturation, Siegel is led to suggest some of the factors that will affect cultural transmission in the school.

> The way in which content is transmitted [from one community to another] is conditioned theoretically by several factors, such as (1) the degree of consistency of the values in each of the subcultures; (2) the extent of agreement of the members of the collectivities on these values; (3) the kinds of role relations established between participants in the several subcultures . . . ; and (4) the perception of one's own roles and of content intended for transmission.

This, then, became a model for the presentation of the data from Nichū with the particular communities of reference determined as the school itself; the local socio-geographic community of people living within the school district; the administrative community of people and organizations having administrative control over and responsibility for the school; and the union-professional community of Japanese teachers, especially the Japanese Teachers Union, which have nonadministrative contact with the school and its administrative staff.

Sociologists tend to write manuals on social research unrelated to specific societies or settings. Anthropologists, on the other hand, write area handbooks for specific cultural areas. If we are going to develop a handbook for educational ethnography, it is obvious that it will have to come out of specific descriptions of ethnographic studies of schools and other educational institutions. Perhaps this paper can help to stimulate the serious discussion of research methodology for educational ethnographers. Someday, then, we will have the basic data which we now lack for a better understanding of the social role of schools in the education of our children and in the structure of our society.

REFERENCES

Bernard Seigel, "Models for the Analysis of the Educative Process in American Communities" in George D. Spindler (ed.) *Education and Anthropology.* Stanford, California: Stanford University Press, pp. 38–49.

John Singleton, *Nichū, A Japanese School.* New York: Holt, Rinehart and Winston, 1967.

Richard L. Warren, "Teacher Encounters: A Typology for Ethnographic Research on the Teaching Experience." Paper presented to the annual meeting of the American Anthropological Association, November, 1968, mimeographed.

21 / Event Description and Analysis in the Microethnography of Urban Classrooms

Jacquetta Hill Burnett

Doing ethnography in the modern city is somewhat like trying to stay afloat on a stormy sea. People, problems, factors, and variables come in waves breaking over the mind, tearing at one's feeble efforts to make sensible statements about attributes, components, or relationships in answer to one's questions. In this circumstance some unit or unitary percept of this sea of data is a minimal necessity to keep one's senses from drowning in disorientation.

The objective of the EPIC (*Estudio de Problemas Interculturales*) is to study the intercultural process and problems in migration, education, and occupation of Puerto Rican youths in Chicago. The first set of questions asked by the researcher concerned whether cultural factors and differences were one major source of the educational problems experienced by Puerto Rican youths in United States schools. A second set of questions asks how the educational problems and cultural factors affect occupational socialization and access to occupations for Puerto Rican youths in an urban setting in the United States. The household of a Puerto Rican youth is regarded as the domain and conservator of a characteristic Puerto Rican culture. At the same time the school, in this case one elementary school comprised of grades one through eight, is viewed as the domain and conservator of a dominant and characteristic North American culture. Peer relations is a third domain, potentially of great relevance to acculturation of youth, but its cultural character or characteristics was an unknown that had to be discovered.

In the urban setting of our research, there were no neighborhood segments or community units that were small enough, bounded clearly enough, or understood sufficiently well for use as a sample system through which to approach our research objectives. A study of families would not necessarily get us into the school. A study of school classrooms and associated families, when each classroom might have thirty-five to forty-four pupils, would overtax our resources. If we were to study cultural factors and differences in vivo, we needed a new research strategy. Our solution, then, was to bring together two separate streams of conceptual development in social anthropology, egocentric network models and event analysis, to develop a new variant on earlier methodological strategies for doing ethnographic studies in urban settings.

We decided to study a sample of egocentric networks. The networks began with thirty egos who were selected by stratified random selection from one grade level, the seventh grade of 1967–68, in one large urban elementary school. We planned to follow the sample of egos and parts of their networks over a period of approximately two and one-half years, from seventh grade through the first year of secondary school (that is, through the ninth grade, which is part of secondary school in our city).

We chose seventh grade because this was the point at which the effects of cultural difference came into full expression, or so the literature and the private accounts of teachers and of Puerto Rican community leaders told us. Moreover, starting with a group at this grade level we could examine the effects of a difference in experience with school cultures. We included in the randomly selected principal sample five girls and five boys who had attended Puerto Rican schools for at least five years of their school careers before coming to Chicago, five girls and five boys from Puerto Rican families who had spent all their school careers in Chicago schools, and five non-Puerto Rican girls and five non-Puerto Rican boys. The last ten provide us with a comparison for sorting out factors that are endemic to the inner city: socioeconomic level, broken homes, etc. It will help to keep us "honest" and self-critical about what is poverty and urbanism and what is cultural difference.

EGOCENTRIC NETWORK ANALYSIS

This paper is mainly concerned with event analysis, but some attention to network analysis is necessary to show the special nature of the methodological linkage between the two areas. The concept of network or egocentric network as developed by Barnes, Bott, Epstein, and Mayer is based on the image of points connected and interconnected by lines in latticelike patterns.* The points represent persons or household groups or other groups. The lines represent relationships of some sort such as person-contacts, friendship, or even a range of several different sorts of relationships. Barnes emphasized the linkages of friendship, acquaintanceship, and kinship of persons with other persons; Bott emphasized whether other persons or households in a network were acquainted or connected with one another as well as with the family of origin—i.e., the point of origin of the network; and Mayer used the concept to depict and explore linkages of political support for three different egos as the relationships were enacted or manifested in an election in Madhya Pradesh State in India.

When we began our study we drew on this development of egocentric network concepts to define where and with whom we should begin. So, in the early stages of the research in the spring of 1968 we selected thirty seventh-grade children, or thirty egocentric networks. We wanted to study their networks; in particular, that part of each network that manifests itself in the household, in the school and classroom, and in relations with peers outside the classroom and school.

After selecting our sample, we followed the plan of the network and contacted

*If you will think of an ego-centered sociogram, this will give you a quick idea of the imagery involved. Given a field of persons represented as points in two dimensional space, select one point as an ego; then draw a line to represent a primary linkage to every person-point with whom he has face-to-face and regular contacts.

the household adults. Moreover, then and now we go only into those classrooms that our sample of egos attend and where we have been doing regular participant observation and taking ethnographic accounts of events. In the households we are doing interviews and trying to establish close enough relations to do participant observation. In our store-front neighborhood research center we have afternoon recreation time to which we have invited our sample and their friends, or more accurately, the youths and their friends in the classrooms we observe.

In our observations and interviews with household adults and teachers we plan to follow out certain secondary linkages, where we can, into the area of the network that is unbounded from ego's point of view. Beginning with links from ego to teacher and then following these secondary linkages of the teacher to other teachers carries us into the study of school culture. The secondary linkages of parents can lead us to relatives, leisure-time companions, and on-the-job relationships. The question of whether the linkages of the household are close-knit or loose-knit networks shall interest us from the point of view of acculturation of household patterns to North American patterns, to maintaining Island patterns, or to developing idiosyncratic family practices. The study of the cultural character of these linkages and of the cultural characteristics of three organizational contexts in which they manifest themselves is the central objective of our study. But we study the linkages and their social contexts through more than interviews; we use participant observation and ethnographic description of observed events to explore the linkages.

While our network sample defined with whom and where we were to begin our study, it still left us with the question of how and what we planned to study. The problem of being explicit on this point loomed larger for us than for most ethnographic studies since the research was being carried out not by a single ethnographer, but by a team of field workers. Moreover, the style of the division of labor led to ethnographic accounts that were interdependent, rather than merely parallel or related. We faced a serious problem of clear intersubjective communication in comparing one classroom with another, a household with a classroom, and life in peer groups with life in a household and in school. We were looking at numerous streams of behavior in various different locales. From the point of view of our egos, we were observing egos and their networks in events—human behavioral events.

EVENTS AS SEGMENTS

Regarding the classroom—where we began the research—as a stream of behavior, we could perceive phases or segments of that stream that seemed to have natural breaks, at least in temporal dimension. Although the concept of event has had a different emphasis and a somewhat more macrocosmic meaning in anthropological literature, for a number of persuasive theoretical reasons the author thought that we would label as "event" that segment with a certain "natural" or "easily developed" sense of integrality to it, and thus preserve what Barker regards as the primary attribute of the behavior stream—its arrangement in time. The event we speak of here is a microevent; but our unit of description can logically and with theoretical significance, be linked to macroevents of the order of a festival, a community ceremonial, a health survey, or longer and more complex constellations of human behavioral processes and elements.

An event begins with the entry into a specific place by a person or sets of persons and their engagement there in actions, including interactions. The event ends when the person, or at least one complete set of the various sets of persons engaged in behavior, changes his place, either by departing from that place, or by manipulating the place-defining objects so that the location is transformed from one place type to another. In Puerto Rico I saw classrooms of students transformed into a partial school assembly by simply moving the partitions between four classrooms and reorienting the chairs toward the stage on one end. On the other hand, the movement of personnel or part of the personnel in and out of a place where an event is occurring doesn't necessarily constitute the end point of an event. This is clearly the case in our urban classrooms where students move in and out of the classroom at a bewildering rate for special classes, monitor duties, service to the school, safety patrol duties, etc. But when one teacher goes out and another teacher comes in, one has completely changed the membership of one set, although there is no change in the actor type of the set. This then amounts to a new event. In like manner, keeping the same teacher in the same place, but changing the class of students entirely, constitutes the ending of one event and the beginning of another. At this time, this is our working definition of the beginning and ending of an event. It has proved usable so far.

Isolating events in an urban school is often an easy matter. For example, as the warning bell ending lunch recess rings, students line up, by room and sex, outside the building and enter together by classroom groups. If the teacher isn't there, they assemble around the door until the teacher comes with the key and they enter to take their seats. After the final bell, as regular as morning prayers in a nunnery, one teacher says, "Girls, put up your wraps," pauses while girls get up and hang up wraps they don't want to wear, then, "Boys, hang up your coats," pauses while boys who have coats put them in the cloakroom. "Now get out your homework papers." And so the new event proceeds. Most regular, recurrent events in the school begin and end with a ritual phase. Other events, such as school assemblies, are highly ritualized throughout.

Let's follow out the stream of behavior over a period of time. After morning recess and the asembling ritual described above, in a given classroom there will be minor changes in personnel from time to time and day to day, but the place is the same and the set of actors and actor types are common from event to event.

As time moves through its cycle, objects, actions, and messages interrelate to produce what we can abstract as activities. Some activities become salient and so the event comes to be named after them—"the spelling hour." A bell near noon initiates a series of actions that begin with "put your books and things away" from the teacher. Pause. Teacher, "Girls, get your wraps and form a line by twos." Action by girls. "Now boys, get your wraps and form a line by twos." The girls and boys form a line at a 45-degree angle to one another, at the corner of the room where the door is. (I've never observed a class in this school where the door is in any other position than in the corner.) The teacher stands near the origin of the angle, waiting for the bell to signal time to lead them out. They move out in a line of twos, usually girls first, then boys. The teacher moves out last, closes the door, and checks to see that it is locked. They move on, stopping at the top of the stairs, then down two flights of stairs, pausing at every landing, and around to the door. As they get near the double door their line disappears into a sea of students surging through the doors. This happens the same way when school is out. At noon, however, the teacher walks them to the door, then turns to her left and goes into the cafeteria.

I compared these events day after day for one classroom I observed regularly. Then I observed another room, another place (but the same place type) and another teacher (but the same actor type), etc. Usually there was a ritual episode to begin an event and a second ritual episode to end an event. The particular event I discussed above was continuous from recess to noon. Other events during the day began with the same ritual episode of entry and later terminated with the ritual episode described above. Sometimes new instances of events were initiated by a change in the teacher, and often the teachers exchanged places. On other occasions a class group terminated one event and began another by shifting from classroom to gym, or to library, or to home mechanics room.

I compared my field-note accounts of events with the accounts of two other field observers. It became clear that while all events in the day did not begin and end in the same way, beginnings and endings were highly regularized for a given event that recurred at the same time, in the same place, and with the same actor sets.

ELEMENTS AND COORDINATES OF EVENTS

We describe an event by describing where it is, what objects are involved, what actions and what interactions occur and who participates, and when these elements appear, in the order of their appearance. Actions are carefully distinguished into verbal action and nonverbal action. The messages of the verbal action are recorded, either in English or in Spanish depending upon which code is used. To get a full verbal account in the classroom, however, a tape recorder is necessary.

In addition to using actions, verbal and nonverbal, as elements in the microanalysis of an event, we used scene coordinates of the actions, that is, the elements that set the scene for the action which include actor types, place-space types, object types, and absolute and relative time. Actor types are defined by physical features, behavioral features, and combinations of both types of features. Object types, too, can be defined by physical or behavioral features, or a combination of both. But object types also help to define place-space. So, for example, the difference in a classroom and a school library may be based on the differences between types of objects present rather than in macro-place features such as room size. However, providing an inventory of all objects or artifacts before entering into descriptions of behavior is probably unnecessarily tedious. The degree of refinement in characterization is necessary to describe behavior, distinguish places, events, and classes of actions intersubjectively.

At the first level of abstraction on action, one can distinguish interaction, the interdependent ordered actions of two or more persons. Thanks to early, careful work on the part of Chapple and Arensberg in developing a data language and system of notation for interaction, we can be fairly precise when we wish to focus on the interaction dimension of the event. We can include a fairly precise account of interaction in the direct observation of events.

We have included on our observation form a place for entering rule guides or paradigms that apply to the action and relations that take place in the event. This is not to be recorded during the observation since such statements are often several logical steps and a few inductive leaps away from direct accounts of the behavior stream. These constructions, however, do provide for the logical, structural account of the system. The provision on the form for placing these formulations in juxtaposition with the descriptive account of the event, readily allows us to index the empirical bases for those constructions.

The conceptualization of *activities* is another reconstruction of descriptive data several logical steps removed and, therefore, at a further level of abstraction from the coordinates of the scene and the stream of action. Goodenough suggests that since activities are organized with reference to intended goals, they, like sentences in speech, have recognizable beginnings and endings which make them readily isolable as natural behavioral entities for analysis. Plainly, they are likely to be behavioral entities that have significance and meaning in the minds of members of a culture. The concept of activity bridges the level of description involved in micro-events with the level of symbolic meaning and manifest function of the culture in which the events take place. Thus, we adopt Goodenough's formulation, that whether the activity is customary (that is, "designed to accomplish recurring purposes . . . where the same means for accomplishing the purpose continues to be available") or whether the activity is ad hoc (that is, "designed to accomplish unusual ends or to deal with conditions where common means are unavailable"), all activities involve these three features: (1) actors of certain types; (2) a set of procedures that can be formulated as recipes and rules; and (3) one or more purposes or goals from the views of the actors. Actors and other people are aware that the effects of goals and purposes contribute to the activity's meaning to them. The effects of purposes, however, whether or not the people are aware of all of them, produce the activity's functions in their lives and in the event.

Making sense out of activities involves relating the action to intended consequences, usually by asking, "Why are you doing that?" or, placing more emphasis on procedure, asking, "Why are you doing that *that* way?" For a given cultural group, finding purpose for activities gives one a picture of the cognitive maps the members of a group have of their physical, social, and even historical environment. These maps are what Lévi-Strauss calls "folk-models." In earlier behavioral science terms, they were labeled the desires and values of a people. So, beyond the descriptive account of the events themselves for our Puerto Rican and non-Puerto Rican egos and their networks in the domains of home, school, and peerdom, we have been inquiring about people's procedures and purposes in their activities and about their perceptions of their own and others' purposes. We have been comparing them with one another to reveal culture differences and unrecognized sources of conflict.

EVENT TYPOLOGIES

Returning once again to the task of event-focused descriptive ethnography, we turn to the questions of the relationships among events and to questions of classes and types. While events are described and characterized by the elements just discussed, the relationships among events can be of several varieties. One important relationship is temporal-spatial scheduling, a relationship that underlies the typology of events we are using at this stage in our research. This typology is discussed below.

Another way of comparing events is through *feature overlap*, or the amount of common features among events which can be specified in terms of actors and actor types; place and place types; actions, interactions, or their abstractions as activities, particularly customary activities; and relevant object-types. It is through feature overlap that we decide whether one instance of an event is sufficiently like another instance of an event to be classed as the "same" event. Events may be *complementary* to one another with respect to features, i.e., they complete one another in some fashion. Thus the actor composite of the school may be divided up among simultaneous events, e.g., teachers in the cafeteria and pupils on the playground during recess.

Events are often *contingent* upon one another, one being instrumental to the other. The contingency relationship is of special interest to us because some of our proposed explanations for commonly known conflicts suggest that events in the households have contingencies with events in the school, and one of our problems is to discover those contingencies. In order for the school to attain certain goals, certain outcomes, it may depend on and require certain contingent conditions to exist in the homes of its students in the form of certain activities or procedures for carrying out activities. When the conditions are not present, or when carried out by different procedures than those assumed in schools the children attend, then schools find themselves unable to meet their goals. They may rationalize the failures by viewing the home as deprived or disadvantaged when in actuality it should be more properly regarded as *different* in customary goals, meanings, and purposes. Another way to view this problem is to view the school as disabled, disadvantaged, and in need of rehabilitation to adapt to the conditions of its parental constituency because its activities are contingent upon the presence of certain activities and certain customary procedures in the homes of its student clientele if it is to attain the goals related to its key social functions. From the point of view of the event typology, contingency of events in different domains points up the practical applications of typology that includes this relationship.

One can analyze events according to how nearly they comprehend or include all the actors and actor types in the system or organization in question. Events that function as rites of intensification for a system should be found to include representatives of all actor types in the system or organization, even if not all the individual actors. The relative frequency of events with different degrees of comprehensiveness might be found to relate to such concepts of group climate as "cohesiveness." Comprehensiveness, of course, can vary from a single-person event, to partial assembly, to full assembly of the complement of actors—both for school, household, and peer network. The composition and frequency of partial assembly relative to full assembly and to single-person event is a numerical relationship of some importance. Another dimension of comparison is event complexity. Complexity of an event varies with the variety of different activities, actor types, semantic domains, sequencing of activities (and episodes), and object types that are involved in the course of an event.

We have adopted temporal scheduling of an event as a basis for our first typology. *Recurrence* refers to the fact that an event type recurs on a cyclical basis such that one can specify its occurrence in that cycle, and at what point in the cycle it will occur—diurnal, weekly, monthly, seasonally, etc. *Regular events* are predictable events, but predictable within stated limits. Speaking in terms of the typology, events are *recurrent-regular* in that they are highly predictable and have a very specific, sequencial place in the cycle. There are events that are *recurrent but irregular* in that one knows they will happen within the interval of a temporal cycle, but just when they will take place in the cycle is uncertain. *Nonrecurrent-regular* events cannot be anticipated in terms of cycle but are predictable within an interval period. Finally, *nonrecurrent-irregular* events are happenings which are unpredictable from within the system. An example of this nonrecurrent-irregular event in our school system was the death of the principal and the memorial event held in his memory. His death with respect to the social system of the school is a nonrecurrent-irregular event.

Using as our basic dimension a schedule of events by cycles of time and by absolute time, we can provide proper time orientation to our model of the behavior stream. We may subdivide any given one of these types according to varieties of place types, actor types, and activity types. Under the general recurrent-regular events, or type 1, we might have subtype *a* events that could be labeled *daily-morning/teacher-student/in-classroom/doing-math event*. Recurrent-regular subtype *b* events might be *daily-afternoon/student/playground/recess*; and subtype *c* event could be scheduled at the same time as subtype *b* where subtype *c* is *afternoon/teacher/cafeteria/drinking-coffee event*. Type 1, subtype *b* and *c*, are related to one another by being complementary to one another.

Recurrent-regular events, or type 2, might have subvarieties as subtype *a*, *weekly/sixth, seventh, eighth, teacher-student-administrator/auditorium/having-program*. The point is that this event subtype will happen sometime during the week, but specification of when it will occur on a smaller time scale, such as a daily time scale or relative time within the daily time schedule is impossible. Within the nonrecurrent-regular event type one might have such subvarieties, *teacher-student/adjustment-office/for sanctioning*. This type happens often and regularly, but not on a recurrent cycle. Several days might go by without the occurrence of this type of event and then three such events like this could occur in one morning.

Nonrecurrent and nonregular events such as the appearance of a crew of research workers on the scene to do ethnographic research, of course, are important types of events that cannot be predicted from internal knowledge of the organization. Another example of this type of event might be a student demonstration that has not as yet become regular, let alone a recurrent kind of event in the school in which we are doing a study. High school students in some of the predominantly black high schools in Chicago did try to put demonstrations on a recurrent weekly basis for a period, but they were not able to maintain recurrent regularity.

We emphasize that we are working toward a usable typology of events by working inductively. Even our four-member typology based on schedule came about inductively because it is important to develop the capability of predicting events in order to be there to observe them, or even to make work plans. We rounded out our typology beyond our inductive recognition of two types by generating four types and discovering real events that fit the theoretical categories. We could develop a theoretical typology based on our event coordinates types and activity types, but by this procedure we would have a grid with many thousands of cells, and types. The most fruitful strategy seems to be that of working from our four schedule types, and on an inductive basis make further decisions about types of event characteristics.

The contour of events in the school is based on a basic pattern of four events that are very similar in beginning and ending episodes, and three other *periods* in which there is a diffusion of *events* into different place-types and among the actor types in the system. The first four we ordinarily call "class"; the other three periods are "recess." Weekly recurrent variations are introduced into the daily cycle, in the form of weekly events in the library, in the gymnasium, in the home mechanics shop, and in the form of a special teacher for art and for music.

While the schoolwork processing events and their cyclical variations are repetitive with respect to beginnings, endings, place types, actor types, and even *procedures of activities*, there *is* great variety in interaction and particularly in the verbal messages that make up the information flow. There is some indication already that household and peer behavior are characterized by proportionately fewer recurrent-regular events. Seemingly there is more recurrent-irregular scheduling of events, and many nonrecurrent-regular events in household and peer relations. One can anticipate, however, less complexity and variability in messages and code, and perhaps even less variation in interaction.

AN EXAMPLE

Perhaps an example can be used here to illustrate our approach. On a particular Wednesday morning in November, I had entered the classroom at 10:45 A.M., as the class returned from recess. My commentary was as follows:

> The boy in the blue shirt wads a sheet of paper up in his hand, swings his knees around under the edge of the desk, gets up, walks to the front of the room, then turns left across the front of the room in front of the desks over to the waste basket under the windows. He walks leisurely and deliberately. He unhurriedly drops the wad of paper into the waste basket, turns and walks slowly back across the front of the room in front of the desks, apparently on his way back to his desk. At this point the teacher says to him, "Julio, *what* are you *doing*?" "Taking that scrap paper to the waste basket, teacher." Teacher says, "You *know* you are not to get up and *wander* around the room. *Remember* that!" Boy in blue shirt (Julio) returns to seat in a less leisurely, but still not completely hurried fashion, puts his hands on his desk and whirls himself around them, throwing himself into the seat and stares up at the teacher momentarily. (I can't see his face or the expression on it.) Then he picks up his pencil and begins writing on a sheet of paper at his desk.

This account includes two activities, one of which interrupted the other. Julio stated his purpose was to throw away waste paper. The teacher may have had a different idea of his purpose. Her actions also follow a definite procedure, a "verbal-spear" with purpose, apparently, of controlling his behavior, and of explicating a rule of behavior.

In the account please note that the actions are described not only in terms of when each occurs relative to other actions, but also how it occurs; for example, in terms of the volume of voice with which certain parts of the message are emphasized. All this is the procedural part of an activity. In giving attention to the *procedure* we are well within the cultural realm, that is, specifying a style or a rule for the style of a set of actions that are interrelated with respect to a purpose. One can move on in the cultural realm here and talk about the conceptualization or cognition of purpose. The teacher, on being interviewed, could specify her notion of Julio's purpose, a statement of purpose that predictably will differ very radically from his. She might have said, "He got up because he seems unable to concentrate and wanted to pass the time." The observer may specify certain goals or a goal that he thinks the behavior leads to; but in addition, he must derive from the verbal messages, or from accounts in interviews, what the actors regard as the explicit goal objectives of the activity's procedure from the actor's point of view. Within his own analysis and concept of a dynamic activity, the observer may have some theory of implicit or latent purposes or objectives which could be served by the procedure of the activity.

An observer's view of purpose, however, should take into account the full course of activity that took place throughout the event he was describing. For example, having observed the activity we have just mentioned in the context of the full event—from the point at which the whole class and the teacher entered the room— I knew that an earlier episode had begun with a "public" remark by the teacher: "Who is using Susan's desk as a waste basket?" Susan, who was absent that day, sits in the desk behind Julio. On top of her desk, around the old-fashioned inkwell, several wads of paper were piled. Very obviously Julio was the culprit. As the teacher stared at him with a pursed-lip, accusing expression, Julio gathered up the wads of paper and quickly walked over to the waste basket, threw them in and walked back to his desk. When later in the course of the same event, Julio got up to take one piece of paper to the waste basket, he may have been responding to the earlier episode. In an interview with Julio one might establish that the earlier episode was part of the context of the episode that we related here.

It is our hunch that most North American female teachers try to establish an interactive style with boys, including older Puerto Rican boys, that challenges the latter's sense of masculinity. This arouses them to do battle with the female teachers in order to maintain their self-concept of having arrived at manhood, in the Puerto Rican terms. If our comparisons suggest that that relationship is plausible, then we can pursue it into the realms of cognition, self-concept, interpersonal identity, etc.

As an example, consider the fact that the episode involving Julio is a kind of activity we have noticed occurring with great frequency between certain teachers and older Puerto Rican boys in the school. When involving Puerto Rican boys of fifteen or sixteen the interaction we described is usually only the first phase of a more extended episode that includes both verbal and physical action on the part of the Puerto Rican boy to defy the directive of the teacher. In contrast, North American boys and younger and smaller Puerto Rican boys generally do not work themselves up to the point of continuing the episode into actions of defiance. They capitulate or at least appear to capitulate, although this does not deny them the privilege of heated and colorful descriptions of their concept of the teacher outside the context of the episode. During these types of encounters with older Puerto Rican boys, suspense builds up over who is going to *win*. As time goes on and more of these episodes occur between a given pair, a teacher and a Puerto Rican boy, the teacher may be forced to take the boy to the office in order to win. But she has "lost" to some degree because she resorted to the larger system of arrangements for social control that is not of her own design.

With respect to the question of conflicts between Puerto Rican boys and North American teachers, our research task is to select a sample of events, *not a sample of individuals*, and to be sure that the events vary according to actor type. We could take a random sample of type 1 recurrent-regular events, e.g., math in the morning, but stratify that sample by the sex of the teacher, e.g., male and female. Or we could collect descriptions of the nonrecurrent-regular event, *teacher-student/ adjustment-office/behavior sanction*, that took place over a given period of time, say a four-week period, and analyze them for actor-type characteristics and for the event type that just preceded the nonrecurrent-regular type that we are sampling. By checking back on the event type that just preceded this nonrecurrent-regular event, we are checking out contingencies, of course.

If we establish the plausibility of this type of interaction and contingency in the school, our next step is to follow the network of those Puerto Rican boys in our principal sample who fit the age range of boys involved in this type of event. We turn to their households and to events in that household in order to see whether the pattern of interaction and the procedural aspect of activities directed toward sanctioning and toward inhibiting violations of behavior rules seem to follow the same procedures as those we have seen in school. In particular, we would want to look at the same activity sequences involving Puerto Rican adult women and Puerto Rican boys to find out if there is a sharp contrast between the procedures in their interactions, with the procedures in activities involving the same Puerto Rican boys and their female teachers. If there is sharp contrast, then we can pursue the question through interviews with informants concerning how these behavioral procedures and their differences affect them and strike them in emotive and in value terms.

We could carry on the analysis of these two episodes and of other episodes in the same event, but I think this example carries the burden of expressing part of our rationale for using behavioral events. As we have specified, it is a segment of the stream of behavior that we can use as an integral context for the behavioral items we are interested in—from object types to the semantic analyses of the messages that occur in the event.

One other very important point should be made in terms of the limitations of sheer human energy. For example, it is important to recognize that within the classroom there are simultaneous currents of activities. The current of activities that involves the teacher can be quite different from the current of activities that involves the students with one another, although both are going on in the course of the same event. Moreover, a teacher may interrupt one activity, introduce another and complete it, and then go back to the first. While an observer may be in the class throughout the course of the day, the amount of attention demanded in the accurate report of the behavior stream would not allow one to continue this kind of close observation necessary throughout the day. So, one's recording may be in terms of *events*. Two carefully described events in the course of the morning while the other events are briefly sketched in according to the order in which they occurred or how they began and ended is, we think, an orderly and sensible way to develop a store of data. Several people are able to orient themselves quickly with respect to each others ethnographic work.

A serial, contingent, and complementary arrangement of events has long been recognized in the analysis of ritual and ceremony. Sometimes a set of serially related microevents has been referred to as *event* in the singular. For our purposes, that collection of microevents is a "serial event set," not a single event. Nor do we wish to simplify events to the point of singling out only one factor, in variant aspects, as the unit. In contrast to that emphasis, the descriptive segment that we call a microevent is a complex of component parts or factors, each of which may take variable form. The component variations amount to cultural difference when they reach a certain order of variation. Our approach is more analogous to a molecular than an atomic approach to units of description.

The level at which the discovery of difference will be a most potent base from which to suggest changes in organization and behavior will be at the level of activities and interactions. We anticipate finding differences between household and school with respect to the conceptual domains of socialization, schooling, and occupational socialization. Feature overlap with respect to activities in an event, that is, the recurrence of similar activities in different instances of an event is one relation out of which an event typology based on activities can be generated. Insofar as our rapport with the households permit us, we are trying to get accounts of streams of behavior in that context to compare with our classroom behavior. We feel it is at this level of activity that we can fruitfully compare patterns of behavior in the home and in the school, both in terms of procedure and in terms of goals and purposes. Moreover, interviews around these activities are the common referent points with respect to which we can compare the cognitive maps and conceptualizations of different members and different segments of the egocentric networks.

A more general but equally important objective of event description and analysis is to secure descriptive data that can be used for cross-cultural comparison of schools, and for comparison of schools in the same cultural system. The criteria for satisfactory description goes beyond that of satisfying our own anthropological research demands, however. We are involved in action-generating research, and eventually we must have descriptions and comparisons that meet and satisfy instrumental criteria for modifying teacher behavior, administrative procedure, and even student behavior so as to make a genuine difference in the satisfaction of Puerto Rican children within United States schools.

To reiterate, a description of event types presented in terms of the time cycles by which they occur can provide one with the general contour of the pattern of schooling, as well as of the household and of peerdom. The main advantage that we derive from the approach outlined here is that the team of field workers has a way of orienting themselves to each other's work. Each has an idea of from where in the complex stream of behavior the other has chosen to draw in order to get a participant observer description. We have intersubjective navigational points, so to speak. The microdescriptions of particular behaviors and verbalization in particular classrooms can then be placed into a temporal sort of macromodel of the organization or of the group into which ego's network has led us.

In summary, we are studying a sample of egocentric networks using participant observation, interviews, and basic ethnographic description; but the accounts are conceptualized as accounts of events. We are studying the linkages in the networks through their manifestations in events. We can follow these egos into the classroom, as well as into household and peer contacts, and do ethnographic accounts of their experience in the classroom. Putting our accounts in terms of a cluster in the stream of behavior that we are calling "events" allows us to study the peer linkages and the teacher linkages as they manifest themselves in these events. Examination of these events may even allow us to study the effects of teachers' secondary linkages on the teachers' primary links with the sample egos. We submit that using this approach to allow us to combine participant observation with network analysis in terms of event description resolves on the one hand the object-sample problem posed by the very complex urban setting, and on the other still permits us to utilize the in vivo observational study of complex processes of acculturation.

22 / Interaction and Adaptation in Two Negro Kindergartens

Carol Talbert

Studies of school systems, as of other societal institutions, generally employ one of two main approaches—macrocosmic or microcosmic. Macrocosmic studies focus on the school system as a whole, as it is articulated with its general socioeconomic and cultural milieu. Such studies often concentrate on the values, or general ideology as expressed in the stated goals of the system, and on the organization of activities designed to achieve these goals. Microcosmic studies, on the other hand, direct their attention to actual events and behaviors in the classrooms.

The predominantly macrocosmic studies of recent decades reveal a great deal about schools as bureaucracies,[1] as forms of secondary socialization under the influences of local communities[2] and about the importance of national ideological orientations such as those exemplified in the Soviet educational system.[3] But it is often difficult in such studies to distinguish the real from the idealized descriptions of teaching patterns, course content, and other aspects of school operations which are presented as if the actual ongoing activities in the classrooms accurately reflected official views and goals.

Recent and growing crises in urban American schools have raised serious questions about the relationships between generalized descriptions and the realities of day-to-day interaction between pupils and teachers. It is increasingly apparent that even when all the features of the "ideal" classroom in the way of equipment, books, trained teachers, potentially capable pupils, and acceptable values are present, very little of the desired learning may be taking place in given situations. There are also a great many schools where there are not enough trained teachers, equipment is lacking, and the general delapidation of the physical setting is far from conducive to learning. These may all be viewed as macrocosmic problems but it is apparent that we must also examine the actual behavior within the classrooms in detail if we are to understand the failures (as well as the successes) of the educational system.

My purpose in this paper is to review briefly several studies by teachers and social scientists who have tackled the problem and then to discuss in greater detail the methods and results of my own study of interaction in two Negro kindergartens in a Midwestern urban area.

AMERICAN TEACHERS LOOK AT THEIR SCHOOLS

A number of writers, including teachers themselves, have described classroom behaviors and interactions. They "tell it like it is" and in the process reveal serious deficiencies in the United States educational practices—so serious in some instances as to call into question the entire educational system. Kohl's perceptions of the realities of classroom and curriculum in a Harlem ghetto are instructive in this connection.[4] His description of the textbook situation is vivid:

> There were twenty-five arithmetic books from one publisher and twelve from another, but in the entire school there was no complete set of sixth-grade arithmetic books. A few minutes spent checking the first day's arithmetic assignment showed me that it wouldn't have mattered if a full set had existed, since half the class barely mastered multiplication, and only one child, Grace, who had turned in a perfect paper, was actually ready for sixth-grade arith-

metic. It was as though, encouraged to believe that the children couldn't do arithmetic by judging from the school's poor results in teaching it, the administration decided not to waste money on arithmetic books, thereby creating a vicious circle that made it even more impossible for the children to learn.[5]

Classroom conditions in the form of broken desks and missing textbooks were bad enough but Kohl felt that the more serious problem lay in the discrepancy between the content of instruction and the life experiences of the ghetto children. Faced with this situation, Kohl embarked on several radical innovations. For example, departing from standard procedure, his class produced a newspaper containing highly creative original poetry, comic strips, and essays which exhibited a degree of realism concerning life in the ghetto with its dope addicts, violence, and despair that the school staff reacted to with horror.

In *Death at an Early Age*, another American teacher dwells on the same contrast between the school situation and the learning patterns that educational administrators desire.[6] He notes the subtle imposition of the Reading Teacher's values on the children.

> We were reading out of the phonics book *Wide Doors Open*, a story which none of them seemed to like very much and several were yawning the whole while. . . . When we were done with the story I asked them whether they had liked it, and the thing that astonished me was that almost every one of them pretended that he had. I said: "What did you think of it?" . . . The answers came back: "Interesting"—"humorous"—"colorful"—"adventurous"—and all the rest of the words on the Reading Teacher's list. I twisted my head and I looked up at the list in the back of the room: There they all were. The words that they had given me were all up in neat order on the permissible list. They had not even begun thinking . . . responding.[7]

Many of the empirical descriptions by teachers are concerned with schools among minority groups or other underprivileged populations. In such cases the educational problems may seem to stem from conditions of poverty, overcrowding, and inadequate financing of the school system.

That similar situations may be found in private schools catering to a more privileged class of children is suggested by another teacher, John Holt.[8] He makes the disturbing claim that in spite of the most enlightened curriculum, access to the latest equipment and materials, and other advantages of a well-financed school, school is largely a place where children learn to be stupid.

Holt goes on to discuss what he terms "strategies" that students develop in reaction to teacher methods. He views these "stupidity generating" strategies as responses to the fear of failure and remonstration and draws examples from his own classroom:

> Most children in school are answer-centered rather than problem-centered. They see a problem as a kind of announcement that, far off in some mysterious Answerland, there is an answer, which they are supposed to go out and find. Some children begin right away to try to pry this answer out of the mind of their teacher. Little children are good at this. They know, especially if they are cute-looking, that if they look baffled or frightened enough, teacher will usually tell them what they need to know. This is called "helping them." Bolder children are ready to sally forth into Answerland in a kind of treasure hunt for the answer. For them, the problem is an answer-getting recipe, a set of hints or clues telling them what to do, i.e., instructions for finding buried pirate treasure—go to the big oak, walk a hundred paces in

line with the top of the church steeple, etc. These producers think. "Let's
see, what did I do last time I had a problem like this?" If they remember
their recipes, and don't mix them up, they may be good at the answer-
hunting game, and the answers they bring home may often be the right ones.[9]

Holt also makes the important point that "what goes on in the classroom is not
what the teacher thinks!"

> For years now I have worked with a picture in mind of what my class was
> like. . . . This reality, which I felt I knew, was partly physical, partly mental
> or spiritual. In other words, I thought I knew, in general, what the students
> were doing, and also what they were thinking and feeling. I see now that my
> picture of reality was almost wholly false.[10]

SOCIAL SCIENTISTS LOOK AT AMERICAN SCHOOLS

Teacher's descriptions are certainly of great value since the teacher, continuously
present in the classroom for several hours every day, knows in detail what goes on.
On the other hand, as a directly involved participant in the classroom scene, the
teacher is obviously not the most ideal candidate for effective objective observation. It would appear, then, that full description and analysis of the teaching
process requires a neutral observer who has no teaching duties and is not directly
responsible to the particular school. An increasing number of studies utilize this
sort of nonparticipant observation.

In his study of social status and scholastic achievement, for example, Deutsch
uses observational data as well as indices of pupil self-evaluation, socioeconomic
status, achievement and intelligence to compare the performance of pupils in two
elementary schools.[11] It is the classroom observations that are of interest here.
The recorders were instructed to concentrate upon each student several times during each observed class period, noting his activity and participation. At other times
they were to note the activities of the teacher. At a later stage (after the accumulation of a body of rich narrative data) the observers concentrated on two variables
in particular: motor activity and verbal teacher-related behavior.

After studying several classrooms, interteacher differences were apparent, although there were some general trends—e.g., 80 percent of the classroom day tends
to be channeled into disciplining and organizational details. Within the overall
picture, however, Deutsch notes two kinds of teachers: the "typical" and the
"better than average." Mrs. A illustrates the former:

> November 5—Mrs. A was yelling at different children and the children were
> yelling at each other. Santiago was sawing wood at the back of the room,
> which did not add to the peace and quiet. Although Mrs. A yelled, I could
> not hear a word she said. The general volume of noise in the room was so
> great that you couldn't hear a person speaking if he were more than a foot
> away. Mrs. A said: "I can't force you to work, but don't think you can leave
> your seat and disrupt all of us," to Albert. He was crying. A took him in
> her arms and tried to soothe him. He broke away, stamped his foot, and
> turned around.[12]

Mrs. B. exemplifies the better than average teacher.

> March 9—There are four reading groups, and B helps them one at a time. She
> compliments the children [Edward and Mareline], who read with good ex-
> pression and tells those who are improving how pleased she is. The speed of
> reading in general is very slow. Most of the children stumble over two-

syllable words and frequently have a hard time reading one-syllable words. B helps them to pronounce the words, but she usually gives the children time to sound them out.[13]

Deutsch uses observations only to supplement or complement more quantitative measures. Other studies, such as that reported by Elizabeth Eddy in *Walk the White Line*, rely primarily on observational data.[14] In that project, a team of researchers observed the behavior of pupils and teachers in nine elementary and junior high schools in a big city slum school district. The observations ranged from "model" classes to the so-called "discipline" classes often referred to as "jungle" classes, "zoos," and other derogatory terms. The author presents behavioral data exemplifying the negative attitudes of teachers and staff toward the latter students as well as their more positive behavior toward pupils in the model classrooms. Observations were also made in such other relevant settings as hallways and school cafeterias. A particularly striking finding of the study is the role of "muscle man" that is given to certain older students who are unable to continue on to high school and remain in the lower schools as a special kind of monitor and disciplinarian, as in the following example:

> . . . [Teacher] threatens him [Angel, a male student] several times with being sent to the principal's office. Now she is threatening several of the children by saying that she is going to get John. She leaves the room. As she does so, the noise level decreases considerably and three of the children say. "Oh, oh." One child says, "Here she comes."
> Mrs. Auslander returns, followed by an older Negro boy from the fifth grade. Meanwhile Angel is seated at his desk, clutching it and crying. Unsuccessfully, she tries to pry him loose but finally asks John to please take him. Angel screams. "Leave me alone, leave me alone," and continues to cling to the desk. John finally pries him loose and drags him screaming from the room as the rest of the class watches. [Teacher explains:] "When I use one for an example, the rest behave. It's the only way."[15]

Jules Henry and his research staff also have carried out a number of observational investigations in both Negro and white classrooms in a Midwestern urban center. They recorded time segments of teacher behavior and teacher/pupil interaction noting especially the verbal content of interaction, as well as such aspects of the classroom environment as noise level, condition of the school equipment, and the amount and quality of pupil/pupil interaction. From these materials, Henry extracts certain recurrent themes such as "learning to be stupid, the witch-hunt syndrome, the importance of whiteness in the Negro school," and other elements which seem to reflect United States value orientations. He expresses this interrelation between the classroom and North American culture as follows:

> The elementary school classroom in our culture is one of the most powerful instruments in this effort, for it does not merely sustain attitudes that have been created in the home, but reinforces some, deemphasizes others, and makes its own contribution, prepares the conditions for and contributes toward the ultimate organization of peer and parent-directed attitudes into a dynamically interrelated attitudinal structure supportive of the culture.[16]

The witch-hunt syndrome is formulated from observations of the following type, in which Henry sees the development of attitudes of competitiveness and guilt among others:

> In the extreme back of the room is a desk called the "isolation ward." A child has been placed there for disciplinary reasons. The Vigilance Club of

the class is holding a meeting. The purpose . . . is to teach children to be better citizens. . . . Each child then takes from his or her desk a booklet entitled, *All About Me*. The vice-president calls the name of the child, gets the child's booklet, and places it on the teacher's desk. The president [asks the child], "———, have you been a good citizen this week?" . . . "Name some of the things you have done." . . . President asks the class if it remembers any good things the child has done . . . [then it is] written in the booklet by the teacher. The president then . . . says. . . . "Name the bad things you have done." . . . Child reports . . . class is asked to contribute information . . . [also] written in the booklet by the teacher, who also reprimands the student, registers horror, scolds, etc. . . . numerous children volunteer . . . the child in the "isolation ward" reported some good deeds he had done; the children report some more, and the isolated child was told he would soon be released.[17]

There are also some studies in which social scientists and teachers have collaborated with each other. Smith and Geoffrey, for example, carried out daily (all day) observations in a single classroom in a lower-class white neighborhood for one semester[18]: Smith, a psychologist, notes as precisely as possible the interaction behaviors of the teacher and the pupils, and the content of their verbal interactions. Geoffrey, the teacher, wrote personal accounts at the end of each day and also administered various sociometric and other tests. The purpose of the study was analysis of the classroom social organization, including the establishment of belief and normative systems, the development of role behaviors, and the decision-making processes of the teacher. From these materials it was possible to construct a "flow of the semester" model describing the processes and structures that organize the classroom and make it into a coherent social system.

The studies discussed in this section are similar in scope in that all of the social scientists are interested in describing events in the classroom. Their treatment of data is therefore geared to chronicling and relating happenings within this arena. The data also enables them to relate classroom events to other psychological, social, or cultural variables. While I do not question the importance of a neutral observer, the inferences drawn from such observational data are not conclusively demonstrated to be "representative" of the empirical reality in any quantitative sense nor are they replicable by future researchers. These facts can be related to methodology, in that the behavioral observations are not systematically operationalized. The observers are not sufficiently specific as to which kinds of concrete behaviors led to their generalizations. Although data obtained by a neutral observer are more systematic and objective than those of a teacher-observer, there nevertheless remains the scientific question of the representativeness and replicability of such observational data.

This is not to suggest that the descriptions in these studies are not based upon analytical categorizations of classroom behavior. Deutsch does define verbal and motor behaviors, Smith defines the types of roles enacted by the pupils, and Eddy defines the attributes of teacher and pupil roles in a school system. Henry, too, defines the broad outlines of American culture which he feels are reinforced via particular types of interactional syndromes within the classroom. But systematic observation of the kinds of behaviors one is looking for within specified segments of time can be integrated with social-ecological studies. Operationalization assures replicability, thereby adding another dimension to the above research by demonstrating not only the existence but the quantitative dimensions of the behaviors of teachers and pupils. Better quantification would also facilitate comparative study by assuring that the categories being compared are in fact the same phenomenon in different settings.

Detailed guidelines for the coding of interactions between teachers or parents and children have been suggested by Roger Barker[19] and Edmond Amidon and

John Hough.[20]   Dyck, utilizing the scheme of Barker, carefully defines the be-havior categories he sets out to observe in classroom and familial interactions, with the aim of investigating the properties of the social contact and its attributes.[21]   He concentrates upon parent/child and teacher/pupil interaction in his quantitative analysis of ritual-related behavior, for which he distinguishes twelve raison d'être categories.   On the basis of twelve days of intensive study of selected children's contacts, Dyck is able to demonstrate statistical differences between parents and teachers in their ritual-related interactions with the children.   Some of these are indicated in the following summarizing paragraphs:

> A finding of considerable importance is that the children generally exceeded their parents in originating social interaction. For the most part parents reacted to what the child said or did in their presence and did not plan or determine in advance the kind of behavior they wished from their children. The picture is strikingly different for teacher/child social contacts to which we shall now turn.
>
> Teachers within the classroom greatly exceeded children in the origination of social interaction and in this respect they differed a great deal from parents in the home. This difference between teachers and parents, we believe, is largely a difference between the demands of quite different situations. Teachers by necessity, have a curriculum to follow and, in conjunction with it, lesson plans to make. Parents exceeded teachers on all except one of the *raison d'être* categories which describe the agent as responding to the child. The one exception to this, "responding to a request for information," . . . showed no significant difference between parents and teachers. Teachers give out most of their information without being asked, but there are occa-sions when the child needs to request information.[22]

INTERACTION AND ADAPTATION IN KINDERGARTEN

The observations made by our research team in four Negro schools in a mid-western urban area permit the use of carefully defined categories with which we are able to quantify various specified types of interaction. These categorical anal-yses are based upon observation and recording of interaction between teacher and pupil as well as descriptions of the social ecology of the classroom. The analysis presented here is necessarily incomplete and tentative, based as it is on observations in two kindergartens during the first year of a long-term study of the education of Negro children. It does suggest, however, the potential value of operationally defined observational measures for describing accurately the amount and type of intersections occurring against the background of unfolding classroom social or-ganization during the kindergarten year.

Furthermore, it was possible to compare an additional variable, the goals of the teacher, with our observations.   From long interviews conducted periodically through the first year it became apparent that a crucial problem from the teachers' viewpoint was what they termed their "discipline problem." The teachers stated frequently that they were unable to teach effectively because of the need for con-tinual strict control in the classroom. When questioned about their teaching goals, the teachers were in agreement that individual instruction is important and also that children need to feel that they are a part of a cohesive group. Ideally, then, the teacher works to decrease disruptive activity so that the children will be able to act as a unit, and she will be free to intensify individual relationships. The follow-ing statements are typical. "Our class is successful if they talk and act as a *group*." "I want them to come to me for help, to be *close* to me" (emphasis added).

Methodology

On the basis of the teacher interviews, the decision was made to compare the interviewees' "ideal teacher image" with the pupil/teacher interaction and pupil adaptational patterns of centrality and peripherality within the classroom. Using the interview data, the following two "ideal teacher" hypotheses were developed. The third hypothesis is based upon teachers' frequent statements of their preference for little girls due to their "maturity," "intelligence," and "acquiescence."

1. Over time the amount of positively toned personal interaction will increase. Conversely, the amount of negatively toned interaction will decrease.

2. Centrality (i.e., movement toward the teacher) will increase. Conversely, peripherality (movement away from the teacher, with or without a tendency to form secondary groups) will decrease.

3. Girls will receive as many or more positive responses than the boys and the boys will receive as many or more negative responses than the girls. Furthermore, because of the favoring attitudes of the teachers toward the girls there will be interactions with more of the girls in the class than boys.

By the latter half of the first year, the research staff was making weekly one and a half hour observations in each of the four kindergartens. There were additional observations in the homes of selected children; and team members also attended meetings of the school staff, Parent-Teacher Association functions, and the like, as well as mixing informally with the teachers—e.g., at lunch time. In the classrooms each observer kept a written record of the verbal and nonverbal activities of the teacher and children, noting the child's name, the exact context of the interaction, the teacher's expression and tone of voice, and the exact wording. From these records, it is possible to identify positive and negative responses and to chart the "drift" of children toward or away from the teacher.

For purposes of this analysis, I have used the observers' records from two of the schools, selecting 21 observational periods (totaling 25½ hours) distributed equally among three time samples (September, January, and April) in order to discover changes through the school year. The following rules for coding interactions indicate the definitional base from which quantitative statements that are comparable from one classroom situation to another are made:

A. *Do* code as an interaction.

Pupil, whose identity must be recorded, initiates an action; teacher responds. The response is then coded as (+) or (−) in accordance with the following guidelines.

Positive (+).

1. Pupil is engaged in disruptive or disapproved behavior, teacher ignores it, though aware of it.

2. Teacher has asked pupil a question, pupil answers, and teacher in response indicates approval.

3. Teacher has asked pupil a question, pupil answers, and teacher indicates approval by asking for further information on the subject.

4. Teacher expresses approval for an action by the pupil which occurred in the past.

Negative (−).

1. Pupil is engaged in disruptive or disapproved behavior, teacher indicates disapproval, verbally or nonverbally.

2. Teacher has asked pupil a question, pupil answers, and teacher in no way indicates approval.

3. Teacher has asked pupil a question, pupil answers, teacher points out what is missing or incorrect.

4. Teacher expresses disapproval for an action by the pupil which occurred in the past.

Example of coding of interaction.

If a child was disturbed by another child and went to tell the teacher it should be coded in the following manner, depending upon the responses of the teacher.

(+) for Child A, who was disturbed, if teacher praises him for being a tattle.

(−) for Child A, if teacher reacts negatively to him saying, for example, "Well, if you hadn't been out of your seat, David would not have hit you."

(+) for Child B, who was snitched on, if the teacher ignores his behavior or signifies approval.

(−) for Child B, if the teacher reacts in any negative manner.

The rationale for the coding system postulates that each interaction of a pupil with the teacher has the inherent possibility for the teacher to handle it in either a supportive or nonsupportive manner. It is assumed additionally that the teacher's negative reaction will lessen the child's motivation for further interaction. The opposite effect will occur in a situation of positive reaction by the teacher. As for the question of the congruence between what the coder calls a positive or negative response and what the pupil interprets as negative or positive, I believe the pupil does, in any case, very quickly learn the teacher's expectations and the "rules of the classroom."

The reliability of the coding procedure proved to be high when three data samples were coded by a second individual. The percentage of agreement was 93.5 percent.

Findings

Certain trends emerge from the interaction frequencies for the two kindergartens. As shown in tables 1 and 2, the absolute number of interactions decreases markedly

TABLE 22.1. TEACHER'S RESPONSES TO CHILDREN IN KINDERGARTEN A IN THREE SAMPLE MONTHS

| | SAMPLE MONTHS | | | | | | |
| | SEPTEMBER | | JANUARY | | APRIL | | |
RESPONSE TYPE	(+)	(−)	(+)	(−)	(+)	(−)	TOTAL
High (*N* = 10)							
Gregory*	4	12	4	5	2	7	34
Regina*	12	5	4	4	0	1	26
Harry*	6	8	4	4	2	0	24
Erna*	1	10	0	0	2	2	15
Malcolm*	0	5	1	3	0	1	10
Anna*	2	6	0	1	0	0	9
Rudy*	2	0	1	4	0	0	7
Jackie*	0	0	4	2	0	1	7
Dinah	0	2	1	2	0	2	7
Ella	0	0	1	4	1	0	6
Medium (*N* = 10) 1–3 Responses per child	3	11	2	3	1	0	20
Low (*N* = 11) 0 Responses per child	0	0	0	0	0	0	0
Response Totals	30	59	22	32	8	14	165

*Children who received 80 percent of the teacher's responses in one or more categories.

TABLE 22.2. TEACHER'S RESPONSES TO CHILDREN IN KINDERGARTEN B
IN THREE SAMPLE MONTHS

| | SAMPLE MONTHS | | | | | | |
| | SEPTEMBER | | JANUARY | | APRIL | | |
RESPONSE TYPE	(+)	(−)	(+)	(−)	(+)	(−)	TOTAL
High (N = 19)							
Norman*	1	7	5	18	0	5	36
Raymond*	1	8	5	3	0	4	21
Benny*	5	12	2	1	0	0	20
Clarence*	1	9	3	6	0	0	19
Henry*	0	10	2	2	0	3	17
Cornelia*	0	0	8	7	0	0	15
Lincoln*	2	4	2	0	1	2	11
Jerome*	0	4	2	3	0	1	10
Hank*	1	1	2	4	0	0	8
Jessica*	1	1	4	1	0	1	8
Oleatha*	2	6	0	0	0	0	8
Dave*	0	2	0	1	1	4	8
Dupree*	2	0	2	0	2	0	6
Leon*	1	0	0	5	0	0	6
DeLara*	4	2	0	0	0	0	6
Hollis	0	2	1	2	0	0	5
George*	2	0	3	0	0	0	5
Eugenia	0	0	3	0	0	1	4
Edith*	4	0	0	0	0	0	4
Medium (N = 21)							
1–3 Responses per child	10	9	10	7	1	8	45
Low (N = 11)							
0 Responses per child	0	0	0	0	0	0	0
Response Totals	37	77	54	60	5	29	262

*Children who received 80 percent of the teacher's responses in one or more categories.

between September and April. By April, a few pupils are receiving the majority of the teachers' interactions. There is a corresponding increase in the number of children receiving no responses. As the school year progresses, the teachers appear to spend relatively more and more time giving negatively toned responses, while decreasing both the number and percentage of positive responses. Figure 1 shows graphically this decrease in response frequencies over time, with an accompanying proportional increase in negative responses.

Looking next at centrality/peripherality, we see an increase of activity on the periphery of the classroom over the time span studied. There are some children around the teacher continually (some are high interactors; others are passive, low interactors), but there are usually others engaged in activities apart from the core around the teacher. The number on the periphery seems to increase through the year, as indicated in tables 3 and 4. The tables summarize two actual story-telling events occurring in September and in the following April. They demonstrate the development of different zones of activity in reaction to the patterning of the

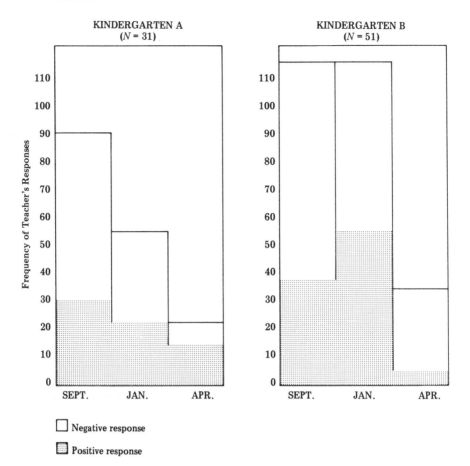

FIGURE 22.1. Frequency of Teacher Responses to Children
in Two Kindergartens in Three Sample Months

teachers' responses. In table 4 especially, we see the action sequence of a small group of boys who drifted in and out of the peripheral zone in a way that is typical of the day-to-day classroom scene in the kindergartens observed.

Finally, table 5 summarizes the data on the teachers' responses in relation to the sex of the child. It is obvious that boys get a larger number and share of the responses in all three sample months, and this is especially true for negative responses. In fact, the boys in Kindergarten B received about five and one-half times as many negative reactions as did the girls, while the boys in Kindergarten A fared only slightly better with almost three times as many negative responses as the girls received.

It is evident that the "ideal teacher" hypotheses derived from interview data are not supported by the observations. Apparently once a stable social structure is established within the classroom, the amount of individual interaction diminishes. The term "stable social structure" in this context appears to refer to a reduction in negative responses by the teacher. If she is being less negative in an overall sense the students must in some way be adjusting to her norms and reacting in an acceptable manner. Tables 1 through 5 and figure 1 indicate that the teacher's in-

TABLE 22.3. CENTRALITY PERIPHERALITY PATTERNS AS TEACHER
TELLS A STORY (SEPTEMBER)

TIME P.M.	TEACHER'S ACTIVITIES[a]	CENTRAL ZONE ACTIVITIES[b]	PERIPHERAL ZONE ACTIVITIES
2:55	gives directions	$N = 40$ all attentive	none
2:56	gives directions	$N = 40$ all attentive	none
2:57	begins narration	$N = 39$ all attentive $\longrightarrow$	*Norman:* walks to piano
2:58	pauses in narration to reprimand Norman	$N = 39$ all attentive	*Norman:* at piano
2:59	continues narration	$N = 40$ all attentive $\longleftarrow$	*Norman:* returns
3:00	concludes narration	$N = 40$ all attentive	to 'C' group none

[a]This kindergarten has combined two classes and has two teachers. During this episode one teacher is in charge and the other is absent.
[b]The attentive boys and girls are seated on the floor in a semi-circle. The teacher is seated on a chair facing them.

teractions focus on fewer children over time and, concurrently, that the absolute magnitude of interaction decreases.

Thus, the ideal goals expressed in interviews are not being actualized within the classroom studied. Moreover, the data show that the teacher never interacts in a personal manner with one-third of the children in one kindergarten and roughly one-fifth of those in the other (see tables 1 and 2). Our other observational data suggest that these children are neither disruptive nor high interactors with the teacher. Some of them actually receive a number of negative responses in the beginning of the school year as the teacher tries to reduce their extreme withdrawal by bringing them back into the group when they leave the classroom, or perhaps hide behind the piano; but the negative responses lessen as the children become able to join the group on their own, e.g., Jay, Billy, Laura, and Rosetta in table 1.

There is a smaller group of children who have high interaction initially with the teacher, but whose subsequent interactions seem to take two general forms. First there are some such as Norman, who interact less with the teacher over time but concurrently engage in many more activities apart from the group around the teacher. Other high interactors (e.g., Regina) begin the year with many positive responses and remain in the central group despite a reduction in responses from the teacher. Whatever the particular pattern, the process can be viewed as the pupil's adaptation to the teacher's responses to them.

The adaptive response we term peripherality has several interesting concomitants. Not only do these individuals (usually boys) remove themselves from the teacher but they generally form a group that engages in its own activities. These boys in the peripheral zone, though often compelled to converse in whispered tones, appear to get a lot of satisfaction from their mutual activities. But these activities further remove them from the teacher and consequently from the center of the teaching process. The decrease in the magnitude of negative responses to children such as Norman (table 2) between February and April indicates that as the child moves to

TABLE 22.4. CENTRALITY PERIPHERALITY PATTERNS AS TEACHER TELLS A STORY (APRIL)

TIME A.M.	TEACHER'S ACTIVITIES[a]	CENTRAL ZONE ACTIVITIES[b]	PERIPHERAL ZONE ACTIVITIES
10:42	continues narration ignoring Raymond	$N = 34$ all attentive	$N = 7$ *Raymond:* goes to teacher, returns to 'P' group *Henry, Leon:* play together *Roy:* isolate *Jerome, Dave, Chad:* wrestle
10:43	pauses in narration to tell Roy to return	$N = 35$ all attentive	N = 6 *Dave, Raymond, Jerome:* talk *Henry, Leon, Chad:* isolates ⟵ *Roy:* returns to 'C' group
10:44	pauses in narration to tell Leon to return	$N = 35$ all attentive	N = 6 *Dave, Henry, Leon:* play together *Jerome, Raymond, Chad:* isolates
10:45	continues narration	$N = 35$ all attentive	N = 6 *Dave, Henry, Leon:* play together *Jerome, Raymond, Chad:* talk together
10:46	continues narration while glaring at Henry and Dave	$N = 38$ all attentive ⟵	N = 3 *Dave, Henry, Leon:* return to 'C' group *Jerome, Raymond, Chad:* talk together
10:47	concludes narration	$N = 38$ all attentive	N = 3 *Jerome, Raymond, Chad:* talk together

[a]This kindergarten has combined two classes and has two teachers. During this episode one teacher is in charge and the other is absent.
[b]The attentive boys and girls are seated on the floor in a semi-circle. The teacher is seated on a chair facing them.

TABLE 22.5. TEACHER'S RESPONSES BY SEX OF CHILD IN TWO KINDERGARTENS IN THREE SAMPLE MONTHS

	SAMPLE MONTHS						
	SEPTEMBER		JANUARY		APRIL		
RESPONSE TYPE	(+)	(−)	(+)	(−)	(+)	(−)	TOTAL
Kindergarten A							
Boys ($N = 14$)	14	31	15	20	5	9	94
Girls ($N = 17$)	16	28	7	12	3	5	71
Kindergarten B							
Boys ($N = 24$)	17	67	30	48	4	25	191
Girls ($N = 27$)	20	10	24	12	1	4	71
Response Total							427

the periphery, the teacher accepts his peer-group interaction probably because it does not disturb the core group in the central zone around her.

Children like Norman in Kindergarten B or Gregory and Regina in Kindergarten A are at first allowed to remain close to the teachers, throughout the day; but as time goes by, their attempts to dominate the teacher's time and attention elicit quite a few negative responses. The problem can be illustrated from a recording of the activities of Regina taken in February during a fifteen-minute period in which the class was being given art instructions. Regina interrupted the teacher ten times and talked with other children three times. The teacher in turn answered Regina five times, interrupted her twice, praised her once, and ignored her three times.

One of the most significant findings of this research is the importance of the pupil's initial kindergarten experiences. If the child does not interact personally with the teacher in September, it is fairly certain that he will not be a high interactor the following April. Similarly, the child who initially receives a high proportion of negative responses will not later be transformed into a recipient of high positive responses. On the other hand, a student receiving high positive interactions in September is likely to remain in the core group around the teacher throughout the year, becoming an active participant in most of the teaching process.

It would appear that there are actually three kinds of learning occurring in the classroom. In the central group are the active learners who, by virtue of their high interaction with the teacher, are able to benefit from instant feedback, immediate reinforcement and the high repetition of the teacher's instructions and directions. Passive members of this central group are also exposed to the lessons presented by the teacher and the behaviors of the "star" performers; these can be labeled vicarious learners. The third group, operating in the peripheral zone, are no doubt learning a great deal, but it is not the kind of learning desired by the teacher since it misses out on crucial areas of socialization. The peripheral learner is not in direct contact with the reading and arithmetic lessons or other necessary teaching experiences essential to later scholastic achievement. Since the general structure of elementary school instruction is based upon a sequential model in which lower levels must be mastered before progression to the next step, these peripheral pupils will almost certainly be severely handicapped when they are expected to meet the requirements of the first and later grades.

At present we can only form tentative hypotheses concerning the cues by which the teachers form an initial judgment of the child. This aspect of pupil/teacher relation will be studied more thoroughly as the project continues, but it seems reasonable to state now that teachers in these schools rarely change their initial perception of the child formed at the beginning of the school year.[23]

CONCLUSION

Though teachers themselves have critically discussed and illustrated the gap between goals and actuality in United States education, it is clear that careful research is necessary in order to generalize about school system and classroom. There have been several classroom studies which, though highly valuable, lack comparability and replicability. Statistical comparison is possible only when the units of behavior under observation have been operationally defined. This permits the testing of clearly specified hypotheses in such a way that others can duplicate the research and be assured that parallel data will be gathered in other settings.

The comparison of two Negro kindergartens discussed in this paper is based upon careful interactional analyses which take the emerging social structural features in which the interactions occur into account. The interdependence of the interactional and socioecological data is seen, for example, in the relation of the higher frequency of positive responses to the children seated closest to the teacher and conversely the decrease in negative responses to those who crystallized into a peripheral group later in the school year.

This interdependence is also demonstrated in the relationship between negative and positive teacher response and pupil identity. The selection of pupil-initiated behavior as the unit of analysis indicated clearly that it is not only "what the pupil is doing" which generates a negative or positive response from the teacher but also "who the pupil is."

Operationalization of the types of behaviors to be coded as negative or positive, as in this study, assures that a parallel and comparative study of not only pupil/teacher, but also child/parent or child/child interactions is possible. Furthermore, information observed and recorded of behaviors such as those labeled "centrality" or "peripherality" could then be related to the interactional data.

The differences between what teachers had expressed in interviews as their goals and their observed actions suggest the desirability of comparative study of the quantitative behavioral data and the perceptions of the teacher. Such a study could compare not only one "real" classroom with another but could also measure quite accurately the gap between the "behavior" of the teacher and the "ideals" of the teacher.

NOTES AND REFERENCES

1. See, for example, Patricia C. Sexton, *The American School, A Sociological Analysis* (Englewood Cliffs, N.J.: Prentice-Hall, 1967); Seymour Harris, ed., *Educational and Public Policy* (Berkeley: McCutchan, 1965); and Robert J. Havighurst, *Education in Metropolitan Areas* (Boston: Allyn & Bacon, 1966).
2. See, for example, Jules Henry, *Culture against Man* (New York: Vintage Books, 1963); Leonard Covello, *The Social Background of the Italo-American School Child* (Leiden, Netherlands: E. J. Brill, 1967); and Edgar Z. Friedenberg, *Coming of Age in America* (New York: Random House, 1963).
3. See, for example, Robert J. Havighurst, *Comparative Perspectives on Education* (Boston: Little, Brown and Co., 1968); John Singleton, *Nichū, A Japanese School* (New York: Holt, Rinehart and Winston, 1967); and Jan Myrdal, *Report from a Chinese Village* (New York: Random House, 1965).
4. Herbert Kohl, *36 Children* (New York: New American Library, 1967). Additional sources are James Herndon, *The Way It Spozed to Be* (New York: Bantam Books, 1968); and Bel Kaufman, *Up the Down Staircase* (Englewood Cliffs, N.J.: Prentice-Hall, 1964).
5. Kohl, *36 Children*, p. 9.
6. Jonathan Kozol, *Death at an Early Age* (Boston: Houghton Mifflin, 1967).
7. Ibid., p. 167.
8. John Holt, *How Children Fail* (New York: Pitman, 1964).
9. Ibid., p. 9.
10. Ibid., p. 21.
11. Martin Deutsch, *Minority Group and Class Status As Related to Social and Personality Factors in Scholastic Achievement*, Society for Applied Anthropology, Monograph No. 2, 1960.
12. Ibid., p. 24.
13. Ibid.
14. Elizabeth M. Eddy, *Walk the White Line* (Garden City, N.Y.: Doubleday, 1967).
15. Ibid., p. 119.
16. Jules Henry, "Attitude Organization in Elementary School Classrooms," in *Education in American Culture*, ed. George Spindler (New York: Holt, Rinehart and Winston, 1963), pp. 192–214.
17. Ibid., p. 195.
18. Louis M. Smith and William Geoffrey, *The Complexities of an Urban Classroom* (New York: Holt, Rinehart and Winston, 1968).

19. Roger G. Barker, ed., *The Stream of Behavior* (New York: Appleton-Century-Crofts, 1963).
20. Edmond J. Amidon and John B. Hough, *Interactional Analysis* (Reading, Mass.: Addison-Wesley, 1967).
21. Arthur J. Dyck, "The Social Contacts of Some Midwest Children with Their Parents and Teachers," in Barker, *Stream of Behavior*, pp. 78–98.
22. Ibid., p. 96.
23. A careful analysis and test of the effect of teacher's perceptions upon pupil performance is found in Robert Rosenthal, *Pygmalion in the Classroom* (New York: Holt, Rinehart and Winston, 1968).

23 / Ceremony, Rites, and Economy in the Student System of an American High School

Jacquetta Hill Burnett

Recently, John L. Fischer described as "common sense" the view that the progress of civilization leads to the reduced importance of ritual.[1] If one changes "progress of civilization" to "urbanization," Fischer's description seems to understate the professional respectability of the proponents of this position. Only five years ago, Max Gluckman expressed the view that "modern urban life" is correlated with the disappearance of the ritualization of social relations.[2] Gluckman said:

> I consider that rituals of the kind investigated by Van Gennep are "incompatible" with the structure of modern urban life.[3]

He goes on to say, with respect to helping people of the secular urbanized world in their transitions from one status to another:

> ...I do not believe that it [i.e., help] can come from the tribal type of *rites de passage* in which social relationships are ritualized to assist persons at what are defined as crises.[4]

On the basis of nearly a year's field work in a small midwestern high school in 1960-61, I wish here not only to present a description of one aspect of the culture of an American secondary school, but also to question on empirical grounds the extinction of ritual as an effective, functional device in urbanized societies.[5] In fact, the empirical extension of the concepts "ceremony" and "ritual" was critical to the analysis of the calendar of events of the high school, although the clearly nonsupernatural character of the symbolism associated with the student's public events placed those data in a rather awkward relationship to the conceptual schema usually employed to analyze ritual and ceremony. By most of the traditional anthropological canons for using "ritual" and "ceremony," many of the most dramatic and behaviorally significant events of the student system would have to be relegated to the analytic insignificance of the general category, "custom." Yet is it not legitimate conceptually to view certain student activities as ceremonies and rituals?

THE CONCEPTUAL RATIONALE

When focusing upon the action dimensions of these high school events, I found practices that readily fit Nadel's action criterion for ritual: "... any type of behavior may thus be said to turn into 'ritual' when it is stylized or formalized, and made repetitive in that form."[6] Moreover, following on careful attention to modes, order, and frequencies of interaction, I found I could readily distinguish "rites of intensification" and "rites of passage" in these events, in accord with the Chapple and Coon criteria.[7] Indeed, Van Gennep's original schema of separation, transition, and incorporation as phases of rites of passage also was helpful analytically when applied to certain parts of the data.[8]

The quandary over the conceptual status of the data is most marked in the consideration of the associated belief system. When one pursues the course, so eloquently and persuasively recommended by Geertz, of concentrating on the symbolic system, one often interviews students in vain for anything more elaborate than "we do it because it's fun" or "we do it because it was done that way last year."[9] This minimal development of myth and belief might cast doubt on the ritual status of the associated events were it not for Kluckhohn's demonstration that, although ritual often is associated with elaborate mythical development, this need not always be the case.[10] More recently, Lévi-Strauss, in his penetrating essay on the totemic illusion, argues that because nonsentient norms, or customs, determine the sentiments of the individuals in whatever society, the individual can rarely assign cause to his conformity, other than to say that "things have always been like this, and he does what people before him did."[11] Feeble elaboration of rationale, then, need not exclude the associated action systems or events from the field of ritual phenomena.

Recently, Jack Goody, Robin Horton, and S. H. Posinsky have made relevant reexaminations of the issue of the conceptual relationships among religion, magic, ceremony, ritual, belief, and action.[12] In particular, Jack Goody's clarification of the definitional problem of religion and ritual seems to justify the conceptual decision to view certain student activities as ritual events. He uses the insight that much magico-religious behavior is nonrational, rather than irrational.

Goody's general purpose is to advance the development of a cross-culturally useful data language, and to advance the concern of anthropological science with the study of conditions under which similar entities recur in different populations. When Goody analyzes magic, religion, science, ceremony, and ritual with respect to one another and with respect to rationality of belief, he is concerned with developing a more powerful etic orientation, or observer's data language and frame of reference.[13] One of the key problems of an adequate etic, or actor's, frame of thought is to develop a system that is sufficiently isomorphic to all emic systems of the world to allow the objective transformation of the latter into the former, and at the same time have an etic system of thought that is sufficiently powerful and discriminating to bring observed phenomena into theoretically significant relationship to other phenomena.

Goody's purpose is particularly salutary with respect to the analytic dilemma of what to do with student behaviors that in action dimension look like ritualistic and ceremonial behavior, but under the more current canons of analysis of ritual and ceremony would not be included there. Goody devotes patient attention to a range of western theorists' positions—Durkheim, Malinowsky, Frazer, Radcliffe-Brown, Parsons, and even others—on the definitions of magic and religion and rational and irrational distinctions in magical and religious phenomena. He finds that our understanding of magic and religious behavior has been confounded by the assumption that certain distinctions are universal to the actor-oriented—or to the emic—standpoint, when as a matter of fact, the distinction is a vestige of our own folk taxonomy intruding upon the observer's frame of reference. He goes to careful lengths to show that such category systems as sacred profane, natural supernatural, rational irrational are not universals to the actor's views within all cultural systems, but are observer frames of reference. Not only have the actor and the observer frames of reference in other cultures been confused with our own emic perspective, or folk taxonomy, with a resultant retarding of the development of cross-cultural theory and an intersubjective data language of religion and ritual with respect to other cultures: it also seems to have inhibited our ability to relate that theory to new emergences in western culture.

In agreement with Radcliffe-Brown, Goody holds that ceremonial has to do with "collective action required by custom." It is an elaborate conventional form of expression of feeling, not confined, however, to religious occasions. It is public in nature and consists of ritual acts. He says

> ... ceremonial may ... be used to refer to those collective actions required by custom, performed on occasions of change in social life. Thus a ceremonial consists of a specific sequence of ritual acts, performed in public.[14]

Goody notes that *ritual* often has wider reference than magico-religious behavior. The fundamental criterion of ritual is the idea of formality of procedure or action that either *is not* directed toward a pragmatic end, or *if so* directed, will fail to achieve the intended aim. Goody notes with approval that Nadel views ritual inclusively to apply to any type of excessively formal action. Religious ritual, however, under which Nadel also includes magic, covers only those excessively formal acts where the means end relationship is deemed inadequate by empirical standards. Goody suggests, however, that incongruous rigidity in itself is also to some extent empirically inadequate. He suggests that Pareto's view that much magico-religious behavior is *nonrational*, rather than irrational, can be used to conceptualize ritual behavior in which the means end relationship is deemed inadequate merely because of its incongruous rigidity.

For Goody, then, ritual is not simply equated with religious action, but is a more general category of action. If ritual activities are addressed to some mystical or supernatural power, they *are* religious activities. Some religious acts may be irrational, as is the case of many forms of sacrifice and prayer, because they have a pragmatic end which the procedures fail to achieve, or achieve for other reasons than the actors suppose. Religious acts may be nonrational, as in many public celebrations. But in both types, the activities are addressed to some mystical or supernatural power. Magical action falls within the general category of ritual, but is essentially irrational in any particular case since it has a pragmatic end which its procedures fail to achieve or achieve for reasons other than the patient, or possibly the practitioner, supposes.

There is ritual which is neither religious, because it does not assume the existence of spiritual beings, nor magic, because it is not aimed at some empirical end. Goody emphasizes that the absence of explicit empirical ends for nonmagico-religious ritual does not preclude its having recognized purpose within the actor's frame of reference, as well as having some "latent" purpose or function from the observer's standpoint.

The nonmagico-religious category of ritual may include such things as civil marriage ceremonies, rituals of birth and death in secular households or societies, and the rituals of family living described by Bossard and Boll, as well as rituals of liquidation as described by Leites and Beraut, and other similar types of formalized interpersonal behavior.[15] I include here also the rituals connected with high school football and basketball homecoming, graduation, junior and senior proms, freshmen initiations, senior trips, and sundry other ceremonial events in the student systems of American high schools. Usually these ritual acts are nonmagico-religious and are nonrational rather than irrational. By accepting the conceptual advances of Kluckhohn, Goody, and others, the public events of the student system fall safely and logically within the perimeter of the concepts of ritual, rite, and ceremony.

Turning now to the culture of the American high school, what are these ceremonial events like? How do they fit with the other aspects of the institutional context to form that set of people, relations, and events which I have called the student subsystem?

RITUAL AND CEREMONIAL IN AN AMERICAN HIGH SCHOOL

The ceremonies and rites of the American high school which I studied were a regular part of extracurricular or student activities. Beyond the formal organization of work and the ubiquitous informal network of clique relationships, there were associational sets (or student clubs) of three general types that sponsored, planned, and carried out the annual calendar of activities. The most dominant type was formed out of the age-grade statuses in the high school. The second type grew out of the subject matter and work of formal courses in the regular curriculum, though the activities of these associations often seemed far removed from that subject matter. Finally, there was a type formed out of participation in interschool sports competition—a type with only one member, the Varsity Club.

Although teachers participated in these associations and activities as advisors and counselors and stressed their importance in teaching students a "sense of responsibility" (i.e., independence of initiative and decision making), participation by the teachers was a matter of tradition and expectation, not of contract. The fact that they, as a body, could have withdrawn from participation, emphasized the semiformal character of this extracurricular sector of the institution.

Although the activities and events of the system were patterned into an annual cycle, for each age-grade or year-class status there was a four-year cycle of changing relationships to the annual cycle of student activities. From freshman initiation through sophomore, junior, and senior years, each year-class group experienced increasing opportunities for mobility in the student prestige hierarchy, increasing access as a group to commercial enterprises of the system, increasing financial affluence of the class-group, increasing political power and responsibility for important ceremonial events, and increasing opportunity to engage in student self-regulation of the subsystem.

The temporal aspect of the student system is diagrammed in figure 1, in which I have tried to summarize the system's time cycles and phases of activities. Moving around the circle clockwise, one band notes the rites of passage, with freshman initiation occurring in September and a cluster of ceremonies in May marking separation of the senior class from the high school system. One group enters in the fall and is incorporated into the student subsystem, and an older group departs during the spring. The next inner band notes the annual cycle of rites of intensification. At several points it is related to the sports seasons and to the traditional seasonal calendar in the center circle. The black bars in the circle $A-G$ show the various significant ceremonies that mark a change in the character of interaction, in the configuration of relationships, and in the nature of activity.

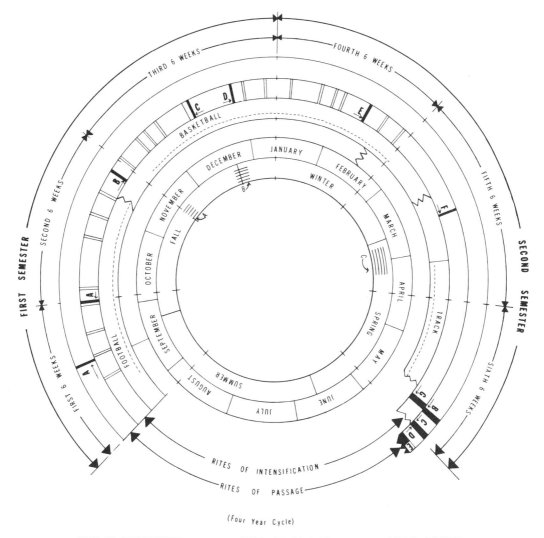

(Four Year Cycle)

RITES OF INTENSICATION	RITES OF PASSAGE	SCHOOL HOLIDAYS
A. HOMECOMING	**A.** FRESHMAN INITIATION	**A.** THANKSGIVING
B. FOOTBALL BANQUET	**B.** BACCALAUREATE	**B.** CHRISTMAS
C. CHRISTMAS DANCE	**C.** GRADUATION	**C.** EASTER
D. NEW YEAR'S EVE PARTY	**D.** ALUMNI BANQUET	
E. SWEETHEART DANCE	**E.** SENIOR TRIP	
F. ATHLETES BANQUET		
G. HONORS DAY		
☐. PEP RALLIES		

FIGURE 23.1. Time Cycles and Phases of Activities

AN ILLUSTRATION OF STUDENT RITUAL

Here we will first consider in some detail one of the ceremonies, the pep rally, to illustrate the criteria and data used in analysis of these ceremonial events. The pep rallies involved full assemblage of the high school body to "work up school spirit," as the explanation usually went, just before an extramural sports event. The pep rally for football season struck me as somewhat more elaborate than the ones preceding basketball. No pep rallies preceded track meets, an incongruity that will be explained later. The rite was a regular, recurrent part of student life and very much a mainstay of the student system.

Chapple and Coon's theory of ritual is very much concerned with crisis in systems and with interaction of participants as the basic component structure.[16] To understand the systemic significance of ritual, one must take note of who interacts with whom and of the regular habitual order, duration, and temporal distribution of their actions with respect to one another. Human social systems are continuously faced with crisis in their need to change the characteristic modes of interaction to carry out the instrumental requirements of a living system, and to meet shifts in their internal aspects as well as in the external environment. Disturbances, or required changes, in an interaction relationship result in crisis and adjustment of the individual or of a group to the new arrangement and frequency of interaction.

Adjustment to change or to crisis may be secured either through associational interaction or through ritual. Associations hold a very special place in the Chapple and Coon theory of institutional equilibrium, but the main points here are that crisis is an everyday reality in social systems and that both associational interaction and ritual interaction can be used to restore effective interactive equilibrium. Rites of passage are used at some points of crisis in the individual life cycle and rites of intensification are used to restore the interactive balance for a group when some change of conditions or disturbance effects all or a part of the members of a system. Through the rituals of the ceremony, rites of passage provide the individual with practice in new orders and distribution of interaction entailed in a change in his status in the system. The ritual in the ceremony of rites of intensification provides group members with a dramatic presentation of habitual relationships associated with the activities of the system. Shifts in required activities bring about crisis through demanding changes in the interaction needed to carry out the activities. A rite of intensification is one functional device for carrying off the shifts in habitual relationships. Pep rallies, then, are ritual means of quickly carrying the students through a transition in interaction from work activity and the everyday relations of daily school life to the characteristically different relationships of extramural athletic events, when students relate to large numbers of members of the community and relate to one another in somewhat different ways.

The course of the events during football season can illustrate the characteristic order and interrelationship of aspects of ceremonial events. Football games were held on Friday evenings around 8:00 P.M. out-of-doors under floodlights. (Basketball games were also held in the evenings, but on Tuesday as well as Friday in a large new gymnasium in a new section of the school building.) During football season, the order of events of the day ran its familiar course until a special bell rang ten minutes earlier than the usual dismissal bell. At this signal, the entire high school population, including teachers, assembled in the old gymnasium. When all were assembled, the school principal called the group to order and made a few announcements. Then the cheerleaders, as a group, trotted before the audience, and in well-practiced formation initiated cheers to the students and led them in highly synchronized cheers, first for the team, then for the coaches. They retired and one or two of the varsity players (always either seniors or juniors in class standing) stood before the group and gave a pep talk on the coming game. The talks always ended on a note of determination to strive to win. The player was greeted with a cheer; his talk was sometimes interrupted with cheers and always closed with a cheer from students. Next, the head coach or assistant coach gave a pep talk always concerned with the reputation of this week's opponent and the good features and improvements in the home team. The coach's talk always closed with a statement of his confidence in the players and their determination to play hard and to play to win. Finally, he usually alluded to the helpfulness toward victory of the spirit and support of the rest of the students. Then, the cheerleaders led the entire student body in more cheers and, as the dismissal bell rang, the students filed out, cheering as they went.

As the girls and boys dispersed to walk home or ride home in bus or car, there was an unusual degree of segregation of boys and girls. The occupants of cars were particularly noticeable for their sexual homogeneity. According to training rules, the players reported to me, the boys on the team were to go straight home to rest and prepare themselves for the game. Those boys were not to engage in interaction with girls from the time they departed from school until after the game. As the boys usually put it, "You aren't supposed to be seen with girls."

The male–female segregation actually began during the pep rally. In the old gymnasium, there were bleachers running the length of the south side of the gym; they were separated into an east and a west side by the entrance and steps leading down into the gymnasium. During pep rallies, the students always sat on the west side of the bleachers; the teachers, except for coaches, always sat on the east side; the coaches sat with their players. The students further segregated themselves; the players sat toward the west end of the west bleachers near the playing floor of the gymnasium; the boys who weren't on the team sat at the back of the west bleachers from the center aisle to the west wall. The girls sat toward the front of the west bleachers nearest the aisle and well separated from the players. The cheerleaders, all girls, sat on the lowest bleachers adjoining the gymnasium floor directly in front of the other girls. The students were further organized spatially through the tendency of students to cluster near one another in clique groups.

During the evening event in the course of the game, the social relations and orders of action that were prominent in the pep rally occurred repeatedly. For example, players were segregated from other students, particularly from girls; cheerleaders initiated and synchronized cheers during the course of the game; and students were not subject to their usual relationship to teachers and other adults. And those who acted as vendors of drink and food, had a different type of relationship with adults.

After home games, a student dance, called a soc hop, was usually held in the gymnasium with music provided on phonograph records. At this event players and females once more interacted with one another. The dances were called "soc hops" because they were held on the sleek, waxed perfection of the basketball court that must not be marred or scratched with ordinary shoes, thus requiring that students remove their shoes and dance in stocking feet.

The mode of activity and interactive relationships characteristic of evening events like this were markedly different from the mode of activity and interaction that characterized the school workday. Clearly, the ritual of the pep rally ceremony could be said to help with the quick transition by organizing, dramatizing, and actively illustrating the change in interaction and relationship.

OTHER STUDENT CEREMONIALS

The football banquet marked the end of football season. The banquet—for football players, their coaches, and the school principal and superintendant—was a boisterous, rowdy, stag affair that signaled a change in the characteristic mode of interaction among players. Relationships with other students, among community members, and between players and spectators did not change enough from football to basketball seasons to require ritual dramatization for student body and community. The rite, therefore, involved only the players and the coaches, who were deeply affected by the cessation of certain modes of relationship and interaction.

The Christmas dance and New Year's Eve dance related to the culture-wide temporal event of the Christmas season. They marked the beginning and close, respectively, of a long recess from schoolwork and from regular modes of interaction among students. The Sweetheart Dance anticipated the end of "soc-hop season," the Friday evening dances that followed home games.

The athletes' banquet, in contrast to the football banquet, was sponsored by parents and attended by parents as well as students and players. It posed an interesting challenge to the view that rites of intensification mark changes in group social relations. One asks why did it occur before, rather than after, track season? The explanation lies in the fact that track meets were held in the afternoon immediately after school rather than later in the evening. Despite several winning track seasons, few students attended, only a handful of adults attended, no money-earning enterprises were operated, and no cheerleaders or other means were used to organize spectator response. Most heads of households drove to nearby cities to their work and, consequently, did not arrive in time for events beginning around half past three in the afternoon. Track meets after school just didn't fit the community time schedule. The significant change in interaction for the community occurred with the cessation of basketball games, which were evening games they could attend. It is this which was marked by a rite of intensification—the community-sponsored athletes' banquet.

Homecoming, which occurred in the fall just a few weeks after the school year began, was an event that brought together students, former students, and the community in general, and that gave expression to every significant relationship in the student subsystem—because successful execution of the ceremony *demanded* the operation of all these relationships. The political dominance of the seniors was reflected in the fact that they were entirely in charge of planning, organizing, and supervising Homecoming. From the building of parade floats, through the ritual beginning of Homecoming with a bonfire and snake dance on Thursday, a parade in town on Friday afternoon, the half-time activities at the football game Friday evening, the decoration of the gymnasium, sponsorship of the Homecoming Dance, to the ritual climax of the Homecoming ceremony with the crowning of the King and Queen of Homecoming, seniors were in charge. But they relied on the cooperation of all the student organizations in the school. By the time the first preparations for Homecoming began in late September, positions in the various associations had been assigned personnel, from presidents to minor standing committees. Homecoming activities were handled within the permanent associations through both special and standing committees. But the structures were not activated and put into motion until Homecoming and its preparation, colored by intensity of feeling, deadline rush, and anxiety for success, touched the whole system with a sense of crisis and the need to mobilize. The organizational system then moved into forward gear as the senior class offered a monetary prize for the best float. The year-class, age-graded associations were the liveliest competitors in that contest. In addition, whether or not they organized to build floats, *all* associations carried out elections to nominate a king and queen candidate—although seniors always won the final crowns. The student council had exercised its function as a control for allocating money-earning enterprises. The community at several points assumed its role of interested, responsive spectator to the knowledge, performances, and products of the high school students.

Details might be added, but it seems clear that Homecoming was a system-wide rite of intensification. The usual role positions of the associations were filled; certain organizations had begun to operate; year-class groups were poised to behave in a new status in relationship to the total system. But without a very dramatic challenge it might have required a long time for the complex interdependencies and synchronization of activity and positional duties to work in smooth, orderly fashion. All these new characteristics of interaction amount to a crisis of the system that is resolved through carrying out a complex event in the form of ritualized, traditional patterns of action and interdependencies. In accordance with Chapple and Coon's view of what a rite of intensification does, everyone gets practice in the patterns of action and interaction that will be characteristic of associational work throughout the rest of the year.

RITUAL, CEREMONY, AND THE STUDENT ECONOMIC SYSTEM

Turning finally to the manner in which the entire ceremonial system was supported by and related to the student economic system, one must consider a special rite of passage: the senior trip. The senior trip was the main objective in the money-earning activities of each year-class. Every year, after going through several ceremonial events that dramatized the separation of the seniors from the high school system, the senior class departed on a three- or four-day trip. Accompanied only by the class sponsor, bus driver, and their respective spouses, the seniors rode to a resort in the Missouri Ozarks where other senior classes from other high schools also gathered for three or four days of "gay abandon." This was the final event of the school year and the final student activity of the seniors' high school career. It showed the characteristic isolation that Van Gennep found associated often with the transition or marginal phase in his tripartite schema.

Though the beliefs associated with most of these ceremonial events mentioned above were skimpy to nonexistent, there was a rather more elaborate development of myth in connection with the senior trip. These myths, told more often by boys than girls, centered on tales of curfew violation, smoking, drinking, and sex. Ex-seniors emphatically declared to me that there was much fiction and little fact in these stories. Perhaps each group found that the outside world of "peerdom"—members of which they met at the resort—was little more marked by drunken busts, nocturnal merry-making, and sexual abandon than their own world. But I think, although I cannot prove, that the myths were perpetuated by young post-high school males of the community.

The senior trip was the keystone of the student economy and the integrating goal of the student system. That this economic goal took priority over all other goals was reflected in the student council's policy of allocating the best and the greatest number of money-making enterprises to the seniors and juniors, in that order. I would not argue that economic motive was the only propelling force of the system. For example, yearning for prestige among their peers and within their immediate social milieu surely impelled students to expend thought, time, and energy in student activities. Yet the economic goal of financing special events of the year welded atomistic desires into group effort. Each student association had a main annual event around which to muster the efforts and economic enterprise of its members. However, the main event around which each year-class association organized its economic activities was the senior trip which was quadrennial rather than annual. By providing motive and direction over a four-year cycle rather than an annual cycle, the senior trip provided the focus for an intergenerational tradition which upperclassmen could transmit to lowerclassmen, thus forming a pattern of enculturation for the student system as a whole.

The most common means of earning money was through selling food, and sometimes services. Except where long tradition had given another association a particularly lucrative resource, class associations, especially seniors, were granted the more profitable enterprises.

The frequent coincidence of entertainment activities and relationships with commercial activities and relationships was a salient characteristic of the system. The most successful entertainment events from the commercial point of view were the athletic events, for the needs of the crowd during the games were fulfilled by the goods sold by student associations. School spirit and school pride notwithstanding, the better the team the bigger the crowd; the bigger the crowd the more popcorn, candy, hot dogs, soda pop, and coffee sold. Thus, a good team, along with star athletes, not only carried responsibility for the reputation of the school *vis-à-vis* other schools; it was an economic asset to the student system.

There were other ways of making money from persons outside the student body than selling refreshments, but most of these required an assemblage of persons from the community. A group could earn money through admissions to dances, but the size of the crowd was critical. The sponsoring group hired an orchestra and a certain minimum attendance was required before the initial investment could be recovered and a profit made. Scheduling the dance after an athletic event was one of the best means of assuring at least this minimum profitable attendance. In light of this relationship it does not seem entirely unwarranted to suggest that between the athletic events and the student systems there was a kind of ecological connection.

Without the participation of adults and community members as spectators, these events would have gradually disappeared from the calendar of events. Through student activities, adults and parents were involved in socialization into that special style we have come to call "independence training." The adult was spectator to the performance, learning, success or failure of the young. Much of this learning was from peers, but is was then tested against the positive or negative response of adults as spectators. The adults in the community, through their interest in local high school athletics and other entertainment events, ultimately influenced and affected the value system of the students in the school—not in a one-to-one, adult-to-young relationship, but through a complex network of influence.

CONCLUSION

At the empirical level, this study challenges the position that rites and ceremonies of "status change" necessarily disappear with the rise of secular urban institutions. The analysis is based on the premise that many current arguments for the disappearance of such rites and ceremonies resemble in certain respects earlier arguments for definitions of totemism that totally divorce primitive institutions from those of modernity.[17] The act of assuming their disappearance places an intellectual blindfold upon the investigation of this aspect of behavior in modern institutions. The cultural patterns and practices of various types of school environments provide a context in modern society where both proponents and opponents of the disappearance of rites of transition can test their ideas empirically in the interest of resolving the problem.

Some may argue that the rural setting of the high school studied here is a survival from the past and that data from this community are not relevant to the modern urban world. Actually, this type of rural community is a necessary part of the urban scene. The mechanized, market-oriented, commercialized agriculture and the salient presence of commuting by nonfarmers to nearby urban centers for employment declare this community's membership in the broad urban scene and the relevance of this study to urban society. This is the agricultural sector of an urbanized society.

The town and school are admittedly small and highly homogeneous. These facts may limit the extension of any generalization from this setting. We know, however, that elaborate ceremonial cycles characterize secondary schools across the United

States, although the interrelationships among ceremonial cycle, the academic work system, clique structure, immediate community, and association structure may vary greatly with the heterogeneity and size of the high school population. But this study does raise the question of what part ritual palys in the multichartered, multi-grouped institutions that educate, socialize, and enculturate young people into modern megalopolises.

NOTES AND REFERENCES

1. John L. Fischer, "Psychology and Anthropology," in B. S. Siegel, ed., *Biennial Review of Anthropology* (Stanford: Stanford University Press, 1965), p. 284.
2. Max Gluckman, "Les Rites de Passage," in M. Gluckman, ed., *Essays on the Ritual of Social Relations.* (Manchester, England: Manchester University Press, 1962), pp. 36–37.
3. Ibid.
4. Ibid.
5. I spent nine months as a participant observer in an American high school of 110 students, 7 teachers, and a teaching principal. Although I presented myself as a researcher, the students and faculty soon interpreted my activities and assigned me the role of guidance counselor. Throughout the nine-month school term, I observed the students during free periods of the day and during school-sponsored and school-related afternoon and evening activities. I gathered data on the relation between academic work and the student system by observing students in the study halls and in and between classes for several hundred hours. Interviews of an extemporaneous kind, semistructured interviews, structured interviews, and several questionnaires based on structured interviews rounded out the data collection techniques.
6. S. F. Nadel, *Nupe Religion* (London: Routledge & Kegan Paul, 1954), p. 99.
7. E. D. Chapple and Carleton S. Coon, *Principles of Anthropology* (New York: Henry Holt, 1942).
8. Arnold Van Gennep, *The Rites of Passage*, trans. Monika B. Vizedom and Gabrielle L. Caffee (Chicago: University of Chicago Press, 1960).
9. Clifford Geertz, "Religion as a Cultural System," in W. A. Lessa and E. Z. Vogt, eds., *Reader in Comparative Religion* (New York: Harper & Row, 1958), pp. 449–512.
10. Clyde Kluckhohn, "Myths and Ritual: A General Theory," in W. A. Lessa and E. Z. Vogt, eds., *Reader in Comparative Religion* (New York: Harper & Row, 1958), pp. 135–51.
11. Claude Lévi-Strauss, *Totemism* (Boston: Beacon Press, 1963), p. 70.
12. Jack Goody, "Religion and Ritual: The Definitional Problem," *British Journal of Sociology* 12, (1961): 142–64; Robert Horton, "A Definition of Religion and its Uses," *Journal of Royal Anthropological Institute* 90 (1960): 201–26; S. H. Posinsky, "Ritual, Neurotic and Social," *American Image* 19 (1962): 375–90.
13. Goody, "Religion and Ritual," p. 160.
14. Ibid., p. 159.
15. J. H. S. Bossard and E. S. Boll, *Ritual in Family Living* (Philadelphia: University of Pennsylvania Press, 1950); N. Leites and E. Bernaut, *Ritual of Liquidation* (Glencoe, Ill.: Free Press, 1954).
16. Chapple and Coon, *Principles*, pp. 484–528.
17. Lévi-Strauss, *Totemism*, eloquently demonstrates how the conceptions of totemism in primitive society have been used to dissociate the thought processes and practices of modern western tradition from the taint of commonality with primitive peoples of the world. With respect to a related set of concepts, Murray and Rosalie Wax ("the Notion of Magic," *Current Anthropology* 4 [1963]: 495–518) show that much the same kind of "protectionist" thinking has dominated the problem of distinguishing among magic, science, and religion.

Part V

Applying Anthropology to Education

24 / A Proposal for the Unification of Secondary School Courses through Anthropology

John H. Chilcott

Since World War II there has been a florescence of interest in anthropology in college campuses, in popular literature, and in governmental and other social agencies; yet secondary schools almost universally have been reluctant to include anthropological topics in their school programs. Part of this lack of enthusiasm for anthropology is derived from an outdated stereotype of an anthropologist as a person who digs up old bones and broken pots and embarrasses dinner guests by describing unmentionable erotic practices of primitive peoples. Another deterrent is the myth that classroom discussion of the evolution of man may cause controversy. Both of these positions are partially created by a lack of anthropology coursework in teacher-education programs. The avoidance of anthropology by secondary schools overlooks the many valuable contributions which this unique science can furnish the secondary school program.

Anthropology may be defined as the science of man and his works. Such a definition readily illustrates the breadth of inquiry of this science. The anthropologist combines in one discipline the interests and methods of both the biological and the social sciences. He is interested both in man as a member of the animal kingdom and in man's behavior as a member of society. Focusing as it does on man, anthropology does not limit itself to any one dimension of man, but seeks to study all aspects of man in order to provide a greater understanding of what man is, does, and thinks. The science of man and his works may be divided into two major branches: physical anthropology, which investigates the structure of man, human evolution, and the origins and types of races; and cultural anthropology, which through archaeology and ethnography investigates the nature of societies, social processes, and the relationship of language to culture (linguistics). Traditionally anthropologists have studied primitive people, since they constitute a rapidly vanishing laboratory; however, many anthropologists have also studied complex and modern societies as well.[1] The comparative studies of cultures basic to anthropology provide understanding of cultural dynamics and knowledge of the basis of cultures. The unity in anthropology comes from the attempt to learn of the origin and development of man. In all his investigations the anthropologist attempts to be as objective as possible, seeking to avoid value judgments even though his results might be in opposition to his own personal and cultural beliefs. Without this objective approach the anthropologist's attempts to understand man and his works would be futile.

Through the unique approach of anthropology a student may acquire a greater understanding of the causes of human behavior. Using the anthropological approach, the student would study instead of the history of Greece or the United States, the dominant cultures in those areas. Included in his studies would be the physical characteristics of the people represented by these cultures; their economy, political and religious systems, social institutions, customs and mores, family life, and social groups; their daily life activities; and the geographical situation in which these people live. In short, the student would study the total environment— physical, biological, and social. By studying what life was like in these cultures at various periods in their development, the student could better understand the changes that took place and the causes of those changes. History would "come to life."

Since the history of culture includes all phases of human endeavor, it integrates fragmented topics by distinguishing their relationship to man. The fragmentary nature of much knowledge presented in the secondary schools would be supplied some cohesiveness through this approach. The current emphasis upon unique events in history and political geography is insufficient to provide an adequate understanding of history. Many historians have recognized this deficiency and have attempted to include more elements of the cultures existing at the period of their discussion. Whereas history emphasizes people in time, anthropology emphasizes people in space and time.

The teacher, in order to furnish a more nearly complete picture and understanding of human history, must present not only an understanding of other peoples but also an understanding of our relationship to other peoples both historically and currently. One useful approach to showing this relationship is to indicate the biological unity of man. In this manner anthropology connects man to history.

The science of man assists the student in understanding world situations. Anthropology seeks to develop an appreciation for the best of other cultures. It can point out that one set of rules in one set of circumstances can be catastrophic in another set of circumstances. In some situations the old set of rules is no longer appropriate in new circumstances. For example, those rules which were appropriate for an extended type of family in an agricultural society of the 1850s are not only inappropriate but may actually disrupt family life in a nuclear type of family which is suited for an urban, industrialized society of today. Those modern parents who are seeking family customs from the past may not only be frustrated, they might become so inflexible that their family might break up. This concept of cultural relativism is another valuable feature of anthropology.

The attention of anthropology on all peoples in the world is especially necessary today when formerly obscure peoples are rising to prominence in the world scene. Cultures which a short time ago were classified as primitive now send representatives to the United Nations. The study of man is not limited to the Western world. Teachers and curricula have traditionally been isolationist in their view of peoples outside the sphere of Western civilization.[2] An administrator seeking a teacher with a world point of view would do better to seek persons trained in anthropology than in any other discipline.

Not only do students need to learn more about other peoples but they need to understand more about themselves. The humanizing nature of anthropology gives the student an idea of his place in the world, both natural and social. He becomes aware of what is involved in his being a human. Through a study of the standards of adulthood in other cultures, the student learns what standards he must meet in order to be an adult in his own society. In many cases he is vaguely aware of what these standards consist, but had never really tried to describe them. The usual comment, "I knew that, but I never thought about it before," is repeated again and again as students study their own culture. The comparison of customs from another culture with those of their own reinforces their understanding of their own society.

Students find the study of man exciting. Teachers have a difficult time making this subject dry and uninviting. There appears to be an innate curiosity about the origin of things, especially man. When describing some customs of peoples in other parts of the world, even the dullest of students becomes interested and sits on the edge of his seat anticipating the next anecdote. Anthropology challenges the interest of students in all levels of capacity, and should not be restricted to only the bright students.

The recent attention to the impact of modern technology on social groupings can better be understood through a study of the evolution of technology, a study to which anthropology can contribute much. Anthropologists have intensively studied the interrelationship of technology, man, and the physical environment. Archaeology has revealed the increasing sophistication of tools from crude hand axes to polished stone axes to metal implements and eventually to complicated machinery. Students become aware of the time span for these improvements to take place and their effect on the existing cultures at the time of their invention. With this perspective they are aware that the need for man's adjustment to the necessary speed of large-scale operations performed in increasingly less time can come only through a better understanding of the role of technology in the past.

Before the reader receives the impression that anthropology is the panacea for all ills and provides the answers to all questions, it is necessary to indicate that unlike some social scientists, anthropologists are very cautious in the development of general statements with respect to human behavior. There are still many questions which anthropologists have been unable to answer. Cultural anthropologists, for example, cannot explain the continued exhaustion of the natural resources in the United States. There is also the danger of deculturation, wherein a student might become attracted to practices in another culture without realizing that what is best for other cultures may not be the best for this culture.

Anthropology's unique content and divergent application provide a framework from which to study human behavior. Although separate courses in anthropology may be found in some private and public schools, a separate course is not the answer to incorporating anthropological content and viewpoint in the secondary school program. The curriculum is already overcrowded with separate courses. Furthermore, it is difficult to find teachers with sufficient background to teach a special course. Or perhaps even more precarious, the course is added during the tenure of a qualified teacher and then taught by a teacher without any background when the qualified teacher leaves. Finally a separate course would not make accessible to all students the understandings provided by anthropology. These understandings need to permeate the present curriculum wherever possible. The development of man and his culture should provide a central theme around which all other subjects are organized.

The famous anthropologist Clyde Kluckhohn once described the present secondary school curriculum as a formal garden with high walls between the various sections. Too often the current curriculum is a collection of fragmentary topics loosely collected into a series of courses which in turn are illogically related to one another. The science of man and his works can provide a framework from which the student may view the increasingly complex development of man both physically and culturally.

The human record started approximately 500,000 years ago with the development of the first man-apes. The student, however, is rarely exposed to anything man did beyond 10,000 years ago. Man's gradual development both physically and culturally is rarely impressed upon youngsters, resulting in many misconceptions such as the rapid development of culture in historical times. To neglect this 490,000-year heritage is to neglect the major steps in the development of man. To study man's evolving physical nature and culture provides a greater appreciation for the current status of man in the modern world.

Science courses tend to become dehumanized by not relating their material to man. As a consequence man's position in the biological and physical world is little understood until years of study at the college level. Not only is evolution slighted in biology courses[3] but the culmination of biological development, the organic origin of man, is many times not included for fear of parental or administrator reprisals. This myth of controversy needs to be exposed, and evolution, especially the evolution of man, needs to take its proper place as the central organizing theme in the biological sciences.[4] Other anthropological topics, such as human genetics, race characteristics, human ecology, and the material basis of culture, need to receive greater emphasis in science courses. Many other anthropological topics can add enrichment and meaning to current science courses, especially the biologically oriented sciences, in junior and senior secondary schools. These topics may vary from the relationship between magic and science to an analysis of the chemical composition of natural poisons used by primitive peoples.

It has already been suggested that the current social studies approach to man is narrowly superficial, isolationist, and extremely limited in scope. The study of the development of culture can provide a framework around which all the related topics included in world history, American history, and geography can be organized. By study of the culture representative of the eras of human history, the understanding of history would be enhanced.

The common stereotype engendered by history books of life in Rome as a life pursued in a columned, resplendent house with much attention given to exotic parties, the arts, and politics is both superficial and misleading. Archaeological reconstruction of life in Rome paints a different picture.[5] The majority of people in Rome lived in plank, two-story tenement houses which were poorly heated; all refuse was thrown in the narrow muddy street; and life was anything but as glamorous as the history books have pictured to generations of students.

Just as in science courses, evolution should provide the central theme for social studies through the study of cultural change and diffusion. The effect of inventions, acculturation, and historical accidents should be illustrated through changes in customs, values, and ethos of the cultures studied. This would presuppose the study of man through dominant cultural themes and their distribution in space rather than a chronological account of man's activities. Only through an approach such as this can the student come to understand how man's former biological evolution continues through man's cultural evolution and idea systems.

Too few of the discoveries of the behavioral sciences have been included in current social studies programs. The emphasis is still upon history with little or no attention directed toward current society. Through the comparison of family life in America, students can better understand the emerging patterns of family life in urban America.[6]

Anthropology provides four approaches to understanding humanity.[7] One approach through prehistory and archaeology furnishes a more nearly accurate understanding of the length of man's cultural evolution and the many significant adjustments that were necessary prior to modern history. This approach also provides a perspective for understanding man's current interrelationship with his fellowman and with his environment. Another approach to understanding humanity is the biological and evolutionary approach, which provides an understanding of man's relationships with other animals and the common unity of all men. Still another approach is through direct comparisons both of cultures and of races. This approach is unique to anthropology and provides an acute awareness of the differences and unity among peoples. The final approach is through a study of social problems, an approach which is particularly appealing since it includes all the social sciences in the solution of the social problems. All too often the historical approach is overlooked when minority problems are being studied. The history of minority peoples provides a much-needed dimension in the consideration of their problems.

All these approaches may be incorporated in the social studies curriculum.

The core program, however, is ideally suited for the study of culture history, for this program permits the crossing of subject matter barriers in order to provide a central theme, a core program might assume the following characteristics: In the seventh grade, students would concentrate on three primitive societies, each selected on the basis of staple food product. A culture such as the Arunta of Australia, the Cheyenne of North America, or the Bushmen of Africa, would be representative of a hunting and gathering economy. A culture such as the historic Navaho of North America, the Kazaks of central Asia, or the Masai of Africa might be used to represent pastoral nomads with domesticated animals. The cultures of the Hopi in the American Southwest, the Dahomeans of Africa, or the Samoans of the western Pacific would be representative of agricultural peoples. Each of these cultures representing a different type of economy would be studied intensively in order for students to get a "feel" for the type of life these people lived. With this background they could then proceed to study the development of culture from the Pleistocene period to the Metal ages in Europe and in the Near East.

During the eighth grade, students would follow the migration of man into the New World, culminating in either the cultures of the Inca or the Maya. Following this they would return to the Eastern Hemisphere to study two literate societies, such as the Greek and the Egyptian. These cultures, however, would be approached through the concept of change and the causes of change. Thus, the students might start with Homeric Greece and then shift to the period of the Golden Age, noting the degree and sources of change. The following grades (9 and 10) would be spent in developing a diffusion chart indicating the development and diffusion of Western culture throughout the world.

During the eleventh grade, students would concentrate on Western civilization in the modern world and its integration with Eastern and primitive societies. The twelfth grade would be devoted to current American value systems,[8] modern American society, and current social problems.

Besides science and social science courses, anthropological topics can contribute to coursework in English and guidance. Too often English teachers overlook the value of literature as representative of folklore, a means of reinforcing cultural traditions. A book is not created in isolation from the culture of the person who wrote it. Without explaining the cultural context in which a book was written, English can degenerate into the narrow approach of style and plot without any attention to developing significance and understanding of what the author is trying to illustrate. In "group" guidance programs the behavior of groups and individuals can be explained in terms of the cultural matrix in which a person matures. By studying behavior in other cultures, through descriptions such as Ruth Benedict's *Patterns of Culture* or the *Ways of Mankind* recordings, students come to realize what types of behavior are appropriate for our society. In the presentation of all these anthropological topics, emphasis should be placed on the nature of culture and the way it motivates human behavior. Just reading books about primitive peoples and the races of man is not enough. Discussion and direction are a necessary component of the teaching process.

So far, anthropology has been a plaything in our secondary schools. Keeping in mind that what's right or wrong in any presentation or school program is determined by our own cultural matrix, the secondary program needs to be reorganized to include anthropological concepts and point of view. Our current secondary school curriculum is a cultural tradition, parts of which need to be changed, parts of which need to be retained, according to the current needs of our society. Many innovations are currently being tried in our secondary schools. It is time to evaluate through research and experimentation the contributions which anthropology can provide both in terms of organization and enrichment of the secondary school program.

NOTES

1. For a recent study of life in suburbia and its implications for education, see John R. Seeley, R. Alexander Sim, and Elizabeth W. Goosley, *Crestwood Heights* (New York: Basic Books, 1956).
2. Clifford Hooker, "To Create an Enduring Society," *Phi Delta Kappan* 42, no. 9 (June 1961): 575.
3. E. R. Laba and E. W. Gross, "Evolution Slighted in High School Biology," *Clearing House* 24, no. 7 (March 1950): 396-99.
4. John H. Chilcott, "Apes, Men and Schoolmarms" (Public lecture), National Science Foundation Summer Institute in Anthropology, University of California, Santa Barbara, July 27, 1961. Mimeographed.
5. Jerome Carcopino, *Daily Life in Ancient Rome* (New Haven: Yale University Press, 1940).
6. Paul Schumann, "Teaching the Course in Family Relations," *Journal of Secondary Education* 36, no. 5 (May 1961): 282-84.
7. James B. Watson, "Roads to Understanding Man," *Washington Education* 72 (January 1961): 6-10.
8. An example of a value "system" may be provided by study of those values associated with family life in the United States. Values provide a basis upon which behavior, objects, and ideas may be either sought or avoided. Their interactions with persons, behavior, objects, and ideas provide a system around which the family relates itself.

SELECTED BIBLIOGRAPHY

California State Department of Education. *Generalizations Relating to Anthropology*. Report of the State Central Committee on Social Studies, Sacramento, Calif. 1959. Pp. 53-60.

Gruber, J. W. "Anthropology and the High School." *American Biology Teacher* 17 (November 1958): 228-30.

Henry, J. "Anthropology in the General Social Science Course." *Journal of General Education* 8 (July 1949): 304-8.

Holmes, L. D. "It's More Than Bones and Old Stones." *Social Studies* 48 (November 1958): 220-22.

Jacobs, M. "Teaching of Anthropology in the Secondary Schools." University of Washington, College of Education *Record*, February 1940. For further comment on this, see *School Review* 48 (May 1940): 323-25.

James, P. E. "New Viewpoints in Geography." *New Viewpoints in the Social Sciences*. 28th Yearbook. National Council for the Social Studies, 1958.

James, P. E. "The Use of Culture Areas as a Frame of Organization for the Social Studies." *New Viewpoints in Geography*. 29th Yearbook. National Council for the Social Studies, 1959.

Lee, D. "Anthropology and American Secondary Education." *Frontiers of Secondary Education*, edited by P. M. Halverson. Syracuse: Syracuse University Press, 1957.

Mead, M. "The High School of the Future." *California Journal of Secondary Education* 35 (October 1960): 360-69.

Nagles, H. "Place of Anthropology in the Biology Course." *American Biology Teacher* 12 (March 1950): 65-67.

Spindler, G. "Anthropology in the Social Studies Curriculum." *National Education Association Journal* 47 (December 1958): 623-27.

Spindler, G. "New Trends and Application in Anthropology." *New Viewpoints in the Social Sciences*. 28th Yearbook. National Council for the Social Studies, 1958.

25 / Anthropology and World History Texts

Rachel Reese Sady

Anthropologists and educators are increasingly concerned with how anthropology can best contribute to the teaching of secondary school social studies courses. One part of this concern is with world history textbooks, both because anthropology and history share the same subject matter and because texts are so influential in molding courses.

The feeling is widespread that anthropology can help improve these texts, but the question is, how? Ordinarily, anthropology enters world history courses at the same point that Neanderthal man rears his heavy-browed head, and leaves it not far from his heels. The recent emphasis on non-Western cultures has led some course designers to turn for particular data to anthropologists who are area specialists. But anthropologists feel that their discipline has a greater potential, a potential that can be proven in the explanation, exploration, and illustration of concepts that students can apply throughout their social studies. To clarify the nature of this potential, five world history textbooks widely used in secondary schools were examined from an anthropological point of view, and eight other texts were skimmed.[1]

The five texts analyzed are good books. They are well organized, well written, and packed with information and interpretation. The task of synthesis and selection of facts involved in writing a secondary school world history is not an easy one, however, and looked at from the particular point of view of anthropology, each text has certain deficiencies. The texts were examined in regard to their scope—that is, "whose world" they consider, their use of anthropological concepts, and their use of anthropological data.

WHOSE WORLD?

The majority of the texts look at the world narrowly, blocking off as insignificant those areas and those times that seem unconnected with the main line of development of Western civilization. These books do not ignore Asia and Africa; neither has Western civilization ignored them. A typical world history starts off with the birth of the earth, skips quickly through the beginnings of life, and then goes on to discuss early man and the development of early civilizations (always in Egypt and Mesopotamia, often in the Indus and Hwang Ho valleys, and more rarely in the American Indian centers). Once Greece is reached, the chapters march on with Western civilization, and the rest of the world is held in abeyance until "discovered," by Europeans, of course. In brief, the main content of a typical text follows the lifeline of Western civilization.

There is nothing wrong with stories of the development of Western civilization. But when a text claims—as most do—to be "the story of mankind," such a strong Western orientation is misleading. The problem arises, just whose world is being described? When an area is discussed in a world history textbook only at the point that it comes in contact with Western civilization, the impression is inevitable that this area is important only because of Western contact. Well over halfway through a very well-written text, this statement occurs:

> Earlier parts of this book concentrated on certain areas on the globe. Even
> the great empire of Rome covered only a section of the earth. In modern

times, history is in the fullest sense *world* history and Part Eight covers events
that affected all lands and peoples.

Part Eight is entitled "Great Power Rivalries," and imperialism is the context in
which India, China, Japan, and Africa are considered. India, China, and Japan
receive backward glances; but Africa is apparently born with the partition of that
continent.

Publishers and textbook writers have not ignored the pleas for history in a wider
context. The book quoted above has a great deal of material on modern world
problems. The most recent edition of a widely used twenty-five-year-old textbook
is a compromise between the old book and new demands: as in previous editions,
there is a chapter each for Great Britain, France, and other European countries or
blocks of countries, but an earlier chapter on Latin America is much expanded and
three new parts have been added in a bow to the modern world—the Far East,
Africa, and India and Southeast Asia. However, these new parts do little to change
the main emphasis of the text, which is on what the Western civilization "owes" to
ancient civilizations, and on the development of nationalism along with Western
civilization.

Efforts to keep up to date with the importance of non-Western areas are obvious
in several volumes. Last chapters are expanded to take into account each new
nation or event. These efforts sometimes founder as when last-minute assessments
conflict with even later news reports. Only two of the books reviewed make a
sharp break with the typical Western-oriented tradition and use an area approach.

In summary, the farsightedness and clearsightedness of historians and educators
about the need for a wider view of the world has resulted in a patching operation
on Western civilization histories in order to bring in the rest of the world, and in
two new approaches to world history in which area organization is important. The
trend is clear, but it is far from complete, and there is still need to emphasize that
world history is not Western history.

THE CONCEPT OF CULTURE

The transformation of "our world" into "the world" brings with it increased use
of anthropological materials. There is some evidence, however, that in the adoption of anthropological concepts in support of world history teaching, there is not
always a clear understanding of those concepts. As the use of anthropology becomes more common, this lack of understanding becomes more serious.

Anthropology is the comparative study of all mankind. It is not restricted to
early man and the American Indians, or to exotic peoples. Except for physical
anthropology, all branches of the study center on culture. Culture is the total way
of life of a people, the content and pattern of their learned behavior and beliefs.
How cultures form and how they change is a major part of history. More than that,
the idea of culture is itself a useful tool in understanding world history because it
explains how peoples act and are likely to act, what values and judgments they employ and are likely to employ. It helps to explain or point out what is universally
human about mankind in its response to basic needs, and to indicate why differences have come about. These explanations all lead toward a greater understanding
of other peoples, and of ourselves.

Many other ideas flow from this fundamental notion of culture. Some of them
are: the way cultures are integrated and their underlying value systems, ethnocentrism and cultural relativism, the distribution of common cultural elements, and
the ways culture spreads and the nature of culture change.

The Other Culture

The concept of culture seems simple, but it is apparently deceptively simple,
from the evidence of the world history textbooks. The fault lies in the etymology

of the word itself, which has accustomed us to think automatically of the artistic or the intellectual life as the "cultured" one. Culture derives from "cultivate," meaning "create." Most people when they think of culture think of those things or ideas consciously created by artistic or intellectual effort. But anthropologists use the term to mean the whole body of institutions, customs, beliefs, and artifacts developing therefrom that have been created by man. The culture of anthropology includes the other "culture," but it also includes all those ways of everyday living that each person acquires from the society into which he is born.

The other "culture" is a significant concept and deserves the attention it receives in the history books. However, it is important not to confuse the two aspects of the word because of the implications of such confusion. When we speak of the other "culture," we are likely to have a ranking of societies against a very specific yardstick, one perhaps marked off in our own aesthetic values. This is a legitimate measurement against which to judge societies, if one cares to use it, and many do. It is not, however, the whole story, and as a descriptive device it omits much that would make the ways of the peoples of the world understandable to us.

What is the evidence from the textbooks about their use of the concept of culture? None makes an attempt, beyond a quick definition, to explore culture as an idea. Most of the definitions are anthropological, but actual use of the word thereafter often does not correspond with the definition. In one text there is a fundamental misunderstanding; the whole brunt of the word's use, in spite of sporadic corrective gestures, is that the economic and political history of a nation is not discussed in terms of culture, and that a nation's "contributions to" or "achievements in" the fields of literature, music, art, philosophy, and science are so discussed. The practical effect of this is evident. We are not asked to admire the first category, whole culture and its history; we *are* asked to admire the "culture" as fine arts. So the gulf between peoples is to be bridged by selective "understanding":

> Many Americans have difficulty finding anything to admire in the political and economic institutions of Communist Russia. But we must not forget that Russian authors, musicians, and scientists have given the world fine books, important ideas, and beautiful music.

This is a good bridge, but not adequate to the traffic.

Of the textbooks studied, the one which does most in the direction of widening the scope of world history and presenting the cultural background of societies uses the term culture prolifically but inconsistently. Culture is defined as "the way of life of a society—the habits, ideas, and practices of its members," and the observation is made that this definition is broad enough to cover any form of human organization. This good definition is marred by the following statement that "a culture, however, ceases to be such and becomes a civilization when it reaches a further state of development." This assumption that culture excludes civilization is not borne out by the text's own further usage.

Moreover, throughout this book the use of culture veers back and forth from the anthropological to the other meaning. At the two extremes are the section on Africa, which is definitely written from an anthropological point of view, and the section on the United States, where the phenomenon termed "mass culture" adds still another meaning. The authors at a few points indicate an awareness that there is a problem of usage, but this never jells into a real understanding, partly prevented by the practice in book organization of treating culture in chapters separate from those on economy and politics. Quite near the end of the volume, cultural differences are discussed:

> The term "culture" as used here does not refer to the arts, such as painting, sculpture, or poetry. Rather, it refers to a people's total way of life—to the way in which they think and believe and act.

Had the text followed this definition throughout, this remarkably successful volume would have been much improved.

Culture Patterns and Values

The pattern of a culture is the way in which cultural elements are integrated—their relationship to each other and to the underlying values or goals of a culture. The texts vary to the extent that they attempt to describe a way of life in terms of that culture's own values. All of them recognize integrating principles in the development of Western civilization, but only some of them discuss the difference between culture as it really is lived and culture as it is supposed to be lived—that is, between real and ideal culture.

One text tends to regard the motivations of African and Asians as replicas of our own, but historically more recent. We are told that "all peoples want a good life," but there is no indication that definitions of the good life may vary. Another text also looks at other cultures with our own values in mind, but occasionally tries to describe the assumptions and values of others' ways. The books organized by area fully appreciate that peoples have developed different ways in response to common needs. One discusses pattern in terms of "style" of civilization and effectively portrays certain societies from the point of view of what those societies consider important.

The old province of anthropologists, the American Indian, does not fare well in any of the texts. In one book with a special Latin American section, Indians are consistently referred to as "poor and barefoot" or living in "ignorance and poverty." The absence of further portrayal gives the impression that poverty and ignorance (of the kind of things that Westerners know) create a vacuum that cannot or need not be described until the things our culture deems important begin to fill it. In other places in all the texts the term "different traditions and customs," without further specifications, is used liberally either because of space or data limitations.

Ethnocentrism and Cultural Relativism

Ethnocentrism means the tendency for a people to take for granted that their way is the human or right way. Cultural relativism is the other side of the coin, and means that the "right way" depends on the culture in which one is brought up, and that peoples should be considered in that light.

No text can or should escape being ethnocentric. Nevertheless, it is desirable that the texts be understanding enough of other cultures and critical enough of our own to provide a basis for some objectivity in facing world problems. As discussed above, all the texts but two exhibit ethnocentrism in their answer to the question, whose world? It is also ethnocentric to be overprotective of our own history, and two of the books seem to err in this direction. Such assessments are a matter of judgment, however, and are bound to vary. The problem of ethnocentrism can be attacked directly by discussion of the idea itself, but none of the texts does this, although all contain illustrations of it, as below:

> ... through the centuries, the Chinese people were taught that China was literally the central country of the universe, and all other lands were merely outlying regions. Hand in hand with this idea went the firm belief that Chinese society was the only good way to live. All other peoples were considered barbarians.

This important concept of ethnocentrism is rarely recognized in connection with other countries, and is particularly missing where needed most—for our own. At best, there are references to the Chinese view of Europeans as "long-nosed barbarians" and this throught-provoking passage in one text:

> Not understanding the native traditions, (the Europeans) felt that the "savage" needed to learn European ways, to become Christian, and to experience the blessings of European medical knowledge and higher standards of living. ... Each of the European nations believed its culture was the most advanced, and each therefore felt it was best fitted to help the natives.

The two volumes that deal with non-Western cultures extensively are both very good in pointing out that these cultures must be regarded from the viewpoint of their own value systems, that behavior is relative to culture.

Culture Areas

The idea of culture area refers to a geographic area—transcending political boundaries—whose populations exhibit in common a number of culture traits. The idea can be used in different ways, depending on how many cultural elements are shared and which of them are considered meaningful. That is, culture areas are not rigid, mutually exclusive divisions of the same degree of commonality. They are useful ways of looking at the world and their extent depends on who has decided what elements or group of elements are important for what particular purpose.

Most of the texts do not use the idea, although history is inevitably discussed in terms of distinct civilizations and the areas encompassed by them. One text pioneers in organization and approach based on large culture areas, but assimilates land mass, regardless of related cultures, to the idea. This volume selects seven "great societies" and then attempts to discuss each one in terms of its roots, a traditional period, and the impact of Western civilization or modern technology. This is an effective scheme, except that current culture areas or societies do not necessarily correspond with prehistoric ones. Fossil man and the American Indians are fitted into niches defensible on the basis of geography, not culture. Another text, partly organized by culture area, solves this problem of "roots" by prefacing the area approach with a chronological exposition.

Culture Change

All histories are a documentation of cultural change, but they vary in their recognition of the processes involved and in the assumptions made about the nature of those processes. In all the texts, culture change is considered against a background of "progress" or "advancement." Progress must be toward something, but the texts usually assume that we know what that something is. In general, one text uses scientific and technological knowhow as a yardstick for progress, another uses achievement of a "better life," and another emphasizes nationalism. In all three, progress and the development of Western civilization are virtually synonymous. Two of the more recent texts have a wider context in keeping with their wider worlds, and it is simply civilization and progress that go hand in hand.

All these texts recognize in final chapters that, from the point of view of modern war and peace, progress and civilization have somehow parted company. This recognition seems to open no doors to doubt about the suitability of coupling the two ideas throughout the rest of history. In other words, all the texts tend to overuse evaluating words as opposed to descriptive words in recounting the development of cultures. If one part of a culture (technology) is valued highly (for efficiency), the assumption is often made that the rest of the culture should be equally rated, although the reason for this is not made clear. While it is important to understand that a culture tends to be integrated, such integration does not mean that the same standards can be applied meaningfully throughout the culture. A list of overt and covert culture traits does not readily fit onto an "advancement" continuum with its assumption of superiority. If it is forced to fit, mistaken connotations occur, understanding is hindered instead of helped, and critical thinking about ourselves and others is hampered. Criteria that are uncertain and descriptive terms that are value laden reduce the usefulness that generalized comments about progress might otherwise have.

It is no belittlement of our own advanced technology and democratic values to realize that if all history is written with progress understood in terms of the values of one culture, naturally other cultures won't be "advanced" until they conform. Pointing this out should not discourage one from making evaluations, since these are necessary as a basis for action, when the standards used are made clear. The fact remains that culture change is not comparable to climbing a ladder, and history can better be understood in terms of the substance of changes than in terms of progress toward unstated goals. It is more important to be clear about the denotations of civilization (urbanization, specialization, and so on) than to assume its connotations (generalized advancement or progress).

The actual processes of culture change—innovation, internal growth, diffusion, the recasting and integration of borrowed elements—are not discussed as such in most texts, but there are many good descriptions of particular changes and the factors involved. Occasionally culture change is described so as to indicate planned change or stubborn resistance to change which may not have been the case. This is undoubtedly merely a matter of writing style, but the result is not a sense of the processes involved, but a sense of unreasoning perversity on the part of the people. Two examples are:

> Yet the Chinese peasant could not be easily persuaded to change the honored ways of his forefathers. Nor would he organize with hundreds of other farmers to meet new conditions with new methods.

> . . . The American Indians did not want to adapt themselves.

Related inversely to these examples are the following:

> [The peoples of Eastern Europe] have often tried to become part of Western European society.

> But Asoka tried a different way of uniting his great empire. He tried the Buddhist religion.

In conclusion about the use of concepts, it is clear that an alert student may very well wring a knowledge of the nature of culture from these books—more easily from some than from others—but the books are not planned to facilitate it, with the exception of some sections of the most recent. A systematic explanation of the concepts themselves is missing.

ANTHROPOLOGICAL DATA

In addition to clarifying the nature of culture so that it can be a useful tool in understanding world history, anthropologists can supply data that illuminate particular areas. The extent to which the texts deal with the wider world has increased their dependence on the kinds of data anthropologists in particular are likely to compile—that is, information about peoples whose cultures vary a great deal from our own.

It is evident from reading through the texts that anthropologists should be more forward in making available their data and that authors and publishers should be more aware of the need for checking data. Errors occur in particular about early man, evolution and race, and linguistics.

Some descriptions of early man are fanciful instead of accurate. One intimates that large-brained Neanderthal man had a small brain-case. Another makes the statement about Heidelberg man, who has been represented since 1907 by a solitary jawbone, that he is "presumed to be the oldest *complete* skeleton yet unearthed." And there is little reason to resort to dinosaurs to pique students' interest. Decorating the beginning page of a section entitled "Old Stone Age Men Were Hunters" in one text are two pictures of dinosaurs. This juxtaposition would fool no high school student in this dinosaur-aware age, but the review question, "What is historically wrong with the comic strip that shows a cave man riding a dinosaur?" might better have been asked about the text's own layout.

Brief explanations of evolution and race are always well intentioned, always inadequate, and usually inaccurate. One text asks a review question, "Why is there no such thing as a pure or superior race?" when the body of the text has given the student no basis at all for thinking about such a question.

Much more care should be taken in the way that identifying labels are applied to groups. Linguistic, physical, national, and cultural names are mixed with abandon, even though—and sometimes immediately after—most texts state very clearly that these are separate categories and not to be confused. For example, after one text has stated that race must not be confused with language, religion, and nation, and that there can be one race and many languages and vice versa, these passages occur:

> It is true that the Jews of Biblical times resided in Palestine and belonged either to the Semitic or Armenoid branches of the Mediterranian Caucasoids.
>
> England . . . was occupied in very early times by Nordics, Mediterraneans, and Alpines. Later it was invaded by Saxons, Norwegians, Danes, and Normans. Thus instead of one physical type in England, we see there is an excellent mosaic of Caucasoid subraces.

In another text, Slavs are variously referred to as being so identified because of race, language, background, or nationality.

One text mistakenly refers to the Ainus of Japan as Indo-European, apparently under the impression that this purely linguistic term means Caucasoid, a physically descriptive term. This error is illustrative of the less obvious kind of misuse of labels that occurs constantly. When the linguistic term Dravidian, for example, is used to apply to "dark-skinned peoples of India," which is a physical description, this is not accurate. It really means that most Dravidian-speaking people in India also have dark skins. The fact that there may be a near coincidence of the linguistic and the physical groups does not diminish the need for distinguishing between the two categories. Racial, cultural, and linguistic relationships have a history too burdened by misunderstanding to add to the confusion in any way.

The examples given above are important only in that they illustrate the kinds of things an anthropological editing might catch. More important, anthropological data on particular cultures can fill in outlines necessarily only sketched in the textbooks.

CONCLUSIONS

In teaching social studies, including world history, the schools wish not only to inform and instruct but to promote good intentions and good works in the world community. To do this, attitudes that question, consider alternatives, and seek information instead of make assumptions are to be encouraged. In the context of world history, a comparative look at world cultures—at the various solutions man has made to the same problems—is essential to the stimulation of critical thinking.

Anthropologists can join historians and social studies teachers in impressing on writers and publishers the need for widening their concept of world history to include the non-Western world. And anthropologists must share the task of providing data on those cultures. As more and more people are won over to this point of view, however—and the trend is evident—anthropologists have a special responsibility to head off confusion about the nature of culture, and to prepare material that will add to our understanding of other peoples and ourselves. The Anthropology Curriculum Study Project of the American Anthropological Association is engaged in this work at present. As material pointed specifically toward social studies in the secondary schools is developed, teachers will be apprised of it.

NOTES

1. The five texts analyzed are: Boak, Slosson, Anderson, and Bartlett, *The History of Our World*, 1959; Maxons and Peoples, *Men and Nations*, 1961; Rogers, Adams, and Brown, *Story of Nations*, 1960; Ewing, *Our Widening World*, 1960; and Stavrianos, Andrews, Blanksten, Hacken, Leppert, Murphy, and Smith, *A Global History of Man*, 1962. The eight other texts were published between 1940 and 1962.
   In order to save space, documentation, even in the case of direct quotations, is omitted. This was done so that examples can be cited without concern for the balanced judgment of the books that only complete documentation could give. Complete documentation is available to those interested from the Anthropology Curriculum Study Project, 5632 Kimbark Avenue, Chicago, Illinois 60637.

26 / Cross-Cultural Teaching of Science

Francis E. Dart and Panna Lal Pradhan

A major theme of our age is the development of science and technology in societies around the world. Leaders in most of the developing countries of Asia, Africa, and South America, where knowledge and utilization of natural resources have remained nearly static over the past several centuries, now recognize that they must move into the era of applied science and technology if provision is to be made for the needs of increasing populations and for improved standards of living.[1] Thus, technology and science are emphasized in their development plans and in the assistance they seek and receive from nations such as the United States.[2] It is generally assumed that this process of scientific and technological development will require very much less time in Asia, Africa, and South America than it did in Europe and North America, and in fact many countries hope to achieve in one or two generations changes comparable to those that occurred in the West over two or three centuries. Their hope is based partly upon the availability of capital assistance from the industrial nations and partly upon the ease and rapidity with which knowledge now at hand can be communicated—knowledge which was originally obtained over a long period in a process involving many errors and confusions that will not have to be repeated. In their optimism they largely ignore the profound social and cultural changes that accompanied the Western development and the social and cultural changes that must accompany this new scientific revolution. Frequently it is found that a country whose leaders are determined to introduce rapid change is not ready to adopt modes of thought and organization that are fundamental to an advancing science and technology, and hoped-for results have been slow to materialize. It should be added that unnecessary ambiguity has sometimes resulted from a failure, in discussions such as this one, to distinguish between technology and science.[3] In what follows we are concerned specifically with science and with problems associated with its introduction.

The difficulties encountered frequently relate to the very nature of the interaction between Western science and non-Western cultures, an interaction that has received little study in spite of the fact that it lies at the very heart of the development process. Western technology developed out of the Western scientific revolution, which, over the last three centuries, has profoundly altered Western man's understanding of, and relation to, nature. The resulting "scientific viewpoint" has become our way of considering reality, and it is so much a part of us that it is taken for granted. The traditional cultures of Asia or Africa, however, are frequently nonscientific—nonrational in their approach to nature—and they do not always provide a ready foundation upon which to build a more scientific view. Of course people of all cultures experience many of the same familiar phenomena of nature and feel that they understand what is real and how knowledge about the real world is to be organized. Interpretations of what is meant by the "real" world, however, vary widely. Major tasks, then, are to determine what constitutes reality for persons of different cultures and to learn how the most meaningful communication about nature can be established among people holding different views of reality. The first of these tasks has been undertaken, with particular attention to science, by Malinowski,[4] Hsu,[5] and others,[6] but our knowledge is far from complete; the second has hardly been touched on, except as it relates to science education within the Western countries.

Science education, in any country, is certainly a systematic and sustained attempt at communication about nature between a scientific and a nonscientific, or a partially scientific, community, and as such it should be particularly sensitive to the attitudes and presuppositions of both the scientist and the student. In fact, however, the teaching of science is often singularly insensitive to the intellectual environment of the students, particularly so in the developing countries, where the science courses usually offered were developed in a foreign country and have undergone little if any modification in the process of export. Why should we suppose that a program of instruction in botany, say, which is well designed for British children, familiar with an English countryside and English ways of thinking and writing, will prove equally effective for boys and girls in a Malayan village? It is not merely that the plants and their ecology are different in Malaya; more important is the fact that the *children* and *their* ecology are also different.

We are convinced that a study of the intellectual environment in which children live can lead to significant improvements in science teaching and science learning. This is of particular importance, moreover, to the developing countries whose environments are very different from those of the West and whose educational resources are so limited as to make any increase in efficiency very desirable. We discuss in this article an initial effort in that direction, some pilot experiments conducted in Nepal during October and November 1965.

EXPERIMENTAL SETTING AND PROCEDURE

Nepal and its people remained effectively isolated from Western intervention or education throughout the entire colonial period of European influence in Asia, the only important exception being the Gurkha mercenary soldiers who returned to their villages after a period of service in the British army, bringing with them the accumulated experiences of several years of travel and contact with foreign places and ideas. Only within the last dozen years has there been any opportunity for Western education or science to reach appreciable numbers of Nepalese communities, and there is now a considerable range in the degree to which they have penetrated into village life and thought. The government is actively supporting the development of education, as to both quantity and quality, through increase in the number of schools, establishment of a modern teachers college, development of a national university, and other measures. These circumstances, together with the practical consideration that one of us (PLP) is a native of the country, with knowledge of the language and customs, dictated our choice of Nepal for our investigations. (It should be added that each of us has spent several years living and working in the other's native country).

We decided to investigate three widely separated ethnic communities having quite different histories of outside contact: the Newars of the Kathmandu Valley, the Limbus of eastern Nepal, and the Gurungs and Chhetris in the west of Nepal. The sacrifice in depth which this decision entails is justified by a need, at least at this early stage, to determine how widely applicable our conclusions might be. The Newars have, for many centuries, been the principal inhabitants of the Kathmandu Valley, where they have developed a rich artistic and literary heritage. They include many skillful artisans and enterprising merchants within a predominantly agricultural economy. They are conservative, adhering rigidly to an inclusive, self-consistent social and philosophical orthodoxy. The Newar town of Panga, where we worked, is a closely packed unit of narrow paved streets and three-story brick houses surrounded by fertile rice fields. Many of its citizens make frequent trips to Kathmandu, the cosmopolitan capital no more than eight kilometers away, and some of them work there regularly, yet Panga is in most respects an island which might just as well be five hundred kilometers or five centuries away. Its people are shy, friendly, and hospitable to strangers, but they express little curiosity about a visitor's thoughts. The town has both primary and secondary schools with trained teachers, but fewer than one-fourth of its school-age children attend school.

In contrast, the Limbu village of Tokma is several days' walk from any motor road, airfield, or city. Its dwellings are scattered widely over a large and fertile hillside, which provides ample income to the inhabitants, all of whom live by farming. There is no school or store or other business establishment in the village itself. The villagers have the reputation, shared by all Limbus, of being proud, quick to anger, and fiercely independent. They have resisted political domination, and they take pride in an independence of mind which resists the importation of orthodoxies from outside. Their religious life combines Hinduism with shamanism and witchcraft, and they maintain unique customs not shared by other Hindus.[7] They are reserved and suspicious of visitors but not hostile, adhering carefully to established rules of courtesy.

Finally, the Chhetri and Gurung people of Armala Dihi are open, friendly, and relatively poor farmers who will sit for hours asking questions about a stranger's experiences and opinions and about the world he comes from. Many Chhetri men serve as Gurkha soldiers, and nearly every village has one or more members who have returned from such service to live in retirement as respected and influential citizens whose pension payments add significantly to the economic well-being of the village. In Armala Dihi there is a small primary school but no store. There is a good middle school about an hour's walk away. Whereas in Tokma we were the guests of a wealthy Limbu landowner for several days without once being invited to enter his house, our host in Armala Dihi insisted that we move into his own room, sleep in his own bed, share his meals, and use the best of everything he could provide.

We sought information about attitudes toward familiar phenomena of nature, and about the sources of knowledge about nature, through interviews with school-age children, typically nine to fourteen years old, and with adults of an age to be these children's parents. The interviewing was kept informal and usually involved small groups of three or four individuals at a time. The main content and order of the interviews was held constant for all groups.

The questions were of three types, designed to reveal (1) how the respondents accounted for various commonly experienced phenomena, such as rain, lightning, thunder, fire, and earthquake; (2) what attitudes the respondents held about the control or manipulation of such phenomena; (3) what were considered to be the origins of knowledge about nature, and what the accepted criteria of validity of such knowledge were. Typical questions are as follows.

Category 1. How do you account for rain? Where does the rainwater originate? What do most people in the village think about rain? What makes an earthquake?

Category 2. How can rainfall be brought about or prevented? Is it appropriate for men to influence the rain? Is there any protection against lightning or thunder?

Category 3. How were these things (about rain, and so on) learned? How does one know if they are true? How might new knowledge about such things be obtained?

In addition, observations were made of the kinds of opportunities available to children for learning and practicing skills of abstraction and manipulation that could later be a help in learning and using science. As a test of ability to represent real situations by means of an abstract model, each respondent was asked to sketch a rough map showing how to get from his house to the school.

For comparison, similar groups of American primary school children aged nine to twelve attending the University of Hawaii Elementary School in Honolulu were interviewed and asked to sketch maps. About half of these children were Caucasian, the others being of Asian and Polynesian origin. All had been brought up in Hawaii among typically Western surroundings of American games and toys, American magazines and television programs, and all the great diversity of intellectual and physical stimuli to be found in a city such as Honolulu.

THE NATURE OF PHENOMENA

Throughout the interviews, in both Nepal and Hawaii, our interest was directed not toward the "correctness" of a response, as judged by accepted scientific or other standards, but rather toward the type of the response itself and the relation to nature that it suggests—whether, that is, it suggests an explanation of phenomena that is mechanistic, supernatural, teleological, and so on. If a given statement can be recognized as referring to a certain religious belief, for example, that recognition serves our purpose, and we are not concerned with whether or not the pertinent religious scripture is accurately quoted or even explicitly referred to.

With very few exceptions we were given both a "folk-oriented" or "myth-oriented" and a "school-explanation of a given phenomenon within a single interview, sometimes by a single individual. Thus, to account for earthquakes, one of a group of four Chhetri boys said, "The earth is supported on the back of a fish. When the fish grows tired it shifts the weight, and this shakes the earth."

All agreed, but another added, "There is fire at the center of the earth. It seeks to escape and sometimes cracks the earth, causing an earthquake." All agreed to this as well.

In a group of Newar schoolchildren (four boys and a girl) these statements were given in answer to the same question:

"The earth is supported by four elephants. When one of them shifts the weight to another shoulder an earthquake results."

"There are fire and molten metal inside the earth which try to escape. They may crack or move the rock of the earth, causing an earthquake."

Again all agreed to both statements.

This pattern is repeated again and again:

"The deities break vessels of water in the sky, causing rain."

"The sun evaporates water from the sea, producing vapor which is cooled by the mountains to make clouds and rain."

"Lightning comes from the bangles of Indra's dancers."

"Lightning comes from the collision of clouds."

"It rains only in the summer [monsoon] season because we need the rain then. In winter we do not need rain."

"It rains in the summer because the sun is hotter then and causes more evaporation."

The replies given by Newars, Limbus, and Chhetris are very similar in content, evidently reflecting a common background of mythology and of school curricula, a similarity which is not very surprising, for the three groups, with all their differences, do in fact have a common school system and, in the main, a common religion. More surprising is the fact that each group nearly always gave answers of both the types illustrated above, and that all the members generally accepted both. Of course there is nothing unusual in the thought that a given phenomenon may result from either of two different causes and hence that, in general, each of these causes may be accepted as potentially valid. However, here the two types of "causes" offered appear to be qualitatively so different as to be mutually incompatible, for they suggest conceptually very different ideas of nature. Examination of the replies quoted shows that they do not admit of the type of synthesis which states, "God is the source of rain. He produces rain by causing the heat of the sun to evaporate water from the sea." It is as difficult for us to accept both as real alternatives as it is to accept them as simultaneously true.

The contradiction is far more apparent to us, however, than to our respondents, who showed no discomfort over it, a fact which should serve to warn the science educator that all is not as it appears on the surface. The philosophies and literature of Asia make great use of paradox, and, to Asians, contradiction may be more intriguing than disturbing. We should not, therefore, discount the possible existence of very deep-rooted patterns of thought not consonant with the "either-or" logic underlying Western science, the logic which makes it so difficult, for instance, for American students to accept the concept of complementarity in modern physics. However, a simpler explanation should also be considered. Much of the teaching and learning in Nepalese schools involved rote memory only and demands very little understanding or conceptualization. Furthermore, many of the teachers and textbook writers belong to the Brahman caste, the priestly class traditionally responsible for the teaching and preservation of orthodox religious beliefs and practices. It is quite possible that, even without any conscious intent on their part, these teachers and textbook writers have taught early "scientific" concepts in such a way as to produce, in combination with a tradition-oriented home environment, a dual view, according to which distinction between myth and science is unnecessary. Even in science teaching in an American elementary school the amount of teleology used is not inconsiderable. In any case, this dual view of nature is a matter that needs to be considered in the planning of revised science teaching methods.

No such duality was evident concerning the control or manipulation of nature (which was always considered appropriate although not always possible). To questions such as, How can rainfall be brought about or prevented? or, Is there any protection against thunder (lightning)?, a single type of reply was always given. Usually control of such natural phenomena is expected to follow from a religious ritual in which it is made explicit that actual control is at the will of a deity who may not always respond. Thus control is uncertain. In some instances, as when the farmers want hail deflected away from crops, the resort is to magic or charms performed by special persons and not associated with a religious ceremony. Charms too may fail, and all such procedures remain ambiguous enough in principle to make convincing empirical tests of their validity hard to manage. Of course there are many common and well-understood technological manipulations of nature which are taken for granted and explained in operational terms. Such is the case, for example, with irrigation, the cooking of food, or the firing of clay vessels.

In no single instance did a member of any one of the groups of Honolulu school-children manifest a comparable duality of viewpoint. The explanations offered in answer to the same questions about rain, lightning, and so on were not always factually correct, but they were always "scientific" in concept and usually mechanical. Lightning is produced "when two clouds collide"; the heat of the sun evaporates and "lifts" water up to make rain; parts of the earth "shift," causing earthquakes, and so on. On two occasions the biblical story of God erecting the rainbow as a promise to the children of Israel was mentioned, and each time the respondent spontaneously pointed out that this is a different kind of statement and not an explanation of rainbows.

None of the members of the comparison groups in Honolulu believed that control or manipulation of natural phenomena of the kinds under consideration was achievable through magical or religious practices; they considered such control either achievable through technological procedures or impossible. Many, but not all, the individuals who said control was impossible suggested that it might in time become possible. Sometimes procedures were described which are not used and would not work, such as the use of lightning rods to convert lightning into ordinary house current, but even these procedures were always presented as scientific, technological processes without any occult or supernatural element.

THE NATURE OF KNOWLEDGE

When our Nepalese respondents were asked to give the source of their knowledge about nature they invariably said that it came "from books" and "from old people." When we asked how the old people found out or how knowledge got into the books they told us it came from earlier generations of "old people" or from other books. When we pressed for some ultimate source, most of our respondents said that these things had always been known, although a few of them referred to legends telling how some particular skill, such as fire building, was given to men by the deities. One Chhetri student suggested that some knowledge might have been obtained by "accidental observations."

We went on to inquire how knowledge hitherto unknown to anyone might be acquired or how it might be sought. We were always told that such new knowledge is not to be expected. Even when we pushed this question so far as to call attention to such "new" discoveries as space travel or transistor radios, which all Nepalese know about, it was held that such things were always known by someone, or else that these are merely new applications of old knowledge. One very tentative exception was offered by a Limbu boy, who suggested that really new knowledge might sometimes come through dreams. We find it hard to believe that more probing would not reveal other exceptions, yet the predominant view is one that pictures human knowledge about nature as a closed body, rarely if ever capable of extension, which is passed down from teacher to student and from generation to generation. Its source is authority, not observation. In fact, experiment or observation was never directly suggested to us as an appropriate or trustworthy criterion of the validity of a statement, or as its source. When one of us stated that a book, after all, is only a more permanent record of someone's observations, the idea was treated as novel and faintly suspect. Given this concept of knowledge, it is no surprise that the schools rely heavily upon rote memory. Memorizing would seem to be the easiest and most efficient way to deal with a closed and limited body of unvarying facts. There are also other well-known and frequently criticized forces embedded within the formal educational system which strongly reinforce this natural tendency.

It should not be thought, of course, that it is only in Nepal or Asia that students try to learn science by memorizing. Our comparison group in Honolulu showed evidence of considerable, though more limited, reliance on the memorizing of facts given in a book or stated by a teacher. However, members of the Honolulu group all stated that the knowledge originated in observation and experiment, and they believed that new knowledge not only can be obtained but continuously is being obtained.

USE OF ABSTRACTIONS

Science as the scientist thinks of it and would like to see it taught consists not of a body of more or less isolated facts to be memorized, but of a system of empirically verifiable relationships between more or less abstract concepts. While the concepts are derived from real phenomena, the relationships of science relate concepts, not real objects, and the theories of science are built around "models" which portray in abstract, often mathematical, terms a selectively idealized representation of real phenomena. It is essential for the science student to learn to be at home, at some level of sophistication, with this process, which must surely appear even to the Western layman to be extraordinarily indirect. Much attention is given to this in the recently developed or improved science courses in the United States, which go to great lengths to give students systematic training and practice in skills of abstraction and inference while striving to maintain contact with the real world by subjecting conclusions to observational verification. Of course, informal learning plays a part in this process. The toys children manipulate, the games they play, the activities of the adults they watch and imitate, the conversations they listen to all contribute to the attitudes and skills they develop.[8] In everything the child does in school there is an echo of his environment at home.

How much more difficult science must be, then, for a child who lives in a Nepalese village or small town, immersed in a very different environment with its own pervasive non-Western influences. Here he lives close to nature in a direct, particularistic relation of planting and harvesting, with little or no abstraction and little need to generalize. He does not play with mechanical toys or build mechanical models; he plays or watches games of skill or chance but knows little about games of strategy; he rarely sees a book in his home; he rarely has occasion or opportunity to deal with derived or inferred properties or concepts. Certainly his society, or any society, contains a great many abstractions, ranging from spoken or written language all the way to a very complex religious cosmology, but these are not all particularly useful in preparing the way for science, which wants to hold to a rather special and verifiable relation to nature. Thus, for example, every Nepalese child will be familiar with abstract representations of certain Hindu or Buddhist deities and heroes of religious myths and legends, yet these are not subject to direct or even indirect observational verification, after the manner of science, and they may not be conducive to a scientific approach.

A thorough analysis of the informal intellectual environment, even in one of the groups we visited, would be a major undertaking which we did not have the resources to undertake. Yet we did want to include some tentative assessment of the effects of informal learning as it might bear upon science learning. For this purpose we asked our subjects to sketch rough freehand maps showing how to get "from your house to the school" (or to some other well-known local landmark). A map is a fairly simple, yet typical, example of a scientific model. It preserves a verifiable one-to-one relation to reality and yet it is an abstraction, useful for what is omitted no less than for what is included. Mapping allows for great variety in the way a given reality is represented, and the relationships and inferences derived from a map, while not totally unrelated to reality, nevertheless actually refer to the model and not to the real world. We believe that the maps which children[9] or adults draw to represent a well-known route or neighborhood will reveal with some accuracy their readiness to understand and use other scientific abstractions.

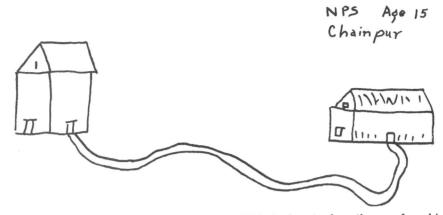

Figure 26.1. Map drawn by a fifteen-year-old Limbu boy to show the way from his house to the school. In fact, the house and school are not on the same street or path.

The "maps" we obtained from the Nepalese respondents are all very similar to each other and to the example shown in fig. 26.1. Always they include a recognizable *picture* of "my house" and of "the school," the two being connected by a line which seems to denote *the process of going* from one to the other, not the spatial relationship of one to the other. Thus, the two buildings represented in fig. 26.1 are not in fact on the same street or path, being separated by several street intersections and other landmarks, none of which appear on the map. In contrast we show (fig. 26.2) a map typical of those drawn by American children in response to the same instructions. Here both house and school are represented by abstract symbols, not pictures, and there is a clear effort to show spatial relationships and to

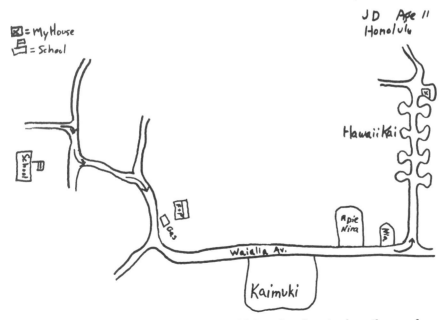

Figure 26.2. Map drawn by an eleven-year-old American boy to show the way from his house to the school. Note the wealth of spatial and directional clues.

provide needed spatial clues. The propensity of the Nepalese for making maps (whether verbal or graphic) which are *sequential* rather than spatial constructs is not limited to schoolchildren. In a land of foot trails, where literacy is too low to justify the use of signs, this propensity has been a source of consternation to more than a few travelers of Western upbringing! We, too, in reply to our inquiries as we traveled, were given instructions or "maps" which, like a string of beads, list in correct sequence the places we should pass through without giving any clue as to distances, trail intersections, changes of directions, and so on. Our interest is not in the accuracy or potential usefulness of this different kind of model but in the light it may shed on a way of thinking which may extend far beyond mere map making. The villagers use no other kind of map; they do not use drawings in constructing a building or a piece of furniture—in fact they hardly use drawings or spatial representation at all (except for records of land ownership, which does not change very frequently), and the lack of spatial models may be very natural. One wonders, however, whether the science teacher will have this in mind when he presents a model of a molecule or the solar system.

VARIATIONS BETWEEN GROUPS

Our observations were the same for all three of the Nepalese groups we visited. No doubt this is partly due to the rather gross nature of the study, which may bring out only the most obvious and general conclusions where a finer-grained, more extensive study could be expected also to reveal characteristics that pertain to one group only. From the standpoint of science education, however, it is useful to start with observations that lead to widely applicable recommendations, and this has been a factor in the design of our study. Certain differences between groups are suggested by the results of our interviews, however, and we mention below two that might well be of further interest.

Although observation was practically never suggested explicitly by any group as a reliable source of knowledge, we did find many indications among Limbu respondents that observation of nature plays an important role in shaping their attitudes, and also that they feel a need for observational support of theories to an extent not found in either of the other groups. Thus, whereas our Newar respondents always had a firm answer to every question, it was not uncommon for a Limbu to give a reply and then add, "it seems so, but we are not sure," or even to admit that he had no explanation of a given phenomenon. All groups described the rainbow as a manifestation which draws water up from lakes or rivers into the sky. However, more than one of the Limbu respondents pointed out to us that a rainbow may be seen in waterfalls when the sun shines on them, "and so it must have something to do with light and water spray or vapor."

Newar respondents always attributed lightning damage to a particular variety of thunder,[10] literally "ax thunder" (we refer to it here as a "thunderbolt"). They describe it as a material object, shaped like an ax, which falls from the sky during a thunderstorm and returns to the sky again, splitting or smashing things on its way. They offer no evidence to support this description, except to refer to the knowledge of old people, if evidence is demanded. When we asked Limbus about thunder and thunderbolts we were told essentially the same thing, with the added information that "thunderbolts" are black in color. We did not question this explanation nor ask for any evidence, yet in a few minutes one of the informants produced a small, black stone artifact shaped like an ax head. He explained that it was a "spent thunderbolt" which had been damaged when it struck the earth and, being imperfect, could not return to the sky. Further inquiry indicates that such artifacts are occasionally found on the ground or in rice paddies. They are not made from locally available stone and are not believed to be of human origin but are always taken to be "thunderbolts." They fit the mythological concept of "ax thunder" closely enough to make identification of them in this way very natural, provided a need for observational support of the theoretical concept is felt. Obviously our informant felt that, in our minds too, this evidence would support his explanation.

This experience was duplicated in every essential detail in the community of Armala Dihi, 300 kilometers to the west, where we were again presented with a stone-age "thunderbolt"! Other evidence of a need for empirical observation was less strong, however, in Armala Dihi than in Tokma.

Finally, there are differences among these three groups in the degree of stress produced as a result of new ideas from the West. All groups and all individual respondents know that change is coming rapidly to Nepal and that many new ideas are reaching the young people through the rapidly expanding school system. Among the Chhetris of Armala Dihi this is evidently a source of much personal and intergroup tension. The adults welcome schools and urge or require their children to attend them, yet they are engaged with the children in a continuing and sometimes strenuous dialogue in defense of the old ideas and cosmology—a dialogue in which both adults and youths did their best to enlist our participation. Although the adults clearly identify themselves with the old order, they are intensely curious about the new. They seem not to tire of asking questions that range widely over a world of ideas just visible over a still-distant horizon. None of our respondents had served as Gurkha soldiers, but, as we have pointed out, the region includes many individuals who have. In contrast, the Newars of Panga, certainly the most conservative of the three communities, show very little curiosity about the world outside Panga and evidence very little concern about what their children may be learning. The Limbus, too, showed little concern about foreign ideas, which they know about but do not perceive as threatening. They seemed to show a similar lack of concern about a number of introduced Hindu rituals which are practiced and yet disclaimed as foreign and of no value. Such patterns of receptivity or rejection of change and the stresses they lead to in individuals or families are, of course, too complicated to be treated here. Yet they are important to the processes of development and education, and they deserve careful study in considerable depth.

IMPLICATIONS FOR SCIENCE EDUCATION

The foregoing observations suggest changes in method or content which might lead to easier and more economical, as well as more effective, teaching of science in Nepal. We believe that some of these changes will be found to apply more or less well in many other developing countries, and we hope that similar, or more refined, studies will be undertaken which will extend and, hopefully, corroborate our conclusions. For the present we shall limit ourselves to a few relatively clearly indicated changes that could be introduced on a pilot scale.

It is clear that the school-age boys and girls among our subjects do not have the attitudes about nature and learning that are most conducive to an understanding of science. Clearly, too, they have not developed much skill in abstract representation, measurement, and so on—skills which contribute not only to scientific experimentation but to conceptualization as well. It is now well accepted that such attitudes and skills can best be developed relatively early in a child's school experience, well before the introduction of formal subject-matter courses like chemistry or physics. We believe that a program of prescience instruction in the elementary grades, similar to programs now under development in the United States,[11] will be both possible and very desirable in Nepal and probably in other developing countries. This instruction may well follow the general guidelines that have been laid down for the American efforts, but it will have to be adapted to conform closely to the particular environment, needs, and available resources of the country and community where it is used, and it should start with the questions children ask there. The project will involve program design and teacher training but no difficult economic problems pertaining to equipment or supplies, for local "phenomena" for observation are best and are abundant; "laboratory material" will consist of leaves and pebbles, sunshine and seeds; and equipment will consist of pieces of bamboo, locally available utensils, and so on. Such a program can certainly present real phenomena and teach real facts, but its fundamental intent is to provide a basis of skills and attitudes and a relation to nature, rather than facts as such. In a school system that relies heavily on memorized factual content this will be a delicate undertaking.

We have noted the prevalence of a dual view of nature or reality which was especially striking because the two views expressed seem to us contradictory, although accepted simultaneously by our subjects. If this paradox is new in Nepal, it is certainly not new to the West. The same ambivalence has run through Western thought at least since the early scientific revolution, and it is still with us. What scientist in the West has not heard the question, But how can you be a scientist and still accept that view? or has not at one time or another agreed to speak on "Science and Religion"?

Yet for the most part we in the West have been able to make our peace with the complementary worlds of matter and spirit, of objects and values. Through careful delineation of boundaries, conscious and unconscious compartmentalization, or reinterpretation, and a variety of intellectual nonaggression pacts, a reasonably secure and peaceful coexistence has been achieved, so that this particular dualism no longer poses serious problems for the Western scientist or student. Can others be helped to achieve or preserve a coexistence that does not violate their cultural values as they try to assimilate our Western science and scientific viewpoint?

We propose, as one step, that science be presented as a "second culture," complementing that already present rather than replacing it, and taught in the spirit in which a second language is taught—to be learned and used, certainly, but not to the exclusion of the student's native tongue. This will require a very different orientation from that commonly found in most Asian schools, or indeed from that characteristic of most Asian-American relationships, even if it does not mean great changes in school curriculum. Beginning with the earliest missionary schools and continuing through the period of colonial schools, the attitude, and often the intent, of Western education has been that a "primitive" or "decadent" civilization is to be replaced with a more modern and "better" one.[12] This attitude tends to continue even though colonialism is no longer a force behind it, and it tends to be particularly strong in science teaching, for science is taken to be the one really unique and powerful offering of the Western world. In fact, however, the purpose of education, whether in Nepal or elsewhere in Asia, is no longer to destroy one civilization, or even one set of ideas, in order to replace it totally with something that is conceived to be better; to proceed in that direction, or with that implicit attitude, is to create unnecessary difficulties along the way. An implacable either-or approach, leading to a direct confrontation between traditional attitudes and a modern and very foreign approach to knowledge, invites conflict both within the student's own mind and between him and his elders in the community.

As has been seen too often, such a conflict results at best in a draw, which alienates from one world without really admitting into the other. We propose to avoid or postpone this confrontation by starting early science instruction with simple observations of ordinary things and events—observations which stimulate and use the child's latent curiosity, which anyone can make, and which demand no special or formal interpretation in cosmological or philosophical terms. Instead, this approach will provide a foundation of skills, of attitudes toward observation, and of specific observations upon which a more formal knowledge of science may later be built. In making this proposal we accept a complementarity of views as natural and perhaps as inevitable.

We are mindful of certain arguments that favor, in principle, the opposite alternative of immersing the student in the Western scientific culture, through study in the West, and demanding that he learn it and conform to it totally. Of course, this "total immersion" would not be possible for most Nepalese children or adults, the vast majority of whom do not in any case expect or wish to become scientists. Beyond this lies the fact that any who were to succeed in such a "total immersion" and then return to work and live in Nepal would be sure to find themselves seriously alienated. To a considerable degree this does happen to Asian graduate students who leave home to study in the United States and then, partly because of the consequent alienation, find themselves unenthusiastic about returning home. Once immersed, one is more comfortable to remain so.

We are mindful, also, of a seeming contradiction in our proposal. If extensive social and cultural changes are bound to accompany the introduction of science, is it wise to ignore this in preparing the child for learning science? We believe that it is. Of course, some kind of accommodation between the scientific revolution and Nepalese culture must and will eventually be reached if science is introduced at all. This is a complex matter which must evolve slowly within the Eastern cultures as it did in the West. Experience suggests that this accommodation will not be most easily achieved simply by substituting the one for the other, and particularly not during the school years when the children are immersed in the intellectual and physical environment of the village. It is important to them and to the village that they remain at peace there. Moreover, an eventual accommodation should be based upon real science well learned rather than on a set of memorized facts and formulas learned under stress.

To refer again to the analogy of language teaching, recent experience seems to show that the attitudes and techniques used in teaching English to, say, Urdu-speaking children, where no question of substitution or conflict arises, are the most effective in teaching a standard English to children, in Hawaii or Georgia, for example, who speak a "substandard" dialect of English. It is easier for these children to learn standard English when it is presented as a second language, not as a substitute for their own "incorrect" dialect, which of course they continue to need in their own community.

ELEMENTARY SCIENCE INSTRUCTION

A detailed program of instruction in science (many might prefer to call it pre-science) is under development in Nepal, partly as a result of the observations reported above. It would be premature at this time to anticipate its final dimensions or content, but we may say a few things about its methods and goals. Emphasis will be on an observational approach to phenomena which are familiar to anyone, or which can readily be produced by anyone, and a progression of skills and experiences will be built up, encompassing classification, measurement, generalization, inference, and quantification, and leading ultimately to the design and execution of elementary but conceptually more or less sophisticated experiments by the students. The material presented will contain some specific information intended for later use, but this will not receive major emphasis and need not be memorized. In addition to the observational material, some history of science will be introduced, in essentially anecdotal form, to show that knowledge of "books and old people" is really a record of observations and interpretations made by real people.

The educational system of Nepal, like that of many other countries, is fairly rigid and is not amenable to rapid change or experimentation. Nevertheless, we see it as necessary that improvements, to be lasting, be developed within the existing system, however time-consuming that may prove to be; hence, such efforts must have the understanding and active support of those persons who are in positions of leadership and authority within the system. The program we are proposing will be developed within the Education Ministry and tried out in the laboratory schools of the College of Education of Tribhuwan University. Further trial and development with the help of Peace Corps teachers, now working in many schools throughout the country, is anticipated. These Peace Corps volunteers are enthusiastic, well accepted, and devoted to the improvement of education. If the program has the endorsement of the government, they will be ready to try it out with very little feeling of hesitancy because the teaching methods are new and different. Moreover, there is reason to hope that the interest in better science teaching which has resulted from the American experimental curricula in secondary school science will result in changes and improvements in Asia, and perhaps in Nepal, affecting the teaching of science at the secondary level. These American courses, as well as other studies,[13] emphasize observation and experiment. We hope that a program such as the one we propose for Nepal at the elementary levels will provide a useful preparation for more formal course changes patterned on the American model. In fact, we believe that some such preparation will be found necessary if science courses based on the American experimental courses are to maintain their spirit and emphasis as they are adapted for use in Asia.

In concluding, we must emphasize that much of what has been said is tentative, based as it is on a limited pilot study. Yet the study does indicate that research of this nature can provide needed perspective for the improvement of science teaching in non-Western countries. We hope it will lead to more study and discussion, with regard both to Nepal and to other developing countries.

NOTES

1. R. Gruber, *Science and the New Nations* (New York: Basic Books, 1961).
2. U.S. Agency for International Development, *Science, Technology and Development: The U.S. Papers Prepared for the United Nations Conference on Applications of Science and Technology for the Benefit of the Developing Nations* (Washington, D.C.: Government Printing Office, 1962-63).
3. F. E. Dart, *Foreign Affairs* 41 (1963): 360.
4. B. Malinowski, in *Science, Religion and Reality*, ed. J. Needham (New York: Macmillan, 1925).
5. F. L. K. Hsu, *Religion, Science and Human Crises* (London: Routledge, 1952).
6. E. E. Evans-Pritchard, *Witchcraft among the Azande* (London: Oxford University Press, 1937); J. Needham, *Science and Civilization in China* (London: Cambridge University Press, 1954).
7. V. Barnouw, *Southwestern Journal Anthropology* 11 (1955): 15.
8. See, for example, J. M. Roberts, M. J. Arth, R. R. Bush, *American Anthropologist* 61 (1959): 597.
9. Here we consider only children old enough to be capable of abstraction. See, for example, B. Inhelder and J. Piaget, *The Growth of Logical Thinking from Childhood to Adolescence* (New York: Basic Books, 1958).
10. Newars refer to four of five different kinds of thunder, of which this is one. Each has a name and is distinguished from others by the quality of sound perceived.
11. R. M. Gagné, *Science* 151 (1966): 49; see also, "Science—a Process Approach," *AAAS* (1965).
12. See, for example, R. J. Crane, in *The Transfer of Institutions*, ed. W. B. Hamilton (Durham, N.C.: Duke University Press, 1964).
13. "Guidelines for the Development of the Laboratory in Science Instruction," *National Acad. Science-Nat. Res. Council Publ. No. 1093* (1962).

27 / An Experimental Ninth-Grade Anthropology Course

Paul Bohannan, Merwyn S. Garbarino, and
Earle W. Carlson

In 1965–66 we initiated a full-year course in anthropology for ninth graders at the North Shore Country Day School in Winnetka, Illinois. The school, a member of the National Association of Independent Schools, has about twenty students in its kindergarten and in each of its first five grades and about forty in each of its sixth through twelfth grades. It is divided, as most independent schools are, into a lower school, middle school (grades six through eight), and an upper school (grades nine through twelve). It is what is commonly called a progressive school because it emphasizes close personal attention to each student, recognizes human capacities beyond the traditional scholarly ones, and tries to train the visual and aural senses as well as the capacities for reading, writing, and computing.

Our students met in two sections, each for forty minutes daily with about eighteen students in each section. These students were "selected" in the sense that their capacities ran from average up. We had a few very bright students but none who were not of at least average capacity and achievement. We think it is an important point that the students of the school are not selected primarily for their scholarly capacities—in fact, that is rather far down the list in the requirements. It is, however, assumed that the students are able to absorb and profit from a good high school education. Therefore, we had no problems with dropouts or with lack of motivation. We had boys with long hair, and, like the rest of the school, we treated it merely as a hairstyle.

The course was undertaken when, in a discussion with the headmaster of the school, Nathaniel S. French, Bohannan criticized several new curricula that used anthropology and sociology as decorations on a course that was basically economics and history. He felt the right way to handle the material was to treat the principles of sociology and anthropology as the fundamentals, history and ethnology as the primary sources of data on human existence, and economics and political science as the two disciplines most helpful in evaluating today's newspapers. French and Bohannan agreed that neither economics nor political science made as much sense without the background of history, sociology, and anthropology as with it.

When an opening occurred in the social studies faculty in the upper school, French suggested that if Bohannan would plan such a course, he (French) would appoint whatever teacher of the course the two of them found satisfactory. Bohannan replied that although he needed a co-worker in this program, he would like to teach part of it himself and would prefer a partnership with a second anthropologist rather than to try directing a program taught by someone else. At that time Garbarino had just finished field work among the Seminole Indians and was writing her dissertation. She agreed to become a partner in this project. Throughout the year the two taught more or less alternate units, one for a few days, then the other for a few days; meanwhile keeping in close touch and exchanging "field notes." We did not find this arrangement difficult, and as far as we know, the students did not find it confusing or objectionable.

From the beginning of the program our goal was to teach students in high school the data, methods, theories, and insights of the behavioral sciences. Although we concentrated on anthropology, we also included a good bit of sociology, no inconsiderable amount of psychoanalytic viewpoint and psychological anthropology, some historical and more prehistorical material, and some theory derived ultimately from economics and political science. Our goal was to provide the best available scaffolding for studying history and comprehending the present-day human situation.

We considered ourselves responsible for the first year. We knew that our students would proceed to at least one more year, and some of them to three more years, of social studies in their high school careers. We wanted to establish a set of viewpoints that would be useful and expandable in the later years with as little as possible to be relearned, unlearned, or jettisoned. We are aware, of course, that ethnographic details will be forgotten. Nevertheless, we are also aware—and our experience proved overwhelmingly—that only good ethnographic factual material can make such a course interesting.

The year was divided into three quarters. In the first quarter we began with American Indians, proceeded to Africa, and reached a caesura with some theoretical material on cultural theory and the structure of society.

The second quarter dealt with human origins. We taught the principles of evolutionary theory (about three-quarters of our students had already studied it in their biology course), the evolution of mankind and the development of man's capacity for culture, and prehistory up to the creation of the ancient civilizations, therefore including the acquisition of agriculture, metalworking, and the like.

In the third quarter we made a comparative study of civilizations. We began with the ancient Near Eastern civilizations and then discussed the history and culture of the civilizations of China and Japan.

What we accomplished could be called a course in non-Western civilizations. Although it was anthropologically based, it was not limited to anthropology.

It is probably necessary here to justify for most anthropologists and teachers our decision to put the cultural anthropology quarter ahead of the human origins' quarter, because it is the reverse of the way it occurred historically. We have never found, either here or in our university teaching, that students are better informed from having gone through a subject in chronological order. On the contrary, we have found, both here and in our university teaching, that if they have some knowledge of the principles of social organization and cultural symbolism, that the entire developmental aspects are easier to teach because the students know what attributes have in fact been acquired and can begin to take a developmental view from the very first. Put another way, if one teaches this material in chronological order, it is necessary to explain the culture and social structure at the same time that you are explaining the development of it. If they already know what social structure and culture are, then we are free to pursue the way in which development took place. We have found that in this way both structural functionalism and evolutionism can be taught in such a way that the students themselves discover the interrelationship between these two sets of theories in terms of historical and archeological facts.

Finally, Bohannan and Garbarino came into this teaching experiment without experience in teaching high school students. (Carlson, who took over in subsequent years, had such experience.) Except for our own children and those of our friends, we had not faced or dealt with teen-agers since we ourselves had been teen-agers. Our basic fear was, How do you teach social science to people who necessarily, because of their age, have limited social experience? We quickly found the answer: You fill them in. And we soon realized that "filling them in" is as good a definition as any other of a liberal education.

FIRST QUARTER: CULTURAL AND SOCIAL ANTHROPOLOGY

We began with Theodora Kroeber's *Ishi in Two Worlds*. We found this a very good book for ninth graders because they read it with interest, consider it an adult book, and react emotionally as well as intellectually to its contents. On the first day they were assigned the Prologue to Mrs. Kroeber's book. Ishi, the last surviving member of the Yahi tribe of Central California, was driven by hunger and fear to a slaughterhouse outside of Oroville, California, where he was discovered one morning in a corral. Because no communication was possible and because he was naked and on the verge of exhaustion, he was taken to the Oroville jail. The anthropologists at the University of California in Berkeley were notified, and T. T. Waterman went immediately to Oroville to see him.

In spite of the fact that Mrs. Kroeber goes to some pains to point out that the sheriff's action in putting Ishi into jail was neither stupid nor brutal, our ninth graders had a serious reaction to it. On the basis, then, of no more than the Prologue, they started a discussion in which they blamed their own people, and in a sense themselves, for being inept and guilty of mistreatment of Ishi and the Indians. When this attitude became evident, we asked them what they thought would happen if the last wild Indian were to wander today out of the Skokie lagoons into Winnetka; what would we do with him? After a few minutes' discussion one boy raised his hand and said, "We would obviously have to put him in jail." We were encouraged by the first session of the class because we were finding the students willing to get involved in both the material we had assigned to them and the discussion of hypothetical situations set in their own community.

The second chapter of *Ishi* gives background material on California Indians. We had the ninth graders make maps, on the basis of the one Mrs. Kroeber gives, and do a little encyclopedia work on the problem of American Indians. Thereafter, we went through this book a chapter a day. The only part of our teaching techniques that might be difficult for someone who is not a professional anthropologist to emulate is that when students asked questions, we answered them with as precise detail and as much theory as we thought necessary to make the details understood.

By the time they had finished *Ishi*, they were well launched into the study of cultural anthropology. It would, perhaps, be possible to write a teacher's guide for this material. It would be vastly preferable, however, for the teacher to have a few good courses in anthropology and to deal with the questions and the material as it comes up. Our two sections brought up different points; yet we think that they were approximately equal in their achievement at the end of the unit. Certainly we could not have achieved so much if *we* had brought up the points and told them what they were to be interested in.

Next we read Alice Marriott's *Ten Grandmothers*. We found this, like *Ishi*, a superb book for teaching ninth-grade social studies. It is an adult book—a factor that cannot be underestimated. With a series of characters running through the story, Dr. Marriott explains the pressures and responses that led the Kiowa Indians to change and develop as they did in the middle nineteenth century. It is fascinating history and superb anthropology and, like all Dr. Marriott's work, well written. On the basis of this material we discussed Plains Indians at length, and some of the students wrote special reports, taking their materials from such standard books as Spencer and Jennings' *The Native Americans* and Driver's *Indians of North America*.

When we took up our third Indian group, the Iroquois, we made a serious mistake. We considered, and still do, Hazel Hertzberg's *The Great Tree and the Longhouse*, a part of the AAA's Curriculum Development Project, a very fine book. It is, however, written for the sixth grade, and we did not realize that our ninth graders would not be willing to adjust to what was for them easy reading. The attitude was best summed up by a girl who asked, "When are we going to get through with this kid stuff and back to books written for just people?" This judgment is not a considered judgment on Mrs. Hertzberg's book; it is a statement that ninth graders, in our experience, are not able to utilize material that is easy for them nearly so well as they are able to cope with material that is difficult for them. Although we have not tested this proposition further, it is our hunch that it is probably true in all groups of ninth graders. We found that they could not consider the book as just a book from which they should study and get information and perhaps write things that would bring it up to their level. They didn't see it that way. They felt that we were trying to keep them in a junior role. We think that they understood the intellectual aspects of the problem, but emotionally they nevertheless felt that this book was not for them; we also have a hunch that they would not feel that any book that was written for the schools was for them. They need and want well-written material that can be of interest to an adult.

After discussion of these three books, we gave a few short lectures on introductory aspects of the theories of cultural anthropology. We told students how to take notes on lectures, showed them how lectures should be organized and how to judge a good one, and tried to get them to evaluate critically the structure of lectures. We graded them on the notes they took on our lectures and found that we had to teach them the outline form.

The lecture material covered the prehistory of the American Indians in a very fast sweep, as well as some statements about the culture areas of North America (we used one created by Garbarino on the basis of all the others available; we think that this makes no difference, and the one in Driver can be utilized with no comparative material at all). For a special project that each student was required to do during the quarter, some of our more advanced students made a study of American Indian origins, basing it primarily on Driver and on Spencer and Jennings. We also led a series of discussions in which the ecology and economic adjustment, the political forms, and the family life of the three peoples we had studied were compared, bringing this into line with other material that the students happened to know, with material they had read for their reports, and with their own experiences in families in the middle and upper middle class in the Middle West.

We then attempted to go over the same general ground, but more briefly and in more depth, for the peoples of Africa. We began with Colin Turnbull's *The Forest People*. This book, about the Pygmies of the Congo, is a superb example of what ought to be written to teach anthropology as a basic subject in the social sciences for high school students. We might add, parenthetically, that the first twelve chapters are, for this purpose, better than the last three, and would suggest that teachers consider skipping the last three chapters unless they plan to use them for considering how a person from one society reacts to geography and social situations that are strange to him. Since we had already explored this idea in *Ishi*, we did not find the last three chapters as useful as the rest of the book.

But *The Forest People* is a hard act to follow. Therefore, rather than try to use material that we thought less suitable, we went directly to a summary position and used Bohannan's *Africa and Africans*. This book (which has fast become obsolete in all except chapters 7–14, although a new edition, with Philip Curtin as co-author, is in the works) was not terribly successful in the ninth grade, because it contains too many generalizations, too much summary, and too few ethnographic examples. What we finally did was take a single point from each one of the chapters around which could be built discussions and outside assignments. Our discussions of slavery, of religion, of witchcraft, and of social organization went very well.

We spent about tens days at the end of the quarter on a summary. We gave lectures on basic ideas and fundamentals of social organization, including the family, political structure, and anthropological ideas of economy and religion. We also assigned Douglas Oliver's *Invitation to Anthropology*. We thought, and still think, that it is a very good, short summary of what anthropology is about. Our students did not concur. The reasons that they gave—and this underscores a point we have made above—was that it was not about anything, by which they meant that there were no ethnographic facts or examples in it.

Our conclusions at the end of the quarter were that if you have a lot of good ethnographic fact, well presented and organized, ninth-grade students are extremely interested in it; they do make an association between the people they read about and their own lives so that the teacher can capitalize on the inherent comparative aspects of anthropology; and they are able to learn and are even willing to help to create cultural and social theory.

SECOND QUARTER: HUMAN ORIGINS AND PREHISTORY

Our course took place before the material created by the Anthropology Curriculum Development Project directed by Dr. Malcolm Collier was available, but Carlson used that material in the second and third years. The biggest problem in the first year was the plethora of material—highly repetitious, but with comparatively few outstanding books suitable for ninth graders. The irony, or perhaps one should say it is the cause, is that human origins and prehistory have attracted more nonprofessionals and more writers of "books for young people" than all the rest of anthropology put together. Some of the nonprofessional summaries are good. Others are worse than misleading.

This particular topic presents a problem we do not know how to combat: the primary question that both the writers of the books and our ninth graders ask is "what happened in prehistory?" They want to be given a more or less precise history of the development of man and of his culture and civilization. Obviously, with each new discovery, or at least with each major new theoretical development, it becomes necessary to reconstruct prehistory all over again. This means that each of the books contains a reconstruction and that the reconstructions all too often do not jibe. The reason for this is sometimes to be found simply in the dates of the books, but it is often due to special pleading by the authors. Solving this problem means that the teacher must give a great deal of factual and theoretical material on the evolution of the human animal and culture. We gave this material in lecture form because we did not find books that could do the task for us. The "technician's books" were almost all to detailed for this grade level and for our task. The "writer's books" hurried over the technical problems to get to the romance. Highly technical books on evolution, such as those of Dobzhansky, we did not even try at this grade level. Perhaps we were wrong. We used *Early Man*, by F. Clark Howell and the editors of *Life*. It was extremely useful, but it is difficult to use without supplementary material because there is too much material in it for a casual reading and too little to go into any one aspect of the problem.

Because of limitations both in time and in students' backgrounds in biology, our intention was to teach the concepts rather than the actual mechanisms of evolution. On this level, it was expected that there would be little reason for students who had not had biology to suffer any real disability.

In teaching biological evolution we had to combat the tendency of all the students to take a teleological view of natural selection. We had hoped, by presenting cultural anthropology first, to avoid the problem of purpose in evolution. That is to say, by first showing the present day range of human behavior and then adding the time dimension, we would avoid the bugaboo of tribal peoples seen as contemporary ancestors and would demonstrate that nonliterate peoples have histories, although not written, as long as that of Western man. We think it helped, but we still had to counteract the idea that the aim of evolution was to produce Western man.

We stressed in lecture and discussion that biological and cultural evolution were inseparable in man's development and that through the evolution of culture man was able to move into many new environmental zones without gross biological changes. Culture is thus shown as the extension of man's senses and his nonbiological means of adaptation, including adaptation to the social environment. Man then differs from the other primates primarily because of his culture.

To demonstrate the concept of adaptation we first discussed the exploitative potential of various environments at different stages of cultural evolution, but we hoped to avoid the pitfall of geographic determinism by presenting the environment as permitting a range of forms within its limits. Therefore, even in an extreme environment such as the circumpolar regions, while shelter is an essential, we found many forms shelter could take.

In terms of our stated aims of teaching concepts rather than mechanisms, we believe we were successful in the following ways. The students demonstrated reasonable grasp of natural selection and adaptation, and (within the limits of the facts available to them) they understood the positive feedback relationship between culture and biological evolution. They also learned the generally accepted sequence of fossil forms of the hominid line.

Growing out of our study of adaptation to environment, we progressed to post-Pleistocene times and to culture changes arising from the domestication of plants and animals. Domestication in our presentation was only one of many regional adaptations in response to a slowly changing climate. In this fashion we hoped to avoid the mental image of the neolithic or agricultural revolution as a sudden insight on the part of an individual—a point of view many students have. Indeed, for one of our weekly written assignments we got a lively, imaginative story about *the* woman who invented agriculture. It is quite likely that many students tend toward a similar picture of domestication, and we wanted to correct that view. We think we did.

It was easy to generate interest in the changes in behavior caused by a change from hunting and gathering to food production. In fact, the very concept of domestication as opposed to taming resulted in lively class discussion, and some students became so interested that they did independent study projects, which they reported to the class. Among the topics studied were the attributes selected for domestication and a comparison of productive usefulness of children in hunting and gathering as opposed to agricultural societies. There was some class amusement at the realization that children were usually burdens to hunters whereas they could contribute importantly to an agricultural community. Our students had never before considered children as anything but assets by their mere existence.

Here a note on independent research might be injected. The limitations of the school library presented a real difficulty. This is not to be taken as a criticism of the particular school we taught in, for it is highly unlikely that any high school would have adequate resource material in either cultural or physical anthropology unless some recent attempt had been made to obtain it. The fact is that library materials must be expanded if anthropology is to be taught, and from our experience it would appear that most of the expansion must be in the direction of college-level literature, *not* adaptations written for high school students.

THIRD QUARTER: COMPARATIVE CIVILIZATIONS

By the end of the second quarter we had reached the point of talking about civilization as a subset of culture marked by certain specific items or traits. The students became interested in the "causes" of civilization, a point we could not have started with. To come up with the necessary and sufficient causes of civilization we turned to the data of the archaic civilizations of the Old and New Worlds—Sumer, Egypt, and Mexico. We went to the various works of V. Gordon Childe, taking his criteria for civilization as a place to start. Then, through discussions with the students, we elicited their ideas of the way these various criteria are to be ranked in importance.

From reading and lectures, discussion ensued, and the students decided that although agriculture was necessary to civilization, it was not sufficient "cause"—that, indeed, no one "cause" was sufficient in itself. That conclusion led to the question of why all agriculturalists did not achieve civilization and to a discussion of social and ecological limitations to evolutionary potential.

During the whole unit on early civilization we had the students compare *culture* and the *special form* of culture that is called a civilization. The result was happily more than just a list of traits. It came close to being a statement of cultural process and increasing structural complexity. Without using such professional jargon, the students came up with the recognition that civilization has more components and greater specialization of the components than the noncivilized society. Briefly, we discussed the greater complexities and possibilities of food production with differentiation of primary producers and full-time labor specialists versus food collecting or producing with very little specialization.

The students decided—as anthropologists have known for over a century, but we do not think that we precooked their decision—that the presence of writing was one of the two most important of the several criteria of civilization. The only new thing about this idea is that they discovered it in terms that were not available in the nineteenth century when it was discovered—undoubtedly rediscovered—by anthropologists. They pointed out that the capacity to store culture created by writing vastly enlarges the choices open to people. At the same time, it reduces the amount of effort it takes to maintain a cultural level. The result is a proliferation of specialist roles and hence the complexification and cultural achievement that civilization exhibits. We had lively discussions about the fact, which they pointed out with no prodding, that the same thing is happening again today because computers provide new kinds of storage mechanisms for culture and that we are only just beginning to feel the effects of them. In our summary we noted that just as speaking means that the demonstrator is not necessary in all situations of learning, and just as writing means that the actively participating teacher is not necessary in all situations of learning, so in the present situation, the written record has been changed out of recognition so that word symbols too are no longer necessary in all situations of learning. It seemed unlikely to our students—and to us—that computers would replace writing any more than writing replaced speaking or speaking replaced demonstration. (We missed, here, an opportunity to explain a Gutmann scale.)

The other item they thought was of fundamental importance was full-time specialization of arts and industries. However, there were many other characteristics of civilization that we discussed, including oral tradition and common expectations as means of social control in homogeneous societies as opposed to the need for a codification of laws in the heterogeneous society that appeared with early urbanization. Urban culture itself, as a new and different set of relationships, was dwelt upon at some length. Without calling it such, we came close to Redfield's rural-urban continuum as a concept useful in describing development over time as well as change in space.

Largely because the class *demanded* some sort of chronology—we think as a result of prior conditioning—we did a time line of invention from 10,000 B.C. to A.D. 1500, comparing Old and New World chronologies. The comparison involved not only the invention of technical improvements, such as the wheel and metallurgy, but also the appearance of major structural change, such as the beginnings of complex village life. The visual stimulus of a time line was important to the students. We think now that throughout the year more visual treatment should have been incorporated, perhaps in the form of films.

We ended the unit on early civilization with a few lectures and some discussion of the European neolithic, the spread of food production into Europe, the Mediterranean influence in the north, and the steppe pastoralists' introduction of the domesticated horse into central Europe. The emphasis here was on the cultural backwardness of Western man during the formative period of civilization and the importance of diffusion and recombination of many ideas from many sources. Once again we tried to avoid the tendency to think of European as the purposive aim of development and tried to stress the importance of interaction in the spread and elaboration of the few very great simplifying inventions and new combinations of old knowledge.

We spent more time on the ideas of civilization than we had originally planned, so we did not have as much time as we had hoped to deal with nonwestern civilizations of the nineteenth and twentieth centuries. The class read two books: Etsu Sugimoto's *Daughter of the Samurai* and Francis Hsu's *Americans and Chinese*.

The *Daughter of the Samurai* is an excellent book, which ninth graders read with great attention. It contains a great deal of ethnographic material, and Mrs. Sugimoto's coming to America, finding the culture strange, and contrasting it with her own makes this good teaching material. Since Bohannan knew some Japanese ethnography and had been in Japan, he was able to fill in the book with materials on Japanese history, the nature of the Meiji Restoration, and how the social structure led to modern economic development in a way that it did not in most other traditional societies. We also went into such things as how properly to sit, stand, walk, and eat. We tried to conduct one class on the floor, sitting Japanese fashion; we lasted about fifteen minutes.

In the case of China, we had Francis Hsu himself come and discuss further some of the ideas in his book. This was an exciting part of the course. At the end, as a summary, we repeated very quickly the criteria for civilization, drawing on Chinese and Japanese examples.

THE FOLLOWING TWO YEARS

Like many another beginner, we tried to put too much into this course, and in the years following it, Carlson (a doctoral candidate at Northwestern), who took the course over from Bohannan and Garbarino, has not proceeded to the third quarter but rather has spread the original material from the first two quarters over the year, finding that in that way, he can get through it without rushing. New materials have also changed the course, and we now use the experimental units of the Anthropology Curriculum Study Project on "Early Man" and "The Great Transformation" of society and culture from hunting and gathering bands to the beginnings of urban civilization.

The basic strategy was, however, left intact: to introduce the students to as much ethnographic material as they could handle in the first half then to proceed to human origins and culture history, with a strong emphasis on archeological methods and reasoning by inference, in the second half.

This plan, like any other that a teacher of such a course may produce, necessarily demanded some modifications. Students discovered that they needed evolutionary concepts, geographical orientations, and biological insights to deal with ethnographic and, particularly, historical material. These were reinserted.

The plan for the first half was much the same as that outlined above for the first quarter. The materials were the same with the following exceptions. Hazel Hertzberg's book was replaced by chapter 9, on the Iroquois, from Wendell H. Oswalt's *This Land Was Theirs*. In the Africa section we followed Turnbull's Pygmies with Elizabeth Marshall Thomas's *The Harmless People*, and we inserted there the material from the ASCP on the Kalahari Bushmen and the materials from *Early Man* in *Life's* Nature Series, edited by F. Clark Howell. This book proved invaluable in this context and later as an introduction to the idea of man's development through the Pleistocene. In the second year talks and discussions on the Tiv were conducted by Laura Bohannan, and her *Return to Laughter* was read by the class. This book proved stimulating to advanced students, but it can be more safely recommended for the upper grades of high school than for the ninth.

In the third year no appreciable changes in materials or approach were made, but as the terminal assignment of the first half, each student worked through a monograph approved in advance. The student reported to the class, then, the essence of what he had read and commented on its special value for our studies. Invaluable for this assignment were the paperback volumes in the Spindler series, Kluckhohn and Leighton's *The Navaho*, and Drucker's *Indians of the Northwest Coast*.

CONCLUSIONS

We think we have proved that the three of us can teach anthropology to middle-class ninth graders as readily as we can to freshmen and sophomores in college. In many ways, indeed, it is easier to teach ninth graders. There is less resistance on the part of the students, which may, of course, be a characteristic of this particular group of students, although we are not convinced that that is the case. There is a great eagerness to learn the bases and techniques of social life. At this particular time of their lives, students are struggling with becoming adult members of society. Besides being an important educational period and the time when most students go through the experiences of puberty and adolescence, high school (and perhaps this continues for the first two or three years of college) is a rehearsal period for adult life; it is something like watching the prepubertal ten- or eleven-year-old boy rehearsing for adolescence. Social science has a great deal to say directly to these people. It tells them about choices in behavior and allows them to ask questions about behavior in their own society and in comparative contexts. Our students, by and large, were not interested in social sciences merely as subject matter or as the basis on which to make reforms and commitments. They were interested in these things, but they were even more interested in creating their own techniques of social living on an adult plane, and for this reason they gave it an attention that goes beyond the specific data, while at the same time the data allow them to compare and contrast their own situations with it. In short, social science is a good way to learn something about life at this time (and perhaps at any other) of one's own life.

On the other side of the coin, there were some problems we did not expect. Statements in class, in texts, in written themes had to be taken *very* seriously in order to convince students that this was not just another assignment but that their communications carried information about themselves and their culture as well as about the subject matter. This care precipitated some crises for students, who thought they were only to say "nice things" about primitive or prehistoric peoples. We found a stubborn sentimentality for the underdog; we did not allow the sentimentality to go unchallenged, but the process of finding that sentimentality can cover prejudice and that they were not as respectful of other human beings as they had thought, or as they tried to make out was sometimes painful. There was a tendency to turn the world into good guys and bad guys; Ishi and Turnbull's pygmies were good guys, and White civilization was the bad guy. We did our best to make them examine these ideas and go deeper than a good-guy/bad-guy dichotomy into the religion, world view, technology, and history of the groups, and somehow to gain respect for groups and individuals still closer to themselves in experience without the kind of guilt (which is systematically taught to them somewhere) that ultimately will cripple their attempts to make reforms. At the age of fourteen the biases of mature Americans are not yet entirely internalized; the problems our students faced can be compared with those faced by youth anywhere. We think that the possibility of penetrating cultural biases through anthropological studies appears greater at this age than at eighteen. However, we also think that the problem is that teachers have been brainwashed into saying "What 'they' do is good for 'them.'" A teacher once told Bohannan in a workshop, "Their ways are as good as ours." He asked, "Good for what?" Her immediate reply was, "Good for them," and she could not get beyond that.

This leads to our conviction that the difficulty in applying this sort of program lies largely with the fact that teachers are not adequately trained in anthropology. Bohannan and Garbarino have worked at training teachers in a summer institute and in an extension course for Northwestern (also treated as "in-service training" in some of the local high schools). We found the task overwhelming, and for two reasons. First of all, the better the teacher, the more difficult it is to retrain him.

We mean this as a compliment, if a rather left-handed one, to successful and good teachers. What such teachers want, and what they should have, is material to add to their already successful courses. They want material to upgrade and enrich their courses, and they often think of using the social sciences from this point of view. We think that such material should be supplied. We would much rather have good teachers using good materials in ways of which we basically disapprove than to have good teachers using bad materials in ways of which we basically disapprove. We would, in fact, much rather have good teachers teaching things of which we disapprove on professional grounds than to have bad teachers teaching materials we think superb. Therefore, we have come to the conclusion that training social-studies teachers should be done in full-blown M.A. programs for teachers who take a year, or even two years off to take M.A.s in one of the social sciences, or else that it should be done before a teacher goes out and begins to set up his courses and his style of dealing with them. We hope their superintendents and school boards can be brought to concur. We are of the opinion that good teachers are legion in the schools of this country, at least in the areas with which we are acquainted, and that what they need is more and better teaching materials and a much freer hand in using those materials.

The second reason that we think the teacher-training task is overwhelming and must be done in undergraduate and MAT programs, is that for the scholar or the school administrator to insist upon it is to earn the resentment of people who consider themselves successful and have some pretty good bases for their opinions. Our schools today are burgeoning with new curricula in the social sciences. The "new social studies" has become a jargon term—and a pejorative one. When one looks at the wide variety of the curricula being produced, it is not to be wondered that the very best teachers are skeptical.

It cannot be said after these three years that we have found *the* curriculum or *the* program for the proper study of man in the ninth grade. We *can* say that we are unanimous in our rejection of certain materials for this level and only a little less wholeheartedly unanimous in those we accept; incidentally, our unanimity includes our students.

The greatest challenge is working out curricula that integrate objectives, methods, and materials into a series of units. It is easy enough to make lists of objectives and lesson plans to develop them over time, but the unpredictable nature of ninth graders makes my plan highly tentative. The rationale for *making* such plans is, of course, that it gives the teacher adequate command of his material so that changes of plans will not throw him for a loss. Carlson found in teaching the ACSP materials that he tended to rely too heavily on following the intricate lesson plans and suggestions uncritically, which means, of course, without reference to the particular students in front of him. Teachers not trained as anthropologists usually find them extremely helpful and rich in material. Carlson often found it profitable to abandon the form while retaining the essence of the ACSP materials; for all that, we all think these are the best prepared materials we know for teaching anthropology in secondary schools.

Our mode of teaching was based on what today's educators are calling "inductive principles" of "discovery." However, we found that ninth graders also have to be filled in; the teacher must allow himself, his information and opinions, and his character to be used as raw material for the discoveries of his students. "Filling in" is best done, in anthropology courses of this sort, by giving facts. The amount of theory that students need can be determined on a "demand" basis. Theoretical presentations should *follow* the facts if the maximum number of students are to gain some appreciation of theory. Stating a theoretical position and then illustrating it is probably poor pedagogy anywhere (except, perhaps, in graduate seminars that are about theory). Certainly it is bad pedagogy in the ninth grade. By the second semester our students had enough sense of theory to apply it to what they were studying and to demand more when they needed it, although, certainly, sometimes we sensed the demand before they did. Obviously, the danger of the "inductive method" is that students may discover things that are either wrong or obsolete. This is an especially great risk in social studies.

Finally, we want to emphasize the vast profit that we ourselves got from teaching this course. We were, in a very real sense, daily driven to the wall. Fourteen-year-olds will not be put off with jargon and expertise. We hope that more of our colleagues will try such courses and that they too will discover that the learning that is part of every teaching experience was never more vivid and more fun than with good high school students. The anthropological point of view is congenial to young people. Young people test the anthropologist's ingenuity and challenge his professional stereotypes.

REFERENCES

Anthropology Curriculum Study Project. *Study of Early Man* and *The Great Transformation.* Chicago: The Project, 1967.

Bohannan, Paul. *Africa and Africans.* New York: Natural History Press, 1964.

Bowen, Elenore Smith (Laura Bohannan). *Return to Laughter.* New York: Natural History Press, 1964.

Driver, Harold E. *Indians of North America.* Chicago: University of Chicago Press, 1960.

Drucker, Philip. *Indians of the Northwest Coast.* New York: Natural History Press, 1963.

Hertzberg, Hazel W. *The Great Tree and the Longhouse.* New York: Macmillan, 1966.

Hoebel, E. Adamson. *Man in the Primitive World: An Introduction to Anthropology.* New York: McGraw-Hill, 1958.

Howell, F. Clark, and the Editors of *Life*. *Early Man.* New York: Time-Life Books, 1965.

Hsu, Francis L. K. *Americans and Chinese.* London: Cresset Press, 1955.

Kluckhohn, Clyde, and Leighton, Dorothea. *The Navaho.* New York: Doubleday, 1962.

Kroeber, Theodora. *Ishi in Two Worlds.* Berkeley and Los Angeles: University of California Press, 1963.

Marriott, Alice. *Ten Grandmothers.* Norman: University of Oklahoma Press, 1945.

Oliver, Douglas. *Invitation to Anthropology.* New York: Natural History Press, 1964.

Oswalt, Wendell, H. *This Land Was Theirs: A Study of the North American Indian*, New York: John Wiley, 1965.

Spencer, Robert F., and Jennings, Jesse D. *The Native Americans.* New York: Harper & Row, 1965.

Spindler, George, and Spindler, Louise. *Case Studies in Cultural Anthropology.* New York: Holt, Rinehart and Winston.

Sugimoto, Etsu, *Daughter of the Samurai.* Garden City, N.Y.: Doubleday, 1934.

Thomas, Elizabeth Marshall. *The Harmless People.* New York: Random House, 1965.

Turnbull, Colin. *The Forest People.* New York: Simon & Schuster, 1961.

28 / Anthropology and Teacher Education

Elizabeth M. Eddy

In recent years, anthropologists have increasingly been asked to contribute their knowledge and skills to the training of teachers and administrators for positions in the public schools. While anthropologists have always taught their own successors in anthropology, it is still rare for them to give serious attention to the preparation of nonanthropological teachers and administrators for the vast educational bureaucracy that attends to the formal socialization and enculturation of the youth of our society.

Although some educators and anthropologists would agree that anthropology has some relevance for training the persons officially appointed as transmitters of culture to successive generations of the young, the currently unanswered question is, What areas of anthropology are most relevant to this function? A second question is, How is anthropology to be presented to educators in a way that conveys its significance to their understanding of formal education in a modern technological society, rather than a collection of interesting and exotic bits of knowledge about primitive peoples far removed from those educators are likely to encounter in modern schools? These questions are not easily answered, and attempts to find answers are made difficult by the field situation within which teacher education occurs. The reader should understand that the comments to be presented here are based on one very limited experience with a teacher-education program, and that this paper is not intended to be a report of research findings, nor a definitive statement about the relationship between all anthropologists and all educators. Rather, the purpose is to suggest what appear to be potential problem areas in the relationship between anthropology and teacher education in some, but not necessarily all situations.

Traditionally, many programs of teacher education have focused on the individual child, who is perceived as one who is to be trained in the knowledge and values of middle-class behavior and the skills which will enable him to occupy family and work roles as an adult in middle-class society. Observations in schools in slum areas indicate, for example, that if the child comes to school with already acquired cultural or subcultural values which differ from those of the middle class, he is viewed as one whose behavior and values must be changed so that they conform with the dominant middle-class expectations of American society.[1] The widespread definition of the slum child as "culturally deprived" is but one indication of the ethnocentric position of those who perceive the educational task as one of providing him with the "culture" to enable him to be more fully accepted by the school and by American society in general. In another type of setting, Wax has recently reported a "vacuum ideology" which enabled educators in Indian reservations to perceive their pupils as possessing nothing positive which could contribute to their education.[2]

Teachers who have been carefully trained to treat each child as an individual, but not in understanding sociocultural factors which contribute to differences in the ways individuals behave, are frequently at a loss when confronted with those who do not share their own sociocultural background and values. Trained to teach middle-class values, but not in how to transmit them to those who come to the school with a different set of values, such teachers are frequently unequal to the task of socializing and enculturating into the mainstream of American life youth from cultures and subcultures viewed as inferior in American society. Often they abandon the attempt—either by withdrawing from these schools entirely or by defining the child as unteachable and emphasizing the custodial disciplinary role of the school rather than the educational role[3].

The problems referred to above are aggravated by the fact that historically, especially in urban settings, schools have drawn heavily on the factory as an organizational model and on psychological stimulus-response models as the basis for an understanding of the teaching-learning process in the classroom.[4] As a consequence, teacher preparation is predominantly concerned with the teaching of methods and techniques designed to help teachers provide external motivations so that the child will cooperate in work activities defined by the educational system as appropriate to his age and ability. Within the formal classroom itself, pupils are usually tested and graded for individual work achievement, the highest honors going to those who receive the best grades. Pupils are encouraged to compete with each other, to do their own work, and to refrain from copying the work of others. Cooperative work activity may be sanctioned in some situations, but the final testing of the pupil is based on his individual work. If he engages in cooperative work with others in the test situation, he is defined as a cheater and suffers severe penalties. Although studies of other types of human organization in modern societies suggest that the organizational model described here has important effects on such things as worker morale, these studies are largely unknown to many educators or ignored in much the same way that studies of the socio-cultural influences on IQ scores and achievement tests have frequently been ignored in the daily operation of the schools.

Some of the prevailing ideologies in teacher-education programs are reinforced by the tradition of selecting from the social sciences only those findings or approaches that support current educational beliefs and practices. The exclusion of specialists in other disciplines who do not have a teaching certificate and experience in teaching in the school system has also contributed, in many instances, to a selective use of social science methods and findings. It is not historically accidental that so much of educational research has been naively concerned with techniques, with little or inadequate understanding of the sociocultural context within which these techniques find their meaning. Currently there are signs that this situation is slowly changing, but resistance to change remains strong in many educational circles.

The professional provincialism expressed by many educators is frequently reinforced by their almost lifelong experience within the formal educational system, sometimes even within the same local school system. In one large cosmopolitan city, for example, most of those who are teachers of teachers have themselves attended the local city schools and are now capping a long successful career as inmates of this local system by teaching those who will succeed them at the lower rungs of the educational hierarchy. Frequently persons who "have come up the hard way," these teachers of teachers (as well as those they teach) are often those for whom education has been a means of upward social mobility and who have a deep sense of loyalty for the local school system. Often, too, they have close ties to their family and ethnic group, which may also be strongly "local" rather than "cosmopolitan" in outlook and experience.

Thus, the way the local school system is operated becomes the only known and experienced way to do things. Local educational folklore and tradition is passed from one generation to the next, and innovations by outsiders are seen as something to be guarded against. Represented in the extreme by teachers who, after attending a local metropolitan college, begin their teaching career in the same school from which they graduated and in which they did student teaching, this type of localism in the urban setting results in a school system dominated by those who have never left the local school; they provide new trainees and teachers on probation with a careful induction into the traditions and practices which have been successful for them. But these traditions are not suited to the needs of children in the contemporary world, particularly the special needs of those who now dwell in the urban slum.

As teachers of teachers, faculty members of the teacher-training situation tend to think that they alone prepare their successors. In actual fact, unlike other professions, induction into the profession of teaching begins in early childhood when one first enters school and becomes a participant observer of classroom life. Unlike trainees for other occupations who have only very limited periods of time (or none) when they observe experienced workers, those preparing to teach have for many years observed how teaching is practiced and are intimately acquainted with what it is that teachers do. This long socialization of teachers into their role provides another source of resistance to change—and this is accentuated for those who return to the same school or system in which they made their observations.

In becoming a teacher of teachers, the anthropologist brings a new and distinctly different approach to the understanding of the educational universe. Strongly committed to the study of behavior by the comparative method, and concerned with all cultural aspects of human behavior, the anthropologist brings an outsider's view of the local educational world that contrasts sharply with that of his teacher training colleagues. Moreover, the anthropologist usually views society more dynamically than educators, who have good reasons for maintaining the *status quo*. Because of his knowledge of child training in many societies, the anthropologist also casts a jaundiced eye on theories of child development and behavior which fail to take sociocultural factors into account.

In light of these and other differences in world view, it is apparent that anthropology and anthropologists must seem strange to educators. By the same token, anthropologists will be wary of "going native" in teacher training institutions and almost necessarily will think of themselves as being in a field situation if they accept employment as a teacher of teachers. It may be anticipated that anthropologists in teacher education programs will experience culture shock as they encounter professional orientations and values different from their own. An antiintellectual bias among many educators is only one of the orientations apt to insult the dedicated scholar. Further, just as his family and friends may regard him as peculiar for going to remote parts of the world, so now his professional colleagues in the academic world may consider him strange for working with educators. Educators themselves regard the anthropologist, at least initially, as an outsider. They are not at first willing to accept and trust him, especially if his salary and research funds come from outside the department or school of education, as is frequently the case today.

Since anthropologists will be increasingly called upon by educators, it would seem appropriate to begin a serious consideration of possible ways to use anthropology effectively in the training of teachers and administrators for the public school system. Ways must be found to recruit anthropologists into the educational field as teachers, researchers, and authors of appropriate books, articles, and curriculum materials. Even more important is the need for strategic placement of anthropological personnel and resources in order to capitalize on those situations which appear likely to yield the best results. Anthropologists who enter the field will need help in understanding their own problems in relating to educators, learning how to work effectively with them, and in acquiring a greater knowledge of American culture than most anthropologists now have. Finally, anthropologists must think about their potential contribution not only in terms of specific new subject matter for teacher training, but also in terms of introducing the anthropological way of looking at the world as a new tool for perceiving and analyzing educational problems from other than the traditional educational perspective. The most crucial need is the development of methods for teaching anthropology to educators in such a way that the training and practice of educators will rest on a more scientific base as they organize our educational system to undertake the task of imparting to the young the cognitive and human skills needed for full participation in a complex, technologically developed, and rapidly changing modern world.

NOTES

1. Elizabeth M. Eddy, *Walk the White Line: A Profile of Urban Education* (Garden City, N.Y.: Doubleday Anchor Books, 1967).
2. Murray L. Wax, Rosalie H. Wax, et al., "Formal Education in an American Indian Community," *Social Problems* (Supplement) 11, 4 (Spring 1964): 67-71.
3. Eddy, *Walk the White Line*.
4. For an historical account of the sacrifice of educational goals to the requirements of business procedures, see Raymond E. Callahan, *Education and the Cult of Efficiency* (Chicago: University of Chicago Press, 1962).

29 / Anthropology and an Education for the Future
Margaret Mead

Today, as we search for a new way of educating men and women who can both understand and cope with our intricate, just emerging universe with its tremendous contradictions, discrepancies, potentialities, and dangers, there is an urgent need for new alignments of subject matter in our undergraduate colleges. It is being increasingly recognized that before a man can become an engineer or a statesman, a production manager, an astronaut, or a poet, he must be made somehow into an educated man; that is, a whole man, to whom nothing in the world is alien, to whom no path of possible exploration is blocked or closed. Our experience since World War II has demonstrated with terrible vividness how few men there are—of any age or from any country—who have such an integrated relationship to all that man has been, is, and may become. The creation of a United Nations Educational Scientific and Cultural Organization was a bold venture in integration at the top, but only a handful of men in the world had the imagination to head it up. The tremendous vogue of C. P. Snow's "two cultures," the restless searching for new formulas—varying from new architecture on the old campus to proposals for floating universities that would visit landfall points in the underdeveloped countries—the plea for the scientist to become familiar with man as well as with the natural order of the universe, for the physician to learn about the heights of man's achievement as well as the failures of his body and mind, the scholar to come out of his library and watch the intricate new patterns which a microscope can reveal, or listen to a real nightingale against a real sky—all of these are signs of the times we live in, and the task that lies before the colleges.

Anthropology is a uniquely situated discipline, related in diverse ways to many other disciplines, each of which, in specializing, has also inadvertently helped to fragment the mind of modern man. Anthropology is a humanity, represented in the American Council of Learned Societies, concerned with the arts of language and with the versions that human cultures have given of the definition of man and of man's relationship to the universe; anthropology is a science, concerned with discovering and ordering the behavior of man-in-culture; anthropology is a biological science, concerned with the physical nature of man, with man's place in evolution, with the way genetic and racial differences, ecological adaptations, growth and maturation, and constitutional differences are implicated in man's culture and achievements; anthropology is a historical discipline concerned with reading the record of man's far past and establishing the links which unite the potsherd and the first inscription on stone, in tying together the threads between the preliterate and the literate world wherever the sequence occurs, in Egypt, in China, in Crete, or in a modern African state. Anthropology is a social science, although never only a social science because in anthropology man, as part of the natural world, as a biological creature, is not separated from man as a consumer or producer, member of a group, or possessor of certain psychological faculties. Anthropology is an art. The research skills which go into good field work are as complex as the skills of a musician or a surgeon; a disciplined awareness of self is as essential.

Partly because anthropology is a late comer on the scene, including a curiously assembled set of subject matters—such as the preliterate past, the body of man, the behavior of preliterate surviving people, the formal study of spoken language—and partly because of the diversity of anthropological interests, it is an uncommitted discipline. Because it includes all of them, it does not fall, with relentless traditionalism, into any category of science or of humanities or of social science. It has sheltered under the wings of philosophy and anatomy, botany and history, aesthetics and geology. Wherever it has been placed it has been restive, not for the simple imperialistic reasons that all part-departments seek to be whole departments but because there was always, when anthropology was placed within any category, such a large part that did not fit. How did a course in primitive art fit into a sociology curriculum, a course in the diffusion of material culture into a psychology department, a course in child training into philosophy?

It is in this very anomalousness that I believe anthropology can make a unique contribution to a liberal education. As a part of liberal education, it is peculiarly fitted to fill a tremendous need.

I should like to review briefly some of the gaps in the knowledge and understanding of modern man, so fragmented, so myopically limited and specialized, even at this very moment when we are journeying into space. Then I will consider how anthropology can be taught not by professional anthropologists alone, but by those who have studied under anthropologists and, like all great teachers of the adolescent mind, are willing to immerse themselves in their material sufficiently to convey it to their students "with the dew still on it."

The gaps in men's minds and imagination which we need to bridge are appallingly conspicuous today: the gap between the understanding of the past, the grasp of the present, and an ability to deal with the future; the gap between the lively pursuit of natural science wherever it leads and the statesmanship which will be able to control the results of such pursuits; the gap between the mathematical and formal analyses of systems and the ability to analyze and predict the behavior of human beings; the gap between the scientist who "understands" a single approach to the natural world and the poet and painter who can find no foothold in modern man's response to changes which he does not understand; the gap between man's knowledge of things and his knowledge of people; between his awareness of the external world, which has never been so great, and his awareness of himself, which has seldom been so impoverished; the gap between our small ethnocentric, narrowly racial, class- and time-bound senses of identity and the grandeur of our membership in one human species, now bound together as denizens of one planet. On the verge of leaving that planet, we still fail to conceive our full place upon it, in time and in space.

The fully educated man, whether he was the young adult male member of a primitive tribe who had learned all that the elders had to tell him; the man of Greece or Rome, thinking about and understanding the known world; Renaissance man stirred to an aware excitement of the ancient world from which he had been cut off, and moved by the new discoveries—the great and the small seen for the first time through telescopes and microscopes—all of these had, in different measure, what we now seek to reestablish for our own time. In contrast, many members of great societies—the peasant, taught for centuries that his is a limited place in the world; the urban proletarian, starved and cynical in his slums near the palace; the bitter contentious member of one of the cults and sects that seek to narrow truth to the limits of their own impoverished emotions and intellects—these have never, no matter how great the civilization within which they resided, been men of a liberal education. The essence of a liberal education is to share the full identity made possible by the state of civilization within which one lives: today that identity stretches back to the beginning of life on this planet, and soon perhaps in other parts of the universe; it comprises all members of the human species, all their work and marvels of hand and brain, heart and eye, the intricacy of their languages, the significance of their myraid experiments in human relationships, the cunningness with which their bodies are made, their relationships to all living creatures—to birds who are bipeds and build nests, and dolphins who, handless and lipless, devise ballets of their own in the sea; it reaches back into the past, out into the present, deeper beneath the sea and farther into the atmosphere than man has ever gone, and onward into a future for which each one of us, and each nation, holds today a terrible responsibility. Modern man is offered today an identity far greater than he has ever known. It is a task of a liberal education to help him develop it.

In order to appreciate fully how anthropology can contribute to this stupendous but rewarding task, something must be said of the way in which an anthropologist is educated, and what he does, when, as a research worker, he goes into the field. Every smallest research report, and every more generalized publication for the layman, bears the stamp of this education, of the presuppositions on which his work is based, and of the methods that, whatever his temperamental bent, he must pursue in the field. It is this experience of the field anthropologist, particularly of the field cultural anthropologist, which provides the possibility of integration. It is not that the anthropologist is widely read in the literature of the world, that he has an encyclopedic grasp of the history of science, that he has traveled and understood the ancient ruins of Angkor Wat or Crete, or undergone the rigorous disciplines of medicine, or one of the arts. His inclusiveness and universality are of quite another order. It is in his education and his research, based as they are in the whole of human history, embedded in the simplest and the most solemn moments of human life, that his integration lies.

In the United States anthropology has remained an inclusive and integrating discipline by successfully resisting the fragmentation which has occurred in most disciplines, which, as they become more specialized, with more workers in more countries of the world, have progressively shattered into mutually noncommunicating parts. Anthropology has kept its own media of intradisciplinary communication. Just as the fragmented and over specialized biological sciences can still communicate through observation of scientific canons of presentation, argument, and experimental style, and the humanists in many tongues can still invoke the names of Plato and Aristotle, or physicians refer to a well-described case and lawyers to a carefully stated legal precedent, so too anthropologists have remained in communication with each other through the concrete materials with which they deal. They work not only with generalizations about culture, but also with the descriptions of particular cultures; not only with generalizations about language, but also with the auditory records of the speech of particular Indians or particular South Sea Island tribes; not only with tables of prehistoric time, but also with the actual artifacts and skeletal bits from which these tables are constructed. In their field work they go to various parts of the world, among living peoples who are different and speak different languages, or at a second remove, to the detailed accounts of those who did travel, and to the concrete specimens that they brought back.

Although it looked during the 1940s as if American anthropology, which had stood for such a unified approach to man in all his aspects, might fragment, it did not fragment. Graduate students in our universities today still learn about man's past, his place in evolution, the remains of his past civilization, the complexity of his languages, the nature of his culture and how to study it, and, increasingly, how to apply this knowledge, professionally, to various contemporary social problems as practitioners. In such an education the student is not lectured about the various parts of the subject but is forced to experience some small part of each, to read monographs about the Chukchee and the Koryak, to learn the shape of a bone, to undergo the discipline of analyzing an unknown language straight from an informant's lips, to arrange an assemblage of potsherd, and/or the contents of a single archaeological dig. Where this ideal is not fully realized, contact with those who have spent many years doing just these concrete things serves, to some extent, as a surrogate for the experience itself.

Along with this integrative, concrete, experiential training, there go certain basic assumptions: the psychic unity of mankind, as one species, with the expectation that because man is one species, all forms of his cultural behavior must have been invented or borrowed; and the recognition that all cultures, as systems of learned behavior within which groups have been able to reproduce and protect themselves over several generations, must be accorded a basic equal dignity, so that the cultural system of the smallest nomadic tribe must in these respects be treated as comparable to the civilization of Egypt or France; the insistence that no behavior, no item, no artifact, can be understood except in a complete ecological context; the expectation that in order to behave like an anthropologist one must be prepared to "go into the field."

There is also intense training in widening the student's expectancy, so that when he meets new forms—a hitherto unknown kinship form; or religious belief, that gods need not be parental figures, but can, as in Bali, be children; or biological anomaly, like the strange, probably genetic disease of *kuru* in the highlands of New Guinea—he will not fail to note them because he is too ready to assimilate them to some older set of categories. This eager alertness to the unknown, the improbable, the unexpected, not only provides the necessary preparation for doing research where each piece of historically vanishing strange behavior is valuable just in proportion to its strangeness, but also provides an ideal state of mind for facing a world that is changing as rapidly as ours.

The young anthropologist, either during graduate training or in his first field experience, becomes aware of himself as a cultural being, each of whose categories for ordering experience bear the imprint of the culture in which he is reared, from such simple matters as the gesture he uses for assent, the way in which he groups colors, to the criteria of reality or illusion, and the position of the future—in front of an American, but behind a Balinese. His cultural ethnocentrism is transformed into a feeling of ability to move in and out of the categories of other peoples, past and present and future, as he expects also to learn to eat their food, sleep on their mats or wooden pillows, speak their language and respond quickly to signs that they are frightened or angry, delighted or bemused.

This attrition of an ethnocentrism which today keeps Americans and many other peoples of the world from learning the languages and responding sensitively and appropriately to the diplomatic maneuvers or technical deficiencies of other peoples is accomplished, not by admonition and preaching against prejudices or for the brotherhood of man, but by the experience of the value, in anthropology itself, of the diversity of human behavior which has been and will be recorded. The recognition of this is central to his becoming an anthropologist, to his professional identity. He is not a believer in the brotherhood of man, who *then* studies a social science to implement the accomplishment of his ideal—although such recruits to anthropology do, of course, exist—but rather, a deeply committed scientist-scholar, who as he works with the material about which he is delighted, curious, and eager learns his universal values as he works, tracing the pattern of a design on the edge of a pot, a myth of origin in its various forms, a wayward gene responsible for difference in blood type among peoples of an island world, or seven divergent spoken tongues back to their cradle land. As a result when the anthropologist teaches, he does not preach, he simply embodies the attitudes toward all human beings that are intrinsic to his work.

In the course of such a graduate training, the anthropologist also learns something about taking into account great wholes, how he must be aware of the context of the problem with which he himself will be immediately dealing. As he deals with the folklore, or the medical beliefs, or the ethnobotany—selected small detailed research elements—in two American Indian tribes, whose languages are related but who now live far apart, he must be aware of our accumulating knowledge of the age of man in North America, and behind that of the age of *Homo sapiens* and the appearance in the Old World of the tools and beliefs of which, under the pressure of a much later wave of historical contact with Europe, his Indians are just now losing the last memory. He must see the horses which those Indians rode to war and to the buffalo hunt, not as a fixed attribute of the Plains Indians, who sit, immutable, with their feathered war bonnets outlined against the sky, but as they were, imported by the Spaniards and traded up to meet the guns which the French and English gave the Indians. Beneath the English within which he now communicates with his informants, he must be prepared to hear the syntax and the cadence and the categories of the Indian language that is not yet quite abandoned, and on the inhabited plains of the present time, criss-crossed by modern highways, he must be able to conjure up a period when in the loneliness of the Indian's vision quest, each encountered living creature became a supernatural messenger. At the same time he must be able, if his problem requires, to analyze the physical evidence for some connection between his two groups, as well as the linguistic, or to take into account the archaeological evidence which has been assembled about early man in North America.

So the context within which he works is not only the context of prehistory, of great migrations, of the overflow of Europeans, Africans, and Asians into the New World, of industrialization and change, which makes Indians today, as change has made so many people in the past, strangers in their own country. He also has to learn to live within an intellectual world of rapid change, of ideas that will come tomorrow from biochemistry or from microbiology, from brain physiology or studies of maturation, from a new method of esthetic analysis or a new vista in the relationship of man's old brain or his unconscious to dreaming and the arts. There will continually be new conceptual tools to work with, and new demands on his field work, to bring back droplets of blood, measurements of skin folds, records of perception, or moving pictures of a method of holding a child. However much of a scholar he is, he cannot be indifferent to science, however much a scientist he cannot ignore the demands for his materials, in all their entirety, undissected and clear; however little he knows of music, he can still collect the musical instruments, film their use, sound record the songs. He is part of a living enterprise, scientific, scholarly, and artistic. The music he brings back may stimulate the tired imaginations of a composer, the carvings may set off a new mode in sculpture; and today his work is also deeply political, as the new nations, so recently only of interest to anthropologists, administrators, missionaries, and traders, proudly plant their flags within the circle of the world's flags at the United Nations. He is forced to deal with the modern political realities, by the exigencies of planning field work, getting a visa, arranging to get his collections out, working with native labor, trying to find educated members of the people he studies, phrasing his results so that they will neither be impounded inside the country in which he has worked, nor forbidden entry to it. He cannot remain in any ivory tower of political unawareness. The record of his own personal vicissitudes becomes automatically part of the record of his work, of why the ethnobotanical specimens were lost or the publication of the second volume postponed.

Today, too, as anthropology is broadening its scope, from the study of primitive and near-primitive people to the study of peasant villages in Southeast Asia or Southern Europe, to mining towns in the British Isles or London neighborhoods, the anthropologist is brought ever more sharply into contact with the whole framework of modern life in all its complexities of technical change, political ferment, and changing bureaucratic structure.

The young anthropologist's growing appreciation of all of these things is gradual: some are learnt in the library, from the written regret of an ethnologist who arrived after the last old man who knew the tribal secrets was dead; some are learnt in the laboratory, working with fragments where wholes are needed and so must be reconstructed; some are learnt from the interpolated personal experience of his teachers in graduate schools, who have all been in the field themselves. But the focus is not on the learning so much as upon getting into the field. Here again the young anthropologist differs from the young scientist who wishes feverishly to find a spot where he can make a new discovery and win, if not fame, at least support for further work; he differs from the young scholar hopefully scouring the last pages of a famous text for new clues or using some new method of reconstructing a past with which many others have worked; he differs from the young artist or writer, wondering if he is, after all, an artist or a writer, or only one who enjoys the arts. He has very little of the preoccupation of the other social scientists—the sociologists, economists, and psychologists—anxiously watching problem and method not only for results but to be certain that their work looks and sounds like Science. His eyes are rather on the whole experience of doing field work or getting into the field. Depending upon the fashions current in different graduate schools or grant-giving institutions, he may set his work up with different kinds of problem orientation, but these are ways of organizing his research rather than ends in themselves. His end purpose is actually an account of some whole living part of man's experience, which will be good enough to generate new hypotheses in the years to come, long after his particular people have put on the blue jeans, the spectacles, the raincoats, and the sack suits of the industrial modern world.

For the anthropologist all of life is his subject matter, with the field the most vivid part of that life. A new costume on the street, a new word or phrase or cadence in the everyday speech, a change in posture, a new theme in popular songs, a new response in American life to some phase of Oriental or European philosophy, change in political stance in a social class, or an emerging architectural style borrowed from a Buddhist temple—all are grist to the anthropologist's mill. He may not be studying these particular things, but his disciplined awareness makes him conscious of them, interested in them, and as he walks the paths of his university campus or rides on a bus to a museum, his latent continuous codifying of human experience is enriched, or given tiny little jolts by the unexpected, that will in time become new questions, new hypotheses, new theories.

In the field itself, the anthropologist undergoes, simply because of his job, most of the experiences which the imagination of experimental educators or the well-filled purse of the traveled cosmopolitan provide for. He travels, and penetrates through several layers of culturally relevant groups of officials, planters, agency officials, police, learning by the need to get through these barriers, something about them. He goes almost always to a new terrain, and the closeness with which his "people" live to the natural world forces him, however abstract-minded he has been, to an awareness of it. His clock will give him scanty help in predicting when an informant will arrive; he must learn the meaning of "I will start when the second bird cries out." All the careful fussiness of oversterilized and fabricated world we live in is stripped off, not by artificial journeys by helicopter to experience the wilderness, or the costly delights of traveling for three days by canoe without a bath, but simply because these are the conditions of his work. The lamented softness of our young people who cannot imagine a world without porcelain latrines and orange juice simply disappears, because if it didn't, he couldn't survive. As he works his way into the community of strangers, very alert not to make some irrevocably false step which may end his work or even his life, his eye and ear become attuned to the significance of a whole new repertoire of sights and sounds, of lifted brows, or shifted betel basket. And, reflexively, he becomes aware of how he sits and stands, feels and thinks; increasing self-awareness goes hand in hand with his knowledge of the people he has come to study.

The world, whole, takes on a new meaning, as he selects a village small enough so that he can know everyone in it well enough to recognize by a change of companions or of pace that something is afoot. He builds his house by the most traveled road and takes events into account as they occur. He lives alone—almost all anthropologists have at least some experience of field work alone—and so comes face to face with himself, without the need to take a special pilgrimage to a Buddhist lamasery. He lives as a whole human being, aware of his body, which he must arrange to feed and shelter and compose into unfamiliar postures and gestures, of his mind, whose conceptualizing and analyzing and synthesizing abilities are invoked every instant, of himself as a human being among other human beings, both companions and counterpoints to his kind of self-realization and identity.

And the wholeness which he lives out is matched by the wholeness of the life he must record. Nothing can be wholly neglected; although some aspects of the culture may be treated sketchily, this very sketchiness must be handled systematically. If one does not map every taro patch in the bush, or count the catch of every canoe, list the gods of every clan, or explore the details of every ceremony, watch every birth, or sit at every death-bed, follow every artist and would-be artist as he works, and sit for hours at the feet of the only mystic or philosopher, one must always know the exact place in the whole of the part that is unexplored, the probable size of the unexplored area, and, most importantly, how it fits in with those things that one is studying in detail. Here the field work model becomes very easily the model for the educated man; it is not that he must know in detail all that there is to know, but he must know the shape of this knowledge and be able to make a reasoned judgement of what he does not know, how it fits in, how long it would take him to master any unknown piece. His mind must carry the imprint of the shape of the whole, however few details of any part of it his memory retains.

Within the culture of a people there is nothing that is alien, nothing that can be wholly ignored. When I went to Samoa to study adolescence, W. C. Handy was also considering a Samoan field trip to study religion. "Never mind, you won't overlap," said the director of the Bishop Museum, a geologist, "he won't be dealing with the mundane things that you are. He is interested in higher things." But, of course, he was wrong, as both Dr. Handy and I well knew, for the nature of the gods is expressed in the way a child is held, and the disposal of the umbilical cord may hold the key to past religious history. Within the web of a whole culture, just as each individual in the society is important and plays a part, be it philosopher or fool of god, so there is no part which can be ranked as "high" or "low." The historical snobberies of our European inheritance, with their distinctions between the aristocratic and the common people, between one race and another, between men and women, between adults and children, between fine art and popular art, epic and lyric, high architecture and domestic, all these inheritances from an earlier age are dissolved by a study of culture. The student who works with anthropological materials without being pushed into taking some new stance, and without the pendulum swings that accompany a snobbery transformed into aggressive egalitarianism, comes to feel the whole of human life as one, to see the shepherd's pipe and the great organ as part of the continuing human attempt to pattern sound and the shaped bit of clay, the David and the Nefertiti as related efforts.

If the emphasis is kept always upon the whole, however, it is possible to make a further and more exciting point—first made, I think, by Ruth Benedict—that rather than compare the simplest bits of primitive music and dance with the great developments of art in high civilizations, it is more fruitful to regard the culture of the simplest people as itself a work of art, its delicate complexity as aesthetically satisfying, as spiritually renewing, as philosophically moving, as any of the great achievements of individual artists.

But, it may be objected, the student on a liberal arts campus will not go into the field, he will not learn to eat dragon flies or translate the language of the drums, he will not be caught by the relationship between a pattern of a song and a pattern of a blanket. He will not have to make a whole from the interrelationships of a carefully observed group of human beings, strange in form and speech. True, but if the anthropology is taught well, taught with a full recognition of the kind of original materials which anthropologists collect and produce, the student will experience something of this. Even if the teacher of undergraduates has never been in the field, it should be a requirement that he should have studied in an anthropological graduate school and been taught by anthropologists. Undergraduate anthropology taught by someone trained in another discipline, with a very different ethos, will not, of course, communicate this to the students, even with the help of the original materials. Anthropology is a discipline of the whole, the whole of man's history, the whole of man's culture, the whole of man's being, and this approach can only be communicated by someone who is himself, or herself, wholly involved, immersed, in it. But I believe the field experience, doubly embodied in the experience of the teacher who has studied under an original field worker and in the materials which have been created by field work, will survive *one generation*. The students of such teachers will not themselves be able to be anthropologists; for this, also, field experience is essential; but they will be able to communicate to under-graduates something of the world view, the integration of man's life on earth, which the practice of anthropology involves.

From the liberal arts colleges students emerge who wish to become various types of practitioners, physicians, lawyers, statesmen, architects, engineers, as well as those who will go on to become pure scientists or poets, bankers or builders, or those who will go to the graduate schools to learn to teach better what they themselves have been taught. Anthropology today offers not only a way of integrating the diversity of our existing knowledge and experience, but also a great variety of implications for the practitioners of the individual or socially healing arts. Applied anthropology is not suitable for undergraduate teaching, in most instances, particularly because those few who are adept at practicing it are too busy even to do their share of teaching in graduate school. But the student's mind can be opened to its possibilities.

And here we meet another contribution which anthropology can make, the full recognition of moral responsibility and the negation of an irresponsible scientism or the advocacy of sterile types of cultural relativity. Cultural relativity in the anthropological sense means that any act, or institution, must be understood as relative to the cultural system in which it occurs. Leaving the aged to die is murder in a society where it would be possible to save them, correct ethical behavior on the part of the aged and their children where saving them would compromise the survival of their grandchildren. And none understand better than anthropologists the unity of mankind, the significance of membership in one species, the levels of interdependence in the world, or the fragility and toughness of human culture; and the need for responsible cultural custodianship. These anthropology cannot escape. Again not because we hold them as dissociated high level values but because they are of the very essence of the work we do. Without them, we could not build the discipline we are so intent upon building. They show through our work, inform its every nook and cranny, and light up the empty spaces where work is still to be done. For characteristically the anthropologist does not say: "We do not know," but rather, "We do not know *yet*."

Finally, a close acquaintance with the cultures of the past can help us make workable models of the future. We have abundant materials on how one people have borrowed from another, house forms, tools, script and architecture, higher mathematics and electronic devices, but we have yet to devise a way in which aspiring men may safely build a model of an unknown future state which itself leaves the future open. Throughout history the attempt to construct desirable future states has been caught between the rock of insipidity and the rock of overcertainty. To build an image of heaven, compelling enough to make men want to go there, but still to interdict religious suicide, has challenged missionaries among peoples who take the vision too literally. Similarly, to build an image of a future culture which will compel men's allegiance without also authorizing a Gestapo to force their fellows to accept it, is equally difficult. A knowledge of many cultures, past and present, is one of the best sources of the cultural creativity which we need today.

From our college campuses must come the poets and builders of tomorrow, the artist's prefigurative vision, the scientific quest for the necessary knowledge, the scientist's experience of how to make the vision real—and not too real, but always open, always allowing for still another future, still a further vision. Today, as we move into new worlds of weightlessness, into space and under the sea, there will be new sources on which men's imagination can feed, as we seek to devise new cultures, which will never become prisons, never be static, but will remain launching platforms into a widening universe.

Part VI

Chronological Bibliographies

Bibliography on Anthropology and Education*

Compiled by Joan I. Roberts and
Sherrie K. Akinsanya

1896

CHAMBERLAIN, ALEXANDER. *Child and Childhood in Folk Thought*. New York: Macmillan.

1897

BARNES, EARL, and BARNES, MARY. "Education Among the Aztecs." In *Studies in Education*, edited by Earl Barnes. Palo Alto: Stanford University Press.

1898

BOAS, FRANZ. "Advances in Methods of Teaching." Discussion before the New York meeting of the American Naturalist and Affiliated Societies. *Science* 9 (December): 93–96.

VANDEWALKER, NINA C. "Some Demands of Education Upon Anthropology." *American Journal of Sociology* 4:69–78.

1904

HEWETT, EDGAR LEE. "Anthropology and Education." *American Anthropologist* 6:574–75.

1905

HEWETT, EDGAR L. "Ethnic Factors in Education." *American Anthropologist* 6, no. 1:1–16.

1907

DRESSLAR, FLETCHER B. "Superstitions and Education." University of California, *Publications in Education* 5, no. 1:1–239.

1909

THOMAS, WILLIAM ISSAC. *Sourcebook for Social Origins*. Chicago: University of Chicago Press.

1913

MONTESSORI, MARIE. *Pedagogical Anthropology*. New York: Lippincott.

TODD, A. J. *The Primitive Family as an Educational Agency*. New York: G. P. Putnam's Sons.

WEBSTER, HUTTON. "Education Among Primitive Peoples." *Monroe's Encyclopedia of Education*, 31–35.

1914

KING, IRVING. *The Social Aspects of Education*. New York: Macmillan.

1923

LEVY-BRUHL, LUCIEN. *Primitive Mentality*. New York: Macmillan.

*This bibliography represents the complete coverage for the time period of all known materials pertaining to anthropology and education with primary emphasis on formalized systems.

1926

HAMBLY, W. D. *Origins of Education Among Primitive Peoples.* London: Macmillan.
LEVY-BRUHL, LUCIEN. *How Natives Think.* London: George Allen & Unwin.

1927

RADIN, PAUL. *Primitive Man as Philosopher.* New York: D. Appleton.

1928

BOAS, FRANZ. *Anthropology and Modern Life.* New York: Norton.
MILLER, NATHAN. *The Child in Primitive Society.* New York: Brentanos.

1929

MALINOWSKI, BRONISLAW. *The Sexual Life of Savages in North-Western Melanesia: An Ethnographic Account of Courtship, Marriage and Family Life Among the Natives of the Trobriand Islands.* New York: New Guinea Eugenics Publishing Co.
MURRAY, A. VICTOR. *The School in the Bush: A Critical Study of the Theory and Practice of Native Education in Africa.* London: Longmans, Green.

1930

MEAD, MARGARET. "Primitive Education." *Encyclopedia of the Social Sciences* 5:399–403.
NICHOLS, CLAUDE A. *Moral Education Among the North American Indians.* New York: Teachers College Press.

1931

HOERNLE, A. A. "An Outline of the Native Conception of Education." *Africa* 4, no. 4:145–63.
STAYT, HUGH A. *The Bavenda.* London: International Institute of African Languages and Cultures, Oxford University Press.

1932

WALLER, WILLARD. *The Sociology of Teaching.* New York: Wiley.

1933

GOLDENWEISER, ALEXANDER. *History, Psychology, and Culture.* New York: Knopf.
————. *Social Education, Stanford Education Conference.* New York: Macmillan.

1934

HELSER, ALBERT DAVID. *Education of Primitive People: A Presentation of Folklore of the Bura Animists with a Meaningful Experience Curriculum.* New York: Fleming H. Ravel.

1935

BLACKWOOD, BEATRICE. *Both Sides of Buka Passage.* Oxford: Clarendon Press.
WIST, B. O. "Ethnology as the Basis for Education: An Experiment in American Samoa." *Social Science* 10:336–47.

1936

LINTON, RALPH. *The Study of Man.* New York: Appleton-Century-Crofts.
MALINOWSKI, BRONISLAW. "Native Education and Culture Contact." *International Review of Missions* 25:480–515.
WILSON, MONICA. *Reaction to Conquest.* London: Oxford University Press.

1937

ERICKSON, E. H. "Observations on Sioux Education." *Journal of Psychology* 7:101–56.
KEESING, FELIX M. *Education in Pacific Countries.* Shanghai, China: Kelly & Walsh.
LI, AN-CHE. "Zuni: Some Observations and Queries." *American Anthropologist* 39:62–77.

1938

BENEDICT, RUTH. "Continuities and Discontinuities in Cultural Conditioning." *Psychiatry* 1:161–67.

1939

BRYSON, LYMAN. "Anthropology and Education." In *So Live the Works of Men*, edited by D. D. Brand and Fred Harvey. Albuquerque: University of New Mexico Press.

EMBREE, JOHN F. *Suye Mura, A Japanese Village*. Chicago: University of Chicago Press.

GILLIN, J. "Personality in Preliterate Societies." *American Sociological Review* 4:681–702.

1940

MEAD, MARGARET. "Social Change and Cultural Surrogates." *Journal of Educational Sociology* 14, no. 2:92–109.

SUMNER, WILLIAM GRAHAM. *Folkways*. Boston: Ginn.

1941

HARLEY, GEORGE W. "Notes on the Poro in Liberia." *Papers of the Peabody Museum of American Archaeology and Ethnology* 19, no. 2.

1942

BURGESS, ERNEST W.; WARNER, W. LLOYD; ALEXANDER, FRANZ; MEAD, MARGARET, eds. *Environment and Education. Human Development Series*. Vol. 1. Chicago: University of Chicago Press.

MEAD, MARGARET. "An Anthropologist Looks at the Teacher's Role." *Educational Method* 21:210–23.

——. "Educative Effects of Social Environment as Disclosed by Studies of Primitive Societies." In *Environment and Education*, edited by Ernest W. Burgess, W. Lloyd Warner, Franz Alexander, and Margaret Mead. Human Development Series, vol. 1. Chicago: University of Chicago Press.

NADEL, S. F. "Education for Citizenship Among the Nupe." *From Child to Adult: Studies in the Anthropology of Education*, edited by John Middleton. Garden City, N.Y.: Natural History Press.

WARNER, W. LLOYD. "Educative Effects of Social Status." In *Environment and Education*, edited by Ernest W. Burgess, W. Lloyd Warner, Franz Alexander, and Margaret Mead. *Human Development Series*, vol. 1.

1943

BENEDICT, RUTH. "Transmitting Our Democratic Heritage in the School." *American Journal of Sociology* 48:722–27.

BOND, HORACE MANN. "Education as a Social Process: A Case Study of Higher Institution as an Incident in the Process of Acculturation." *American Journal of Sociology* 48:701–9.

HERSKOVITS, MELVILLE J. "Education and Cultural Dynamics." *American Journal of Sociology* 48:737–49.

JOHNSON, CHARLES S. "Education and the Cultural Process: Symposium, with Introduction." *American Journal of Sociology* 48:629–32.

MALINOWSKI, BRONISLAW. "Pan-African Problems of Cultural Contact." *American Journal of Sociology* 48:649–65.

MEAD, MARGARET. "Our Educational Emphasis in Primitive Perspective." *American Journal of Sociology* 48:633–38.

MEEKEL, SCUDDER. "Education, Child-Training and Culture." *American Journal of Sociology* 48:676–81.

POWDERMAKER, HORTENSE. "The Channelling of Negro Aggression by the Cultural Process." *American Journal of Sociology* 48:750–58.

REDFIELD, ROBERT. "Culture and Education in the Midwestern Highlands of Guatemala." *American Journal of Sociology* 48:640–48.

WATKINS, MARK HANNA. "The West African 'Bush' School." *American Journal of Sociology* 48:666–75.

WURTH, LOUIS. "Education for Survival: The Jews." *American Journal of Sociology* 48:682–91.

1945

REDFIELD, ROBERT. "A Contribution of Anthropology to the Education of the Teacher." *School Review* 53:516–25.

1946

MEAD, MARGARET. "Professional Problems of Education in Dependent Countries." *Journal of Negro Education* 15:346–57.

——. "Research on Primitive Children." In *Manual of Child Psychology*, edited by Leonard Carmichael. New York: Wiley.

PETTITT, GEORGE A. "Primitive Education in North America." *California University Publications in American Archaeology and Ethnology* 53:1–182.

SPINDLER, GEORGE. "Anthropology May Be an Answer." *Journal of Education* 44:130–31.

TAX, SOL. "The Education of Underprivileged Peoples in Dependent and Independent Territories." *Journal of Negro Education* 15, no. 3:336–45.

WOOTON, FLAUD G. "Primitive Education in the History of Education." *Harvard Educational Review* 16, no. 4:235–54.

1947

EHRLICH, ROBERT W. "The Place of Anthropology in a College Education." *Harvard Educational Review* 42:57–61.

GRANQUIST, HILMA. *Birth and Childhood Among the Arabs: Studies in a Muhamedan Village in Palestine*. Helsingors: Soderstrom.

HOLLINGSHEAD, AUGUST B. *Elmtown's Youth*. New York: Wiley.

OPLER, MORRIS E. "Cultural Alternatives and Educational Theory." *Harvard Educational Review* 17, no. 1:28–44.

REDFIELD, ROBERT. "The Study of Culture in General Education." *Social Education* 11:259–64.

1948

HERSKOVITS, MELVILLE J. "Education and the Sanctions of Custom." In *Man and His Works: The Science of Cultural Anthropology*. New York: Knopf.

1949

KEESING, FELIX H. "Experiment in Training Overseas Administrators." *Human Organization* 8, no. 4.

1950

FIRTH, J. R. "Personality and Language in Society." *Sociological Review* 42:8–14.

MEAD, MARGARET. "Cultural Traditions and Educational Process." An Inaugural Lecture delivered at the University of London, Institute of Education, London, June 19.

——. *The School in American Culture*. Cambridge, Mass.: Harvard University Press.

PITJE, B. M. "Traditional Systems of Male Education Among Pedi and Cognate Tribes." *African Studies* 9, no. 2:53–76.

RICHARDS, AUDREY I. "The Teaching Process." In *A Handbook for College Teachers*, edited by Bernice Cronkhite. Cambridge, Mass.: Harvard University Press.

WEDGEWOOD, CAMILLA H. "The Contribution of Anthropology to the Educational Development of Colonial Peoples." *South Pacific* 4, no. 5:77–84.

1952

REDFIELD, ROBERT. "Primitive World View." *Proceedings of the American Philosophical Society* 96:30–36.

1953

BECKER, HOWARD S. "The Teacher in the Authority System of the Public School." *Journal of Educational Sociology* 27 (November).

KENYATTA, JOMO. *Facing Mount Kenya: The Tribal Life of the Gikuyu*. London: Secker & Warburg.

1954

ENGLE, SHIRLEY. "The Culture Concept in the Teaching of History." Ph.D. dissertation, University of Illinois.

KROEBER, A. L. "The Place of Anthropology in Universities." *American Anthropologist* 54:764–67.

ROSENSTIEL, ANNETTE. "Educational Anthropology: A New Approach to Cultural Analysis." *Harvard Educational Review* 24:28–36.

1955

BRAMELD, THEDORE. "The Meeting of Educational and Anthropological Theory." In *Education and Anthropology*, edited by George D. Spindler. Palo Alto: Stanford University Press.

DU BOIS, CORA. "Some Notions on Learning Intercultural Understanding." In *Education and Anthropology*, edited by George D. Spindler. Palo Alto: Stanford University Press.

HART, C. W. M. "Contrast Between Prepubertal and Postpubertal Education." In *Education and Anthropology*, edited by George D. Spindler. Palo Alto: Stanford University Press.

HENRY, JULES. "Docility, Or Giving Teacher What She Wants." *Journal of Social Issues* 11:33-41.

HOEBEL, E. ADAMSON. "Anthropology in Education." *Yearbook of Anthropology*, 391-95.

KIMBALL, SOLON T. "Anthropology and Communication." *Teacher's College Record* 57, no. 2:64-71.

———. "Education: The Foundation of International Cooperation." *Teacher's College Record* 57, no. 5:252-64.

———. "The Method of Natural History and Educational Research." In *Education and Anthropology*, edited by George D. Spindler. Palo Alto: Stanford University Press.

LEE, DOROTHY. "Discrepancies in the Teaching of American Culture." In *Education and Anthropology*, edited by George D. Spindler. Palo Alto: Stanford University Press.

MEAD, MARGARET, ed. *Cultural Patterns and Technical Change*. Paris: World Federation for Mental Health, UNESCO.

METRAUX, RHODA. "Implicit and Explicit Values in Education and Teaching as Related to Growth and Development." *Merrill-Palmer Quarterly* 2:27-34.

QUILLEN, I. JAMES. "Problems and Prospects." In *Education and Anthropology*, edited by George D. Spindler. Palo Alto: Stanford University Press.

READ, MARGARET. *Education and Social Change in Tropical Areas*. London: Thomas Nelson & Sons.

———. "Education in Africa: Its Pattern and Role in Social Change." *Annals of American Academy of Political and Social Science* 298:170-79.

SIEGEL, BERNARD J. "Models for the Analysis of the Educative Process in American Communities." In *Education and Anthropology*, edited by George D. Spindler. Palo Alto: Stanford University Press.

SPINDLER, GEORGE D. "Anthropology and Education: An Overview." In *Education and Anthropology*, edited by George D. Spindler. Palo Alto: Stanford University Press.

———. *Education and Anthropology*. Palo Alto: Stanford University Press.

———. "Education in Transforming American Culture." *Harvard Educational Review* 25:145-56.

SPIRO, MELFORD E. "Education in a Collective Settlement in Israel." *American Journal of Orthopsychiatry* 25:283-92.

TABA, HILDA. *School Culture: Studies of Participation and Leadership*. Washington, D.C.: American Council on Education.

USEEM, JOHN, and USEEM, RUTH HILL. *The Western Educated Man in India. A Study of His Social Roles and Influence*. New York: Holt, Rinehart & Winston.

ZBOROWSKI, MARK. "The Place of Book Learning in Traditional Jewish Culture." In *Childhood in Contemporary Cultures*, edited by Margaret Mead and Martha Wolfenstein. Chicago: University of Chicago Press.

1956

BROOKOVER, WILBUR. "Sociology Contributes to the Analysis of the Educative Process." *Educational Leadership* 14:484.

EGGAN, DOROTHY. "Instruction and Affect in Hopi Cultural Continuity." *Southwestern Journal of Anthropology* 12:347-70.

HERSKOVITS, MELVILLE J. *Man and His Works*. New York: Knopf.

KIMBALL, SOLON T. "Anthropology and Education." *Educational Leadership* 13:480-83.

———. "The Role of Education in Community Development." *Teacher's College Record* 57, no. 6:386-91.

MANNHEIM, CARL. *Essays on the Sociology of Culture*. London: Routledge & Kegan Paul.

1957

BRAMELD, THEODORE. *Cultural Foundations of Education: An Interdisciplinary Exploration*. New York: Harper & Brothers.

EGGAN, FRED. "Social Anthropology and the Educational System." *School Review* 65:247–59.

HARTSHORNE, EDWARD Y. "Class Aspects of Undergraduate Society." In *Education and the Social Order*, edited by Blaine E. Mercer and Edwin R. Curr. New York: Rinehart.

HENRY, JULES. "Attitude Organization in Elementary School Classrooms." *American Journal of Orthopsychiatry* 27:117–33.

LEE, DOROTHY. "Anthropology and American Secondary Education." In *Frontiers of Secondary Education*, Vol. 2, edited by Paul Halverson. Syracuse: University of Syracuse Press.

MAIR, L. P. *Studies in Applied Anthropology.* London: Athlone Press.

MEAD, MARGARET. "Our Educational Emphases in Primitive Perspective." In *Education and the Social Order*, edited by Blaine E. Mercer and Edwin R. Curr. New York: Rinehart.

MERCER, BLAINE E., and CURR, EDWIN R. *Education and the Social Order.* New York: Rinehart.

MILLER, HENRY. "A Problem of Acculturation." In *Education and the Social Order*, edited by Blaine E. Mercer and Edwin R. Curr. New York: Rinehart.

STEPHENSON, RICHARD. "Education and Stratification." In *Education and the Social Order*, edited by Blaine E. Mercer and Edwin R. Curr. New York: Rinehart.

TABA, HILDA. "Educational Implications in the Concepts of Culture and Personality." *Educational Leadership* 15:183–86.

THELEN, HERBERT A., and GETZELS, JACOB W. "The Social Sciences: Conceptual Framework for Education." *School Review* 65:339–55.

WYLIE, LAURENCE. *Village in the Vaucluse.* Cambridge, Mass.: Harvard University Press.

1958

BRAMELD, THEODORE. "Explicit and Implicit Culture in Puerto Rico: A Case Study in Educational Anthropology." *Harvard Educational Review* 28:197–213.

CLARK, HAROLD F., and SLOAN, HAROLD S. *Classrooms in the Factories.* Rutherford, N.J.: Institute of Research, Fairleigh Dickinson University.

DAHLKE, H. O. *Values in Culture and Classroom.* New York: Harper & Brothers.

FRANK, LAWRENCE. *The School as Agent for Cultural Renewal.* Cambridge, Mass.: Harvard University Press.

HANKS, LUCIEN M., JR. "Indifference to Modern Education in a Thai Farming Community." *Human Organization* 17:9–14.

HOLMES, LOWELL D. "It's More Than Bones and Old Stones." *Social Studies* 48:220–22.

JAMES, PRESTON E. "New Viewpoints in Geography." *New Viewpoints in the Social Sciences.* Twenty-eighth Yearbook of the National Council for the Social Studies: Washington, D.C.

KIMBALL, SOLON T. "Problemas e Pesquisas Educasionais." *Educacao e Ciencias Sociais* 3:65–81.

MONTAGU, ASHLEY. *Education and Human Relations.* New York: Grove Press.

SPINDLER, GEORGE. "Anthropology in the Social Studies Curriculum." *National Education Association Journal* 47:626–27.

——. "New Trends and Applications in Anthropology." *New Viewpoints in the Social Sciences.* Twenty-eighth Yearbook of the National Council for the Social Studies: Washington, D.C.

1959

BRAMELD, THEODORE. "Modern Society's Challenge to Education: The Philosopher's View." *Rhode Island College Journal* 1:17–25.

——. *The Remaking of a Culture: Life and Education in Puerto Rico.* New York: Harper & Brothers.

——. "Review of Montagu's *Education and Human Relations.*" *Harvard Educational Review* 29:154–57.

CALIFORNIA STATE DEPARTMENT OF EDUCATION. *Generalizations Relating to Anthropology.* Sacramento: Department of Education: 53–60.

EGGAN, FRED. "An Anthropologist Looks at Discipline." *Grade Teacher* 76:93–95.

FLOUD, JEAN, and HALSEY, A. H. "Education and Social Structures: Theories and Methods." *Harvard Educational Review* 29:289–96.

GRINAGER, PATRICIA. "A Plea for Educanthropology." Paper presented to the American Anthropological Association, Washington, D.C., December.

HENRY, JULES. "The Problems of Spontaneity, Initiative, and Creativity in Suburban Classrooms." *American Journal of Orthopsychiatry* 29:266-79.

HOFFENBACHER, HAROLD. "Putting Concepts from Anthropology into the Secondary School Program," Dearborn, Michigan. Mimeographed.

JAMES, PRESTON. "The Use of Culture Areas as a Frame of Organization for the Social Sciences." *New Viewpoints in Geography.* Twenty-ninth Yearbook of the National Council for the Social Studies: Washington, D.C.

LANDY, DAVID. *Tropical Childhood: Cultural Transmission and Learning in a Rural Puerto Rican Village.* New York: Harper & Row.

LEE, DOROTHY. "Personal Significance and Group Structure." *Freedom and Culture.* Edited by Clark Moustakas and David Smillie. Englewood Cliffs, N.J.: Prentice-Hall.

MEAD, MARGARET. *People and Places.* Cleveland: World.

——. "A Redefinition of Education." *National Education Association Journal* 48:15-17.

ONG, WALTER. "Latin Language Study as a Renaissance Puberty Rite." *Studies in Philology* 56, no. 2 (April): 103-24.

ROSENSTIEL, ANNETTE. "Anthropology and Childhood Education." *School and Society* 87:482-83.

SIEGEL, BERNARD J. "Review of Brameld's Cultural Foundations of Education." *American Anthropologist* 48:118-20.

SPINDLER, GEORGE. "Learning in Culture: An Anthropological Perspective." *Educational Leadership* 16:394-97.

——. *Transmission of American Culture.* Cambridge, Mass.: Harvard University Press.

1960

BROOKS, NELSON. "Teaching Culture in the Foreign Language Classroom." In *Linguistic-Cultural Differences and American Education*, edited by Alfred C. Aarons, Barbara V. Gordon, and William A. Stewart. *Florida FL Reporter* 7, no. 1:20-28.

CHILCOTT, JOHN H. "The Place of Anthropology in the American Public School Curriculum." *Kroeber Anthropological Society Papers* 22.

EHRLICH, ROBERT. "Anthropology and Liberal Arts Education." Paper presented to the Symposium on Anthropology in General Education held at the New York Academy of Sciences. New York: Brooklyn College Press. Mimeographed.

ELLISON, JACK L. "Anthropology Brings Human Nature into the Classroom." *Social Education* 24:313-16, 328.

GOLDSCHMIDT, WALTER, ed. *Exploring the Ways of Mankind.* New York: Holt, Rinehart & Winston.

HAWTHORN, HARRY B.; BELSHAW, C. S.; and JAMIESON, S. M. *The Indians of British Columbia.* Berkeley: University of California Press.

HENRY, JULES. "A Cross-Cultural Outline of Education." *Current Anthropology* 1, no. 4:267-305.

HILGER, I. *Field Guide to the Ethnological Study of Child Life.* New Haven, Connecticut: Human Area Relations Files.

KIMBALL, SOLON T. "Darwin and the Future of Education." *Educational Forum* 20, no. 1:59-72.

——. "Primary Education in Brazil." *Comparative Education Review* 4:49-54.

——. "The Teaching of Anthropology: Graduate Professional Education." Paper presented to the Symposium on Anthropology in General Education at the New York Academy of Science. New York: Columbia University, May. Mimeographed.

LEE, DOROTHY. "Freeing Capacity to Learn." In *Papers and Reports from the Fourth ASCD Research Institute*, edited by Alexander Frazier. Washington, D.C.: Association for Supervision and Curriculum Development.

LEEDS, ANTHONY. "Some Considerations of the Possibilities of Anthropology in the High School Curriculum: An Experiment on Teaching Anthropology." Paper presented to the Symposium on Anthropology in General Education at the New York Academy of Science. New York: City College, May. Mimeographed.

MANDELBAUM, DAVID G. "The Teaching of Anthropology in the United States: A review of the Symposia of the Project in Educational Anthropology." New York: Werner Gren Foundation for Anthropological Research. Mimeographed.

MEAD, MARGARET. "The High School of the Future." *California Journal of Secondary Education* 35:360-69.

PETTITT, GEORGE A. "Educational Practices of the North American Indian." In *Exploring the Ways of Mankind*, edited by Walter Goldschmidt. New York: Holt, Rinehart & Winston.

WEST, JAMES. "Childhood Education in Rural America." In *Exploring the Ways of Mankind*, edited by Walter Goldschmidt. New York: Holt, Rinehart & Winston.

1961

BECKER, HOWARD S. "Schools, and Systems of Stratification." In *Education, Economy, and Society*, edited by A. H. Halsey, Jean Floud, and C. Arnold Anderson. New York: Free Press.

BECKER, HOWARD S.; GEER, BLANCHE; HUGHES, EVERETT C.; and STRAUSS, ANSELM L. *Boys in White: Student Culture in Medical School.* Chicago: University of Chicago Press.

BRAMELD, THEODORE. "Anthropology and Education." *Review of Educational Research* (February): 70–79.

———. *Education for the Emerging Age: Newer Ends and Stronger Means.* New York: Harper & Brothers.

BURTON, WILLIAM L. "History of Civilization as a Core Course in Teacher Education." *Social Studies* 52:181–85.

CLIFT, VIRGIL A. "Social and Cultural Factors Relating to Education in the Middle East." *Journal of Educational Sociology* 35:18–26.

DUNLAP, ROBERT L. "Teaching Anthropology in the High School." *Education Digest* 26:52–53.

ELONEN, ANNA S. "Culture Components as a Significant Factor in Child Development." *American Journal of Orthopsychiatry* 31:505–12.

GOODENOUGH, WARD H. "Education and Identity." In *Anthropology and Education*, edited by Frederick C. Gruber. The Martin G. Brumbaugh Lectures, fifth series. Philadelphia: University of Pennsylvania Press.

GRUBER, FREDERICK C. *Anthropology and Education.* The Martin G. Brumbaugh Lectures, fifth series. Philadelphia: University of Pennsylvania Press.

HENRY, JULES. "More on Cross-Cultural Education." *Current Anthropology* 2:260–64.

HOYT, ELIZABETH E. "Integration of Culture: A Review of Concepts." *Current Anthropology* 2:407–26.

HUUS, HELEN. "Education: Intellectual, Moral, Physical." *Proceedings of Forty-eighth Annual Schoolmen's Week.* Philadelphia: University of Pennsylvania Press.

KIMBALL, SOLON T. "An Anthropological View of Learning." *National Elementary Principal* 40:23–27.

KRAESTEFF, KRASTYU. "Anthropology in the Secondary School." *School and Community* 48:8–9.

LEE, DOROTHY. "Autonomous Motivation." In *Anthropology and Education*, edited by Frederick C. Gruber. The Martin G. Brumbaugh Lectures, fifth series. Philadelphia: University of Pennsylvania Press.

MEAD, MARGARET, and HILL, HENRY H. *American Culture in the Sixties. Your AASA in 1960-1961.* Official Report. Washington, D.C.: American Association of School Administrators. Department of the National Education Association.

MURDOCK, GEORGE P. *Outline of Cultural Materials.* New Haven, Conn.: Human Relations Area Files.

PAULSEN, F. ROBERT. "Cultural Anthropology and Education." *Journal of Educational Sociology* 34:289–99.

SIERSKMA, F.; WAX, MURRAY; and WOOD, EVELYN. "More On Cross-Cultural Education." *Current Anthropology* 2:255–59.

VAN DALEN, D. B. "Cultural Impact on Physical Education." *Journal of Health, Physical Education, Recreation* 32:15–17.

WALLACE, ANTHONY F. C. "Schools of Revolutionary and Conservative Societies." In *Anthropology and Education*, edited by Frederick C. Gruber. Philadelphia: University of Pennsylvania Press.

1962

BIENENSTOK, THEODORE, and SAYRES, WILLIAM C. *Contributions of Sociology and Anthropology to Education.* Albany, N.Y.: University of the State of New York.

BLUMENFELD, RUTH. "Community Influences on Children." *Childhood Education* 38:409–11.

BUSHNELL, JOHN H. "Student Culture at Vassar." In *A Psychological and Social Integration of Higher Learning*, edited by Nevitt Sanford. New York: Wiley.

CHILCOTT, JOHN H. "A Proposal for the Unification of Secondary Courses Through Anthropology." *Clearing House* 26:387-93.

CONDON, PAUL U. "A Study to Estimate Amenability of Citizens Toward Certain Reconstructionist Concepts Proposed for Application to Their Public High School." Ph.D. dissertation, Boston University.

EISELEY, LOREN. *The Mind as Nature*. New York: Harper & Row.

FOSTER, GEORGE M. *Traditional Cultures and the Impact of Technological Change*. New York: Harper & Row.

GANS, HERBERT J. *The Urban Villagers: Group and Class in the Life of Italian Americans*. New York: Free Press of Glencoe.

GOODMAN, MARY ELLEN. "Culture and Conceptualization: A Study of Japanese and American Children." *Ethnology* 1:374-86.

GROSS, CARL H.; HANSON, JOHN; and WRONSKI, STANLEY,P.; eds. *School and Society: Readings in the Social and Philosophical Foundations of Education*. Lexington, Mass.: Heath.

HELLMAN, ROBERT A. "A Case for Anthropology in Public School Curricula." *Phi Delta Kappan* 44:43-44.

HERZOG, JOHN D. "Deliberate Instruction and Household Structure: A Cross-Cultural Study." *Harvard Educational Review* 32, no. 3:301-42.

HODGKINSON, HAROLD. *Education in Social and Cultural Perspectives*. Englewood Cliffs, N.J.: Prentice-Hall.

Journal of Secondary Education. "Symposium: Each Pupil's International Responsibility: Implications for Secondary Schools." *Journal of Secondary Education* 37:157-92.

KIMBALL, SOLON T. "Social Science Research and Higher Education." *Human Organization* 21, no. 4:271-79.

———, and McCLELLAN, JAMES E., JR. *Education and the New America*. New York: Random House.

LLOYD, JOHN. "British and American Education in Cultural Perspectives." *Comparative Education Review* 6:16-24.

McMACKIN, LORIN. "The Function of Culture in Isaac Berkson's Theory of Education." *Educational Theory* 12:106-9.

MEAD, MARGARET. "The Social Responsibility of the Anthropologist." *Journal of Higher Education* 23:1-12.

MILLER, STANLEY N. "The World Cultures Course." *Social Education* 26:69-80.

MONTAGU, ASHLEY. *The Humanization of Man*. Cleveland: World.

RAMSEY, ROBERT R., JR. "A Subcultural Approach to Academic Behavior." *Journal of Educational Sociology* 35:278-83.

SEAGOE, MAY V. "Children's Play as an Indicator of Cross-Cultural and Intra-Cultural Differences." *Journal of Educational Sociology* 35:278-83.

SNYDER, ELDON E. "The Social-Cultural Approach to Intergroup Education at the Secondary School Level." *Journal of Educational Sociology* 35:236-39.

TAGLIACOZZO, GIORGIO. "Culture and Education. General Education: Mirror Culture." *American Behavioral Scientist* 6:22-25.

WOLMAN, MARIANNE. "Cultural Factors and Creativity." *Journal of Secondary Education*, 37:454-60.

1963

ALBERT, ETHEL H. "Value Aspects of Teaching Anthropology." In *The Teaching of Anthropology*, edited by David G. Mandelbaum, Gabriel W. Lasker, and Ethel M. Albert. Berkeley: University of California Press.

BARKER, ROGER G., ed. *The Stream of Behavior. Exploration of Its Structure and Content*. New York: Appleton-Century-Crofts.

BROWN, INA CORRINE. "Anthropology in the Humanities." *Educational Leadership* 20:256-58.

DRIVER, HAROLD E., and DRIVER, WILHELMINE. *Ethnography and Acculturation of Chichimeca-Jonaz of Northeast Mexico. Folklore and Linguistics*. Publication 26. Bloomington: Indiana University Research Center in Anthropology.

DU BOIS, CORA. "The Curriculum in Cultural Anthropology." In The *Teaching of Anthropology*, edited by David G. Mandelbaum, Gabriel W. Lasker, and Ethel M. Albert. Berkeley: University of California Press.

FISCHER, JOHN L., and FISCHER, ANN. "The New Englanders of Orchard Town, U.S.A." In *Six Cultures: Studies of Child Rearing*, edited by Beatrice B. Whiting. New York: Wiley.

GOODENOUGH, WARD H. *Cooperation in Change: An Anthropological Approach to Community Development.* New York: Russel Sage Foundation.

GUTHRIE, GEORGE M. "Structure of Abilities in a Non-Western Culture." *Journal of Educational Psychology* 54:94–103.

HENRY, JULES. "American Schoolrooms: Learning the Nightmare." *Columbia University Forum* 6, no. 2:24–30.

———. *Culture Against Man.* New York: Random House.

HERTZBERG, HAZEL W. "Grasping the Drama of a Culture." *National Education Association Journal* 52:44–46.

KIMBALL, SOLON T. "Anthropology and Administration." In *The Social Sciences and Educational Administration*, edited by Lawrence W. Downey and Frederick Enns. Alberta, Canada: University of Alberta.

———. "Cultural Influences Shaping the Role of the Child." In *Education and Culture*, edited by George D. Spindler. New York: Holt, Rinehart & Winston.

LANDES, RUTH. "An Anthropologist Looks at School Counseling." *School Review* 10, no. 1:14–19.

MANDELBAUM, DAVID G. "A Design for an Anthropology Curriculum." In *The Teaching of Anthropology*, edited by David G. Mandelbaum, Gabriel W. Lasker, and Ethel M. Albert. Berkeley: University of California Press.

MANDELBAUM, DAVID G.; LASKER, GABRIEL W.; LASKER, ETHEL M.; eds. *The Teaching of Anthropology.* Berkeley: University of California Press.

MEAD, MARGARET. "Anthropology and an Education for the Future." In *The Teaching of Anthropology*, edited by David G. Mandelbaum, Gabriel W. Lasker, and Ethel M. Albert. Berkeley: University of California Press.

———. "Cultural Factors in Community-Education Programs." In *Education and Culture*, edited by George D. Spindler. New York: Holt, Rinehart & Winston.

———. "Socialization and Enculturation." *Current Anthropology* 6, no. 2:184–88.

MOREHOUSE, WARD. "Strengthening the Study of Neglected Cultures." *Journal of Higher Education* 34:311–17.

NICHOLS, PETER W. "Sources in Anthropology for High Schools." *School and Community* 49 (February): 11.

SPINDLER, GEORGE D. "The Character Structure of Anthropology." In *Education and Culture*, edited by George D. Spindler. New York: Holt, Rinehart & Winston.

———. "Current Anthropology." In *Education and Culture*, edited by George D. Spindler. New York: Holt, Rinehart & Winston.

———, ed. *Education and Culture.* New York: Holt, Rinehart, & Winston.

———. "Personality, Sociolcultural System, and Education Among the Menomini." In *Education and Culture*, edited by George D. Spindler. New York: Holt, Rinehart & Winston.

———. "The Role of the School Administrator." In *Education and Culture*, edited by George D. Spindler. New York: Holt, Rinehart & Winston.

———. "The Transmission of American Culture." In *Education and Culture*, edited by George D. Spindler. New York: Holt, Rinehart & Winston.

TABA, HILDA. "Cultural Orientation in Comparative Education." *Comparative Education Review* 6:171–76.

TAGLIACOZZO, GIORGIO. "Culture and Education. The Origins." *American Behavioral Scientist* 6:8–13.

WAX, MURRAY L. "American Indian Education as a Cross-Cultural Transaction." *Teacher's College Record* 64:693–704.

WERNER, FRED H. "Acculturation and Milieu Therapy in Student Transition." In *Education and Culture*, edited by George D. Spindler. New York: Holt, Rinehart & Winston.

WHITING, BEATRICE B., ed. *Six Cultures: Studies of Child Rearing.* New York: Wiley.

ZINTZ, MILES V. *Education Across Cultures.* Dubuque, Iowa: William C. Brown.

1964

ATWOOD, M. S. "Small-scale Administrative Change: Resistance to the Introduction of a High School Guidance Program." In *Innovation in Education*, edited by Matthew B. Miles. New York: Teachers College, Columbia University.

BULL, WILLIAM E. "The Use of Vernacular Languages in Education." In *Language in Culture and Society: A Reader in Linguistics and Anthropology*, edited by Dell Hymes. Evanston: Harper & Row.

CARLSON, RICHARD O. "Environmental Constraints and Organizational Consequences: The Public School and Its Clients." In *Behavioral Science and Educa-*

tional Administration, edited by Daniel E. Griffiths. Chicago: Sixty-third Year-book of the National Society for the Study of Education.

COHEN, YEHUDI A. "The Establishment of Identity in a Social Nexus: The Special Case of Initiation Ceremonies and Their Relation to Value and Legal Systems." *American Anthropologist* 66: 529–52.

———. *The Transition from Childhood to Adolescence*. Chicago: Aldine.

EISENSTADT, S. N. *From Generation to Generation: Age Groups and Social Structure*. Glencoe, Ill.: Free Press.

FUCHS, ESTELLE. "The Compatibility of Western Education with Ibo Culture: An Examination of the Complex Dynamics Involved in the Successful Diffusion of Literacy and Schooling to the Ibo of Eastern Nigeria." Ph.D. dissertation, Columbia University.

GUMPERZ, JOHN J., and HYMES, DELL. "The Ethnography of Communication." *American Anthropologist* 66, no. 6 (December): 2.

GUSSOW, ZACHARY. "The Observer-Observed Relationship as Information About Structure in Small-Group Research." *Psychiatry* 27:230–47.

HODGKIN, MARY C. "Cross-Cultural Education in Anthropological Perspectives." *Anthropological Forum* 1:232–47.

LANGEVELD, M. J. "Anthropologie und padagogik inzwei kurslich erchienenen deutshen buchern." *International Review of Education* 9, no. 4:448–54.

LAWSON, DAVID. "Culture and Education: Definitions and Relations." *Educational Forum* 28:449–56.

LYONS, R. G. "Philosophy and Anthropology in the Study of Mankind." *Social Education* 28:405–06.

MINTURN, LEIGH, and LAMBERT, WILLIAM W., eds. *Mothers of Six Cultures: Antecedents of Child Rearing*. New York: Wiley.

MONTAGU, ASHLEY. "To Think and To Feel." *National Education Association Journal* 53.

REDFIELD, ROBERT. *Education and the Social Sciences*. Chicago: Publications of the Anthropology Curriculum Study Program, American Anthropological Association.

SADY, RACHEL R. "Anthropology and World History Texts." *Phi Delta Kappan* 45:247–51.

SHUNK, WILLIAM R., and GOLDSTEIN, BERNICE Z. "Anthropology and Education." *Review of Educational Research* 34:71–84.

SPINDLER, GEORGE D. "The Education of Adolescents: An Anthropological Perspective." *Proceedings of the Fifteenth Annual Conference of the California Association of School Psychologists and Psychometrists*. Riverside, Calif.: The Association.

STULL, E. G. "Reading Materials for the Disadvantaged: From Yaki to Tlingit to Kotzekive." *Reading Teacher* 17:522–27.

WAX, MURRAY L., and WAX, ROSALIE H. "Indian Education for What?" *Mid-continent American Studies Journal* 6:164–70.

———; WAX, ROSALIE H.; DUMONT, ROBERT V., JR. "Formal Education in an American Indian Community." *Social Problems* 11, no. 4:1–126.

WAX, ROSALIE H., and WAX, MURRAY L. "Dropout of American Indians at the Secondary Level." Final Report, U.S. Office of Education. Mimeographed.

WHIPPLE, GERTRUDE. "Multiculture Primers for Today's Children." *Education Digest* 29: 26–29.

1965

BIXBY, PAUL. "The United States and the Non-Western World." *National Elementary Principal* 64, no. 4:25–31.

BRAMELD, THEODORE. Anthropotherapy—Toward Theory and Practice." *Human Organization* 24:288–97.

———. *The Use of Explosive Ideas in Education*. Pittsburgh: University of Pittsburgh Press.

BREMBECK, COLE. "Education for National Development." *National Elementary Principal* 64:32–39.

CHRISTIAN, CHESTER C. "Acculturation of the Bilingual Child." *Modern Language Journal* 49:160–65.

DORE, RONALD P. *Education in Tokugawa Japan*. Berkeley: University of California Press.

EDDY, ELIZABETH. *Walk the White Line: A Profile of Urban Education*. Garden City, N.Y.: Doubleday.

FOSTER, PHILIP. *Education and Social Change in Ghana*. Chicago: University of Chicago Press.

———. "Essay Review: Education and Culture." *School Review* 73:66–73.

GALLAHER, ART, JR. "Directed Change in Formal Organization: The School System. Change Processes in the Public Schools." *Educational Administration* 3: 35–51.

HAMBLIN, F. "Oak Tree and Education." *National Elementary Principal* 44: 20–24.

HANVEY, ROBERT G. "Anthropology in the Schools." *Educational Leadership* 22 (February).

HOBART, C. W., and BRANT, C. S. "Eskimo Education, Danish and Canadian: A Comparison." *Canadian Review of Sociology and Anthropology* 3, no. 2: 47–66.

HONIGMANN, JOHN J., and HONIGMANN, IRMA. *Eskimo Townsmen.* Ottawa: Canadian Research Centre for Anthropology.

KHLEIF, B. B. "A Sociolcultural Framework for Training Teachers in a School Mental Health Program." *School Review* 73 (Spring).

KIMBALL, SOLON T. "Anthropology and Teacher Training." In *Five Fields and Teacher Education,* edited by D. B. Gowin and Cynthia Richardson. Ithaca, N.Y.: Cornell University Press.

———. "Education and the New South." In *The South in Continuity and Change,* edited by John C. McKinney and Edgar T. Thompson. Durham, N.C.: Duke University Press.

———. "The Transmission of Culture." *Educational Horizons* 43:161–86.

KNELLER, GEORGE F. *Educational Anthropology: An Introduction.* New York: Wiley.

LANDES, RUTH. *Culture in American Education: Anthropological Approaches to Minority and Dominant Groups in the Schools.* New York: Wiley.

LEE, DOROTHY. "Cultural Factors in the Educational Process." In *Perspectives on Educational Administration and the Behavioral Sciences,* edited by W. W. Charters, Jr., Burton R. Clark, Jack A. Culbertson, Daniel E. Griffiths, Werner Z. Hirsch, Dorothy Lee, and Nicholas A. Masters. Eugene, Ore.: Center for the Advanced Study of Educational Administration, University of Oregon.

MONTAGU, ASHLEY. "What Anthropology Is." *The Instructor* 35:48–49.

ROHNER, RONALD P. "Factors Influencing the Academic Performance of Kwakiutl Indian Children in Canada." *Comparative Education Review* 9:331–40.

SCHMIDT, NANCY J. "Orthodox Judaism: A Minority Within a Minority." *Jewish Journal of Sociology* 7, no. 2:176–206.

SPINDLER, GEORGE D. "Comment on Theodore Brameld." *Human Organization* 24:293–95.

1966

ADAMS, DONALD K., ed. *Introduction to Education: A Comparative Analysis.* Belmont, Calif.: Wadsworth.

BETTELHEIM, BRUNO. "Does Communal Education Work: The Case of the Kibbutz." In *Introduction to Education: A Comparative Analysis,* edited by Donald K. Adams. Belmont, Calif.: Wadsworth.

BROKENSHA, DAVID. *Social Change at Larteh, Ghana.* London: Oxford University Press.

BROPHY, W. A., and ABERLE, S. D. "Education." In *The Indian: America's Unfinished Business.* Commission on Rights, Liberties, and Responsibilities of the American Indian. Norman, Okla.: University of Oklahoma Press.

DIAMOND, STANLEY, and others. *Culture of Schools.* Report to the U.S. Office of Education. ERIC System: U.S. Office of Education.

EDDY, ELIZABETH M. "Anthropology and Guidance." In *Interdisciplinary Roots of Guidance,* edited by T. C. Hennessy. New York: Fordham University Press.

FRANKLIN, BENJAMIN. "Remarks Concerning the Savages of North America." In *Introduction to Education: A Comparative Analysis,* edited by Don Adams. Belmont, Calif.: Wadsworth.

FUCHS, ESTELLE. *Pickets at the Gate.* New York: Free Press.

HANVEY, ROBERT G. "Anthropology in the High Schools: The Representation of a Discipline." In *Concepts and Structure in the New Social Science Curricula,* edited by Irving Morrissett. West Lafayette, Ind.: Social Science Education Consortium.

KAPLAN, ROBERT B. "Cultural Thought Patterns in Intercultural Education." *Language Learning* 16:1–20.

KHLEIF, B. B. "A Socio-Cultural Framework for Studying Guidance in Public Schools." In *Guidance in American Education: Needs and Influencing Forces,* edited by Edward Landy and Arthur M. Kroll. Cambridge, Mass.: Harvard University Press.

LANDSCHEERE, G. "Anthropologie Culturelle et Education Comparee." *International Review of Education* 12:61-72.

PETTIT, GEORGE A. "Anthropology Gives an Opinion—Adult Education." *Adult Leader* 15:124-38.

WILLIAMS, THOMAS RHYS. "The Study of Change as a Concept in Cultural Anthropology." *Theory Into Practice* 5:12-19.

1967

BAIN, R. E. "Missionary Activity in the Bahamas." In *Educational Policy and the Mission Schools: Case Studies from the British Empire*, edited by Brian Holmes. New York: Humanities Press.

BARDIS, PANOS. "Influence of Anthropological Education in International and Interracial Social Distance." Paper presented at World Congress of the Association Internationale de Sociologie, Paris.

BEALS, ALAN R.; SPINDLER, GEORGE; and SPINDLER, LOUISE. *Culture in Process.* New York: Holt, Rinehart & Winston.

BRAMELD, THEODORE. "Adventure in Educational Anthropology: Puerto Rico as a Laboratory." *Journal of Education* 150, no. 2 (Special Issue):3-56.

CONNOR, WILLIAM H., and SMITH, LOUIS M. *Analysis of Patterns of Student Teaching.* Washington, D.C.: U.S. Office of Education, Bureau of Research.

DART, FRANCIS. "Cross-Cultural Teaching of Science." *Science* 155:649-56.

GANS, HERBERT J. *The Levittowners.* New York: Pantheon.

GAY, JOHN, and COLE, MICHAEL. *The New Mathematics and an Old Culture. A Study of Learning Among the Kpelle of Liberia. Case Studies in Education and Culture.* New York: Holt, Rinehart & Winston.

HOLMES, BRIAN, ed. *Educational Policy and the Mission Schools: Case Studies from the British Empire.* New York: Humanities Press.

HORINOUCHI, ISAO. *Educational Values and Preadaptation in the Acculturation of Japanese Americans.* Sacramento, Calif.: Sacramento Anthropological Society, Sacramento State College.

IANNI, FRANCIS A. J. *Culture, System, Behavior: The Behavioral Sciences and Education.* Chicago: Science Research Associates.

JONES, N. G. BLURTON. "An Ethological Study of Some Aspects of Social Behaviour of Children in Nursery School." In *Primate Ethology*, edited by Desmond Morris. Chicago: Aldine.

KIMBALL, SOLON T. "Culture, Class, and Educational Congruency." In *Educational Requirements for the 1970s: An Interdisciplinary Approach*, edited by Stanley Elam and William P. McLure. New York: Praeger.

KING, A. RICHARD. *The School at Mopass: A Problem of Identity.* New York: Holt, Rinehart & Winston.

KLUCKHOHN, FLORENCE R. "Variations in Value Orientation as a Factor in Educational Planning." In *Behavioral Science Frontiers in Education*, edited by Eli M. Bower and William G. Hollister. New York: Wiley.

MODIANO, NANCY, and MACCOBY, MICHAEL. *Final Report: Cultural and Sociological Factors Relating to Learning Development.* Project No. 6836. Washington, D.C.: U.S. Office of Education.

MOORE, G. ALEXANDER. *Realities in the Urban Classroom: Observations in Elementary Schools.* Garden City, N.Y.: Doubleday.

SINGLETON, JOHN. *Nichū: A Japanese School.* New York: Holt, Rinehart & Winston.

———. "Urban-Rural Comparisons in Japanese Education." *International Review of Education* 13:470-82.

SMITH, LOUIS M. "The Microethnography of the Classroom." *Psychology in the Schools* 4:216-21.

SPINDLER, GEORGE D. "The Transmission of Culture." In *Culture in Process*, edited by Alan Beals, George D. Spindler, and Louise Spindler. New York: Holt, Rinehart & Winston.

STENHOUSE, LAWRENCE. *Culture and Education.* New York: Weybright & Talley.

STONG, C. L. "An Indian Mound is Excavated by High School Archaeologists." *Scientific American* 217 (December).

WARREN, RICHARD L. *Education in Rebhausen: A German Village.* New York: Holt, Rinehart & Winston.

WAX, ROSALIE H. "The Warrior Dropouts." In *Education: Readings in the Processes of Cultural Transmission*, edited by Harry M. Lindquist. Boston: Houghton Mifflin.

————. "Ogalala Sioux Dropouts and Their Problems with Educators." In *Education and School Crisis: Perspectives on Teaching Disadvantaged Youth*, edited by Everett T. Keach, R. R. Fulton, and W. E. Gardner. New York: Wiley.

WEEKS, SHELDON G. *Divergence in Educational Development: The Case of Kenya and Uganda.* New York: Center for Education in Africa, Teacher's College Press.

WOLCOTT, HARRY F. "Anthropology and Education." *Review of Educational Research* 27, no. 1:82-95.

————. *A Kwakiutl Village and School.* New York: Holt, Rinehart & Winston.

1968

BAILEY, WILFRED. "Preparation of Elementary School Units on the Concept of Culture." *Human Organization* 27:6-10.

BECKER, HOWARD S.; GEER, BLANCHE; and HUGHES, EVERETT S. *Making the Grade: The Academic Side of College Life.* New York: Wiley.

BERRY, BREWTON. *The Education of American Indians: A Survey of the Literature.* Washington, D.C.: Government Printing Office.

BRAMELD, THEODORE. *Japan: Culture, Education, and Change in Two Communities.* New York: Holt, Rinehart & Winston.

BRUNER, JEROME S. "Culture, Politics, and Pedagogy." *Saturday Review*, May 18.

BURGER, HENRY G. "Ethnopedagogy." *A Manual in Cultural Sensitivity with Techniques for Improving Cross-Cultural Teaching by Fitting Ethnic Patterns.* Albuquerque, N.M.: Southwestern Cooperative Educational Laboratory.

BURNETT, JACQUETTA HILL. "School Culture and Social Change in the City." *Educational Leadership* 26 (October).

————. "Event Analysis in the Micro-Ethnography of Urban Classrooms." Paper presented at the Annual Meeting of the American Anthropological Association, Seattle, Washington. Urbana: Bureau of Educational Research, University of Illinois. Mimeographed.

CAZDEN, COURTNEY B. "Subcultural Differences in Child Language: An Interdisciplinary Review." In *Disadvantaged Child*, edited by Jerome Hellmuth. Vol. 2. New York: Brunner/Mazel.

CHILCOTT, JOHN H. "The School as a Cultural System." In *Readings in the Socio-Cultural Foundations of Education*, edited by John H. Chilcott, Norman C. Greenberg, and Herbert B. Wilson. Belmont, Calif.: Wadsworth.

————. "Some Perspectives for Teaching First Generation Mexican-Americans." In *Readings in the Socio-Cultural Foundations of Education*, edited by John H. Chilcott, Norman C. Greenberg, and Herbert B. Wilson. Belmont, Calif.: Wadsworth.

————, and others, eds. *Readings in the Socio-Cultural Foundations of Education.* Belmont, Calif.: Wadsworth.

COLLIER, MALCOLM, and DETHLEFSEN, EDWIN S. "Anthropology in the Pre-Collegiate Curriculum." *Human Organization* (Spring): 11-16.

DOW, PETER B. "Man: A Course for Study: An Experimental Social Science Course for Elementary Schools." *Man: A Course of Study. Talks to Teachers.* Cambridge, Mass.: Education Development Center.

DUNN, ETHEL. "Educating the Small Peoples of the Soviet North: The Limits of Cultural Change." *Arctic Anthropology* 5:1-31.

EDDY, ELIZABETH. "Anthropology and Teacher Education." *Human Organization* 27, no. 1:17-20.

EMMONS, FRANCES, and COBIA, JACQUELINE. "Introducing Anthropological Concepts in the Primary Grades." *Social Education* 32 (March).

FREEDMAN, DANIEL G., and OMARK, DONALD R. "Ethology, Genetics, and Education." In *Proceedings: The National Conference on Anthropology and Education*, edited by Frederick O. Gearing. Miami Beach, Fla.: The Conference.

GEARING, FREDERICK O. "Why Indians?" *Social Education* 32 (February).

————. *Proceedings: The National Conference on Anthropology and Education.* Miami Beach, Fla.: The Conference.

GOLDSTEIN, MARCUS. "Anthropological Research, Action, and Education in Modern Nations. With Special Reference to the U.S.A." *Current Anthropology* 9, no. 4:247-69.

GREENBERG, NORMAN C. "Cross-Cultural Implications for Teachers." In *Readings in Socio-Cultural Foundations of Education*, edited by John H. Chilcott, Norman C. Greenberg, and Herbert B. Wilson. Belmont, Calif.: Wadsworth.

HAVIGHURST, ROBERT J. *Comparative Perspective on Education.* Boston: Little, Brown.

HENRY, JULES. "Educating for Stupidity." *New York Review of Books*, May 9.

HERSKOVITS, MELVILLE J. "Education and the Sanctions of Custom." In *Readings in the Socio-Cultural Foundations of Education*, edited by John H. Chilcott, Norman C. Greenberg, and Herbert B. Wilson. Belmont, Calif.: Wadsworth.

JACKSON, PHILIP W. *Life in Classrooms*. New York: Holt, Rinehart & Winston.

KIMBALL, SOLON T. "Education and Developmental Change." In *Perspectives in Developmental Change*, edited by Art Gallaher, Jr. Lexington: University of Kentucky Press.

———. "The Method of Natural History and the Social Studies." *Social Education* 32, no. 2:123-27.

LAURIA, ANTHONY, JR. "Power, Schools, and Puerto Rican Society." Paper presented at the Annual Meeting of the American Anthropology Association, Seattle, Washington.

LAWTON, DENNIS. *Social Class, Language and Education*. London: Routledge & Kegan Paul.

LEACOCK, ELEANOR. "The Concept of Culture and Its Significance for School Counselors." *Personnel and Guidance Journal* (May): 844-51.

———. "Personality and Culture Theory in the Field of Education." *Proceedings of the Eighth International Congress of the Anthropological and Ethnological Sciences*. Vol. 2. Tokyo: Science Council of Japan.

———. *Teaching and Learning in City Schools: A Comparative Study*. New York: Basic Books.

LEVINE, STUART, and LURIE, NANCY O., eds. *The American Indian Today*. Deland, Fla.: Everett Edwards.

LINDQUIST, LAURENCE W. "The Civic Responsibility of Anthropologists to Public Education." *Human Organization* 27, no. 1 (Spring): 1-4.

NICHOLSON, CLARA K. *Anthropology and Education*. Columbus, Ohio: Charles E. Merrill.

OXAAL, IVAR. *Black Intellectuals Come to Power: The Rise of Creole Nationalism in Trinidad and Tobago*. Cambridge, Mass.: Schenkman.

PARMEE, EDWARD A., ed. *Formal Education and Culture Change. A Modern Apache Indian Community and Government Education Programs*. Tucson: University of Arizona Press.

———. "Factors Affecting the Education of Apache Youth." In *Formal Education and Cultural Change: A Modern Apache Indian Community and Government Education Programs*, edited by Edward A. Parme. Tucson: University of Arizona Press.

PARSONS, THEODORE W. "Psycho-cultural Determinants of Teaching Behavior: A Southwestern Example." In *Proceedings: The National Conference on Anthropology and Education*, edited by Frederick O. Gearing. Miami Beach: The Conference.

POTTERFIELD, J. E. "An Analysis of Elementary Children's Ability to Learn Anthropological Content at Grades Four, Five, and Six." *Journal of Educational Research* 61 (March).

RICE, MARION J. "Materials for Teaching Anthropology in the Elementary School." *Social Education* 32 (March).

ROSENFELD, GERARD L. "Anthropology as Social Studies in the Elementary School." *Teacher's College Record* 69 (May).

SINDELL, PETER S. "Some Discontinuities in the Enculturation of Mistassini Cree Children." In *Conflict in Culture: Problems of Developmental Change Among the Cree*, edited by Norman A. Chance. Ottawa: Canadian Research Centre for Anthropology, Saint-Paul University.

SINGLETON, JOHN. "The Ethnography of a Japanese School: Anthropological Field Technique and Models in the Study of a Complex Organization." Paper presented at the Annual Meeting of the American Anthropological Association, November. Pittsburgh, Pa.: International and Development Education Program, University of Pittsburgh. Mimeographed.

SMITH, LOUIS M., and GEOFFREY, WILLIAM. *The Complexities of an Urban Classroom. An Analysis Toward a General Theory of Teaching*. New York: Holt, Rinehart & Winston.

Social Education. "The Elementary School: Focus on Anthropology." Special Issue, *Social Education*.

STEUBING, CARL. "Some Role Conflicts as Seen by a High School Teacher." *Human Organization* 27:41-44.

TAX, SOL; DIAMOND, STANLEY; RAINWATER, LEE; MANGIN, WILLIAM; and BHARATI, AGEHANANDA. *Notes and Essays on Education for Adults*. Anthropological Backgrounds of Adult Education, No. 57. Boston Center for the Study of Liberal Education for Adults.

VALENTINE, CHARLES A. *Culture and Poverty: Critique and Counter-Proposals.* Chicago: University of Chicago Press.

WARREN, RICHARD L. "Teacher Encounters: A Typology for Ethnographic Research on the Teaching Experience." Paper presented to the Annual Meeting of the American Anthropological Association, Stanford, California: Stanford Center for Research and Development in Teaching, November. Mimeographed.

———. "The Role of Anthropology in Elementary Social Studies." *Social Education* 32 (March).

WAX, MURRAY L., and WAX, ROSALIE H. "Indian Education for What?" In *The American Indian Today*, edited by Stuart Levine and Nancy O. Lurie. Deland, Fla.: Everett Edwards.

WEEKS, SHELDON G. *An African School: A Sociological Case Study of a Day Secondary School in Uganda.* Cambridge, Mass.: Harvard University Press.

WINTROB, RONALD M. "Acculturation, Identification, and Psychopathology Among Cree Indian Youth." In *Conflict in Culture: Problems of Developmental Change Among the Cree*, edited by Norman A. Chance. Ottawa: Canadian Research Centre for Anthropology, Saint-Paul University.

———, and SINDELL, PETER S. *Education and Identity Conflict Among Cree Indian Youth. A Preliminary Report.* Annex 3 of the Final Report, McGill Cree Project. Ottawa: Rural Development Branch, Department of Regional Economic Expansion.

WOLCOTT, HARRY F. "An Ethnographic Approach to Studying School Administration." Paper presented to the Annual Meeting of the American Anthropological Association, November. Mimeographed.

———. *Methodology: The Observer and the Observed.* Eugene, Oregon: Center for the Advanced Study of Educational Administration. Mimeographed.

1969

AARONS, ALFRED C.; GORDON, BARBARA Y.; STEWART, WILLIAM A., eds. "Linguistic-Cultural Differences and American Education." Special Anthology Issue. *Florida FL Reporter.*

ABRAHAMS, ROGER D. "Black Talk and Black Education." In "Linguistic-Cultural Differences and American Education," edited by Alfred C. Aarons, Barbara Y. Gordon, and William A. Stewart. *Florida FL Reporter* 7, no. 1:10–12.

ALLEN, VIRGINIA F. "Teaching Standard English as a Second Dialect." In "Linguistic-Cultural Differences in American Education," edited by Alfred C. Aarons, Barbara Y. Gordon, and William A. Stewart. *Florida FL Reporter* 7, no. 1:123–29.

BAILEY, BERYL L. "Language and Communicative Styles of Afro-American Children in the U.S." In "Linguistic-Cultural Differences in American Education," edited by Alfred C. Aarons, Barbara Y. Gordon, and William A. Stewart. *Florida FL Reporter* 7, no. 1:46.

BARATZ, JOAN C. "Who Should Do What to Whom . . . and Why?" In "Linguistic-Cultural Differences in American Education," edited by Alfred C. Aarons, Barbara Y. Gordon, and William A. Stewart. *Florida FL Reporter* 7, no. 1:75–77.

BARATZ, STEPHEN S., and BARATZ, JOAN C. "Negro Ghetto Children and Urban Education: A Cultural Solution." In "Linguistic-Cultural Differences in American Education," edited by Alfred C. Aarons, Barbara Y. Gordon, and William A. Stewart. *Florida FL Reporter* 7, no. 1:13–14.

BOHANNON, PAUL. "An Experimental Ninth Grade Anthropology Course." *American Anthropologist* 71:409–20.

BURGER, HENRY G. *Ethnics on Education.* Albuquerque, N.M.: Southwestern Cooperative Education Laboratory.

BURNETT, JACQUETTA HILL. "Ceremony, Rites, and Economy in the Student System of an American High School." *Human Organization* 28:1–10.

CARSE, WILLIAM. "Teacher Education in Culture Change." In *Culture Change, Mental Health, and Poverty*, edited by Joseph C. Finney. Lexington, Ky.: University of Kentucky Press.

CAZDEN, COURTNEY B., and JOHN, VERA P. "Learning in American Indian Children." In *Anthropological Perspectives on Education*, edited by Murray Wax, Stanley Diamond, and Fred Gearing. New York: Basic Books.

CHANCE, NORMAN A. "Premises, Policies, and Practice: A Cross-Cultural Study of Education in the Circumpolar North." Conference on Cross-Cultural Education in the North, Montreal, Canada.

COHEN, ROSALIE A. "Conceptual Styles, Culture Conflict, and Nonverbal Tests of Intelligence." *American Anthropologist* 71:828–56.

DUMONT, ROBERT V., JR., and WAX, MURRAY L. "Cherokee School Society and the Intercultural Classroom." *Human Organization* 28 (Fall): 217-26.

EDDY, ELIZABETH M. *Becoming a Teacher.* New York: Teachers College Press.

FISHMAN, JOSHUA. "The Breadth and Depth of English in the U.S." In "Cultural-Linguistic Differences in American Education," edited by Alfred C. Aarons, Barbara Y. Gordon, and William A. Stewart. *Florida FL Reporter* 7, no. 1:41-43.

FORBES, JACK D. *Education of the Culturally Different: A Multi-Cultural Approach.* California: Far West Laboratory for Educational Research and Development.

FUCHS, ESTELLE. "Education and the Culture of Poverty." In *Poverty: New Interdisciplinary Perspective,* edited by Thomas Weaver and Alvin Magid. San Francisco: Chandler.

———. *Teachers Talk: Views from Inside City Schools.* New York: Doubleday.

GRAHAM, GRACE. *The Public School in the New Society.* New York: Harper & Row.

JOCANO, F. LANDA. *Growing Up in a Phillipino Barrio. Case Studies in Education and Culture.* New York: Holt, Rinehart & Winston.

KAPLAN, ROBERT B. "On a Note of Protest (in a Minor Key): Bidialectism vs. Bidialecticism." In "Linguistic-Cultural Differences in American Education," edited by Alfred A. Aarons, Barbara Y. Gordon, and William A. Stewart. *Florida FL Reporter* 7, no. 1:86.

KING, THOMAS. "Archaeological Materials in Secondary Education." Paper presented at the Annual Meeting of the American Anthropological Association, New Orleans, Louisiana.

KOCHMAN, THOMAS. "Culture and Communication: Implications for Black English in the Classroom." In "Linguistic-Cultural Differences in American Education," edited by Alfred A. Aarons, Barbara Y. Gordon, and William A. Stewart. *Florida FL Reporter* 7, no. 1:89-92.

———. "Social Factors in the Consideration of Teaching Standard English." In "Linguistic-Cultural Differences in American Education," edited by Alfred C. Aarons, Barbara Y. Gordon, and William A. Stewart. *Florida FL Reporter* 7, no. 1:87-88.

LABOV, WILLIAM. "A Note in the Relation of Reading Failure to Peer Group Status in Urban Ghettos." In "Linguistic-Cultural Differences in American Education," edited by Alfred C. Aarons, Barbara Y. Gordon, and William A. Stewart. *Florida FL Reporter* 7, no. 1:54-57.

———. "The Logic of Non-Standard English." In "Linguistic-Cultural Differences in American Education," edited by Alfred C. Aarons, Barbara Y. Gordon, and William A. Stewart. *Florida FL Reporter* 7, no. 1:60-74.

LALIBERTE, CECILE, and LEFEBVRE, MADELEINE. "Teaching Social Sciences at the Elementary Level." Paper presented at the Annual Meeting of the American Anthropological Association, New Orleans, Louisiana.

LUTZ, FRANK W., and IANNACCONE, LAWRENCE. *Understanding Educational Organizations: A Field Study Approach.* Columbus, Ohio: Charles Merrill.

MODIANO, NANCY. "Where Are the Children?" In "Linguistic-Cultural Differences in American Education," edited by Alfred C. Aarons, Barbara Y. Gordon, and William A. Stewart. *Florida FL Reporter* 7, no. 1:93-94.

OLSON, JOHN A. "Mapping: A Method for Organizing Data About Your School Attendance Area." *Oregon School Study Council Bulletin* 12, no. 7.

POVEY, JOHN F. "Cultural Self-Expression Through English in American Indian Schools." In "Linguistic-Cultural Differences in American Education," edited by Alfred C. Aarons, Barbara Y. Gordon, and William A. Stewart. *Florida FL Reporter* 7, no. 1:131-32.

SADY, RACHEL R. *Perspectives from Anthropology.* New York: Teachers College Press.

SINDELL, PETER S. "Anthropological Approaches to the Study of Education." *Review of Educational Research* 39:593-605.

SMITH, LOUIS M. "Teacher Awareness: Social Cognition in the Classroom." *School Review,* 245-55.

———, and POHLAND, PAUL A. "Grounded Theory and Educational Ethnography: A Methodological Analysis and Critique." St. Ann, Mo.: Central Midwestern Regional Education Laboratory. Mimeographed.

SPINDLER, GEORGE D. "Urbanization and Education in a Rural German Village." Stanford University. Mimeographed.

STEWART, WILLIAM A. "Language Teaching Problems in Appalachia." In "Linguistic-Cultural Differences in American Education," edited by Alfred C.

Aarons, Barbara Y. Gordon, and William A. Stewart. *Florida FL Reporter* 7, no. 1:58–60.

———. "Urban Negro Speech: Sociolinguistic Factors Affecting English Teaching." In "Linguistic-Cultural Differences in American Education," edited by Alfred C. Aarons, Barbara Y. Gordon, and William A. Stewart. *Florida FL Reporter* 7, no. 1:50–53.

STOREY, EDWARD. "Black Schools and 'Tom' Anthropology." Paper presented at the Annual Meeting of the Society for Applied Anthropology, Mexico City.

TUCKER, C. ALLEN. "The Chinese Immigrant's Language Handicap: Its Extent and Effects." In "Linguistic-Cultural Differences in American Education," edited by Alfred C. Aarons, Barbara Y. Gordon, and William A. Stewart. *Florida FL Reporter* 7, no. 1:44–45.

WARREN, RICHARD L. "Teacher Encounters: A Typology for Ethnographic Research on the Teaching Experience." School of Education, Stanford University (March).

WAX, MURRAY L.; DUMONT, ROBERT V., JR.; DICKEMAN, MILDRED; and PETTIT, PATRICK F. *Indian Education in Eastern Oklahoma: A Report of Fieldwork Among the Cherokee.* Kansas: University of Kansas.

WILLIAMS, THOMAS RHYS. *A Borneo Childhood: Enculturation in Dusun Society.* New York: Holt, Rinehart & Winston.

WILLOWER, DONALD J. "The Teacher Subculture and Rites of Passage." Paper presented at the Annual Meeting of the American Educational Research Association, Los Angeles, California.

WISSOT, JAY. "Manipulating Ethnic Pride in English as a Second Language Class." In "Linguistic-Cultural Differences in American Education," edited by Alfred C. Aarons, Barbara Y. Gordon, and William A. Stewart. *Florida FL Reporter* 7, no. 1:130.

WOLCOTT, HARRY F. "Concomitant Learning: An Anthropological Perspective on the Utilization of the Media." In *Educational Media: Theory into Practice*, edited by Raymond L. Winan and Wesley C. Meierhenry. Columbus, Ohio: Merrill.

———. "The Elementary School Principal: Notes from a Field Study." Eugene: Center for Advanced Study of Educational Administration, University of Oregon. Mimeographed.

———. "The Teacher as Enemy." Eugene: Center for the Advanced Study of Educational Administration, University of Oregon. Mimeographed.

1970

AURBACH, HERBERT; FUCHS, ESTELLE; and MACGREGOR, GORDON. *The Status of American Indian Education.* University Park: Pennsylvania State University.

BELSHAW, CYRIL S. "Anthropology, Development, and Education." *Council on Anthropology and Education Newsletter* 1, no. 2:11–14.

BHARATI, AGEHANANDA. "Formal Education as Tradition-Enhancing Input in Modern India." Paper presented at the Annual Meeting of the American Anthropological Association, San Diego, California, November.

BROPHY, J. E., and GOOD, T. L. "Teachers' Communication of Differential Expectations for Children's Classroom Performance." *Journal of Educational Psychology* 61:365–74.

BURGER, HENRY G. "'Ethno-Janus': Utilizing Cultural Heritage to Plan for Future Employment." *Practical Anthropology* 17 (November–December): 241–52.

———. *Ethnic Live-In: A Guide for Penetrating and Understanding a Cultural Minority.* Kansas City: University of Missouri.

———. "The Furnivall Effect (Ethnic Disinvolvement) vs. Compensatory Education." *Urban Education* (October): 238–52.

BURNETT, JACQUETTA H. "Culture of the School: A Construct for Research and Explanation in Education." *Council on Anthropology and Education Newsletter*, 1 (May): 4–13.

———. *Pattern and Process in Student Life: A Study of Custom and Social Relationship Among the Students in an American High School.* New York: Teachers College Press.

COHEN, YEHUDI A. "Schools and Civilizational States." In *The Social Sciences and the Comparative Study of Educational Systems*, edited by Joseph L. Fischer. Scranton, Pa.: International Textbook.

DI BONA, JOSEPH. "Role Stability and Change in an Indian University." In *The Social Sciences and the Comparative Study of Educational Systems*, edited by Joseph L. Fischer. Scranton, Pa.: International Textbook.

DUMONT, ROBERT V., and WAX, MURRAY L. "The Cherokee School Society and the Intercultural Classroom." In *Education: Readings in the Processes of Cultural Transmission*, edited by Harry M. Lindquist. Boston: Houghton Mifflin.

EMERSON, GLORIA. "The Laughing Boy Syndrome." *School Review* 79, no. 1: 94-103.

EPSTEIN, ERWIN H., ed. *Politics and Education in Puerto Rico: A Documentary Survey of the Language Issue*. Metuchen, N.J.: Scarecrow Press.

ERICKSON, DONALD A. "Custer *Did* Die for Our Sins!" *School Review* 79, no. 1:76-93.

——, and SCHWARTZ, HENRIETTA. *Community School at Rough Rock: An Evaluation for the Office of Economic Opportunity*. Document No. PB 184571. Springfield, Va.: Clearinghouse for Federal Scientific and Technical Information.

FIRTH, RAYMOND. "Education in Tikopia." In *From Child to Adult: Studies in the Anthropology of Education*, edited by John Middleton. New York: Natural History Press.

FISCHER, JOSEPH L., ed. *The Social Sciences and the Comparative Study of Educational Systems*. Scranton, Pa.: International Textbook.

GEARING, FREDERICK O. *The Face of the Fox*. Chicago: Aldine.

——. "Toward a Mankind Curriculum: From Kindergarten Through Twelfth Grade." *Today's Education* 59 (March).

GLADWIN, THOMAS. *East Is a Big Bird: Navigation and Logic on Puluwat Atoll*. Cambridge, Mass.: Harvard University Press.

GOODMAN, MARY ELLEN. *The Culture of Childhood: Child's-Eye View of Society and Culture*. New York: Teachers College Press.

GUSFIELD, JOSEPH. "Educational and Social Segmentation in Modern India." In *The Social Sciences and the Comparative Studies of Educational Systems*, edited by Joseph L. Fischer. Scranton, Pa.: International Textbook.

GUYOT, JAMES F. "The Clerk Mentality in Burmese Education." In *The Social Studies and the Comparative Study of Educational Systems*, edited by Joseph L. Fischer. Scranton, Pa.: International Textbook.

HAVIGHURST, ROBERT J. "The Education of Indian Children and Youth." *National Study of American Indian Education* 10, no. 6.

HOWARD, ALAN. *Learning to be Rotuman*. New York: Teachers College Press.

JAHODA, GUSTAV. "A Psychologist's Perspective." In *Socialization: The Approach from Social Anthropology*, edited by Philip Mayer. New York: Tavistock.

JOHN, VERA P., and HORNER, VIVIAN M. "Bilingualism and the Spanish-Speaking Child." In *Language and Poverty*, edited by Frederick Williams. Chicago: Markham.

JOHNSON, KURT W.; STOREY, EDWARD; and others. *Curriculum Development: Problems and Prospects*. Symposium held at the Annual Meeting of the American Anthropological Association, San Diego, California.

KIEFER, CHRISTIE W. "The Psychological Interdependence of Family, School, and Bureaucracy of Japan." *American Anthropologist* 72 (February).

KIMBALL, SOLON T. "Education." In *Anthropology and the Behavioral and Health Sciences*, edited by Otto von Mering and Leonard Kasden. Pittsburgh: University of Pittsburgh Press.

KUPER, LEO. "The Intellectuals." In *Education: Readings in the Processes of Cultural Transmission*, edited by Harry M. Lindquist. Boston: Houghton Mifflin.

LACEY, COLIN. *Hightown Grammar: The School as a Social System*. Manchester: Manchester University Press.

LA FONTAINE, J. S. "Two Types of Youth Groups in Kinshasa (Leopoldville)." In *Socialization: The Approach from Social Anthropology*, edited by Philip Mayer. New York: Tavistock.

LEACOCK, ELEANOR BURKE. "Education, Socialization, and the Culture of Poverty." In *Schools Against Children: The Case for Community Control*, edited by Annette Rubinstein. New York: Monthly Review Press.

LÉVI-STRAUSS, CLAUDE. *The Savage Mind*. Chicago: University of Chicago Press.

LEWIS, CLAUDIA LOUISE. *Indian Families of the Northwest Coast*. Chicago: University of Chicago Press.

LINDQUIST, HARRY. *Education: Readings in the Processes of Cultural Transmission*. Boston: Houghton Mifflin.

——. "Teacher Preparation: Anthropological Contributions." Symposium held at the Annual Meeting of the American Anthropological Association, San Diego, California.

——. "Traditional Education and Untraditional Demands: Autobiographical Case Studies from Contemporary Taiwan." In *Education: Readings in the Processes of Cultural Transmission*, edited by Harry M. Lindquist. Boston: Houghton Mifflin.

LITTLEFORD, MICHAEL S. "An Anthropological Study of the Internal Structure of An Experimental 'Problems in Democracy' Class in an All-Black High School." Ph.D. dissertation, University of Florida.

MAYER, PHILIP. *Socialization: The Approach from Social Anthropology*. New York: Tavistock.

———, and MAYER, IONA. "Socialization by Peers: The Youth Organization of the Red Xhosa." In *Socialization: The Approach from Social Anthropology*, edited by Philip Mayer. New York: Tavistock.

MEAD, MARGARET. *Culture and Commitment: A Study of the Generation Gap*. New York: Doubleday.

MIDDLETON, JOHN, ed. *From Child to Adult: Studies in the Anthropology of Education*. Garden City, N.Y.: Natural History Press.

MOORE, ALEXANDER G. "An Anthropological View of Urban Education." *Education and Urban Society* 2:423-39.

MUSKRAT, JOSEPH. "The Need for Cultural Empathy." *School Review* 79, no. 1:72-75.

NASH, MANNING. "Education in Burma: An Anthropological Perspective." In *The Social Sciences and the Comparative Study of Educational Systems*, edited by Joseph L. Fischer. Scranton, Pa.: International Textbook.

NORTON, DAVID L. "The Rites of Passage from Dependence to Autonomy." *School Review* 79, no. 1:19-42.

OLSON, JOHN A. "Ecological-Demographic Considerations for Educational Planning: A Micro-Study of a Suburban Elementary School Attendance Area." Ph.D. dissertation, University of Oregon.

"Patterns in Human History. A new multi-media course designed for use within the school anthropology program." *Council on Anthropology and Education Newsletter* 2, no. 1 (February).

SADY, RACHEL R. *Indians View Americans, Americans View Indians: Cultures in Contrast*. Hartsdale, N.Y.: Olcott Forward.

School Review. Special Issue, "Skirmish at Rough Rock," edited by Benjamin D. Wright and Ruth Eckdish. *School Review* 79, no. 1 (November).

SCHWARTZ, AUDREY J. *Traditional Values and Contemporary Achievement of Japanese-American Pupils*. Los Angeles: Center for the Study of Evaluation, University of California.

SHIMAHARA, NOBUO. "Enculturation: A Reconsideration." *Current Anthropology* 11:143-48.

SINGLETON, JOHN. "Cross-Cultural Approaches to Research on Minority Group Education." *Journal of the Steward Anthropological Society* 2 (Fall): 35-50.

———, and EBUCHI, KAZUKIMI. "The Study of Japanese Education." *Rice University Studies*, LVI (4) (Fall).

SMITH, LOUIS M., and KLEINE, PAUL F. "Teacher Awareness: Social Cognition in the Classroom." *School Review* 79, no. 1 (November).

SPINDLER, GEORGE D. "Studying Schooling in Schonhausen." *Council on Anthropology and Education Newsletter* 1, no. 2:3-10.

STOREY, EDWARD. "Concomitant Outcomes: Change Strategies and Their Sociostructural Consequences." Paper presented at the Annual Meeting of the American Educational Research Association, Minneapolis, Minnesota.

———. "The Classroom and Its Cultural Discontents: Some Practical Alternatives for Teachers of English." Paper presented at the Annual Meeting of the National Council of Teachers of English, Atlanta, Georgia.

TALBERT, CAROL. "Interaction and Adaptation in Two Negro Kindergartens." *Human Organization* 29, no. 2 (Summer): 103-13.

THELAN, HERBERT A. "Secularizing the Classroom's Semisacred Culture." *School Review* 79, no. 1 (February): 1-18.

WALKER, WILLIAM. "The Retention of Folk Linguistic Concepts and the Teacher Caste in Contemporary Nacireman Culture." *American Anthropologist* 72, no. 1 (February).

WASSERMAN, MIRIAM. *The School Fix: New York City, U.S.A.* New York: Outerbridge & Drenstfrey.

WATSON, WALTER. "Anthropology and In-Service Education." Paper presented at the Annual Meeting of the American Anthropological Association, San Diego, California.

WAX, MURRAY L. "Gophers or Gadflies: Problems of Indian School Boards." *School Review* 79, no. 1:62-71.

WAX, ROSALIE H. "The Warrior Dropouts." In *Education: Readings in the Processes of Cultural Transmission*, edited by Harry M. Lindquist. Boston: Houghton Mifflin.

WOLCOTT, HARRY F. "An Ethnographic Approach to the Study of School Administrators." *Human Organization* 29, no. 2:115–22.

WRIGHT, BENJAMIN D., and ECKDISH, RUTH. "Which Way at Rough Rock?" *School Review* 79, no. 1:59–61.

ZANOLI, NOA VERA. *Education Towards Development in Tanzania: A Study of the Educative Process in a Rural Area*. Basil, Switzerland: Phasos Vertage.

1971

AVEDON, ELLIOTT M., and SUTTON-SMITH, BRIAN. *The Study of Games*. New York: Wiley.

BENDER, BYRON. *Linguistic Factors in Maori Education: A Report*. Wellington, New Zealand: Council for Educational Research.

BRACE, C. F.; GAMBLE, G. R.; and BOND, J. T. *Race and Intelligence*. Washington, D.C.: Anthropological Studies No. 8.

BURGER, HENRY G. "Diachrony and Arbitrage: Neglected Factors in Operant Behaviorism." *Current Anthropology* 12:179–80.

———. "'Ethno-maieutics': Adapting Curricula for Cross-Cultural Teaching." *Journal of Educational Thought* 5, no. 2:69–79.

CASTRO, JANET. "Untapped Verbal Fluency of Black Schoolchildren." In *The Culture of Poverty: A Critique*, edited by Eleanor Leacock. New York: Simon & Schuster.

COHEN, YEHUDI A. "The Shaping of Men's Minds. Adaptations to Imperatives of Culture." In *Anthropological Perspectives on Education*, edited by Murray Wax and Stanley Diamond. New York: Basic Books.

COLE, MICHAEL; GAY, JOHN; GLICK, J. A.; and SHARP, D. W. *The Cultural Context of Learning and Thinking*. New York: Basic Books.

DICKEMAN, MILDRED. "The Integrity of the Cherokee Student." In *The Culture of Poverty: A Critique*, edited by Eleanor Leacock. New York: Simon & Schuster.

DRUCKER, ERNEST. "Cognitive Styles and Class Stereotypes." In *The Culture of Poverty: A Critique*, edited by Eleanor Leacock. New York: Simon & Schuster.

EBUCHI, KAZUKIMI. "Trends in Educational Anthropology." *Japanese Journal of Ethnology* 36 (September): 157–74.

FUCHS, ESTELLE. "The Danish Friskoler and Community Control." In *The Culture of Poverty: A Critique*, edited by Eleanor Leacock. New York: Simon & Schuster.

GOLDSTEIN, RHODA, ed. *Black Life and Culture in the United States*. New York: Crowell.

GREEN, THOMAS F. "Citizenship or Certification." In *Anthropological Perspectives on Education*, edited by Murray Wax, Stanley Diamond, and Fred Gearing. New York: Basic Books.

HENRY, JULES. "Education of the Negro Child." In *Anthropological Perspectives on Education*, edited by Murray Wax, Stanley Diamond, and Fred Gearing. New York: Basic Books.

———. "Is Education Possible?" In *Anthropological Perspectives on Education*, edited by Murray Wax, Stanley Diamond, and Fred Gearing. New York: Basic Books.

HORTON, DONALD. "The Interplay of Forces in the Development of a Small School System." In *Anthropological Perspectives on Education*, edited by Murray Wax, Stanley Diamond, and Fred Gearing. New York: Basic Books.

HOSTETLER, J. A., and HUNTINGTON, G. E. *Children in Amish Society: Socialization and Community Education*. New York: Holt, Rinehart & Winston.

HYMES, DELL, ed. "On Linguistic Theory, Communicative Competence, and the Education of Disadvantaged Children." In *Anthropological Perspectives on Education*, edited by Murray Wax, Stanley Diamond, and Fred Gearing. New York: Basic Books.

IANNI, FRANCIS A. J. "The Art and Science of Teaching." In *Anthropological Perspectives on Education*, edited by Murray Wax, Stanley Diamond, and Fred Gearing. New York: Basic Books.

JOHN, VERA P. "Language and Educability." In *The Culture of Poverty: A Critique*, edited by Eleanor Leacock. New York: Simon & Schuster.

JONES, J. A. "Operant Psychology and the Study of Culture." *Current Anthropology* 12, no. 4:171-79.

KHLEIF, BUD B. "The School as a Small Society." In *Anthropological Perspectives on Education*, edited by Murray Wax, Stanley Diamond, and Fred Gearing. New York: Basic Books.

KIMBALL, SOLON T. "An Anthropological Perspective for Social Studies." *Council on Anthropology and Education Newsletter* 2, no. 3:9-12.

KING, KENNETH JAMES. *Pan-Africanism and Education*. Oxford: Clarendon Press.

KUPFERER, H. J., and FITZGERALD, T. K. *Culture, Society, and Guidance*. Guidance Monograph Series. Series VI: Minority Groups. Boston: Houghton Mifflin.

LABELLE, THOMAS J. "The School: Center of Cultural Conflict and Learning." *Teachers College Record*.

LEACOCK, ELEANOR B. "At Play in African Villages." *Natural History Magazine* 13, no. 10:60-65.

————. *The Culture of Poverty: A Critique*. New York: Simon & Schuster.

————. "Theoretical and Methodological Problems in the Study of Schools." In *Anthropological Perspectives on Education*, edited by Murray Wax, Stanley Diamond, and Fred Gearing. New York: Basic Books.

LEAVITT, RUBY. *The Puerto Ricans: Culture and Language Deviance*. Viking Foundations Publications in Anthropology.

MEAD, MARGARET. "Early Childhood Experience and Later Education in Complex Cultures." In *Anthropological Perspectives on Education*, edited by Murray Wax, Stanley Diamond, and Fred Gearing. New York: Basic Books.

MODIANO, NANCY. "Teaching Personnel in the Indian Schools of Chiapas." *Council on Anthropology and Education Newsletter* 2, no. 2:9-11.

OWADA, YASUKUKI; GLEASON, ALAN H.; and AVERY, ROBERT W. "Taishu Danko: Agency for Change in a Japanese University." *Council on Anthropology and Education Newsletter* 2, no. 1:9-12.

PEOPLE WATCHING: *Curriculum and Techniques for Teaching the Behavioral Sciences*. New York: Behavioral Publications, Inc.

PHILLIPS, CLAUDE S., JR. "Education for Mankind: A Struggle for Meaning." *Current Anthropology* 12, no. 1 (February).

ROBERTS, JOAN. *The Scene of the Battle: Group Behavior in Urban Classrooms*. Garden City, N.Y.: Doubleday.

ROHLEN, THOMAS P. "Seishin Kyarku in a Japanese Bank: A Description of Methods and Consideration of Some Underlying Concepts." *Council on Anthropology and Education Newsletter* 2, no. 1:3-8.

ROSENFELD, GERRY. *"Shut Those Thick Lips": A Study of Slum Failure*. New York: Holt, Rinehart & Winston.

ROSENSTIEL, ANNETTE. "The Changing Focus of Native Education in Alaska." *Artic and Alpine Research* 3, no. 3:187-97.

SAFA, HELEN ICKEN. "Education, Modernization, and the Process of National Integration." In *Anthropological Perspectives on Education*, edited by Murray Wax, Stanley Diamond, and Fred Gearing. New York: Basic Books.

SINGLETON, JOHN. *Contributions of Anthropology to Basic Research in Education*. Philadelphia: American Association for the Advancement of Science.

SMITH, LOUIS M., and KEITH, P. *Anatomy and Educational Innovation*. New York: Wiley.

SPINDLER, GEORGE D. *Being an Anthropologist: Fieldwork in Eleven Cultures*. New York: Holt, Rinehart & Winston.

————. "Prospects of Anthropology and Education." *Council on Anthropology and Education Newsletter* 2, no. 1 (February): 1-2.

STOREY, EDWARD, ed. *Anthropology and Education: A General Bibliography*. Atlanta: Department of Anthropology, Georgia State University.

VALENTINE, CHARLES A. "'The Culture of Poverty': Its Scientific Significance and Its Implications for Actions." In *The Culture of Poverty: A Critique*, edited by Eleanor Leacock. New York: Simon & Schuster.

————. "Deficit, Difference, and Bicultural Models of Afro-American Behaviour." *Harvard Educational Review* 41:137-57.

VIDICH, ARTHUR J., and MCREYNOLDS, CHARLES. "Rhetoric versus Reality: A Study of New York City High School Principals." In *Anthropological Perspectives on Education*, edited by Murray Wax, Stanley Diamond, and Fred Gearing. New York: Basic Books.

WARD, MARTHA C. *Them Children: A Study of Language Learning*. New York: Holt, Rinehart & Winston.

WASHBURN, SHERWOOD. "On the Importance of the Study of Primate Behavior for Anthropologists." In *Anthropological Perspectives on Education*, edited by Murray Wax, Stanley Diamond, and Fred Gearing. New York: Basic Books.

WAX, MURRAY L. "Comparative Research Upon the Schools and Education: An Anthropological Outline." In *Anthropological Perspectives on Education*, edited by Murray Wax, Stanley Diamond, and Fred Gearing. New York: Basic Books.

———. *Indian-Americans: Unity and Diversity*. Englewood Cliffs, N.J.: Prentice-Hall.

———. "School and Peer Society Within Indian Communities." *Council on Anthropology and Education Newsletter* 2, no. 3:1-4.

———; DIAMOND, STANLEY; and GEARING, FRED O., eds. *Anthropological Perspectives on Education*. New York: Basic Books.

WAX, MURRAY L., and WAX, ROSALIE H. "Cultural Deprivation as an Educational Ideology." In *The Culture of Poverty: A Critique*, edited by Eleanor Leacock. New York: Simon & Schuster.

———. "Federal Programs and Indian Target Populations." In *Majority and Minority: The Dynamics of Racial and Ethnic Relations in the U.S.*, edited by Norman R. Yetman and C. Hoy Steele. Boston: Allyn & Bacon.

———. "Great Tradition, Little Tradition, and Formal Education." In *Anthropological Perspectives on Education*, edited by Murray L. Wax, Stanley Diamond, and Fred O. Gearing. New York: Basic Books.

WOLCOTT, HARRY F. "Handle With Care: Necessary Precautions in the Anthropology of Schools." In *Anthropological Perspectives in Education*, edited by Murray Wax, Stanley Diamond, and Fred O. Gearing. New York: Basic Books.

ZABARENDO, LUCY, and WILLIAMS, ELLEN. "The Computer Center as a Subculture." *Council on Anthropology and Education Newsletter* 2, no. 3:5-8.

1972

ABRAHAMS, ROGER D., and TROIKA, RUDOLPH G. *Language and Cultural Diversity in American Education*. Englewood Cliffs, N.J.: Prentice-Hall.

BATY, ROGER. *Reeducating Teachers for Cultural Awareness: Preparation for Educating Mexican-American Children in Northern California*. New York: Praeger.

BOGGS, STEPHEN T. "The Meaning of Questions and Narratives to Hawaiian Children." In *Functions of Language in the Classroom*, edited by Courtney B. Cazden, Vera P. John, and Dell Hymes. New York: Teachers College Press.

BURGER, HENRY B. "Behavior Modification and Operant Psychology: An Anthropological Critique." *American Educational Research Journal* 9, no. 3:343-60.

CAZDEN, COURTNEY B. *Child, Language and Education*. New York: Holt, Rinehart & Winston.

———; JOHN, VERA P.; HYMES, DELL, eds. *Functions of Language in the Classroom*. New York: Teachers College Press.

COLE, MICHAEL, and GAY, JOHN. "Culture and Memory." *American Anthropologist* 74, no. 5:1066-84.

DILLARD, J. L. *Black English: Its History and Usage in the United States*. New York: Random House.

DOBBERT, MARION L. "Teaching and Undergraduate Anthropology: Problems, Solutions, and Experiments." *Council on Anthropology and Education Newsletter* 3, no. 1 (February): 14-17.

DUMONT, ROBERT V., JR. "Learning English and How to Be Silent: Studies in Sioux and Cherokee Classrooms." In *Functions of Language in the Classroom*, edited by Courtney B. Cazden, Vera P. John, and Dell Hymes. New York: Teachers College Press.

FITZGERALD, THOMAS K. "Education and Identity: A Reconsideration of Some Models of Acculturation and Identity." *New Zealand Journal of Educational Studies* 7, no. 1:45-58.

FOSTER, PHILIP. "Review of Anthropological Perspectives on Education." *American Journal of Sociology* 78:489-92.

FUCHS, ESTELLE, and HAVIGHURST, ROBERT J. *To Live on This Earth. American Indian Education*. New York: Doubleday.

GRINDAL, BRUCE. *Growing Up in Two Worlds: Education and Transition Among the Sisala of Northern Ghana*. New York: Holt, Rinehart & Winston.

GUMPERZ, JOHN J., and HERNANDEZ-CHAVEZ, EDWARDS. "Bilingualism, Bidialectalism, and Classroom Interaction." In *Functions of Language in the Classroom*, edited by Courtney B. Cazden, Vera P. John, and Dell Hymes. New York: Teachers College Press.

HENRY, JULES. *On Education*. New York: Vintage Books.

HERZOG, JOHN D. "The Anthropologist as Broker in Community Education: A Case Study and Some General Propositions." *Council on Anthropology and Education Newsletter* 3, no. 3 (November): 9-14.

HOSTETLER, JOHN A. "Amish Schooling: A Study of Alternatives." *Council on Anthropology and Education Newsletter* 3, no. 2 (June): 1-14.

HYMES, DELL. "Introduction." In *Functions of Language in the Classroom*, edited by Courtney B. Cazden, Vera P. John, and Dell Hymes. New York: Teachers College Press.

IANNI, FRANCIS A. J., and CAESAR, PATRICIA. "Social Organization, Socialization and Cultural Mediation in Formal Learning Situations." Paper presented at the Symposium on Anthropological Perspectives of Educational Phenomena. American Association for the Advancement of Science, Washington, D.C., December.

JOHN, VERA P. "Styles of Learning—Styles of Teaching: Reflections on the Education of Navajo Children." In *Functions of Language in the Classroom*, edited by Courtney B. Cazden, Vera P. John, and Dell Hymes. New York: Teachers College Press.

KOCHMAN, THOMAS. "Black American Speech Events and a Language Program for the Classroom." In *Functions of Language in the Classroom*, edited by Courtney B. Cazden, Vera P. John, and Dell Hymes. New York: Teachers College Press.

KOCHMAN, THOMAS, ed. *Rappin' and Stylin' Out: Communication in Urban Black America.* Urbana: University of Illinois Press.

LABELLE, THOMAS J. "An Anthropological Framework for Studying Education." *Teachers College Record* 73:519-38.

——. *Education and Development: Latin America and the Caribbean.* Los Angeles: University of California Press.

LEACOCK, ELEANOR BURKE. "Abstract vs. Concrete Speech: A False Dichotomy." In *Functions of Language in the Classroom*, edited by Courtney B. Cazden, Vera P. John, and Dell Hymes. New York: Teachers College Press.

——. *Primary Schooling in Zambia: Preliminary Report on a Study Sponsored by the Institute of African Studies.* University of Zambia and Bureau of Research, U.S. Office of Education.

MARRIOTT, MCKIM. "Kishan Garhi Village, A Generation of Change: Technology, Society, and Culture." *Council on Anthropology and Education Newsletter* 3, no. 3 (November): 25.

MCLEAN, HOPE, and others. *A Review of Indian Education in North America.* Toronto, Ontario: Ontario Teacher's Federation.

MISHLER, ELLIOT G. "Implications of Teacher Strategies for Language and Cognition: Observations in First-Grade Classrooms." In *Functions of Language in the Classroom*, edited by Courtney B. Cazden, Vera P. John, and Dell Hymes. New York: Teachers College Press.

ORTIZ, RAFAEL CINTRON. "A Colonial Experience: Schools in Puerto Rico as Agents of Domination." *Critical Anthropology* 2, no. 2: 104-12.

OTAALA, BARNABAS. *The Development of Operational Thinking in Primary School Children: An Examination of Some Aspects of Piaget's Theory Among the Iteso Children of Uganda.* New York: Teachers College Press.

PESHKIN, ALAN. *Kanuri Schoolchildren: Education and Social Mobilization in Nigeria.* New York: Holt, Rinehart & Winston.

PHILIPS, SUSAN U. "Participant Structures and Communicative Competence: Warm Springs Children in Community and Classrooms." In *Functions of Language in the Classroom*, edited by Courtney B. Cazden, Vera P. John, and Dell Hymes. New York: Teachers College Press.

ROSENFELD, GERARD L. "What We Do to Kids." In *An Uncertain America: Anthropological Approaches to Domestic Crises*, edited by Edward Storey. Boston: Little, Brown.

SANDAY, PEGGY R. "The Relevance of Anthropology to U.S. Social Policy." *Council on Anthropology and Education Newsletter* 3, no. 3:1-8.

SCHWARTZ, GARY. *Youth Culture: An Anthropological Approach.* Reading, Mass.: Addison-Wesley.

SMITH, LOUIS M., and POHLAND, P. A. "Education, Technology, and the Rural Highlands." *American Educational Research Association Evaluation Monograph Series*, No. 8. Chicago: Rand McNally.

SPRADLEY, JAMES P., and MCCURDY, DAVID W. *The Cultural Experience: Ethnography in Complex Society.* Chicago: Science Research Associates.

TENENBERG, MORTON S., and DETHLEFSEN, EDWIN S. *Students and Teachers: Strategies for Discussion—What Is Anthropology?* Anthropology Curriculum

Study Project. Teacher Service Materials, Washington, D.C.: American Anthropological Association.

Two-Way Mirror: Anthropologists and Educators Observe Themselves and Each Other. Washington, D.C.: American Anthropological Association.

VALENTINE, CHARLES A. *Black Studies and Anthropology: Scholarly and Political Interests in Afro-American Culture.* Reading, Mass.: Addison-Wesley.

———. "Models and Muddles Concerning Culture and Inequality." *Harvard Educational Review* 42:97-108.

WALKER, ROB, and ADELMAN, CLEM. *Toward a Sociography of Classrooms.* London: Center for Science Education, Chelsey College of Science and Technology.

WALLACE, ANTHONY F. C. "Paradigmatic Processes in Culture Change." *American Anthropologist* 74, no. 3:467-78.

WAX, MURRAY. "How Should Schools Be Held Accountable?" *Council on Anthropology and Education Newsletter* 3, no. 3 (November): 26.

———. "Social Structure and Child-Rearing Practices of North American Indians." In *Nutrition, Growth and Development of North American Indian Children,* edited by William M. Moore, Marjorie M. Silverberg, and Merrill S. Read. Washington, D.C.: National Institute of Health.

WOLCOTT, HARRY F. "Feedback Influences on Fieldwork, or A Funny Thing Happened on the Way to the Beer Garden." Center for the Advanced Study of Educational Administration, University of Oregon. Mimeographed.

———. "Field Study Methods for Educational Researchers." Eugene, Oregon. Mimeographed.

———. "The Ideal World and the Real World of Reading: An Anthropological Perspective." Education Resources Information Center. Clearinghouse on Reading and Communication Skills: Bloomington, Indiana. Mimeographed.

1973

AL-RUBAIY, ABDUL A. "A Case Study of Unsuccessful Political Integration: The Education of the Kurdish Minority in Iraq." Paper presented at the Comparative and International Education Society, San Antonio, Texas, March.

AOKI, T. "Toward Devolution in the Control of Education on a Native Reserve in Alberta: The Hebbema Curriculum Story." *Council on Anthropology and Education Newsletter* 4, no. 2:1-6.

AYABE, TSUNEO, ed. *Education and Culture in a Thai Rural Community.* Fukuoka, Japan: Research Institute of Comparative Education and Culture, Kyushu University.

BARATZ, STEPHEN S., and BARATZ, JOAN C. "Early Childhood Intervention: The Social Science Base of Institutional Racism." In *To See Ourselves: Anthropology and Modern Social Issues,* edited by Thomas Weaver. Glenview: Scott, Foresman.

BERNSTEIN, BASIL, ed. *Class, Codes, and Control: Applied Studies Toward a Sociology of Language.* Boston: Routledge & Kegan Paul.

BRUCKMAN, JAN. "Language and Socialization: Child Culture and the Ethnographer's Task." In *Learning and Culture: Proceedings of the 1972 Annual Spring Meeting of the American Ethnological Society,* edited by Solon T. Kimball and Jacquetta H. Burnett. Seattle: University of Washington Press.

CAZDEN, COURTNEY B. "Subcultural Differences in Child Language: An Inter-Disciplinary Review." In *Cultural Relevance and Educational Issues: Readings in Anthropology and Education,* edited by Francis A. Ianni and Edward Storey. Boston: Little, Brown.

CHANCE, NORMAN A. "Minority Education and the Transformation of Consciousness." In *Learning and Culture: Proceedings of the 1972 Annual Spring Meeting of the American Ethnological Society,* edited by Solon T. Kimball and Jacquetta H. Burnett. Seattle: University of Washington Press.

CLARK, WOODROW W., JR. "Violence as an Event in the Context of Public Schools." *Proceedings of the Ninth International Congress of Anthropological and Ethnological Sciences, August–September.* Chicago: Mouton Press.

COHEN, ROSALIE. "School Reorganization and Learning: An Approach to Assessing the Direction of School Change." In *Learning and Culture: Proceedings of the 1972 Annual Spring Meeting of the American Ethnological Society,* edited by Solon T. Kimball and Jacquetta H. Burnett. Seattle: University of Washington Press.

COLE, MICHAEL. "Toward an Experimental Anthropology of Thinking." In *Learning and Culture: Proceedings of the 1972 Annual Spring Meeting of the*

American Ethnological Society, edited by Solon T. Kimball and Jacquetta H. Burnett. Seattle: University of Washington Press.

COLLIER, JOHN, JR. *Alaskan Eskimo Education*. New York: Holt, Rinehart & Winston.

COMITAS, LAMBORS. "Education and Social Stratification in Contemporary Bolivia." In *Cultural Relevance and Educational Issues*, edited by Francis A. J. Ianni and Edward Storey. Boston: Little, Brown.

CUSICK, PHILIP A. *Inside High School: The Student's World*. New York: Holt, Rinehart & Winston.

EARLY, JOHN D. "Education via Radio Among Guatemalan Highland Maya." *Human Organization* 32, no. 3:221–30.

ERICKSON, FREDERICK. "What Makes School Ethnography 'Ethnographic?'" *Council on Anthropology and Education Newsletter* 4, no. 2:10–19.

FISHER, A. D. "White Rites versus Indian Rights." In *To See Ourselves: Anthropology and Modern Social Issues*, edited by Thomas Weaver. Glenview, Ill.: Scott, Foresman.

FITZGERALD, THOMAS K. "The Role of the Anthropologist in Experimental College Evaluations: Some Personal Observations." *Proceedings of the Ninth International Congress of Anthropological and Ethnological Sciences, August–September*. Chicago: Mouton Press.

FONER, NANCY. *Status and Power in Rural Jamaica: A Study of Educational and Political Change*. New York: Teachers College Press.

FREEDMAN, DANIEL G., and OMARK, DONALD R. "Ethnology, Genetics, and Education." In *Cultural Relevance and Educational Issues: Readings in Anthropology and Education*, edited by Francis A. J. Ianni and Edward Storey. Boston: Little, Brown.

GALLAHER, ART, JR. "Directed Change in Formal Organizations: The School System." In *Cultural Relevance and Educational Issues: Readings in Anthropology and Education*, edited by Francis A. J. Ianni and Edward Storey. Boston: Little, Brown.

GEARING, FREDERICK O. "Where We Are and Where We Might Go: Steps Toward a General Theory of Cultural Transmission." *Council on Anthropology and Education Newsletter* 4, no. 1:1–10.

——. "Why Indians?" In *Cultural Relevance and Educationsl Issues: Readings in Anthropology and Education*, edited by Francis A. J. Ianni and Edward Storey. Boston: Little, Brown.

GEARING, FREDERICK O, and others. "Outline: A General Cultural Theory of Education." *Proceedings of the Ninth International Congress of Anthropological and Ethnological Sciences*. Chicago: Mouton Press.

GLASER, ROBERT. "The New Aptitudes and Adaptive Education." *Council on Anthropology and Education Newsletter* 4, no. 2:27–32.

GOMEZ, ANGEL I., and CHILCOTT, JOHN H. *Outline of Mexican American Education*. New York: Basic Books.

GONZALEZ, NANCIE S. "Applied Anthropology and the Grade Schools." *Human Organization* 32, no. 3:295–304.

HARKINS, ARTHUR. "Rules for Anthropologists I: The Future Is Now." *Council on Anthropology and Education Newsletter* 4, no. 2:27–32.

HARRINGTON, CHARLES. "Pupils, Peers and Politics." In *Learning and Culture: Proceedings of the 1972 Annual Spring Meeting of the American Ethnological Society*, edited by Solon T. Kimball and Jacquetta H. Burnett. Seattle: University of Washington Press.

HEATH, KATHRYN G. "Legislation: An Aid in Eliminating Sex Bias in Education." *Proceedings of the Ninth International Congress of Anthropological and Ethnological Sciences, August–September*. Chicago: Mouton Press.

HOLZBERG, CAROL SUE. "Friendship: The Affective Manipulation." In *Learning and Culture: Proceedings of the 1972 Annual Spring Meeting of the American Ethnological Society*, edited by Solon T. Kimball and Jacquetta H. Burnett. Seattle: University of Washington Press.

HOWARD, ALLAN. "Education in 'Aina Pumehana': The Hawaiian-American Student as Hero." In *Learning and Culture: Proceedings of the 1972 Annual Spring Meeting of the American Ethnological Society*, edited by Solon T. Kimball and Jacquetta H. Burnett. Seattle: University of Washington Press.

IANNI, FRANCIS A. J. "Cultivating the Arts of Poverty." In *Cultural Relevance and Educational Issues: Readings in Anthropology and Education*, edited by Francis A. J. Ianni and Edward Storey. Boston: Little, Brown.

——, and STOREY, EDWARD. *Cultural Relevance and Educational Issues: Readings in Anthropology and Education*. Boston: Little, Brown.

ILLICH, IVAN. "The Futility of Schooling in Latin America." In *To See Ourselves: Anthropology and Modern Social Issues*, edited by Thomas Weaver. Glenview, Ill.: Scott, Foresman.

KALEB, M. "Monastic Education, Social Mobility, and Village Structure in Cambodia." *Proceedings of the Ninth International Congress of Anthropological and Ethnological Sciences*, Chicago: Mouton Press.

KIMBALL, SOLON T., and BURNETT, JACQUETTA H. "Perspectives on Learning and Culture." In *Learning and Culture: Proceedings of the 1972 Annual Spring Meeting of the American Ethnological Society*, edited by Solon T. Kimball and Jacquetta H. Burnett. Seattle: University of Washington Press.

KLIENFELD, J. *A Long Way From Home: Effects of Public High School on Village Children Away From Home.* Fairbanks: Center for Northern Educational Research/Institute of Social, Economic and Government Research, University of Alaska.

LEACOCK, ELEANOR BURKE. *Primary Schooling in Zambia.* Final Report. Education Resources Information Center Document Reproduction Service, Bethesda, Md.

——. "Education in Africa: Myths of 'Modernization.'" *Proceedings of the Ninth International Congress of Anthropological and Ethnological Sciences, August–September.* Chicago: Mouton Press.

LESSER, ALEXANDER. "Education and the Future of Tribalism in the United States: The Case of the American Indian." In *Cultural Relevance and Educational Issues: Readings in Anthropology and Education*, edited by Francis A. J. Ianni and Edward Storey. Boston: Little, Brown.

MEAD, MARGARET. "The High School of the Future." In *Cultural Relevance and Educational Issues: Readings in Anthropology and Education*, edited by Francis A. J. Ianni and Edward Storey. Boston: Little, Brown.

MERING, OTTO VON. "Iterative Activity and Behavioral Piety in Private Places." In *Learning and Culture: Proceedings of the 1972 Annual Spring Meeting of the American Ethnological Society*, edited by Solon T. Kimball and Jacquetta H. Burnett. Seattle: University of Washington Press.

MODIANO, NANCY. *Indian Education in the Chiapas Highlands.* New York: Holt, Rinehart & Winston.

——. "Kerem Looks At His School." *Proceedings of the Ninth International Congress of Anthropological and Ethnological Sciences, August–September.* Chicago: Mouton Press.

MOORE, G. ALEXANDER, JR. *Life Cycles in Atchalan: The Diverse Careers of Certain Guatemalans.* New York: Teachers College Press.

——. "The Validation of Ascribed Status: Gentry Careers in Guatemala." In *Learning and Culture: Proceedings of the 1972 Annual Spring Meeting of the American Ethnological Society*, edited by Solon T. Kimball and Jacquetta H. Burnett. Seattle: University of Washington Press.

MUSGROVE, FRANK. "Education and the Culture Concept." In *Cultural Relevance and Educational Issues: Readings in Anthropology and Education*, edited by Francis A. J. Ianni and Edward Storey. Boston: Little, Brown.

PARMEE, EDWARD A. "Factors Affecting the Education of the Apache Youth." In *Cultural Relevance and Educational Issues: Readings in Anthropology and Education*, edited by Francis A. J. Ianni and Edward Storey. Boston: Little, Brown.

PAULSTON, ROLLAND G. "Non-Formal Education in Peruvian National Development." In *New Strategies for Educational Development: The Cross-Cultural Search for Non-Formal Alternatives*, edited by Cole Brembeck. Lexington, Mass.: Heath.

POIRIER, FRANK E. "Socialization and Learning Among Nonhuman Primates." In *Learning and Culture: Proceedings of the 1972 Annual Spring Meeting of the American Ethnological Society*, edited by Solon T. Kimball and Jacquetta H. Burnett. Seattle: University of Washington Press.

PORATH, D. R. "The Role of the Anthropologist in Minority Education: The Chicano Case." *Proceedings of the Ninth International Congress of Anthropological and Ethnological Sciences, August–September.* Chicago: Mouton Press.

ROSIN, THOMAS. "Gold Medallions: The Arithmetic Calculations of an Illiterate." *Council on Anthropology and Education Newsletter* 4, no. 2:1-9.

SABEY, RALPH H. "The Preparation of Culturally Sensative Curriculum Material for Canadian Schools: An Overview." *Council on Anthropology and Education Newsletter* 4, no. 2:7-10.

SINGLETON, JOHN. "The Educational Uses of Anthropology." In *To See Ourselves: Anthropology and Modern Social Issues*, edited by Thomas Weaver. Glenview, Ill.: Scott, Foresman.

———. "Schooling: Coping with Education in a Modern Society." In *To See Ourselves: Anthropology and Modern Social Issues*, edited by Thomas Weaver. Glenview, Ill.: Scott, Foresman.

SPINDLER, GEORGE D. *Burgbach: Urbanization and Identity in a German Village.* New York: Holt, Rinehart & Winston.

STENT, MADELON D.; HAZARD, W. P.; and RIVLIN, H. N. *Cultural Pluralism in Education: A Mandate for Change.* New York: Appleton-Century-Crofts.

TALBERT, CAROL. "Studying Education in the Ghetto." In *To See Ourselves: Anthropology and Modern Social Issues*, edited by Thomas Weaver. Glenview, Ill.: Scott, Foresman.

———. "Anthropological Research Models." *Research in the Teaching of English* 7:190-211.

TATE, SEAN. "Anthropological Perspectives on Evaluation in Development Education." *Interchange* 4, no. 4:24-32.

WARREN, RICHARD L. "The Classroom as a Sanctuary for Teachers: Discontinuities in Social Control." *American Anthropologist* 75, no. 1:280-91.

WAX, ROSALIE H., and WAX, MURRAY L. "The Enemies of the People." In *To See Ourselves: Anthropology and Modern Social Issues*, edited by Thomas Weaver. Glenview, Ill.: Scott, Foresman.

WAX, MURRAY. "Cultural Pluralism, Political Power, and Ethnic Studies." In *Learning and Culture: Proceedings of the 1972 Annual Spring Meeting of the American Ethnological Society*, edited by Solon T. Kimball and Jacquetta H. Burnett. Seattle: University of Washington Press.

WELKE, ROBERT J. "The 'Greening' of the American College of Switzerland: A Descriptive Study of the Radicalization of a Conservative Community." *Proceedings of the Ninth International Congress of Anthropological and Ethnological Sciences.* Chicago: Mouton Press.

WILSON, CLYDE H. "On the Evolution of Education." In *Learning and Culture: Proceedings of the 1972 Annual Spring Meeting of the American Ethnological Society*, edited by Solon T. Kimball and Jacquetta H. Burnett. Seattle: University of Washington Press.

WOLCOTT, HARRY F. *The Man in the Principal's Office: An Ethnography.* New York: Holt, Rinehart & Winston.

1974

AKINSANYA, SHERRIE KROSKE. "'Silence: We Speak English Here!' Ethnicity, Status and Network in Lagosian Schools." Ph.D. dissertation, University of Wisconsin.

BARNHARDT, RAY. "Being a Native and Becoming A Teacher." *Council on Anthropology and Education Newsletter* 4, no. 4:13-19.

BLANCHARD, KENDALL. "Basketball and the Culture-Change Process: The Remrock Navajo Case." *Council on Anthropology and Education Newsletter* 4, no. 4:8-13.

BRENNAN, PAMELA. "Biculturalism Through Experiential Language Learning." *Council on Anthropology and Education Newsletter* 5, no. 3:15-19.

BURNETT, JACQUETTA H. (With the collaboration of SALLY W. GORDON and CAROL J. GORMLEY). *Anthropology and Education: An Annotated Bibliographic Guide.* New Haven: Human Relations Area File Press.

CALHOUN, CRAIG J. "General Status: Specific Role." *Council on Anthropology and Education Newsletter* 5, no. 2:16-20.

CHRISMAN, NOEL J. "The Social Organization of High Schools." *Council on Anthropology and Education Newsletter* 5, no. 2:21-22.

CLIGNET, REMI. *Liberty and Equality in the Educational Process. A Comparative Sociology of Education.* New York: Wiley.

COLFER, C. "An Ethnography of Leaderlong Indian School." Ph.D. dissertation, University of Washington.

COLE, MICHAEL, and SCRIBNER, SYLVIA. *Culture and Thought: A Psychological Introduction.* New York: Wiley.

COUNCIL ON ANTHROPOLOGY AND EDUCATION. "Participant Observation." *Council on Anthropology and Education Quarterly* 5, no. 23.

DE VOS, GEORGE A. *Socialization for Achievement.* Denver: University of Colorado Press.

ERWIN-TRIPP, SUSAN M. *Language Acquisition and Communication Choice.* Palo Alto: Stanford University Press.

GOETZ, JUDITH P., and HANSEN, JUDITH F. "The Cultural Analysis of Schooling." *Council on Anthropology and Education Newsletter* 5, no. 4:1–8.

HENDRICHS, GLENN. *The Dominican Diaspora.* New York: Teachers College Press.

HOLLOMAN, R. "Ritual Opening and Individual Transformation Rites of Passage at Esalen." *American Anthropologist* 76:265–80.

HENRY, JULES, and HENRY, ZUNIA. *Doll Play of Piluga Indian Children.* New York: Random House.

IANNI, FRANCIS A. J. "Social Organization Study Program: An Interim Report." *Council on Anthropology and Education Newsletter* 5, no. 2:1–8.

KIMBALL, SOLON T. *Culture and the Educative Process.* New York: Teachers College Press.

KING, A. R. "The Teacher As A Participant Observer: A Case Study." In *Education and Cultural Process*, edited by George D. Spindler. New York: Holt, Rinehart, & Winston.

LEACOCK, ELEANOR. "Learning: African Style." *Notes From Workshop Center for Open Education* 3:2–9.

LITTLEFORD, M. S. "Anthropology and Teacher Education." *Educational Forum* 38:285–89.

LOPATE, C. "Approaching School Change: An Anthropologist's View." *Urban Review* 7:227–36.

MEAD, MARGARET. "Grandparents as Educators." *Teachers College Record* 76:240–49.

———. "What I Think I Have Learned About Education, 1923–1973." *Education* 94:291–406.

MULLER, M. "Visual Anthropology in Teacher Education." *Audio-Visual Instruction* 70:30.

NASH, M. "Rural Education For Development: Burma and Malaysia, a Contrast in Cultural Meaning and Structural Relations." *World Yearbook of Education*, 337–49.

OGBU, JOHN V. *The Next Generation: An Ethnography of Education in an Urban School Setting.* New York: Academic Press.

ONG, WALTER J. "Agonistic Structure in Academia: Past to Present." *Daedalus* 103, no. 4:229–38.

RABIN, A. I., and HAZAN, BERTHA, eds. *Collective Education in the Kibbutz.* New York: Springer.

RUBIN, VERA, and SCHAEDEL, RICHARD. *The Haitian Potential.* New York: Teachers College Press.

SERRANO, RODOLFO G. "Ethnography of a Contemporary Chicano Community: A Brief Description." *Council on Anthropology and Education Newsletter* 5, no. 3:3–7.

SINGLETON, J. E. "Schools and Rural Development: An Anthropological Approach." *World Yearbook of Education*, 117–36.

SPINDLER, GEORGE D. *Education and Cultural Process.* New York: Holt, Rinehart & Winston.

TRUEBA, HENRY T. "Bilingual-Bicultural Education for Chicanos in the Southwest." *Council on Anthropology and Education Newsletter* 5, no. 3:8–15.

VARENNE, HERVÉ. "From Grading and Freedom of Choice to Ranking and Segregation in an American High School." *Council on Anthropology and Education Newsletter* 5, no. 2:9–16.

WILSON, DAVID. "Towards an Anthropology of Educational Planning in Developing Nations." *Educational Planning* 1, no. 2:18–28.

1975

BLANCHARD, JOSEPH D., and WARREN, RICHARD L. "Role Stress of Dormitory Aides at an Off-Reservation Boarding School." *Human Organization* 34, no. 1 (Spring): 41–51.

CLINTON, CHARLES A. "The Anthropologist as Hired Hand." *Human Organization* 34, no. 2:97–205.

COLFER, CAROL J. PIERCE. "Bureaucrats, Budgets, and the BIA: Segmentary Opposition in a Residential School." *Human Organization* 34, no. 2:149–57.

EDDY, ELIZABETH M. "Educational Innovation and Desegregation: A Case Study of Symbolic Realignment." *Human Organization* 34, no. 2:163–73.

EVERHART, ROBERT B. "Problems of Doing Fieldwork in Educational Evaluation." *Human Organization* 34, no. 2:205–15.

FEER, MICHAEL. "Informant-Ethnographers in the Study of Schools." *Human Organization* 34, no. 2:157-63.

FITZSIMMONS, STEPHEN J. "The Anthropologist in a Strange Land." *Human Organization* 34, no. 2:183-97.

HENDRICKS, GLENN. "University Registration Systems: A Study of Social Process." *Human Organization* 34, no. 2:173-81.

Human Organization. Special Issue. "Ethnography of Schooling," edited by Harry F. Wolcott. *Human Organization* 34, no. 2.

KILEFF, CLIVE. "The Rebirth of Grandfather's Spirit: Shumba's Two Worlds." *Human Organization* 34, no. 2:129-39.

WARREN, RICHARD L. "Context and Isolation: The Teaching Experience in an Elementary School." *Human Organization* 34, no. 2:139-49.

WOLCOTT, HARRY F. "Criteria for an Ethnographic Approach to Research in Schools." *Human Organization* 34, no. 2:111-29.

Anthropological Studies of Enculturation*

1887

STEVENSON, MATHILDA C. *Religious Life of the Zuni Child.* Fifth Annual Report. Washington, D.C.: Bureau of American Ethnology.

1888

FLETCHER, ALICE C., and LA FLESCHE, FRANCIS. "Glimpses of Child-Life Among the Omaha-Tribe of Indians." *Journal of American Folklore* 1:115-23.

1891

DORSEY, J. OWEN. "Caddo Customs of Childhood." *Journal of American Folklore* 18:226-228.

1896

CHAMBERLAIN, ALEXANDER. *Child and Childhood in Folk Thought.* New York: Macmillan.

1899

WHITE, JOHN. *The Ancient History of the Maori: His Mythology and Tradition.* Wellington: G. Didsbury.

1900

LA FLESCHE, FRANCIS. *The Middle Five: Indian Schoolboys of the Omaha Tribe.* Madison: University of Wisconsin Press.

1904

SPENCER, BALDWIN, and GILLEN, FRANCIS J. *The Northern Tribes of Central Australia.* New York: Macmillan.

1906

KIDD, DUDLEY. *Savage Childhood: A Study of Kafir Children.* Westport, Conn.: Negro Universities Press.

PARSONS, ELSIE WORTHINGTON CLEWS. *The Family: An Ethnographical and Historical Outline with Descriptive Notes.* New York: Putnam's.

1913

JUNOD, HENRI P. *The Life of a South African Tribe.* Vol. 1. New Hyde Park, N.Y.: University Books.

——. *The Life of a South African Tribe.* Vol. 2. New Hyde Park, N.Y.: University Books.

1922

LINCOLN, HARRY, and MICHELSON, TRUMAN. "How Meskwaki Children Should Be Brought Up." In *American Indian Life*, edited by E. C. Parsons. New York: B. W. Huebsch.

1923

MADDOX, JOHN L. *The Medicine Man. A Sociological Study of the Character and Evolution of Shamism.* New York: Macmillan.

*This bibliography incorporates only selected references and is less complete in coverage for the last three years.

1927

MALINOWSKI, BRONISLAW. *Sex and Repression in a Savage Society*. New York: Harcourt, Brace & World.

1928

MEAD, MARGARET. *Coming of Age in Samoa*. New York: William Morrow.
MILLER, NATHAN. *The Child in Primitive Society*. New York: Brentanos.

1929

MALINOWSKI, BRONISLAW. *The Sexual Life of Savages in North-Western Melanesia: An Ethnographic Account of Courtship, Marriage and Family Life Among the Natives of the Trobriand Islands*. New York: New Guinea Eugenics Publishing Co.

1930

MEAD, MARGARET. *Growing Up in New Guinea*. New York: William Morrow.

1931

HOGBIN, H. I. "Education on Ontong Java, Solomon Islands." *American Anthropologist* 33, no. 4:601–15.
STAYT, HUGH A. *The Bavenda*. London: International Institute of African Languages and Cultures, Oxford University Press.

1932

DRIBERG, JACK H. *At Home With the Savage*. London: Routledge & Sons.
POWDERMAKER, HORTENSE. *Life in Lesu*. New York: Norton.

1934

HELSER, ALBERT DAVID. *Education of Primitive People: A Presentation of Folklore of the Bura Animists with a Meaningful Experience Curriculum*. New York: Fleming H. Ravel.
MAHLOBO, G. W. K., and KRIGE, E. J. "Transition from Childhood to Adulthood Amongst the Zulus." *Bantu Studies* 8, no. 1:157–91.

1935

BLACKWOOD, BEATRICE. *Both Sides of Buka Passage*. Oxford: Clarendon Press.
HECKEL, BENNO. "The Yao Tribe: Their Culture and Education." *University of London Institute of Education Studies and Reports* 4: 9–53.

1936

FIRTH, RAYMOND. *We, the Tikopia*. Boston: Beacon Press.

1937

EVANS-PRITCHARD, EDWARD EVAN. *Witchcraft, Oracles, and Magic Among the Azande*. Oxford: Clarendon Press.
JOSEPH, ALICE. *Desert People: A Study of the Papago Indians*. New York: Russell & Russell.
MEAD, MARGARET. *Cooperation and Competition Among Primitive People*. New York: McGraw-Hill.

1938

FORTES, MEYER. *Social and Psychological Aspects of Education in Taliland*. London: Oxford University Press.
WEDGEWOOD, C. H. "The Life of Children in Manam." *Oceania* 9, no. 1:1–29.

1939

EMBREE, JOHN F. *Suye Mura: A Japanese Village*. Chicago: University of Chicago Press.
HOGBIN, H. I. *Experiments in Civilization*. London: Routledge & Kegan Paul.
PERISTIANY, J. G. *The Social Institutions of the Kipsigis*. London: Routledge & Kegan Paul.
WHITING, JOHN W. M. *Becoming a Kwoma: Teaching and Learning in a New Guinea Tribe*. New Haven: Yale University Press.

1940

RAUM, OTTO F. *Chaga Childhood: A Description of Indigenous Education in an East African Tribe*. London: Oxford University Press.

1941

JOHNSON, CHARLES SPURGEON. *Growing Up in the Black Belt: Negro Youth in the Rural South*. Washington, D.C.: American Council on Education.

OPLER, MORRIS E. *An Apache Life-Way.* Chicago: University of Chicago Press.

THOMPSON, LAURA. *Guam and Its People: A Study of Culture Change and Colonial Education.* Studies of the Pacific, No. 8. San Francisco: American Council Institute of Pacific Relations.

1942

COVARRUBIAS, MIGUEL. *The Island of Bali.* New York: Knopf.

NADEL, SIEGFRIED F. *Black Byzantium: Kingdom of Nupe in Nigeria.* Fair Lawn, N.J.: Oxford University Press.

1943

ERIKSON, ERIK. *Observations on the Yurok: Childhood and World Image.* Los Angeles: University of California Press.

1944

MCPHEE, COLIN. *A House in Bali.* New York: John Day.

1945

SIMONS, LEO W. *The Role of the Aged in Primitive Society.* New Haven: Yale University Press.

1946

PETTITT, GEORGE. "Primitive Education in North America." California University *Publications in American Archaeology and Ethnology* 43:1-182.

1947

GRANQUIST, HILMA. *Birth and Childhood Among the Arabs: Studies in a Muhamedan Village in Palestine.* Helsingfors: Soderstrom.

HOLLINGSHEAD, AUGUST B. *Elmtown's Youth.* New York: Wiley.

1948

FOX, LORENE K. *A Rural Community and Its School.* New York: King's Crown Press.

1949

GORER, GEOFFREY. *The People of Great Russia: A Psychological Study.* London: Cresset Press.

MEAD, MARGARET. *Male and Female: A Study of the Sexes in a Changing World.* New York: William Morrow.

SAPIR, EDWARD. *Culture, Language, and Personality.* Berkeley, California: University of California Press.

1950

GRANQUIST, HILMA. *Child Problems Among the Arabs.* Helsingfors: Soderstrom.

PEARSALL, MARION. "Klamath Childhood and Education." *Anthropological Records* 9, no. 5:339-51.

1951

MEAD, MARGARET. *Growth and Culture: A Photographic Study of Balinese Childhood.* New York: Putnam's.

WILSON, MONICA. *Good Company.* London: Oxford University Press.

1952

HILGER, I. (Sister M. Inez). *Arapaho Child Life and Its Cultural Backgrounds.* St. Clair Shores, Michigan: Scholarly Press.

REDFIELD, ROBERT. "Primitive World View." *Proceedings of the American Philosophical Society* 96:30-36.

1954

AMMAR, HAMED. *Growing Up in an Egyptian Village.* London: Routledge & Kegan Paul.

LAYE, CAMARA. *The Dark Child: The Autobiography of an African Boy.* New York: Farrar, Straus & Giroux.

1955

GOUGH, KATHLEEN. "Female Initiation Rites on the Malabar Coast." *Journal of the Royal Anthropological Institute* 75:45-80.

MEAD, MARGARET. *Childhood in Contemporary Cultures.* Chicago: University of Chicago Press.

1956

BRUNER, EDWARD M. "Cultural Transmission and Cultural Change." *Southwestern Journal of Anthropology* 12:191-207.
———. "Primary Group Experience and the Process of Acculturation." *American Anthropologist* 58:605-23.
MEAD, MARGARET. *Cultural Patterns and Technical Change*. Paris: World Federation for Mental Health, UNESCO.
———. *New Lives for Old: A Cultural Transformation—Manus, 1929-1953*. New York: William Morrow.
RICHARDS, AUDREY I. *Chisungu*. London: Faber & Faber.
TAX, SOL. "The Freedom to Make Mistakes." *America Indigena* 16, no. 3:171-77.
WHORF, B. L. *Language, Thought and Reality*. New York: Wiley.
WILLIAMS, THOMAS R. "Socialization in a Papago Indian Village." Ph.D. dissertation, University of Syracuse.

1957

SEARS, ROBERT R.; MACCOBY, ELEANOR E.; and LEVIN, HARRY. *Patterns of Child Rearing*. Evanston, Ill.: Harper & Row.

1958

EARLE, MARGARET J. *Rakau Children from Six to Thirteen Years*. Wellington, New Zealand: Victoria University of Wellington.

1959

LEE, DOROTHY. *Freedom and Culture*. New York: Prentice-Hall.

1960

DUBOIS, CORA A. *People of Alor*. Cambridge, Mass.: Harvard University Press.
HAWTHORN, H. B.; BELSHAW, C. S.; and JAMIESON, S. M. *The Indians of British Columbia*. Berkeley: University of California Press.
KAUFMAN, HOWARD. *Bandknad: A Community Study in Thailand*. Locust Valley, N.Y.: J. J. Agustin.
KEUR, JOHN. *Windward Children*. Assen, Netherlands: Royal Van Gorcum.
LANTIS, MARGARET. *Eskimo Childhood and Interpersonal Relationships: Nunivak Biographies and Genealogies*. Seattle: University of Washington Press.
OPIE, PETER, and OPIE, IONA. *The Lore and Language of School Children*. London: Oxford University Press.
THOMPSON, LAURA, and JOSEPH, ALICE. "The Education of the Hopi Child." In *Exploring the Ways of Mankind*, edited by Walter Goldschmidt. New York: Holt, Rinehart & Winston.

1961

BENEDICT, RUTH. *Patterns of Culture*. Boston: Houghton Mifflin.
———. *Chrysanthemum and the Sword*. Boston: Houghton Mifflin.
DERIDDER, JACOBUS C. *The Personality of the Urban African in South Africa*. London: Routledge & Kegan Paul.
KAPLAN, ROBERT B., ed. *Studying Personality Cross-Culturally*. New York: Harper & Row.

1962

KAYE, BARRINGTON. *Bringing Up Children in Ghana*. London: George Allen & Unwin.
PIAGET, JEAN. *Language and Thought of the Child*. New York: Humanities Press.
ROBERTS, JOHN M., and SUTTON-SMITH, BRIAN. "Child Training and Game Involvement." *Ethnology* 1, no. 2:166-85.
SACRE-COEUR, SISTER MARIE-ANDRE DU. *The House Stands Firm: Family Life in West Africa*. Milwaukee: Bruce.

1963

BROWN, JUDITH K. "A Cross-Cultural Study of Female Initiation Rites." *American Anthropologist* 65:837-53.
FISCHER, JOHN L., and FISCHER, ANN. "The New Englanders of Orchard Town, U.S.A." In *Six Cultures: Studies of Child Rearing*, edited by Beatrice B. Whiting. New York: Wiley.
MINTURN, LEIGH, and HITCHCOCK, JOHN T. "The Rajputs of Khalapur, India." In *Six Cultures: Studies of Child Rearing*, edited by Beatrice B. Whiting. New York: Wiley.

NYDEGGER, WILLIAM F., and NYDEGGER, CORINNE. "Tarong: An Ilocos Barrio in the Philippines." In *Six Cultures: Studies of Child Rearing*, edited by Beatrice B. Whiting. New York: Wiley.

OSWALT, WENDALL. *Napaskick: An Alaskan Eskimo Village*. Tucson: University of Arizona Press.

RITCHIE, JAMES E. *The Making of a Maori*. Wellington: A. H. and A. W. Reed.

ROGERS, EDWARD S., and ROGERS, JEAN H. "The Individual in Mistassini Society From Birth to Death." *Contributions to Anthropology*, Part II. Bulletin 190, National Museum of Canada. Ottawa: Department of Northern Affairs and National Resources.

ROMNEY, KIMBALL, and ROMNEY, ROMAINE. "The Mixtecano of Juxtlahuaca, Mexico." In *Six Cultures: Studies of Child Rearing*, edited by Beatrice B. Whiting. New York: Wiley.

WHITING, BEATRICE B., ed. *Six Cultures: Studies of Child Rearing*. New York: Wiley.

1964

BLACKING, JOHN. *Black Background: The Childhood of a South African Girl*. New York: Abelard-Schuman.

COHEN, YEHUDI A. *The Transition from Childhood to Adolescence*. Chicago: Aldine.

EISENSTADT, S. NOAH. *From Generation to Generation: Age Groups and Social Structure*. Glencoe, Ill.: Free Press.

KUPER, HILDA. *The Swazi: A South African Kingdom*. New York: Holt, Rinehart & Winston.

MADSEN, WILLIAM. *The Mexican-Americans of South Texas*. New York: Holt, Rinehart & Winston.

MINTURN, LEIGH, and LAMBERT, WILLIAM. *Mothers of Six Cultures. Antecedents of Child Rearing*. New York: Wiley.

1965

AUSUBEL, DAVID P. *Maori Youth*. New York: Holt, Rinehart & Winston.

GATHERU, R. MUGO. *Child of Two Worlds: A Kikuyu Story*. Garden City, N.Y.: Doubleday.

HONIGMANN, JOHN J., and HONIGMANN, IRMA. *Eskimo Townsmen*. Ottawa: Canadian Research Centre for Anthropology.

LANDY, DAVID. *Tropical Childhood: Cultural Transmission and Learning in a Rural Puerto Rican Village*. New York: Harper & Row.

NEUBAUER, PETER B. *Children in Collectives: Childrearing Aims and Practices in the Kibbutz*. Springfield, Ill.: Charles C Thomas.

PHILLIPS, HERBERT P. *Thai Peasant Personality: The Patterning of Interpersonal Behavior in the Village of Bang Chan*. Berkeley, Calif.: University of California Press.

RABIN, ROBERT. *Growing Up in the Kibbutz*. New York: Springer.

SPIRO, MELFORD E. *Children of the Kibbutz: A Study in Child Training and Personality*. Cambridge, Mass.: Harvard University Press.

THOMPSON, LAURA, and JOSEPH, ALICE. *Hopi Way*. New York: Russell & Russell.

YOUNG, FRANK W. *Initiation Ceremonies: A Cross-Cultural Study of Status Dramatization*. New York: Merrill.

1966

BRIM, ORVILLE, and WHEELER, STANTON. *Socialization After Childhood: Two Essays*. New York: Wiley.

CASTLE, E. B. *Growing Up in East Africa*. London: Oxford University Press.

GUTHRIE, GEORGE, and JACOBS, PEPITA. *Child Rearing and Personality Development in the Philippines*. University Park, Pa.: Pennsylvania State University.

HILGER, I. *Field Guide to the Ethnological Study of Child Life*. New Haven, Conn.: Human Relations Area File Press.

KAYIRA, LEGSON. *I Will Try*. London: Longmans, Green and Co.

LEVINE, R. A., and LEVINE, B. B. *Nyansongo: A Gusii Community in Kenya*. New York: Wiley.

SCHAPERA, I. *Married Life in an African Tribe*. Evanston: Northwestern University Press.

1967

FOX, LORENE K. *East African Childhood*. New York: Oxford University Press.

GOODMAN, MARY ELLEN. *The Individual and Culture*. Homewood, Ill.: Dorsey Press.

HOTCHKISS, JOHN C. "Children and Conduct in a Ladino Community of Chiapas Mexico." *American Anthropologist* 69:711-18.
MEAD, MARGARET. *Sex and Temperament in Three Primitive Societies.* New York: William Morrow.

1968

EARTHY, EMILY DORA. *Valenge Women.* London: Frank Cass.
READ, MARGARET. *Children of Their Fathers: Growing Up Among the Ngoni of Malawi.* New York: Holt, Rinehart & Winston.
TAX, SOL; DIAMOND, STANLEY; RAINWATER, LEE; MANGIN, WILLIAM; and BARATI, AGEHANANDA. *Notes and Essays on Education for Adults.* Anthropological Backgrounds of Adult Education, No. 57. Center for the Study of Liberal Education for Adults, Boston University.
WHITING, JOHN W. M. "Socialization: Anthropological Aspects." *International Encyclopedia of the Social Sciences* 14:545-49.

1969

CHIANG, YEE. *A Chinese Childhood.* New York: Norton.
DRIVER, HAROLD E. "Girl's Puberty Rites and Matrilocal Residence." *American Anthropologist* 71:905-8.
———. *Indians of North America.* Chicago: University of Chicago Press.
EVANS-PRITCHARD, EDWARD. *Nuer: A Description of the Modes of Livelihood and Political Institutions of a Nilotic People.* Fairlawn, N.J.: Oxford University Press.
GRAVES, NANCY B. *City, Country, and Child-Rearing in Three Cultures.* Boulder, Colo.: University of Colorado.
HIPPLER, ARTHUR E. *Barrow and Kotzebue: An Exploratory Comparison of Acculturation and Education in Two Large Northwestern Alaska Villages.* Minneapolis: Training Center for Community Programs, University of Minnesota.
LEIGHTON, DOROTHEA, and KLUCKHOHN, CLYDE. *Children of the People.* New York: Octagon.
OPIE, PETER, and OPIE, IONA. *Children's Games in Street and Playground.* London: Oxford University Press.
PELLETIER, WILFORD. "Childhood in an Indian Village." *This Magazine Is About Schools* 3, no. 2:6-22.
WILLIAMS, THOMAS RHYS. *A Borneo Childhood: Enculturation in Dusun Society.* New York: Holt, Rinehart & Winston.

1970

AL-ISSA, IHSAN, and WAYNE, DENNIS. *Cross-Cultural Studies of Behavior.* New York: Holt, Rinehart & Winston.
AMMAR, HAMED. "The Aims and Methods of Socialization in Silwa." In *From Child to Adult: Studies in the Anthropology of Education*, edited by John Middleton. Garden City, N.Y.: Natural History Press.
BRONFENBRENNER, URIE. *Two Worlds of Childhood: U.S. and U.S.S.R.* New York: Russell Sage Foundation.
GOODMAN, MARY ELLEN. *The Culture of Childhood: Child's-Eye View of Society and Culture.* New York: Teachers College Press.
GOODY, ESTHER. "Kinship Fostering in Gonja: Deprivation or Advantage?" In *Socialization: The Approach from Social Anthropology*, edited by Philip Mayer. New York: Tavistock.
HARRINGTON, CHARLES G. *Errors in Sex-Role Behavior in Teen-Age Boys.* New York: Teachers College Press.
HOGBIN, H. I. "A New Guinea Childhood: From Weaning Till the Eighth Year in Wogeo." In *From Child to Adult: Studies in the Anthropology of Education*, edited by John Middleton. Garden City, N.Y.: Natural History Press.
HOWARD, ALAN. *Learning to be Rotuman.* New York: Teachers College Press.
LITTLE, KENNETH. "The Social Cycle and Initiation Among the Mende." In *From Child to Adult: Studies in the Anthropology of Education*, edited by John Middleton. Garden City, N.Y.: Natural History Press.
LLOYD, BARBARA B. "Yoruba Mothers' Reports of Child Rearings: Some Theoretical and Methodological Considerations." In *Socialization: The Approach from Social Anthropology*, edited by Philip Mayer. New York: Tavistock.
LOUDON, J. B. "Teasing and Socialization on Tristan da Cunha." In *Socialization: The Approach from Social Anthropology*, edited by Philip Mayer. New York: Tavistock.
MAYER, PHILIP. *Socialization: The Approach from Social Anthropology.* New York: Tavistock.

MAYER, PHILIP, and MAYER, IONA. "Socialization by Peers: The Youth Organization of the Red Xhosa." In *Socialization: The Approach from Social Anthropology*, edited by Philip Mayer. New York: Tavistock.

MEAD, MARGARET. *Culture and Commitment.* New York: Doubleday.

———. "Girls Puberty Rites: A Reply to Driver." *American Anthropologist* 72: 1450–51.

MIDDLETON, JOHN. *From Child to Adult: Studies in the Anthropology of Education.* Garden City, N.Y.: Natural History Press.

RAUM, OTTO F. "Some Aspects of Indigenous Education Among the Chaga." In *From Child to Adult: Studies in the Anthropology of Education*, edited by John Middleton. Garden City, N.Y.: Natural History Press.

RICHARDS, AUDREY I. "Socialization and Contemporary British Anthropology." In *Socialization: The Approach from Social Anthropology*, edited by Philip Mayer. New York: Tavistock.

SHIMAHARA, NOBUO. "Enculturation: A Reconsideration." *Current Anthropology* 11: 143–48.

SPENCER, PAUL. "The Function of Ritual in the Socialization of the Samburu Moran." In *Socialization: The Approach from Social Anthropology*, edited by Philip Mayer. New York: Tavistock.

WARD, BARBARA E. "Temper Tantrums in Kau Sai: Some Speculations Upon Their Effects." In *Socialization: The Approach from Social Anthropology*, edited by Philip Mayer. New York: Tavistock.

WILDER, WILLIAM. "Socialization and Social Structure in a Malay Village." In *Socialization: The Approach from Social Anthropology*, edited by Philip Mayer. New York: Tavistock.

WILLIAMS, THOMAS RHYS. "The Structure of the Socialization Process in Papago Indian Society." In *From Child to Adult: Studies in the Anthropology of Education*, edited by John Middleton. Garden City, N.Y.: Natural History Press.

1971

AVEDON, ELLIOTT M., and SUTTON-SMITH, BRIAN. *The Study of Games.* New York: Wiley.

HOSTETLER, JOHN A., and HUNTINGTON, GERTRUDE E. *Children in Amish Society: Socialization and Community Education.* New York: Holt, Rinehart & Winston.

1972

DENG, FRANCIS MADING. *The Dinka of the Sudan.* New York: Holt, Rinehart & Winston.

DENNIS, WAYNE. *The Hopi Child.* New York: Arno.

ISAACS, SUSAN. *Social Development in Young Children.* New York: Schocken Books.

LEIS, PHILIP E. *Enculturation and Socialization in an Ijaw Village.* New York: Holt, Rinehart & Winston.

PESHKIN, ALAN. *Kanuri Schoolchildren: Education and Social Mobilization in Nigeria.* New York: Holt, Rinehart & Winston.

1973

DEVOS, GEORGE A. *Socialization for Achievement: Essays on the Cultural Psychology of the Japanese.* Berkeley: University of California Press.

GAY, JOHN. *Red Dust on the Green Leaves: A Kpelle Twins' Childhood.* Thompson, Conn.: Interculture Associates.

HARRINGTON, CHARLES. *Cross-Cultural Approaches to Learning.* New York: MSS Information Corporation.

MATANE, PAULIAS. *My Childhood in New Guinea.* New York: Oxford University Press.

MILLS, RICHARD. *Young Outsiders: A Story of Alternative Communities.* New York: Pantheon.

ONON, URGUNGE. *My Childhood in Mongolia.* New York: Oxford University Press.

SUTTON-SMITH, BRIAN. *The Folkgames of Children.* Austin: University of Texas Press.

TCHERNAVIN, TATIANA. *My Childhood in Siberia.* New York: Oxford University Press.

VARKEVISSER, CORLIEN N. *Socialization in a Changing Society: Sukuma Childhood in Rural and Urban Mwana, Tanzania.* The Hague: Center for the Study of Education in Changing Societies.

1974

GALLIMORE, JOAN W. B. and CATHIE JORDAN. *Culture, Behavior and Education: A Study of Hawaiian-Americans.* Beverly Hills, Calif.: Sage Publishing Company.

HOLLOMAN, R. "Ritual Opening and Individual Transformation: Rites of Passage at Esalen." *American Anthropologist* 76: 265–80.

HUGHES, CHARLES C. *Eskimo Boyhood: An Autobiography in Psychosocial Perspective.* Lexington: University of Kentucky Press.

LEBRA, WILLIAM P., ed. *Youth, Socialization and Mental Health.* Honolulu: University of Hawaii Press.

MONTAGU, ASHLEY, ed. *Culture and Human Development: Insights into Growing Human.* Englewood Cliffs, N.J.: Prentice-Hall.

OGBU, JOHN U. *The Next Generation: An Ethnography of Education in an Urban Neighborhood.* New York: Academic Press.